Reintroducing Macroeconomics

Reintroducing Macroeconomics

A CRITICAL APPROACH

STEVEN MARK COHN

M.E.Sharpe
Armonk, New York
London, England

Library of Congress Cataloging-in-Publication Data

Cohn, Steve.
   Reintroducing macroeconomics : a critical approach / Steven Mark Cohn.
     p. cm.
   Includes bibliographical references and index.
    ISBN-13: 978-0-7656-1450-6 (cloth : alk. paper); ISBN-13: 978-0-7656-1451-3 (pbk.: alk. paper)
    ISBN-10: 0-7656-1450-2 (cloth : alk. paper); ISBN-10: 0-7656-1451-0 (pbk.: alk. paper)
  1. Macroeconomics. I. Title.

HB172.5.C635 2007
339—dc22
                                         2006011877

Printed in the United States of America

The paper used in this publication meets the minimum requirements of
American National Standard for Information Sciences
Permanence of Paper for Printed Library Materials,
ANSI Z 39.48-1984.

∞

BM (c) 10 9 8 7 6 5 4 3 2 1
BM (p) 10 9 8 7 6 5 4 3 2 1

For Nancy

For Maury and his generation, and

For all economists trying to make the world a better place rather than
explain why it cannot be different than it is

DETAILED CONTENTS

TABLES, FIGURES, AND BOXES

TABLES

FIGURES

BOXES

PREFACE

Socrates argued that "an unexamined life is not worth living," and the same can be said of textbooks: an unexamined argument is not worth reading. This book is about philosophical debates in economics. It critiques conventional economic theory and standard introductory economics textbooks. It is designed to make you think.

Conventional textbook economic theory is based on many assumptions. We will explore these assumptions and suggest when they may be unreasonable. Conventional textbook economic theory tells a lot of stories. We will look critically at these stories and analyze when they seem analogous to real life and when they may be misleading. Conventional textbook economics also offers a framework for designing public policy. We will explore when it seems wise and unwise to listen to conventional economists' policy recommendations.

In short, we will offer a different pair of glasses with which to look at economic issues from the spectacles provided by conventional economics, or what is called *neoclassical economics.*[1] Our pair of glasses draws on ideas from many different schools of thought, including institutionalist economics, radical economics, Post Keynesian economics, Marxian economics, feminist economics, and ecological economics.[2] We will term this lens *heterodox economics* and offer a more precise definition of the perspective in chapter 2. Our claim is not that conventional economics is totally wrong, but that its assumptions and ways of reasoning are valid in much more limited contexts than it implies. We will try to define the terrain upon which neoclassical theory should and should not be used.

Hopefully many of you will find that the book gives you a new way of seeing the world and that will be exciting. The book should give those preferring to retain old glasses more powerful vision through them. To paraphrase John Stuart Mill, a famous philosopher and economist of the nineteenth century, one who only understands one's own position and not that of competing perspectives does not understand one's own position very well.

Perhaps the most important idea that the book can impart is the idea that learning involves competing theories and active choices about how to think about things. A good education gives you many sets of glasses and a disciplined mind to choose among them.

WHERE WE ARE GOING

We begin with three introductory chapters. Chapter 1 discusses the nature of philosophical debates in economics. Chapters 2 and 3 develop an alternative approach to economic theory from that offered in conventional introductory textbooks. Subsequent chapters apply the ideas outlined in chapters 2 and 3 to the topics of conventional textbooks.

ROLE OF THE ENDNOTES

Many chapters have a lot of endnotes. These endnotes offer elaborations of points made in the text. The chapters are designed to be fully intelligible without the endnotes. If you are curious about the sources of information behind an assertion or would like further elaboration of a point raised in the text, you might want to look at the endnotes.

FINAL WORD

Theories are like tools; they are generally designed to be used, to address some question, and to aid in accomplishing some end. This book is animated by the desire to understand economic outcomes so that a more equal and humanly satisfying economy can be created.

NOTES

1. Is it fair to judge neoclassical economics by its introductory textbooks, which necessarily simplify the theory in order to teach it to beginning students? Is it possible that most of the criticisms of textbook economics presented in this commentary are attacks on a straw man, easily parried by his older brother, "prof-man"? I don't think so. Although the mathematics gets more complicated and the applications of the theory more ingenious, the basic ideas of Econ 101 echo in upper-level undergraduate courses, graduate courses, and scholarly journals. Introductory textbooks necessarily focus on the central ideas of a theory. What is included (or excluded) in neoclassical introductory texts often reveals more about the underlying ideas of neoclassical theory than the structure of advanced graduate courses. Because most standard introductory economics texts do capture the core of neoclassical theory, the authors are not shy about offering unqualified public policy recommendations based on the simplified analyses presented in the texts.

2. Among other sometimes overlapping schools comprising heterodox economics are humanistic economics, social economics, socio-economics, neo-Ricardian economics, and contextual economics.

ACKNOWLEDGMENTS

It is a great pleasure to thank the many people who have helped me put this book together. Their generosity and insights were bountiful. I of course am solely responsible for any errors.

Several colleagues read large portions of the manuscript and gave me helpful feedback. Detailed comments from Jim Crotty, Peter Dorman, and Fred Lee very much improved the book. Many other colleagues and friends offered helpful comments or other kinds of assistance, including: David Amor, Sam Bowles, Dean Baker, Jared Bernstein, Dan Eberhardt, Gerald Epstein, Susan Feiner, Nancy Folbre, Ellen Frank, Karen Kampwirth, Marc Linder, John Marchica, Michele Naples, Stephen Resnick, Maliha Safri, Geoffrey Schneider, Janet Spitz, Lori Sundberg, Charles Whalen, and Marty Wolfson.

Early on in the project, I directed a two-semester seminar series at the University of Massachusetts in Amherst that reviewed heterodox critiques of standard textbooks. The seminar also contributed to the development of a new heterodox microeconomics textbook, *Microeconomics in Context* by Neva Goodwin, Julie A. Nelson, Frank Ackerman, and Thomas Weisskopf. The seminar was funded by the Global Development and Environment Institute (GDAE) and benefited from presentations by a number of faculty members and many graduate students in the Department of Economics at the University of Massachusetts in Amherst. The U. Mass. Economics Department is a very special institution and I am grateful for my associations with it. Its legacy is on every page of this book. Yahya Madra and Maliha Safri were especially helpful in making the seminar work.

I would also like to thank participants at two other GDAE-sponsored seminar series on principles textbooks: faculty and graduate students from the Department of Economics at the University of Memphis (especially professors Julie Heath and David Ciscel) and faculty from the Department of Economics at Bucknell University (especially professor Geoffrey Schneider).

I would like to thank GDAE and Neva Goodwin (codirector of GDAE) for support of my research financially and intellectually. Her work helped turn my attention to the question of what we mean by economic well-being.

At Knox College, Clark Bernier, David Ferris, Melissa Hoffman, Taimur Kahn, and Veronica Kehoss were very helpful research assistants. Susan Massey, Brittany Leggans, and many other Knox students also offered helpful feedback on draft chapters of the book used in class.

I would like to also thank Knox College for research funds. The Knox library and computer center staffs were helpful as always. I thank my colleagues in the economics department, Roy Andersen, David Gourd, Jonathan Powers, and Richard Stout for productive chats in the hallways about economic issues and for adjusting to scheduling and other burdens attendant with my research leaves.

I would like to thank Redefining Progress and the Exploratorium for permission to use some of their graphics in this book. I also would like to thank Steuart Pittman for help with several of the text's illustrations.

I thank Lynn Taylor of M.E. Sharpe for her confidence in the book and help in bringing it to fruition. I would also like to thank Anna Kaltenbach for thoughtful and timely copyediting, and Amy Odum for overseeing the book's journey through the publication process.

This list is necessarily incomplete as one incurs intellectual debts to informal conversations and other kinds of assistance during a long project that elude formal lists. But a thanks just the same to these anonymous helpers.

Finally I'd like to thank my wife Nancy for much help of all kinds.

NOTE TO INSTRUCTORS

Ways to Use This Book

ORIGINS AND PURPOSE OF THE BOOK

It is often said that the purpose of introductory economics classes is to "teach students to think like economists." What is usually meant by this claim, however, is to teach students to think like *neoclassical* economists. My aim in introductory classes has been broader. It has been to teach students both neoclassical and heterodox approaches to economics. I have found this goal hard to achieve. This book grew out of my frustration with using reserve readings to present the ideas of heterodox economics alongside a mainstream macroeconomics textbook.

Although there are many excellent and accessible articles on different aspects of heterodox economics that can be assigned in a principles course, I was never able to assemble a collection that adequately conveyed the broad logic of heterodox alternatives to neoclassical theory. Regardless of the particular articles I chose, the articles did not cross reference each other, did not build an argument in the seamless way the textbook did, did not offer a sustained alternative to the textbook, and were not read as diligently as the textbook. Although some students were excited by the heterodox readings, even these students seemed to have trouble generating heterodox arguments in new contexts. Many other students treated the reserve readings as an afterthought.

As a result of this experience I decided to try to write a commentary that offered a heterodox critique, on a chapter-by-chapter basis, of standard introductory economics textbooks. This book is the first result of that project. It critiques introductory macroeconomics textbooks. A volume critiquing introductory microeconomics textbooks may follow.

The project rests on two key assumptions: that there is a generic neoclassical macro principles textbook and that there is enough common ground among heterodox economic paradigms to construct a common heterodox alternative. The first assumption is uncontroversial. David Colander's observation that principles texts can not diverge more than 15 percent from standard fare and survive in the market characterizes the tendency for homogenization fairly well.

The second assumption deserves more attention. I believe a broad common ground exists across a wide range of heterodox critiques of neoclassical principles texts, including, among others, the work of many institutionalist, radical, Marxist, feminist, Post Keynesian, socioeconomic, humanistic, and ecological economists. Chapters 2 and 3 outline what constitutes this shared terrain. Subsequent chapters use the methodological arguments developed in chapters 1 to 3 to critique neoclassical textbooks.

INTENDED AUDIENCE

This text is primarily intended for use in introductory macroeconomics courses, but because of the significant overlap between introductory micro- and macroeconomics classes and because of the special topic chapters included in the book, significant parts of the text may be of interest to professors and students in a wider array of courses (see below).

The book could be used in two different ways, as required reading assigned by a course professor or as independent reading by students interested in gaining a heterodox perspective on their course material.

TO PROFESSORS USING THE BOOK FOR ASSIGNED READINGS IN INTRODUCTORY MACROECONOMICS COURSES

Core Chapters

Like most textbooks, the commentary includes more material than can be covered in a single term. The core chapters are chapters 1 through 12 and 17 and 18. Chapter 1 discusses the nature of paradigm debates in social science. It lays out the epistemological rationale for the existence of competing theories of economics. Chapters 2 through 6 critique the standard introductory chapters found in neoclassical micro and macro textbooks. Chapters 7 and 8 focus on the national income accounts and other measurement issues in macroeconomics. Chapter 9 critiques textbook discussions of Keynesian Cross income determination models. Chapters 10 and 11 deal with the Federal Reserve and the monetary sector. Chapter 12 critiques textbook discussions of the Aggregate Supply–Aggregate Demand (AS-AD) framework. Chapters 17 and 18 analyze current debates in macroeconomics from a heterodox perspective. The book concludes with suggestions on where to look in the library and on the internet for further information about heterodox economics.

Special Topics Chapters

Chapters 13–16 can be thought of as special topics chapters. Chapter 13 looks at heterodox alternatives to the AS-AD framework. Chapter 14 deals with international economic issues. Chapter 15 focuses on the macroeconomics of inequality and chapter 16 looks at macroeconomics and the environment.

Pedagogical Strategies

The commentary emphasizes the methodological basis of heterodox objections to textbook economics. My aim was to illustrate how the same kinds of objections can be raised in different contexts. Following Thomas Kuhn's ideas about how students learn new paradigms, I have tried to present classic examples of heterodox objections to neoclassical economics and demonstrations of how subsequent critiques can be seen as analogous to the original critique. My goal has been to enable students to draw similar analogies when encountering neoclassical analyses of new topics.

I have used much of the book in my own classes. I have tried different teaching strategies. One strategy is to follow each textbook chapter with the corresponding critique chapter. Another approach is to bundle together a number of textbook chapters (such as the intro chapters) and then read a group of chapters in the commentary. A third approach is to discuss heterodox ideas at the end of the term. Each approach has advantages and disadvantages.

The risk of the first method is that students may not have consolidated the neoclassical material when you begin to critique it. This can lead to muddled thinking. In the early part of the term, the chapter-by-chapter critique strategy seems to work best if students have already had an introductory microeconomics class. I have found the second approach the most effective. The risk of the third approach is that students are very used to looking through neoclassical glasses by the time you begin to suggest alternative ways of seeing the economy. This can make it difficult for them to rethink economic analysis. In addition, if you fall behind the syllabus, the time left for critique can be cramped.

USING THE BOOK IN CLASSES OTHER THAN INTRODUCTORY MACROECONOMICS

Chapter 1

I assign the first chapter of the book on the nature of paradigm debates in economics in every course I teach. Besides laying the groundwork for understanding paradigm competition in economics, it introduces students to sociology of knowledge questions that apply to numerous other fields.

Using the Book in Introductory Microeconomics Courses

Along with chapter 1, chapters 2 through 5 (on basic concepts in economics), chapter 14 (on international economics), chapter 15 (on economic inequality), chapter 16 (on environmental economics), and the last part of chapter 18 (on where to find more information on heterodox economics) might be used in an introductory microeconomics class.

Using the Book in Public Policy and Area Studies Classes

A course in introductory economics is often required for public policy majors and many interdisciplinary programs, such as environmental studies, black studies, women's studies, and American studies. Some of the students in these classes are familiar with more sophisticated philosophical and social theories than the logical positivism and methodological individualism that underlie neoclassical economics. Many students in these courses also have personal intuitions that make them skeptical of the free-market orientation of neoclassical economics. The students lack, however, a language and formal framework to express their ideas and identify what it is about neoclassical analysis that generates the disturbing conclusions. This commentary is designed to help such students explore the contestable assumptions behind neoclassical thinking. Chapters 1, 2 through 5, and 15 would be especially relevant for public policy courses and interdisciplinary studies. The addition of chapter 16 on macroeconomics and the environment would work well in an environmental economics class.

I would very much welcome feedback on what sections of the book were useful to instructors and suggestions for topics to cover in future editions.

Reintroducing Macroeconomics

PHILOSOPHICAL DEBATES IN ECONOMICS

A RIDDLE

A man and his son are driving to a championship football game. It is late December and the roads are covered with snow. They hit a patch of ice and crash into a telephone pole. The father is killed instantly. An ambulance rushes the son to a nearby hospital and operating room. The doctor walks in and says, "I can't operate, that's my son." How could this be true?

Whatever your answer is to the riddle, assume that it is incorrect and come up with a second answer. We will return to this riddle shortly.

PARADIGMS IN ECONOMIC THEORY (OR WHY ECONOMISTS DISAGREE)

Definitions

A paradigm is a conceptual framework, a context for organizing thought. It is like a pair of theoretical spectacles used to observe and think about the world. There are competing paradigms for understanding the economy, competing frameworks for organizing economic theory. This chapter explores why competing paradigms (such as neoclassical economics, Marxist economics, and ecological economics) exist.

Thinking is hard. Thinking about thinking (epistemology) is even harder, but that is where we must begin if we are to fully understand economic debates. Epistemology refers to the study of the nature of knowledge, including how we determine what is true and even what we mean by "truth." We shall begin by comparing two simple models of knowing: the "blank slate" theory of knowledge and the "paradigmatic" or gestalt[1] theory of knowledge. Page constraints require that we skip over many subtle and fascinating issues, but if our brief inquiry whets your appetite, you might think about enrolling in a philosophy course that reads thinkers such as Descartes, Locke, Hume, Popper, and Kuhn.

Blank Slate Theory of Knowledge

Most people in our society, including most economists, accept a blank slate theory of knowledge, often without explicit recognition. For many people, blank slate claims seem commonsensical and self-evident. The blank slate theory of knowledge is often associated with empiricist philosophers. It imagines that the mind confronts the world directly. Individuals have experiences from which they generate ideas. It is as if ideas were imminent or pregnant in experience. You stick your hand in a fire and generate the idea "hot." You look at a rose and generate the idea "beautiful." Your mind reflects the world as if it were a mirror. The world writes on you as if you were a blank slate.

The world's scribblings and reflections, however, are not always easy to interpret. After sticking your hand in a fire, you might, for example, mistakenly think that orangeness causes pain. Blank slate theories of knowledge thus require that all imminent ideas be treated as hypotheses and elevated to the status of provisional knowledge only after having survived experimental tests. The idea that orangeness causes pain, for example, would presumably be jettisoned after eating your first orange.

There is often an implied universality to blank slate knowledge claims. According to this reasoning everyone can in principle do the same experiments. Therefore all thinkers should eventually arrive at the same ideas. Variants of blank slate epistemology lie behind many popular expositions of the "scientific method." Science is said to "command" our belief because it generates falsifiable (testable) propositions from experience and logical deductions. All scientists should, according to this view, eventually reach the same conclusions.

Conventional economic theory tends to adopt blank slate epistemology. It thinks of itself as a science, whose conclusions command belief. We shall see shortly why some economists disagree.

Paradigmatic Theory of Knowledge

In contrast to the blank slate view of the mind, the paradigmatic view of knowledge argues that the mind never perceives the world directly or experiences sensations innocently, that is, untranslated, or unmediated by a person's prior conceptual framework. According to paradigmatic theories of knowledge everyone is always wearing theoretical spectacles and thinking within some paradigm. What one sees is a product of what "is out there" *and* the lens used to study it. The accompanying picture provides a simple (and perhaps dangerously oversimplified) introduction to this idea. Look at it and write down what you see. Assume it came from a book about a young woman drinking wine.

I suspect that most of you saw an attractive young lady. Some of you saw an old lady. Why? If you look closely at the picture you should be able to see both versions of the person. The picture represents a classic example of figure-ground reversal, a topic studied in perceptual research. Although looking at the same picture, we perceive different scenes. By organizing the lines in different ways in our minds, we can "see" different things. In much more subtle ways, paradigmatic theories of knowledge claim that economists and other social theorists in competing paradigms "see" different things and understand the workings of the social world differently.

From a paradigmatic perspective, observation and thinking are *active rather than passive* processes. Instead of simply *reflecting* what is "out there," the observer partially *constructs* what she sees. As a first approximation, it is helpful to think about paradigms influencing thought in four main ways, by their impact on: (1) the data attended to, (2) the abstractions used to organize data, (3) the language used to convey ideas, and (4) the way in which new theories are tested.

Data Attended To

As the philosopher William James notes, without editing sensations (that is, without focusing on some sensory inputs and ignoring others), the world would be a "bloomin' buzzin' confusion."

Figure 1.1 **Old Woman or Young Lady?**

Old woman or young lady?

Adapted with permission from an Exploratorium postcard [http://www.exploratorium.edu/exhibits/postcard_illusions/] originally rendered by W.E. Hill. The illusion, sometimes referred to as the Young Girl–Old Woman illusion, is based on a 1915 cartoon in an American humor magazine, which in turn was based on an 1888 German postcard. See mathworld.wolfram.com and Al Seckel's web site (http://neuro.caltech.edu/~seckel) for additional information about this and other optical illusions. Thanks to all of these people and web sites for helping me utilize this image.

People's conceptual frameworks help provide that editing, by telling people, "look here, and not there." One's theory of the mind, for instance, helps determine what psychologists and other counselors "hear" when they interview people.

For example, consider the idea of a "Freudian slip." According to Freudian psychology, the mind is multidimensional, including conscious and unconscious levels. Occasionally, instinctual energy from the unconscious bubbles into overt behavior, circumventing subconscious and conscious censors in devious ways. What a non-Freudian might treat as an inconsequential typographical error or slip of the tongue becomes for a Freudian a key piece of data, a window into the unconscious. When Freudian counselors "listen" to their patients, they often listen more for the silences (censored utterances) and irregularities (Freudian slips) than for explicit remarks. Non-Freudians listen and hear differently.

Similarly, some contemporary physicists build special instruments to explore the nature of matter. The instruments exist because of the presence of a theory that implies the existence of special particles (solar neutrinos) that can be measured by the instruments. Without the theory we would not have the instruments or data about the particles. We would not "see" them. In fact, we never do "see" them; we record some effects, which, given our theory, we interpret as their "reflections."

As we shall discover shortly, different economic paradigms allow one to "see" different things. The paradigms orient us to different data and to different questions about the data. Conventional gross domestic product (GDP) statistics, for example, attempt to measure national economic output. They leave out, however, the value of things produced in the home for family use (because they are not priced in markets) and the value of social maintenance (that is, the cultivation of interpersonal ties that transform a group of people into a community). Feminist economists note that such oversights are not random; they often exclude the experiences and contributions of women in the economy.

Ecological economists have criticized GDP statistics for their incomplete treatment of "natural capital" (such as exhaustible resources or the earth's capacity to absorb wastes). We will explore exactly what this means in the text. The point here is that even the numbers that economists use to "describe" the level of a country's economic activity reflect paradigmatic visions. There is no neutral, objective, "theory-less" scale with which to measure economic activity.

Abstractions Used to Organize Data

Even when two observers "see" similar objects, people from different paradigms may organize their observations differently. People's conceptual frameworks provide the categories (the concepts or abstractions) for linking and integrating observations. Marxist and feminist economists, for example, organize economic observations about inequality with respect to the customs and institutions of a social system. They knit together their analysis with categories that link individual actions to culturally given social roles. Neoclassical economists talk about individuals rather than social systems and have few categories or concepts linking individual behaviors to social structures. (Precisely what this distinction means will occupy us in chapter 2).

Language Used

Almost all paradigms develop specialized languages by using familiar words in special ways and occasionally creating new terms. Just as a paradigm's abstract concepts are linked together, its language is interactively constructed. Groups of words are often used reciprocally to define each other, much like cross-referencing in a dictionary.

The language of a conceptual framework inevitably shapes how questions are posed and how events are understood. Even when "jargon" appears to be absent because of the presence of familiar words, the paradigm's specialized use of these words imposes its voice on the discussion. Religious language, business language, military language, and the language of network news, for example, all frame the subjects discussed in particular ways; all presuppose a particular kind of reality in the way they talk about it.

This book will try to point out to you how your main textbook is shaping your thinking through its paradigmatic use of language. By emphasizing the "constitutive impact" of language on thought, paradigmatic epistemology challenges the tendency of blank slate epistemology to treat language as a neutral medium for conveying prior and universal ideas.

One of the problems in attempting to compare paradigms is the tendency for participants in one paradigm to translate the ideas from another paradigm into their own language. When this happens, the translated ideas can lose the meaning that they had in their original language. Learning a second paradigm is like learning a foreign language, since you do not really have full command of the alternative paradigm until you learn to think in it directly, without translating. Because learning a new paradigm is a major investment, most neoclassical economists are relatively unfamiliar with the "real" content of heterodox paradigms.[2] This commentary will try to point out where the "quick and dirty" translations offered in conventional macroeconomic textbooks of heterodox ideas break down. Because of most readers' lack of background in alternative paradigms, even our discussion will lose some of the richness of alternative economic theories.

Ways of Testing Theories

People holding blank slate ideas about epistemology can accept that paradigms *initially* influence the data attended to and the abstractions used to organize data without abandoning many blank slate conclusions. The key question is whether paradigms condition the way theories (and paradigms themselves) are tested and evaluated. From a blank slate perspective, it seems relatively easy to discredit incorrect paradigms. Experiments can be designed to test whether one conceptual framework explains the world better than another. The results can be evaluated objectively and all observers quickly converted to a common paradigm.

From a paradigmatic perspective, things are trickier. People's conceptual frameworks inevitably influence how they test their theories. People tend to respond to failed predictions or data that challenges their ideas by making minor modifications within their existing conceptual frameworks. People seldom shift conceptual frameworks. When doctors become baffled by a new disease, for example, they do not discard the germ theory of disease; they try to refine it so it can be applied to the anomalous case. When a Freudian psychoanalyst's treatment of a patient's phobia fails to "cure" the patient, the analyst does not give up Freudian theory; he or she tries to find another explanation for the person's behavior *within* Freudian theory. Even when answers are not found for anomalous cases, most thinkers tolerate the anomalies on the assumption that *answers will be found in the future.*

We shall see the same tendency to search for answers *within existing paradigms* in economics when, for instance, economists mis-predict inflation and unemployment rates. A group of economists known as classical economists, for example, have historically asserted that markets automatically produce full employment without government assistance. During the Great Depression (~1929 to 1940) the U.S. economy averaged more than 17 percent unemployment for nearly a decade. The unemployment rate peaked at about 25 percent in 1933. How did classical economists respond to this apparent failure of their theory to predict what happened? Rather than reject the notion of automatic full employment, the "new classical" economists made minor changes in their models that allowed them to explain the depression without giving up their full-employment, laissez-faire policy conclusions.

In contrast with classical economists, a group of economists known as Keynesians have argued that capitalist economies *can* have unemployment problems. In the 1960s the Keynesians argued that too little aggregate demand caused unemployment and too much aggregate demand caused inflation. The stagflation (simultaneous unemployment *and* inflation) of the late 1970s appeared as devastating for existing Keynesian theory as the Great Depression had been for classical economic theory. However, just like the new classical theorists, the New Keynesians made modest changes *within* Keynesian theory that allowed it to explain stagflation without abandoning its basic ideas.

Similarly, orthodox Marxist economists have appealed to their own adjustments to reconcile their failed predictions (for example that profit rates have a tendency to fall in mature capitalist economies) to the data. These adjustments (by Marxists, Keynesians, classical economists, etc.) are not constructed in bad faith. They are not debating tricks devised by partisans to save face. Rather, they reflect a reasoned way of seeing the world from within a particular conceptual framework.

Let us return now to the riddle about the doctor and the football game. I have asked it for twenty years in my introductory economics classes. There tend to be two sets of answers. The first group offers couplets, like:

1. The doctor gave his sperm to a sperm bank and the boy was fathered from the bank.
2. The doctor was God.

Box 1.1
Paradigmatic Reasoning

Thomas Kuhn provides the classic example of paradigmatic reasoning in his study of the history of earth-centered astronomy. From before the second century B.C.E. until about 1500 C.E., astronomers, philosophers, and educated observers believed that the sun rotated around the earth. This belief was part of a larger conceptual framework that linked ideas about the natural world with religious beliefs and ideas about the nature of human society.

The science of the period sought to explain *how* things worked and *why* the universe took the form it did. Astronomers predicted the motion of the heavenly bodies fairly accurately with models that assumed the planets orbited the earth in circular fashion. They felt this was because the circle was the most perfect form and the earth the most important object in the universe. These thinkers would have rejected any explanation of the motion of the planets that did not include a coherent reason for why the planetary system took the form it did.

Like modern scientists, the astronomers were accountable to the facts. When observations contradicted their predictions, as they did as telescopes improved, they amended their theory to make it consistent with the facts. As Figure 1.2a illustrates, the appearance of an unexpected observation challenged the assumption of circular orbits. After satisfying themselves that the anomalous or puzzling data was not due to mismeasurement, the astronomers attempted to revise their theories to incorporate the new information. Their answer: the universe was even more perfect than they had realized. The heavenly bodies orbited the earth in circles on circles, or **epicycles** (see Figure 1.2b and Figure 1.2c). When even better telescopes discovered continuing divergences from predicted epicyclic orbits, the astronomers theorized epicycles on epicycles. Thomas Kuhn has demonstrated that such a system can in fact "explain" (successfully predict) relatively well the appearance of astronomical motions in the night sky. The model flourished for about 1700 years.

Modern science has rejected an earth-centered astronomy in favor of a sun-focused solar system with elliptical orbits. It has also given up the project of explaining why the universe has its particular set of "natural laws." Modern science attempts to explain the workings of

Figures 1.2a, b, and c: Epicycles

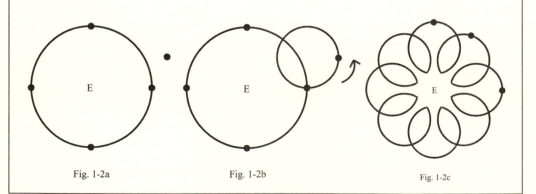

Fig. 1-2a   Fig. 1-2b   Fig. 1-2c

Box 1.1 *(continued)*

"natural law," and not its origins. Astronomers, for example, do not argue that the ellipse is a more perfect form than the circle. They ignore the question of *why* gravity or matter take the form they do. They try instead to model how gravity and matter behave.[1] As this shift suggests, one of the major battles between different paradigms often concerns debates over what are legitimate and important questions. Conventional economics, for example, argues that asking where consumers' tastes and preferences come from is not a legitimate question for economics. Other paradigms of economic theory disagree.

1. Modern physics has similarly given up Einstein's pursuit of a deterministic physics and posits that the world is probabilistic at the subatomic level. Given exactly the same preconditions quantum mechanics implies that different outcomes are possible, implying a fundamental randomness to the universe. Einstein believed that the apparent randomness was due to incomplete information and demanded that physics search for the hidden cause of different outcomes. The debate over whether the universe is deterministic or stochastic is ultimately an aesthetic debate and not really resolvable by appeal to data. Economists, in much the same way, debate whether macroeconomics can be fully grounded in microeconomics, or whether human action can be formally modeled.

---

1. By using this tack he [the doctor] wants to increase his wage . . .
2. His mother may have married twice.

1. The doctor is very confused.
2. The boy was messed up beyond recognition.

1. It was a supernatural event. . . .
2. The doctor [is] . . . a part time priest.

1. Boy's dead father was adoptive father.
2. Father in car was Catholic priest.

The second group includes the possibility that the doctor is the boy's mother. There is no reason to assume that this is the case, but the interesting thing about the riddle is the degree to which traditional gender stereotypes prevent some people *from even considering* the possibility. Many students (both male and female) make revision after revision in their answers (epicycling) without conceiving of the possibility that the doctor may be a woman. Such is the power of paradigms; they assert themselves before you think and before you "see." To some extent, they think and see for you.[3] We shall find that this is clearly the case for economic paradigms. To some extent the purpose of this book is to problematize or denaturalize neoclassical economic theory, so you can *choose* whether to think within or outside of its boundaries.

Normal Science and Scientific Revolutions

Thomas Kuhn, the most famous historian and philosopher of science of the twentieth century, provides a very useful way of thinking about the impact of paradigms on scientific research. He distinguishes between "normal science," which takes place within the dominant existing paradigm, and "scientific revolutions," which involve paradigm shifts. The latter resemble gestalt shifts. They go beyond integrating new information into a preexisting conceptual framework;

they redefine the meaning given to old information, much like the figure/ground shift in perception depicted in Figure 1.1.

From a blank slate perspective, it would be imagined that the causes of a scientific revolution are the accumulation of intolerable contradictions within the old framework and the emergence from the data of a self-evidently superior new framework. Kuhn's historical studies paint a more complex picture. The superiority of new frameworks often appears only after the jettisoned paradigm has atrophied. The superiority may be as much a *result* of the scientific revolution as its cause. It is not clear that the boundaries of older systems could not have been stretched to compete with the triumphant framework.

The allegiance of obvious geniuses, such as Albert Einstein, to "defeated" paradigms suggests that choices are not simple matters of logical deduction. As with many human judgments, there often appear to be cultural and sociological factors involved in determining what seems a reasonable way to think about something.

A paradigm is like a language. It evolves through shared use. The community of people who work within a paradigm determine how it develops. Their judgments are usually influenced by the projects they wish to pursue. As we will see in chapter 2, neoclassical and heterodox economists have often wanted to pursue very different projects and, as a result, have taken economic theory in distinctly different directions. The result is the paradigm debate described in this book.

SOME STUDY QUESTIONS

Simple Review Questions (Making Sure You Got the Basic Ideas)

1. What is meant by the term "paradigm"? Compare and contrast paradigmatic and blank slate epistemologies.
2. How does a paradigm influence thinking?
3. What is meant by the terms: "normal science," "epicycle," and "scientific revolution"?

More Thought-Provoking Discussion Questions

1a. Adherents of a blank slate theory of knowledge often imagine that history (and a college history course) is like a movie about the past. The course "plays back" what happened as if the instructor or the textbook were a camcorder that recorded and later replayed the events that transpired. What alternative cinematic metaphors for the telling of history might a paradigmatic theorist use?
1b. Why, according to the paradigmatic perspective, is the writing of history (say, the history of the United States from 1700 to 1900) more than narrative reporting?
2. Read pages 1–9 in Thomas Kuhn's famous book *The Structure of Scientific Revolutions*. What is the image of science that Kuhn is attacking?
3. Kuhn asserts that facts and theories are not "categorically separable" (Kuhn 1970, 7). What do you think he means by this?
4. Kuhn argues that empirical data limits scientific theories, but adds "they cannot alone determine a particular body of such belief. An apparently arbitrary element, compounded of personal and historical accident, is always a formative ingredient of the beliefs espoused by a given scientific community at a given time" (Kuhn 1970, 4). What do you think he means by this?

5. Assess the following claims from the perspective of paradigmatic epistemology:

    • "The problem is that everyone is limited by their paradigm. What we need to develop is a paradigm-free science. Then we could free ourselves from bias."
    • "I know we interpret the world differently, but let's look at the facts."

6. Simple computers can offer definitions of words in a foreign language. Why might the task of designing a "translating machine" be a complicated one (i.e., why can't you use the computer's massive memory to simply match each foreign word with the appropriate English word)? What does the complexity of translation suggest about the nature of knowledge?

LEARNING NEW PARADIGMS

How do people learn new paradigms, such as neoclassical, institutionalist, or Marxist economics? That is, how do people learn to see and to think in new and distinctive ways? The answer to this question will tell us a lot about the logic and structure of your macro textbook.

The goal of introductory economics classes is frequently stated as "to teach students to think like economists" (read, neoclassical economists). This means teaching students to approach economic questions in a certain way, to think within a particular conceptual framework, and *not* to think like a historian, an anthropologist, or a non-neoclassical economist. In other words, *the goal of your textbook is to initiate you into the neoclassical paradigm.*

Learning a paradigm involves learning abstract principles and concrete examples of their application, what Thomas Kuhn calls "shared exemplars." Kuhn notes that by studying a series of examples, students learn to see new problems as variants of these previously solved problems. Thus, learning a paradigm can be said to involve learning to draw the *appropriate analogies,* to highlight *certain* characteristics of two situations and to suppress others. In teaching neoclassical economics, introductory texts teach students what to attend to, and what to ignore, in economic analysis; what questions to ask, and what questions to suppress.[4]

Teaching a paradigm resembles sharing a worldview. The goal is to construct a context within which certain "stories" can be told, knowing that the audience will fill in the gaps with expected background. The capacity to draw appropriate analogies and supply the necessary background is sometimes called "tacit knowledge."

Your textbook is designed to cultivate that knowledge, by the topics selected for discussion, by the examples offered, and even by the jokes shared in the text and in class. All are geared toward teaching you how to fit a multidimensional reality into the boxes offered by neoclassical economics. This chiseling of the world into a paradigmatic narrative is attempted by *all* paradigms and is not a flaw in the neoclassical approach. In order to study reality, we must simplify it and look at it from some angle. Paradigm debates are about what simplifications and angles of vision to use, not about whether to use simplifications.

In criticizing the angle of vision offered in your textbook we will critique all of the techniques by which your text constructs the neoclassical paradigm. In particular:

1. We will criticize the abstract principles the text explicitly offers for analyzing economic activity.
2. We will dissect the text's "shared exemplars" and try to show why these examples may miss fundamental aspects of the topics they claim to illuminate.

3. We will examine the system of analogy that the text tries to develop and we will attempt to show why the "shared exemplars" may not generate fertile offspring even when they are helpful for thinking about their original problem.
4. We will draw attention to the questions ignored and subjects suppressed in economics by the adoption of a neoclassical perspective.
5. We will critique the language and metaphors used by the textbook to conform discussion to neoclassical ways of thinking.

In sum, we will critique the "tacit assumptions" underlying neoclassical analysis and its basic framework. We will try to problematize the arguments your textbook tries to naturalize by suggesting alternatives to what the text portrays as the natural way to see the world. We will give special attention to the stories and imagery conjured up by neoclassical language, for as McCloskey notes (quoting Rorty), "'It is pictures rather than propositions, metaphors rather than statements, which determine most of our philosophical [and economic] [*and economic* in McCloskey] convictions'" (McCloskey 1985, 75).

CONCLUSION: SOME IMPLICATIONS OF A PARADIGMATIC THEORY OF KNOWLEDGE FOR SOCIAL SCIENCE AND ECONOMICS

Centrality of Paradigms to Research Results

The paradigmatic model of knowledge emphasizes the impact of conceptual frameworks on research findings. It recommends focusing carefully on the basic assumptions that define a paradigm's organization of inquiry. Because these assumptions are frequently taken for granted and only "tacitly" acknowledged, it is often difficult to realize the limitations of the frame of reference one is learning. This book tries to remind you of the limitations of the glasses you put on whenever you look at the world like a conventional neoclassical economist.

Distinguishing Between Inter- and Intra-Paradigm Debates

The paradigmatic framework also suggests that it is very helpful to distinguish between inter- and intra-paradigm debates. Debates between members of the same paradigm (intra-paradigm debates) are much more easily resolved by empirical data because the participants are wearing the same glasses and asking similar questions. Inter-paradigm debates are frequently mired in confusion. It is often as if an accountant asked a poet which is larger, the letter "k" or the number "6."

Indeterminacy of Paradigm Debates

Because proponents of different paradigms epicycle within their own conceptual frameworks, it is difficult to resolve paradigm debates. This problem is confounded by the fact that each paradigm tends to define what the important issues are a bit differently, so what appears a devastating gap to one observer may be an acceptable anomaly to another.

Pedagogical Implications

The paradigmatic framework has interesting implications for how people learn new ideas. It envisions a two-step process. Any new paradigm must initially be learned within the language and categories of an old paradigm. This is inevitably unsatisfying as some of the categories of the new paradigm do not really fit in the existing paradigm's categories. Eventually, after enough of the new paradigm has been absorbed, however imperfectly, within the categories of the old paradigm, a paradigm shift can occur. The new ideas are reconfigured in line with their own logic. This reorganization is often characterized as the "A-ha!" experience, and represents a gestalt shift. It is an exciting moment. I hope you experience it as you study heterodox economics.

FINAL QUESTIONS FOR DISCUSSION

1. For each of the blank slate characterizations listed below offer a paradigmatic alternative and explain your reasoning.

   Table 1.1

   Competing Theories of Knowledge

Category	Blank Slate Concept	Paradigmatic Alternative
Nature of observation	Descriptive	
Nature of language	Neutral medium	
Nature of "the knower"	Passive	
Nature of truth	Objective, universal	

2. Evaluate the statements below from a paradigmatic perspective.
   a. "We all agree on the important questions in economics, but different paradigms come up with different answers to these questions."
   b. "While the examples of economic reasoning in introductory texts are helpful in introducing students to economic ideas, the neoclassical paradigm could be conveyed entirely by detailing its abstract principles."
3. According to Kuhn, why would the world appear "a bloomin' buzzin' confusion" without paradigms (Kuhn 1970, 13)? Why might a scientific revolution be described as "picking up the other end of the stick" (Kuhn 1970, 85)?
4. Explain what Kuhn means in the following quote from *The Structure of Scientific Revolutions.*

   [O]ne of the things a scientific community acquires with a paradigm is a criterion for choosing problems that, while the paradigm is taken for granted, can be assumed to have solutions. To a great extent these are the only problems that the community will admit as scientific or encourage its members to undertake. Other problems, including many that had previously been standard, are rejected as metaphysical, as the concern of another discipline, or sometimes as just too problematic to be worth the time. A paradigm can, for that matter, even insulate the community from those socially important problems that are not reducible to the puzzle form, because they cannot be stated in terms of the conceptual and instrumental tools the paradigm supplies (Kuhn 1970, 37).

5. Put on blank slate glasses and review your answers to questions 1–3. What problems do you see with the paradigmatic viewpoint?

NOTES

1. A gestalt is an interconnected context that tends to define its parts in a cross-referenced way. Loosely used, the term implies an integrated way of seeing, akin to a worldview.

2. In contrast, because of the dominance of the neoclassical paradigm in contemporary economics, all heterodox economists must take the time to become fluent in its language. This gives heterodox thinkers a bilingual perspective that can leave them more open to new ideas than neoclassical economists.

3. I have had several interesting experiences telling this riddle. On one occasion one of my male students repeated the riddle back to me to make sure he understood it. When he came to the end of the riddle the young man said, "And the doctor walks in and he says I can't operate that's my son." I indicated that he had the riddle just about right, but not exactly right, and repeated the story with the correct phrasing at the end ("And the doctor walks in and says I can't operate that's my son." The student could not identify the difference between our renditions of the riddle. I narrowed the focus to the last phrase, but the student remained unable to hear my description without inserting the word "he" in his reproduction. It was a powerful example of the impact of preconceived notions on the data attended to.

About twenty years ago I told the riddle to two female medical students. They did not include the boy's mother in their answer. One can speculate about what this implied about their medical school's treatment of women.

The fluctuations in student responses to the riddle over the last twenty years are interesting. For the first five to ten years the percentage including "the doctor is the boy's mother" grew, peaking at a little more than half. More recently the number has been falling.

4. McCloskey (1985) offers a helpful discussion of the impact of paradigms on economic reasoning in her analysis of the role of metaphors and analogy in economics. She writes (quoting from Perelman and Olbrechts-Tyteca), "'the acceptance of an analogy . . . is often equivalent to a judgment as to the importance of the characteristics that the analogy brings to the fore'" (82–83). She thusly analyzes Gary Becker's characterization of children as durable goods, like refrigerators. "A beginning at literal translation would say, 'A child is costly to acquire initially, lasts for a long time, gives flows of pleasure during that time, is expensive to maintain and repair, has an imperfect second-hand market. . . . the list of similarities could be extended further and further, gradually revealing the differences as well . . .'" (McCloskey 1985, 76–77).

While no neoclassical economist would equate a refrigerator with a child, the paradigm does assert the priority of that metaphor over, for example, the metaphor of a child as a "Thou" in Martin Buber's language, a presence with which people can have "human" as opposed to "object" relations. What neoclassical theory does with its metaphors, models, and analogies is to give priority to thinking about the world in a particular way. Students and other potential users of economic paradigms have to decide whether the language and categories of neoclassical theory are an adequate framework for organizing analysis of the economy. Heterodox economists find the language lacking.

THINKING DIFFERENTLY

Neoclassical Versus Heterodox Economics

TEXTS, SUBTEXTS, AND BASIC ORIENTATIONS

> *The best kept secret in economics is that economics is about the study of capitalism.*
> —Robert Heilbroner (quoted in Palley 1998, 15)

> *I use the concept "elite folk science" to explain how a discipline can have functions other than those of the increase of positive knowledge. . . . Such other functions can be in the ideological sphere, providing reassurance for a general world view. . . . Mainstream academic economics has . . . flourished in recent decades largely as such an elite folk science.*
> —Jerry Ravetz (1995, 165)

> *Part of this [ideological] service [of economics] consists in instructing several hundred thousand students each year. Although gravely inefficient this instruction implants an imprecise but still serviceable set of ideas in the minds of many and perhaps most of those who are exposed to it. They are led to accept what they might otherwise criticize; critical inclinations which might be brought to bear on economic life are diverted to other and more benign fields. And there is great immediate effect on those who presume to guide and speak on economic matters. Although the accepted image of economic society is not the reality, it is what is available. As such it serves as a surrogate for the reality for legislators, civil servants, journalists, television commentators, professional prophets—all, indeed, who must speak, write or act on economic questions.*
> —John Kenneth Galbraith (1973, 7)

INTRODUCTION AND CHAPTER OVERVIEW

This chapter outlines the most basic differences between heterodox and neoclassical economists over how to study economics. It describes the different "theoretical spectacles" each group uses to view the economy. It introduces in general or abstract terms several key objections to neoclassical economics that will be elaborated in later chapters through concrete examples.

Chapter 2 is divided into five sections. This first section (Introduction) outlines the chapter. The second section (Well-Being) explores the different conceptions of successful economic performance organizing neoclassical and heterodox analysis. The third section (Implied Readers) contrasts the different vantage points used by neoclassical and heterodox economics for viewing the economy. The fourth section (Methodological Individualism [MI] vs. Holism [H]) explores one of the great divides in social science, linking neoclassical theory to "methodologically individualistic" explanations for societal outcomes and heterodox economics to "holist" explanations of societal outcomes. The concluding section (Texts and Subtexts in Economics) ties many of the above topics together, contrasting the different philosophical assumptions and practical agendas animating neoclassical and heterodox economics.

WELL-BEING

Some of the key differences between neoclassical and heterodox subtexts are related to different conceptions of well-being. Most neoclassical textbooks devote little attention to analyzing the nature and causes of human well-being. They strongly imply, however, that there is a close positive correlation between gross domestic product (GDP), or output, and national well-being. Although most texts briefly acknowledge that several factors might complicate the link between output and well-being, they spend little time exploring these complexities.

Most heterodox economists find the link between economic growth and well-being more complicated than implied in neoclassical texts. They urge more attention to issues of well-being in introductory courses in order to clarify what we might want from the economy and how we might get it.

Economist Richard Easterlin's work is very interesting in this area. He notes that over the last fifty years numerous surveys about human happiness have reported surprisingly similar results. They have usually found that within a society the rich are, on average, happier than the poor, but richer societies are not happier than poorer societies. Easterlin reports that

1. In the United States since World War II, real per capita income [i.e., income adjusted for inflation] has more than doubled. The average level of happiness, however, is the same today as it was in the late 1940s.
2. The story is similar for Europe. There are nine European countries for which happiness-type measures go back at least two decades. Between the 1970s and 1990s real income per capita rises substantially in all of these countries, by amounts ranging from 25 to 50 percent. In five of the nine countries, happiness is unchanged; in two it goes up, and, in two, it goes down. Net change in happiness for all nine countries: zero.
3. The experience of Japan is of special interest. . . . Between the 1950s and late 1980s Japan had the most phenomenal economic growth ever witnessed. Consumer durables, like refrigerators, washing machines, and TVs, were virtually nonexistent at the start of the period; by the end, almost every household had them. Car ownership rose from 1 to 60 percent of households. In only three decades real income per capita multiplied by an incredible *five-fold*. What happened to happiness during this period of unparalleled income growth? The answer is, no change (Easterlin 2000, p. 5).

The implications of Easterlin's research are largely ignored by neoclassical economists and standard textbooks. Many heterodox economists, however, have tried to explain Easterlin's paradox of happiness, often using the concept of "positional goods." Positional goods are goods whose value includes a significant status effect, such as a diamond ring or a college degree from a "better than average" college. As a society becomes more affluent, it appears that positional goods make up an increasing percentage of consumption.

The problem with positional goods from the point of view of maximizing well-being is that they undermine the wisdom of the invisible hand. Rather than *increasing* human happiness, producing more elaborate positional goods may simply increase the level of expenditure necessary to achieve the *same* social status. To the extent that individuals use real resources (hours of labor, lost leisure, barrels of oil) to acquire positional goods, it is possible for well-being to even decline as output rises. To the extent that positional competition influences economic behavior, national output (GDP) statistics will tend to overrate the payoffs to increased economic growth.

Easterlin (2003) notes that "(t)he reason preferences are excluded from policy consideration by mainstream economics is because each individual is assumed to be the best judge of his or her own interests. But if individuals are making decisions in ignorance of the effect that . . . social comparison will have on their aspirations, this assumption no longer holds. Once it is recognized that individuals are unaware of some of the forces shaping their choices, it can no longer be argued that they will successfully maximize their well-being. It is, perhaps, time to recognize that serious attention is needed to devising measures that may contribute to more informed preferences" (11, 182).

Echoing Easterlin, heterodox economists call for increased attention to the implications of positional competition in economics courses. Heterodox economists also argue that introductory textbooks should give increased attention to several components of economic well-being currently overshadowed by the texts' preoccupation with GDP statistics. Among these economic outcomes are an economy's sustainability, quality of work life, level of economic security, and degree of inequality.

Heterodox economists also call for greater attention in the textbooks to the implications of macroeconomic outcomes for various social and cultural goals, such as the maintenance of democracy and the nurturing of community. The impact of economic outcomes on these social phenomena can be considered a "meta-externality." The word *externality* implies that these impacts are not considered by economic agents when they buy or sell goods and services. The impacts are accidental byproducts or unintended consequences of actions taken for other reasons. The prefix "meta" implies that these consequences can affect the broad contours of societal life.

Because these outcomes are not included in the decisions made by economic agents, there is no reason to expect that market outcomes will automatically produce optimal results. Heterodox economics recommends that economic theory and economic policy analyze and respond to meta-externalities. Exploring these issues tends to expand the potential area for social governance of the economy and is at odds with the "let the market work" perspective often favored in standard texts.

In sum, heterodox economists want introductory economics classes to pursue a much more complicated image of the bases for societal well-being than is offered in most introductory textbooks. We will return to issues of well-being in much more detail in chapter 7 when we discuss neoclassical texts' treatment of GDP statistics and other measures of economic activity.

IMPLIED READERS

Another way of trying to think about the differences between neoclassical and heterodox economics and the projects that motivate their respective textbooks is to ask: Who is the implied reader for each text and from what angle is this reader viewing the economy? Neoclassical texts imply that the viewer has no particular vantage point, that the viewer is everyone and anyone. Heterodox critiques often disagree, finding that the assumed reader for most neoclassical texts is a person in one of two roles—that of a *consumer* (shopping) or a *manager* (organizing and supervising the labor of others).

The consumer focus is reflected in standard texts' penchant for illustrations involving retail choices. The typical economic experience in these texts occurs in the department store rather than on the shop floor. What is missing is attention to the experience of people on the assembly line or behind the counter. This is significant because, although people frequently experience choice and relative autonomy in consumption, they often experience subordination in the workplace. By drawing their examples from one realm of people's experience but not the other, the textbook picture of the economy highlights autonomy and downplays subordination.

When the world of work does enter the textbook, it is mainly from the perspective of *employers* rather than *employees*. This is consistent with neoclassical economics' treatment of management as the medium through which market forces operate. From the perspective of management, labor is an input to production, like steel or electricity. From the employee's perspective, however, labor is a lived experience. By viewing work predominantly from only one of these perspectives we lose important information.

The presumed reader is also often male. The signs here are more subtle and I invite you to search for them. One key piece of evidence is the subject matter. The following topics, for example, receive very little coverage in a typical macroeconomics textbook: the impact of macroeconomic outcomes on the household economy and human capital formation (e.g., children's education); the economic contribution of people (usually women) who make organizations work (from families to corporations) by knitting together social relationships; the role of altruism, as opposed to narrow self-interest, in economic life; and the economics of elder care. These activities, which are responsible for a significant chunk of any economy's output and quality of life, are dwarfed in most introductory textbooks by the discussion of topics like corporate finance, foreign trade, and the auto industry.

In drawing attention to these discrepancies, the point is not that the latter topics do not belong in an introductory economics course, but that the former do as well. The point is not that women are not interested in the topics included in standard textbooks, but that other areas of economic life, frequently related to women's experience, are being neglected and devalued. The point is not that people don't often act out of self-interest, but that this is an incomplete organizing principle for understanding economic action.

Heterodox texts tend to add perspectives, such as those derived from women's and workers' experience, to the narrower habits of view offered in neoclassical texts. I invite you to keep track of the topics covered in your textbook and to judge for yourself whether it looks at the economy from as universal a position as it claims.[1]

METHODOLOGICAL INDIVIDUALISM (MI) VERSUS HOLISM (H)

Introduction

Many famous thinkers of the mid-twentieth century (such as the eminent economist John Maynard Keynes[2] and the psychologist Abraham Maslow) predicted that once the economy had satisfied people's basic needs for commodities, human energies would shift from materialist agendas to "higher needs." Futurists foresaw shorter work weeks and increased leisure time for projects oriented toward "self-actualization," inter-personal relationships, and learning. But this predicted shift has not occurred. In fact, the focus on acquiring income to purchase more commodities has if anything accelerated with affluence. From 1973 to 2000, for example, despite nearly a doubling in labor productivity, the number of hours worked by the average American increased by about five weeks per year (de Graaf 2003).[3] The material standard of living deemed minimally acceptable has constantly escalated.

Why has this occurred? Is it likely to continue? Do the answers lie in the nature of human nature or elsewhere, perhaps in the nature of society? The holist methodologies of heterodox economics invite this question, as well as attention to the broader issue of where tastes and preferences come from. The methodologically individualistic approach of neoclassical economics, on the other hand, discourages this question and rules out inquiry into the origins of tastes and preferences.

The difference between holist (H) and methodologically individualistic (MI) approaches to economics is one of the most important methodological distinctions for many heterodox critiques of neoclassical economics.[4] It is either not discussed at all in neoclassical texts or briefly alluded to in a manner that treats the MI perspective as an objective, paradigm-free view of the world. On the simplest and most practical level, the distinction bears a resemblance to the "nature-nurture" debate over the origins of human behavior. Holists tend to come down on the nurture side and MI theorists on the nature side. While this analogy is a reasonable entry point for talking about the H/MI distinction, the issues involved are more subtle.

Methodological Individualism (MI)

Because the MI position is more familiar to most people, we will look at it first. Methodological individualism refers to an approach to studying and explaining societal outcomes. It should not be confused with the colloquial meaning of "individualism" and value judgments about the merits of nonconformist behavior.

MI theorists conceive of society as composed of units akin to atoms. The atoms are individuals. In order to understand societal outcomes, social scientists are directed to study and explain individual behavior. Societal outcomes are portrayed as nothing more than the aggregation of these behaviors. As former British prime minister Margaret Thatcher put it, "there is no such thing as society. There are individual men and women, and there are families."[5] At first glance this seems like a commonsense strategy, a truism that no one could disagree with, and this is largely the way the approach is portrayed in neoclassical texts. We will see shortly why the issue is more complicated and paradigmatic.

Although it is not logically necessary for MI theory, most MI economists tend to think of individuals as the bearers of a human nature that leads them to try to maximize their isolated self-interest in a rational way. But how do people decide what is in their best interest and how to protect that interest? A key aspect of MI economics is an extreme reluctance to reflect upon what is responsible for individuals' definitions of their self-interest, their conception of appropriate ways to pursue that interest, and their ways of understanding the world and processing information.

Neoclassical economists attempt to model economic behavior as a "maximization subject to constraint" decision. People are said to maximize "utility" (a fancy word for happiness) given their tastes and preferences and available options. Where a person's tastes and preferences come from (for example, *why* someone likes Coca Cola or whole wheat bread) is not deemed part of economics. I would be surprised, for example, if there are more than five pages out of five hundred in your textbook on the topic of marketing.

For MI theory to work best, individuals have to be born whole, with their tastes and preferences intact—like Athena leaping out of Zeus's head in Greek mythology or Hobbes's mushroom

Figure 2.1   **Methodologically Individualistic vs. Holist Metaphors**

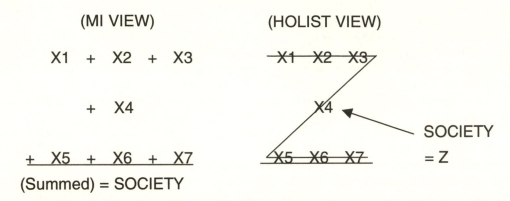

men who spring up overnight from the earth.[6] Once you allow the individual to be at least partially socially constructed, that is, to be partially a product of a particular social context, MI theory is an insufficient methodology for understanding the world.[7]

Metaphorically one can illustrate the MI view of the world by the left half of Figure 2.1, where each of the X's represents a different individual.

From an MI perspective, what the discipline of economics studies is how markets "add up" these individual maximizing choices. Other social sciences (for example, political science) look at how other mechanisms (such as the electoral process) aggregate maximizing choices.

Holism (H) (or Holist Structuralism [HS])

Instead of beginning with a focus on the "natural" or "given" individual, holism begins with a focus on the social structure (or structures) of society, or the implicit Z in the right half of Figure 2.1.[8] The basic idea of holist theory is that social wholes need to be studied as structured entities (particular kinds of societies or kinds of economies or kinds of families, etc.), rather than as aggregations of a priori individuals. The key claim is that there is a "coherence" or structure at a higher level of integration than the individual that reproduces itself over time. The process of reproduction is not akin to photocopying. Social structures do not produce exact copies of themselves; they evolve and change. They persist, however, as organized contexts for human action. Explaining societal outcomes requires an understanding of the logic of experience induced by social structures as well as an exploration of how particular individuals act and react within these structures.[9]

Although holism may seem to be a very hard concept to grasp formally, it is analogous to more intuitive notions about the persistence of "American culture" or the endurance of an institution such as the Catholic Church. The claim is that there is a cluster of social roles, institutions, and beliefs that evolve collectively over time. This cluster creates the context within which individuals experience the world. It also creates the incentive structures, organizational vehicles, opportunities for group action, distributions of power, and so forth that bring about change in the world.[10]

A holist approach to social theory (to explaining societal events) suggests a different view of the individual than an MI perspective does. Rather than conceiving of society as composed of individuals who exist prior to society and come together to form it (left picture in Figure 2.1), in holist theory the individual is thought of as a participant in a social system (the components of the Z in the right picture). Individuals are born into a way of life (the Z) and participate in the world through a shared language, in both a literal sense (they learn to speak their native tongue) and a figurative sense (they learn the language of local experience and culture). They are concurrent with, rather than prior to, society. Individuals may take adversarial nonconforming positions toward their culture, family, traditions, and so on, but they do so in a socialized or historically specific way.

To understand events from a holist perspective, it is necessary to study the logic of a social system. And to study *economics* from a holist perspective, it is necessary to study the logic of American society as an industrial society, and/or a capitalist society, and/or any combination of other organizing categories (patriarchal, secular, etc.) that illuminate economic behavior. This strategy tends to put the big questions in social theory back on the agenda for economics classes, questions such as: Why is there massive inequality in the world and in the U.S. economy? How can we develop lifestyles and an economy that are sustainable and protect the environment? What is the relationship between economic growth and human happiness? And why has the division of labor tended to concentrate women's work in certain jobs and household tasks?

Although aspects of these topics are sometimes briefly discussed in neoclassical introductory texts, the larger questions are generally pushed aside. Most students soon give up asking big questions. This commentary encourages you to keep these questions alive.

Holist theory also tends to encourage situating issues in a historical context. MI theory asks, "How can we understand economic outcomes as the result of maximizing decisions by given individuals in given circumstances?" Holist theory asks, "What were the historical circumstances that led these individuals to make the particular economic decisions that they did?" In fact, one tip-off as to whether your text favors an MI or a holist perspective is the amount of historical discussion in the text. If less than 10 percent of the text is historical, it is probably not a holist text.

If you are like most Americans you are less interested in history than you are in current issues. However, what holism suggests, and what I will try to convince you of in this text, is that if you want to understand current issues (including economic issues), you must study history. This is because it is largely through history that you can get an understanding of the dynamic motion of a social system. You need to view things over time in order to perceive the logics of change.

TEXTS AND SUBTEXTS IN ECONOMICS

A "subtext" is a book's underlying message and guidance for human action. Subtexts are what animate economics books, transforming the lifeless logic of cause and effect into a kind of practical and moral calculus for human action.

Economic subtexts are built upon tacit and unprovable assumptions about how the world works (such as assumptions about human nature) and reflect beliefs about the kinds of questions and projects that are important for economists to work on. Subtexts influence what topics are covered in introductory texts and how complex ideas are simplified to make them accessible to beginning students. Many simplifying (but unrealistic) assumptions are tolerated in introductory textbooks as long as the analysis gets the "fundamental" story "correct." What counts as "fundamental" and "correct," of course, is a paradigmatic judgment and usually echoes a paradigm's subtexts.

Subtexts are rarely stated explicitly. You have to tease them out of a book's structure, its rhetoric, and its pattern of examples. Heterodox and neoclassical textbooks are usually animated by very different subtexts, as the two sample lists below demonstrate. As the term progresses, you should try to determine what subtexts animate your own textbook as well as this commentary.

Illustrative Neoclassical Subtexts

Most neoclassical introductory textbooks (also called "principles" texts) include some or all of the following subtexts:

(i)   *On Epistemology* (the nature of knowledge): Neoclassical economics is a scientific theory with claims on belief similar to modern physics.

(ii) *On Ontology* (the nature of being): There is no independent entity called society. There are only individuals. Economics needs to study how individuals make choices and how various institutions like markets add them up.

(iii) *On Human Nature:* Most people have insatiable consumer appetites, reflecting human nature. Markets permit the harnessing of self-interest in the service of the common good. Capitalism is successful, in part, because it offers an incentive system that builds on "human nature."

(iv) *On the Contribution of Economic Theory to Human Well-Being:* The purpose of economic theory is to promote economic efficiency and economic growth, as both provide a basis for human happiness and the solution to many of our social problems. Many troubling aspects of market outcomes, such as inequality or concentrated economic power, are tolerable because of their contribution to economic growth.

(v)   *On Markets:* Market outcomes reflect free choice and produce outcomes that make all parties in an exchange better off. Markets are generally self-regulating. They automatically find the price that equates supply and demand and spur institutional innovation when social changes are needed for economic expansion.

(vi) *On Socioeconomic Choices:* TINA (There Is No Alternative [to capitalism]). The failure of the former Soviet Union implies that socialism, totalitarian or democratic, and other attempts at more egalitarian and planned economies cannot work. The message of the twentieth century is "let (capitalist) markets work." The burden is on the government to justify any "intervention" in the market.

You may agree or disagree with these claims. For the moment, that is not the issue. What is important is to realize that there are two threads weaving through your textbook; one is explicit and usually involves the appearance of formal reasoning. The second is informal and involves a chain of subtexts like those listed above. The latter claims are not explicitly argued. They are asserted indirectly through asides and anecdotes and the kinds of examples that are chosen to illustrate analytic points. They are present in the texts' near silences on certain subjects as well as the texts' repeated pronouncements on others. The subtexts are sometimes qualified, but there is a tendency to "note but ignore" these qualifications.

The fact that your textbook is animated by subtexts is not in itself nefarious. Most intellectual work in any field is motivated by a belief that the ideas pursued are worth knowing. Subtexts provide the context for knowing, that is, they provide a backdrop that situates the knowledge in relationship to the projects it is intended to facilitate (i.e., they show how the knowledge might be used). In this sense, *neoclassical economics both studies and celebrates markets. It is designed to reveal the wisdom of markets and to make them work better.* There is a tendency to view what "is" as what "ought to be." Simply put, the primary subtext of neoclassical textbooks is that most of the time *markets optimize*.

Illustrative Heterodox Subtexts

Let us now look at some alternative subtexts found in heterodox economic writings:

(i) *On Epistemology:* Economic analysis is paradigmatic. It contains much more "subjective" or "stylized" content[11] than is acknowledged in neoclassical texts. If you are uncomfortable with a conclusion that rests on textbook economic theory, it may be productive to think about the broader assumptions that underlie the textbook's analysis of the issue and whether these assumptions are appropriate.

(ii) *On Ontology:* Economic analysis cannot be limited to studying individual behavior because there are logics to individual behavior that are generated at the societal level. Hence, economic analysis needs to be situated within a broader analysis of the relevant social system; in America that social system is modern capitalism.

(iii) *On Human Nature:* There is less "natural" individual behavior and more socially constructed behavior involved in economic activities than is often suggested by neoclassical theory.

(iv) *On the Contribution of Economics and Economic Growth to Human Well-Being:* The link between economic growth and human well-being is much more complicated than is implied in neoclassical textbooks and this link has weakened considerably in the advanced economies. Equity and environmental concerns, as well as the nature of the nonmarket economy (for example, the household economy) deserve increased attention in economic analysis and are often mistakenly devalued in relationship to market efficiency and growth concerns in neoclassical introductory texts.

(v) *On Markets:* While extremely useful social institutions, markets cannot meet the full range of human needs. Markets offer both "free" and "coerced" choice,[12] and have dysfunctional as well as self-regulating moments. A good society needs to reflect more carefully on the areas within which markets should and should not organize human activity than is generally invited by textbook economics.

(vi) *On Socioeconomic Choices:* Capitalist economies need to be embedded in a system of social governance to meet human needs (and for a subset of heterodox theorists: alternatives to capitalism need to be explored).

There are, of course, some variations in subtexts across neoclassical and heterodox textbooks. There are also additional subtexts in principles books besides those listed above. Nevertheless, the aforementioned examples should be sufficient to suggest why the competing subtexts of neoclassical and heterodox economics generate a different agenda for introductory textbooks.

STUDY QUESTIONS

Review Questions

1. Happiness surveys appear to indicate that at any given moment in time those with higher income, on average, report higher levels of happiness than those with lower income. Over time, however, as societies increase their real (inflation adjusted) per capita in-

come, average happiness does not appear to rise. What explanations have been given for this seemingly odd combination of outcomes? What kind of policy implications might be drawn from these results?

2. Explain the basic difference between methodologically individualistic and holist social science. What extra questions and subject matter do holist approaches to social science put on the agenda for economic inquiry?
3. What is a subtext? According to heterodox economists, how do subtexts influence economic theories and economic textbooks?
4. Compare and contrast orthodox and heterodox subtexts from a heterodox perspective.

Discussion Questions

1. If you were going to devise an index to measure economic well-being in order to guide economic policy making, what phenomena would you include in the measure? Why?
2. There are many more women athletes in the classes that I teach now than there were in the classes that I took as a student many years ago. Speculate on the kinds of differences that might distinguish methodologically individualist from holist structuralist approaches to researching and explaining the increase in women's athletics.
3. Do you think it is possible to resolve the debate over whether holism or methodological individualism is a better way to study economics by appeal to empirical data? Why or why not?
4. Explain what Gunnar Myrdal (winner of the Nobel Prize in Economics in 1974) means in the quote below. Try to illustrate his claim with specific examples. Discuss what you think are the strengths and weaknesses of this perspective.

Valuations are always with us. Disinterested research there has never been and can never be. Prior to answers there must be questions. There can be no view except from a viewpoint. In the questions raised and the viewpoint chosen, valuations are implied. Our valuations determine our approaches to a problem, the definition of our concepts, the choice of models, the selection of observations, the presentations of our conclusions—in fact the whole pursuit of a study from beginning to end. (Myrdal 1978, pp. 778–79)

5. Criticize Myrdal's remarks from a "blank slate" (tabula rasa) perspective.

NOTES

1. Oddly, drawing attention to the particularized perspective found in standard economics texts is sometimes perceived as "politicizing" economics, while de-emphasizing women's experience or that of workers is seen as "normal." Part of the power of ideology is its capacity to define what constitutes polite conversation and what are legitimate topics for academic inquiry.

2. See, for example, "Economic Possibilities for Our Grandchildren" in *Essays in Persuasion* (Keynes [1931] 1963).

3. See Schor 1991 (especially pp. 28–32) for a detailed analysis of working hours for the period 1969–1987. Schor finds that the average employed man worked about two and one half weeks longer in 1987 than 1969, while the average employed woman added an extra seven and a half weeks to her working year (Schor 1991, 29).

4. Holism is central to Marxist and radical economics, and an important part of many, but not all, institutionalist, feminist, Post Keynesian, and ecological economic analyses. Most recently, "complexity theory" has emerged as a new framework for developing holist analysis. See, for example, O'Hara 2003b.

5. Brian Deer web site, http://briandeer.com/social/thatcher-society.htm.

6. Image borrowed from Barker and Feiner 2004, 5.

7. Some neoclassical economists, such as Nobel Prize winner Douglass North, have tried to test the limits of methodological individualism by trying to derive institutional arrangements, social norms, and other cultural practices in a methodologically individualist way. Although these efforts seem to me deeply flawed, they did produce some interesting ideas. For students interested in studying economic history from an MI perspective, I would recommend reading North's *Structure and Change in Economic History*. For a holist analysis of similar historical issues see Perry Anderson's *Passages from Antiquity to Feudalism*. For a brief summary of heterodox objections to methodological individualism see Geoffrey Hodgson's "Behind Methodological Individualism" (Hodgson 1986).

8. "Social structure" is a concept absent in MI theory or discourse. The absence can be analogized to the absence of the concept of the unconscious in many pre-Freudian theories of behavior, or the absence of the idea of a divine being in most economic discussions. The implicit justification for the absence of these concepts in various discourses is that they are either confused concepts or irrelevant to the topics considered (i.e., the conclusions reached without attention to these categories are true, regardless of the merits of thinking about the excluded topics). In other words, to draw a religious example, there may or may not be a God, but according to modern economic theory one need not think about that question to explain economic outcomes.

9. The attempt to explain complex entities by breaking them down into their component parts is often called reductionism. Holism challenges the reductionist project and asserts the need to study the whole at the level of the whole as well as in terms of its parts. As Geoffrey Hodgson (1986) has observed, it is not enough to argue that the whole is more than the sum of its parts, implying that when you put things together you get an outcome that is qualitatively different from the parts by themselves. The key claim is that the whole is infused in and constitutive of the parts. See also Wilber and Harrison (1978).

Different heterodox approaches develop this concept in different ways. In Marxist theory, for example, the concept of dialectics is introduced to explain the relationship between the whole and its parts. Institutional economics uses many evolutionary metaphors and the image of cumulative causation. Each heterodox paradigm generally has its own vocabulary and metaphors for asserting a holist perspective.

10. This need not imply a determinist view of history. Within any conjuncture, more than one outcome may be possible. What actually happens may depend upon the idiosyncrasies of individual actions and agency. The approach does imply, however, that historical contexts limit possible outcomes. American society is not likely to become a feudal society tomorrow or a variant of Japanese or Egyptian society.

11. By subjective or stylized content I mean thinking that is dependent upon posing issues in a particular way.

12. By "coerced choice" I mean decisions that are formally free, like the decision to seek wage labor, but are practically imposed by a lack of alternatives. Having become an employee, many individuals find significant limitations on their personal freedom, from the minor constraints of corporate dress codes, to the more burdensome detailed organization of one's working day, to the imposition of forced overtime. Similarly, many business leaders may find they are unable to avoid polluting the environment if competitors are already doing so.

COMPETING ASSUMPTIONS, METHODS, AND METAPHORS

The composition of this book has been for the author a long struggle of escape, and so must the reading of it be for most readers . . . a struggle of escape from habitual modes of thought and expression. The ideas which are here expressed so laboriously are extremely simple and should be obvious. The difficulty lies, not in the new ideas, but in escaping from the old ones, which ramify, for those brought up as most of us have been, into every corner of our minds.
—John Maynard Keynes ([1936] 1964, viii)

INTRODUCTION

In chapter 2 we outlined some of the most basic differences between neoclassical and heterodox economic analysis, such as the difference between "holist" and "methodologically individualistic" social science. In this chapter we compare the two approaches to economics along some additional dimensions. The first section (Methodological Critiques) develops additional heterodox concerns about the approach taken to economic analysis in standard textbooks. Section two (Threads) illustrates how heterodox thinking applies to three selected topics (distributional, gender, and environmental issues) that will receive special attention in many chapters of this book. Section three (Telling Other Stories) illustrates how heterodox economists critique the stories and metaphors, as well as the formal logic, used in neoclassical textbooks.

METHODOLOGICAL CRITIQUES

The discussion below briefly outlines a number of methodological debates between heterodox and textbook economics. It is intended to alert you to these issues, rather than fully elaborate them. We will explore the debates in much greater detail later in the text.

Heterodox Objections to Excessive Abstraction: The Fallacy of Misplaced Concreteness

Heterodox economists often criticize neoclassical textbooks for posing economic issues too abstractly, that is, for leaving out important institutional and contextual information. Most introductory textbooks, for example, ignore the difference between goods that are desired for their use value (like a warm coat) and goods that are desired for their status value (like expensive jewelry). The distinctiveness of ecological phenomena, such as the earth's climate system or species diversity, is similarly subsumed under more general categories like factors of production or consumer goods. This systematic loss of concrete information has been called the "fallacy of misplaced concreteness" by ecological economists Herman Daly and John B. Cobb.

Since all economic theory must simplify reality in order to analyze it (especially in introductory textbooks), the problem from a heterodox perspective is not that "details" are missing. Rather, the problem is that necessary information, information whose inclusion might alter the conceptual framework organizing the discussion, is absent.

Neoclassical economists contend that mathematical reasoning is a paramount sign of scientific rigor. In order to represent economic relationships mathematically, they argue, it is often necessary to abstract from contextual phenomena and treat a wide variety of cases as formally identical. Institutional information, they claim, can be added later after the basic economic relationships have been established rigorously and mathematically.

Heterodox economists find that the textbooks' stripped-down models, such as the aggregate supply and aggregate demand model that will be discussed later in the book, offer an illusion of rigor (bordering at times on rigor mortis). While not anti-mathematical, heterodox economists refuse to sacrifice an appropriate level of institutional specificity for the option of mathematical modeling.[1] Heterodoxy endorses a pluralism of methods in economics, ranging from detailed case studies to bare-bones mathematical models. Neoclassical theory tends to privilege mathematical models.

Heterodox Critiques of *Homo Economicus* ("Rational Economic Man" or REM)

Many heterodox economists criticize neoclassical textbooks for relying on an oversimplified picture of human beings. The textbooks' assumption of "rational economic man" (REM, or *homo economicus*) posits that all economic behavior reflects individuals' efforts to rationally pursue their preexisting desires. The textbooks portray individuals as isolated units of desire, programmed by *exogenous* and stable tastes and preferences. *Exogenous* in economics means something is taken as *given to* the economy. The variable or phenomenon is external to the economy and beyond economic analysis. Exogenous variables determine economic outcomes and are not determined by the economy.

Neoclassical economists often admit that real people are more complicated than their models suggest and that economic phenomena might influence some of the variables that the textbooks treat as exogenous. They argue, however, that adding such real-world complexities would not "fundamentally" change the analysis offered.

Heterodox economists disagree. They urge economics to adopt a richer image of human behavior, one that includes but is not limited to the REM model. They find the economic analysis and intellectual agendas facilitated by assuming "rational economic man" to be limiting and often misleading.

For example, heterodox economists ask: Why does "rational economic man" get caught time and again in speculative manias and financial panics? Why does rational economic man *purchase* cigarettes or repeatedly save insufficiently for a rainy day? Does not the well-being of other people enter into an individual's own sense of well-being, either negatively (as with the envy associated with "positional competition") or positively (as with displays of altruism and solidarity)? Where is *homo reciprocans* (the persona motivated by a sense of reciprocity in exchange) in economics? What is the role of culture and social convention in shaping individuals' responses to uncertainties? The distinctly different answers to these questions offered in heterodox and neo-classical textbooks suggest some of the objections to *homo economicus* that will be raised in later chapters.

Heterodox Objections to Neoclassical Theory's Treatment of Work and the Labor Process

There is a tendency in neoclassical textbooks to ignore the qualitative difference between human labor and other inputs to production in order to treat labor markets as analogous to other markets. While this lends neoclassical theory an appealing symmetry, it also invites Daly and Cobb's criticism of "misplaced concreteness." That is, it tends to confine or restrict discussions of "labor markets" to categories and issues that are also relevant for thinking about nonhuman "inputs to production." From a heterodox perspective, this misses a lot.

The organization of work has profound feedback effects on the rest of society. The particular kind of work people do, for example, partially structures their experiences and shapes their imaginations. Hence, while labor produces goods and services in neoclassical economics, it also produces "laborers" (doctors, assembly line workers, craft workers, teachers, soldiers, etc.) in heterodox economics. The economy's division of labor also influences the structure of many noneconomic institutions, such as schools and families, as well as the distribution of political and social power. Heterodox economists want to study these feedback effects in order to give public policy the opportunity to influence them.

Heterodox economists also stress the special "human contingencies" involved in labor markets. When firms buy other inputs, they automatically receive the services of those commodities. For example, if a factory purchases 100 gallons of oil, it knows precisely the amount of thermal energy it can expect to mobilize from the oil. When a firm hires workers, however, it buys "labor power" or "labor potential" rather than actual labor. The sensitivity of labor output to many sociological phenomena, such as the workers' sense of being treated fairly or unfairly, introduces all sorts of social conventions into labor market dynamics that do not apply when dealing with other kinds of inputs. These social conventions are consequential; they can divert market outcomes in significant ways from the results suggested by supply-and-demand models. The relative neglect of these conventions in standard textbooks has led to many gaps in the texts' discussion of wage determination and unemployment.

Heterodox Perspectives on How Markets Work

The next five methodological criticisms of neoclassical macro principles texts made by heterodox economists raise more technically oriented kinds of objections to standard textbook economics than the broad philosophical critiques discussed above. Pooled together these five objections imply that the automatically self-regulating, basically stable view of market economies that is projected in principles texts is an incomplete and at times misleading picture of the economy.

(1) Heterodox Objections to Perfect Information Assumptions

The first of these objections criticizes neoclassical introductory texts for generally assuming "perfect information" on the part of everyone in the economy. Consumers, for example, are always assumed to know exactly what they want to buy, as well as the price of all available alternatives. Firms are assumed to know all possible ways of producing their products, as well as the level of future demand for their products. Following a "note but ignore" rhetorical strategy, many neo-classical textbooks acknowledge that there is greater uncertainty in the real world. The textbooks imply, however, that models assuming perfect information can be used to analyze the economy with only a modest loss of accuracy.

Heterodox economists disagree, emphasizing that the neoclassical model works best when applied to the most trivial choices, such as daily decisions taken in relatively fixed circumstances involving short time horizons (for example, deciding which route to take from home to the office). The assumption of perfect information serves us badly, however, for modeling more important choices, such as what technology to invest in as a firm or what to major in as a student. In chapters 5 and 6 we will begin exploring how adding uncertainty to economic analysis changes the context and content of the analysis.

(2) Heterodox Objections to Static Formats of Analysis

Heterodox economists criticize neoclassical textbooks for relying excessively on "static" as opposed to "dynamic" analyses of economic activity. The difference between static and dynamic analysis is a little like the difference between a snapshot and a movie. If you have ever tried to learn a dance step from a series of still drawings, you have a sense of the limitations of static analysis.

The problem is that the drawings leave out key information about how to get from one position to another. If the drawings were based on an actual dance performance, the ambiguities accompanying the drawings might be frustrating for students trying to learn the dance, but the drawings would not necessarily misrepresent the dance. The problem could be more severe, however, if the drawings were based on a hypothetical performance, with dance positions drawn that seemed perfectly reasonable as discrete steps, but that did not work out as a continuous motion.

For example, imagine a dance that called for a 270-degree spin, followed by a step that required the dancer to balance on one leg. The drawings would show the dancer in three positions, before the spin, after the spin, and balanced on one leg. All three positions would represent reasonable moments in a dance. The fact that the momentum of the spin might make it impossible for the dancer to balance in the way represented by the third drawing would be missed in static analysis. This impossibility would be highlighted in dynamic analysis, however, since dynamic analysis looks at how adjustment processes work.[2]

Most heterodox approaches give greater attention to dynamic questions than neoclassical textbooks do. This is due in part to heterodoxy's holist methodology, which focuses analysis on how systems of feedback work in an economy and society. Heterodoxy's related tendency to situate market outcomes in a historical context also encourages heterodox economists to look for patterns of movement rather than static states.

(3) Heterodox Objections to Neoclassical Texts' Abstraction from the "Monetary Character" of the Economy

By the "monetary character" of the economy we refer to the fact that money is used to carry out exchanges. Long-term agreements (like debts) are also calculated in monetary terms. In our economy, goods usually cannot buy goods directly. Workers are not paid in units of a firm's output, nor can they usually purchase goods with their labor time.

Objections to ignoring this monetization may seem strange to people studying economics for the first time. You might ask, "how can you think about the economy without treating it as a monetary economy?" This is a good question and leads to an interesting discussion. Most economists think of the economy as a web of exchanges. All participants in the economy are trading real things (like hours of labor, or tons of iron) for other real things, like bundles of consumer goods. From this perspective, money is a kind of scorecard for keeping track of people's claims on each other. Workers do not actually work for money; they work for what that money can buy (e.g., goods and services). Owners of mineral resources do not trade their assets for pieces of paper; they exchange their goods for claims on other goods.

Economists sometimes find it helpful to "abstract" from the monetary form of exchange and analyze the underlying "real sector" trade that is occurring. Economists ask, for example, what is the exchange ratio between unskilled labor and gasoline (i.e., how many gallons of gas will one hour of unskilled labor purchase), or the exchange ratio between chickens and apples (how many pounds of apples will a pound of chicken trade for), and so on.

This "real sector" focus is very helpful for understanding some issues. Unfortunately, abstracting from the monetary form of exchange is unhelpful for understanding other issues. For example, in a true barter economy, goods exchange directly for other goods. When a person "sells" (i.e., trades) a good they automatically "buy" another good. In a monetized economy, however, a person can sell without buying. This is done by selling and holding money. The potentially troubling implications of such behavior for maintaining enough demand in an economy to achieve full employment can be obscured by the use of barter-like metaphors for economic activity.

(4) Heterodox Objections to the Treatment of the "Coordination Problem" in Neoclassical Macro Texts

One of the central topics in macroeconomics is the "coordination problem." This refers to the question of whether all the economic choices made by participants in the economy can fit together in a stable and consistent way that maintains full employment. The macro economy is a very complicated and interconnected whole. What one person buys is another person's sale. One person's expenditure becomes another person's income. For a long time macro economists have tried to construct a framework that explains how all of these economic decisions fit together. The version of this coordinating framework that appears in neoclassical textbooks (and with which heterodox economists take issue) is known as *general equilibrium [GE] theory*.

In the model of the economy proposed by GE theory, everything fits together. There is no unemployment. The employees and owners of the auto industry, for example, buy the services of the medical industry, whose employees and owners purchase automobiles. It can be demonstrated (with certain restrictive assumptions) that a bundle of prices, production techniques, and outputs exists that would allow supply to equal demand in all markets and guarantee full employment. The problem with this model is that there is no assurance that if the economy is not already in this state, it will move there. For example, if there are currently some unemployed people, it is not clear that the goods they would have bought had they been employed will be produced. And in turn, it is not clear that the income from the goods the unemployed would have bought will be available for spending by the hypothetical recipients to employ the unemployed. We will examine this problem more rigorously many times, beginning in chapter 5.

(5) Heterodox Critiques of the Perfect Competition (PC) Assumption in Textbook Economics

Economists have devised numerous models to characterize the relationships among firms. The simplest case is that of "perfect competition." This model assumes that there are many small firms in a market and that they engage in vigorous price competition. Your textbook probably also briefly discusses the behavior of firms in monopoly markets (markets with only one firm) and oligopoly markets (markets with a small number of large firms). It is generally easier to use popular mathematical techniques to analyze how firms behave in perfectly competitive markets than in other types of markets.

Most neoclassical textbooks have traditionally assumed perfect competition when building models of the economy. Unfortunately, this assumption was probably more valid in the nineteenth century than it is now. While many textbook authors acknowledge that the assumption of perfect competition is unrealistic, they claim that conclusions derived from the assumption also apply to other kinds of market structures that lack perfect competition. Heterodox economists disagree. They find that firms in imperfectly competitive markets can behave in ways that undermine conclusions derived from perfectly competitive models. Firms may be slower to lower prices, for example, when goods are not selling well. This can lead to greater declines in production and employment than forecast in standard models.

In this commentary I will use the abbreviation "PC" to stand for the assumption of perfect competition since, in a sense, the assumption is the "politically correct" (rather than the empirically accurate) assumption to make in *neoclassical economics* textbooks. In subsequent chapters I will try to convince you why this is so.

THREADS

Many upcoming chapters will give special attention to distributional, gender, and environmental issues in illustrating heterodox critiques of textbook economics. By focusing on these topics in a variety of contexts we will be able to weave some additional unifying threads across chapters.

Distributional Issues

Many heterodox paradigms criticize neoclassical texts for giving insufficient attention to equity issues, that is, to how the products of the economy (income, wealth, leisure, meaningful work, economic security, self-esteem, etc.) are distributed. Principles textbooks generally try to separate "equity" and "efficiency" issues and routinely de-emphasize equity matters. Heterodox economists challenge this devaluation and find many more cases where equity and efficiency issues need to be thought about together.

For example, consider a winning sports team. Part of the secret to many organizations' success (from basketball teams to computer companies) is the ability of team members to take pleasure in shared success. Part of the payoff for team members is the comradeship, and part of the payoff to the bottom line is increased productivity. Perceptive analysis requires understanding how equity and efficiency are much more complexly intertwined than is often implied in neoclassical texts. The latter tend to presume a pervasive negative relationship between increased equity and economic efficiency, due to the alleged dulling of incentives when output is distributed more equally. We will give much more attention to legitimate and illegitimate claims of an "equity/efficiency tradeoff" than is usually given in neoclassical texts.

Gender Issues

By gender issues, I mean both the treatment of issues related to women's economic experience and issues raised by "feminist economics," a distinct heterodox paradigm. Economics has generally evolved in a very male-dominated environment. This is certainly true for neoclassical economics. Some statistics, drawn from Ferber and Nelson's excellent anthology *Beyond Economic Man: Feminist Theory and Economics* (1993b), can help convey the gendered profile of economics.

- In 1986, Mark Blaug's *Who's Who in Economics* listed the 1,000 most cited economists; 969 were men. (2)
- Through 1993 there had been thirty-four Nobel prizes awarded in economics; all had gone to men. (2)
- From 1886 to 1993, a period of over 100 years, the leading professional association of American economists, the American Economic Association (AEA), had had only one female president. (2)
- Through 1989, less than 2 percent of the AEA's prestigious research awards had been awarded to women. (2)
- In 1989 only three percent of the full professors at universities with graduate programs were women. (3)

Things have improved, but only modestly, since the time of Ferber and Nelson's analysis, which ended in 1989. Twenty-seven more Nobel prizes have been shared in economics, and all have gone to men. The AEA has had fourteen more presidents; thirteen have been men. The AEA has given seven more Clark medals (the association's most coveted honor for economists under forty years of age) and all have gone to men. In 1995, 7.5 percent of the full professors and 24.2 percent of the untenured assistant professors at economics departments granting Ph.Ds were women. In 2003, 9.4 percent of the full professors and 26.5 percent of the untenured assistant professors were women (CSWEP 2004, 5). There has yet to be a female chair of the Federal Reserve Board.[3]

Many chapters of this text will explore how the research agenda nurtured in the above environment has reflected a gendered bias. It is obviously not the biological identity of economists that matters; it is the outlook of economists. But in the context of gendered experiences, the dominance of a profession by one sex can have substantive implications.

Most textbooks give relatively little attention to areas of economic life traditionally associated with women's experiences, such as household production, child rearing, and elder care. In the 1980s, a survey of twenty-one leading introductory textbooks found that less than 1.5 percent of all pages referred to women and/or minorities (Feiner and Roberts 1990, 160–61). Though things improved a little in the 1990s, under-coverage of women's experience continued (Robson 1999). For example, a survey of nine leading introductory texts in the early 1990s reported that more than half failed to discuss the influx of married women into the labor force, one of the major developments in the economy since World War II (Ferber 1997, 149; Bartlett 1995, 363).

This inattention to women's experiences has tended to be present even when economists have ventured into areas involving activities traditionally performed by women. Neoclassical economists, for example, have developed the interesting concept of "human capital" to analyze the development of human skills. They have often given little attention, however, to the role of women in nurturing such skills in the family, focusing instead on how job training or formal education programs might increase human capital. This oversight has led to some poor policy recommendations for economic development in the third world. As we review each neoclassical chapter, I will try to point out similar gaps in the topics covered that are the result of a male bias in the text.

Besides coverage issues, feminist economists have raised a series of interesting methodological challenges to textbook economics. While many of these objections are variants of more general heterodox critiques of neoclassical theory, by putting them in the context and language of feminist theory new insights are possible. When feminist economists speak of "women's work," or "women's ways of knowing," they are not referring to biologically given tasks or ways of thinking. They are referring instead to jobs and habits of mind that have traditionally been associated with women, but can be, and are, available to men. The tendency to devalue these sorts of experiences in Western thought has discouraged academic interest in methodological techniques associated with women. This has reduced the richness of economic analysis.

For example, empathy is a personal characteristic and human skill that in our society is often associated with women. It implies an ability to imagine what someone else feels. The implications of empathy for human behavior and for economic analysis are downplayed in neoclassical economics. This has contributed to, among other things, macroeconomic textbooks' relative neglect of issues related to inequality.

For example, the textbooks assert the "law of diminishing marginal utility," which means that the more you have of a good, the less you value another unit of it. The textbooks extend the law to money, implying that the value of the millionth dollar received by a millionaire is less than the value of the thousandth dollar received by the same millionaire. The textbooks stress, however, that these valuations all apply to the *same* individual. The textbooks go out of their way to emphasize that nothing "scientific" can be said about "interpersonal utility comparisons." By this they mean that nothing can be said about the potential utility received by a millionaire from an extra dollar compared to the utility received by a poor person from an extra dollar. It is thus impossible to scientifically determine whether redistributing income from the very rich to the very poor would increase average well-being. Many feminist economists find this a case of false modesty. While no one can know exactly what anyone else feels, we can make reasonable inferences about others' feelings in many cases.

Appealing to the limitations involved in making interpersonal utility comparisons, neoclassical textbooks tend to retreat from discussing the potential impact of income redistribution on societal well-being. Although the textbooks allocate dozens and probably hundreds of pages to discussing how different economic policies can increase social well-being by increasing the efficiency and level of production, they give very little attention to how societal well-being might be increased by redistributing output. Heterodox economists tackle this question, and we shall do so in chapter 15.

Many other heterodox concerns can also be reexpressed in feminist terms, such as heterodox claims that textbook economics overemphasizes abstract and mathematical forms of analysis compared to embedded and concrete forms of analysis. Feminist economists also tend to challenge the textbooks' image of *homo economicus* in feminist terms, replacing "the separative self" of the textbooks with agents linked together by feelings of empathy, sympathy, envy, and imitation. We will highlight the reexpression of heterodox ideas in feminist terms in the gender "thread" at the end of most chapters.

Environmental Issues

It is especially fitting that heterodox critiques of textbook economics should focus on environmental issues, as these are among the major challenges facing humanity in the twenty-first century. Many of the concerns about neoclassical theory embodied in the methodological critiques

---

Box 3.1
Women and Economics

This is a special plea to women in introductory economics classes who are reading this book. Economists have acknowledged for some time that economics has a problem attracting women students. For example, while 48.3 percent of all graduating math majors in 1988–1989 were women, only 32.5 percent of graduating economics majors were women.[1] Many research papers have attempted to understand why women are not attracted to economics. We have argued that this problem reflects, in part, the legacy of male dominance in the field. Along with other factors, this dominance has led to the use of methodologies that do not adequately analyze many subjects of interest to women students.

But, this is not true for all of economics! If you become disenchanted with your economics class, before deciding not to take another economics course see if you can find a class in feminist economics or another branch of heterodox economics. The field of economics very much needs talented women teachers and researchers. There are many exciting projects to work on, in part because of the neglect of important topics by the dominant paradigm. You could make a difference in this field, and I urge you to consider it.

1.   Ferber 1997, 148. From approximately 1985 to 1997 the female share of students graduating with a B.A. in economics fell from about 35 percent to 30 percent. The ratio averaged around 30 percent from 1990 to 1997 (Siegfried 1999, 326). Since 1997 the female share of economics graduates has rebounded to the 1985 level of approximately 34 percent (CSWEP 2004, 4).

---

raised earlier in this chapter can be illustrated with environmental topics. Let me give a few examples.

Neoclassical theory's commitment to methodological individualism prevents attention to what some theorists see as the underlying cause of environmental problems, namely, our economic system's tendency to cultivate insatiable desires for commodities. The textbooks' subtext of market optimality also discourages thinking about the troubling implications of competitive consumption and "positional competition" for environmental welfare.

The tendency of neoclassical economics to abstract from the specificity of environmental phenomena can also reduce its usefulness in analyzing some environmental issues. For example, the textbooks tend to treat nature and the environment as commodities, that is, as phenomena whose value can (and should) be established by market forces. Their distinctiveness as, perhaps, a source of meaning (transcendentalism), a basis for group identity (sense of place), a living system to which we have obligations, and the basic context for life whose use should be governed by a "precautionary principle" is de-emphasized and sometimes obscured in textbook economics.

The notion that people might make different choices about environmental policies as citizens (in the context of the voting booth) rather than as consumers (in the department store) is similarly absent or de-emphasized in neoclassical texts. The environmental goal of most neoclassical economists is to create efficient markets in environmental amenities. The environmental agenda of most heterodox economists is broader. It includes increasing market efficiency, but also asks whether markets (even perfected ones) are always the best institution for organizing economic interactions with the environment.

TELLING OTHER STORIES: HETERODOX CRITIQUES OF NEOCLASSICAL METAPHORS AND STORIES

As was explained in chapter 1, economics textbooks necessarily rely on metaphors and stories to convey economic theory as much as they rely on formal reasoning, graphs, and mathematics. It is as if the textbooks' sparse formal arguments were dots on a canvas. The accompanying metaphors and stories connect the dots in a particular way and thereby dissolve inherent ambiguities. Any critique of neoclassical textbooks must, therefore, critique both its formal and its informal arguments. I would like to illustrate the latter kind of critique here with two examples.

Robinson Crusoe and Friday

When I was a student, economics courses often made reference to the story of Robinson Crusoe.[4] The classic tale seems less popular today, but still appears in a number of texts, course lectures, and supplemental readings. For those of you who are unfamiliar with Daniel Defoe's novel, it is the fictitious story of a rugged, rationally oriented British adventurer in the seventeenth century named Robinson Crusoe. The images of the book that are usually invoked in economics classes concern Crusoe's life as a shipwrecked survivor on an isolated island where he encounters another individual whom he calls Friday. The two men, who are the sole inhabitants of the island, work together to survive and, in so doing, specialize in different tasks. Their division of labor has traditionally been alluded to by neoclassical economists to illustrate the "natural occurrence" and benefits of economic specialization and trade.

Defoe's story is much richer, however, than indicated by the simplistic images drawn from it in neoclassical allusions. Distinguishing between the actual story and the textbooks' moral tale about the naturalness and benefits of trade can help illustrate some heterodox critiques of neoclassical habits of argument. In the neoclassical version of the story, the division of labor between Crusoe and Friday is presented as primarily a reflection of each man's different abilities. In the actual novel, however, the division of labor between Crusoe and Friday also reflects the relative power each man can mobilize. Crusoe has a gun and Friday does not. Crusoe, a former slave trader, subordinates the dark-skinned Friday in colonial fashion. Crusoe takes the name "Master" for himself and eventually indoctrinates Friday into a colonialist expression of Christianity. Although total output may have increased on the island through Crusoe and Friday's specialization, the growth was accompanied by a permanent subjugation of Friday to Crusoe's rule. The construction and implications of the island's division of labor are thus much more complicated than the benign and functionally determined picture offered in the textbooks.

The key point of "deconstructing" the images of the textbook story is to counter the neoclassical habit of looking at behaviors independent of their social context. In a similar spirit, heterodox economists frequently object to contemporary arguments in favor of global "free trade" that fail to analyze issues in a larger context.

It is also worth noting that in using Robinson Crusoe's island experiences as illustrative of the "universal" category of "rational economic man," neoclassical authors retreat into a world without women. There are also no children. If Crusoe and Friday were to have children, the social process through which social systems renew and reproduce themselves would be more visible. Its presence might invite analysis about what is an efficient and fair social order alongside the prevailing neoclassical attention to how existing individuals make decisions.

Final Image

I would like to end this chapter with an image that conveys the main critique this book will make of neoclassical textbooks.[5] Most of you have probably heard the story of "The Emperor's New Clothes," in which some tricksters convince a foolish emperor that they have made a beautiful garment for him that only the wise and noble can see. Fearful that he will be thought unwise and ignoble, the emperor (and all of his advisers) pretend to see a make-believe garment. Finally, during a parade to show off his new robes, a child cries out, "the emperor has no clothes!" and the illusion is broken.

In economics, the story is slightly different. The "emperor" (neoclassical economics) has some clothes and they serve him well in certain circumstances. The problem is that the emperor wears the same clothes everywhere and so is often dressed inappropriately. Neoclassical economics uses basically the same analysis in the bedroom as in the boardroom, in labor markets as in grain markets, and in the twenty-first century as in the seventeenth century. It is the behavior of an *emperor with a limited wardrobe*, and this is the image that animates heterodox critiques of neoclassical economic theory.

STUDY QUESTIONS

Review Questions

1. Briefly explain what heterodox critics of orthodox theory mean by the "fallacy of misplaced concreteness." How does one know whether a neglected topic is a "detail" or a fundamental aspect of a subject? (Hint: think about the nature of paradigm debates and keep in mind that there is no simple answer to this question.)
2. What does the assumption of *homo economicus* imply? What kinds of objections have heterodox economists raised to this assumption?
3. Why do heterodox economists argue that it can be misleading to treat labor markets in the same way as markets for inanimate inputs?
4. Heterodox economists have raised five major objections to how textbook economic theory depicts the way markets work. List these five objections. (We will develop the ideas behind these concerns in later chapters so do not worry if you do not yet fully understand them. The purpose of this chapter was simply to alert you to watch for these topics in future chapters.)
5. Why do some economists argue that economics is a "gendered" and specifically male discipline? In what ways might it be claimed that the subject matter of economics has reflected a male bias? What kinds of methodological objections to textbook economics have been raised by feminist economists?

Discussion Questions

1. Economics is relatively unique among the social sciences and humanities in claiming that most important economic activity can be explained by assuming that people make rational decisions that maximize their self-interest. Think about your own decisions, your friends' decisions, and your perception of other people's decisions. How accurate do you think the assumption of *homo economicus* is? What do you see as the strengths of this assumption? Where does it seem to work? Where or when do you think the assumption goes astray?

2. If we wanted to insure we had a healthy democracy by insuring we had a citizenry whose life experiences prepared them for participation in a democracy, what kind of division of labor and organization of work might we try to promote?

3. Try to identify a subject that you think men and women tend to approach differently, or think of a situation in which men and women might notice and/or attend to different things. Can you see any ways in which these differences might affect how groups of men and women might go about studying the economy?

NOTES

1. See Keen 2002, chapter 12, for a good discussion of the use and misuse of mathematics in economics.

2. Let us look at some economic examples. Neoclassical textbooks do a lot of what is called "comparative static analysis," that is, they start with an initial situation and analyze how the economy is likely to behave in that situation. They then imagine the same economy with one variable altered (for example, an increase in taxes) and ask how that economy is likely to behave. They then conclude that if taxes were increased in the first economy it would look like the second economy. What this approach misses is the impact of the momentum from the first economy on the outcome in the altered economy. Sometimes this oversight leads to imagining that the economy can balance on one leg, when it cannot.

Let us look at a more concrete example. If there is a shock to the economy, such as a surprise cutback in oil supply by the OPEC cartel, neoclassical textbook analyses recalculate what the economy would look like in the new state if everyone had had perfect information in advance about OPEC's decision and the higher price of oil. There is very little attention to how this correction would be accomplished, that is, how the economy would move from its original position to its new "corrected" position. The possibility that the dynamics of the adjustment process (for example, the bankruptcy of some firms who had been expecting lower oil prices) could alter economic outcomes is de-emphasized in the analysis.

3. The situation is similar globally. Only 2.2 percent of the board of governors of the IMF (the International Monetary Fund) and 5.5 percent of the governors of the World Bank are women (May 2002, p. 47).

4. For extended heterodox critiques of the use of the Robinson Crusoe story in economic argument see: (1) Hymer 1971; (2) Hewitson 1999, chapter 5; and (3) White 1982.

5. This endnote is directed primarily to instructors, though much of it should be intelligible to beginning students. There are many ways to present heterodox economics and each choice has its advantages and disadvantages. The common ground I have tried to carve in chapters 2 and 3 distinguishes heterodox from neoclassical economics along several axes, such as the difference between holism and methodological individualism, the difference between neoclassical and heterodox subtexts, and the difference between doing economics "in context" and "out of context."

Many heterodox economists might find four other axes surprisingly absent. First, it is often helpful to distinguish between heterodox and neoclassical economics by the former's attention to and the latter's neglect of issues of power in the economy. While I agree with this distinction and find it useful, I have chosen to derive the different treatments of power in economic paradigms from other differences. The primary reason for this is that discussions of power in the abstract can be fairly amorphous and require quite a bit more elaboration than is possible in this chapter.

I have also not used the language of "class analysis" to distinguish heterodox from orthodox economics. While I think this approach has many advantages, most of the insights it offers can be subsumed under other categories developed in the chapter. Instructors interested in using class analysis can develop it as a particular form of holism that stresses the role of classes in defining social wholes. Feminists, institutionalists, and other paradigms can similarly use different social logics to define their vision of the social whole.

In a similar vein, I have not distinguished heterodox and neoclassical economics by the former's attention to the concept of "social surplus." Some heterodox paradigms focus on how different kinds of societies (with different class structures) generate and distribute a social surplus. These paradigms often give special attention to the process of accumulation (roughly, investment) in a capitalist economy, and the complicated linkages between economic growth, income distribution, employment, and finance. Rather than thinking about the economy in terms of the implications of isolated consumer choices, analyses organized around the dynamics of surplus generation look for structural relationships in the way societies reproduce an interrelated pattern of inputs and outputs. To draw a rough analogy, a surplus approach looks at the dynamics of an expanding ecosystem, while a consumerist approach looks at isolated members of the ecosystem at a moment in time. I decided not to highlight this approach because I thought it would require too much specialized discussion. Many of the insights derived from a surplus approach are developed in other ways throughout the commentary.

Finally I have chosen to highlight issues of gender, rather than race and gender, in the thread section due to space limitations. I have focused on gender rather than race because I think the topic raises broader concerns methodologically. This strategy has some serious drawbacks, as one cannot understand U.S. economic history without understanding racial dynamics.

NEW BEGINNINGS

Heterodox Critiques of the Introductory Chapters in Neoclassical Principles Texts

INTRODUCTION

Most neoclassical micro and macro textbooks begin with more or less the same topics. The introductory material defines economics in ways that both limit analysis to neoclassical methodologies and support neoclassical subtexts. The chiseling of economics into neoclassical boxes is done without fanfare or attention to alternative ideas, leaving many interesting questions about how to study economics unasked. In this chapter, I will try to pose some of these questions, illustrate heterodox answers, and critique neoclassical positions.

IS NEOCLASSICAL ECONOMIC THEORY A SCIENCE?

Is economics a science? Are economists scientists? Are neoclassical economic ideas akin to the findings of modern physics? Do economists "test" their ideas in ways similar to the "hard sciences"? The answer to the first question depends on what you mean by science. Heterodox answers to the last two questions are negative.

Neoclassical texts often use the mantle of science to try to command belief and silence competitors. It is implied that the text's neoclassical conclusions meet the canons of the scientific method that emphasize empirical testing. Some of the texts even refer to the authors as scientists. There are sweeping claims for enduring truths expressed in the passive voice (i.e., as the necessary embodiment of reason or data, rather than the judgment of an individual or group of particular individuals, such as neoclassical economists). See if you can find such claims in your text.

As explained in chapter 1, heterodox ideas about the nature of knowledge reflect a paradigmatic rather than a blank slate (or positivist) view of knowledge. While demanding that economic arguments be logical and reconciled with empirical data, heterodox economists believe that multiple systems of explanation can meet these criteria. This is due in part to our limited ability to do controlled experiments in economics. It also reflects the fact that human experience is influenced by the meaning people give things, rather than the simple (objective) character of naked circumstances. This makes interpreting economic events difficult because you have to make assumptions about what is going on in people's heads.

Partially because of the impossibility of basing economics on the same experimental footing as the hard sciences, economics necessarily relies on many forms of reasoning besides those permitted in the textbook portrayal of science. For example, economists often argue by analogy or through case studies. They make inferences about the real economy based on extremely simple models. They argue by introspection (that is, by asking individuals to reflect on what they would do in a situation, and assessing the reasonableness of their model by how consistent it is with their own subjectivity). All of these forms of reasoning are legitimate forms of argument. Neoclassical economists have nothing to be ashamed of in using these techniques. What is troubling is their misrepresentation of their methodology in order to deny attention to competing analogies.

What is the implication of this for your textbook and economics course? Be on the lookout for improper invocations of scientific authority. When economists claim to have "proved" something, make sure you look at the details of the study and the data underlying the claim. For the most important propositions in economics you will usually find that the "proof" rests on reasonable but debatable assumptions and interpretative leaps. Try to see where your text argues by analogy and whether other analogies might work as well or better. Always ask what questions are being ignored. Learning to do this is hard, as once you get inside a way of thinking it is difficult to get out. Let me offer an example close to student experience to illustrate what I mean by thinking outside of the "neoclassical box."

The neoclassical model of behavior has been applied by Nobel Prize winners such as Gary Becker of the University of Chicago to analyze criminal behavior. In a nutshell, Becker argues that criminal activity can be reduced by increasing the expected costs to criminals of committing crimes. This reasoning can be applied to the problem of cheating on exams. The implication of Becker's work is that colleges and universities could decrease cheating by increasing the penalty for cheating and the probability of getting caught (as it is the penalty adjusted for the probability of detection that is the relevant cost of cheating).

Increasing apprehension rates and penalties requires resources. Proponents of Becker's theory recommend spending to the point where the extra reduction in crime is no longer valued more than the costs of the program necessary to reduce crime. Becker's reasoning applied to the cheating problem suggests that colleges set the level of exam monitoring at the point where the costs of proctoring exams (mainly the implicit cost of faculty time) equals the benefits of the expected decline in cheating.

Becker's approach seems to combine common sense with formal economic reasoning (much of which is expressed mathematically). How could anyone disagree with his conclusions? How could you conceptualize the problem differently? At Knox College, where I teach, we have an honor code. The code forbids cheating but exams are not proctored. Students are on their honor not to cheat. Given Gary Becker's view of the world, you might expect that cheating would be rampant. Although some cheating occurs, it is not rampant. Why is this?

Becker's analysis misses a crucial point about human behavior. People's attitudes, their subjective assessment of the meaning of different actions, and their calculation of the costs and benefits of cheating are to some extent socially constructed. While the honor code at Knox reduces the probability of getting caught cheating (as there is no proctoring),[1] it also alters students' sense of what it means to cheat. By helping to create a college community and a feeling of academic responsibility, it discourages cheating in a way different from Becker's incentive system, which is built around crude notions of economic man. Thinking about cheating from a culture-creating point of view is thinking outside of the neoclassical box. It is the kind of thinking you will need to do to escape the bounded rationality of neoclassical theory.

THE POSITIVE/NORMATIVE DISTINCTION

Your textbook has probably drawn a sharp distinction between positive and normative claims. *Positive claims* are defined as issues of fact, such as judgments about cause and effect. *Normative claims* are said to involve value judgments. Positive claims are said to be objectively true or false. Normative claims are said to be subjectively right or wrong. Positive claims are held amenable to scientific assessment. Normative claims are portrayed as matters of opinion and not a fit topic for a scientific discipline like economics. For this reason, it is common for economics courses to deflect moral discussion to other classes. This can be unfortunate as it might appear to indicate that moral issues are relatively unimportant in economics.

Heterodox economists treat the positive/normative distinction more complexly than neoclassical textbooks do. Because the reasons for choosing one paradigm over another are subjective (somewhat analogous to the reasons for choosing one academic major over another), the allegedly objective status of "positive" analysis within a paradigm is already heavily infused with the subjectivity of paradigm choices. Three important conclusions follow.

1. It is helpful to think about the values, goals, and subtexts that animate different paradigms as these can easily color "positive" appearing claims.
2. Because of the subtlety of paradigmatic influences, it is useful to look at questions from several different perspectives.
3. It may be especially wise to look at perspectives that challenge the status quo.

Once economic knowledge is treated as the product of reason "in context," it is possible to reflect on the kinds of "biases" most likely to infiltrate "positive" analysis. There is strong precedent for expecting social systems to produce cultural and ideological justifications for their social hierarchy.[2] Medieval feudalism had ideas about "natural law" behind the inherited status of lords and serfs and the subordinate role of women in society. Europe's "divine right of kings" in the fifteenth century and the notion of the "white man's burden" in the nineteenth century supported the periods' political hierarchies. The Soviet Union's official version of Marxism justified the economic privileges and political power of its ruling bureaucracy. All imperialist projects have had their ideological justifications for colonialism. Slave societies (including the American South) have explained their hierarchy in terms of religious principles, natural law, inherited biological differences, historical necessities, and so on.

Given this history, it seems wise to be extra careful when assessing intellectual systems that tend to justify the status quo. A famous British statesman, Edmund Burke, took the opposite position, endowing existing institutions and social outcomes (like inequality) with functional legitimacy. Their very existence, in Burke's mind, suggested they helped the society function in some tried and tested way. One might suspect that "organic conservatism" (i.e., the claim that what exists is functional and natural in some way) resonates more in upper- than lower-class neighborhoods.

Much of textbook economics tends to justify the status quo, implying, for example, that markets usually produce optimal outcomes, corporations have little power, the consumer is sovereign, workers are paid their marginal product, people are naturally competitive and self-interested, and equity/efficiency tradeoffs seriously limit sensible income redistribution. Although all of these conclusions could conceivably be true, a healthy skepticism calls for careful listening to contrary claims. Barker and Feiner (2004) cite a similar "hermeneutics of suspicion" among feminist thinkers, especially feminist theologians, about the social construction of ideas about women in all fields of study, from economics to religion (p. 8).

WHAT IS ECONOMICS?

Most textbooks begin with a definition of economics. Your text probably offers a variation or combination of two standard definitions: (1) economics studies how societies allocate scarce resources among competing ends; (2) economics studies how individuals make choices. The second definition is more expansive than the first. Its advocates often apply neoclassical models involving *homo economicus* to areas of life not traditionally thought of as part of economics, such as romance and political behavior.

Many students skim quickly over introductory definitions, finding them dry and a bit vacuous. They are dry, but not vacuous. They paradigmatically define and constrict the subject of economics and often smuggle in many assumptions about the way the world works as well. The scarcity definition of economics (standard definition 1) implies that goods are inherently scarce and desires are inherently infinite. The definition is linked to several other terms or concepts introduced very early in neoclassical textbooks, such as the notion of "opportunity costs" and the dictum "there is no such thing as a free lunch." All of these concepts participate in the "growth subtext" of neoclassical texts.

At first glance this view of economics seems reasonable and in some ways it is. *Part* of economics should involve attention to issues of economic efficiency and economic growth. The problem with the textbooks is that they take what should be part of economic analysis and turn it into all of economic analysis. The neoclassical strategy discusses individual choice in ways that foreclose attention to other important topics.

I would like to substitute a third definition of economics (which, unfortunately, will probably also seem dry until fleshed out later). *Economics studies the way groups of people reproduce the material basis for life and the complicated interaction between the economy and the rest of societal life.* This interaction involves both the feedback from the economy to other aspects of society (such as cultural values and distributions of power) and the feedback from social contexts (such as ideological beliefs) to economic outcomes. This definition of economics is consistent with holist ideas of how societies work and permits analysis of the full impact of economic phenomena on social structures.

Some textbooks offer an engineering-oriented definition of economics that portrays the discipline as a "tool kit." This approach muddies the waters. In reality, the choice of tools reflects a prior choice of subjects. The tool kit metaphor tries to avoid acknowledging this choice and its inherent subjectivity. The textbooks imply that neoclassical tools can operate on all potential economic topics. To do this the textbooks have to define economic topics and economic questions in a narrow way.

For the neoclassicals, economic behavior involves the rational pursuit of self-interest by people with preexisting tastes and preferences and individual, rather than socially constructed, perceptions of available choices. The neoclassical model rules out attention to many possible economic topics, such as where the tastes and preferences come from that people are trying to satisfy or how social contexts might condition the information considered by individuals when making choices. Only after narrowing the field in this way can economics be thought of as a bundle of techniques, usually mathematical techniques, that illuminate how people make rational choices among competing options. Heterodox paradigms challenge this delimiting of economic topics.

THE LIMITS OF SCARCITY AND EFFICIENCY DISCOURSE

Paul Samuelson is the father of modern economics textbooks. His book *Economics* (now coauthored with William Nordhaus) enjoyed its fiftieth year of publication and sixteenth edition in

1998. His posing of "scarcity discourse" has served as a model for two generations of textbook writers. To give us a common text illustrating scarcity-efficiency discourse, I will quote a bit from Samuelson and Nordhaus's text (hereafter SN) and suggest some heterodox critiques. SN define economics as:

> the study of how societies use scarce resources to produce valuable commodities and distribute them among different people.
>
> Behind this definition are two key ideas in economics: that goods are scarce and that society must use its resources efficiently (4). . . .
>
> Goods are limited, while wants seem limitless. Even after two centuries of rapid economic growth, production in the United States is simply not high enough to meet everyone's desires. . . .
>
> The essence of economics is to acknowledge the reality of scarcity and then figure out how to organize society in a way which produces the most efficient use of resources. That is where economics makes its unique contribution . . . .
>
> The ultimate goal of economic science is to improve the living conditions of people in their everyday lives. Increasing the gross domestic product is not just a numbers game. Higher incomes mean good food, warm houses, and hot water. (Samuelson and Nordhaus 1998a, 4–7)

Most texts' opening chapters go on to develop a number of interrelated concepts that facilitate discussion of scarcity and efficiency in a neoclassical manner. Among these concepts are those of (1) opportunity costs, (2) the production possibilities frontier, (3) Pareto optimality, and (4) the gains from specialization and trade. As noted above, all of these concepts participate in the texts' growth subtext, which prioritizes economic growth and economic efficiency as mechanisms for meeting human needs.

Critiquing this packaging of economics is tricky, as on first glance it seems an eminently reasonable approach. Why not measure the success of an economy by the level of output (GDP) it produces, treating GDP as a proxy for the ability of people to pursue their own definitions of well-being? Why not orient economic theory toward analyzing economic efficiency and economic growth? Why not use the cluster of concepts associated with scarcity discourse to found economic analysis?

Heterodox economists offer several reasons for not doing so. The first problem with the textbooks' methodologically individualistic analysis is that it retreats from thinking holistically about the origins of scarcity, that is, the origins of "human wants." It implies an innate insatiability to human material desires and treats a sense of scarcity as a definitive aspect of being human. It deflects attention from the massive apparatus nurtured within modern economies to create consumer demand. It discourages reflection on what efficiency means if the economy partially creates the needs it satisfies.

The textbook approach to scarcity-efficiency discourse also assumes much too simple a picture of economic growth. It unreflectively conflates changes in national income with changes in national well-being. It ignores data like that highlighted in Easterlin's happiness surveys and pays no attention to the wastefulness of positional competition. It contracts the scope of economic analysis from a broad inquiry into what is responsible for national economic well-being to a narrower focus on how to maximize GDP.

The scarcity-efficiency package also excessively separates equity and efficiency issues and devalues distributional concerns. The early highlighting in many neoclassical texts of the concept of "Pareto optimality" in defining economic efficiency is especially revealing. An economy is said to be "Pareto efficient" if no one can be made better off without making someone else worse off. In the broadest sense, an efficient economy has exhausted all possible gains from voluntary exchange. While this criterion is one plausible aspect of an efficient use of resources, it limits thinking about economic efficiency to a narrow set of issues. It distracts attention from more complicated questions about societal efficiency and, in tandem with another theme of neoclassical economics (the inability to make interpersonal utility comparisons), discourages integrating equity and efficiency concerns.

For example, prioritizing Pareto efficiency in assessing market outcomes discourages thinking about economic outputs in terms of basic needs. An economy that fails to provide basic nutrition for a large portion of its children, health care for its elderly, or education for its young people can be judged efficient in neoclassical terms (Pareto optimality) if it meets the demand of those with purchasing power (even if that demand is used to "make a fashion statement"). Most neoclassical textbooks also discourage reflection on the "efficiency" of different income distributions. As noted in chapter 3, the texts argue that it is impossible to make "rigorous *interpersonal* utility comparisons."

The lens of Pareto optimality also precludes thinking about the implications of positional competition. According to the logic of Pareto optimality, macroeconomic policies that benefit the wealthy enormously with little or no effect on the bulk of the population would be efficient and desirable. But would they be? Consider the following tale. Some economists from outer space visit your living room and indicate that through their policies the U.S. economy can be immediately restructured so that the top 10 percent of the income ladder would quadruple their wealth, with no wealth changes for anyone else. Would the change be beneficial? According to the logic of neoclassical theory and the principle of Pareto efficiency, the answer is an unambiguous yes! When one adds in equity and distributional concerns, however, the issue is more debatable. There are good reasons for not wanting to broaden the class divide in the United States or to increase the relative power of an economic elite.[3] Neoclassical theory tends to preclude discussion of this issue.

What about the concepts of "opportunity costs," "production possibility frontiers," and "the gains from trade"? By themselves these concepts offer important insights into the nature of tradeoffs and exchange in an economy. There is nothing inherently objectionable in raising them early in an introductory text. The main concern of heterodox economists involves the lack of a dynamic or holistic perspective in the way they are presented. Their elaboration within a scarcity-efficiency discourse tends to cast them in a static light devoid of institutional contexts.

For instance, it has been customary in economics to illustrate the gains from trade by citing Ricardo's famous example of the division of labor between England and Portugal, wherein England specialized in textiles and Portugal in wine. The textbooks imply that the emergence of this division of labor reflected the "comparative advantage" of the two countries (the relative ease with which either country could produce either good). However, as Harry Magdoff has pointed out (Magdoff 1971), this is, at the very least, an incomplete explanation. In fact, the arrangement was imposed on Portugal by the British navy and a series of commercial treaties reflecting each country's relative military power. Over time, the dynamic implications of the arrangement cemented the advantages of the British manufacturing industry over its Portuguese rivals.[4]

There are many other cases where global trading patterns reflect the geopolitical construction of a system of trade (a system of interconnected production possibility frontiers) rather than a priori comparative advantages. The textbooks tend to deflect attention from these examples, preoccupying readers with demonstrations of static efficiency. You might reasonably ask, are these neglected topics going to be addressed later in neoclassical textbooks? Are these introductory concepts going to be complemented in future chapters by a richer discussion of well-being, the social context of the division of labor, and so on? The answer is usually no. The introductory materials in neoclassical principles texts define the terrain upon which the rest of the game will be played. These other topics will be usually given minimal attention, most likely through a "note but ignore" reference. You can judge this for yourself. When the term ends think about what kinds of questions and concerns your textbook has led you to think about when discussing the "efficiency" of economic outcomes and the goals of economic analysis.

MARGINALISM

Most opening chapters in neoclassical texts emphasize that economic decisions "are made at the margin." This is a very important insight, but can be taken too far and out of context in neoclassical textbooks. Prior *structural choices* form the context for many current marginal choices. How structural choices are made is often neglected in neoclassical texts. Structural choices refer to system choices, for example: (1) the choice between an automobile and a mass transit–based transportation system; or (2) the choice between a full-employment economy with long-term relationships between workers and firms and a "slack economy" with more temporary employment relationships.

Because the costs and benefits of many activities are sensitive to the number of people doing them, private choices often depend on the context for action set by group choices. "Network externalities," for example, make the benefits of using a good increase as more people use it (as with e-mail and instant messaging). "Economies of scale" in production make the per-unit costs of producing a good, and its price to consumers, fall as output increases. Neoclassical theory has some interesting things to say about how group and structural choices are made, which invite interesting critiques. Unfortunately, these potential debates are obscured in neoclassical introductory texts due to a lack of attention to structural choices.

The reasons for this inattention re-illustrate how methodological leanings and subtexts help define the topics covered in introductory courses. Thinking about structural choices invites a more holistic and institutionally detailed analysis of economic evolution than routinely welcomed in neoclassical theory. The topic also raises the troubling possibility that market outcomes can be inefficient (even if most people are making rational choices) if the economy gets started down the wrong road. This possibility can complicate the "let the market work" subtext of introductory courses and is not usually a welcome complexity in neoclassical classes.[5] The history of nuclear power in the United States offers a particularly interesting example of the dangers of the economy's getting locked into a poor variant of an emerging technology. Endnote number 6 explores how early developments in the nuclear sector channeled the industry into what in retrospect appears to have been a particularly dangerous and uneconomic form of nuclear energy.[6]

THE CETERIS PARIBUS (ALL THINGS EQUAL) ASSUMPTION

One of the hardest things for many introductory economics students to learn is how to reason under the *all things equal* (ceteris paribus) assumption. In the actual world there is a great deal of interconnectedness. If the price of gasoline tripled, for example, many things might happen. Congress might threaten to investigate the oil industry. The United States might pressure OPEC to increase production. Automobile companies might increase advertising to offset the disincentive to buy a new car from higher gas prices, etc. It is sometimes useful to ignore these contingencies (to hold the existing context for the gasoline market constant) and ask, "If all other things were equal (i.e., the same) and the price of gasoline tripled, what would happen to the demand for gasoline?" This kind of focus allows a complicated problem to be broken into manageable parts.

From a heterodox perspective there tend to be two main concerns about how the ceteris paribus (CP) assumption is used in neoclassical texts. The first involves assuming "all things equal" when it is logically inappropriate to do so. The classic example of this involves the tendency for macroeconomic textbooks to assume that an increase in unemployment will not effect aggregate demand, or, put more broadly, that the economy's "momentary" disequilibrium will not alter its final equilibrium "resting point." (We will look at this problem in the next chapter.)

The second problem is more general and relates to holist criticisms of methodological individualism. The habit of "assuming all things equal" tends to divert neoclassical analyses from attention to holist or systems issues. For example, you may recall that Keynes expected that materialist pressures would subside once most people had a certain level of consumer goods. Given the level of needs and social expectations in the 1900s this seemed reasonable. What Keynes had not anticipated was that modern capitalism has powerful mechanisms to incite demand and renew preoccupation with material acquisitions. In a sense, Keynes used a camera to take a snapshot of individual consumption when he should have used a camcorder to take a dynamic picture of a consumer society.

THE CIRCULAR FLOW: DIRECTIONS

The traditional circular flow diagram implies that causality in the economy runs entirely from households to firms. The image obscures the causal or agency role that firms play in the economy. The diagram conceals the exercise of corporate power. Although consumer signals do influence production, the needs of corporations to reproduce themselves also shape economic outcomes. This side of a capitalist economy is nearly absent in introductory economics texts.

The clockwise circular flow in textbook economics also misses the relentless pressures for expansion that the need to invest idle capital imparts to the economy.[7] This pressure helps make a capitalist economy like a bicycle. It is only stable when it is in motion (i.e., expanding). This motion can impose tremendous burdens on the natural environment, which supports economic activities. The interplay between the economy and its resource base tends to be "cropped" by the picture frame of the circular flow.[8]

SOME LOUD SILENCES

Another way of summarizing many heterodox objections to the introductory chapters in neoclassical textbooks is to note the pages' relative silence on:

1. the paradigmatic nature of economic knowledge
2. the difference between methodological individualism and holism
3. the nature of capitalism as a social system
4. the importance of historical perspectives on economic issues
5. the importance of institutional contexts
6. the significance of the household sector
7. the goals of economic activity and
8. the importance of ecological contexts.

TEXTBOOK IMAGES AND METAPHORS

Heterodox critiques of the textbooks' early chapters also challenge the metaphors employed and offer some heterodox alternatives. Some of the important images challenged are listed below.

Consumer Sovereignty

Three thought-provoking statistics: (1) By the age of 18, the average American has spent about as much time in front of the TV and its advertisers as in school (Goodwin, Ackerman, and Kiron 1997, xxxiii). (2) In 2000 about the same sum was spent on advertising in the United States as on higher education.[9] (3) The average American is exposed to 3,600 commercial impressions daily.[10] Given this data, is it adequate to treat consumers as "the monarchs of the market"? The issue is not whether consumer "choice" is part of the picture; it definitely is. The question is whether it is the whole picture.

Free Markets and Voluntary Exchange

Neoclassical textbooks are usually peppered with images of freedom: free enterprise, free markets, free choice, free trade, etc. Heterodox critiques are more careful in their use of the word *freedom*. They note, for example, that the labor process within firms is very unfree. Most people do not work within worker-owned firms that they help govern. "The boss" has significant power. Most people are not in situations that permit them to avoid this subordination.

One way of summarizing heterodox critiques of the language of freedom in neoclassical texts is to note the distinction between "freedom to" and "freedom from." Standard texts emphasize freedom from. No one can force anyone to take a job that subordinates them to someone else. Heterodox economists ask whether most households have the resources necessary to exercise their potential freedom (freedom to).

The Invisible Hand

There are two messages left by the metaphor of the invisible hand for students. The first is that market outcomes reflect the independent actions of millions of isolated individuals. The second is that self-interest can, and usually does, promote the general interest in a market economy. For example, in his popular macro principles text N. Gregory Mankiw writes,

> One of our goals in this book is to understand how this invisible hand works its magic. . . . [P]rices are the instrument with which the invisible hand directs economic activity. . . .
>
> There is an important corollary to the skill of the invisible hand. . . . When the government prevents prices from adjusting naturally to supply and demand, it impedes the invisible hand's ability to coordinate the millions of households and firms that make up the economy. . . . [This] explains the failure of communism. In communist countries, prices were not determined in the marketplace but were dictated by central planners. These planners lacked the information that gets reflected in prices when prices are free to respond to market forces. Central planners failed because they tried to run the economy with one hand tied behind their backs—the invisible hand of the marketplace (Mankiw 2001, 9–11).

From a heterodox perspective the invisible hand needs to be attached to a much more complicated body. The atomized picture suggested by the invisible hand insightfully describes aspects of some economic activities in competitive markets. In many other areas (as in the nuclear industry discussed in endnote 8) there are concentrations of economic power and high-level planning by corporate, financial, and government decision makers. The metaphor of the invisible hand conceals this.

More importantly, the invisible hand does not always craft ideal outcomes. Sometimes everyone's pursuit of their separate self-interest prevents anyone from achieving their self-interest (see The Prisoner's Dilemma below). Even more perplexing, the organization of the economy on the basis of greed and "all against all" sometimes creates a society we would not want to live in (see Meta-Externalities below).

Numerous qualifying images complement the invisible hand in heterodox writings. Among these are "the implicit handshake," "the invisible fist," "the planning sector," "path dependency," and "the prisoner's dilemma." All of these images offer a much more complicated and sometimes less sunny image of economic coordination in capitalism than suggested by the benevolent invisible hand. We will explore these alternative heterodox images in detail in later chapters.

Mankiw's appeal to the invisible hand to explain the collapse of the former Soviet Union is a good example of oversimplified textbook economic analysis. It illustrates the TINA subtext ("There Is No Alternative" to contemporary capitalism) of most neoclassical textbooks. Sweeping conclusions are offered with little analytical or empirical discussion to support them. Although Mankiw's opinion is plausible, it is hardly "scientific," and it is only one of many viable hypotheses. Its glib presentation as indisputable truth leads some critics of neoclassical textbooks to see them as ideological exercises.

SOME ALTERNATIVE HETERODOX IMAGES

People as Citizens and Family Members as well as Consumers

The textbooks tend to portray all human experience as a variant of consumption (or its negation: unpleasant work). While not necessarily going as far as the "new economics," which treats decisions about having a child, being a friend, or committing a crime in much the same way as decisions about buying a refrigerator, the textbooks treat "the consumer" as an all-purpose image of what constitutes a person and "consumption" as an all-purpose description of experience. This decision treats *homo economicus* as omnipresent. This is questionable. It is sometimes useful to ask how our understanding of society and the economy might be different if we viewed economic participants as citizens and/or people with kinship ties, as well as consumers.

The textbooks imply that we could best recognize and meet human wants if we set up markets for virtually everything, from genetic codes to geodesic orbits. The recourse to markets implicitly posits people as consumers. If we instead imagine people as kin or citizens, the organization of life through markets becomes less automatic. Many people would be hesitant, for example, to organize a family Thanksgiving dinner, romantic relationships, or political activities (e.g., vote selling) through market mechanisms. Thinking about what lies behind this hesitancy can illuminate why it can be misleading to treat people solely as consumers, even in economic activities.

The Prisoner's Dilemma

The prisoner's dilemma refers to a famous paradox in decision making, where the participants' isolated pursuit of self-interest prevents them from achieving their self-interest. While there are many variants of the tale, the basic story involves two prisoners who have been arrested for two crimes they did commit. The prosecutor has enough evidence to convict each person for the lesser offense but not for the more serious crime. Each prisoner is given the following choice: either confess and implicate the other in the more serious crime, or stonewall (not confess). If both confess, the prosecutor promises they will each get five-year sentences. If one confesses and the other does not, the confessor will serve only three months' time and the non-confessor will serve fifteen years. If both refuse to confess, they will both serve one year. The prisoners are not allowed to communicate with each other. It is also assumed that "it is a one-time game," implying that there is no opportunity for retaliation or gratitude on the part of either prisoner toward the other after the declarations.

If each prisoner were to independently pursue their own self-interest they would both confess. No matter what the other party does (confess or stonewall) the second prisoner gets a lighter sentence by confessing. If the other prisoner does not confess, the second prisoner reduces a one-year sentence to three months by confessing. If the other prisoner does confess the second prisoner reduces a potential fifteen-year sentence to five years by confessing. In this case the invisible hand breaks down. By pursuing their own private interest the prisoners ensure that they will each serve five years of jail time. If they had cooperated they could have reduced their jail time to one year.

Discussion of the prisoner's dilemma is usually limited in neoclassical introductory textbooks to a chapter or two in introductory microeconomics textbooks on game theory and corporate competition. The metaphor is not generalized across chapters or used to think about market outcomes more broadly. The subject is usually given even less attention in introductory macroeconomic textbooks. Its implications for assessing the efficiency and social desirability of market outcomes are rarely pursued.

From a heterodox perspective, the prisoner's dilemma raises the possibility that the economy is running on steroids. For example, we may be allowing unregulated competition in labor markets to lower the quality of work life below what most workers would voluntarily choose if making decisions as a group. We may similarly be squandering environmental resources in competitive consumption. As in a military arms race, each individual decision may be rational, but the outcome may be a huge waste of resources. Heterodox economics wants to explore these possibilities.

Meta-Externalities

You may recall from chapter 2 that meta-externalities refer to the unintended consequences of economic activities on the structure of society and culture. Heterodox economists attend to meta-externalities while neoclassical economists ignore them. The differing treatment of Adam Smith's famous pin factory example in the two approaches nicely illustrates this difference.

Samuelson and Nordhaus's well known introductory text, for example, reports "[Smith] pointed to the great strides in productivity brought about by specialization and the division of labor. In a famous example, he described the specialized manufacturing of a pin factory in which 'one man draws out the wire, another straightens it, a third cuts it,' and so it goes. This operation allowed 10 people to make 48,000 pins a day, whereas if 'all wrought separately, they could not each of them make twenty . . . '" (Samuelson and Nordhaus 2001a, 30).

What Samuelson and Nordhaus ignore is Smith's subsequent comments on the meta-externalities of labor specialization. As many heterodox economists note, Smith went on to write,

> In the progress of the division of labour, the employment of . . . the great body of the people, comes to be confined to a few very simple operations, frequently to one or two.

> But the understandings of the greater part of men are necessarily formed by their ordi-
> nary employments. The man whose whole life is spent in performing a few simple opera-
> tions . . . has no occasion to exert his understanding. . . . He naturally loses, therefore, the
> habit of such exertion, and generally becomes as stupid and ignorant as it is possible for
> a human creature to become. . . . His dexterity at his own particular trade seems, in this
> matter, to be acquired at the expence of his intellectual, social, and martial virtues." (Smith
> [1776] 1965, 734–35)

Smith goes on to lament the implications of these changes for the organization of society.

Rethinking Incentives

All economic texts discuss the role of "incentives" in the economy. The standard textbook message is that "people respond to incentives, and if you want to alter their behavior, you need to alter
the incentive structure." This is a reasonable, if not subtle, idea and deserves some attention. The
problem with standard discussions of incentives is their lack of a holist perspective and their
excessive abstraction from specific contexts.

Let me give an example. Switzerland has had a problem finding sites for nuclear waste dumps.
The logic of neoclassical theory suggests that paying residents to accept the waste would be the
rational and efficient way to find new sites. Surveys of citizen opinion, however, revealed the
issue to be more complicated. When citizens were asked if they would accept a waste site in their
community, the number saying yes fell when the site was tied to compensation. Many people
apparently were willing to "do their share" to solve a national problem, but unwilling to accept
the waste for the compensation offered, based on self-interest (Kahan 2002). Similar findings
have been reported with respect to blood donation (Hausman and McPherson 1996, 215–19).[11]
The textbooks' overly simplified portrayal of human motivation tends to make anticipation of
these results difficult.

Heterodox economists also criticize neoclassical discussions of financial incentives for ignoring the "meta-externalities" of incentive systems. For example, Herman Daly and E.F. Schumacher,
two well-known ecological economists, have warned that transforming some additional intercon-
nections between people into forms of self-interested exchange may erode the basis for voluntary
cooperation.[12] Besides being an extremely valuable economic asset, this capacity is one of the
cultural bases for friendship and community.

Some economists have used the concept of "social capital" to refer to a society's ability to
mobilize trust, reciprocity, and other forms of voluntary cooperation. They suggest that economists think about the net change in social capital brought about by different kinds of economic
activities and add these changes to the costs or benefits of a course of action. Using such an
accounting system, it may be possible to tell when it is wise or unwise to use financial incentives
to achieve societal goals.

Summary: "If You Have a Hammer . . ."

Most heterodox objections to neoclassical metaphors involve their systematic incompleteness
and extension to inappropriate contexts. As noted earlier, it has been said that if you have a hammer, the whole world is a nail. From a heterodox perspective, neoclassical economists frequently
use a hammer when a screwdriver would be more appropriate, and nail together boxes that are too
small for the topics they contain.

THREADS

We will conclude this chapter by looking at the implications of some of the ideas we have discussed for thinking about gender, environmental, and distributional issues. For the gender and environmental threads we have selected quotes from leading feminist[13] and ecological economists.

Gender Thread

[E]conomics, like any science, is socially constructed [p. 132]. . . .

Economics is often defined as the study of processes by which things—goods, services, financial assets—are exchanged. By this definition, most of the traditional nonmarket activities of women—care of the home, children, sick and elderly relatives, and so on—have been considered "noneconomic" and therefore inappropriate subjects for economic research [p. 141]. . . .

Rather than using marketization as the criterion for demarcating economics—or using the rational choice model . . . —a broader definition of economics as concerned with "provisioning" could delineate a subject matter without using sexist assumptions about what is and what is not important [p. 142]. . . .

Feminist scholarship suggests that economics has been made less useful by implicitly reflecting a distorted ideal of masculinity in its models, methods, topics, and pedagogy. Feminist scholars argue that the use of a fuller range of tools to study and teach about a wider territory of economic activity would make economics a more productive discipline. (Nelson 1995, 146)

Environmental Thread

Standard growth economics ignores finitude, entropy, and ecological interdependence because the concept of throughput is absent from its preanalytic vision, which is that of an isolated circular flow of exchange value . . . as can be verified by examining the first few chapters of any basic textbook. . . . The focus on exchange value in the macroeconomic circular flow also abstracts from use value and any idea of purpose other than maximization of the circular flow of exchange value. (Daly 1996, 33–34)[14]

Distributional Thread

As we've repeatedly noted, heterodoxy calls for greater attention to equity and other distributional issues than is usually present in neoclassical textbooks. Heterodox economists emphasize the tendency of social systems to generate ideas that legitimize their social hierarchies and urge a special skepticism toward theories that portray economic inequality as inevitable and/or socially necessary.

STUDY QUESTIONS

Discussion Questions

1. What do you think the purpose of economics should be; that is, what questions do you think the discipline should help answer? What social issues or social problems do you

think economics might help clarify? Try to keep the questions you want answered in front of you as the term progresses. Ask yourself whether your textbook addresses these questions. If not, what is the textbook's rationale for neglecting your questions? Is this rationale convincing? To jump-start the process, you might want to thumb through the index at the back of your textbook and note what topics are in it and what topics are absent.[15]

2. Neoclassical texts often discuss how the market optimally rations goods through the price mechanism. Consider the following goods: food, beaches, drinking water, housing, parking downtown, seats in an oversubscribed college course, and any other commodity you would like. What criteria, implicit or explicit, are currently used to distribute these goods in the economy? Under what circumstances do you think the market's willingness to pay principle is a good rationing device? Under what circumstances do you think it is inappropriate? If there were a very worn but useful copy of lecture notes that could not be duplicated for this course, how should access to them be rationed? Why?

3. Heterodox economists have criticized many of the "stories" told in standard textbooks. What is similar about heterodox objections to textbook treatments of Robinson Crusoe, the economics of crime (Gary Becker), and the origins of the division of labor between Portugal and England in the seventeenth and eighteenth centuries?

4. Match the images or metaphors listed below to either textbook or heterodox economics and indicate why the imagery seems to fit better in the camp you chose: (a) people as citizens as well as consumers; (b) consumer sovereignty; (c) the invisible hand; (d) meta-externalities.[16]

Review Questions

1. Neoclassical principles texts often contain a section warning students against several logical fallacies common in economic argument, such as the Post Hoc Fallacy ("after, therefore because of") and the Fallacy of Composition. Many heterodox critiques of neoclassical textbooks add additional fallacies. Briefly explain what is meant by the following fallacies from a heterodox perspective.
    a. Fallacy of Paradigm-Free Knowledge
    b. Fallacy of Scientism
    c. Fallacy of Misplaced Concreteness
    d. Fallacy of Innate Scarcity
    e. Fallacy of Static Analysis
    f. Fallacy (or misuse) of the Ceteris Paribus Assumption

2. What kind of objections do heterodox economists raise to standard textbooks' discussion of "economics and science"? How do you think a neoclassical economist would respond to these objections?

3. Explain the difference between "positive" and "normative" judgments and what is meant by the "fact"/"value" distinction. What modifications do heterodox economists favor for conceptualizing objectivity and subjectivity in economics?

4. How do neoclassical and heterodox definitions of economics differ?

5. What role does "scarcity" play in standard textbooks and neoclassical economics? What kind of objections do heterodox economists raise to approaches to economics that put "scarcity" at the center of economic inquiry? How do these objections illustrate some of the underlying differences between heterodox and orthodox economics?

6. What is meant by "Pareto optimality"? What kinds of objections do heterodox economists raise to making the achievement of Pareto-optimal outcomes the central task of
   economic theory?

7. Neoclassical economics and standard textbooks emphasize the importance of examining and explaining economic activities in terms of "behavior at the margin" (for example, the decision to buy or sell one more unit of a good). While acknowledging the
   power of "marginalist" analysis, heterodox economists urge more attention to what other
   aspect of economic choices? How does the heterodox position re-illustrate some of the
   basic differences between heterodox and orthodox economic analysis?

NOTES

1. Students can still be found guilty of cheating if material evidence demonstrates plagiarism (as with
submitting papers purchased off the Internet) or if other students observe them cheating and bring a case
before the honor board. The chances of being detected, however, are much lower than in a system where
exams are proctored.

2. In Marxist language these justifications reflect "false consciousness," a systematic distortion in people's
understanding of their own circumstances that tends to accompany those circumstances. In John Kenneth
Galbraith's less-threatening language of institutionalist economics, they represent "convenient social virtues" (Galbraith 1973, chapter iv), convenient, of course, for the powerful. One of the major ways that
ideologies shape belief is by making certain questions seem inappropriate. Thus even asking them sounds
shrill and pursuing them appears a waste of time. I highly recommend Galbraith's work for its ability to
liberate readers to ask suppressed questions. People with an interest in the natural sciences might also enjoy
Stephen J. Gould's wonderful book *The Mismeasure of Man,* which offers an especially good account of the
recurring pattern of spurious biological justifications for dominant groups' privileged positions.

3. See Frank 2005a for an interesting discussion of why middle-class citizens might reject the restructuring.

4. As David Colander has pointed out, standard textbook portrayals of production possibility frontiers
(PPFs) (e.g., the guns and butter trade-off) tend to concentrate excessively on examples that assume the law
of diminishing returns for the two goods represented. A more dynamic approach, emphasizing positive
feedback (or what is termed *increasing returns*) would not have the concave shape found in the textbooks.
Discussions of the PPF become much more complicated and realistic when increasing returns to scale,
learning by doing, discontinuous choices, and irreversibilities are added to the analysis (Colander 2000,
132–33). A key implication is that "path choices" rather than "marginal choices" may dominate outcomes—
and thus distributions of power and other factors influencing path choices may infuse economic outcomes.
Walter Rodney has argued this case with respect to Europe's underdevelopment of Africa since about 1500
through the forcible imposition of unfavorable trade patterns (such as slave trading) on the African economy.
See Rodney 1981.

5. Illustrating these concerns, Peter Dorman (a radical/institutionalist-oriented economist) writes,
"[M]ultiple equilibria are . . . widespread. . . . Residents of a metropolitan area might be in equilibrium with
many cars and a weak system of public transportation, or vice versa. . . .

The problem of multiple equilibria should be given a prominent place in the principles course, because
it raises fundamental questions about the limitations of markets. . . . [M]arket analysis promises to explain
the what, how, and by-and-for-whom of economic life by reference to equilibrium, but if there are many
equilibria the explanation falls short. We would need to know . . . which equilibrium the economy settled at
and why" (Dorman 2001, 329).

6. During the early years of the cold war, the United States had a very successful crash program to
develop nuclear submarines and aircraft carriers. Several of the navy's private contractors wanted to cash in
on their near monopoly over nuclear expertise in civilian markets. In 1954, Westinghouse, with the help of
the local utility near its Pittsburgh headquarters, put an aircraft carrier reactor on land and the nuclear power
industry was born.

"There are basically two approaches to nuclear safety; either (1) tolerate the hypothetical possibility of
major accidents, but include in the plant's design enough [engineered] safeguards to make the probabilities
of serious accidents approach zero; or (2) build reactors that are prohibited by design from having serious

accidents (such as very small reactors with minimal amounts of nuclear fuel). . . .

"To draw an analogy, imagine an electric stove with a tea kettle. In designs that follow the first approach, steam explosions are inhibited by a pressure gauge, an automatic feedback control on stove temperature, a kettle whistle and myriad other mechanisms that signal the user to remove the teapot from the stove and/or lower the burner's temperature. In designs that follow the second approach, the maximum temperature the stove's electric coils can ever reach is insufficient to boil the water (though, presumably high enough to make the tea)" (Cohn 1997, 205–6). The second designs are said to be "passively" or "walk-away" safe. Nothing has to operate in order to prevent a steam explosion.

In building submarine reactors, the U.S. Navy followed the first strategy. By the early 1960s naval contractors Westinghouse and General Electric had an enormous head start over other firms in reactor designs using the navy's "active safeguard" strategy. But the companies feared technological competition. As the GE vice president in charge of the company's "Growth Council," John McKitterick, recalls, "We had a problem like a lump of butter sitting in the sun. . . . If we couldn't get orders out of the utility industry, with every tick of the clock it became progressively more likely that some competing technology would be developed that would supersede the economic viability of our own. Our people understood this was a game of massive stakes, and that if we didn't force the utility industry to put those stations on line, we'd end up with nothing" (Demaree 1970, 93).

As a result, Westinghouse and GE offered the utilities completed nuclear plants at "loss-leader" prices (that is, prices below costs) in order to move further down the learning curve for nuclear power plant fabrication, lay the groundwork for capturing economies of scale, and discourage competing reactor designs. The companies also offered the utilities other generous incentives, such as subsidized uranium prices. All told the companies absorbed multi-billion-dollar losses. The loss-leader strategy succeeded, however, in discouraging alternative reactor designs and eventually locked the U.S. nuclear sector into a technological strategy based on active safeguards.

Many observers believe that the inability to ensure and "prove" nuclear safety with an active safeguard system was responsible for the collapse of the nuclear industry. Something can always go wrong with safety systems: emergency core cooling pipes can break, power outages can disable pumps, mechanical failures can disable backup pumps, and so on. Many unexpected failures have occurred and the industry has been forced to add expensive new safety systems to existing plants. Even more seriously, fears of new unanticipated accidents have caused significant portions of public and expert opinion to oppose new nuclear plants. Forty years of marginal changes within an active safety trajectory appear to have cost the U.S. economy tens and possibly hundreds of billions of dollars. Any resurgence of nuclear power would seem to require passive safety designs.

7. Barbara Garson, in her book *Money Makes the World Go Around* (2002), uses the image of a "hot potato" to describe the pressures emanating from the financial sector (banks and other credit institutions) to find investment outlets for liquid funds. Garson traced the journey of her bank deposit from her local bank, to the big city bank where it was redeposited, to various loan recipients.

8. Ecological economists emphasize this neglect in their criticism of the textbook's circular flow imagery. This criticism is pursued further in chapter 16's discussion of macroeconomics and the environment. See also Daly and Farley 2004, chapter 2, esp. pages 26–29, and Daly 1996, 45–60.

9. The U.S. Census Bureau indicates that in 2000 $236 billion was spent on advertising and $257 billion on higher education. Of the latter, about $160 billion was spent on public colleges and universities and $98 billion on private colleges and universities (*Statistical Abstract of the United States: 2001,* Table 1271, p. 777 on advertising expenses; Table 206, p. 133 on higher education funding). Estimates of advertising expenses are sensitive to the definition of advertising employed. Media spending for advertising totaled ~$125 billion in 2003 (TNS Media Intelligence/CMR Reports: http://www.tnsmi-cmr.com/news/2004/030804.html). Tallies adding direct mail, Yellow Pages, and other formats totaled ~$235 billion in 2002 (Worldwatch, *Vital Signs 2003,* 48, 128).

10. Sut Jhally, *Advertising and the End of the World* (video); summarized at http://hope.journ.wwu.edu/tpilgrim/j190/adendofworldvidsum.html.

11. A similar result was reported by Gneezy and Rustichini (2000). They found that when a day care center instituted a fine for parents picking up their children later than scheduled, the number of tardy parents increased. It would appear that people had initially felt a social obligation not to impose on the caregivers. People seem to have treated the fine as if it were a price for overtime and felt less compunction about imposing on the day care staff. The behavior appears to indicate the importance of social norms in regulating economic interactions.

12. It is worth noting that non-market mechanisms of cooperation and coordination (such as "convenient social virtues") can rely on oppressive structures that spread burdens very unequally. Women, in particular, often get the short end of the stick.

13. The term *feminist economics* tends to refer to a more diverse group of economists than some other paradigmatic labels do. Some feminist economists, for example, are comfortable with the basic structure of neoclassical economics but want to apply it more actively to topics involving women's experience, such as child care and domestic activities. Other feminist economists reject neoclassical methodology. The commentary's analysis tends to emphasize the latter group.

14. See the Developing Ideas interview with Herman Daly, available at www.iisd.org/didigest/special/daly.htm.

15. Thanks to Jim Craven for this suggestion.

16. Thanks to Ellen Frank for many of these questions.

REINTRODUCING SUPPLY AND DEMAND

A Heterodox Micro Foundation for Macroeconomics

Act One: Scene 1: Equilibrium!
(Starring Danny DeVito as the Auctioneer)

The scene opens at a gigantic auction. Every single participant in the economy is there. All consumers know exactly how much of each good they would buy at different prices to maximize their "utility." All firms know how much they would produce at different prices to maximize their profits.

There is excitement in the air as the auctioneer (Danny DeVito) rapidly calls out an experimental list of prices for every good in the economy. All market participants write down how much they would want to buy (demand) or sell (supply) at these prices. The auctioneer collects these lists and adds them up. If supply is greater than demand for any good the auctioneer lowers the experimental price of that good. If demand is greater than supply, the auctioneer raises the experimental price. After all the adjustments are made the auctioneer calls out a new price list.

Once again everyone writes down what they would want to buy and sell at the announced prices. The lists are collected and prices adjusted for excess supply and/or excess demand. New prices are announced, new buy and sell totals tallied, and more price adjustments made. Finally, the "equilibrium" list of prices is discovered, where supply equals demand in all markets (*general equilibrium*). With a sense of satisfaction, Danny DeVito calls out the final list of prices, hits a big gong, and says, "TRADE." The economy purrs along in general equilibrium.

No, let's start over.

Act One: Scene 1: Disequilibrium
(Starring Harrison Ford as the chief executive officer of General Motors)

The scene opens with Ford sitting at a large desk poring over sheets of paper and looking frantic (in the way only Harrison Ford can). There are two other people in the room. A thin, stylishly dressed woman indicates that she thinks the economy is healthy and that GM should continue production at high levels to maintain market share. A heavyset man interrupts. He urges modest production cutbacks to prevent GM from building up unsold inventories.

Ford grimaces and indicates he is going to shut down 15 plants and lay off 200,000 workers. He thinks things are far worse than either of them imagines. Everyone looks worried.

The camera fades; a newspaper headline spins into view, "GM Cuts Back 200,000 jobs, Goodyear Tire and U.S. Steel Follow Suit." The screen fades out. Next month's newspaper spins into view. The lead article begins, "Sears, Wal-Mart, and K-Mart, fearing falling worker incomes, have cut back on consumer durable orders. Whirlpool and GE have announced factory closings." The screen fades. We are back in the GM boardroom. Ford is still frantic. GM's announcement seems to have spurred larger production cutbacks across the economy than anticipated. Even after cutting 200,000 jobs, Ford fears GM is producing more cars that it can sell. He is not sure what to do.

The scene shifts to the floor of the New York Stock Exchange. There is pandemonium. GM stock plummets 20 percent, then rises 20 percent, then falls again. Some investors have made a lot of money. Others have lost fortunes.[1]

INTRODUCTION

Most principles texts have an early chapter introducing the basic concepts of supply, demand, and equilibrium price determination. The critique in this chapter assumes that you have read and understood that material. We will begin by looking at heterodox critiques of "equilibrium" models and then raise some objections to the way the supply and demand curves are developed.

DISEQUILIBRIUM CRITIQUES

Many key assumptions of neoclassical macro theory are introduced in standard textbooks' initial chapter on supply and demand with little attention to their contestable nature. The most important of these is the texts' cultivation of an equilibrium view of market outcomes. This view emphasizes markets' "self-regulating" characteristics and generally discourages government "intervention" in markets.

Equilibrium economics offers an incomplete rather than incorrect view of the economy. It is often, but not always, a helpful way to think about markets. It is easy to give examples of how equilibrium models work and tempting to ignore disequilibrium variations. Serious problems can arise, however, when students and policy makers attempt to apply the lessons of equilibrium economics to disequilibrium situations, as happened during the Great Depression in the 1930s or in the deep recession of 1980–1982. The neglect of disequilibrium dynamics offers another example of how the optimality subtext of neoclassical texts narrows economic education and impoverishes the emperor's wardrobe.

The Logic of Equilibrium Models

Most neoclassical textbooks begin their introduction to supply and demand by deriving the supply and demand curves in ways that generate downward sloping demand curves and upward sloping supply curves. For the time being we shall work with curves of this kind. The combination gives us the familiar X diagram.

Most neoclassical textbooks illustrate the logic of supply and demand with reference to markets for consumer goods. All households are assumed to know how much they would demand (buy) at every price in order to maximize their utility. All firms are assumed to know how much they would supply (sell) at every price in order to maximize profits. Both firms and households

Figure 5.1 **Supply and Demand**

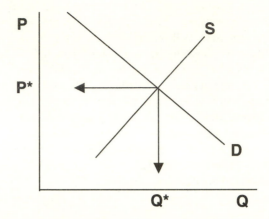

bring these mental schedules to the marketplace, which aggregates them into market demand and market supply curves. The key challenge is to explain how all of these maximizing calculations (what people would choose to supply and demand at different prices) resolve themselves into a single equilibrium market price and market quantity of output (P* and Q*).

Textbook economics relies on three lines of reasoning to explain why market forces always produce equilibrium outcomes: (1) the assumption of perfect information; (2) the auctioneer metaphor; and (3) the assumption of instantaneous adjustment to equilibrium values.

The "perfect information" assumption implies that all market participants have perfect information about the position of the market supply and demand curves. In this case no consumer would be willing to pay more, or producer willing to accept less, than the equilibrium price.

The "auctioneer metaphor" is illustrated by the Danny DeVito vignette at the beginning of this chapter. The metaphor was developed by one of the founders of neoclassical economics, Leon Walras, and remains central to modern neoclassical theory. Rather than assuming that all market participants begin with perfect information, the auctioneer metaphor implies that market processes generate perfect information. The auctioneer metaphor embodies this knowledge in an imaginary person who only allows trading at equilibrium prices.

The "instantaneous adjustment" assumption is usually given the most attention in neoclassical textbooks. This explanation for why markets generate equilibrium prices and quantities asks what would happen if nonequilibrium prices and quantities arose in the market. Given firms' and households' initial mental supply and demand schedules, any price below P* is predicted to generate excess demand and pressures for price increases, while any price above P* is predicted to generate excess supply and pressures for price decreases (see Figure 5.2). These pressures only cease when they force the economy to its equilibrium point. The key claim is that the adjustment process takes place so fast (virtually instantaneously) that it mimics the auctioneer metaphor.

All three of these equilibrium-generating stories are plausible accounts for how markets work in some situations. Unfortunately, the orthodox Walrasian framework overlooks important disequilibrium cases. Heterodox economics challenges this oversight. As we shall see in later chapters, this challenge reflects heterodox concerns about the implications of: (1) "imperfect information"; (2) the "coordination problem"; (3) the "monetary" rather than barter character of the economy; (4) the need for dynamic rather than static models of economic behavior; and (5) the misuse of the "ceteris paribus" assumption.

Figure 5.2 **Equilibrium Adjustments**

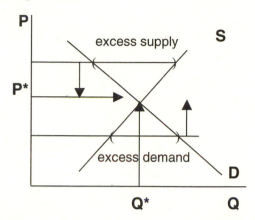

The Logic of Disequilibrium Models

Exacerbating Errors Models

Let us begin with the familiar *X* diagram. We shall assume it represents market supply and market demand in the automobile industry.

Because firms lack perfect information, it is possible for them to misestimate consumer demand for their product. In this case we shall assume that the auto manufacturers underestimate consumer demand, mistakenly expecting it to look like D2 rather than D1 (see Figure 5.3). They therefore only produce the quantity Q2 of cars and price them at P2 in the market. In the textbook model, the low price creates excess demand, which drives up the price of cars and induces higher output levels. While this scenario can occur in heterodox models, it is also possible for the initial error to compound itself.

The latter is the story presented in the Harrison Ford vignette at the beginning of this chapter. The automobile manufacturers' excessive pessimism spreads to other industries in the automobile sector. The lower levels of output lead to layoffs and reduced consumer spending in the economy. Anticipating this contagion, department stores like Wal-Mart cut back on consumer durable orders and layoffs spread to other industries.

The process can feed on itself and create what heterodox economists call a "downward spiral." The problem is precluded in textbook economics (though unfortunately not in the real world) by either the perfect information assumption or the implicit claim that there are no ripple effects from initial "imperfect information mistakes" in the economy. Under the auctioneer and instantaneous adjustment assumptions, initial "errors" are corrected before they can spread.[2]

The neoclassical textbook model of the economy lacks important dynamic features. Imperfect information is not permitted to influence the market's ultimate destination. Shocks to the economy smoothly resolve into new equilibrium outcomes. When firms' output levels fall (represented as backward shifts of the supply curve), the demand curve generally remains fixed. While this may be a reasonable assumption when we are dealing with the paper clip industry, it is not reasonable when we are dealing with large parts of the economy, like the automobile sector or the labor market.

One of the unfortunate impacts of textbook economics is that students learn to "see" the economy in terms of equilibrium pictures. If you ask someone who has had an introductory economics

Figure 5.3 **Market Correction**

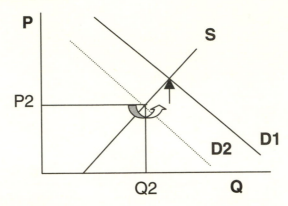

Figure 5.4 **Downward Spirals**

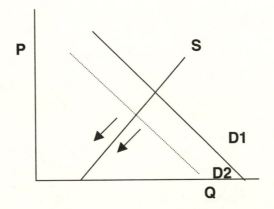

course what would happen if a fall in business confidence or any other economic shock caused a backward shift of the supply curve for automobiles, almost all students will jump from the first *X* intersection of the old supply and demand curves to a second *X* intersection of the new supply curve and old demand curve, without any concern for potential dynamic effects of the adjustment process on the two curves. Students have learned *not to see* dynamic complications. They have learned *to see* through a static supply and demand lens. They have also learned *to see* all other variables remaining the same when thinking about the impact of a change in a single variable on the rest of the economy. These habits can be "blinding" at times.

All Other Things Are Not Always Equal: Challenging the "Ceteris Paribus" Assumption

Although it is often useful in microeconomics to model economic behavior by holding all variables in the economy constant but one, this assumption frequently runs into trouble in macroeconomics. In microeconomics, one might ask what would happen to the price of an *NSYNC CD if the quantity of *NSYNC CDs produced fell by 10 percent assuming all other phenomena that might affect the demand for and price of an *NSYNC CD (such as advertising expenditures or the economy's unemployment rate) remained the same. In this case the drop in employment in

Figure 5.5 **Elastic Price Expectations and Downward Spirals**

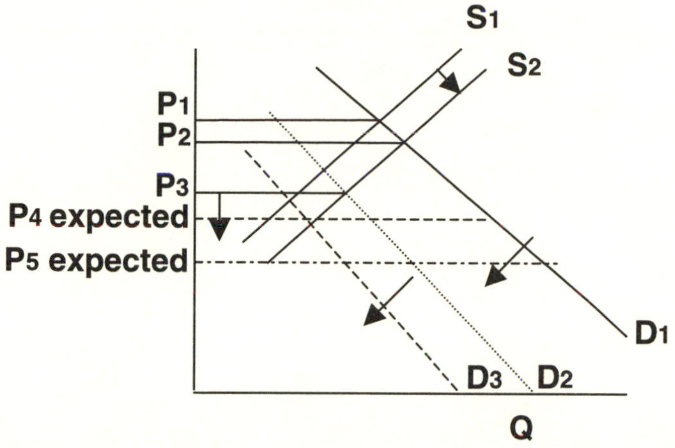

*NSYNC factories could be reasonably assumed to have an infinitesimal impact on the demand for *NSYNC CDs.

This would not be the case, however, if we replaced *NSYNC with the manufacturing sector in a macro model. In this case a fall in the quantity of output produced (and the number of workers employed) might affect the quantity of output demanded. This kind of interplay is foreclosed in most textbook discussions by the ceteris paribus assumption.[3] To understand why unemployment can persist, it is often necessary to abandon the ceteris paribus assumption when thinking about the behavior of a system of markets rather than a single market.

Elastic Price Expectations

Given the absence of perfect information, heterodox economists argue that shifts of the supply or demand curves can cause disequilibrium price expectations. Market participants can assume, for example, that prices will continue to move in the direction they have recently moved (elastic price expectations). This is equivalent to assuming that falling prices can induce backward shifts of the demand curve (i.e., at every existing price people demand less in anticipation of future price declines), which can induce further price declines and new backward shifts of the demand curve— ad infinitum[4] (see Figure 5.5).

For example, assume that the supply of labor has increased, creating a new equilibrium wage below last period's equilibrium wage. Rather than hiring additional workers at this reduced wage, employers might wait for wages to fall further. This could create a self-fulfilling prophecy by reducing labor demand. The new drop in wages could induce expectations of even larger future declines and start its own downward spiral.

Inelastic Price Expectations and Other Forms of Wage and Price Stickiness[5]

It is generally accepted that wages and prices are "sticky" in the economy.[6] Recent research by Alan Blinder, former vice chair of the Federal Reserve, for example, suggests that the median firm changes prices only 1.4 times a year. About half of all firms seem to review prices only once a year (Blinder et al. 1998, 84–85).

Figure 5.6 **Inelastic Price Expectations and Unemployment**

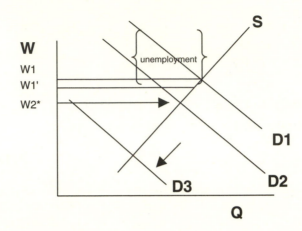

This means that, contrary to the auctioneer assumption, shifts in supply or demand do not always quickly produce price changes that equalize supply and demand. Instead, shifts in supply or demand can, at least initially, produce mainly quantity changes (see figure 5.6). We shall turn shortly to the reasons for sticky prices, but will look first at the implications of sluggish price changes.

Figure 5.6 depicts the impact of a fall in the demand for labor in the presence of wage stickiness. Rather than falling to W2, the maintenance of W1 (or a modest fall to W1´) results in unemployment. The same kind of result emerges in goods markets when prices fail to fall when demand falls.[7]

The implication of these graphs is that economic shocks (phenomena that shift the supply and demand curves) can cause periods of unemployment and unused productive capacity. The most serious problems arise if we combine the short-run disequilibrium potential of sticky wages and sticky prices with the dynamic potential for destabilizing shocks to produce downward spirals.

Why might wages and prices be sticky? There are many different reasons, depending on the industry and direction of the price change. The variety of causes suggests why it is important to look at "markets in context," rather than markets in the abstract. Among the most important causes of sluggish price adjustments are:

1. Long-term contracts with fixed prices, such as year or multiyear labor agreements and long-term rental contracts. About one-quarter of all prices appear to be governed by such contracts (Blinder et al. 1998, 94).
2. "Implicit contracts," that is, informal understandings that limit price changes. These appear to be especially important in discouraging wage cuts in labor markets (due to a desire to maintain labor morale) and price increases in goods markets where cultivating customer relationships is important. We will explore these phenomena in more detail in chapter 12.
3. Uncertainty about whether perceived market conditions are temporary or permanent. This is the inverse of the "elastic expectations" case discussed above where firms mistakenly overestimate the magnitude of equilibrium price changes. In this case market participants have "inelastic price expectations" and mistakenly expect a return to prior prices.

4. Fears that price cuts may be interpreted by customers as signals of quality declines. This effect is probably concentrated in markets with especially poor information about quality, such as some consumer (as opposed to business) product markets.

5. The cost of changing prices, often termed "menu costs" (capturing the image of the cost to restaurants of reprinting their menus).

6. The disincentives for price changes introduced by collusive behavior in markets with a small number of firms.

There are other reasons for anticipating price sluggishness in the economy, which we will review in later chapters. The key point to grasp at this time is that the simple equilibrium picture conveyed in the early chapters of many macro texts is an incomplete and inadequate micro foundation for understanding macroeconomics.

Integrating Equilibrium and Disequilibrium Dynamics: The Auctioneer and the Casino Metaphors

Because of imperfect information and potential disequilibrium moments, firms and consumers, borrowers and lenders, and other participants in the economy must make choices amid uncertainty. In a sense, they have to bet on this or that option. Firms have to guess future consumer demand and which technology will be competitive long after their investment in new productive capacity is fixed in concrete. Households have to decide whether to buy a car or a house or wait for lower mortgage rates or better prices. Students have to guess whether there will be jobs in this or that field five to ten years from now. In this sense the economy is like a casino and its participants are like gamblers.

Most of the time people make pretty good bets and the economy fulfills common expectations. Sometimes it does not. Heterodox economic models emphasize that the economy has both equilibrium and disequilibrium moments. Markets exhibit, in Jim Crotty's words, "conditional stability," that is, temporary stability as long as expectations remain reasonably stable. Situations can arise, however, when expectations are volatile and in these circumstances markets can be volatile too.

In later chapters we will explore many more avenues by which uncertainty and imperfect information can destabilize an economy, especially with respect to monetary phenomena like liquidity crises, financial panics, speculative bubbles, and credit crunches. Once we have developed these arguments, it will be difficult to look at the economy solely through equilibrium glasses. Economic theory needs both the auctioneer metaphor and the casino metaphor to capture the richness of economic activity.

HETERODOX CRITIQUES OF TEXTBOOK DEMAND AND SUPPLY CURVES

In an effort to claim the mantle of science, neoclassical textbooks often portray economic behavior as if it were the predictable actions of inanimate objects, such as pool balls on a table or planets in the heavens. Many textbook introductions to supply and demand try to mimic the language of the physical sciences. There are references to "the law of demand," "the law of diminishing marginal utility," "the law of supply," "the law of diminishing returns," and "the law of supply and demand." In later chapters we will come across similar language embodied in phrases like "the natural rate" of unemployment or "the inevitable" trade-off between equity and efficiency.

In many ways this language is misleading. The so-called laws are not constant, natural relationships. They are observations about certain tendencies in popular behavior in certain contexts. The "laws" are "violated" more often than suggested by the texts. For example, there are some goods for which the demand curve does not slope downward because the price of the good is part of its appeal. Firms producing "status goods" know that if they lower prices they may lose "snob appeal." In addition, some buyers may assume the fall in price is associated with a decline in quality. (How many of you hesitate to buy a less expensive product or visit a less expensive doctor, for fear of shoddiness or inexpertness?) Similarly, for many, and perhaps most, goods, the supply curve is probably flat or falling, rather than upward sloping as suggested by the "law of supply." Although some of these complications are briefly acknowledged in neoclassical textbooks, the qualifiers have a "note but ignore" feel to them, leaving students with an oversimplified view of the economy.

Heterodox economists challenge the static and naturalist image of supply and demand that animates many neoclassical texts. This image paints the demand curve as a reflection of natural consumer tastes and the supply curve as a technologically determined reflection of the costs of production. The market is portrayed as a mechanism for linking together human and physical nature.

Heterodox economists prefer a more dynamic and socially constructed view of supply and demand. Recall, for example, the different treatment of the "circular flow" in neoclassical textbooks and heterodox critiques. In the standard textbook picture of the circular flow, the consumer is sovereign. Consumer signals spur firms' production plans, which in turn galvanize supply and demand in input markets.

The heterodox picture is more complex. Causal forces come from both the consumer and the firm sides of the market. Owners of financial wealth strive to create as well as to find investment outlets for their accumulated money. Corporations strive to create as well as to respond to consumer desires as they struggle to grow and earn a rate of return on past investments. Firms engaged directly in production and firms engaged in financing production develop long-run business plans involving labor policies, supplier relationships, product development, consumer advertising, political lobbying, and competitive strategies. To a significant extent "supply and demand" are the products of, as much as the determinants of, these activities.

Rather than simply linking together human and physical nature through the signaling of supply and demand, market capitalism reconstructs the social and physical world in line with the competitive struggle for growth in a capitalist economy. Supply and demand can be very useful concepts but they need to be situated within a dynamic analysis of how firms compete and shape supply and demand.

Like politics, economic debate sometimes makes strange bedfellows. Both heterodox economists and business economists tend to find the models of market outcomes offered by textbook economics missing the blood and guts (that is, the contingent, dynamic, and strategic aspects) of real-world business. For example, the logic of textbook economics suggests that the price of electricity and the amount used in the economy is automatically determined by the supply and demand for electricity. While business strategies might shift the supply and demand curves a bit, their intersection dances around a natural center of gravity. This anchor is determined by technological phenomena on the supply side and the desires of consumers on the demand side of the electricity market. Heterodox models are more complex.

In heterodox analyses the supply and demand for electricity are situated within a dynamic study of the energy sector. When this is done, a fascinating story emerges. It is a tale of technological triumphs and corporate growth strategies (such as pricing nuclear power below cost to create a market for nuclear-fired electricity, as detailed in note 8 in chapter 4). It is a tale of successful political campaigns to subsidize electric energy sources and penalize nonelectric energy sources (including energy conservation). It is a tale of risk shifting from private to public shoulders and marketing campaigns to increase the demand for electricity. As historian Richard Hirsh (1989) reports,

> [G]rowth constituted an essential element of the grow-and-build strategy. Individually and collectively . . . utilities pursued the goal of growth by engaging in a series of publicity and propaganda activities throughout the years (p. 33). . . .
>
> The biggest concerted promotional push began in 1956 with the "Live Better Electrically" campaign. Conceived of by the General Electric Company (p. 51). . . .
>
> Utility journals exhorted, "Sell or Die!" and "Sell—and Sell—and Sell." . . . Meanwhile in a famous "Inventing Our Future" speech in 1964, Sporn [a leading electric utility executive] noted that "the most important elements that determine our loads [demand for electricity] are not those that happen, but those that we project—that we invent—in the broad sense of the term 'invention.' You have control over such loads: you invent them, and then you can make plans for the best manner of meeting them." (p. 53)

What is the bottom line here? What is at issue? What is the above example meant to show? The heterodox answer is that supply and demand are insufficient as tools of analysis if used without linkage to a deeper sense of how capitalist economies evolve and how market competition works. The point is not that supply and demand are irrelevant concepts, but that they have to be used "in context," within a dynamic analysis that looks at the forces responsible for their shape and position.

To draw an analogy, one could explain the outcome of an election by saying that more people wanted one candidate than another because they agreed with his or her stance on the issues. Or one could look at the way one of the candidates was able to define the issues in order to create a sense of common purpose. The first position implies that there existed an a priori matching between the electorate and one of the candidates. The second position sees the matching as somewhat contingent. The heterodox view of supply and demand is more like the second perspective. The market and its participants are seen as partially creating a pattern of supply and demand rather than simply discovering it.

CONCLUSION

We will elaborate many of the ideas raised in this chapter later in the text. The two key concepts you should keep in mind are: (1) the importance of imperfect information and uncertainty in market economies and the resulting potential for disequilibrium (as opposed to equilibrium) dynamics; and (2) the importance of situating economic analysis and the use of supply and demand concepts within an institutionally specific and dynamic analysis of the nature of competition in a capitalist economy.

IN THEIR OWN WORDS

> Ceteris Paribus is a method that has its uses in micro theory. When the same assumptions are carried over to macro, however, they can foment what I call the "cet par trick." If one firm lays off workers, it is reasonable to assume that its demand curve is not affected. If the average firm lays off workers or cuts wages, it is trickery of the worst sort to assume that the

economy's level of demand is unaffected or that the average firm's demand curve does not shift downwards. Yet this is what is assumed in neoclassical theory.

—Jim Crotty[8]

[S]upply and demand analysis is not sufficient to answer the most interesting and important questions, even at the level of introductory economics.

—Dorman (2001, 332)

One proposal for representing more closely, in the abstract, the real-world variability in prices and quantities is to draw, or imagine, graphs that use thick curves. Thick supply and demand curves represent the fact that a variety of prices and quantities may be possible even within the same market (9–25). . . .

[T]hick curves may present an accurate picture of supply and demand, without being precise. . . .

The pursuit of precision at the expense of accuracy may give us a false confidence about how much of the real world can actually be understood through elegant simplifications.

—Goodwin et al. (2003, 9–27)

STUDY QUESTIONS

Discussion Questions

1. Chapter 5 begins with two different images of economic activity. What do you think the comparison is meant to convey?
2. What assumptions, lines of reasoning, or "stories" are used in standard supply and demand analysis to explain why markets operate at equilibrium values?
3. What assumptions, lines of reasoning, or "stories" are used in heterodox analysis of supply and demand to generate "nonequilibrium outcomes?"
4. Compare and contrast what might happen in an economy when very pessimistic expectations cause a major industry to underestimate the demand for its product according to the logic of equilibrium and disequilibrium analysis.

Review Questions

1. Explain what is meant by the following terms or concepts: (a) the auctioneer metaphor; (b) elastic price expectations; (c) inelastic price expectations; (d) natural law vs. socially constructed supply and demand curves.
2. What metaphor takes the place of the auctioneer in disequilibrium models?
3. Explain why the presence of elastic price expectations can cause economic problems in disequilibrium models of supply and demand.
4. Under what circumstances might falling wages be unable to quickly eliminate unemployment according to the logic of disequilibrium models of supply and demand?
5. Why might inelastic price expectations cause economic problems in disequilibrium models of supply and demand?
6. What are some of the reasons given by heterodox economists for why wages and prices might be "sticky" in the economy (i.e., slow to change even when there is excess supply or excess demand in the economy at existing prices)?

NOTES

1. This scenario is not without recent examples. On October 19, 1987, the Dow Jones Industrial stock average fell a record 508 points, for a decline of 22.6 percent. From July 17 to August 31, 1998, the Dow Jones Industrial average fell 19.26 percent (MD Leasing Corp, http://www.mdleasing.com/djia.htm, June 26, 2003). Some individual stocks suffered even larger percentage declines than the average.

2. In more formal language, textbook economics rules out "false trading," that is, trading outside of equilibrium.

3. Jim Crotty of the University of Massachusetts at Amherst has argued this point especially well. He notes that in neoclassical macro models, households make consumption decisions assuming that they can sell all of the labor they want at the market wage. In effect, the models generate automatic full employment, by assuming it. In contrast, in heterodox models, households may assume they cannot sell all of the labor they want at the market wage due to unemployment. The existence of unemployment (or even the fear of unemployment) can limit consumption demand. The market may therefore fail to record the potential demand that would occur if the economy were at full employment. This shortfall may cause firms to produce less than full-employment levels of output and to demand less than full-employment numbers of workers, weakening the forces pushing the economy toward full employment.

4. This problem worried economists in the spring of 2003, as Paul Krugman wrote in the *New York Times*. "Once an economy is caught in such a trap . . . nasty things (what the I.M.F. calls 'adverse dynamics') begin to happen. Falling prices induce people to postpone their purchases in the expectation that prices will fall further, depressing demand today" (*New York Times*, May 24, 2003).

5. In later chapters we will see how some neoclassical textbooks (those with "New Keynesian sections) attempt to append "sticky price" behaviors to a perfect information model of the economy. Although better than the total neglect of the implications of imperfect information, this strategy fails to capture the full force of disequilibrium dynamics. It is sometimes akin to the "note but ignore" strategy used in textbook economics to handle many "inconvenient" exceptions to the neoclassical model.

6. See for example, Blinder et al. 1998, pp. 4 and 298 for evidence of wage-price stickiness.

7. While some non-price adjustments in product quality, delivery time, and so on may narrow the gap between sticky disequilibrium market prices and equilibrium prices, significant differences can persist.

8. Personal correspondence with the author, July 2004.

FROM MICRO TO MACRO ANALYSIS

Heterodox Critiques of the Initial Macro
Chapters in Principles Texts

INTRODUCTION

This chapter concludes our critique of the introductory chapters in most macro principles text-books. Up until now the material covered in many standard microeconomics and macroeconomics textbooks is quite similar. This chapter comments on the first specifically macroeconomic discussion found in many textbooks.

KEYNES AND THE HISTORY OF MACROECONOMICS

Modern macroeconomics was born as a separate field in economics during the Great Depression. The founding father was John Maynard Keynes. In many textbooks his influence has been reduced to a "box" describing his dazzling achievements as a currency, commodity, and stock speculator; mathematician; adviser to the British Treasury Department; chairman of a life insurance company; a director of the Bank of England; overseer of the endowment of Kings College; editor of England's most influential economic journal; author of many classic works in economic theory; professor at Cambridge University; and chief architect of the major economic institutions of the post–World War II global economy, such as the International Monetary Fund (IMF), the World Bank, and the Bretton Woods system of exchange rates.

Having drawn this engaging picture, most textbooks proceed to ignore Keynes's ideas or recast them in ways that drain them of their major insights and tension with textbook economics. Our approach will be different. About one-quarter of this book is focused on translating Keynes's insights into a critique of textbook economics.

MACRO-MICRO DISTINCTION

Fallacy of Composition

Most neoclassical textbooks begin their overview of macroeconomics with the preface that microeconomics deals with individual firms, households, and markets, while macroeconomics

---

Box 6.1
Two Views of Keynes

Keynes Is Dead

Question: "Should students of macroeconomics still read the *General Theory* [by Keynes]?"
Answer: "No."
Question: "Did Keynes send everyone off down the wrong track?"
Answer: " . . . Keynes . . . thinks that permanent stagnation can result from demand deficiencies. Samuelson's neoclassical synthesis reclaimed [from Keynes] the long run for neoclassical analysis. . . . Now Samuelson's students—my whole generation—are trying to get the short run back, too! . . .

The 1930s sent all of us off on the wrong track, starting with Keynes."
—Brian Snowdon and Howard Vane's interview with Nobel Prize–winning economist Robert E. Lucas Jr.[1]

Keynes Restored

Question: "How do you see the shifting thinking among economists?"
Answer: " . . . The whole thrust of the intellectual revolution led by Robert E. Lucas, Jr. . . . was to tie up all the theoretical strings in nice, neat mathematical bows. . . .

That theory is not applicable to the real world; its predictions are very far off base. In reality, the economy is not a very rapidly self-regulating system, and recessions are not short-lived adjustments. . . ."
Question: "When we talked last in 1984 . . . you were pretty optimistic that a Keynesian restoration was in place. Now eight years have passed, how do you see things?"
Answer: " . . . A Keynesian restoration is not just a hope any more; it has happened."
—Alan Blinder, former assistant chairperson of the Federal Reserve[2]

1. Snowdon and Vane 1999, 148–49. See also Mankiw 1992, esp. pp. 560–61.
2. Blinder 1992, 17–18.

---

deals with the overall economy. What is distinctive about the shift to aggregate outcomes is not explained. Given the textbooks' lack of guidance, it is easy for students to imagine that one can generalize from supply and demand in one market to supply and demand in all markets, that is, from partial equilibrium to general equilibrium models. From this perspective, macroeconomics is merely the summation of a lot of supply and demand curves.

Unfortunately, the world is more complicated. The comfortable optimism of general equilibrium theory suffers from the *fallacy of composition*. It suggests that what is true for the part is automatically true for the whole. This does not always follow. If I am at a concert and I stand up, I will probably see better. If everyone stands up everyone will probably not see better; so too for the macro economy. If I lower my prices, I may sell more. If everyone lowers their prices, things are more ambiguous. Everyone may not sell more. We may, for example, simply get deflation (a fall in the price level).

At the center of many macro controversies is the "coordination question." Oddly, this puzzle is ignored in many neoclassical textbooks. The problem resembles the simultaneity problem posed in the age old question "Which came first, the chicken or the egg?" In order to buy, people must have purchasing power. In order to have purchasing power, others have to buy. As long as everyone is buying, everyone is able to buy, but what ensures everyone is buying?

As you may recall from chapter 5, the auctioneer guarantees everyone is buying in equilibrium theory. There is no such deus ex machina in Keynesian theory. As a result, Keynes warned that pessimistic expectations could precipitate downward spirals in the economy. His perception that macro outcomes depended on peoples' expectations (investors' "animal spirits," consumers' "confidence," wealth holders' "liquidity concerns," etc.) and that pessimistic clusters of expectations could stall economic activity by weakening effective demand is one of the great insights in the history of economic thought. The claim invites a rethinking of many basic ideas derived from equilibrium theory, from the nature of price adjustments (see chapters 5 and 12), to the nature of money (see chapters 10 and 11), to the relationship between savings and investment (see chapter 9), to the nature of unemployment and the labor market (see chapters 12 and 13). The claim implies that theories appropriate for understanding how markets work in isolation may not be adequate for understanding how a system of interconnected markets works. The realization legitimates the existence of a separate field of macroeconomics.

In a nutshell Keynes asked, if we do not *assume* the existence of general equilibrium (GE) (that is, the simultaneous equality between intended supply and intended demand in every market), through a dubious metaphor like the auctioneer, how do we know we are in general equilibrium? Or alternatively, how do we know that we will always return to general equilibrium, if we are not there? There are arguments that can be raised to address Keynes's concerns. Although I do not find them compelling, they are reasonable ideas to discuss. The debate is absent, however, in most introductory texts. There is usually a sentence warning students about the fallacy of composition, but no link of the fallacy to Keynesian problems of insufficient demand. The overall message is "note but ignore."

Micro Foundations for Macro Theory or Macro Foundations for Micro Theory?

The relationship between micro- and macroeconomic theory is a fascinating subject. Most neoclassical texts (following their commitment to methodological individualism) argue for "microfounding" macroeconomics. At first glance this may seem quite reasonable. The neoclassical project argues that economic theory should try to model and explain the maximizing logic underlying individual actions in individual markets and then add them up to explain macro outcomes. Many textbooks imply that if this is done, traditional Keynesian disequilibrium ideas do not fare very well. This result occurs, however, only when the logic of general equilibrium theory is used to model micro outcomes.

You may recall from chapter 5 that GE models assume an auctioneered economy. With this micro foundation, you do not get Keynesian economics. With a more realistic micro theory that includes the possibility of disequilibrium as well as equilibrium dynamics, you get a Keynesian world. We will look at the characteristics of this world in more detail in chapter 9.

The relationship between the micro and macro levels in a Keynesian world is more complicated than that suggested in the GE world of the auctioneer. The irony of the latter world is that its micro theory is really macro founded. In the textbook story, general equilibrium necessarily emerges from the aggregation of millions of isolated maximizing decisions by consumers and firms. The micro decisions precede the macro outcome. The problem with this story is that it includes a hidden assumption about the context of individual decision making. It is only by assuming that each household and firm makes its maximizing decisions as if it were in a general equilibrium macro economy that all the decisions add up to produce that general equilibrium economy. If economic agents have non-GE expectations, or projects they would like to orient the economy toward, you need not arrive at a GE outcome. To some extent, GE theory confuses hypothetical proofs of the possible existence of general equilibrium with practical claims for its actual existence.

In a Keynesian world, macro outcomes are still built upon micro behaviors, but those behaviors assume certain things about the macro environment. In a heterodox, Keynesian world there are "path choices" and clusters of institutions and interconnected expectations that influence or condition individual calculations. Thus, a Keynesian model has continuous feedback between the micro and macro levels, or, put another way, the macro level infuses the micro level, which constructs the macro level.

For example, during the 1960s, the U.S. economy was organized by a set of institutions that included a manufacturing sector with oligopoly industries (industries with a few large firms) and unionized workforces, a government commitment to Keynesian policies to maintain full employment, and other regulations and institutions that reduced speculation in financial markets. Collectively, these policies created a planning context that presupposed high aggregate demand in the economy and encouraged high corporate investment. Market outcomes (macro outcomes) thus represented the aggregate decisions of individual agents (micro choices), but these decisions were predicated on certain assumptions about and characteristics of the macro environment.

Heterodox economics studies how "planning contexts" are created (see chapter 13). Standard textbooks tend to ignore these contexts. Some of the most interesting work in heterodox macroeconomics currently involves efforts to study what have been termed "social structures of accumulation," or SSAs. Social structures of accumulation are interrelated institutions, and expectations nurtured by those institutions, that provide a stable context for long-term economic decisions. Social structures of accumulation represent a kind of institutional response to uncertainty that provides a backdrop for investment decisions and business strategy.

Heterodox economists criticize neoclassical economists for often jumping from the theoretical conclusions of a "micro-founded" auctioneer model of the macro economy to laissez-faire oriented policy recommendations that minimize the role of government in the economy. They find the neoclassicals' demand for "micro foundations" a rhetorical strategy that often trumps real-world institutional details and messy disequilibrium problems with hypothetical models of auctioneered behaviors. Many equilibrium economists today and in Keynes's time have dismissed Keynesian concerns with the claim, "in the long run the economy returns to full-employment equilibrium." To which Keynes is reported to have replied, "In the long run we're all dead" (i.e., disequilibrium is real).

Levels of Aggregation

In both the more complicated "macro-micro fusion" world of heterodox economics and the elegant auctioneered micro-founded macro world of the textbooks, the ideal explanations of macro outcomes involve detailed analyses of micro units in the economy (firms, households, etc.). In reality, however, practical difficulties mitigate against this completeness. It is simply impossible to adequately model 250 million people's interactions across numerous dimensions. In response to this impossibility, many standard "micro-founded" textbooks fall back on the implications of abstract auctioneered models of macroeconomics. In contrast, Keynesian texts often try to build models of the economy based on aggregated behaviors without detailed exploration of the individual actions making up the aggregates. For example, Keynesian economists often model the relationship between changes in the money supply and changes in the level of economic activity at an aggregate level. They do not construct these relationships from a summation of individual actions by households and firms. It is not specified, for example, to what degree increasing the money supply increases economic activity by making credit cheaper or making credit more widely available at the existing interest rate. It is not exactly specified how increasing the money supply effects long-term interest rates. Only end results are modeled, e.g., the relationship between the money supply and interest rates. Practitioners of aggregate analysis argue that this is the best that we can do with the data and complexity of the problem.

The hidden debate in this highly abstract controversy often involves how to understand macro coordination. The auctioneer–micro foundations model implies that markets work wonders by themselves and calls for laissez-faire policies. The Keynesian model raises the risk of coordination failures and recommends government responses. The heterodox model emphasizes the role of institutions in coordinating economic decisions and also recommends government oversight of the market.[1]

TOPICS AND CONCERNS FOR MACROECONOMICS

Most neoclassical textbooks describe macroeconomics as the study of the determinants of GDP, GDP growth, unemployment, and inflation, with secondary attention to other aggregate outcomes such as interest rates, the balance of trade, and exchange rates. The goals of macro policy are identified as maximizing current GDP and future economic growth and maintaining low and stable unemployment and inflation rates.

As explored in detail in the next chapter, heterodox economists offer a much broader list of macroeconomic policy goals. Among these are concerns about: (1) economic security, (2) the quality of work, (3) environmental sustainability, (4) the distribution of income and wealth, (5) the well-being of many nonmarket economic activities organized within the household and community sectors of the economy, and (6) the impact of macroeconomic activity on "meta-externalities" (such as the viability of democracy and community).

The textbooks' narrowing of macroeconomic outcomes tends to privilege neoclassical methodologies and subject matter in determining macroeconomic policy. The old adage "out of sight, out of mind" encourages the acceptance of numerous trade-offs in pursuit of higher GDP.

THE CONFUSING WORLD OF AGGREGATE SUPPLY AND AGGREGATE DEMAND: TWO CURVES IN SEARCH OF A THEORY

Professor to student caught sleeping in class:
"What do you think, Joe?"
Joe: "I didn't hear the question, but I think I know the answer: Supply and Demand."

In the last two decades neoclassical textbooks have introduced the Aggregate Supply (AS) and Aggregate Demand (AD) framework in earlier chapters than they did in the past. As we shall see, there are serious problems with the framework and these are exacerbated by its early introduction in the texts without adequate explanation. If you felt a bit puzzled by your text's discussion of AS and AD, or felt that you only "sort of understood how the framework worked," the problems may be with the framework and not your comprehension of it.

One of the ideas that most introductory econ texts rightly emphasize is that a graph is meaningless without labels on the axes. Millions of students have lost points on exams for leaving out the "P" on the vertical axis and the "Q" on the horizontal axis for microeconomic supply and demand graphs. Surprising as it might seem, at least one major intro textbook offers AS and AD graphs as organizing logos without labeled axes. This is probably because the variables on the axes are quite confusing (the price level and real income). The "logo" strategy appeals to students' established acceptance of supply and demand metaphors to offer a familiar organizing framework for discussing macroeconomics (with the ever-present "note but ignore" warning that they are not typical supply and demand curves).

Most of the time all of the texts do put the "price level" on the vertical axis and real income on the horizontal axis. But there is little explanation of what it means to put the price level on the vertical axis, or why the entire economy should be described in terms of the effect of the "price level" on economic behavior. The introductory texts sometimes seem to appeal to students' understanding of microeconomic supply and demand to suggest that employers want to sell more at high prices (so the AS curve slopes upward) and consumers want to buy more at low prices (so the AD curve slopes downward), but this has almost nothing to do with the logic of the AS and AD curves and is a misleading analogy. For example, when the price level falls, the real cost of consumer goods remains constant (i.e., goods may be 10 percent cheaper but wages and incomes are also 10 percent less).

As we shall see in chapter 12, the standard reasons offered for the curves' slopes are quite different from the intuitions appealed to in students to motivate acceptance of the curves early in the term. It is hard to raise criticisms of the framework at this point in the commentary, however, because the explanation for the curves is so incomplete in the text. The point for now is simply to be wary of this framework and its equilibrium format.

CONCLUSION

Prior to Keynes, macroeconomics did not exist as a separate field of study. The first known juxtaposition of the terms *microeconomic* and *macroeconomic* dates from only 1941.[2] Heterodox macroeconomics challenges the general equilibrium foundation of conventional macro theory and its odd transformation into the aggregate supply and aggregate demand framework (see chapters 12 and 13). In its place heterodox macroeconomics stresses the implications of uncertainty, institutional contexts (especially in terms of, but not limited to, responses to uncertainty), and a number of other features ignored or deemphasized in standard theory. Heterodox macroeconomics also broadens the discussion of macroeconomic outcomes from the textbooks' relatively narrow focus on GDP and the national income accounts (see chapter 7).

IN THEIR OWN WORDS

[I]n the end, what makes macroeconomics a viable subject is that the microeconomic decisions which you get from all the micro foundations do not add up. You have a fallacy of composition. If you do not admit the fallacy of composition, do Walras [i.e., GE].
—Victoria Chick (Snowdon, Vane, and Wynarczyk 1994, 403)

For years after the Spanish dictator actually died, the mock television newscast on "Saturday Night Live" was periodically interrupted with a "news flash" informing viewers that "General Franco is still dead!" This served . . . to suggest that after many decades of taking an absolute ruler for granted, the world needed more than one reminder that he was no longer alive and well.

Much the same is true for general equilibrium theory. . . . It has successfully colonized much of macroeconomics . . . . [and] is widely cited . . . in textbooks . . . as providing the rigorous theoretical version of Adam Smith's invisible hand. . . .

Yet those who follow the news about microeconomic theory have known for sometime that general equilibrium is not exactly alive and well any more.

—Frank Ackerman (1999, 1)

STUDY QUESTIONS

Discussion Questions

1. Why do heterodox economists argue that macroeconomics is more than adding up the implications of microeconomics?
2. Standard textbooks and general equilibrium theory offer powerful reasons for expecting markets to tend toward equilibrium values. What do heterodox economists find objectionable about generalizing from the implications of partial equilibrium analysis (i.e., the tendency for individual markets to move toward equilibrium values) to general equilibrium analysis?
3. GE theory claims it is necessary to micro found macro outcomes. Many heterodox economists, especially post Keynesian economists, argue that it is necessary to understand the macro foundations for micro outcomes. What do the latter claims mean?

Review Questions

1. What is meant by the fallacy of composition and the coordination problem?
2. What is meant by a social structure of accumulation (SSA)? How is the concept used in heterodox theory to operationalize the notion of macro-founding micro outcomes?
3 What are the main goals of macro policy identified in standard textbooks? What additional goals are emphasized in heterodox analysis?

NOTES

1. David Colander's edited volume *The Complexity Vision and the Teaching of Economics* (2000) is an especially helpful source for thinking through complexity issues.

2. Stiglitz 1997, p. 592, citing *The New Palgrave: A Dictionary of Economics*, 1987, 3: pp. 461–63.

REMEASURING ECONOMIC ACTIVITY

Heterodox Critiques of GDP Accounting

> What you measure depends on what you see
> And what you see depends on what lens you look through.

> *Economics is not solely concerned with income and wealth but also with using those resources as means to significant ends, including the promotion and enjoyment of long and worthwhile lives. If . . . the economic success of a nation is judged only by income . . . as it so often is, the important goal of well-being is missed.*[1]
> —Amartya Sen, winner of the Nobel Prize in Economics, 1998

INTRODUCTION

Almost all neoclassical macro textbooks have an early chapter (or chapters) with titles like "Measuring National Output" or "Measuring Economic Activity." The chapters discuss the construction and meaning of macroeconomic statistics. Although the chapters may seem little more than a collection of definitions, they carry expansive subtexts, asserting: (1) the "scientific" and "objective" character of textbook economics and textbook statistics, (2) the centrality of GDP growth to economic well-being, and (3) the wisdom of a "steady as you go" economic program to maintain GDP growth.

The next two chapters of this commentary challenge these claims. The chapters demonstrate how the topics you need to discuss in order to assess economic performance and the statistics you need to construct in order to measure economic activity change when your image of the economy changes. Chapter 7 critiques the textbooks' discussion of GDP. Chapter 8 discusses labor market statistics and price indices.

GDP: THE TEXTBOOKS' YARDSTICK

GDP is probably the most important statistic showcased in neoclassical macro texts. Most authors are careful not to *explicitly* claim that GDP or GDP per capita are measures of economic welfare. In fact, the GDP chapters usually include one or two pages that quickly list some limitations of GDP as a measure of national well-being. Following a "note but ignore" motif, however, these warnings are diluted by repeated assertions of the centrality of GDP statistics for measuring eco-

Figure 7.1   **The "Genuine Progress Indicator"**
An Alternative Measure of U.S. Economic Output

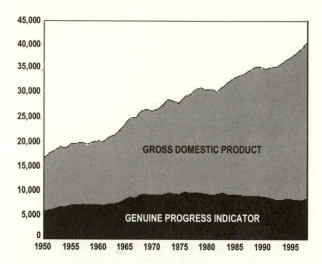

Source: Reprinted with permission from Redefining Progress (http://www.rprogress.org/publications/gpi1999/gpi1999.html). Redefining Progress (http://www.rprogress.org/) is a think tank that addresses issues of economic well-being.

nomic performance, quick-and-dirty comparisons between countries based on GDP, and a relative neglect of dimensions of well-being uncaptured by GDP statistics. The take-away message is that GDP, with all of its blemishes, is an excellent proxy for national economic well-being and maximizing GDP is an excellent strategy for maximizing national well-being (Nordhaus and Kokkelenberg 1999, 27).

Heterodox economists find some GDP-related statistics, such as median national income, useful inputs for constructing broader measures of the economy's performance. Heterodox economists also find GDP and other data in the national income accounts helpful for measuring the level of market activity and aggregate demand in the economy, which is a separate task from measuring the level of well-being produced by the economy. What heterodox economists object to is the reduction of the multidimensional nature of economic activities to the unidimensional measure of GDP. To draw an educational analogy, heterodox objections to the textbooks' treatment of GDP resemble some educators' objections to the use of GPA (grade point average) or scores on standardized tests to measure the "output" and achievements of students and schools. Like the skeptical educators, heterodox economists criticize the related tendency to "teach to the test," that is, to organize education to maximize test scores and to organize the economy to maximize GDP.

INADEQUACIES OF GDP AS A MEASURE OF ECONOMIC WELL-BEING

Overview

Heterodox economists find GDP an inadequate measure of national economic well-being due to: (1) its neglect of the value of nonmarket economic activities, such as household production and leisure time; (2) its neglect of the implications of "positional competition"; (3) its failure to debit the economy for the "production of bads" (such as pollution)[2] and increasing "intermediate goods" requirements (such as lengthier commuting); (4) its failure to debit the economy for its drawdown of exhaustible resources; (5) its inattention to distributional issues; (6) its failure to credit or debit the economy for changes in the quality of work life; and (7) its inattention to "meta-externalities."[3]

If the magnitude of the above items were small or constant, these oversights might be acceptable. The magnitudes are large, however, and growing. They make maximizing GDP an inadequate strategy for guiding macroeconomic policy. We look next at some of these deficiencies in more detail.

Neglect of Nonmarket Activities

It is difficult to calculate the precise economic value of leisure or the goods and services produced in the household or voluntary sectors of the economy.[4] By all accounts it is large. Common estimates for the value of household production range from 25 percent to more than 50 percent of GDP.[5] Neglecting nonmarket productive activities and leisure can thus give a misleading picture of what is happening economically.

For example, just looking at GDP statistics for the last thirty years can paint an excessively rosy picture of economic advance. From 1973 to 2000, real median family income in the United States increased by about 25 percent (Mishel, Bernstein, and Boushey 2003, 37). Almost half of this increase, however, could be attributed to longer working hours, as average family work time per year in the United States increased by about five weeks.[6] Americans now work longer hours than many foreign workers, including the Canadians, Germans, and Japanese.[7] Forty-four percent of employees in a major national survey in 2004 felt overworked (Galinsky et al. 2005, 2). Many people reported they had insufficient time for family, household chores, and/or leisure.[8]

In addition to working longer, Americans appear to be working harder than they did twenty years ago. While some workers' increased effort is voluntary and personally satisfying, some of the increase is unwelcomed and due to "speed up" imposed from above (Bond, Galinsky, and Swanberg 1998, 9).[9] Surveying these changes, the Families and Work Institute warned, "For a significant group of Americans, the way we work today appears to be negatively affecting their health" (Galinsky et al. 2005, 1).[10] None of these problems show up in the GDP statistics measuring the economy's performance over the last quarter century. Few are highlighted in neoclassical texts, upwardly biasing impressions of recent economic performance.

On the other hand, if one thought that the productivity of household labor had increased at the same rate as market labor, the GDP statistics might underestimate positive changes in economic well-being.[11] Two other overlapping areas neglected by the national income accounts are the underground economy (illegal productive activities) and its more benign sibling, the informal economy.

Neglect of Positional Competition

As you might recall from chapter 2, positional competition refers to the struggle to "keep up with the Joneses." Some goods, such as expensive wedding rings or elite brands of liquor, are bought, at least in part, to gain social status. The irony is that when many people succeed in acquiring traditional status goods, they lose much of their positional value. It thus takes ever fancier and more expensive cars, houses, clothes, and so on to capture the same level of social status. Like the mutually draining expenses of an arms race, the spending for positional competition is inherently wasteful. This waste is not recognized in the GDP statistics or in neoclassical texts.

This waste and commodity devaluation does not occur for "functional goods." My pleasure in good health, for example, is not diminished by your attainment of good health. Heterodox economists want to explore the implications of the difference between functional and positional goods for measuring and maximizing national well-being.

How important is positional competition? This is a difficult question to answer, but a lot of evidence suggests that people are quite concerned about relative economic standing. As noted in chapter 2, many surveys across countries and time periods have found that people's sense of what they need to be happy and what is a minimally acceptable standard of living depends on their relative rather than absolute income (R. Frank 1999, 74). This dependence helps explain the otherwise surprising finding that increasing levels of average income do not seem to increase reported levels of happiness (R. Frank 1999, 72–73; see also Kahneman and Krueger 2006).

In one particularly interesting study, researchers asked respondents to choose between two macroeconomic outcomes: one where they received $100,000 in current purchasing power and everyone else received $90,000, and another where they received $110,000 in current real purchasing power and everyone else received $200,000. About half of all respondents preferred having the lower real but higher relative income (Solnick and Hemenway 1998, 378). In another 1998 study, different researchers explored the relationship between work hours and positional competition by looking at the labor market behavior of sisters. They found that "a woman is 16 to 25 percent more likely to work outside the home if her sister's husband earns more than her own husband" (R. Frank 1999, 116).

There are several reasons why the amount and wastefulness of competitive competition has grown during the last thirty years. Positional goods seem to account for a greater share of people's spending as average real income rises and basic material needs are satisfied (Hirsch 1976; see also Krueger 2005).[12] The decline in neighborhood life and the expansion of the mass media also seem to have shifted the reference group that households compare themselves with from similarly provisioned neighbors to the upscale families portrayed on television (Schor 2000). The relaxation of cultural mores against the display of wealth and the tilt of national income toward the very rich also seem to have spurred imitative consumption. All of the above have been reinforced by the continuing spread of consumer culture and commercial advertising.

A number of other factors have discouraged people from opting out of positional consumption. Some formerly free or inexpensive goods (like a clean environment) have become linked to more expensive consumer purchases (like a home in a "good neighborhood"). If you are only interested in a modest house, but would like to ensure your children attend a "good" public school, you may have to purchase a very large house in an expensive part of town. If you do not have a cell phone or show up for a job interview dressed in an inexpensive suit, you may be less competitive for the position. If many of your neighbors buy expensive SUVs, your smaller automobile is suddenly less safe on the highway.[13]

Increasing positional competition has probably contributed to a decline in leisure, a fall in savings rates, an increase in household debt, a drain of resources from the public to the private sector, and increased political support for sacrificing nonmarket commodities (such as environmental protection) to the drive for greater consumer income (R. Frank 2005a). From the perspective of many heterodox economists, these outcomes invite the construction of economic statistics that would make the dilemmas posed by competitive consumption more visible. Neoclassical texts retreat from this task.

As highlighted in chapter 4, Adam Smith's invisible hand animates neoclassical introductory

---

Box 7.1
What Is Economic Waste?

Radical and Marxist economists have approached the topics of intermediate goods, defensive expenses, and bads in a slightly different way. They group together expenses that are not inherently necessary for production but are required by the logic of existing corporate production, such as the need to "manage" a potentially adversarial workforce and the pressures to sell people goods they do not really need.

The logic behind their claims can be illustrated by drawing an analogy to production within a country ruled by a corrupt authoritarian regime. For the sake of argument, let us assume that firms in this country's extractive industries (the oil, natural gas, and iron ore industries) have to pay large bribes to government officials in order to gain extractive licenses. These bribes are used by the government to support a large police force and propaganda activities that help maintain the government's hold on power. The activities of the police and public relations people have no direct effect on production, but funding these bureaucracies is part of the costs of doing business in this society. From a radical and Marxist perspective, expenses attributable to the specific social form of production should be separated from expenses directly involved in production.

This separation is often easier to draw in theory than in practice and is fraught with methodological difficulties. Nevertheless, there seems to be some merit in the distinction between expenses required functionally by production and expenses necessitated by the social form of production. (Somewhat similar themes are echoed in the distinction between "productive" and "unproductive" labor in Marxist economics and are pursued in Shaikh and Tonak 1994.)

Reflecting the radical perspective, Bowles, Gordon, and Weisskopf claim that "the United States has in fact become increasingly burdened by economic waste. . . .

(continued)

---

texts. Behind the metaphor is the idea that the private pursuit of self-interest serves both public and private interests. The dynamics of competitive consumption challenge the universality of this conclusion. Heterodox economists would like to see a more balanced discussion, one in which the invisible hand confronts the prisoner's dilemma.[14]

Neglect of "Bads" and Increasing Intermediate Goods Requirements

The largest negative side effects of current economic activities are probably environmental damages, such as the long-term effects of global warming. Other significant "bads" associated with current production include the costs of automobile accidents, lengthier commuting times, and perhaps declining neighborhood security. Expenditures required to offset the bads produced by economic activity, such as medical bills from commuting accidents, are sometimes called "defensive expenditures."

The core national income accounts mismeasure the impact of these bads on well-being. The accounts erroneously treat some defensive expenditures, such as clean-up costs for an oil spill, as additions to GDP.[15] In the same way, the accounts often treat increases in intermediate goods (such as public safety spending) as increases in final goods (neighborhood security), mistaking an increase in costs for an increase in output. The accounts also fail to

Box 7.1 *(continued)*

"The state of the auto industry in the early 1980s provides a graphic example. . . . For every worker engaged in the production of cars and trucks and busses, there were nearly two additional employees engaged either in supervising the productive workers or in selling cars. Car dealers and their employees alone outnumbered production workers in the auto industry by a considerable margin. . . .

"The cars themselves embodied additional waste. During the halcyon days of the 1950s . . . 25 percent of the cost of the average U.S. car and 20 percent of the cost of the gasoline needed to run it were attributable to annual style changes, to increases in horsepower and weight, and to advertising. . . .

"The auto industry is hardly unique. We argue that *waste pervades our economy.* . . . We point to waste on both the 'demand side' and the 'supply side' of the economy.

"*Demand-side waste* results from a failure to operate the economy at full employment and full capacity. . . .

"Supply-side waste . . . has recently brought us burgeoning costs of supervising and monitoring workers; increasing diversion of corporate resources to legal counsel, financial speculation, and advertising; rising costs of environmental cleanup and occupational illness; and bloated military expenses" (Bowles, Gordon, and Weisskopf 1990, 12–14).

Bowles, Gordon, and Weisskopf estimate that as much as 30 percent of current inputs are wasteful and that the average work week could be reduced to three and one-half days without loss of output if alternative production arrangements were pursued (ibid., 183; see also Hawken, Lovins, and Lovins 1999, chapter 3, especially 57–58, and Perelman 2000).

Neoclassical economists reject the entire argument, asserting that almost any expense incurred by a surviving business is "necessary," due to the ruthless logic of efficiency in competitive markets.

debit GDP for the decline in welfare caused by uncorrected bads (such as the continuing damage caused by acid rain).

While there are large uncertainties involved with pricing the harm caused by particular bads, their burden as a group is certainly quite large, and may total 5 percent or more of GDP.[16] A 1989 study estimated "defensive expenditures" for the West German economy at more than 10 percent of GNP (Ackerman et al. 1997, 376). Many economists have offered lower damage estimates. The debate is an important one, but is generally absent or de-emphasized in macro principles courses.

Neglect of Depletion of "Natural Capital" and Other Problems with Capital Accounting

Net Domestic Product (NDP) is defined as Gross Domestic Product (GDP) minus the depreciation of the nation's capital stock. It indicates the level of sustainable income produced in an economy in a given year. If you did not adjust GDP for depreciation it would be akin to combining what you earned or produced in a year with what you spent from your inheritance. Although the core national income accounts currently subtract depreciation of physical capital from GDP to calculate NDP, the core accounts do not make a similar adjustment for the drawdown of "natural capital," that is, the depletion of the earth's stock of natural resources.

There are lively debates among economists over how to translate the consumption of natural resources into a depreciation charge against natural capital. Using an innovative and controversial measuring technique, two leading ecological economists, Daly and Cobb, estimate that in 1990 the United States consumed nonrenewable resources valued at about 16 percent GDP and destroyed farmland and wetlands valued at about 3 percent GDP (Daly and Cobb 1994, 463).[17] Daly and Cobb's cost estimate is much larger than the actual market price of the resources consumed. It is based on the cost of replacing the services provided by exhaustible resources through the use of renewable resources (Daly and Cobb 1994, 482–87). Since this is a forward-looking cost, it is open to much debate.[18]

One of the most significant controversies in this field is whether to treat the discovery of new reserves as additions to natural capital. Many neoclassical economists favor this approach and suggest that its adoption minimizes the implications of past neglect of natural capital. Samuelson and Nordhaus, for example, cite U.S. Department of Commerce statistics indicating that depletions and discoveries of natural resources matched each other for the U.S. economy from 1958 to 1991 (Samuelson and Nordhaus 2001a, 449). Many heterodox economists challenge this reasoning. They claim that using exhaustible resources draws down natural stocks whether we have discovered new reserves or not.

Many ecological economists fear that existing economic statistics fail to alert people to the possibility that current production is borrowing from the future in unsustainable ways. They favor national income statistics that highlight the depletion of nonrenewable resources. They criticize most macro textbooks for giving insufficient attention to this debate.[19] We will return to this issue in chapter 16's discussion of macroeconomics and the environment.

Neglect of Distributional Issues

From 1973 to 1992 real wages for the bottom 60 percent of male year-round full-time workers fell by about 20 percent. By 1992 real wages were also falling for women workers with less than four years of college. Over the same twenty-year period GDP per capita increased 33 percent (Thurow 1996, 23–24). Where did the money go? "In the decade of the 1980s, all of the gains in male earnings went to the top 20 percent of the workforce and an amazing 64 percent accrued to the top 1 percent. . . . The pay of the average Fortune 500 CEO goes from 35 to 157 times that of the average production worker" (Thurow 1996, 21).

In this context, conventional GDP statistics can give an especially misleading picture of what is happening to most people's economic well-being. While GDP was going up, most people's economic well-being was going down. Heterodox economists want macroeconomic statistics to reflect this. While there are many different statistical ways to accomplish this adjustment, they all involve weighting the value of an extra dollar accruing to a rich person at less than that of a dollar received by a poor person. This weighting is based on the assumption of a "declining marginal utility of money" and the notion that there is a distinction between needs and wants.

Because neoclassical economics rejects such a distinction and retreats from distributional issues (arguing that nothing can be said "scientifically" about interpersonal utility comparisons), the subject is generally downplayed in macro principles texts.

Taking a heterodox approach, Daly and Cobb adjust GDP numbers by a formula that gives special weight to the level of income received by the bottom 20 percent of the income distribution. The effect of their algorithm is to reduce national income increases from 1966 to 1990 by about 20 percent (Daly and Cobb 1994, 461–62). In the late 1990s there was a reduction in income inequality, and heterodox GDP statistics include positive adjustments for that shift.[20]

Besides adjusting GDP for distributional concerns, heterodox economists would like to see macro chapters on economic measurement include explicit statistics about the distribution of output. Neoclassical texts typically treat distributional issues as a "specialty topic" in microeconomics rather than a central aspect of macroeconomics. The extra statistics that would be included in heterodox macro texts are discussed in chapter 15, "Reintroducing the Macroeconomics of Inequality."

Neglect of Changes in the Quality of Work Life

Most people spend more time at work or in activities related to work (such as commuting or job-related schooling) than in any other venue except the home. Both working conditions and the quality of work (measured in terms of job security, health and safety standards, interestingness, opportunities for advancement, degree of autonomy, collegiality, etc.) are key inputs into personal happiness and well-being. Changes in job quality are difficult to measure. In recent years there have been obvious improvements in some areas of work, such as increased air-conditioning in clerical offices, less exposure to pesticides among agricultural workers, more career opportunities for women, and, perhaps, increased sensitivity to the scheduling needs of workers caring for children and/or aging parents. On the other hand, average levels of on-the-job autonomy and job security have probably fallen.[21] As previously noted, many jobs seem to have also become more demanding and onerous to perform. Radical and Marxist economists have paid particular attention to the organization of work. They fear that declining unionization, increased global competition, and corporate-directed technological change have darkened the workday for many people. Heterodox economists acknowledge that aggregating these changes in working conditions is difficult, but call for more attention to the task in economic theory and introductory textbooks.

Neglect of Meta-Externalities

Although almost all of the adjustments to the national income accounts noted above are hard to measure, taking into consideration the economy's meta-externalities is even more difficult. Recall that meta-externalities refer to the impact of economic activities on various social and cultural goals, such as the maintenance of democracy, personal freedom, and popular capacities for voluntary cooperation. Some of these meta-externalities are often characterized as forms of *social capital*. This is because they generate a flow of services over time that contribute to economic and social well-being.

Heterodox economist Fred Hirsch worried eloquently about "the erosion of social capital," warning

> [T]he principle of self-interest is incomplete as a social organizing device. It operates effectively only in tandem with some supporting social principle. . . . The attempt has been made to erect an increasingly explicit social organization without a supporting social morality. . . .
>
> A system that depends for its success on a heritage that it undermines cannot be sustained. . . . (Hirsch 1976, 12)

Daniel M. Hausman and Michael McPherson add,

> The honesty, trust, and sense of fair play that help economies to function well are not givens that are fortunately abundant or unfortunately scarce. They are not comparable to geological formations or biological necessities. They grow or wither depending on the institutions

within which people live and the shared understandings of these institutions. Their content varies widely from individual to individual and from society to society. Economists need to be concerned not only to nurture these vital moral resources, but also to improve them. (Hausman and McPherson 1996, 220)[22]

Echoing similar themes, ecological economist E.F. Schumacher concluded,

If human vices such as greed and envy are systematically cultivated, the inevitable result is nothing less than a collapse of intelligence. . . . After a while, even the Gross National Product refuses to rise any further, not because of scientific or technological failure, but because of a creeping paralysis of non-cooperation. (Schumacher 1973, 29)

Almost all heterodox economists acknowledge that defining economic well-being and setting economic goals are subjective and political tasks. Different heterodox economists have offered different bundles of goals against which to assess macroeconomic performance. Radical economists, Bowles and Edwards, for example, recommend yardsticks that measure the economy's success in terms of its efficiency (~GDP), fairness, and the promotion of democracy. Goodwin and other advocates of "contextual economics" offer a longer list of goals, involving the economy's success in satisfying basic physical needs and in promoting happiness, self-realization, good social relations, fairness, freedom, participation, and ecological balance (Goodwin et al. 2003, 1.6–1.7). Ecological economists have often stressed the importance of sustainability and community[23] while Marxist economists have emphasized the importance of meaningful work in defining well-being. The key point is not the merits of any particular criterion, but the need for economic discussion (and eventually economic policy) to explore economic goals. The foreclosing of this discussion in traditional macro courses seriously limits the character of economic analysis and possible policy recommendations.

NEOCLASSICAL RESPONSES TO HETERODOX CONCERNS: "DÉJÀ VU ALL OVER AGAIN": THE "NOTE BUT IGNORE" MOTIF

As noted earlier, most neoclassical economists accept many of the above objections to GDP as a measure of national well-being. They acknowledge, for example, that the core national income accounts (1) neglect household production, voluntary activities, and leisure; (2) mistreat bads like environmental pollution; and (3) fail to depreciate natural capital. Why then is GDP so heavily highlighted in neoclassical textbooks as the yardstick for measuring macroeconomic performance? Why are the topics ignored or mismeasured by existing statistics not given more attention in neoclassical textbooks? Why are only some kinds of heterodox objections accepted?

Neoclassical economists defend their use of GDP as the main instrument for measuring economic well-being on the grounds that the statistic gets the "basic story right." This claim reflects their belief that the invisible hand works and that market-priced economic growth is the foundation for economic well-being. This assumption suggests that any comprehensive, revised indicator will be correlated with GDP, making adjustments to the national income accounts and further discussion in introductory textbooks unnecessary.

Defenders of neoclassical textbooks also emphasize that it is extremely difficult to measure many of the important phenomena omitted from the core national accounts and that no consensus exists on how to do so. They urge patience and a bracketing of these concerns until more research has clarified how to address them. It is easy to get the impression from standard macro principles texts:

- that heterodox critiques have only recently come to the attention of neoclassical theorists and that most will soon be addressed through mechanisms such as the "augmented national income accounts" without challenging neoclassical methodology,
- that many of the remaining issues of concern to heterodox economists are beyond measurement and cannot be productively integrated into economic assessment, and
- that when estimates have been made of the implications of many of the concerns raised by heterodox economists they do not appear to alter the basic message delivered by naked GDP statistics. This last point is almost always made implicitly rather than explicitly.[24]

HETERODOX REBUTTALS

Novel Difficulties or Topical Disinterest

As you might surmise, heterodox economists challenge these impressions. They note, for example, that most heterodox concerns are not new and were actively discussed at least thirty years ago.[25] Although including heterodox concerns in the national accounts would in many cases significantly complicate the measuring task, the lack of attention to these concerns is not primarily due to measurement problems. The existing accounts already include some goods that are not bought and sold in markets and that are difficult to value. For example, the accounts impute a value for the "housing services" provided by owner-occupied homes, for the food raised and consumed on farms, and for the value of banking services received by savers in lieu of higher interest on their deposits.[26] Similar efforts could have been made to impute a value for household labor. The lack of neoclassical attention to heterodox concerns about the national income accounts is due as much to the irrelevance or hostility of these concerns to key neoclassical subtexts as to the technical difficulties involved in addressing them.

What is fundamental or basic in economics is, of course, paradigmatic. The tendency of neoclassical textbooks to de-emphasize problems with GDP as a measure of economic well-being reflects the neoclassical paradigm's subtexts (e.g., that "markets work" and economic growth is the basis for societal advance). Heterodox economists are animated by different subtexts and attach the invisible hand to a much more complicated body. They have a more complex theory of social well-being and its measurement. They are as a result more interested than the neoclassicals in exploring the limitations of GDP as an economic indicator and the potential need for social governance of the economy.

Threshold Effects: Disabling Old Correlations

Heterodox economists also challenge the textbooks' confidence that any revised measure of well-being will be correlated with GDP. They find that the economy has passed several environmental and sociological thresholds over the last quarter century that invalidate old relationships. For example, the environment can assimilate certain levels of waste products, like greenhouse gases, without harm. As this capacity is exceeded, however, the ecological constraints on economic activity become more and more pressing. Beyond some level of materials use, efforts to contain environmental burdens may simply shift them in unforeseen ways to new sectors. Similarly, once many basic needs have been met, increasing GDP may have diminishing returns as more and more output is dissipated in positional competition. Some heterodox economists believe that exponential growth in consumption also threatens excessive depletion of the earth's resources.[27]

A number of other developments in the last twenty-five years, such as the dramatic increase in inequality, the apparent reduction in economic security, and a surprising decline in leisure, have also increased the importance of preexisting problems with GDP measures of national economic well-being. Taken together, all of these factors help explain the shape of the graph at the beginning of this chapter. Key indicators of economic well-being may now move in different directions from GDP statistics, implying that use of the latter may give an especially misleading picture of macroeconomic performance (see, for example, Costanza et al. 1997, 136–37).

ALTERNATIVE INDICATORS OF ECONOMIC PERFORMANCE

Heterodox economists favor giving more attention to "alternative indicators" of national economic well-being than provided in standard neoclassical textbooks. The first set of indicators we will discuss emphasize the concept of basic needs and the distinction between needs and wants. These indicators are most useful for assessing the economic progress of developing economies. Two examples of these indicators are the Physical Quality of Life Index (PQLI) and the Human Development Index (HDI).

The PQLI measures a nation's economic success in terms of its literacy rate, infant mortality rate, and life expectancy at age one. The HDI, constructed by the United Nations Development Program, measures economic development in terms of adult literacy and school enrollment, life expectancy at birth, and per capita GDP (using a weighting system for national income that gives little credit for per capita incomes beyond the world's median income). While Brazil and Costa Rica appear at similar levels of economic development using GDP/capita statistics, Costa Rica appears significantly better off when ranking countries with the HDI (Folbre 2001, 74). The goal of the HDI's designers and users is to encourage development efforts along the dimensions measured by HDI rather than GDP.[28]

A second set of indicators attempt to address some of the technical problems recognized by neoclassical economists with GDP measures of well-being. We will look at two such indicators: MEW and IEESA.[29] MEW (Measure of Economic Welfare) is perhaps the earliest of these efforts and was constructed about thirty years ago by Yale economists James Tobin and William Nordhaus. Its pioneering revisions of the national accounts included: (1) adding to GDP the value of household labor and leisure; (2) subtracting from GDP the "disamenities of urbanization" (e.g., congestion); and (3) reclassifying some output as intermediate rather than final goods.[30] The latter adjustment can be illustrated with respect to defense spending. Tobin and Nordhaus argued that the final good that defense spending provides is national security. The latter's value does not change if the cost to provide it changes. As such, higher defense spending can reflect a kind of inflation in the national security sector rather than an increase in national output. In much the same way, higher spending for personal safety in response to higher crime rates would not be counted as an increase in GDP. Overall, Nordhaus and Tobin estimated that intermediate and defensive expenditures increased from 8 percent to 16 percent of GNP from 1929 to 1965.

Aspects of MEW, such as its exploration of the difference between final and intermediate goods, pushed the limits of neoclassical methodology. Little work was done in the next twenty years to expand these initiatives. There are disagreements about how to interpret MEW's empirical results. Neoclassical economists have tended to find MEWs numbers close enough to traditional GNP/GDP calculations to justify continued reliance on the older index to measure economic well-being. Nordhaus and Tobin, for example, concluded, "MEW has been growing more slowly than per capita NNP (1.1 per cent for MEW as against 1.7 per cent for NNP, at annual rates over the period 1929–65). Yet MEW has been growing. The progress indicated by conventional national accounts is not just a myth that evaporates when a welfare-oriented measure is substituted." (Nordhaus and Tobin 1972, 13)[31]

Heterodox economists have tended to read the results differently. A number of leading ecological economists argued in 1997, for example, that "during the postwar period 1947–1965 . . . per capita GNP rose about six times as fast as per capita sustainable MEW." After noting how several plausible adjustments to MEW (suggested by Nordhaus and Tobin) could replace GNP's 48 percent increase (1947–1965) with a declining MEW, the ecological economists conclude that "With their own figures Nordhaus and Tobin have shed doubt on the thesis that national income accounts serve as a good proxy measure of economic welfare" (Costanza et al. 1997, 130–32).

Attempts to reform the GDP statistics within an accounting framework consistent with neoclassical methodology got a second burst of energy from the environmental and women's movements and have found expression in the Commerce Department's Integrated Environmental and Economic Satellite Accounts, or IEESA.[32] The accounts are set up to complement, rather than revise, GDP, permitting it to remain the premier statistic for public discussion about the economy. The accounts give special attention to the costs of depleting natural resource stocks and environmental damages from pollution.[33]

The two alternative indictors most relevant to many heterodox concerns are Daly and Cobb's Index of Sustainable Economic Welfare (ISEW) and its offspring, the Genuine Progress Indicator (GPI). Both of these measures combine reforms that fit within a neoclassical framework (e.g., including household labor in GDP) with a few revisions that challenge neoclassical methodology (such as adjusting income for distributional concerns). For the most part, however, the implications of more methodologically radical heterodox concerns, such as attention to the waste of competitive consumption (positional competition), or the character of work life, are absent. One of the largest empirical adjustments to traditional GDP statistics is the ISEW's inclusion of rather large and speculative estimates for the long-term costs of current environmental pollution.[34]

Internationally, there seems to be a growing interest in reducing GDP's dominance of measures of national well-being. Both Britain and Canada, for example, have plans for new indices of well-being that include social and environmental indicators (such as crime rates, the incidence of mental illness, and measures of environmental quality) alongside income statistics (Revkin 2005).[35]

CONCLUSION

One of the main conclusions that emerges from the literature about alternative indicators is that it is probably best to rely on a collage of different kinds of indicators, rather than a single aggregate indicator like GDP, to get a picture of what is happening in the economy. National income statistics that focus solely on market-generated activity, for example, may be quite useful for analyzing some aspects of business cycle behavior or mobilizing resources during wartime (the tasks for which the accounts were originally designed), but inappropriate for measuring national economic well-being. The IEESA may help address some shortcomings and deserves increased funding. Broader databases and indices of well-being that include heterodox concerns should also be developed. We will link measurement issues to our usual threads at the end of chapter 8's discussion of labor market and inflation statistics.

STUDY QUESTIONS

Discussion Questions

1. What is the purpose of the existing national income accounts? What do you think a measure of national economic welfare should include? What kind of statistics might help policymakers measure how the economy is doing?
2. "Maximizing GDP per capita should be the major goal of macroeconomic policy." Offer reasons for and against this proposition.
3. What economic activities have you or your family engaged in that are (counted/not counted) in the GDP statistics? Would changes in your family's annual income adequately capture changes in your family's economic well-being?
4. Bring in a newspaper article or something from the internet that uses the term *GDP* and examine how it is used (e.g., is it treated as a measure of national economic well-being?).
5. Recall the survey comparing two different macroeconomic outcomes alluded to above. In the first case you earn $100,000 and everyone else earns $90,000. In the second case you earn $110,000 (a 10 percent real increase in income), while everyone else's income more than doubles. Which situation would you prefer? Why? What do you think the implications of your choice are for designing measures of national well-being and economic performance?
6. What is meant by economic waste? How do heterodox and textbook approaches to this question differ?
7. Neoclassical textbook authors often acknowledge the validity of many heterodox critiques of GDP accounting, but feel these concerns are not important enough to merit greater discussion in macro principles textbooks or courses. Give the best reasons for and against this claim.

Review Questions

1. Briefly explain what heterodox economists find objectionable in the textbooks' discussion of the national income accounts (i.e., GDP statistics) with respect to the following subjects: nonmarket activities, positional competition, bads, intermediate goods, natural capital, distributional issues, work life, meta-externalities, and social capital.
2. Briefly outline how defenders of the textbooks respond to the heterodox concerns you listed in question 1. How have heterodox economists replied to these responses?
3. Briefly describe some alternative indicators of economic performance to GDP.

NOTES

1. Cited in R. England 1997, 387.

2. The bads not included in market calculations are termed negative externalities in neoclassical economics. The GDP statistics also leave out "positive externalities," which would raise the value of market outputs.

3. Heterodox and many neoclassical economists have also noted that GDP calculations fail to address a few more specialized concerns, such as the buildup of foreign debt to finance current production and consumption.

4. Some heterodox economists, such as Fred Lee of the University of Missouri at Kansas City, feel it is inappropriate to measure nonmarket activities in price terms. While arguing for greater attention to the

performance of these sectors, they reject market-oriented measures of their output. Other heterodox econo-mists, such as Peter Dorman, emphasize that the GDP accounts probably undervalue some public-sector outputs by valuing them at their cost of production.

5. See, for example, Ackerman et al. (1997, 348, 357, 361, and 382); Folbre (2001, 67); R. Bartlett (1997, 131); Eisner (1988, 1674); Goodwin et al. (2003, 2–17); and Barker and Feiner (2004, 39–40).

6. The increase was 199 hours (de Graaf 2003, A13). As might be expected, the average workload in-crease is even higher when the sample is limited to dual-earner couples. A 2002 survey by the Families and Work Institute found that combined work hours increased from 81 to 91 hours a week in these families from 1977 to 2002. At the same time, the proportion of married wage and salaried employees in dual-earner couples increased from 66 percent to 78 percent (Bond et al. 2003, 2). Juliet Schor has disaggregated the increase in labor time by gender for the 1969–1987 period. During these years the average fully employed man's paid work time increased by about 2.5 weeks per year and women's paid work time grew by 7.5 weeks (Schor 1991, 29; see also Mishel, Bernstein, and Boushey 2003, 97–112). If one shifts from the experiences of fully employed people to the entire population, the average growth in labor hours from 1969 to 1987 drops from 163 hours to 117 hours (Schor 1991, 35–36).

7. CNN, August 31, 2001, citing United Nations Statistics (www.cnn.com/2001/CAREER/trends/08/30/ilostudy/index.html). The average Norwegian currently works fourteen weeks a year less than their Ameri-can counterpart (de Graaf 2003). The average income in Norway is 16 percent less than in the United States.

8. See also Mishel, Bernstein, and Boushey (2003, 112); Miringoff, Miringoff, and Opdycke (2001–2002, 82); and R. Frank (1999, 50). A 1997 survey by the Families and Work Institute found that 70 percent of parents felt they did not have enough time with their children (Bond, Galinsky, and Swanberg 1998, 6). Interestingly, because fathers increased their time caring for children on workdays by about thirty minutes per day (1977–1997) to 2.3 hours and mothers' time spent with children remained about 3.2 hours (1977–2002), total parental time with children has increased. What has declined significantly for moms and dads is personal free time, falling to 1.2 hours per day for men and 0.9 hours per day for women (ibid.). Robert Frank has cited some troubling statistics on declining hours of sleep (1999, 50–51).

9. The Families and Work Institute's 1997 national survey, for example, reported, "many workers indi-cate that they have to work very fast (68 percent), have to work very hard (88 percent), and do not have enough time to finish everything that needs to get done on the job (60 percent)—much higher proportions than 20 years ago" (Bond, Galinsky, and Swanberg 1998, 9). Increased demands for multitasking over a common period seem to be especially burdensome.

10. The Families and Work Institute's 2004 national survey found that employees feeling overworked were six times more likely to report the kinds of stress levels associated with physical health problems than colleagues not feeling overworked (Galinsky et al. 2005, 3). Employees feeling overworked were also two and a half times more likely to exhibit symptoms of clinical depression (ibid.).

11. Interestingly, despite time reductions from labor-saving technological change (such as microwave ovens and food processors), Schor reports that total household labor hours for fully employed persons were almost unchanged (889 versus 888) from 1969 to 1987 (Schor 1991, 35). Within the household women are doing less and men more, though the imbalance between women's and men's contribution remains large.

12. When annual income rises above $10,000 to $20,000 per year, the link between rising income and rising happiness seems to weaken significantly (Revkin 2005).

13. A 2003 study by the National Highway Traffic Safety Administration, for example, found that light trucks including SUVs are three times as deadly to the driver of a struck vehicle in head-on collisions and twenty times as deadly in side-impact crashes as car designs (Wikipedia, crash incompatibility). In 1997, 81 percent of the fatalities from collisions between cars and light trucks and vans (a category that includes SUVs) were occupants of the car (Hampton C. Gabler and William T. Hollowell, "The Crash Compatibility of Cars and Light Trucks," *Journal of Crash Prevention and Injury Control* [January 2000]).

14. You may recall the prisoner's dilemma from chapter 4. The prisoners' isolated pursuit of their own self-interest undermines their self-interest. The logic of positional competition suggests a similar loss of well-being in the economy from the private pursuit of self-interest in competitive consumption.

15. Of course, if one debited GDP statistics for the original spill, it would be fine to credit abatement efforts with undoing some of this harm.

16. A few statistics can convey the potential magnitudes of the bads. The United States currently spends about 2.5 percent of its national income on pollution abatement. Many conventional estimates of the benefit of pollution expenditures range from 2.5 percent to 3.5 percent of GDP. Some estimates, however, are much higher.

The annual residual damages caused by continuing pollution are also large. Herman Daly, senior economist in the Environmental Department of the World Bank from 1988 to 1994, placed the immediate costs of the damages caused by air, water, and noise pollution in 1990 at about 2 percent of GDP. Daly estimated the long-term costs of the environmental damages incurred in 1990 at about seven times this amount, acknowledging the highly speculative aspect of such cost estimates due to uncertainties about phenomena like global warming (Daly and Cobb 1994, appendix, esp. p. 463). Recent updates by the think tank "Redefining Progress" for 1998 estimate long-term environmental damages at about 15 percent of GDP and short-term damages due to air, water, and noise pollution at about 1.5 percent of GDP ("Why Bigger Isn't Better: The Genuine Progress Indicator—1999 Update," pp. 4–6; www.rprogress.org/pubs/gpi1999.html). There is wide debate over these numbers. Most estimates are lower.

17. Updated figures for the United States for 1998, calculated by the think tank Rethinking Progress, were even higher. Researchers at the World Resources Institute, focusing on the Indonesian economy, calculated that about half of the country's 7 percent growth rate was purchased at the expense of future output (i.e., built on drawing down the nation's resource stocks) (Daly and Cobb 1994, 444). Both of these groups' calculations are on the high end of conventional adjustments of GDP statistics for depleting natural capital.

18. Economists have devised many different ways to estimate the "scarcity value" of exhaustible resources. Many neoclassical economists favor using market-generated statistics, such as estimates of the "user cost" that resource owners are earning to compensate them for giving up the option to sell their asset in the future. For reasons explored in more detail in chapter 16, Daly and Cobb find these market signals unreliable.

19. Critics of the national income accounts have raised several other thoughtful objections to how the distinction between current income and expenditures and changes in the economy's capital stock are handled. Some of these issues deal with the treatment of consumer durable goods, human capital, and government spending for infrastructure. The basic claim is that the existing accounts give insufficient attention to other forms of capital investment than private business investment. For example, the accounts generally fail to note the difference between government spending for public consumption goods (like recreation sites) and government spending for roads and education, which add to the economy's productive capacity.

20. The "Genuine Progress Indicator" increased GDP estimates for 1998 (a year when the income distribution became more equal) by about 1.5 percent (Redefining Progress, "Why Bigger Isn't Better: Genuine Progress Indicator 1999 Update"). The GPI designers use Gini coefficients (rather than the quintile ratios used by Daly and Cobb) to adjust GDP figures for distributional concerns. (See chapter 15 for an explanation of Gini coefficients.)

21. See, for example, Mishel, Bernstein, and Boushey (2003, 262–76), and Engemann, Friedberg, and Owyang (2005), on job security. Offering a contrary position, Bond, Galinsky, and Swanberg (1998) find workers' autonomy at work increasing.

22. Interestingly, Milton Friedman, a conservative neoclassical economist, has taken the concept of social capital and endogenous cultural practices in a different direction. Friedman celebrates what he perceives to be the modern economy's extension of individual choice into more and more areas of life. He implicitly credits the economy with the cultivation of life styles of "freedom" (economic freedom, political freedom, intellectual freedom, etc.). Friedman's use of a holist methodology in some of his political economic writings (such as his classic text, *Capitalism and Freedom*), however, is inconsistent with the reductionist and methodologically individualistic approach he takes to micro- and macroeconomics. Friedman's ad hoc comments typify the way neoclassical theory addresses social feedback from the economy.

23. See, for example, Daly and Cobb 1994. Costanza et al. (1997, chapter 3) recommend the work of Manfred Max-Neff, who offers a matrix of private and social needs.

24. Samuelson and Nordhaus, for example, write: "Considerable progress has been made in recent years in developing augmented national accounts, which are accounts designed to include both nonmarket and market activities. . . .

"Environmental critics have argued that America's wasteful ways are squandering our precious natural capital. Many were surprised by the results of this first assay into green accounting. The estimates take into account that discovery adds to our proven reserves while extraction subtracts from or depletes these reserves. In fact, these two activities just about canceled each other out . . . from 1958–1991. . . .

"There is much further work needed in this area" (Samuelson and Nordhaus 2001b, 103).

25. Many of these concerns were actively raised at the 1971 Conference on Income and Wealth (Ruggles 1983, 31–32).

26. Ruggles indicates that imputed output totaled about 8 percent of GNP in 1983 (Ruggles 1983, 40). Some definitions of "imputation" imply even higher percentages.

27. This risk partly reflects the unusual logic of exponential growth, which threatens to overwhelm traditional scarcity signals. For example, at a constant 7 percent annual growth rate in resource use, the global economy would consume as many resources in the next ten years as it has in all of human history. Heterodox concerns also involve more technical debates (such as disagreements over the appropriate discount rate to use for comparing inter-temporal situations), which cannot be addressed here.

28. The UN also has a gender-sensitive index of development that disaggregates economic outcomes in order to examine the impact of development on women.

29. Robert Eisner's Total Incomes System of Account (TISA) was another early and important alternative indicator of this kind. TISA focused especially on the GNP accounts' problems with measuring and defining investment, but covered many other issues as well, including concerns about the accounts' treatment of nonmarket activities, intermediate goods, and some de facto consumer services provided employees at work (R. England 1997, 381–82). Two more recent quality of life indices are the annual Index of Social Health put together by Marc Miringoff and others at the Fordham Institute for Innovation in Social Policy, and the Levy Institute's Measure of Economic Well-Being (LIMEW).

30. The index also included a few other important modifications, which are ignored here.

31. Five years after MEW's initial publication, Nordhaus reiterated his interpretation of the instrument's results, asserting, "Although GNP and other national income aggregates are imperfect measures of the economic standard of living, the broad picture of secular progress that they convey remains after correction for their most obvious deficiencies" (Costanza et al. 1997, 132). The sentence is a classic example of neoclassical theory's "note but ignore" review of itself. Whether the link between MEW and GNP could withstand correction of MEW's less-obvious limitations and what is meant by the "broad picture" of "secular progress" is unclear. The deference to neoclassical subtexts about the assumed benefits of market organized expansion does seem clear.

One of the things that paradigms do to influence research results is to signal researchers to look at different kinds of information and to pursue different kinds of leads. As Daly and Cobb note, although the MEW statistics reveal a striking difference in behavior between the 1929–1947 period and the 1947–1965 period, Nordhaus and Tobin "never refer to the remarkable difference between those two periods. . . . To do so would have required them to explain why the growth rate for per capita sustainable MEW had flattened out, even as per capita NNP kept rising" (Daly and Cobb 1994, 80–81). According to Daly and Farley, from 1929–1947 MEW increased by one unit for every three-unit increase in GDP; from 1947–1965, the ratio fell to one to six and by 1980 the link had all but disappeared (Daly and Farley 2004, 233–35).

32. The acronym for the accounts is sometimes also written as ISEEA (Integrated System of Environmental and Economic Accounts).

33. By potentially assigning higher costs to resource use and environmental damage, the accounts may influence how people think about economic activities. Thus it is not surprising that political battles have erupted over control of the accounting process. The Commerce Department's research on how to expand the national income accounts to include more environmental and resource costs began in earnest in 1992. It was suspended by a vote of Congress in 1994 until an expert review of the problem could be conducted. The commissioned study was finally finished in 1999. Like most such studies, the results were fairly sensitive to the "experts" empanelled. Although made up of extremely talented individuals, the panel does not seem to have included many voices outside the neoclassical paradigm. It was led by William Nordhaus. It recommended thoughtful reforms within the neoclassical paradigm.

34. See Richard England (1997) for a thoughtful review of the strengths and weaknesses of ISEW.

35. The king of Bhutan, a small third world country near Nepal and India, is well known for his attempts to develop a Gross National Happiness indicator. See Revkin 2005.

REMEASURING ECONOMIC ACTIVITY

Labor Market and Inflation Statistics

The penalties of unemployment include not only income loss, but also far-reaching effects on self-confidence, work motivation, basic competence, social integration, racial harmony, gender justice, and the appreciation and use of individual freedom and responsibility.
—Amartya Sen, Nobel Prize in Economics 1998 (Sen 1997, 168)

In its preoccupation with questions of resource allocation under equilibrium conditions, the conventional analysis gives short shrift to the critical importance of employment in determining individual and family well-being. . . .
—Alfred Eichner (1985, 95)

INTRODUCTION

In this chapter we compare and contrast neoclassical and heterodox ideas about the presentation of labor market and inflation statistics. Neoclassical textbooks imply that the primary goal of economic policy should be the maximization of current and future GDP. Labor is treated as one of several inputs to production and its efficient use, along with the prudent use of other resources, is highly valued. There is only modest attention, however, to labor as a human activity with special significance for the nature of society and people's well-being. It is thus not surprising that standard macro textbooks usually explore how GDP is measured in much more detail and earlier in the term than they discuss measurement issues involving unemployment.

Heterodox economists challenge this weighting. They urge much earlier and more detailed attention to labor market issues, especially unemployment. The discussion below illustrates the kind of background information heterodox economists recommend including alongside information about GDP, as a frame for subsequent thinking about the logic and goals of macro policy. Some of the definitional points noted below are covered, with less emphasis, in standard texts. You may want to look in the index of your text for the pages in which similar issues are addressed, if they have not yet been raised in your course.

Heterodox economists often emphasize that the "standard" unemployment rate excludes "discouraged workers" (people who have given up looking for jobs because they are pessimistic about finding them in depressed economic conditions) and involuntary part-time workers (those who are working part-time because they cannot find full-time work). The "underemployment rate," which

includes discouraged workers, involuntary part-time workers, and other marginally employed workers, is generally about 1.8 times the official unemployment rate (Bernstein and Baker 2003, 101).

In December 2005, for example, the official unemployment rate was 4.9 percent. If discouraged workers, other "marginally attached" workers, and involuntary part-time workers were added,
the total would have been 8.6 percent.[1] This number probably undercounts important "disadvantaged" subgroups of the population, such as young African American males and older workers
who should be but are not included in the "discouraged worker" category. They are not counted
because they have "dropped out of the labor force." On the other hand, the 8.6 percent figure
includes some people who are not seriously looking for jobs and others who are working, but
doing so in the informal sector where income is not reported.

The 8.6 percent figure also excludes people who are employed but earning poverty-level wages.
Probably the most useful measure of the health of the labor market, from a heterodox perspective,
would be a statistic that combined the number of people underemployed with those earning wages
insufficient to maintain them and/or their families above the poverty line. In 2001, 24.4 percent of
all workers had hourly wages less than $8.78 (the wage rate necessary for a full-time worker to
raise a family of four above the poverty line) (Mishel, Bernstein, and Boushey 2003, 353). Actual
poverty rates were about half this level, because most families rely on more than one wage earner.

THE COSTS OF UNEMPLOYMENT

Overview

Most mainstream textbooks allocate less than 1 percent of their 500 or so pages to exploring the
effects of unemployment. The costs of unemployment can be divided into four categories: (1) lost
output, (2) lost income to working families, (3) psychological and sociological burdens, and (4)
increases in social inequality. Standard texts are generally pretty good at addressing the problem
of lost output. The books usually appeal to a variant of "Okun's Law" (a 1 percent increase in the
unemployment rate decreases real output by ~2 percent) to represent the wastefulness of unemployment. The books are usually much less successful in addressing the other effects.

The texts frequently list in a paragraph or two a series of serious personal and social patholo-
gies that appear to be correlated with unemployment, ranging from suicide and increased racial
tensions to, in extreme cases, the rise of fascism. The discussion is surprisingly brief. There is
minimal exploration of when the harms occur, how much they occur, and under what circumstances the more severe implications arise. The lack of discussion is even more puzzling because
the texts often suggest that macro policy makers occasionally face decisions that involve unemployment trade-offs in the short and even long run.

Standard texts give almost no attention to the impact of unemployment on the level of social
inequality. Heterodox analysis often highlights these effects, looking at the implications of unemployment for power relations in the workplace, the distribution of income between labor and
capital, and the general level of inequality in society.

The next three sections explore how heterodox economists fill in the gaps in standard texts'
discussion of the costs of unemployment.

The Cost of Lost Income to Working Families

The average duration of unemployment from 1975 to 2000 varied between eleven and twenty
weeks and averaged about three and one-half months (*Economic Report of the President* 2000,

356).[2] Because of the tendency of official statistics to exclude discouraged workers, the real duration was probably higher.[3] Despite the high level of consumption in the U.S. economy most working people have very little financial savings. The bottom half of the income ladder would be unable to maintain a standard of living 25 percent above the poverty line by relying on their financial savings for even two months.[4] Although many families have more than one wage earner and other survival options (such as loans from relatives, home equity loans, high-interest credit card debt, and expanded household production), the financial burden of unemployment can obviously be quite high.[5]

The social support system for the unemployed has two major components, unemployment insurance and the social safety net. Over the last twenty-five years there has been a reduction in unemployment insurance. From 1980 to 1999, coverage fell from 43.9 percent to 37.2 percent of the unemployed. State unemployment insurance payments fell from 36.6 percent to 31.6 percent of lost wages.[6] Because there have been many different changes in the social safety net, it is difficult to say how the overall level of social insurance has changed. If we use "government expenditures for income-tested benefits" as a proxy for safety net spending, it appears the net strengthened a bit.[7]

Psychological and Sociological Impacts of Unemployment

Unemployment often has serious psychological impacts in addition to its economic burdens. A recent review of empirical research on happiness in the *Journal of Economic Literature* reported that "Happiness research suggests that unemployment strongly reduces subjectively self-reported well-being, both personally and for society as a whole. This is . . . in line with the view that unemployment is involuntary for the bulk of people affected" (Frey and Stutzer 2002, 428).

Voices of the Unemployed

Bouts of long-term unemployment can be devastating. Studs Terkel's (1970) interviews with people unemployed during the Great Depression (*Hard Times*) provide a classic window on this trauma:

> I'd get up at five in the morning and head for the waterfront. . . . [O]utside the gates, there would be a thousand men. You know dang well there's only three or four jobs. The guy would come out with two little Pinkerton cops: "I need two guys for the bull gang. Two guys to go into the hole." A thousand men would fight like a pack of Alaskan dogs to get through there (30). . . .
>
> Everybody was a criminal. You stole, you cheated through. You were getting by, survival . . . . (34)
>
> [I]t created a coyote mentality. (34)

More recent interviews and studies (Maurer 1979; *New York Times* 1996) paint a similar picture:

> It's affected my outlook on life a lot. I don't dress so hot anymore. I just put on anything I have. . . . I mean, when you don't feel too good inside and there is no money in your pocket, it's no use getting into a suit. I guess it affected the way I walk, the way I dress, and where I go. . . . I became more lonesome. . . . So it's really a bad psychological state. I don't feel too good about myself. But I try not to be bitter. That bitterness is just going to eat me up inside. . . . I can't just go out and start punching people in the nose. "You didn't give me a job." (Maurer 1979, 59)

Nearly three-quarters of all households have had a close encounter with layoffs since 1980, according to a new poll by the *New York Times*. In one-third of all households, a family member has lost a job, and nearly 40 percent more know a relative, friend, or neighbor who was laid off.

One in 10 adults—or about 19 million people . . . acknowledged that a lost job in their household had precipitated a major crisis in their lives . . . . (5)

The job apprehension has intruded everywhere, diluting self-worth, splintering families, fragmenting communities. . . .

White-collar, middle-class Americans in mass numbers are coming to understand first hand the chronic insecurity on which the working class and the poor are experts.

All of this is causing a pronounced withdrawal from community and civic life. . . .

[T]he effects billow beyond community participation. People find themselves sifting for convenient scapegoats . . . and are adopting harsher views toward those more needy than themselves . . . . (7–8)

The economists I interviewed by telephone advised me not to go to Dayton. . . . Dayton was doing well, they said. The economic indicators seemed to prove it. My editors told me to go to Dayton and see for myself. I stayed five weeks. The first thing I learned was that the statistics were only part of the story about Dayton. Everyone I met in Dayton talked about their anxiety about jobs and the economy and the fraying of community ties. (*New York Times* 1996, 232–33)

High levels of job insecurity seem to be continuing in the U.S. economy, though the duration of recent unemployment seems relatively short for many workers. Roughly one in four workers earning less than $40,000 were laid off from full- or part-time jobs from the spring of 2000 to the spring of 2003 (Magdoff and Magdoff 2004, 26).

Emotional Costs of Unemployment

Many studies have linked prolonged unemployment to serious emotional problems. Different rationales have been offered to explain the impact of unemployment. "Some . . . argue that work is psychologically supportive, imposing a structure on the day, providing contacts, experience and goals . . . and giving status and identity to the individual. . . . Others . . . [point to] financial anxiety, insecurity, rejection and loss of control over one's life. . . ." (Piachaud 1997, 53) Many research studies have linked prolonged unemployment to reduced self-esteem, depression, and weaker motivation to look for work. Other studies have linked unemployment to higher rates of suicide, mental illness, and alcohol abuse (Darity and Goldsmith 1996, 122–26; Wray and Pigeon 2000, 834; Brenner 1979).

Social Costs of Unemployment

The impact and burden of unemployment extends past the unemployed themselves. Researchers have found increased rates of infant mortality, emotional problems among children, and marital tensions in the families of the unemployed.[8] In the early 1980s, for example, when Michigan led the nation in long-term unemployment (due to widespread layoffs in the automobile industry), there was a significant rise in reported child abuse and a large increase in caseloads for psychological counselors of children in some Michigan communities (Riegle 1982, 1114–15).

Researchers have also found that unemployment has a negative psychological impact on workers who retain their jobs in firms with layoffs. Besides fearing that they might be next, some job retainers seem to suffer from survivor guilt (Darity and Goldsmith 1996, 124). Many managers report declines in employee morale and productivity after layoffs.

There is an extensive literature linking rates of unemployment and rates of crime. One study, for example, estimated that falling unemployment was responsible for about a third of the drop in crime in the 1990s (Bernstein and Baker 2003, 59–60; Piachaud 1997, 55; Brenner 1979). The sharp rise in unemployment in the mid-seventies has been linked to the jump in crime during that period.[9]

While suggestive, quantitative estimates of the impact of unemployment on societal outcomes should probably be treated more as qualitative than quantitative data. The psychological impact of unemployment on individual behavior depends on a large number of factors, including the strength of a person's social support system, local cultural traditions, and the government's social safety net. There are also uncertain lag times between unemployment and its behavioral impact. It is very difficult to tease precise relationships from the data.[10]

William Julius Wilson's (1996) work has emphasized the destructive impact of concentrated unemployment on neighborhood life in the African American community. He writes,

> The consequences of high neighborhood joblessness are more devastating than those of high neighborhood poverty. A neighborhood in which people are poor but employed is different from a neighborhood in which people are poor and jobless. Many of today's problems in the inner-city ghetto neighborhoods—crime, family dissolution, welfare, low levels of social organization, and so on—are fundamentally a consequence of the disappearance of work (xiii). . . .
>
> [T]he residents of . . . jobless black poverty areas face certain social constraints on the choices they can make in their daily lives. These constraints, combined with restricted opportunities in the larger society, lead to ghetto-related behavior and attitudes (52). . . .
>
> The problems associated with the absence of work are most severe for a jobless family in a low-employment neighborhood because they are more likely to be shared and therefore reinforced by other families in the neighborhood through the process of accidental or nonconscious cultural transmission. One of these shared problems is a perception of a lack of self-efficacy. (75)

The impact of unemployment on African Americans deserves special attention and is pursued in the next section.

Unemployment and Social Inequality

The unemployment rate has four major impacts on social inequality. Increases in the unemployment rate tend to (1) be especially damaging to African Americans, (2) increase income inequalities in general, (3) shift power in the workplace from workers to employers, and (4) increase the social leverage of employers and owners of capital in the broader community. We explore each of these effects below.

Racial Inequalities

For the last fifty years changes in African American unemployment rates have tracked national unemployment rates quite closely. The main difference is that African American rates have been about double the white rate.[11]

Table 8.1

Race and Unemployment

Year	National Rate	White Rate	Black Rate (until 1972 entitled Black and Other)
1955	4.4	3.9	8.7
1960	5.5	5.0	10.2
1965	4.5	4.1	8.1
1970	4.9	4.5	8.2
1975	8.5	7.8	14.8
1980	7.1	6.3	14.3
1983	9.6	8.4	19.5
1985	7.2	6.2	15.1
1990	5.6	4.8	11.4
1995	5.6	4.9	10.4
2000	4.0	3.5	7.6
2001	4.7	4.2	8.6
2002	5.8	5.1	10.2
2003	6.0	5.2	10.8
2004	5.5	4.8	10.4

Source: Economic Report of the President (2/2005, 260), (2/2000, 354).

As many observers have noted, the high African American unemployment rates have had disastrous effects on the black community. This was true forty years ago when the "Moynihan Report" documented the burden of unemployment rates and it was true in the 1990s when William Julius Wilson revisited the issue. Declines in the unemployment rate tend to be especially helpful to African American communities.[12] Although many analysts have attributed high unemployment rates in African American communities to "supply side" problems (e.g., skill deficits), the sensitivity of African American unemployment rates to the business cycle suggests that if the jobs are there, unemployment will fall.

David Piachaud looks at the flip side of racism and unemployment, the potential for white workers to blame minority groups and immigrants for high unemployment. Although his discussion focuses on Europe, it may echo in the United States. Piachaud warns, "There can be no doubt that one of the most far-reaching and evil consequences of mass unemployment in the 1920s and 1930s was the growth of racism" (Piachaud 1997, 55).

Unemployment and Wage Dispersion

Declines in unemployment frequently have the greatest benefit for less-skilled and less-educated workers. For example, during the last five years of the 1990s expansion, unemployment fell more rapidly for high-school dropouts than any other education group[13] (Bernstein and Baker 2001). The expansion also reversed the long decline in income for the bottom of the wage ladder. From 1973 to 1995 real hourly earnings for low-wage male workers fell 20 percent. From 1995 to 2000 real wages grew at 1.5 percent per year (Bernstein and Baker 2001). To paraphrase heterodox economists Dean Baker and Jared Bernstein, skills matter, but full employment is a working person's best friend.

Institutionalist economist James K Galbraith has emphasized the key relationship between unemployment and economic inequality, estimating, for example, that nearly 80 percent of the variation in wage inequality can be explained by variations in the unemployment rate (Galbraith 2000, 147). His

research also finds that 5.5 percent unemployment can be treated as a macroeconomic hinge for forecasting changes in economic inequality. When unemployment is above 5.5 percent, inequality tends to
rise; when unemployment is below 5.5 percent, inequality tends to fall (Galbraith 2000, 148–49).

Unemployment and Power Relations in the Workplace

As noted above, tight labor markets tend to shift power relations in the workplace in labor's favor.
Sagging labor markets tend to shift power to employers. As Marc Linder reports, "'job security is
more important than job safety' during recessions." According to an OSHA inspector, "'workers
don't ask questions when a foreman tells them to do something that might be dangerous.' The
resulting rise in injuries may be concealed by the circumstance that workers may keep working
during such periods of high unemployment for fear that employers will replace them. . . ." (Linder
1994, 81).[14] Similar dynamics probably affect other amenities in the workplace, such as access to
flex time and grievance procedures.

Chronically high unemployment may also shift power from people as workers to people as
consumers. Competition among workers and communities for jobs in an economy with serious
unemployment problems (or fears of unemployment) can encourage the sacrifice of the environment, workers' rights, and other amenities for better job prospects. Firms with excess capacity
may pass on resulting cost savings to consumers. A full-employment economy may tilt power the
other way. Thus macro institutions may influence the pattern of tradeoffs between consumption
levels and other dimensions of well-being in the economy.

Unemployment and Power Relations in the Community

Heterodox economists argue that the threat of unemployment gives enormous social leverage to firms
and owners of financial capital. Workers face an "all-or-nothing" trade-off over jobs. Local environmental conditions, zoning regulations, working conditions, and so on are all held hostage to "jobs."

Textbook economic theory suggests that competition between communities to attract jobs
produces net benefits in the long run. Heterodox economists see the competition as risking "a race
to the bottom." What is behind this disagreement? Textbook economic theory portrays all prices
as reflecting competitive market outcomes. No one exercises any power. The level of local environmental protection, for example, reflects the logic of supply and demand for environmental
services. Local communities trade off the marginal benefit of an additional unit of environmental
protection against the marginal benefit of other economic objectives, such as economic growth.
The market allocates jobs to those areas with the least environmental damage (based on people's
valuation of the environment as measured by their "willingness to pay" for its protection).

Heterodox economists see a more complicated world. The logic of the labor market in modern
capitalist economies frequently creates more supply than demand for labor at existing wages in
many labor markets. There are many different theories for why this occurs, but there is consensus
that it does occur. Within neoclassical economics these theories include ideas about "efficiency
wages," "insider/outsider differentials," and "implicit contracts." Within heterodox theory explanations include reference to the need for a "reserve army of the unemployed," the impact of dual
labor markets, the logic of internal labor markets, and other issues involving institutional phenomena (many of which will be discussed in later chapters). Regardless of the rationale for its
persistence, the existence of excess labor supply endows employers with power and puts enormous pressure on local governments to attract jobs.

Low unemployment reduces employer power and alters the terms of social trade-offs across the economy, increasing the quality of life in numerous areas. Many heterodox economists believe that a program of guaranteed public employment at the "social minimum wage" (the government employment wage) would weaken employers' bargaining position with communities and encourage more desirable trade-offs. The option of public employment is also expected to have beneficial "dynamic" effects on the economy that would orient firms' planning to technological and management strategies that take the "high road" of high-wage jobs.

The danger, of course, is that a high-road economy will lead to lower private-sector employment and expanded public-sector employment at the social minimum wage. Let us assume a relatively pessimistic outcome for the moment and look at its implications. Assume that the presence of guaranteed public employment (at a social minimum wage sufficient to maintain a family of four above the poverty line, ~$9.50/hr, plus $1.75 in benefits) increased the private sector's unemployment rate by 25 percent or about 1.5 percentage points. Let us also assume that on average 2 percent of the workforce currently counted as unemployed pursued public employment. The cost of guaranteed employment would be about $100 billion.[15] The net costs of the program to the U.S. government would be significantly less due to reduced spending for unemployment compensation and other means-tested social programs. The final price tag would be significant but manageable within existing government budgets. In the year 2000, for example, federal government receipts (excluding social security receipts) tallied ~1.8 trillion (*Economic Report of the President* 2000, 399).

Furthermore, those in expanded public-sector jobs would be producing something, so the real economic cost of the program is the difference between what they would have produced in the private sector compared to what they will produce in the public sector. There has been a strong ideological campaign to convince people that the private sector (populated by IBM, but also by Enron; by ATT, but also by WorldCom; by Arthur D. Little consulting, but also by Arthur Anderson) is much more efficient than the public sector (populated by public school teachers, sanitation workers, police and firefighters, public health workers, park workers, etc.). Heterodox economists are skeptical about this portrayal and doubt that the real economic costs of expanded public-sector production would be high. In fact, many heterodox economists believe that the social payoffs to expanding the production of local government services, such as park services and school aides, are often higher than for increased private-sector production.

Implications of the Costs of Unemployment

The chief conclusion of heterodox analyses of the costs of unemployment is that they are huge. A 2 percent rise in the unemployment rate is not the same thing as a fall in national income by 2 percent or even 4 percent. The social meaning and impact of unemployment are different. Heterodox economists emphasize the path-dependent and enduring feedback effects of unemployment on individuals, neighborhoods, and business strategies. Darity and Goldsmith, for example, conclude:

> Orthodox macroeconomics is largely independent of time. Cultural, social and institutional evolution is neglected. For instance, it is commonly asserted that an exogenous shock to the macroeconomy leading to unemployment can be offset by an appropriate policy stimulus that returns to the economy to its original point. This description of events ignores the social psychological consequences of exposure to unemployment. These factors are likely to affect personal productivity, motivation, attitudes toward participation in the labor force and relations with acquaintances, spouses, offspring and friends. (Darity and Goldsmith 1996, 136–37)

These conclusions imply that potential trade-offs between unemployment and other economic variables, such as inflation or economic growth, have to be weighed very carefully. It also recommends looking for innovative macroeconomic policies for maintaining high employment levels.

PRICE INDICES

Conceptual Debates

Most chapters on economic measurement in principles texts include a section on measures of inflation, such as the consumer price index (CPI). Heterodox critiques of these discussions often resemble heterodox objections to the textbooks' treatment of GDP statistics. In both cases heterodox concerns often involve disagreements with the textbooks about what is being measured.

In the GDP case, heterodox economists criticize the textbooks for not adequately discussing the limitations of GDP as a measure of economic well-being. The problems with the CPI are more complex. Heterodox economists fault the textbooks for not fully exploring the tension between two different uses and conceptions of the CPI. One conception treats the CPI as a "cost-of-living" index. In this role the CPI is used for socioeconomic accounting tasks, such as adjusting social security payments to maintain a constant level of benefits. The second conception of the CPI treats it as a measure of the changing purchasing power of a constant sum of money. In this role the CPI is used as a macroeconomic indicator, often to help manage the size of the money supply. While these roles seem similar, they are not the same.

When used as a cost-of-living indicator, the CPI seeks to measure the changing costs of a constant set of outcomes. The latter comes closest to measuring the everyday notion of "the cost of living." The difficulty in this case involves defining what is meant by a "constant set of purchases or outcomes" due to ambiguities about what is being bought. The question returns us to the vexing distinction between intermediate and final goods that muddied the GDP waters.

For example, if there is an increase in crime and households require twice the number of locks on outer doors to achieve the same level of security and the price of locks falls 10 percent, did the cost of living rise or fall?[16] The same ambiguity can be seen by an example closer to student experience. In many ways colleges today offer a much better product to students than they did forty years ago. The multimedia resources of libraries and computer centers have expanded dramatically. Most colleges have much more elaborate athletic facilities. Modern "fitness centers," for example, have significantly more equipment than "weight rooms" did forty years ago. Average tuition has also increased dramatically. How should these tuition increases affect the CPI?

The answer may be that we need several cost-of-living indices. One could attempt to hold constant the social meaning of expenditures (treating college attendance as a prerequisite for participation in many areas of American life) and report large increases in the cost of college and the cost of living in America. Another index could adjust for quality changes and report much less of an increase in the cost of educational commodities, tying most price increases to higher quality. Analysts could use either index depending on its relevance to the question addressed.

Recent Debates

Recalibrating the CPI

The history of recent controversies within and outside the economics profession over the correct way to measure the CPI provides some interesting insights into the nature of economic theory and its relationship to larger social forces. In the mid-1990s concerns over the size of the federal government's budget deficit and the indexing of many federal spending programs, such as social security, to the CPI[17] spurred the Senate Finance Committee to appoint a commission to study the CPI. The panel was chaired by Stanford economics professor Michael Boskin. Professor Boskin was the head of former president George Bush's Council of Economic Advisers and an associate of the Hoover Institute, a conservative think tank. The panel included four other prominent economists. Each had previously expressed the opinion that the CPI overstated inflation. No heterodox economists or experts who took a different view, such as former Bureau of Labor Statistics commissioner Janet Norwood, were appointed (Baker 1996; Palley 1997). The preexisting orientation of the commission's members is very rarely noted in introductory textbooks.

The commissioners pointed to many factors they believed upwardly biased estimates of the CPI, highlighting insufficient adjustments for quality increases, the impact of new products, and a shift in consumer spending from higher to lower priced goods and from traditional retailers to discount chains like Wal-Mart. Despite very complex estimating problems, the commission quickly released findings indicating that the CPI overstated inflation by between 0.8 percent and 1.6 percent per year, with a best-guess estimate of 1.1 percent. The commission's quick rendering of quantitative judgments calls into question the oft-heard claim that failures to estimate the missing parameters in GDP (like the contribution of household labor to national output) reflect the difficulty of the task.

The commissioners indicated that their revisions resulted in a much rosier picture of the country's economic performance over the preceding two decades, noting that if they were right, "Over the last quarter-century, average real earnings have risen, not fallen, and real median income has grown not stagnated. The poverty rate would be lower . . . [and] real GDP growth . . . understated" (Boskin et al. 1998, 4). In addition, in the next twelve years the federal budget deficit could be cut by about 1 trillion dollars due to less indexed spending for programs like social security.

Despite the acknowledged presence of many speculative calculations and information gaps, the commission's findings quickly became the new orthodoxy. Modest attention was given to dissenting opinions, and that almost always within the neoclassical framework. Dean Baker, among others, offered very thoughtful critiques of the commission's findings from a heterodox perspective.[18] His critique suggests that the kinds of concerns that get integrated into government statistics are influenced by the aims of the users of those statistics.[19]

While agreeing with the commission's claim that several phenomena imparted an upward bias to the CPI, Baker and other critics offered thoughtful reasons for why the panel's estimation of the "product-substitution," "outlet-substitution," "quality-change," and "new-product" biases were too large.[20] Baker emphasized that "virtually no effort" was made to examine the ways in which the CPI might understate inflation.[21] He noted that costs like higher co-pays in medical insurance programs or increased household spending for legal services were not counted as price increases in the CPI. In like fashion, declining personal attention in medical treatment or increasing inconveniences in air travel were not included as quality declines.[22] Increases in defensive spending, such as the need to shift from tap water to bottled water due to pollution concerns, are also generally overlooked in CPI calculations.

Baker also emphasized that "price increases attributed to quality adjustments are not counted as price increases in the index, even though many consumers might not pay for them if they had the choice."[23] Numerous socioeconomic changes, such as the decline of public transport and pay phones in public spaces, have similarly increased the cost of participation in mainstream American life. It thus seems likely that many price increases for "basic" services, from automobiles to medical treatment, have increased "the cost of living" for people at the bottom of the income ladder in ways that are not detected by the CPI.

One of the most striking arguments Baker makes is that if the commission's estimate of the upward bias in the CPI were correct, real wages would have grown much faster than current statistics indicate, implying that past wage levels were much lower than previously realized. In fact, Baker writes, "The *average* hourly wage in 1960 would have been less than $5.50 an hour, measured in today's dollars, compared to over $16.00 an hour at present [italics in original]" (Baker 1998b, 84). The gap between the two seems much larger than commonsense comparisons of living standards in the two periods.

Implications of the CPI Debate

What can we learn from the CPI debate about macro textbooks? Once again, a key message is the centrality of subtexts in framing economic inquiry. Heterodox economists reject the neoclassicals' faith that maximizing market-measured growth is a prerequisite to maximizing societal well-being. Heterodox economists do not treat each additional dollar advance in GDP as equivalent, and they lack the sense of excitement about these advances that animates neoclassical economists.

In responding to heterodox concerns, the Boskin Commission members wrote, "While we certainly are concerned about the economic well-being of our least well-off citizens, it is important to understand how dramatically improved the standard of living of even those poorest in the population has been. It is simply incorrect to argue that quality improvements and new products accrue only to the rich, rather than broadly throughout the population. As noted earlier, there are 47 million cellular telephone subscribers in the United States and over 100 million Americans receive a telephone call initiated on a cellular phone" (Boskin et al. 1998, 23). Heterodox economists question the juxtapositioning of "dramatic improvements in standards of living" and the number of cellular phone calls received.

The neoclassical aesthetic, celebrating the "tectonic" shifts in quality of life brought about by consumer goods, can be re-illustrated by a comment from William Nordhaus's 1998 article "Quality Changes in Price Indexes." Nordhaus writes, "Ponder the tectonic shifts in the economy that occurred as railroads replaced muddy cow paths . . . as television replaced dark and lonely nights. . . ." (Nordhaus 1998, 62). Heterodox economists question the implication that people before TV sat facing empty walls on a sofa (a la a famous Gary Larson cartoon, "The World Before TV"). Although obviously some of the changes Nordhaus cites, like improvements in public health, have made enormous differences in human well-being, his lack of attention to qualitative differences among technological advances troubles heterodox economists. It is precisely the distinction between the shift from black-and-white to color TV (also highlighted by Nordhaus) and the discovery and diffusion of the polio vaccine that heterodox economists want to emphasize and neoclassicals resist.

THREADS

Environmental Issues

The Ecological Economic Paradigm

Although the shared methodology of heterodox economics leads to some common stances on environmental issues, there are variations among heterodox economists. The discussion in this section emphasizes the views of ecological economists, a relatively new heterodox economic paradigm. We will explore many of the ideas noted in this section in more detail in chapter 16, "Reintroducing Macroeconomics and the Environment."

Reflecting concerns about misplaced concreteness, ecological economists criticize neoclassical textbooks for failing to emphasize the uniqueness of "natural capital," both in the form of natural resources (such as fossil fuels) and environmental resources (such as species diversity and the earth's climate system). Ecological economists criticize standard textbooks for giving insufficient attention to debates about how to measure the costs of environmental hazards and how to calculate depreciation charges for the drawdown of natural resources.

Ecological economists also fault the textbooks for failing to convey the potential seriousness of the environmental risks that accompany modern production techniques and the large uncertainties involved in putting a price tag on these risks. They urge the adoption of the *precautionary principle* for estimating the economic costs of environmental hazards. This principle gives special weight to the high end of risk estimates when dealing with hazards that have large potential costs that are irreversible.[24]

Ecological economists stress the difference between uncertainties for which we know the underlying probability distribution (like the probability of different numbers arising from a single roll of dice), and uncertainties for which we don't have a probability distribution, such as the name of the most popular new CD ten years from now or the effects of global warming. They urge the adoption of the precautionary principle for assessing the latter's hazards and criticize neoclassical texts for inadequate discussion of these uncertainties.

Among the issues that take center stage in ecological economics is whether the market's valuation techniques provide acceptable estimates of the costs of depleting the world's resources. Ecological economists offer several reasons for suspecting they do not. We will investigate these reasons in chapter 16.

Viewing the economy from the perspective of ecological economics invites the construction of an accounting system geared toward the information needs of a sustainable economy. Traditional GDP statistics would be given less attention and the Commerce Department's Integrated Environmental and Economic Satellite Accounts greater attention in heterodox measurement chapters. Information about scarcity constraints, such as data about aquifer depletion or declining fishing stocks (as published annually in the Worldwatch Institute's "State of the World" volumes) would similarly be highlighted.

In Their Own Words. Perhaps the best way to get a feel for ecological economists' orientation toward economic measurement is to quote from two textbooks by several leading ecological economists, *An Introduction to Ecological Economics* (Costanza et al. 1997) and *Ecological Economics* (Daly and Farley 2004).

> *On Paradigms.* "Where conventional economics espouses growth forever, ecological economics envisions a steady-state economy at optimal scale. . . .
>
> "In other words ecological economics calls for a 'paradigm shift' in the words of philosopher Thomas Kuhn . . . ." (Daly and Farley 2004, 23)
>
> *On GDP/GNP.* "When economists or political leaders forget that what is measured by GNP is quite distinct from economic welfare, and when they then draw conclusions from the GNP about economic welfare, the fallacy of misplaced concreteness appears again." (Costanza et al. 1997, 114)
>
> "Perhaps the classic instance of the fallacy of misplaced concreteness in economics is 'money fetishism.' . . . [I]f money balances can grow forever at compound interest, then so can real GNP . . . ." (Daly and Cobb 1994, 37)
>
> "Ecological economics challenges today's standard emphasis on growth [226]. . . .

"[F]or the United States since 1947, the empirical evidence that GNP growth has increased welfare is weak, and since 1980 probably nonexistent. . . . [T]he 'great benefit,' habitually used to justify sacrifices of the environment, community standards, and industrial peace, appears, on closer inspection likely not even to exist. . . ." [234]

"[T]he blind pursuit of positional wealth and consumption places substantial demands on our time and resources, and leaves us with a decreasing ability to meet our other human needs." (Daly and Farley 2004, 237)

On Uncertainty. "[W]e need to be especially cognizant of the inherent uncertainty in our ability to predict the future. The 'precautionary principle' is beginning to achieve a degree of consensus as the basic approach to uncertainty. . . . [T]he focus should be on policies that are aimed at assuring sustainability over as wide a range of future conditions as possible." (Costanza et al. 1997, 106)

Gender Issues

Basic Themes

Heterodox critiques of the measurement chapters in neoclassical principles texts also have important implications for gender issues.

1. Heterodox economists criticize neoclassical texts for not giving more attention to statistics about household production, which has been traditionally, and still is predominantly, performed by women. This oversight mirrors the general erasure of women's role in the economy in the history of economic thought. Even when attempts have been made to include women's domestic labor in economic output, the worth of that labor has often been underestimated. Valuation methods have treated domestic labor as unskilled labor and priced it at the minimum wage, failing to include the "planning and managerial" dimensions of "homemaking," as well as the role of parents in human capital formation.

2. Heterodox economists also criticize textbook chapters on economic measurement for their neglect of the voluntary and informal sector, where women's roles have also been large. One of the important effects of increased female participation in the market sector has been a loss of women's labor in key areas of community life, such as support services for the public schools, informal neighborhood systems of after-school childcare, care of the elderly and infirm, and aid to numerous community groups, from the local library to the local zoo. The national income accounts give little information to social planners on what's happening in these areas.

3. Women's labor has traditionally been involved in knitting people together, be it families, neighborhoods, or social organizations. The tendency for economists to overlook these functions has meant that not enough is known about the contribution of such labor to economic productivity. Even as more women have entered economics, they have tended to adopt traditional research agendas in order to advance in the profession. Research on areas of production traditionally dominated by women has not generally been thought "interesting" by the profession. This is changing very slowly.

4. Feminist economists have also criticized the national income accounts for treating expenditures on health and education (which contribute to human capital formation) as categories of consumption rather than investment.

In Their Own Words

> [T]he major policy-related problem lies, not so much with underaccounting for household production in GDP, but in taking GDP numbers too seriously as a measure of welfare. . . . Measurement of welfare . . . is fundamentally multidimensional. . . . I see a key role of the feminist critique to be in questioning the methodological reductionism of (in spite of the weak 'we know it's not a welfare measure' paragraph in the introduction to every macroeconomics textbook) focusing so much attention on a single number. . . .
>
> —Nelson (1996, 119–20)

> Standard discussions of human capital formation . . . start with a discussion of secondary schooling; they ignore the socialization and education processes undertaken at home as well as the care from birth (or even from before birth, as in maternal health and nutrition) devoted to creating and developing a child's capacities.
>
> —Ferber and Nelson (1993a, 5)

> The goal is not counting and measuring for its own sake, but gathering information that will enable us to understand how the unpaid/informal economy functions and integrates with the cash/market. . . .
>
> [F]or example, we expect that expenditure cutbacks in health and education services transfer work from the market to the home, threatening women's jobs in the public sector, and increasing their unpaid workload in the home. This does not eliminate the costs of these services but renders the cost invisible and imposes it on women.
>
> —MacDonald (1995, 184)

Distributional Issues

As noted previously, heterodox economists tend to value equality in economic life as an end in itself, that is, as a feature of a good society. As a result they call for economic statistics that include more distributional information than commonly present in neoclassical macro texts. Since we will analyze many of these statistics in chapter 15's discussion of the macroeconomics of inequality, we offer only a brief sketch here.

Heterodox economists would adjust GDP and CPI statistics for distributional characteristics, weighting lower-income dollars more heavily than upper-income dollars. They would give greater attention to more dimensions of inequality than neoclassical texts, such as: (1) inequalities within the household vis-à-vis the production and distribution of economic output; and (2) inequalities within the workplace, vis-à-vis levels of personal autonomy (e.g., percentage of people self-employed) or levels of "workers' rights" (opportunities for collective bargaining, participatory decision making, profit sharing, access to grievance procedures, job security, etc.). Heterodox economists' interest in intergenerational equity issues would invite heightened attention to statistics on sustainability.

In Their Own Words: Heterodox Remarks on Distributional Statistics

> [W]e should develop an alternative to the Dow Jones, one that better describes what's happening to ordinary people. It could measure some combination of changes in unemployment, wages, and benefits like health insurance—the overall average of what people are earning [64]. . . .
>
> [C]onsider how little we know about Dolly Jones, the representative working mother.

We can trace improvements in her labor market earnings over time, but we know little about the organization or outcome of activities that occupy fully half of her total work time—cooking, cleaning, shopping, networking, managing, chauffeuring, volunteering, etc.

Nor do we know exactly how successful Dolly has been at persuading her male family members and friends to assume a greater share of these responsibilities as she has increased her paid work time. . . . It would help if the government collected systematic time-use data along the lines of its current surveys of consumer expenditure and labor force participation. Then the evening news could report the Dolly Jones index along with the . . . Dow [Jones Index]. (Folbre 2001, 67)

CONCLUSION: THE "SO WHAT" QUESTION

Policy Implications

Heterodox economists believe that the national income accounts and GDP statistics are important tools for discussing the level of market activity. As we will see in chapter 9, heterodox analyses often use GDP data to analyze the level and composition of aggregate demand. Heterodox economists object, however, to confusing the level of market activity and GDP with the level of economic well-being. They strongly criticize textbook chapters on macroeconomic measurement for giving insufficient attention to (1) the implications of positional competition, (2) the distinction between intermediate and final goods, (3) the economic relevance of nonmarket activities, (4) the quality of work life and the costs of unemployment, (5) the depletion of natural resources and costs of environmental hazards, (6) distributional issues, (7) the accumulation or depreciation of social capital and other meta-externalities, and (8) alternative economic indicators. These oversights tend to magnify the net benefits of increasing GDP and encourage public policies that "let the market work" in the name of economic growth. The oversights and "note but ignore" qualifiers reflect the neoclassical paradigm's subtexts and bottom-line commitment to market measured growth as the prerequisite for meeting most societal challenges.

Heterodox concerns about broader phenomena, such as social inequality, economic sustainability, and meta-externalities, challenge this subtext and invite attention to a broader range of statistics than highlighted in the core national income accounts and macro textbooks. These amplified indicators paint a much more complicated picture of the implications of market-led growth, and often invite a more active government role in the economy to achieve *both* individual and social objectives than implied by neoclassical textbooks.

Consider, for example, the implications of giving greater attention to the growing importance of positional competition. Although it is not usually highlighted in neoclassical texts, many societies, including our own, have experimented with different ways of resolving the prisoner's dilemma and minimizing the waste of destructive competition. Among well-known responses are: social norms against conspicuous consumption, arms control agreements, limitations on campaign spending, agreements requiring compulsory arbitration rather than limitless legal conflicts, limitations on athletic teams' practice times or use of steroids, and mandatory safety standards for the workplace and athletic field. In a similar spirit, we legislate "forced savings" in the form of social security taxes. The latter helps reduce the pressures on individuals to sacrifice retirement security for current social position.

Among the additional policies that heterodox attention to positional competition might recommend are (1) luxury good taxes; (2) limitations on advertising;[25] (3) the shift of resources from the private to the public sector for non-positional goods such as public safety, public health, environmental protection, primary and secondary education, and caregiving activities (such as support for the disabled); and (4) increased incentives for shorter work weeks (such as stronger regulations requiring higher rates of pay after a prescribed number of hours of labor per day or week).

Giving greater attention to measuring the costs of unemployment similarly invites greater policy attention to reducing unemployment. Prioritizing full employment as a macro goal has major implications for macro policy, as we will see in chapters 10 to 18. Increased attention to the uncertainties surrounding the risks of environmental hazards and resource depletion might likewise encourage tighter restrictions on pollution and public policies to reduce the use of exhaustible resources.[26] There are of course a wide range of policies that could redistribute income in the economy. We will defer discussion of this topic to chapter 15.

The lack of data on heterodox concerns also hinders policy makers and students from understanding some important features of the current economy. For instance, inattention to the household sector obscures the time squeeze occurring in many dual-income families and the general problems arising from the growth of the market sector at the expense of the voluntary sector.

STUDY QUESTIONS

Discussion Questions

1. Why is "economic measurement" a complicated task? In other words, why aren't measuring "economic well-being," the "costs of unemployment," or "the cost of living" straightforward tasks like weighing a sack of potatoes?
2. See if you can find an annual record of tuition and room and board charges at your college or university over the last twenty years. Assume they match every other college or university in the country. Also assume that higher education counts for about 2.5 percent of national expenditures. Explain how you would calculate the implications of this price history for the CPI.
3. Compare and contrast the treatment of the costs of unemployment in heterodox and neoclassical economic analyses. Why do many heterodox economists tend to find the costs of unemployment higher and deserving of more attention in macro textbooks than most neoclassical economists?
4. What aspects of the different treatment of the costs of unemployment by heterodox and neoclassical economists can be linked to basic methodological differences between heterodox and neoclassical economists?
5. What changes might occur in your life if you, your spouse, or your parents got laid off?
6. What are the policy implications of heterodox critiques of the GDP accounts? Or, put slightly differently, how might attention to heterodox discussions of GDP accounting lead to different economic policy initiatives?

Review Questions

1. Briefly identify some of the most serious psychological and social problems that have been correlated with unemployment.
2. Briefly discuss some of the links that heterodox economists have drawn between unemployment and inequality.
3. What has been the traditional relationship between white and African American unemployment rates?

4. What is the "hinge" rate of unemployment with respect to wage inequality according to James Galbraith?

5. Explain the difference between using the CPI as a measure of the "cost of living" and as a measure of the "purchasing power of money."

6. What concerns have heterodox economists raised about the adequacy of the CPI as a measure of the cost of living?

7. What are the major concerns raised by ecological economists about the costs and benefits of economic growth and the measurement of environmental and natural resources in neoclassical textbooks? (Hint: Why might ecological economists tend to value another dollar of GDP less than neoclassical economists and another unit of resource conservation or environmental protection more than neoclassical economists?)

8. What kinds of concerns have feminist economists raised about the treatment of women's productive activities in textbook chapters on economic measurement?

NOTES

1. U.S. Department of Labor, "Employment Situation," January 6, 2005, Table A-12, "Alternative Measures of Labor Underutilization." In 2004, the corresponding numbers were 5.4 percent and 9.3 percent.

2. The median duration was about seven weeks.

3. Government unemployment statistics indicate that in 1999 only 12 percent of the unemployed were out of work for more than twenty-seven weeks (*Economic Report of the President* 2000, 356). Although partially correct, these statistics probably exaggerate the brevity of unemployment due to the neglect of discouraged workers. This problem is especially acute for African Americans and older Americans, where low labor force participation rates probably give a truer picture of labor market problems than unemployment rates. Wray and Pigeon (2000), for example, note that about 14 million more people would be in the labor force if people aged twenty-five to sixty-four without a college education had the same labor force participation rate as college-educated Americans (831). Obviously not all of this group should be counted as underemployed. There are many reasons besides insufficient demand for why low- and semiskilled workers might have lower labor force participation rates than skilled workers. Nevertheless, it is likely that some of these 14 million people are discouraged workers. Monica Castillo's research, for example, found that 10 percent of those out of the labor force wanted a job (ibid., 829). Schmitt and Baker (2006) have also offered persuasive evidence for expecting that current sampling techniques significantly overestimate the employment rates (and, by extension, underestimate the labor market problems) of young black men and Hispanic women due to the way the surveys treat nonresponders.

4. The bottom 20 percent of the income ladder have no financial reserves. The next 40 percent of the population could not, on average, sustain their consumption at 125 percent of the poverty level from financial savings for two months. Even the families in the sixtieth percentile to eightieth percentile of the income ladder could not sustain their families, on average, at 125 percent of the poverty line from their financial savings for more than nine months (Wolff 1998, 144–45).

5. The unemployed also tend to incur job search costs, potential relocation costs, reductions in their credit rating, and the loss of "firm-specific human capital" (which means the loss of compensation for skills they have developed that are only applicable in the firm they previously worked for) (Schutz 2001, 111–12).

6. *Statistical Abstract of the United States 2001,* Table 537, p. 351.

7. Government assistance (excluding medical benefits) increased by about 30 percent in real terms (compared to about a 25 percent increase in population) from 1980 to 2000 (*Statistical Abstract of the United States 2004–2005,* Table 523, p. 346; Table 2, p. 7). Government spending for medical benefits grew at an even faster rate. "Income-tested benefits" refer to benefits that require recipients to have incomes below certain thresholds to qualify for aid.

8. Schutz (2001, 113), citing John W. Lynch, George Kaplan, and Sarah J. Shema, "Cumulative Impact of Sustained Economic Hardship on Physical, Cognitive, Psychological, and Social Functioning," *New England Journal of Medicine* 337, 12/25/97, 1889–95; also International Health Program, "Health and Income Equity," University of Washington and Health Alliance International. Web site: http://depts.washing3ton.edu/eqhlth (August 2000); Riegle (1982), and Wray and Pigeon (2000).

9. See, for example, Tom Wicker, "Jobs and Crime," *New York Times,* April 25, 1975, 30.

10. See for example, Feather (1990). Darity and Goldsmith (1996) indicate that some of the statistical problems with earlier estimates of unemployment effects have been corrected without altering basic conclusions about unemployment's destructive impact.

11. In many past business cycles, the impact of rising economic activity has also tended to increase labor force participation rates among African American teenagers more than whites, suggesting that standard unemployment data may understate the benefits of economic expansions to African Americans. Several convincing reasons have been advanced for why African American unemployment rates fall further than white rates during expansions: the last hired, first fired effect; the higher percentage of African Americans in industries sensitive to business cycle conditions; and the relatively lower education levels of African Americans (which tends to result in lower levels of firm-specific job skills, making it easier for firms to hire and fire African American workers).

12. During the 1980s economic expansion (1983–1989), the national unemployment rate fell 4.3 percentage points, the African American unemployment rate fell 8.1 percentage points, and the unemployment rate among African American males aged sixteen to nineteen fell 16.9 percentage points. As labor markets tightened from 1994 to 2000, the national unemployment rate fell 2.1 percentage points, the African American unemployment rate fell 3.9 percentage points, and the unemployment rate among African American males aged sixteen to nineteen fell 11.4 percentage points (*Economic Report of the President* 2004, 334–35).

13. The ability of full-employment policies to eliminate the worst inequalities in the economy should not be taken too far. Even at the peak of the last expansion, when the official unemployment fell below 4 percent, high school dropouts and those without any college attendance had significant problems finding jobs.

14. Boone and Ours report similar findings about workers' reluctance to report injuries during periods of high unemployment in their forthcoming article "Are Recessions Good for Workplace Safety?" in the *Journal of Health Economics,* May 2006. More than 150 years ago, John Stuart Mill, one of the great economists of the nineteenth century, offered a similar observation, writing, "when the supply of labour so far exceeds the demand . . . [t]he more revolting the occupation, the more certain it is to receive the minimum remuneration, because it devolves on the most helpless and degraded" (quoted in Linder [1994, 87]). High unemployment greatly expands the number of "helpless and degraded" applicants.

15. Calculations assume an increase in public employment of 4.65 million people (0.035 times the 1999 civilian labor force of 133 million) at $9.50/hour plus $1.75/hour in benefits for 2000 hours/year. Hopefully, the guaranteed public employment wage could be gradually increased to approach "living wage" levels.

16. Similar questions arise when trying to define a poverty line. At one point in America's history indoor plumbing was a luxury. The absence of it would not have signaled poverty status; today it would. Does this mean that the cost of living has gone up, or has the cost of living gone down with a fall in the costs of indoor plumbing, even if the latter has become a necessity? This issue is pursued in more detail in chapter 15's discussion of relative and absolute definitions of poverty.

17. When a program is indexed to the CPI it means that its expenditures are adjusted upward for inflation as measured by the CPI.

18. See, for example, Baker (1998a,b; 1996), Devine (2001), and Palley (1997). Baker is currently codirector of the Center for Economic and Policy Research (CEPR) and was formerly a senior economist at the Economic Policy Institute. He has written widely on CPI and social security issues and is the author of *Getting Prices Right: The Debate over the Consumer Price Index.*

19. The politics of the CPI resurfaced in October 2001 in debates about the appointment of a new director of the Bureau of Labor Statistics, which establishes the definition of the CPI. ("BLS Chief on Verge of Becoming a Statistic: Administration Looking to Replace Commissioner," by John M. Berry, October 5, 2001, *Washington Post*). Interestingly, political debates have surrounded the CPI and the construction of price indices since their inception due to their impact on wage negotiations. See for example Persky 1998.

20. Baker (1998b, 1996) notes, for example, that the "outlet bias" may be five to ten times too high. Hulten (1997) provides thoughtful reasons why the commission's quality bias may be too high.

21. Norwood (1997, 41) echoes this judgment.

22. Everett Ehrlich adds other potential quality declines in the areas of public education (due to the loss of talented women to the private sector) and housing quality, while still agreeing with the Boskin Commission's finding of CPI bias (Ehrlich 1997, 21).

23. Baker (1996) gives a nice example using automobiles. He indicates that from about 1970 to 1996 the average cost of a new car increased by about 400 percent, while the CPI's price for cars increased by about

150 percent. The differential was due to quality improvements. In 1970 it was possible to buy a new Volkswagen beetle for about $2,000. Despite the CPI's claim that the increase in automobile prices since 1970 is only 150 percent, it is impossible to find a new car for anywhere close to $5,000 today. Although contemporary automobiles are no doubt superior to the 1970 beetle, some people might find the bells and whistles insufficient compensation for the higher real price. Hulten (1997) notes that almost half of some years' actual price increases have been erased by quality adjustments.

24. In order to get a sense of the order of magnitude of the contribution of natural systems to the human economy, some ecological economists have recently attempted to put a dollar value on the services of the earth's ecosystems. The breadth of estimates is very large, ranging from three to fifty-four trillion dollars a year (Costanza et al. 1997; Roush 1997). U.S. GDP in 2004 was about $11.5 trillion. Although very interesting, the numerous gaps and heroic leaps involved in the estimates suggest that using traditional economic methodologies to attempt to "value the earth" may not be helpful.

25. Illustrative of such policies might be limitations on commercial intrusions into public spaces, like public schools, or higher postal rates for bulk mailings.

26. These policies might include higher taxes on resource extraction and more restrictive access to public lands.

9

REINTRODUCING AGGREGATE DEMAND

The celebrated optimism of traditional economic theory . . . is also to be traced,
I think, to their having neglected to take account of the drag on prosperity
which can be exercised by an insufficiency of effective demand.
—John Maynard Keynes ([1936] 1964, 33–34)

(T)he Walrasian auctioneer does not really exist, and . . . "as if" stories about the
auctioneer are a fiction that has too long misled the [economics] profession.
—Bruce Greenwald and Joseph Stiglitz (winner of the Nobel Prize in
Economics in 2001) (Greenwald and Stiglitz 1993, 42)

INTRODUCTION

What is the logical structure behind the next several chapters in neoclassical textbooks? Why
are they there? What do they have in common? What questions are they trying to answer?
The chapters generally have titles like "Consumption," "Investment," "Fiscal Policy," and
"The Multiplier Model." They have a common focus on what determines the level of spending for final goods and services in the economy and are usually integrated through the geo-
metric device of the "Keynesian Cross." Why is this lens used to organize inquiry into
macroeconomic outcomes?

The question is puzzling from the equilibrium perspective offered in neoclassical texts.
The question is easier to answer from the disequilibrium perspective we developed in chapter 5. In the casino (rather than the auctioneer) economy and in markets with sticky (rather
than smoothly adjusting) prices, reductions in demand can cause the economy to sputter.
Declines in consumer confidence can weaken consumer spending. Pessimistic business expectations can contract investment. Initial declines can lead to downward spirals that mire
the economy in depressed conditions. The next several chapters in your text focus on the
domestic "components of aggregate demand" (consumption, investment, and government
spending) because of historic concerns about the problem of "insufficient aggregate demand"
in capitalist economies.

Over the last twenty-five years, the dominant voices in the neoclassical paradigm have
downplayed potential macroeconomic difficulties, eliminating many Keynesian concerns from
introductory textbooks. As we shall see in later chapters, several appendages have been added to
earlier Keynesian models that minimize their disequilibrium implications. Like archaeological
ruins, however, the current textbooks' structure hints at the presence of older ideas.

REENCOUNTERING KEYNES

To understand the reasoning behind the structure of your textbook it is helpful to talk a bit more about John Maynard Keynes, the father of modern macroeconomics. As noted earlier, he was a colorful figure and digressions about him are almost always interesting.[1]

Keynes's Life

The defining macroeconomic event in Keynes's life (1883–1946) was the Great Depression (1929–1940), which saw unemployment reach 25 percent in the U.S. and average more than 17 percent for a decade. Keynes found equilibrium economics unable to explain the causes of the Great Depression and questioned its laissez-faire, "do-nothing" policy recommendations for responding to high unemployment.

Keynes was a reformer rather than a radical.[2] His aim was to repair, rather than replace, capitalism. He pictured macroeconomists as mechanics or medics for the body politic, suggesting, "the economic problem . . . should be a matter for specialists—like dentistry" (Lekachman 1966, 50). His goal was to write a repair manual, a macroeconomic theory that would tell policy makers how to prevent or minimize the damage caused by economic depressions.

The brief and selective biographical sketch of Keynes's life below provides some insights into the new directions he took macroeconomics.[3] See if you can anticipate some of the challenges his life experiences posed for equilibrium economics.

Keynes learned his economics from the giants of orthodox theory, Alfred Marshall and A.C. Pigou at Cambridge University in England. Early in his career, he was the author of a highly praised book on mathematical probability. One of the goals of his research was to understand how people reasoned amid uncertainty. He amassed a personal fortune by speculating in financial markets, turning a few thousand British pounds into 400,000 pounds. He similarly increased the value of Kings College's endowment tenfold (Heilbroner 1967, 236). He served on the boards of several insurance companies and was a director of the Bank of England. Keynes was also a member of the avant-garde British intellectual group known as the Bloomsbury Group, which celebrated unorthodox thinking.

One of Keynes's early works was *The Economic Consequences of Peace*. In this book he attacked the Treaty of Versailles that concluded World War I. He argued that the reparations and other economic punishments imposed on the defeated countries would cripple their economies. This result would rebound to the disadvantage of their trading partners (the victorious allies) and injure the world economy. Although the treaty writers rejected his views, the subsequent collapse of the European economy in the 1930s seemed to vindicate his perspective.

Keynes spent much of his early career studying monetary phenomena, such as banking panics, runs on currencies, and people's fluctuating desire to be "liquid" (i.e., hold money). All of these interests ultimately found their way into the economic argument constructed in Keynes's great book, *The General Theory of Employment, Interest and Money*. In the *General Theory,* as the work has come to be called, Keynes argued that economic analysis had to include both equilibrium economics, which implied a tendency for automatic full employment, and disequilibrium economics, which implied the potential for serious unemployment and unused productive capacity. He gave special attention to the impact of imperfect information, uncertainty, and speculation on economic behavior and explored how volatile expectations could disrupt the economy.

Keynes worried especially about collapses in investment demand. He believed that investment decisions were fraught with uncertainty as they stretched over long time horizons and involved judgments about things one could only guess at. The decisions were also frequently irreversible, or if amendable, only at great economic loss. Investors in modern nuclear power plants, for example, have to decide whether to risk several billion dollars on the expectation that over the next fifty years nuclear energy will prove cheaper than as-yet unimagined alternatives. Even investors in seemingly healthy technologies like computer chips have to make guesses about the level of future demand for their industry, the nature of their competition, and the implications of new technologies. Reflecting this situation, Keynes argued:

> Most, probably, of our decisions to do something positive, the full consequences of which will be drawn out over many days to come, can only be taken as a result of animal spirits. . . . [I]f the animal spirits are dimmed and the spontaneous optimism falters, leaving us to depend on nothing but a mathematical expectation, enterprise will fade and die;—though fears of loss may have a basis no more reasonable than hopes of profit had before. . . .
>
> We should not conclude from this that everything depends on waves of irrational psychology. . . . [T]he state of long-term expectation is often steady. . . . We are merely reminding ourselves that human decisions affecting the future . . . cannot depend on strict mathematical expectation, since the basis for making such calculations does not exist. . . . (Keynes [1936] 1964, 161–63)

A fall in business confidence and a decline in investment demand, by themselves, need not cause economic problems. For example, if pessimism about future investment opportunities were accompanied by a decline in the savings rate (which implies an increase in current consumption), investor pessimism need not reduce aggregate demand. Keynes believed that, unfortunately, the way savings, consumption, and investment behaved in the modern economy did not ensure smooth adjustments to declining investor expectations. Later in this chapter we will look at each of these activities (savings, consumption, and investment) and explore how heterodox analysis highlights potential problems for the economy that are obscured in standard textbooks.

Keynesian Doubts of Full-Employment Guarantees

In order to explain Keynes's reasoning it is helpful to outline the mechanisms by which full employment is restored after a contraction in aggregate demand according to the logic of equilibrium theory. We can then zero in on Keynes's objections to these arguments. For illustrative purposes, we shall assume an initial decline in aggregate demand caused by a fall in investment, as this has often been the case historically. We could have begun just as well, however, with other demand shocks.

Perhaps the most important equilibrating mechanism in equilibrium theory is a decline in the interest rate. This is expected to restore aggregate demand by increasing investment, decreasing savings, and increasing consumption. It is automatically precipitated by an excess of desired savings over desired investment.

Keynes and other heterodox economists have raised several objections to this rosy scenario, often based on attention to the implications of uncertainty. The first objection involves situations where business expectations are so pessimistic (as in the Great Depression) that falling interest rates cannot spur significant new investment. The second involves situations where interest rates are inhibited from falling (or at least falling far enough to stimulate significant investment). Their stickiness can be due to many factors. For example, lenders may require high interest rates to compensate them for increased uncertainty in a weak economy. Or lenders may expect interest rates to rise in the future and be reluctant to part with their savings at significantly lower rates today.[4] Keynes concludes that in these circumstances changes in national income, rather than changes in interest rates, will equilibrate savings and investment.

Keynes argues that as long as savings is greater than investment, there will not be enough purchasing power in the economy to buy back all of the goods produced. The buildup of unsold goods will eventually lead to production and employment cutbacks. As output and national income declines, however, so will savings. Eventually the economy will come to rest at a level of output where the lower level of savings equals the lower level of investment that initiated the downward spiral.

"Not so," reply the equilibrium theorists. They argue that even if declining interest rates are unable to offset reductions in aggregate demand, other automatic adjustment mechanisms will be able to maintain full-employment levels of output. Firms and workers in a recessed economy, they claim, will offer their goods and labor at lower prices. This reaction should increase sales and employment.

We will look more closely at the behavior of labor and product markets in chapters 12 and 13, but it is helpful to briefly explore some key issues at this time. Keynes had two concerns about the ability of lower product prices to spur higher sales and output levels. The first revolved around the empirical observation that prices tend to be sticky. The consumer price index, for example, has not fallen since 1955, despite the fact that there have been eight recessions since then, with unemployment reaching 11 percent in the 1980s. (In chapter 5 we noted some of the reasons that have been offered for the existence of sticky prices.)

But Keynes's argument went beyond this observation and actually suggested that flexible prices might in some cases exacerbate rather than eliminate contractionary pressures. For one thing, although an individual firm may sell more if it lowers its prices, it is not clear that any firm will sell more if all firms lower their prices. One likely outcome is simply deflation, that is, a fall in the price level. The issue then becomes whether deflation can stimulate the economy.

It is possible that exports might increase if the price level of a country fell in relationship to that of others. When global economic conditions are synchronized (as in the Great Depression and perhaps today), however, this restorative mechanism fades. Several other arguments have been offered by neoclassical economists for why deflation might automatically stimulate aggregate demand and restore full employment. These arguments are very weak. One of the most well known is the "real balance effect." It suggests that as the price level falls owners of U.S. government debt will feel richer (as the real purchasing power of their savings grows) and increase their consumption. As many authors have pointed out, any deflation large enough to spur serious increases in consumption would probably bankrupt many households and firms obligated to pay off old debts in much more expensive dollars. Bankruptcies of this magnitude would likely have very destabilizing and contractionary effects.

"OK," say the equilibrium theorists, "there are still other mechanisms that would automatically restart a stalled economy. Unemployed workers would offer themselves at lower wages and firms would increase their employment levels. Spending by these workers would increase aggregate demand and restart the economy."

Heterodox economists also question the reliability of this restorative mechanism. First of all wages might be sticky, due to long-term contracts or implicit understandings between employers and employees to avoid wage cuts. Even if money wages did fall, firms might simply pass this savings on to customers, lowering output prices. The resulting deflation might leave the real wage (the money wage adjusted for inflation) unchanged, and thus have no effect on employment. And the *coup de grace*: Even if real wages fell, Keynes feared that employment might not increase.

The latter is really the main problem. Falling real wages could increase employment in two ways. Firms could increase production levels or substitute labor for other inputs at current output levels. As Keynes emphasized, it is possible that firms' expectations of future sales would be unaffected (or even harmed) by falling real wages. It is also likely that there is limited capital/labor substitution in many production processes. Firms have fixed machinery, for example, and it is not clear that falling wages can significantly alter the mix of inputs used to produce goods in the short run (say several years). Thus, in the absence of altered expectations about aggregate demand, falling wages may not lead firms to hire more workers. Falling wages may simply increase profits and tilt national income toward the upper-income groups. In an economy with weak aggregate demand this could exacerbate the problem of excess savings. Another way of putting this is to note that the economy's problems did not begin in the labor market (they arose from insufficient aggregate demand in the goods market) and thus may not always be resolvable in the labor market.

Still another way of getting a handle on the inability of falling wages to resolve aggregate demand problems is to note that workers cannot be paid in units of output. Firms must pay workers in dollars, which means that they must sell the output in order to compensate workers. If the firm were like a roadside apple orchard that paid itinerant workers in apples, it could hire apple pickers without concern about aggregate demand. It could take a cut of their harvest and pay them in apples. Some neoclassical models of the labor market imply a similar independence from demand expectations. The models implicitly assume that workers can always be paid their marginal physical product. The chronic unemployment of the 1930s belies this point. To paraphrase Jim Crotty, firms would love to hire workers if only sales would rise first; and workers would love to buy goods if only employment and wages would rise first.

Keynes also gave much attention to how uncertainty surfaced in "the monetary sector" of the economy, that is, how it affected phenomena such as credit flows. We will defer discussion of these issues until chapter 10's analysis of monetary phenomena.

The bottom line of all of these scenarios is a situation where pessimistic expectations create self-fulfilling prophecies of economic contraction. Once stalled, the economy might not be able to restart itself. Keynes did not think that the combination of factors necessary to disable an economy characterized the normal state of the economy. He did think, however, that the conditions arose frequently enough to warrant economic analysis and public policy responses. To draw a medical analogy, most people are healthy most of the time. Most illnesses cure themselves. Nevertheless, a biological theory that focused solely on explaining how a healthy body works would not be very useful to doctors. What is needed is a "General Theory" that covers both well and ill moments. This is what Keynes tried to provide and the task continues to occupy heterodox economists.

It is often hard for neoclassical textbooks to address macroeconomic failures as the stories, metaphors, and simple models of textbook theory are built around equilibrium assumptions, such as perfect information or the characteristics of a barter economy. In the former case, there is no role for volatile and pessimistic expectations. In the latter case (a barter economy), supply automatically creates demand (the purchase of a new good).[5] There is no impulse to hold money and interrupt exchange.

As the term progresses the disequilibrium ideas underlying Keynesian theory will probably disappear from your textbook, leaving the motivation behind analytical devices like the Keynesian Cross a bit puzzling. If this happens, you may want to return to the early chapters of this commentary to refresh your memory of an alternative way of understanding the economy.[6]

Keynesian Policy Implications

Keynes believed that the economy did not have to remain mired in depression or recession after a downward spiral in aggregate demand. The same dynamic that resulted in idle workers not being able to buy goods from idle factories could be run in reverse. Expansionary government policy could "prime the pump," increase aggregate demand, reemploy people who would re-spend their incomes and induce new production to reemploy others, and so on.

From Keynes's perspective, what blocked this recovery were the laissez-faire doctrines of orthodox economics that assured everyone that the economy would automatically right itself in the long run. In exasperation Keynes offered his famous remark, "In the long run we are all dead" (Yates 2003, 20, 265) and half-seriously suggested in 1936:

> If the Treasury were to fill old bottles with bank notes, bury them at suitable depths in disused coal mines which are then filled up to the surface with town rubbish, and leave it to private enterprise on well-tried principles of *laissez-faire* to dig the notes up again . . . there need be no more unemployment and, with the help of the repercussions, the real income of the community, and its capital wealth also, would probably become a good deal greater than it actually is. It would, indeed, be more sensible to build houses and the like; but if there are political and practical difficulties in the way of this, the above would be better than nothing. (Keynes [1936] 1964, 129)

The Great Depression continued throughout the 1930s. What rescued the U.S. and English economies was massive government spending to fight World War II. With the onset of the war Keynes turned his attention from depression economics to wartime economics, and finally toward reconstruction economics. After the war ended there was widespread concern that the global economy would sink back into prewar depression. The time was right for a debate over Keynesian economics. Unfortunately, Keynes died of a heart attack in 1946, before he could participate in that debate.

INTERMISSION: A BREAK FOR DISCUSSION

Can you see a link between Keynes's life and his previous economic research and the logic of the *General Theory?* For example, would it be possible for anyone to make a fortune as a speculator in a world of perfect information? Would anyone want to hold their wealth in money rather than interest-bearing assets in a world with perfect information? What does this imply about the demand for money?

EROSION OF KEYNESIAN THEORY

Over the next fifty years the heterodox message of Keynesian economics was eroded. By the year 2000 most introductory macroeconomics textbooks sounded more like pre-Keynesian than Keynesian textbooks in their macro analysis and policy recommendations. Nearly all concern about potential problems in aggregate demand had disappeared. Concerns about "animal spirits" and "liquidity crises" (one of the foci of our next two chapters), for example, are gone. Keynes is dismissed.[7]

The only debate recognized in most textbooks is over how "sticky" some prices are and how fast the economy automatically returns to full employment. This posing of Keynesian concerns misses the essence of Keynes's thinking and narrows economic debate. We will try to widen the debate and put "Keynes" back into Keynesian economics.

THE KEYNESIAN CROSS

The Purpose of the Keynesian Cross

The simple Keynesian Cross model in your textbook finds "equilibrium income" by graphically determining where the C+I+G line (the aggregate demand line) intersects the 45-degree line. If the intersecting level of output is below the level of output necessary for full employment, the economy is said to have a "demand gap." The model can be used to show how demand shocks to the economy, such as pessimistic swings in investor and consumer confidence, can cause downward economic spirals and rising unemployment. Any reasonable use of the model, however, needs to demonstrate why negative demand shocks do not trigger full-employment adjustments. We have just presented Keynes's answer to that question. The absence of similar analysis in most neoclassical textbooks allows later chapters to ignore and/or undo the challenge to automatic full employment posed by the Keynesian Cross.

The Road Ahead

In the next few sections we look at ways of constructing the Keynesian Cross that capture the insights of Keynesian and heterodox economic theory. We will follow the table of contents of standard texts, which focus sequentially on consumption behavior, savings behavior, and investment behavior. The textbooks follow this agenda because the original logic of Keynesian theory implied that the way households make consumption and savings decisions, coupled with the way firms make investment decisions, could create problems of insufficient aggregate demand in the economy and involuntary unemployment. The Keynesian cross was designed to illuminate these problems.

TEXTBOOK AND HETERODOX DISCUSSIONS OF CONSUMPTION

Overview

Standard textbook discussions of consumption include both macroeconomic phenomena and more general neoclassical claims about the nature of economic behavior. This section critiques both aspects of the texts' discussion. It demonstrates how the paradigmatic lens of neoclassical theory has shaped and limited the texts' analysis of consumer behavior.

Heterodox discussions of consumption explore the implications of uncertainty and social contexts for household decisions about savings and consumption. Heterodox economists stress the significance of consumer confidence for aggregate demand and the tendency of consumers to fall back on social conventions and habits when making consumption decisions amid uncertainty. By focusing on uncertainty, consumer confidence, and social conventions, heterodoxy comes to different conclusions from the textbooks about the reasons for volatility and stability in consumer demand.

Neglect of the Social Dimension of Consumer Demand

Heterodox economists criticize neoclassical textbooks for giving insufficient attention to the impact of social contexts on consumer desire; the information available to consumers about products, prices, and economic conditions; and the conventions used by consumers to respond to inherent uncertainty. Before taking on long-term obligations (like a mortgage or car payments) families have to estimate their future income and define "prudent" spending habits. Faced with imperfect information and information overload (an inability to process all available information), households often utilize traditional rules of thumb and socially popular conventions to make decisions. In most cases, individuals follow the norms of their peer group.

People tend to follow the herd, not because they are stupid or the herd is especially wise, but because this economizes on time and information needs. The strategy also reduces the risks of being "left out" and offers the security of one's potential problems being common problems. Households exhibit *bounded rationality,* that is, they tend to explore a set of options that are *socially highlighted,* rather than peruse all hypothetical options for the ideal outcome. Like "culture" in the broadest sense, this strategy also confers a sense of orderliness to the external world, an orderliness that may be necessary for mental health.[8]

This strategy tends to stabilize consumer behavior. People do not usually change their consumption patterns very much in response to modest price changes or moderate fluctuations in their income. From a heterodox perspective it is the inertia encouraged by social conventions, rather than the auctioneer or rapid price adjustments, that often stabilizes the economy.[9]

Occasionally, the logic of group behavior can lead to economic discontinuities. Moderate economic shocks can generate positive feedback that amplifies rather than reduces the destabilizing impact of the initial shock. Dramatic shifts in behavior can arise when waves of optimism or pessimism among consumers reverse themselves. Textbook models of consumer demand tend to downplay this possibility.

Subtexts and Subjects

Many heterodox analyses of consumption are not logically precluded in neoclassical theory. The textbooks' neglect of these ideas reflects instead the topics' lack of congeniality with, or relevance to, neoclassical subtexts.[10] As we have seen, neoclassical economists tend to judge economic models to be "illuminating" (and thus significant enough to be included in introductory texts) if they (1) teach or reveal economic behavior and market outcomes to be the result of rational individual optimizing decisions, or (2) generate precise results. Neoclassical textbooks tend to be relatively disinterested in economic models and ways of thinking that (1) undermine claims of rational behavior and market optimality,[11] or (2) lead to "sociological" and "indeterminate" models of behavior.

The privileging of models that generate precise results is often tied to claims that such models can be tested empirically. The problem with this claim is that the information necessary to test the models is frequently (and often inherently) unavailable. The hypothetically testable nature of the model thus has more rhetorical than practical consequence.

Isolated or Social Consumers: Alternative Consumption Functions

Underlying most textbook analyses of consumer demand is the image of an isolated consumer making private consumption decisions without reference to anyone else's consumption choices. The idea that what I want to buy is affected by what you are buying, and vice versa (formally described as the *interdependence* of consumer preferences) is generally deemphasized in neoclassical textbooks.

Addressing interdependency invites attention to the "social logic" organizing behavior in a capitalist economy; makes simple mathematical models of consumers' activity almost impossible; and undermines claims about market rationality and market optimality. Not surprisingly, the topic tends to be explored more fully in heterodox than in neoclassical economics. In earlier chapters we discussed interdependency primarily in terms of "positional competition." We noted how the textbooks' neglect of the futility and wastefulness of positional competition can lead to serious gaps in thinking about economic welfare and economic trade-offs. The discussion below explores the implications of interdependency for the behavior of aggregate demand.

Although much of the work on interdependency has been done by heterodox economists, such as Thorstein Veblen, John Kenneth Galbraith, and Fred Hirsch,[12] important contributions were made fifty years ago by two neoclassical economists, James Duesenberry and Harvey Leibenstein of Harvard University. The fate of their work is illustrative of the treatment of heterodox ideas within neoclassical theory. The work died on the vine. Few seeds reproduced in the subsoil (the subtext) of the neoclassical paradigm.

Leibenstein suggested that the relationship between price and quantity demanded was much more complicated than suggested by textbook theory. Under the "bandwagon effect," the demand for a good can increase because of its popularity (as, for example, the demand for a movie that people are already talking about). Under the "snob effect," declining prices can lower the perceived value of a good because lower prices lower the value of the good as a status symbol. Both cases imply that the market demand curve cannot simply be a summation of individual demand curves. Both effects imply that consumer demand needs to be studied in a social context.

Duesenberry's work is the most relevant to our discussion of aggregate demand. It arose in the context of an empirical puzzle about consumer demand. If you look at a "cross section" of different income groups in the population at a moment in time, the rich have lower marginal propensities to consume (mpc) and higher marginal propensities to save than the poor. Over time, however, richer societies have not had lower mpcs than poorer societies. How can this be?

Three major theories emerged to answer this question: Milton Friedman's "permanent income hypothesis," Franco Modigliani's "life cycle hypothesis," and James Duesenberry's "relative income hypothesis." The first two theories contributed to the authors' receipt of the Nobel Prize in Economics. Duesenberry's work has remained in the shadows of neoclassical economics.[13]

Both the permanent income and life cycle hypotheses model consumers' consumption decisions as the aggregation of isolated individual consumption choices. The life cycle hypothesis suggests that people attempt to smooth out their consumption over their lifetime. The permanent income hypothesis comes to about the same conclusion within a shorter time horizon. Both theories imply that the apparent inverse relationship between income levels and the marginal propensity to consume is due to timing rather than enduring differences between the spending habits of the rich and the poor.[14]

Duesenberry approaches the paradox in a different way. He argues that people's consumption behavior is influenced by other people's consumption behavior. More particularly, he argues that a person's mpc is a function of both their relative and their absolute income. People in the lower income brackets tend to emulate the consumption patterns of higher income brackets and thus consume a higher percentage of their income. When all incomes rise proportionately, the aggregate mpc does not fall because relative incomes remain unchanged.

Duesenberry also argues that consumption is a learned activity and that consumer tastes tend to "ratchet" upward after income increases. This implies a tendency for mpcs to rise during periods of income decline (as consumers seek to hold on to their newly revised lifestyles) and to fall in periods of rapid income increases (before consumers acquire new tastes). Duesenberry's theories draw attention to the importance of distributional issues and positional competition. They also open the door to potential challenges to the optimality of "perfect market" outcomes.

Not much of Duesenberry's thinking remains in the textbooks. The erasure of Duesenberry's work has little to do with empirical evidence. The data is at least as consistent (and probably more so) with his thinking as textbook theory. The erasure is paradigmatic. Duesenberry's approach did not fit well within the neoclassical project.

For example, Robert Frank of Cornell University (1985) reports,

> Though Duesenberry's explanation was persuasive to many . . . it is fair to say that many economists felt uncomfortable with what they regarded as a sociological theory of the consumption function. To many economists, the notion of consumers' being strongly influenced by demonstration effects in consumption must have seemed troublingly at odds with the postulate of rational pursuit of self-interest. It is hardly surprising, therefore, that the profession later so warmly embraced Milton Friedman's permanent income hypothesis (1957) and the life cycle hypothesis of Franco Modigliani and Richard Brumberg (1955). Without relying on vague constructs borrowed from other branches of the social sciences, these theories provided clear a priori reasons, carefully grounded in utility-maximizing behavior, for the observed pattern of average propensities to consume in time-series and in cross-section data.
>
> There is no question that the phenomena addressed by the permanent income and life cycle theories are real and important. But these theories simply cannot account fully for the positive relationship between savings rates and incomes we observe in cross-section samples of individuals. The life cycle and permanent income theories of saving both insist that if the influence of life cycle differences and transitory earning could be eliminated, we would then see that high-income persons save the same fractions of their incomes as do low-income persons. *In study after careful study, however, this prediction has failed to find empirical support* [emphasis added] (109). . . .
>
> The evidence on the savings vs. income relationship is so strong and so consistent that it would appear difficult for proponents of the permanent income and life cycle theories to continue to insist that savings rates are unrelated to income. Yet these claims persist in most major undergraduate and graduate texts in macroeconomics. (110)

Revisiting the issue twenty years later, Frank summed up the textbooks' treatment of macro theories of consumption as "an intriguing cautionary tale in the sociology of knowledge," adding that "Most economists it appears, just never wanted to believe the relative income hypothesis—perhaps because it suggests the possibility of wasteful spending races" (R. Frank 2005b).[15]

THE SAVINGS FUNCTION

Heterodox critiques of the treatment of savings in standard macro principles texts repeat many of the objections raised to the treatment of consumption. There is, for example, a lack of attention to uncertainty and the role of social conventions and institutional contexts in determining savings behavior. There is also a tendency to neglect topics uncongenial with neoclassical subtexts. We will look at four examples.

Insufficient Attention to Business Savings

Perhaps the most glaring problem in neoclassical textbooks is the tendency to imply that national savings is primarily determined by household decisions to save or consume their disposable in-

Table 9.1

U.S. Savings Behavior (in billions of historical dollars)

Year	Gross Savings	Gross Private Savings	Social Security & Gross Government Savings	Medicaid Savings
2001	1,662	1,399	263	694
2000	1,808	1,372	436	653
1999	1,704	1,356	348	612
1998	1,647	1,375	272	572
1997	1,502	1,344	159	539

Source: *Economic Report of the President 2/2003*, pp. 314, 371.

Table 9.2

Disaggregating U.S. Savings Behavior (in billions of historical dollars)

Year	Gross Savings	Gross Private Savings	Personal Savings	Gross Business Savings	Undistributed Corporate Profits*	Business Consumption of Capital**
2001	1,662	1,399	170	1,230	123	1,107
2000	1,808	1,372	202	1,171	153	1,018
1999	1,704	1,356	174	1,182	230	947
1998	1,647	1,375	302	1,074	190	884
1997	1,502	1,344	253	1,091	261	832

Source: U.S. Executive Office of the President 2003, 314.
*This refers to retained earnings
**This refers to corporate income used to offset capital depreciation

come. This focus is consistent with the image of consumer sovereignty that animates neoclassical texts. Over the last fifty years, however, household savings have accounted for only one-third of private savings. Recently, personal savings have accounted for less than 20 percent of private savings. The dominant factor has been business savings in the form of retained earnings and funds to cover capital depreciation (see Tables 9.1 and 9.2).[16] The factors determining business and household savings are different and require distinct analysis.

Insufficient Attention to Institutional Factors

Heterodox explanations of savings behavior generally give more attention to institutional variables than neoclassical texts do. For example, there is usually more emphasis in heterodox than textbook theory on the impact of socially constructed conventions, expectations, and institutions (like pension plans and social security) on savings rates. As tables 9.1 and 9.2 indicate, this attention reflects the relative magnitude of savings streams. Government-required household saving for social security and Medicare, for example, was about three times the size of non-social-security savings in recent years. There is similarly more attention in heterodox than orthodox texts to the role of consumer credit mechanisms, such as installment plans for the purchase of consumer durables or the increased availability of credit cards, in explaining households' inter-temporal spending practices. There is greater focus on the role of government tax policies and financial institutions, such as the Federal National Mortgage Association (Fannie Mae) in mobilizing savings for home purchases.[17]

It is not formally difficult to integrate many institutional topics into neoclassical discussions. What is resistant to change, however, is the individualistic optimizing message that the standard chapters convey. Heterodox images of the determination of savings and consumption behavior stress their grounding in institutional systems. Market outcomes lose their de-novo (out-of-nothing) origins and their automatic optimality. The task of economists and economic textbooks becomes more centered on understanding the institutional context of economic activities than on deriving abstract conclusions about ahistorical individual actions.

Insufficient Attention to Suboptimal Behaviors

Heterodox analyses of savings behavior also note the potential for the logic of positional competition and the illogic of irrational behavior to produce suboptimal savings rates, in terms of both the well-being of individuals and the construction of a good society. Interestingly, standard textbook discussions of savings rarely discuss the rationale for the largest savings plan in the United States, the "forced savings" of the social security system. Under this system, most workers are *required* to have about 15 percent of their wages contributed to an old age, disability, and medical insurance system. We shall ignore the current debate over whether these funds should be invested in market assets, to address an even more fundamental issue. What is the basis for *required* savings? The practice would seem to contradict the assumption of individual rationality and market optimality that underlies neoclassical economics. This tension is rarely addressed in standard macro textbooks.

The best neoclassical rationale for forced saving under the social security system is related to the free rider problem. From a neoclassical perspective, if one assumed that the public was inevitably going to provide a minimum safety net for elderly or disabled workers, it would be tempting for some people to take advantage of that generosity and not save for their own retirement. Anticipation of this behavior might justify requiring all citizens to participate in a social security system.

This is a reasonable argument, but clearly not the whole story. A key additional reason for requiring universal participation in the social security system is widespread recognition that relying on private decisions would produce insufficient savings. The pressures of positional competition for current consumption and predictable errors of judgment, like shortsightedness, would lead many people to save less than they would have preferred to save retrospectively. Although this judgment fits easily within heterodox theory, it borders on heresy within neoclassical texts.[18] Heterodox economists find the contribution of economic education to current debates over social security disappointing and dangerously likely to contribute to the dismantling of a successful insurance system in the name of spurious market optimality.

Insufficient Attention to Distributional Issues

As noted earlier, cross-sectional studies of savings behavior indicate that richer households tend to have higher savings rates than poorer households and that consumption out of wages tends to be higher than consumption out of non-labor income (profits, rental payments, and interest payments, collectively known as property income) due to the latter's concentration in upper-income groups. One implication of differential savings rates is that the level of consumer demand in the economy may fluctuate with changes in the share of national income going to labor and property

Table 9.3

Macroeconomic Volatility

Time Period	Annual Real Change in GDP	Annual Real Change in Consumption	Annual Real Change in Gross Private Investment
1980–1989	−1.9% to +7.3%	0% to +5.4%	−3.7% to +17.6%
1990s	−0.2% to +4.5%	0.1% to +5.3%	−4.9% to +12.7%

Source: U.S. Executive Office of the President 2000, 311.

income. Some heterodox theories of the business cycle explain economic downturns partially in terms of the impact on aggregate demand of cyclical shifts in the ratio of labor to property income. This topic is commonly de-emphasized in neoclassical texts.

Another implication of differential savings rates is that tax cuts and transfer programs designed to increase the income of lower-income groups may be more effective in increasing aggregate demand than tax cuts accruing mainly to upper-income groups. The latter might be more effective in increasing savings.

INVESTMENT

Impact of Uncertainty and Expectations

Most heterodox concerns about textbook treatments of consumption and savings reappear in heterodox critiques of textbook discussions of investment demand. Investment decisions usually involve longer time periods and less complete information than consumption decisions do. They are also more open to change. Although households have some discretion over whether and when to purchase some commodities, especially durable goods, people do not decide to stop eating or cease heating their homes. Corporations can decide, however, to postpone investing. The impact of uncertainty, "animal spirits," and fluctuating economic expectations thus tends to be greater on investor than consumer decisions. (See Table 9.3) Although neoclassical textbooks usually mention expectations as a factor in investment decisions, the texts tend to offer relatively automatic theories of investment, mechanically linking the level of business spending to the interest rate and a few other variables.

Savings, Consumption, and Investment Relations in a Demand-Constrained Economy

Because standard texts basically adhere to an equilibrium picture of the economy, the discussion of most economic relationships assumes full employment of capital and labor. Many conclusions based on this assumption do not hold in a disequilibrium economy. For example, in an economy fully using its productive resources, the only way to increase investment is to decrease consumption, which requires increasing savings. In a fully employed economy savings leads to investment.

In a demand-constrained economy the relationship can be reversed. In a demand-constrained economy an increase in investment can increase aggregate demand. The latter can increase national income and thereby increase savings. Thus, instead of savings generating investment, investment can generate savings. This is often briefly noted in standard texts in discussions of "the paradox of thrift."

The full implications of the paradox, however, are seldom pursued. For example, in economies suffering from insufficient aggregate demand, the paradox implies that tax breaks for poorer families may increase national savings more than tax cuts for richer families, despite the lower propensity to save among the poor. This surprising conclusion results from the ability of increases in aggregate demand to simultaneously increase national income, overall consumption, aggregate savings, and aggregate investment.

Neglect of Institutional Phenomena

Perhaps the biggest single difference between heterodox and neoclassical treatments of investment is heterodox theory's stress on the need to analyze the institutional context within which investment decisions are made. Among other things, this requires analyzing (1) the structure of the firm (especially the nature of the modern corporation); (2) the market structure of different industries (for example the degree and kind of competition); and (3) the character of financial-credit institutions.

The firm is often treated as a mechanical profit maximizer in neoclassical macro principles texts. Its actions are derived mathematically from its "production function" and price signals in the market for inputs and outputs. The firm is portrayed as a "price taker," a "technology taker," and a handmaiden to consumer preferences. In a sense there really is not a firm in neoclassical macro principles texts. There is simply a passive reflex, which responds to consumer tastes and technological possibilities.

Heterodox analyses offer a much richer analysis of firms. First of all there are different kinds of firms in different kinds of industries. We shall focus in this section on heterodox analyses of investment decisions by large firms. Heterodox analyses employ an "active" rather than a "passive" image of corporations. The firm in heterodox theory is interested in growth. It is the main source of private savings in the economy, not households. It seeks to develop and market new products. It seeks to influence consumers' tastes and preferences. The question for the firm is not whether to grow, but how and when to grow.

The large firm in heterodox theory is governed by managers. The managers are constrained by the need to return acceptable profits to stockholders, but their planning is often most focused on institutional expansion. Because stock ownership is dispersed and because there has frequently been a correlation between corporate expansion and profitability, the managers' pursuit of institutional growth is generally not resisted by stockholders.

This perspective suggests that the economic history of capitalism is partially a history of firms' growth strategies. A key task for economic theory is to understand how these strategies are developed and what factors influence their shape and success. The picture of investment that emerges is less like the accounting exercise often presented in principles texts and more like military campaigns depicted in history courses or battles for species survival depicted in evolutionary biology classes.

Firms' growth strategies depend on their corporate cultures and their competitive environment, which involves, among other things, their industry's structure (e.g., perfectly competitive or oligopolistic), the firm's current labor policies and relationships with creditors, macroeconomic conditions, and government macro policies. The firm's decision makers frequently rely on "rules of thumb" for pricing and other kinds of decisions (such as investment spending) because of the impossibility of acquiring all of the information necessary to make the "optimizing" decisions celebrated in the textbooks. The rules of thumb employed tend to reflect social conventions, as they are the product of historically woven routines and broader social contexts rather than the handiwork of isolated individuals. Even when "cultural change" occurs, when paradigm shifts reorient firms' reproductive strategies, the direction of change is influenced by each corporation's institutional culture and larger cultural conversations.

Heterodox theories of investment include the familiar variables cited in principles texts, such as the interest rate, current sales, inventory levels, tax rates, and so on. They situate these factors, however, within a strategic rather than mechanical model of investment. It is a story with more "blood and guts," fewer claims of automatic optimality, and more claims of path dependency and historical conjunctures than the neoclassical textbook story. It is also a more interesting story.

Case Study: Investment Strategies in the "New" and "Old" Economies

What might a heterodox analysis of investment look like? The example below is built around Keynesian and Marxist concepts. It is based on research by James Crotty, a professor of economics at the University of Massachusetts in Amherst, analyzing the reasons for the recent slowdown in global economic growth. Professor Crotty describes two different contexts within which large firms have developed investment strategies over the last half century. From roughly 1945 to 1970, he argues there was:

1) *An active government role in the economy* that (a) maintained aggregate demand through government spending, tax, and credit policies; (b) maintained stable financial markets through limits on speculative activities; and (c) regulated cross-border economic interactions.

2) *Generally secure oligopoly profits for most large American firms,* due to: (a) healthy aggregate demand; (b) institutional arrangements that reduced uncertainty; (c) an implicit agreement among firms to refrain from mutually destructive forms of competition (such as predatory pricing and "capital investment wars"); and (d) limited foreign competition, due to America's dominant economic position at the end of World War II.

3) *A tendency for oligopoly profits to be used for "high-road" economic development policies,* including: (a) high levels of research and development (R&D) spending; and (b) semi-cooperative labor policies, built around implicit promises of job security and shared gains from technological change (i.e., wage increases).

Crotty argues that these practices combined to produce a *virtuous cycle.* High R&D levels and high-road labor policies, for example, promoted productivity increases and relatively high wages. This boosted worker morale, labor productivity, and consumer demand. The latter contributed to solid corporate earnings. Corporate investment was financed largely from retained earnings and funded expanding markets in new products and new technologies without excessively depreciating the value of prior investments.

Unfortunately, events culminating in the mid-seventies shifted the U.S. economy from a "virtuous" to a "vicious" cycle. The new environment was marked by less government intervention in the economy. Firms also faced weaker aggregate demand and cutthroat competition, often from overseas companies. This competition encouraged many American firms to reduce job security and cut wages in order to cut prices. Firms also had to deploy new technologies before amortizing old ones [19] and invest in new plants in industries suffering from excess productive capacity. The result, until the 1990s, was often a fall in corporate profits, a buildup of corporate debt, reduced job security, and a decline in real wages or real wage growth.[20] The degeneration of competition into destructive forms represents an economic failure akin to the prisoner's dilemma.

Crotty ties the fall in global aggregate demand to stagnant or falling wages, a shift in government macroeconomic priorities in the advanced countries from maintaining aggregate demand to fighting inflation, and the imposition of similar priorities on the developing nations by the International Monetary Fund (IMF) and the World Bank.

He ties the tendency for destructive "overinvestment" in core industries[21] to the competitive logic of the emerging global economy. He notes that these industries are generally characterized by large economies of scale, frequent technological change, and the lure of long-run oligopoly profits. The large multinational firms of the advanced countries have traditionally dominated these markets domestically and wish to do so in the future. The increasing integration of the world market, however, has thrown into flux who the survivors will be on a global scale. It has also added new players from the developing world who wish to enter these industries in order to move up the perceived technological ladder of economic growth.

Crotty's analysis suggests that many firms are playing a high-stakes game of chicken, hoping that other firms will drop out of these overcrowded markets. The need to capture economies of scale encourages each firm to build large facilities, which collectively would far exceed market demand if all firms went ahead with their investments. The companies' sunk costs in physical terms (other existing factories, etc.), in human terms (employee skills), and in intangible assets (marketing networks, name recognition, etc.), discourage exit from the industry. Too many firms thus try to hang on, creating excess capacity and low profit rates. This leads to draconian labor policies (firings, wage and benefit cuts, speed ups, etc.) further weakening global aggregate demand. Finally, the free-market ideology that dominates current economic thinking discourages serious government responses.

Crotty (2000b) uses various industries to illustrate his argument. He writes,

> Consider, for example, the global auto industry. *Business Week* recently reported that at least three quarters of the globe's forty auto makers are "drowning in debt and glutted with factory capacity: the industry can make 20 million more cars and trucks a year than it can sell." The global market is plagued by "cost pressures and cutthroat pricing on top of overcapacity problems" (January 25 1999: 69). Yet firms continue to invest in the face of disastrous industry conditions.[22] . . . (366)
>
> Price-profit pressures *force* firms that have decided to "stay in the game" to build plants where labor and other costs are cheapest and market growth strongest—and Neoliberalism has offered them the whole world as potential investment sites. They invest to shed and more tightly control labor, to gain economies of scale, and to acquire best practice technology for both cost reduction and quality reasons. Finally, they invest to get inside the borders of expected high growth developing markets. . . . (366)
>
> This process of coerced investment appears to be irrational and for this reason it does not exist in the world of Neoclassical theory. From the perspective of the economy or society as a whole it *is* irrational. *But it is not irrational for the affected firms.* Under their "natural" oligopolistic organization, these industries are exceptionally profitable. Thus, every firm wants to be one of the survivors. . . . (366)
>
> The point that must be stressed is that *sluggish aggregate demand growth and chronic excess aggregate supply reinforce one another in a vicious circle.* The more competitive pressures develop, the more they force firms to cut wages, smash unions, substitute low for high wage labor, and pressure governments to cut spending and generate budget surpluses.

But these actions constrain global aggregate demand even more tightly, creating yet stronger competitive intensity—and so on. (366–67)

Crotty's work was written in the late 1990s, before the onset of the most recent recession and recovery. It predicted the U.S. and global macro economy faced a difficult period. Only time will tell whether he was right or wrong.

THREADS

Distributional Issues

As noted above, heterodox analyses tend to give greater attention to the impact of distributional variables on consumption and savings behavior than neoclassical texts do. The "under-consumptionist" school of heterodox theory has stressed the potential problems of insufficient demand that can arise from a shift in national income toward upper-income groups in the absence of optimistic investment expectations. Numerous heterodox economists have explored how periodic shifts in the ratio of labor to property income can help explain some aspects of business cycles.

Many heterodox economists call for "industrial policies" that would encourage investment in industries with positive social externalities. They stress the path dependency of technological and institutional change and argue that public policy needs to attempt to define development paths with desirable distributional characteristics.

Gender Issues

Feminist economists have often criticized neoclassical textbooks for neglecting the role of social conventions and emotion in explaining economic behavior. Keynesian analyses of the implications of uncertainty for understanding investment behavior fit neatly within a feminist framework. In relentlessly relying on "rational actor" models of mechanical maximizing behavior, neoclassical texts convey a hyperrational image of economic activity. Alan Greenspan's concept of "irrational exuberance," Keynes's notion of herd behavior, and Crotty's claim that investors necessarily rely on social conventions are left in the shadows in standard texts and illuminated by feminist economics.

Feminist economists have also stressed the need to treat spending for child care (especially government support) as an investment rather than a consumer good. The failure to do so often leads to characterizing social programs supporting children (such as the Head Start and subsidized school lunch programs) as luxury goods we cannot afford, rather than investment goods we need for economic development.

Environmental Issues

The themes of chapter 9 touch on environmental issues tangentially. These links are explored in chapter 16.

COMPETING METAPHORS AND STORIES

The juxtapositions in Table 9.4 illustrate the different images found in neoclassical and heterodox analyses of aggregate demand.

Table 9.4

Competing Metaphors

Textbook Economics	Heterodox Economics
Auctioneer	Casino
Flexible prices	Sticky prices
Hyperrationality	Bounded rationality
Static analysis	Dynamic analysis
Marginal focus	Structural focus
Ahistorical analysis	Historical analysis

CONCLUSION

This chapter critiqued the section of standard neoclassical textbooks discussing consumption, savings, and investment behavior, and the construction of the Keynesian Cross model of aggregate demand. We made six main points.

1. Neoclassical textbooks give insufficient attention to the implications of uncertainty and unstable expectations for investment, savings, and consumption decisions. This oversight leaves them unable to convey key dimensions of the disequilibrium logic underlying the Keynesian Cross framework and its explanation for unemployment in terms of insufficient aggregate demand. Heterodox economists stress the impact of uncertainty on long-lasting and irreversible decisions involving large sums of money, such as investments in physical capital or the granting of long-term credit. Once fundamental uncertainty is added to macroeconomic models, a much different picture emerges from the auctioneered world of automatic full employment. Heterodox theory offers a "general theory" that includes both equilibrium and disequilibrium dynamics.

2. Neoclassical textbooks give insufficient attention to the impact of institutional arrangements and bounded rationality on consumption, savings, and investment behaviors. The textbooks' focus on how rational households maximize utility by allocating income to savings and consumption misses key elements that determine an economy's savings rate, such as the role of large firms' retained earnings and the impact of habits and social conventions. The neglect of routine behavior also misses some of the key factors responsible for the stability of economic life.

3. Neoclassical textbooks' passive image of the firm and static framework for analyzing economic activity fails to convey the key role played by firms' growth strategies in determining investment and "creating" rather than "discovering" economic development paths and macroeconomic outcomes.

4. The textbook model of macroeconomic activity is excessively "deterministic." It suggests that market outcomes inevitably converge on results dictated by preexisting consumer tastes and firms' technologically determined cost schedules. In contrast, heterodox models are path dependent. The economy can end up in several different conditions (multiple equilibria in formal language), depending on contingent expectations and strategic decisions by firms. There is no inherent optimality to current market outcomes.

5. Neoclassical texts usually fail to discuss important qualitative issues involving savings and investment decisions, such as (1) what do we mean by the optimal rate of savings? Is

it what a "perfect market" summing up individual decisions would produce? (2) What do we mean by the optimal level and pattern of investment? Is it necessarily consistent with summing up firms' growth strategies? These kinds of questions become very important when discussing topics like social security and technological change.

6. Although it is possible to include some heterodox ideas within modified versions of neoclassical economics, doing so would often challenge the subtext of market optimality that animates standard principles texts. The neglect of these heterodox topics reflects judgments about what are important and/or interesting topics to raise in an introductory course.

IN THEIR OWN WORDS

On Paradigms in Macroeconomics

I have called this book The *General Theory of Employment, Interest and Money,* placing the emphasis on the prefix *general*. The object of such a title is to contrast the character of my arguments and conclusions with those of the *classical* theory of the subject, upon which I was brought up and which dominates the economic thought, both practical and theoretical of the governing and academic classes of this generation. . . . I shall argue that the postulates of the classical theory are applicable to a special case only . . . . Moreover, the characteristics of the special case assumed by the classical theory happen not to be those of the economic society in which we actually live, with the result that its teaching is misleading and disastrous if we attempt to apply it to the facts of experience.

—John Maynard Keynes ([1936] 1964, 3)

[I]t is possible to conceive of an economics which is based upon feminist notions of knowledge, an economics which takes the thought processes upon which agents base their decisions to be both socially and emotionally constituted. . . . [P]ost-Keynesian theory proves especially amenable to this feminist epistemological approach. . . .

The Keynesian concept of uncertainty is linked not only to the primacy of convention in determining agent knowledge but is connected, as well, to the importance of emotion. . . . [B]ecause of . . . the unmitigated uncertainty which characterizes the nature of things . . . the knowledge of agents is inherently social and it is inalterably impacted by emotion.

—Lee Levin (1995, 110, 112)

On Investment-Led Savings

It is Enterprise which builds and improves the world's possessions. . . . If Enterprise is afoot, wealth accumulates whatever may be happening to Thrift; and if Enterprise is asleep, wealth decays whatever Thrift may be doing.

—Keynes (quoted in Heilbroner 1967, 244)

The system and the individual face different conditions. For the individual, high consumption now must come at the expense of high consumption later. . . . Savings is the key to growth, for individuals. But not for the system as a whole. Savings is simply not spending; saving is a withdrawal from the stream of circulation. Consumption is demand, and demand is the key to production; investment occurs only when there is an expectation of further pressure on the facilities of production; or when there is pressure to innovate to keep up with the competition. . . . Hence high current demand is required to provide business with a stimulus to invest, and it is chiefly through such investment that technical progress takes place. Thus high consumption and high public spending not only mean investment in human beings, making for a more productive, healthier, better educated labour force; they also stimulate investment in physical plant and equipment, bringing technical improvements and better organization.

—Edward Nell (1996, 112)

On the Nature of Consumer Behavior

A new interdisciplinary area of research on consumption has emerged in the last 10–15 years, drawing contributions and participants from sociology, anthropology, history, philosophy, literature, and marketing. . . . Yet despite the central role that consumption plays in economic theory, economics has been one of the least important contributors to the new wave of research. . . .

[This] largely reflects the rigidity of the conventional economic theory of consumer behavior. That theory, of course, assumes that consumers come to the market with well-defined, insatiable desires for private goods and services; those desires are not affected by social interactions, culture, economic institutions, or the consumption choices or well-being of others.

—Frank Ackerman (1997a, 651)

[R]ules of thumb, the acceptance of social conventions, and reliance on the hopefully better informed opinion of others. . . . are the only [kind of] sensible answer to an environment characterized by bounded knowledge and computational capabilities, time constraints and fundamental uncertainty. . . . It could also be called the principle of *reasonable rationality*. The purpose of economics ought not to define an ideal consumer that would have all the nice mathematical properties that are required by an elegant theory; rather the purpose should be to define realistic behaviour.

—Marc Lavoie (2004, 643)

The use of rules, customs, and conventions brings in organicism, holism and intersubjectivity. In post-Keynesian economics, individual behavior is interdependent. Individuals are influenced by their social environment. . . . By contrast, the mainstream neoclassical agent is generally seen as an atomistic being. . . .

—Marc Lavoie (2003, 190)

STUDY QUESTIONS

Discussion Questions

1. Should the Social Security system be abolished? Why? Why not? If you think that a system of "forced savings" is wise, what does this imply about the a priori optimality of market outcomes? How might a neoclassical economist defend the continuation or termination of the social security system?
2. Read chapter 25 in John Steinbeck's *Grapes of Wrath* dealing with the Great Depression. What is the economic message of the chapter?[23]

Review Questions

1. What aspects of Keynes's vision of economic activity led Keynesians to develop the Keynesian Cross model of income determination?
2. What did Keynes mean by his suggestion that economists should be thought of as dentists?
3. What did Keynes mean by "animal spirits"? Contrast this image with a corresponding image of economic motivation in textbook economics.
4. Outline the arguments Keynesian economists offer for why market adjustments might not be able to eliminate unemployment after a fall in business confidence.
5. Why did Keynes think that burying money in garbage dumps might help the economy?
6. Compare and contrast the treatment of consumer demand in textbook and heterodox economics. How do the different images of consumer behavior in heterodox and textbook economics illustrate the basic differences between the two approaches to economic analysis? How do the differing treatments of consumption relate to the different subtexts animating textbook and heterodox economics? Illustrate your answer with reference to the consumption theories of Friedman, Modigliani, and Duesenberry. Why might the different images of consumer behavior lead to different attitudes toward government involvement in the economy?
7. Compare and contrast the treatment of savings in textbook and heterodox economics. How do the different images of savings behavior in heterodox and textbook economics illustrate the basic differences between the two approaches to economic analysis? How do the differing treatments of savings relate to the different subtexts animating textbook and heterodox economics? Why might the different images of savings behavior lead to different attitudes toward government involvement in the economy?
8. Compare and contrast the treatment of investment demand in textbook and heterodox economics. How do the different images of investment behavior in heterodox and textbook economics illustrate the basic differences between the two approaches to economic analysis? How do the differing treatments of investment relate to the different subtexts animating textbook and heterodox economics? Why might the different images of investment behavior lead to different attitudes toward government involvement in the economy?
9. Why does Crotty think that the U.S. economy may experience weak employment and wage trends in the coming decades?

NOTES

1. There have been many excellent biographical portraits of Keynes. A few especially accessible to students are: Robert Heilbroner's engaging chapter on Keynes in *The Worldly Philosophers* (1967, 225–61), Robert Lekachman's *The Age of Keynes* (1966), and for really ambitious readers *John Maynard Keynes 1883–1946: Economist, Philosopher, Statesman* by Robert Skidelsky.

2. See Heilbroner (1967, 255) and Lekachman (1966, 49) for some telling quotes from Keynes.

3. Much of the material in this section comes from the first two books cited in note 1.

4. Other reasons have been offered for the potential insensitivity of the level of savings and investment to changes in the interest rate. Empirically, household savings seems to depend primarily on the level of household income. Although a modest percentage of people do seem to save less when interest rates fall (due to the lower reward for savings) about the same number of people seem to save more, as they need to accumulate a larger target sum to achieve some accumulation goal (say, financing a child's college education). Although it is hard to isolate different variables' independent effects on the savings rate, it is worth noting that after the Reagan tax cuts in the 1980s significantly increased the after-tax return to savings,

personal savings as a percent of disposable income fell by about 2 percent (from roughly 9 to 10 percent of income to about 7 to 9 percent) (*Economic Report of the President 2000*, 343).

On the investment side, many production techniques seem to involve fixed relationships among inputs. Thus a fall in the price of capital (the interest rate) may not cause firms to utilize more capital inputs in production.

5. In the history of economic thought this is known as "Says Law" and has been roundly criticized by heterodox economists.

6. Keynes's explanation for chronic unemployment can be expressed in different ways. We have chosen to characterize it as a disequilibrium critique of the automatic adjustments assumed to guarantee full employment in neoclassical theory. Some Keynesians might reasonably object to the disequilibrium label. According to Keynes a contracting economy can evolve in three ways. It can free fall in a downward spiral indefinitely; rebound to full employment; or stabilize at a level of output with significant unemployment. Some authors have called the latter case an unemployment equilibrium. In our terms this outcome would be a "disequilibrium-equilibrium"; a disequilibrium because all who want work at the going wage are not able to find it, and an equilibrium because there are no pressures for change that guarantee movement toward full employment.

One of Keynes's great contributions was to show how patterns of actual expectations and institutional responses to economic shocks (rather than hypothetical general equilibrium potentials) can generate chronic unemployment. Whether we term the latter "an unemployment equilibrium" or "disequilibrium unemployment" makes little difference, as long as we ground the outcome in patterns of expectations that produce disequilibrium outcomes in the labor market.

7. Perhaps most significant is the retreat from Keynesian theory by economists reputed to be Keynesians. For example, Mankiw writes, "one might suppose that reading Keynes is an important part of Keynesian theorizing. In fact, quite the opposite is the case. . . . If new Keynesian economics is not a true representation of Keynes's views, then so much the worse for Keynes. . . .

[C]lassical economics is right in the long run. Moreover, economists today are more interested in the long-run equilibrium. The long run is not so far away . . ." (Mankiw 1992, 560–61; see also Davidson 1996).

8. Jim Crotty has offered the phrase "necessarily psychologically complex individual" as an alternative to the neoclassicals' assumption of perfectly informed rational economic man. David Colander similarly notes, "individuals accept conventions, and these institutional constraints upon their actions. These imposed institutional constraints create the sufficiently stable environment within which individuals can operate" (Colander 1996b, 7; see also Lavoie 2004, 1994).

9. "If individuals were globally rational, the economy would be unstable. . . . In Walrasian [mainstream neoclassical] economics institutional constraints on individuals prevent the attainment of optimality; in Post Walrasian macroeconomics [another kind of heterodox economics] the constraints are systemic requirements for stability. Without the institutional constraints, there would be no functioning economy" (Colander 1996b, 7).

10. For a short history of paradigm debates about consumer demand see Ackerman 1997c.

11. This does not mean that neoclassical texts do not address some market failures, such as externalities in micro theory and sticky prices in macro theory. The problem is with the breadth and depth of treatment and the tendency for a "note but ignore" stance toward the implications of "market imperfections."

12. See for example, Veblen's *The Theory of the Leisure Class* ([1899] 1973), Galbraith's *The Affluent Society* ([1958] 1998), and Hirsch's *Social Limits to Growth* (1976).

13. For some interesting comments on Duesenberry, see Ackerman (1997c), R. Frank (2005b; 1985, 109–10), Bober (2001, 80–81), and Hodgson (1998, 170–73).

14. Interestingly, and characteristic of neoclassical theory, permanent income theorists tend to define future or permanent income in terms of a weighted average of present and past income (all known) rather than contingent expectations about future income. Even when the analysis is forward (future) looking, as with "rational expectations" models, there is a strong tendency to assume that people behave as if they had perfect information about future general equilibrium prices and quantities. Insights from social psychology about the persistent irrationalities of some consumer expectations and behavior are ignored. Heterodox models tell a messier but more accurate story. They highlight the contingency and volatility of consumer expectations about future income.

15. British economist Geoff Hodgson similarly notes, "Much empirical data in economics are consistent with the prevalence of habitual activity. . . . Consider, for example, the now neglected theory of the consumption function developed by James Duesenberry (1949). This theory was heavily influenced by Veblen and

stressed the role of habit in consumer behavior. Duesenberry's theory did not fall out of favor because it did badly on empirical tests. In fact it predicted rather well. Instead, the theory was discarded primarily because it was not seen to conform with the presumptions of rational choice theory" (Hodgson 1998, 170).

16. It is possible to argue that business savings reflect the desires of consumers who own the firms, but this is a stretch. It ignores, for example, the institutional factors governing corporate savings decisions and the independent role firms and their managers play in the economy.

17. These publicly sponsored organizations have channeled savings into home building by organizing a secondary market for home mortgages and appearing to partially insure them.

18. The conclusion also fits comfortably within the findings of behavioral economics, a school of economics that challenges the assumptions of *homo economicus* by studying people's actual behavior in the economy. See, for example, the entry "Behavioral Economics" by Mullainathan and Thaler in the *International Encyclopedia of the Social and Behavioral Sciences*.

19. Interestingly, Crotty suggests that markets can introduce technological changes at too fast a rate. Paralleling arguments for patents, which allow companies to enjoy protection from competition for a span of years in order to recover R&D outlays on new technologies, Crotty argues that "corespective competition" allowed firms to spend R&D monies with an implicit understanding that routine competition would not obsolete them before they recovered their investment. In an ironic twist, Crotty suggests that informal limits on short-run technological change may actually accelerate long-run technological change by encouraging and enabling firms to spend on R&D.

20. The U.S. economy experienced a temporary respite from contractionary pressures in the late 1990s. This expansion, however, was based on unsustainable factors (such as an enormous speculative bubble in the stock market) and ended in 2001. Labor market problems have endured.

21. Among the industries Crotty considers core industries are autos, airplanes, computers, semiconductors, electric appliances, steel, ship building, and machine tools.

22. R. Brenner (2003) develops a similar argument. On January 20, 2005, the *Wall Street Journal* reported that global surplus capacity in the auto industry was estimated to have reached 24 million vehicles. Despite this glut, a $3-billion bailout of nearly bankrupt Mitsubishi Motors, by linked Japanese firms, seemed likely to keep that company in the game (p. 1, "Repair Job," by Sapsford and Shirouzu). A different article in the same *Wall Street Journal* reported that General Motors was facing falling profit rates and had plans to increase its market share (p. A-4, "GM Net Falls 37% . . . ," by Hawkins).

23. Thanks to Randy Wray for this suggestion.

10

REINTRODUCING MONEY

Basic Concepts

Textbooks: "Despite the important role of enterprises and money in our actual economy, and despite the numerous and complex problems they raise, the central characteristic of the market technique of achieving co-ordination is fully displayed in the simple exchange economy that contains neither enterprises nor money."
—Milton Friedman (1982, 14)

Heterodoxy: "[I]t is my belief that the far-reaching and in some respects fundamental differences between the conclusions of a monetary economy and those of the more simplified real-exchange economy have been greatly underestimated by the exponents of the traditional economics."[1]
—John Maynard Keynes

INTRODUCTION AND OVERVIEW

Your text probably has a separate section, consisting of two or three chapters, entitled something like "Money and Banking" or "The Financial Sector." These chapters usually discuss the history of money, the nature of the money supply (Ms) and money demand (Md), the determination of the interest rate by the intersection of Ms and Md, and the nature of financial markets, such as the stock market. The textbook chapters usually focus on the role of the Federal Reserve (Fed) and the banking system in "creating money," and the logic of monetary policy. This initial discussion is frequently complemented by a later chapter in a different section of the textbook focusing on current debates over monetary policy. Our analysis in the next two chapters will offer a heterodox critique of the initial monetary chapters in standard textbooks. We will revisit current debates over monetary policy later in the text (chapter 17).

Chapter 10 outlines heterodox economists' major objections to textbook treatments of money. The chapter focuses on the insufficient attention given to:

1. the implications of uncertainty
2. the consequences of a monetized (rather than barter) form of exchange
3. the limitations of *homo economicus* for understanding behavior in the monetary sector
4. the impact of institutional structures on financial markets
5. the distributional impacts of monetary policy

Chapter 11 illustrates heterodox monetary theory by applying it to important topics in monetary theory. The first section of chapter 11 discusses heterodox analyses of financial markets, such as the stock market. Section two offers a heterodox analysis of the Federal Reserve, while section three reviews the general policy implications of heterodox monetary theories. As is often the case, exploring heterodox topics tends to undermine images of market optimality and invites more social governance of the economy.

Chapter 11 concludes with our usual threads: (a) looking at the implications of heterodox analyses of the monetary sector for distributional, gender, and environmental themes; (b) juxtaposing orthodox and heterodox metaphors regarding the monetary sector; and (c) illustrating some heterodox economists' ideas in their own words.

Many heterodox objections to standard textbook treatments of money are interconnected. These linkages make initial presentations of heterodox theory difficult, because each topic discussed quickly raises issues linked to other topics, which in turn do the same. To respond to this interconnectedness, we begin with a skeletal discussion of some key issues and move to higher levels of integration in later analyses of overlapping topics.

THE IMPLICATIONS OF UNCERTAINTY

"Like Hamlet Without the Prince"

Heterodox economists' major objection to the treatment of "money" in standard textbooks involves the insufficient attention given to the implications of uncertainty. Neglect of the full impact of imperfect and incomplete information on economic behavior can be especially harmful when discussing the monetary sector. This is because uncertainty in the real sector is often deflected to and surfaces in the monetary sector. What we mean by deflection will be clarified shortly.

What do we mean by the "real" and "monetary" sectors? The real sector involves the flow of material goods and services (e.g., labor hours, gallons of oil, loaves of bread, etc.). The monetary sector involves the flow of money and other pieces of paper representing ownership claims on the real sector. You may recall the circular flow model of the economy introduced in the early chapters of your textbook. (See Figure 10.1.) The inner circle of Figure 10.1 depicts the economic activity of the real sector. Households supply and firms demand material inputs in the input market; while firms supply and households demand material output in the output markets. The outer circle depicts monetary flows. These move in the opposite direction of the flow of real goods and services. In the textbooks, the monetary circle is simply a mirror image (or displaced shadow) of the real sector.

In the textbook story, economic activity is about the exchange of real things for real things. People trade their labor for a bundle of commodities. Owners of apples trade for oranges, owners of oranges trade for apples, and so on. No one works for "money" per se, or relinquishes what they own for small pieces of green paper. People "keep score" in money, but what is "actually" going on is a series of exchanges of real things for real things. Paper flows in the monetary sector (dashed arrows in Figure 10.1) are simply shadows of the flow of real goods (continuous arrows in Figure 10.1).

In the textbooks, the relative value of all goods is determined in the real sector by people's tastes and preferences for the goods and the real costs of producing them. The monetary sector (involving the supply and demand for money) influences only the price level (e.g., you may earn $10.00/hour and face gasoline costs of $1.50/gallon and milk costs of $2.00/gallon or earn $15.00/hour and face gas costs of $2.25/gallon and milk costs of $3.00/gallon).[2]

Although there is a lot of truth in the textbook's story, it is not the whole story or the whole truth.

Figure 10.1   **Circular Flow Models of the Economy: Real and Monetary Sectors**

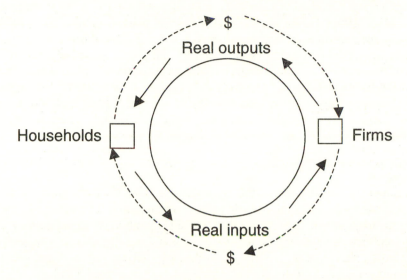

Because it is a perceptive view of part of the story, however, it is easy to mistake it for the whole story. As we have emphasized, the textbook picture of the economy generally abstracts from uncertainty. People are assumed to have perfect information when they trade, or, more accurately, the texts imply that the market can be modeled "as if" people had such information, without losing anything important. In chapter 9 we challenged this claim. We explored how uncertainty can create problems of insufficient aggregate demand that can cause voluntary unemployment, excess capacity in the business sector, and personal and business bankruptcies. In this chapter we explore how uncertainty can influence the relationship between the real and monetary sectors.

Heterodox Focus on Liquidity

Once the potential for insufficient aggregate demand and economic contraction is recognized (and it is widely perceived by participants in the market, if not in the textbooks), it is reasonable to expect economic decision makers to try to protect themselves against unexpected events and the consequences of economic contractions. Faced with uncertainty, many economic decision makers may try to increase their economic flexibility by increasing their "liquidity."

By *liquidity* is meant the ability to turn an asset into something else quickly and without loss of monetary value. The metaphor of liquidity captures the ability of liquids to take whatever form they are poured into. Money is the most liquid of assets, as it can be transformed into anything at the current price of the asset. Physical assets, like a piece of machinery, tend to be among the least liquid of assets. It is hard to get your money back for a shoe-making machine once you have installed it in your factory. It is much easier to recover your money from your checking account. A sudden rush for liquidity can disrupt the real sector. Firms can hesitate to build new factories or buy new machines and consumers may hesitate to buy new cars.

The financial sector serves three main functions: (1) it provides a medium of exchange for economic transactions; (2) it manages credit and mobilizes savings for investment; and (3) it reshuffles risks. Most standard textbooks give insufficient attention to risk management due to their tendency to minimize the implications of uncertainty. Many activities in the financial sector involve attempts by market participants to "buy insurance." The form of insurance can get quite complicated, but the basic idea is simple. To grasp it, however, you have to acknowledge the presence of uncertainty. Here are some examples. Futures markets in agricultural products shift the potential gains and losses from fluctuations in future agricultural prices facing farmers and firms purchasing agricultural inputs (such as bakers and textile manufacturers) among themselves and to financial speculators acting as middle traders. The secondary market in mortgage and credit card debt (which resells these promised payments to new buyers) similarly reshuffles default risks. Insured bonds shift the risk of default (for a price) from lenders to the insurance company, and so on. Modeling the monetary sector without highlighting uncertainty is like directing Shakespeare's play *Hamlet* without focusing on the prince.

Reconceptualizing Money Demand and Money Supply

When the economy is in equilibrium at full employment, all assets (such as factories, office space, productive machinery, agricultural land, etc.) are earning equilibrium revenues. Firms that took on debts to buy the assets (based on what they would be worth in an economy in equilibrium at full employment) are able to meet their debt obligations and make a profit. In a sense all goods are like money, in that they trade at "par," that is, at their equilibrium values. If you bought a car in such an economy you could resell it for the same price that you bought it and use the proceeds to buy something else.

Once the possibilities of disequilibrium and economic contractions are acknowledged, however, "illiquid" purchases become more risky. No goods are like money. Forced sale at inopportune times (e.g., when everyone else is trying to sell similar assets to acquire money) can lead to a collapse in asset prices. If firms or households must sell an illiquid asset to meet living expenses or debt obligations during a serious economic downturn, they can suffer deep losses. In order to avoid such difficulties, people in uncertain times may resist purchasing new physical assets. This behavior will appear in the real sector as a slowdown in aggregate demand and appear in the monetary sector as an increase in the demand for money. The latter will increase the interest rate and add to recessionary pressures.[3]

Most neoclassical textbooks concentrate on money's role as a medium of exchange and the related *transaction demand for money*. Heterodoxy complements this discussion with increased attention to money's role as a store of value and the associated *liquidity demand for money*.

On the supply side, standard textbooks treat the size of the money supply as primarily determined by the Federal Reserve (with modest inputs from private banks' decisions about the level of excess reserves and the public's currency to deposit ratio, which together determine the so-called "money multiplier"). Heterodoxy implies much more "endogeneity" to the size of the money supply. When economic activity increases and the demand for credit expands (along with the creditworthiness of borrowers due to stronger economic times), banks seek out new deposits (often in creative ways, such as borrowing in the Euro dollar market or offering certificates of deposits, which enjoy lower reserve ratios). The money supply thus expands, independently of the Fed. Similarly, in a downturn the demand for credit by firms can decline (along with their creditworthiness), thereby reducing banks' incentives to extend loans. This partial endogeneity of the money supply is pro-cyclical and adds to macroeconomic volatility.

Bankruptcy and Disequilibrium Dynamics

When some firms and some households go bankrupt (announce they cannot meet their debt obligations), the effects can be widespread and unpredictable. For example, if a major customer of a profitable firm went bankrupt, it could cause serious financial difficulties for the otherwise-solvent firm, especially if the bankrupt company owed it a lot of money. If the first default caused the second firm to go bankrupt, a similar crisis could spread to its creditors and laid off workers (and their credit card companies), and so on. Fear of this contagion could cause firms to deny or reduce trade credit to companies who traditionally enjoyed a grace period between the receipt of goods and payment for them. This could disrupt their businesses and reduce the sales and revenues of many firms, again spreading bankruptcy risks. As defaults mount, a major credit institution (e.g., banks who had loaned the defaulting businesses money) could fail. These bankruptcies could reduce other firms' access to credit and add to contractionary pressures. Even if banks do not fail, increased levels of perceived risk can cause lending institutions to be more restrictive in "rolling over" or renewing existing debt. Such caution caused a "credit crunch" in New England in the early 1990s that shook small and medium-sized businesses.

The problem of bank failures and banking panics is one of the most interesting and important kinds of financial crises. Although most people have little to fear from their bank failing (as the Federal Deposit Insurance Corporation [FDIC] insures all deposits less than $100,000), larger depositors, such as money managers, are at risk. In a banking panic, depositors can create a self-fulfilling prophecy. A mass rush to withdraw funds from even solvent banks (as occurs in the movie *It's a Wonderful Life*) can push many banks into a liquidity crisis. This is because a widespread forced sale of previously good assets to repay depositors can depress asset prices and turn a positive balance sheet into a negative one.

As your textbook probably noted, the Federal Reserve's discount window often acts as a "liquifier of last resort," loaning money to banks with temporary liquidity problems. This assistance helps banks avoid the forced sale of assets in depressed markets and allows them to provide credit to firms suffering similar liquidity problems. Because most textbooks do not stress the importance of uncertainty when discussing the monetary sector, this aspect of the Fed's role in the economy is probably treated separately from the analytics of the money market. This is unfortunate, as the discount window offers an excellent vantage point from which to the view the centrality of liquidity and uncertainty dynamics in the financial sector.

To some extent, risks can be shifted but not destroyed in a market economy. Risks circulate like hot potatoes. For example, Caterpillar builds a new factory in Peoria and seeks a line of Citibank credit to protect it against unforeseen financial risks. Citibank sells large certificates of deposit (CDs) to raise funds to pay for the loan. Caterpillar also sells new shares of stock to raise funds. The stock purchasers borrow money from stockbrokers, who in turn get credit from the banking system. If things go sour, Caterpillar can go belly-up and threaten the solvency of its creditors.[4] Alternatively, the tax payers can bail out the banks, who bail out Caterpillar and the stock brokers, who bail out the stock purchasers. More often than not, when the potato hits the ground it was last touched by the taxpayers or a small investor. This drama is missing or deemphasized in standard texts. It is obscured and very much upstaged by the dominant images of equilibrium, rationality, and market efficiency in standard accounts, making markets seem much more placid than they are and economics much duller than it is.

THE "MONETIZED" NATURE OF A CAPITALIST ECONOMY

Heterodox analyses stress the irreducibly monetary character of capitalist economies. Buying and selling can proceed only when the conditions for monetized (as opposed to bartered) exchange are met. Commodities must be paid for in money, not in goods. Neither workers nor input suppliers can be paid in units of physical product. Workers need to purchase commodities with money, not labor hours. Nearly all long-term agreements are denominated in money and require their fulfillment in money. All of these preconditions suggest that disturbances in the monetary sector (such as a rush to hold money for liquidity reasons or a sudden decline in credit) can disrupt and otherwise influence the real sector.

(C-M-C′) Versus (M-C-C′-M′)

Heterodox analyses often organize the flow and logic of economic activity differently from mainstream texts. Standard textbooks emphasize consumer sovereignty, both in terms of the origins of people's tastes and preferences and the underlying projects that motivate the economy. The economic circuit involves the sale (or transformation) of a commodity (C) (such as labor) into money (M) and the subsequent retransformation of money into a new commodity (C′) (such as videos). The flow is thus: C-M-C′. Money appears as a "lubricant" for exchange, not as an "end" in itself.

Many heterodox economists, especially Marxist and Post Keynesian economists, analyze the economy in terms of M-C-C′-M′. Financial capital (M) buys real input commodities (C), such as flour, eggs, and labor. These are then transformed in production into another commodity (C′), such as bread. The latter is sold and reconverted into money (M′). In this case, the animating energy is the expansionary drive of financial capital. Production is organized by financial capital for the purpose of increasing financial capital. The organizing goal is not consumption, but the enlargement of bank balances at the end of the period.[5] Of course, many participants in the circuit are engaging in a C (labor) → M (wage) → C′ (consumer goods) circuit, but the organizing logic is governed by M-C-C′-M′.

This model captures *the limitless drive for expansion* within a capitalist economy better than the C-M-C′ model of the textbooks. It also captures the centrality of monetary forms of economic behavior. In an economy based on consumption, no one saves without planning to buy. But in an economy energized by the drive to accumulate more financial capital, saving need not lead to future consumption or by extension to a justification for investment. The key role played by controllers of money balances in capitalist economies leads to a much more fragile economic flow than a system of exchange among direct producers.[6]

Credit

If we combine the concept of a monetized economy embodied in the M-C-C′-M′ cycle with Keynes's emphasis on the role of "animal spirits" in mobilizing investment, we can generate a much more dynamic picture of the role of credit in a capitalist economy than is common in the textbooks. Heterodox economic theory emphasizes how market pressures can "create money" during an economic expansion (in response to an increase in the demand for credit), and destroy money during an economic contraction, when credit disappears. The pro-cyclical behavior of credit can add to the volatility of business cycles. Heterodox theory thus emphasizes both the importance of credit to capitalist economies' routine functioning and the potential volatility of credit.

The Complicated Relationship Between
Savings and Investment

Because of the endogenous creation of credit, capitalist economies can create purchasing power for investors prior to savings decisions by households. The mobilization of bank credit (rather than the acquisition of preexisting savings) can bring new resources into production or bid resources away from the consumer sector. In heterodox models, investment can, in effect, create savings. If the economy is at a less than full-employment level of output, the growth in income spurred by investment can generate the savings required to finance investment. Although some of these ideas also appear in standard texts, the tone is different. Monetary images are ultimately dwarfed by real-sector stories that assume full employment and the monetary sector's passive shepherding of preexisting household savings into investment.

BEYOND *HOMO ECONOMICUS*

Textbook models of market outcomes tend to assume that people utilize all available information efficiently to make rational choices.[7] These models can be especially misleading when applied to the financial sector because of the important role that nonrational factors often play in financial decisions. In addition, the information required for making financial choices (such as whether to buy or to sell a share of stock) often involves speculative judgments about other people's subjective thinking (e.g., "what do I think other people think other people think the value of this stock will be?"). In this context, the characterization of thinking as rational or irrational may be less meaningful than explorations of the cultural construction of reasonable thought.

The textbook assumption of rational economic man (*homo economicus*) tends to support laissez-faire attitudes toward financial markets by endowing them with the sweet smell of reason. Heterodox analysis complicates this story and in so doing undermines the textbook's image of automatic market optimality.

Heterodox economics assumes a much more psychologically complicated economic actor than neoclassical economics does. As we have seen, feminist and institutional economists have been especially active in criticizing "economic man," but their objections are echoed in many writings by Post Keynesians, radicals, and neo-Marxists. In earlier chapters we discussed heterodox objections to "the separative self" of standard textbooks. These objections challenge the tendency of neoclassical theory to abstract from (1) the socialization of individuals, (2) people's penchant for comparing their economic standing with others (which can spur envy and positional competition), and (3) the positive interdependency of aspects of human well-being suggested by feelings of empathy and altruism. We have also noted heterodoxy's tendency to (4) give greater weight to the role of emotion, habits, and conventions in organizing human behavior than given in neoclassical theory.

When people's tendencies for social referencing and habitual behavior are combined with the uncertainty that often surrounds financial sector choices, a new context emerges for understanding financial sector behavior. In order to explore the implications of this context for understanding financial markets, we have to analyze the role of institutions in solidifying and coordinating habits, and organizing human behavior. In chapter 11 we will develop a model of behavior in the financial sector that anticipates the speculative bubbles and anxious panics observed in actual financial markets. This behavior challenges the seemingly cold rationality implied by *homo economicus*.

INSTITUTIONS AND "MISPLACED CONCRETENESS"

As we have seen in earlier chapters, heterodoxy tends to analyze economic outcomes with greater attention to concrete circumstances and institutional formats than orthodox economics does. Heterodox economists frequently warn against blurring fundamental differences among concrete phenomena, such as "apples," and "money," when applying tools like supply and demand to explain economic outcomes. Where neoclassical theory sees and celebrates parsimony (the ability to apply the same simplifying assumptions to a broad range of phenomena), heterodoxy often sees and criticizes "misplaced concreteness" and the triumph of subtexts over subjects.

In order to apply the tools of textbook economics to the financial sector, the phenomena studied often has to be chiseled into forms initially designed to deal with simpler entities, such as physical commodities, barter economies, self-employed producers, and small firms. When analyzing topics like money, this whittling can be inappropriate. Heterodox economists tend to be more sensitive to this mismatch than neoclassical economists do.

The latters' research methods tend toward the manipulation of axiomatic models (i.e., the positing of a few simple behavioral assumptions, such as utility maximization, and the mathematical deduction of their implications) to generate hypotheses about financial markets. It is the goal of the textbooks to teach students to approach economic subjects in a similar fashion. "Thinking like an economist," in this context, means generating simple models with hypothetically (though often not realistically) testable hypotheses. Analysis of the actual institutions organizing financial flows and the implications of fundamental uncertainty can be glossed over in introductory courses because they are not "as important" as model building.

Heterodox economists dissent and are more likely to engage with empirical data at an earlier stage of inquiry. Institutionalist economists, for example, might recommend that economists studying financial markets engage in "participant observation" in a Wall Street brokerage firm prior to model building in order to generate hypotheses about bull and bear markets. Thinking like an economist, from this perspective, does not impose a priori frames of rational actors. Thinking like a heterodox economist requires investigation of actual historical contexts.[8]

In addition to "valorizing the concrete," heterodoxy's interest in studying institutional arrangements also reflects holist concerns about the limits of methodological individualism. The key claim is that the activities of institutions (conceived of as bundles of collective behaviors, subcultures, and social relationships) often need to be studied at the level of the institution. This contrasts with the tenets of methodological individualism, which imply that individuals always precede and constitute institutions. If the holists are right, the logic of individual behavior is infused by the whole. It is thus necessary to explore how institutions reproduce as institutions in addition to studying how individual maximizing behaviors occur within institutions. For the monetary sector this invites efforts at understanding how financial sector outcomes reflect, in part, the interactive strategies of major organizations (like industrial corporations, large banks, public bureaucracies, etc.) to reproduce themselves.

In Marxist hands, holism leads to a reorientation of economics from the study of individual choice to the study of capitalism as a social system. Marxists argue that it is necessary to understand the "laws of motion" of capitalism as a reproducing social system in order to explain individual behavior or subsystems of the economy like financial markets. The Marxist approach calls for "macro-founding" micro behaviors. For other heterodox paradigms, like institutionalism, holism invites more modest efforts at understanding how institutions work and how market outcomes reflect, in part, the interactive strategies of major organizations (like industrial corporations, large banks, public bureaucracies, etc.) to reproduce themselves. Galbraith's work (e.g., *Economics and the Public Purpose,* 1973) tends to blend the Marxist and institutionalist projects, offering a kind of institutional matrix for how the economy as a whole reproduces itself.

DISTRIBUTIONAL ISSUES

Many heterodox economists reject neoclassical economics' theory of what determines a country's income distribution.[9] Different heterodox paradigms offer different reasons for this rejection and different alternative theories. Although space limitations preclude discussing the reasoning behind most of these theories, it is helpful to outline their basic claims in order to understand some heterodox ideas about how monetary policy might affect income distributions.

At the heart of many heterodox theories of income distribution is the idea that the exercise of power (economic, political, institutional, ideological, etc.) is involved with the determination of income and economic reward. In this section we will focus on one example of this approach, wage/profit squeeze theories of the business cycle, in order to illustrate the flavor of heterodox thinking. We will revisit this issue in a bit more detail in chapter 12's discussion of labor markets.

The most general form of wage/profit squeeze theories implies that moderate rates of unemployment benefit employers by putting downward pressure on wages. As the economy nears full employment, wages and unit labor costs begin to rise. As a result prices begin to rise, but usually not as much as wages. This dynamic squeezes the profits of firms and harms creditors, whose assets (debtors' IOUs) are devalued by inflation. Thus, while relatively high levels of employment are in almost everyone's interest (as they benefit the owners of firms by supporting high levels of capacity utilization, benefit financial capital by increasing the demand for credit and the solvency of borrowers, and benefit labor by increasing employment and wages), this may not be true for permanently "high" or "full-employment" levels of output. While full employment benefits most working people, radical theories of the wage-profit squeeze and Marxist theories of the function of the "reserve army of the unemployed" imply that permanent full employment conflicts with the interests of corporate and financial capital.

Summarizing the Marxist perspective, Michal Kalecki argued,

> The assumption that a Government will maintain full employment in a capitalist economy if it only knows how to do it is fallacious (138). . . .
> [T]he *maintenance* of full-employment would cause social and political changes which would give a new impetus to the opposition of the business leaders. Indeed, under a regime of permanent full employment, "the sack" would cease to play its role as a disciplinary measure. The social position of the boss would be undermined and the self assurance and class consciousness of the working class would grow. Strikes for wage increases and improvements in conditions of work would create political tension. . . . [C]lass instinct tells them that lasting full employment is unsound from their point of view and that unemployment is an integral part of the normal capitalist system. (Kalecki 1971, 138–41)[10]

In the next chapter we will explore the implications of these claims for analyzing the Fed's conduct of monetary policy.

STUDY QUESTIONS

Discussion Questions

1. Why do heterodox economists characterize textbook discussions of the monetary sector as akin to Hamlet without the prince?
2. Why do heterodox economists find *homo economicus* an inadequate psychology for understanding monetary sector behavior?
3. Why do heterodox economists foresee political battles over how tightly to run the economy?

Review Questions

1. Briefly explain what is meant by the distinction between the real and monetary sectors.
2. What is meant by liquidity?
3. Why do heterodox economists prefer to represent the flow and logic of economic activity by M-C-C'-M' rather than C-M-C'?
4. Who plays the role of "liquefier of the last resort" in the economy? Why is this an important role?
5. How can investment generate savings?
6. Heterodox economists typically criticize neoclassical textbooks for insufficient attention to institutional details and the use of an overly simple theory of human nature (*homo economicus*). How do these objections apply to the monetary sector?

NOTES

1. Quoted in Dow 1996, 175.

2. This view is most explicitly stated in the "quantity theory of money" (which your text probably discusses a little later in the term). The perspective also dominates the texts' depiction of the long run. The claim that outcomes in the real sector are determined independently of events in the monetary sector is sometimes called "dichotomous market" theory. The inability of the supply and demand for money to alter long-run outcomes in the economy is termed "money neutrality." These theories are challenged by heterodox theory.

3. It is worth noting that the rise in the interest rate is not due to an increase in money demand due to a higher level of economic activity (i.e., an increase in the transaction demand for money). It is due to an increase in liquidity demand.

4. For a recent example of shifting and persisting risks with derivatives and hedge funds see the *Wall Street Journal* (May 12, 2005), C1, C7; (May 15, 2005), C7; and *Business Week* (May 23. 2005), 96–97.

5. Dow, for example, writes, "Keynes perceived individuals' motivation within a capitalist society to be determined by the nature of its social arrangements: an important motivating force was the accumulation of monetary wealth. . . . Far from questioning individuals' motivation, general equilibrium theorists present the accumulation of wealth as being rational, reflecting a choice in favour of future consumption, at the expense of present consumption. Keynes in contrast observed rather accumulation without any particular consumption plans in mind. This he viewed as irrational . . ." (Dow 1996, 100).

Keynes writes, "The 'purposive' man' [i.e., the capitalist] . . . . does not love his cat, but his cat's kittens; nor, in truth, the kittens, but only the kittens' kittens, and so on forward for ever to the end of cat-dom" (Keynes 1963, 370). A similar drive for "free-floating" expansion arises from units of industrial capital as corporations strive to reproduce themselves.

6. In the M-C-C'-M' scenario it is easier to imagine banks "pushing loans" and seeking out lending opportunities than in the C-M-C' economy. It is also easier to imagine rivalry dynamics leading to imprudent loans (as illustrated by the drive to recycle petro-dollars after the first OPEC price shock). In the M-C-C'-M' model, financial capital appears like a "hot potato." Its owners strive to "get rid of it," to lend it to others who must inject it into the real cycle of production. This memorable metaphor is developed by Barbara Garson in her book *Money Makes the World Go Around* (2002).

7. Neoclassical economists admit that real people are more complicated than neoclassical models suggest, but argue that adding real-world complexities would not "fundamentally" change the analysis offered. They often celebrate, in fact, how much can be explained and, by implication, how little lost, through the assumption of rational economic man (REM).

8. Some neoclassical economists have begun to do this in limited contexts under the label of "behavioral economics." Like most neoclassical tilts in heterodox directions, however, the adjustment is generally treated as an aside by most other neoclassical economists and not allowed to alter the basic general equilibrium picture of markets at the heart of textbook theory.

9. Neoclassical economics' explanation of the distribution of income is based on "marginal productivity theory," which asserts that all factors of production are paid according to their productivity. Thus the distri-

bution of income reflects the distribution of ownership of the factors of production and their relative productivity. Different workers get paid different amounts of money because they contribute different values to production. The owners of land and capital are similarly compensated (with rents and interest) for the contribution that their factors of production make to output. Although "market imperfections" may cause minor divergences in incomes from productivity, neoclassical analyses typically imply that these differences can be ignored with little import.

10. Radical economists Raford Boddy and James Crotty (Boddy and Crotty 1975) develop similar themes. From their perspective macro policy becomes a battleground for class and sector interests. Some Post-Keynesian economists seem sympathetic to this interpretation, emphasizing the tendency for full employment to erode capitalist control within the workplace. Other Post-Keynesian economists imply that most major nonfinancial corporations can pass on cost increases (and perhaps even increase their markups) during booms, shifting the distributional burden to creditors holding financial assets with fixed nominal rates of return.

11

APPLICATIONS OF
HETERODOX MONETARY THEORY

INTRODUCTION

We are now in a position to combine several themes of heterodox monetary theory into an applied framework for critiquing standard textbooks' treatment of the way financial markets work, the character of the Fed, and the nature of monetary policy. We begin by taking a heterodox look at the way financial markets work.

FINANCIAL MARKETS

Introduction

In the rational-actor model underlying mainstream principles texts, buyers and sellers of financial assets, such as bank loans and shares of stock, follow unambiguous and rational decision rules in making economic choices. The "correct decision" is knowable and grounded in stable fundamentals from the real sector. Mainstream texts acknowledge that the "real world" is more uncertain and complex than suggested by perfect information models. Some texts briefly illustrate this complexity in "boxes" or other asides. Ultimately, however, the market optimality subtext of standard texts prevails and a "note but ignore" motif qualifies the disequilibrium asides. The books' take-away message (often conveyed as much by omission as commission) is that financial markets are basically stable, rational, and efficient (meaning that they allocate capital to its most productive use).

When doing formal analysis standard textbooks generally condense the monetary sector into the supply and demand for money. The other financial markets, such as the stock market, are dealt with in descriptive sections and "boxes," usually without formal analysis. This may be because of the difficulty in winning student acceptance of the rational-actor approach to these markets.

Heterodox analyses offer a more complicated and volatile picture of financial markets, one with individuals making decisions with limited information, limited expertise, and heavy reliance on popular imagery. Heterodox stories are populated by raging bulls, panicked bears, and people who defer to social conventions, as well as the purely rational agents of neoclassical theory. Heterodox analysis gives greater attention to the possibility of dysfunctional market behavior (e.g., markets with capricious price swings that can disrupt the real economy, or markets that fail to allocate capital to the most beneficial uses) than the textbooks do.

Sample Financial Crises

Macroeconomic history resonates with heterodox images.[1] Among the major financial crises of the last twenty-five years, for example, are:

The Silver Crisis

In 1980 two Texas oil men (Bunker and Herbert Hunt) speculated massively in the silver market with their own wealth and borrowed funds. For two months of 1980 the Hunts' borrowing to finance silver market purchases accounted for 13 percent of all U.S. business loans. When prices in the silver market fell unexpectedly the brothers were unable to meet their debt obligations and the banks and brokerage firms who had loaned them money were threatened with bankruptcy. This in turn threatened to seriously disrupt the banking system and its ability to extend credit to other borrowers.[2]

The Third World Debt Crisis

In the late 1970s and early 1980s many U.S. banks made very speculative and seemingly irrational loans to third world governments.[3] These loans eventually tallied more than twice the invested capital of the nine largest U.S. banks (Greider 1987, 433). When it became obvious that the governments could not repay the loans, the solvency of some of these banks was threatened, along with a possible unraveling of credit markets in the United States. Bailouts from the International Monetary Fund (IMF), the World Bank, and the Federal Reserve, financed heavily by U.S. taxpayers, defused the crisis.[4]

Booms and Busts in the Real Estate and Junk Bond Markets

The boom and bust cycle (Wolfson 1994a, 109) in the real estate market in the mid- to late 1980s produced a glut of commercial real estate.[5] The same dynamics in the junk bond market saddled many reorganized corporations with debt levels that undermined real-sector investment (Crotty and Goldstein 1993).[6] Both markets ultimately bankrupted many firms and their creditors in the banking sector (Wolfson 1994a, 117, 125–30; Crotty and Goldstein 1993).

The 1980s Stock Market Bubble and Crash

On October 19, 1987, the stock market lost 22 percent of its value, or half a trillion dollars, in one day (Wolfson 1994a, 121; Shiller 2001, 94). As Fed chairman Alan Greenspan put it, "Stock prices finally reached levels that stretched to incredulity expectations of rising real earnings. . . . Something had to snap. . . . The market plunge was an accident waiting to happen" (Wolfson 1994a, 121). About a decade later, Greenspan would again lament the "irrational exuberance" of the stock market, which would bubble and burst at the turn of the century, spraying parts of crashing "dot-coms" all across the financial landscape. From July 2000 to October 2002 the S&P index fell by about 45 percent and the Nasdaq index by about 75 percent (Crotty 2003, 275).

The 1980s Savings and Loan Crisis

Resolving this crisis saddled U.S. taxpayers with a bailout bill for bankrupt savings and loan institutions of about 200 billion dollars (Henwood 1997, 86; Stiglitz 2002, 81).

The Generic Crisis

John Kenneth Galbraith, a leading institutionalist economist, has offered a blueprint for what he calls "financial dementia" (John Kenneth Galbraith 1994, 106). His analysis emphasizes the 300-year period from 1635 to 1935, but applies equally well to more recent events.[7] The boom market generally starts with enthusiasm for some underpriced and frequently novel-appearing financial asset. As people begin to make money from its price increase, others jump aboard, generating a bandwagon psychology that pushes prices still higher. At this point, Galbraith argues, an interesting psychological dynamic develops. Both the enriched participants in the boom market and "expert" observers endow the participants and the market with impeccable foresight in valuing the asset. Just when prudent skepticism might be expected, according to textbook theory, runaway optimism prevails. With surprising consistency, Galbraith and others find repeated talk of "a new economy" in the rhetoric of boom markets, a rhetoric that drowns out memories of past boom and bust cycles.[8]

Explaining Financial Crises

How are we to understand these episodes? There have been attempts to reconcile textbook images of *homo economicus* with the erratic behavior of financial markets. These explanations tie market volatility to shifting events in the real sector that cause reasonable revaluations of economic assets. These explanations are not very persuasive, however, as they deny the self-evident impact of "irrational exuberance" during economic expansions and the panicked selling that shadows economic contractions. They also have trouble explaining the dramatic collapse of the stock market on October 19, 1987, without an equally dramatic change in the real sector.[9] In retaining *homo economicus,* the textbook story imposes the well-ordered narrative of economic theory on a much messier economic reality.

Heterodox explanations of financial market volatility take a different approach, focusing on the implications of: massive uncertainty, alternative psychologies to *homo economicus,* and the impact of institutional arrangements on individual behavior. As noted earlier, heterodox economists often stress the difference between "probabilistic" uncertainty, where decision makers have reasonable knowledge of the odds of different outcomes (as with rolling dice), and "fundamental" uncertainty, where the underlying probabilities are unknown (as with the question, what will be the title of the most popular song in January 2010?). Heterodoxy emphasizes the practical and psychological problems posed for financial investors by the necessity of making some momentous choices amid fundamental uncertainty.

Faced with this dilemma and recognizing the tenuousness of their own judgment, heterodox economists argue, decision makers often fall back on group conventions and social rules of thumb. They also tend to follow the crowd. Robert Shiller of Yale University cites interesting psychological research demonstrating the tendency of people to defer to group opinion and/or expert opinion even when it seems logically inconsistent and contradicts other beliefs they continue to hold (Shiller 2001, 150–51, 162–64). Shiller also emphasizes the tendency for background impressions, such as the image of stock holding as relatively riskless over the long term, to heavily influence and homogenize people's behavior. He notes that these impressions are often as much the product of the media's attempt to attract viewers and financial firms' attempts to attract customers, as the product of rational review of the prudence of stock ownership.

Some heterodox economists, such as Crotty (1994) and Levin (1995), argue that financial investors frequently adhere to an irrational faith that the future will be like the present,[10] and adjust their expectations in herd-like fashion. This deference to "groupthink" can impart an inertia to financial markets that elongates and elevates expansions and deepens contractions. It can also cause sudden dramatic shifts in market behavior (such as the 22 percent decline in stock prices on October 19, 1987) when the gap between groupthink and reality finally implodes.

Crotty analogizes the deference given conventional rules of thumb and popular opinion in financial decisions to the sway culture has over everyday behavior. Besides affecting investor judgments, these tendencies also tend to bias information environments, making it difficult for analysts to develop independent opinions. Crotty's portrayal is consistent with the historical accounts sketched by Galbraith and Kindleberger (Kindleberger [1978] 2000, 26, 37, 218).

Kindleberger argues, for example, that people have a tendency to screen out information that is at odds with their preconceived notions (Kindleberger [1978] 2000, 218). He writes, "People may experience cognitive dissonance, defined as the capacity to filter, massage, manipulate, or otherwise process information to make it accord with strongly held internalized beliefs" (Kindleberger [1978] 2000, 218).

The neoclassicals respond to heterodox claims with a very good question. They ask, if investors' errors are regular and predictable, "why aren't you rich?" Why don't heterodox economists, and other astute observers, use their knowledge to take advantage of predictable market errors and buy when assets are underpriced and sell when they are overpriced (and in the process smooth out market fluctuations)?

The answer to this question is as complicated as human beings. One can similarly ask why people in different cultures adhere to different religious beliefs (which to an external observer do not seem very credible) or why most people do not reflect upon their mortality and continue savings behaviors that contradict the life-cycle hypothesis of levelized spending. The answer to the original question (of why heterodox economists are not rich, and why predictable errors are not corrected) appears to have an individual and an institutional dimension. Individually, people seem to face asymmetric payoffs from being right or wrong, with or against the crowd. Both psychologically and professionally, the costs of being wrong with everyone else are much lower than the cost of being wrong alone. It is easier to forgive oneself, for example, for making conventional errors rather than one's own errors. While there is cachet in being right when everyone else is wrong, it probably does not outweigh the insurance of group identity.

On an institutional level, there seem to be similar "conservative" principles at work. Galbraith, for example, emphasizes the tendency of bureaucracies to promote safe choices to leadership positions. He writes, "In practice, the individual or individuals at the top of these [financial] institutions are often there because, as happens regularly in great organizations, theirs was mentally the most predictable and, in consequence, bureaucratically the least inimical of the contending talent. . . . In the 1970s, it was the greatest of the New York banks and bankers that, praising their own success in recycling Arab oil revenues, made those durably unfortunate loans to Latin America and to Africa and Poland" (John Kenneth Galbraith 1994, 15–16).

Galbraith's picture matches the assessment of the big New York banks offered by Anthony Solomon, a former president of the New York Federal Reserve Bank. Solomon laments, "What I don't understand is why the major commercial banks pay so little attention to their own country-risk assessments. My guess is that it isn't the country-risk experts who are too optimistic. It's the top lending officers of the banks, the senior officers themselves. They watch what other banks are doing. They rely too much on imagery, not enough on risk analysis. . . .

"[T]hey are consoled by fashion. If everyone else is lending to sovereign LDCs, they feel a little better even if their own country-risk department is suggesting otherwise" (Greider 1987, 434).

Solomon's view seems to have been shared by the politically conservative and enormously influential chair of the Federal Reserve (1979–1987) Paul Volcker, who, according to one of his close associates, saw "bankers as subject to fad and whim, almost incapable of making short-term sacrifices for their own long-term interest." The Federal Reserve Board governor overseeing the Fed's committee on banks similarly lamented, "You look at the bank's portfolio and try to point out the potential problems. . . . When this was done in 1980 and 1981, our examination people were told: 'You don't understand the situation. We know better than you.' There was almost no decent response from the banks—until, of course, their loans got into great difficulty" (Greider 1987, 438–39).

Finally, it is one thing to argue that financial markets are frequently rampant with speculation or panic and quite another to know when herds are likely to shift directions. Because the self-fulfilling logic of financial optimism or pessimism can validate itself for quite a while, it is necessary to take a fairly long view in order to cash in on perceptions of market excesses. The pressures on many financial decision makers to produce short-term successes reduces the incentive for taking such long-term views. It is thus difficult for "prudent observers" to drive out less-astute observers who will do quite well in the early parts of most speculative booms. In fact, it is the few lucky speculators who ride the wave and randomly happen to guess its turning point who get rich. Heterodox forecasters are likely to be comfortable, but not rich. They are also unlikely to "reform" the market.[11]

Sample Heterodox Analyses of Financial Markets

What kind of findings emerge from heterodox analyses? Where do these arguments lead? Although there is no single outcome, some destinations are very different from the optimized world of the textbooks. Heterodoxy adds disequilibrium moments and institutional contingencies to the equilibrium pictures of standard theory. The discussion below looks at the findings of two heterodox inquiries, Hyman Minsky's theory of business cycles and structuralist theories of financial arrangements.

Minsky Cycles

Minsky contends that economic expansions often breed overly optimistic business forecasts. These expectations encourage investors to buy overpriced financial assets with borrowed funds. The run-up in asset prices is frequently termed a *speculative bubble*. Unrealistic optimism can also lead corporations to finance excessive investment in new productive capacity with borrowed funds. When the day of reckoning comes, firms can have difficulty repaying past debts. Bankruptcies can spread in unpredictable ways, disrupting the credit system and crippling the real economy.

More specifically, Minsky argues that during a boom corporations gradually assume more debt in order to take advantage of perceived profit opportunities. Building upon objectively attractive investment possibilities, business optimism acts as a self-fulfilling prophecy. Buoyant business confidence spurs investment, which in turn increases aggregate demand and corporate profits, thereby reinforcing business confidence and initiating a new round of expansion. Even though debt increases, the relative burden of debt seems unimposing. This is because lenders and the borrowing firms' managers place increasingly higher values on the companies' assets (expressed in rising stock prices). Unfortunately, Minsky argues, bandwagon markets tend to push stock prices to unrealistic levels, which conceal the firms' growing debt burdens. As a boom progresses, firms may also anticipate easy refinancing and shift borrowing from long- to short-term loans, to gain lower rates. This reliance on short-term financing leaves them quite exposed to sudden increases in interest rates when they need to renew a loan.

As the boom matures, the run-up in asset prices can create a "get rich quick" culture on Wall Street and Main Street that entices new less-savvy players into financial markets (such as the stock, real estate, and options markets). At this point, larceny can add to the economy's financial

Figure 11.1   **Minsky Business Cycle Model of Financial Markets Fluctuations**

Box IV
Peak of expansion
Collapse and decline
Burst of speculative bubble
Rush for liquidity
Tighter credit conditions
Decline in real-sector investment

Box III
Mid–late expansion
Bandwagon dynamics
"Irrational exuberance"
Overshooting
Excess real-sector investment
Speculative excesses in financial markets
Inflated stock prices, rising debt levels

Box V
Early–mid contraction
Continued fall in real-sector investment
   (working off excess capacity)
Difficult credit conditions (high debt levels,
   increasing risk premiums)
Contagious business pessimism

Box II
Early–mid Expansion
GDP up, capacity utilization up
Employment up
Profits up
Low debt levels
Stock prices up
Low liquidity demand

Box VI
Mid–late contraction
Serious collapse with credit crunch
   and debt-induced bankruptcies OR
Gradual recovery with declines in
   excess capacity, debt levels, and
   interest rates and
Stabilization in asset prices

Box I
Bottom of last contraction
Renewal and recovery

Box VII
Bottom of contraction
Renewal and
recovery

weakness. Households can be lured by careless and/or self-interested advisors to spend life savings (or second mortgages) on all sorts of questionable assets, from worthless Florida real estate to overpriced "dot-com" stocks. Firms may engage in "creative accounting" to disguise the fact that profits are much lower than required to justify the companies' high stock prices, accumulated debt levels, and continued access to credit.

This practice was taken to new heights in the late 1990s by Enron (years after Minsky's prediction), but has often accompanied boom markets. As Arthur Levitt Jr., former chair of the Securities and Exchange Commission, has noted, "'Booms bring out situations that breed financial scandal. . . . A culture of what-can-we-get-away-with takes hold.' . . . When that happens . . . regulators come to be viewed as 'professional naysayers and doomsday predictors, and they lose credibility'" (Gosselin 2002).

Although the self-fulfilling prophecy aspect of business expansions and speculative booms in asset prices can continue for quite a while, doubts eventually emerge about the ability of debt-burdened corporations to meet their financing obligations. Once this happens, risk premiums increase, interest rates rise, equity values fall, debt/equity ratios increase, real investment falls, aggregate demand declines, and economic contraction occurs. Corporations burdened with debt find it difficult to refinance short-term obligations at favorable rates, bankruptcies loom, and confidence falls. The credit process that fueled the expansion runs in reverse.[12] Figure 11.1, drawn to look like the expansion and contraction phases of a business cycle, sums up the Minsky Model.

Heterodox economists argue that the troubling image of Minsky cycles is muted in standard texts. This facilitates each decade's "end of the business cycle," "efficient markets," "new economy" rhetoric, and weakens efforts to dampen market speculation through government regulation.

Structuralist Analyses of Financial Arrangements

Adding Institutional Details. As noted earlier, heterodox economists emphasize the need to develop a habit of inquiry that includes institutional detail at a very early stage of analysis. Standard textbooks argue that students are better served by learning a few simple abstract models that they can apply on their own to explain all economic activity. Heterodoxy challenges this vision, claiming it oversimplifies economic activity in order to homogenize it. By so doing, it can encourage readers to place excessive faith in the implications of simple models (as is often the case with arguments for "totally free trade," "shock therapy" for transition economies, and unregulated capital markets).

Thus, rather than simply modeling the credit market with abstract supply-and-demand curves, heterodox analyses explore the concrete institutional arrangements that assemble and distribute credit. Market outcomes are tied to both the logic of inherited institutional contexts and the calculus of individual maximization decisions. As discussed in more detail in chapter 13, the logic of institutional contexts is tied in turn to larger historical and cultural phenomena, such as "social structures of accumulation" in radical and neo-Marxist theory, or "institutional conjunctures" in institutionalist economic theory. We will illustrate heterodox discussions of finance by looking at the implications of the difference between the "bank-centered" financial systems of Germany and Japan and the "stock-market-centered" systems of the United States and the United Kingdom.[13]

Bank- Versus Stock Market–Centered Financing System. German and Japanese firms have usually financed their long-term operations through retained earnings and loans from banks with whom they maintain relatively permanent relationships. These banks frequently have strong representation on the corporations' governing bodies. They are well informed about the firms' prospects and often have a great deal of influence over corporate strategy and personnel policy (Himmelweit, Simonetti, and Trigg 2001, chapter 17).

In the Anglo-American case the relationship between banks and firms is more detached. When companies borrow from banks, they generally do so on a loan-by-loan basis. Banks do not own corporate stock and generally do not have significant representation on corporate boards. Firms in the United States and United Kingdom are also more likely to use equity financing (the issuance of stock) to raise capital than are Japanese or German firms.

Traditionally, bank-based, relational financing seems to encourage decision makers to take a long-term perspective, as most participants have long-term ties to the corporation. Equity-based systems can encourage short-run preoccupations with stock prices, although they may also offer greater stimulus for innovation by promoting venture capital spending.

The above differences in corporate finance tend to be related to differences in corporate governance. The German and Japanese systems appear to encourage "stakeholder participation" in corporate management. Among the groups represented in the German and Japanese systems are workers, industry suppliers, customers, and financiers. Stakeholder governance has many causes, including regulatory requirements (such as the "codetermination system" in Germany that legally requires that employees be represented on corporate boards of directors) and cultural traditions (such as the Japanese custom of lifetime employment in core firms, which has encouraged managers to feel a sense of community with fellow employees).

As Himmelweit, Simonetti, and Trigg indicate, "In the Anglo-Saxon economies . . . wealth has been seen essentially as a commodity rather than enmeshed with rights and obligations" (Himmelweit, Simonetti, and Trigg 2001, 481). In 1998 American and Japanese managers were asked, "'Do you agree that corporations are the property of the shareholders and employees merely one of the factors of production?' In the United States 67 percent of managers agreed; in Japan only 9 percent" (Wade 2005, 36).

The Anglo-American stock market model of corporate governance tends to leave corporate control in the hands of current management or hostile takeover teams. Although offering less participation to the different constituencies affected by corporate decisions than the German and Japanese systems do, the U.S.-U.K. approach seems less likely to encourage the concentration of economic power that accompanies the German and Japanese systems (interlocking directorship, closed finance-industrial complexes, etc.).

The different systems of finance and management help shape the maximizing decisions of participants within and outside the firm by influencing expectations, the cost of different forms of collective action, and people's tastes and preferences (by offering them different experiences). Understanding monetary sector outcomes in the United States, the United Kingdom, Germany, and Japan thus requires a solid understanding of the institutional histories of these economies.

One could construct alternative comparative analyses or extend the discussion to many other topics, such as the particular institutional networks and arrangements governing housing or electric utility financing in the United States. My research on the history of the nuclear power industry (Cohn 1997), for example, found that the financing of nuclear power plants was dominated by institutional variables. Both lenders and borrowers for nuclear projects believed that utility regulators would increase electricity rates to cover the construction cost of nuclear plants and an allowable rate of return. This belief, rather than the faceless working out of supply and demand, mobilized capital for nuclear plants. One could similarly explore the importance of the social security system, private pension systems, and corporate management's control of retained earnings for the determination of savings.

The key implication of these examples is that formal models of financial markets abstracted from social contexts are inadequate to understand the workings of the monetary sector. Students need to know as much history and institutional theory as mathematics to understand financial markets. This message is obscured in most mainstream textbooks. Although institutional detail is sometimes provided, it comes across as fluff, pleasant background information that can be ignored when deriving important conclusions about market optimality, deregulation, and the efficiency of capital markets. Heterodox analysis challenges this loss of context and automatic endorsement of relatively unregulated market outcomes.

THE FED

Technocratic or Political Policy Making?

All macro textbooks highlight the role of the Fed in the monetary sector. Virtually all neoclassical texts portray the Fed as a "technocratic" institution, that is, an institution administered by apolitical experts who attempt to promote the general welfare. Policy debates are portrayed as theoretical debates over how the economy works. There is little attention to the possibility that policy debates might reflect the conflicting interests of different political economic groups.

The alignments in public discussion and political lobbying, however, suggest the presence of distributional conflicts. Voices representing labor groups generally press for more expansionary monetary policy than is favored by bankers and other lenders. The reasons for this alignment are consistent with profit squeeze theories of the business cycle, as outlined at the end of chapter 10 and elaborated in chapter 12's discussion of labor markets.

Heterodox theories of the Fed suggest it anticipates a tilt in national income from capital to labor as the economy approaches full employment. In response, it attempts to "cool off" the economy. Why does the Fed do this? Heterodox theory suggests two reasons: (1) deference to the functional role of unemployment in maintaining macroeconomic stability and (2) deference to the economic interests of the owners of bonds (sometimes referred to as financial capital) and the owners of firms (sometimes referred to as nonfinancial or industrial capital), though this distinction is blurring.

Functional Role of Unemployment

The first reason resembles, but is not identical to, the rationale offered in most mainstream textbooks. The Fed acts to slow down the economy as it nears full employment in order to avoid even sharper contractionary forces that would arise if the economy reached and maintained full employment. Unchecked by economic policy, full-employment booms frequently lead to declines in investment, as falling profit margins and labor's increasing power sour investment expectations. Reduced profits and falling aggregate demand (due to collapses in investment demand) can bankrupt marginal firms and, in unpredictable ways, cripple firms doing business with profit-squeezed firms. All sorts of debt and credit-related problems can subsequently spread throughout the economy.

In a variation on this theme, full employment leads to rising labor costs, but rather than squeezing profits these costs are passed on as price increases. In this case, the Fed acts to slow down the economy in order to prevent inflation. It is implied that even mild inflation threatens to evolve into accelerating inflation, which would cripple the economy or require much more draconian monetary contraction.

Although more bloody than the standard textbook metaphor of "taking away the punch bowl just as the party gets going," this account of the Fed's role in the economy is somewhat compatible with the textbook vision. The main difference is that heterodox theorists make explicit the idea that capitalist economies need unemployment in order to "control" labor. Heterodox analyses of cyclical unemployment thus shift responsibility from the failings of individual workers to the dynamics of the market. Rather than talking in terms of the "natural rate of unemployment," as mainstream textbooks do, radical and Marxist theories suggest the notion of "disciplinary unemployment."

Heterodox theory invites attention to whether alternative ways can be found to avoid inflation or investment collapses from reliance on the threat and/or reality of unemployment. Heterodox analyses emphasize the large societal benefits of tight labor markets, including (1) employment of the most disadvantaged workers at the end of the labor queue, (2) increases in training and human capital formation within firms, (3) reductions in wage inequalities, and (4) support for stable families and communities.[14]

Low unemployment rates seem likely to have virtuous path-dependent effects (hysteresis) quite different from the vicious cycle of economic downturns. An economy with relatively low levels of unemployment encourages employers to engage in long-run labor management strategies—often called the invisible handshake strategy. Firms keep workers on during mild periods of low aggregate demand and do not slash wages in order to win the loyalty of workers for normal periods of tight labor markets. This strategy becomes less viable in an economy with cyclical periods of serious downturns, during which firing or squeezing workers can be profitable and even necessary for business survival. Thus, to some extent, "macro regimes" may condition micro strategies.[15] This point is explored further in chapter 13.

Dual labor market theory suggests that there is feedback not only between macro conditions and firms' internal labor market policies but also between macro conditions and community institutions. A high unemployment economy has much greater potential for disrupting stable work habits and corroding community institutions built around those habits (such as stable families and strong neighborhood organizations) than a low unemployment economy does.[16]

Interest Group Politics

In addition to maintaining macro stability, heterodox theory suggests that the Fed cools off the economy to protect the balance sheets of corporate and financial capital. In other words, the Fed slows the economy in order to prevent profit squeeze pressures from tilting income toward labor. It helps to take a closer look at the governance of the Fed in order to understand why it might behave this way.

As noted in most mainstream texts, the two most powerful organs of the Fed are the Board of Governors and the Federal Reserve Open Market Committee (FOMC). Many mainstream texts describe in some detail the twelve-district, decentralized bank structure of the Fed, the appointment process for the Board of Governors, and the composition of the FOMC. Oddly and perhaps revealingly, almost none of the texts say much about how the presidents of the district banks of the Fed are chosen, despite the fact that these presidents fill five of the twelve seats on the FOMC and oversee the staffs of the district banks that provide much of the economic information used by the Fed's planning bodies.[17]

The process of appointment is quite interesting and illustrates the economic bias inherent in the Fed's structure. Each district bank has a nine-member board of directors. The board appoints the bank's president, subject to approval by the Fed's Board of Governors.[18] Partially by statute and partially by tradition, three members represent the banking system (typical members are private bank officials), three members represent borrowers (typical members are major corporate executives), and three members represent the public. What the latter means is somewhat ambiguous. Sometimes independent individuals, like university and foundation presidents, fill these slots; sometimes individuals related to the first two groups, such as business leaders and the lawyers who represent them, fill these slots.[19]

Similar, though less formally structured, biases shape the selection of Fed chairs. Fully cognizant of their self-interest, corporate and financial capital (colloquially referred to as "the capital markets") lobby hard for sympathetic Fed chairs. Rumors of choices at odds with their interests (e.g., candidates likely to promote prolonged full employment) bring concerns about inflationary pressures and profit squeezes. These anticipatory concerns threaten higher current interest rates and lower current investment, putting tremendous political pressure on presidents to appoint "conservative" chairs (e.g., Greenspan, Volcker, Burns, McMartin) who will "reassure" the capital markets that the Fed is in good hands.

The main argument is not that the Fed governors are lackeys of Wall Street, but that the selection process elevates people who believe what is good for Wall Street is good for America. The people who make it through the selection process generally accept as part of their role an implicit contract with creditor interests to protect their financial investments. They do not feel bound by similar implicit contracts with small businesses or other participants in the weaker parts of a dual economy.[20] As Nobel Prize–winning economist William Vickrey notes, "[M]onetary authorities

seem to be afflicted with an inherent bias stemming from the close association of those responsible for monetary policy with financial interests, and their relative remoteness from the grim
realities of unemployment" (Vickrey 1993, 5).

The ideological influence of the Fed is widespread. Besides its priestly contribution to economic discourse at the highest level (academic papers) and the most public level (the evening
news and the *Wall Street Journal*), it is probably the largest employer of economists in the world
and generates an enormous volume of free informational materials that stock the library shelves
of economics departments across the country.

William Grieder's book *Secrets of the Temple* (1987) paints a complicated and at times moving picture of the pained acceptance by the Fed governors of the economic ruin they were inflict-
ing on various groups to curb inflationary pressures (1979–1982). The Fed's decision makers
(and staff economists) generally carried general equilibrium (GE) and "market cornucopia" views[21]
with them to the table, independent of whatever personal feelings they might have had. They
tended to consider only certain kinds of economic policies. The process of selection (representing
broader features of the U.S. social structure) endows these views with control of monetary policy.
The practitioners are not necessarily "bad people," but their views can have painful distributional
and systemic consequences.[22]

One can go even further when analyzing the wider public debate over monetary policy and
identify the implications of self-interest in the voices representing the banks, bond holders, and
corporations. These voices are represented in the Fed's governance through the district bank
presidents. The textbooks' failure to acknowledge this misleads students.

The textbooks' usual portrayal of the governance debate as a choice between the current
system of allegedly disinterested experts and a more politicized alternative confuses the issue.
The current process already includes aspects of self-interest and ideology alongside disinterested expertise.

POLICY IMPLICATIONS

We turn now to the public policy implications of heterodox critiques of the treatment of monetary
sector issues in neoclassical textbooks. The discussion draws together ideas scattered throughout
earlier sections and covers some new ground. As is often the case, heterodox critiques tend to
undermine the "let the market work" subtext of neoclassical textbooks.

Monetary Policy

Goals

Mainstream texts usually limit the debate over monetary policy to arguments between the new
(soft) Keynesians and different groups of GE theorists (such as the monetarists, new classicals,
and real-business-cycle theorists). By highlighting the differences between these positions, the
text gives the appearance of exhausting serious opinion, without including heterodox alternatives.

The macro fluctuations anticipated and policy responses invited by standard neoclassical texts
are more modest than those explored in heterodox theory. There is little discussion of the merits
of using monetary policy to push unemployment low enough to alter the balance of power in
labor markets. There is virtually no discussion of how to reduce the influence of banking and
corporate interests on Fed policy (such as altering the way district bank presidents are selected).
The textbooks do little to tarnish the media's elevation of Alan Greenspan and other Fed chairs to

sainthood, which helps convince students of the wisdom of apostolic succession: from "the market," to Fed chairs, to public policy.[23] Heterodoxy challenges these boundaries.

Responses to Inflationary Pressures

The dominant image of inflation in neoclassical textbooks is "too much money chasing too few goods." Monetary restraint is pictured as bringing the growth of the money supply in line with the growth of the real sector. Although there is modest debate in the textbooks over whether sticky prices will cause monetary contractions to be temporarily accompanied by higher rates of unemployment, the increase in unemployment is not treated as a necessary part of the adjustment process.

In heterodox theory, inflation is frequently tied to cost push pressures. Contractionary monetary policies are thought to reduce inflation by increasing unemployment and lowering capacity utilization rates, thereby reducing pricing pressures. In heterodox theory, the Fed's macro control variable is the short-term interest rate, rather than the size of the money supply. By raising the federal funds rate, monetary cures for inflation create slack in the economy and thereby reduce pricing pressures. In other words, there is almost always an unemployment price for monetary answers to inflation.[24]

Because of the large social costs of unemployment outlined in chapter 8, heterodox economists look especially hard for innovative ways to contain cost push pressures without reducing employment and high-capacity utilization rates. Among the measures explored are incomes policies and pattern bargaining, which create mechanisms for setting wages and prices that share the economy's productivity gains between wages and profits in noninflationary ways.[25]

Heterodox economics usually gives greater attention to the distributional impacts of monetary policy than textbook economics does. For example, heterodox economists analyze the impact of different monetary policies on labor's share of national income, on working conditions, and on the viability of small businesses and family farms. Building on the work of "dual economy theorists," heterodox economists often stress the extra burden that contractionary monetary policy places on small, as opposed to large, businesses in fighting inflation. Nobel Laureate William Vickrey, in particular, was an outspoken critic of Fed policies that contracted the money supply whenever unemployment fell within a 4-to-6 percent range in the name of fighting inflation. He wrote, "while 5 percent unemployment might be barely tolerable if it meant that everyone would be taking an additional two weeks vacation every year without pay, it is totally unacceptable as a social goal when it means unemployment rates of 10 percent, 20 percent, or even 40 percent among disadvantaged groups, this phenomenon being accompanied by increases in poverty, homelessness, poor health, drug addiction and crime" (Vickrey 1993, 10).

Financial Markets Policy

The neoclassicals' faith in market optimality and a tendency to "note but ignore," the importance of institutional choices for economic outcomes have animated many recent models of financial markets. Among the most popular theories have been the "efficient market" hypothesis, which asserts the wisdom of financial markets, and "Modigliani-Miller" notions of the independence of investment outcomes from institutional choices of stock or bond financing. There has been strong neoclassical support for financial deregulation, warnings against government credit channeling, and a cautious interest in privatizing aspects of social security. Although there are also neoclassical critics of these positions, the spirit of neoclassical theory and its textbooks constantly argues for public policies that "let the market work." The relevant debates are usually between the status quo and more market independence.

The takeaway message of most mainstream texts is that existing financial markets work quite well. The deregulation of domestic credit markets is portrayed as a success. There are nods given to patching up a few flaws (perhaps through better accounting practices), but the general theme is, "if it ain't broke, don't fix it" and "if it is broke, find market solutions to market problems."[26]

Heterodox economists tend to favor more activist public policies, such as regulatory efforts to curb the harmful effects of financial speculation. Heterodox economists tend to favor retention of the social security system and oppose replacing it with a market-oriented, individually managed stock portfolio. Among the reasons for this opposition is a fear that privatization would lead to a more arbitrary and unequal distribution of wealth and retirement outcomes.

Industrial Policy

Heterodox economists put industrial policy on the agenda of monetary policy makers. Industrial policy attempts to channel economic development in socially desirable directions. Among the kinds of monetary policies targeted for discussion by heterodox economists are:

- The use of variable reserve requirements to channel bank loans to projects with positive societal impacts like home mortgages and loans to small farmers and students.
- The use of similar and more powerful incentives (such as favorable tax treatment) to channel credit to industries with desirable employment characteristics (such as good blue-collar jobs) or positive environmental benefits.
- The use of legislation such as the Community Reinvestment Act (which created incentives for banks to meet the credit needs of low- and moderate-income neighborhoods in their service area) to recycle local deposits in communities with significant low-income populations.

Many of these policies attempt to internalize the positive meta-externalities accompanying the cultivation of social capital, a heterodox category given relatively little attention in mainstream analyses.

In the mid-1970s and early 1980s there was increasing public discussion of expanded economic planning in response to the difficulties faced by rust-belt industries due to heightened foreign competition (Shoch 1994, 177). Echoing its traditional "free-market" hostility toward economic planning, the economics profession tended to weigh in against industrial policy. As Jim Shoch writes, "Perhaps most important in turning the tide of elite and public opinion against industrial policy in the Fall of 1983 was the offensive against the doctrine mounted from within the economics profession, especially by economists affiliated with conservative and liberal-think-tanks" (Shoch 1994, 180–81).[27] Principles texts tend to echo this dismissal of industrial policy, as much by omission as by commission.

Heterodox theorists want to put industrial policy on the agenda of economic inquiry and macro principles courses. Although there are some reasons to question the feasibility of industrial policy (especially as it might be practiced by the Export-Import Bank in the service of corporations like Enron and Exxon), it is one thing to raise objections to the idea and another to silence or minimize discussion of it.

THREADS

Distributional Threads

As noted above, heterodox economists tend to give greater attention to distributional issues than standard texts do, both in terms of the unequal effect of Fed credit policies on different groups (like big and small business), the unequal leverage of different groups on Fed policy, and the implications of high and low unemployment for social inequality.

Gender Threads

Feminist economists endorse heterodoxy's concern about the distributional effects of contractionary monetary policies. Linda Manning and Patricia Graham, for example, note that credit crunches generally burden small businesses owned by women more severely than large corporations (Manning and Graham 1999, p. 27).

With ideas surprisingly similar to Keynes's behavioral psychology (though expressed in a very different voice), many feminist economists reject the textbooks' attempt to explain financial sector behavior by relying solely on the assumptions of rational, isolated, economic man. Like Keynes's thinking, feminist models of socially referenced and emotionally complex behavior are able to explain recurring speculative bubbles and financial panics that seem anomalous in the textbooks' rational-actor model of behavior. As Marc Lavoie (2003) writes, "there are tight methodological links between post Keynesian economics . . . and feminist economics (189). . . . [Feminist economics] points toward Keynes's notion of animal spirits and conventions, which are recurrent themes along with fundamental uncertainty and liquidity preference in post-Keynesian economics" (191).

Feminist ideas about the importance of analyzing economic activities within institutional contexts and with reference to the impact of these activities on systems of social relationships also have interesting implications for analyzing monetary issues. They invite, for example, a skepticism toward simple theories of the monetary sector, such as the quantity theory of money that abstract from institutional contexts. Feminist ideas also recommend caution before adhering to mechanical theories of monetary policy that recommend large doses of unemployment to fight inflation.

Parts of William Greider's book *Secrets of the Temple,* detailing the history of the Federal Reserve, offer a fascinating example of feminist thinking about monetary policy. Greider details the opposition of Nancy Teeters, the first woman member of the Board of Governors of the Federal Reserve, to the Fed's "shock therapy" to fight inflation from 1979 to 1982. Greider writes,

> Nancy Teeters, almost alone, resisted. Month after month, as the economy spiraled downward, she repeatedly urged her colleagues to back off. . . . "I told them: 'You are pulling the financial fabric of this country so tight that it's going to rip. You should understand that once you tear a piece of fabric, it's very difficult, almost impossible, to put it back together again'" (465). . . .
>
> The feminist critique was aimed in part at the masculine moral perspective, a mind-set that seemed narrow and mechanical, driven by abstract formulations that excluded social complexities and was insufficiently attentive to human loss. (Greider 1987, 466)

Greider argues that Teeters's greater attention to the costs of severed social relationships led her to disagree with her male colleagues about the wisdom of the Fed's extreme monetary stringency. Although the other governors regretted the unemployment and bankruptcies that their policies were causing, they deemed this tradeoff necessary to break the back of double-digit inflation. Teeters disagreed because she thought the costs were higher than realized. Greider adds,

> When Harvard psychologist Carol Gilligan explored these gender-related moral differences in her study, *In a Different Voice,* she used the same metaphor that Nancy Teeters had used before the Federal Open Market Committee. Women, Gilligan wrote, will usually seek to

Table 11.1

Textbook Versus Heterodox Images of Monetary Phenomena

The Auctioneer Model of the Economy	The Casino Model
Perfect information	Imperfect information
Certainty	Uncertainty
Probabilistic uncertainty	Fundamental uncertainty
Barter economy	Monetized economy
Dichotomous real and monetary sectors	Integrated real and monetary sectors
C-M-C′	M-C-C′-M′
Static equilibrium	Dynamic expansion
Rational isolated man	Socially embedded people
Random walks and efficient markets	Anxious forays and speculative excesses
The short long run	The long short run
The divine Fed	The bankers' Fed

avoid "the fracture of human relationships that must be mended with its own thread" (Greider 1987, 466). [Greider continues,] Boys were taught to believe in rules, a hard and concise form of justice that could be calculated. Girls were taught to negotiate and compromise, to avoid harsh judgments that might fracture relationships. . . .

This difference, one could say, was approximately parallel to what divided Teeters from her colleagues at the Fed. She was willing to abandon the arbitrary money "rules" that the Federal Reserve was following rather than allow even greater destruction to unfold. (Greider 1987, 467–68)

Environmental Threads

There are some interesting issues related to the monetary sector that are relevant to environmental concerns. Some of these issues involve the way in which financial markets establish the "discount rate" (which is the annual percentage by which economic costs or benefits received in future years are reduced to an equivalent "present value"). Because analysis of these issues requires more background discussion than would be appropriate in this chapter, we will defer that discussion to chapter 16, which focuses on macroeconomics and the environment.

Ecological economists Herman Daly and Joshua Farley have also noted that the use of money tends to obscure natural limits to growth. Although money balances can hypothetically grow exponentially forever, real output cannot, due to physical limits to growth.

COMPETING STORIES AND METAPHORS

As we have emphasized, learning economics is like learning a language and its system of metaphor. The juxtapositions in Table 11.1 compare some of the different metaphors used by neoclassical textbooks and heterodox analysis to discuss monetary sector phenomena. Rather than totally erasing the metaphor, the heterodox alternative often adds an image to the textbook picture.

IN THEIR OWN WORDS

The circumstances that induce the recurrent lapses into financial dementia have not changed in any truly operative fashion since the Tulipomania of 1636–1637. . . .

[T]he speculative episode, with increases provoking increases, is within the market itself. And so is the culminating crash. . . .

The final question that remains is what, if anything, should be done. Recurrent descent into insanity is not a wholly attractive feature of capitalism. . . .

The only remedy . . . is an enhanced skepticism. . . . Let the following be one of the unfailing rules by which the individual investor . . . [is] guided: there is the possibility, even the likelihood, of self-approving and extravagantly error-prone behavior on the part of those closely associated with money.

—John Kenneth Galbraith (1994, 106–9)

[Keynes's] work on probability suggested that reason had to act on limited knowledge, and thus on subjective assessments of probability. . . . Keynes emphasized the problems of decision-making under conditions of uncertainty. . . . Lacking the capacity in many instances to form predictions, even in probabilistic terms, individuals employ conventions which rely heavily on group behaviour.

—Sheila Dow (1996, 99–100)

Keynes assumed that *agents are socially and endogenously-constituted human beings* [italics in original], not autonomously constituted, lifeless Walrasian calculating machines. . . . The theory of agent choice, therefore, must reflect both the social constitution of the agent (which is contingent on, and changes with, the institutions, values, and practices specific to time and place) as well as the psychological complexity of the human-being-in society. . . .

[B]ecause they are fully human, agents have a deep psychological need to create the illusion of order and continuity even where these things may not exist. . . .

[W]e have a psychological need to calm our anxieties, to remove the constant stress created by forced decision making under inadequate information, a need that is neither irrational nor socially or economically dysfunctional. . . . We have good reason, in other words, to try to "overlook this awkward fact" that the reproduction of our economic and social status requires a knowledge of things that, in fact, "we simply do not know." . . .

To help us accomplish this calming of our nerves, Keynes argues, we collectively develop a "conventional" process of expectations and confidence formation. Keynes's concept of conventional decision making is a sine qua non of Keynesian macrotheory. It is also one of Keynes's most important and most radical theoretical innovations.

—James Crotty (1994, 119–120)

[A]gents know the economy is naturally unstable. This is why uncertainty plays a role in their decisions . . . and why liquidity matters. . . .

Money is endogenously supplied, and bankers live in the same expectational environment as everyone else. If the value of liquidity is lowered, this increases the willingness of "lenders" to also reduce their own liquidity. . . .

Big Government is necessary and countercyclical deficits are necessary to put a floor on aggregate demand. . . . The Big Bank is necessary and lender of last resort intervention is necessary to put a floor on asset prices to prevent debt deflation. . . . A variety of institutions are needed to constrain the inherent instability—they don't all have to come from government, but many must.

—Dimitri B. Papadimitriou and L. Randall Wray (1999, 11)

An unrepresentative and unresponsive elite has extensive control over the financial system. . . .

I propose a dramatically different approach: transforming the Federal Reserve System (the "Fed") into a public investment bank. . . .

The Fed would make credit more expensive for lenders that finance speculative activities such as the mergers, buyouts, and takeovers that dominated the 1980s.

The Fed would also give favorable credit terms to banks that finance decent affordable housing rather than luxury housing and speculative office buildings. It would make low-cost credit available for environmental research and development. . . .

Finally, the Fed would give preferential treatment to loans that finance investment in the United States rather than in foreign countries.

—Robert Pollin (1999, 8–9)

STUDY QUESTIONS

Discussion Questions

1. Neoclassical textbooks portray debates about the governance of the Fed as debates about the benefits of democratic versus expert decision making. How do heterodox analyses of the Fed alter this portrayal?
2. Compare and contrast heterodox and neoclassical metaphors for discussing the monetary sector and financial markets.
3. Discuss the major policy implications of heterodox critiques of textbook analyses of financial markets and the monetary sector.

Review Questions

1. List some of the major financial crises of the last twenty-five years.
2. Outline the stages of Minsky's theory of financial crises.
3. Briefly explain Galbraith's theory of financial crises.
4. From a heterodox perspective what are the main problems with the depiction of financial markets in neoclassical textbooks?
5. Why do boom and bust cycles persist in the monetary sector according to Hyman Minsky? Briefly outline the stages in the cycle according to Minsky.
6. Heterodox economists typically criticize neoclassical textbooks for insufficient attention to institutional details and the use of an overly simple theory of human nature (*homo economicus*). How do these objections apply to analyses of the financial sector?

NOTES

1. See, for example, Wolfson (1994a), John Kenneth Galbraith (1955, 1994), and Kindleberger ([1978] 2000).

2. This assessment comes from the Securities and Exchange Commission (Wolfson 1994a, 68–75). The crisis was averted when the silver market turned around.

3. Drawing on extensive interviews with high-ranking officials in the Federal Reserve, William Greider (1987) offers a fascinating look at the puzzling behavior of leading private bankers with respect to risky loans to third world countries in the 1970s and early 1980s. Arthur Levitt Jr., former chair of the Securities and Exchange Commission, has made similar observations about the tendency of market booms to dull economic and moral judgment (Gosselin 2002).

4. The Federal Reserve's decision to allow the banks to carry inflated values on their balance sheets for third world loans also helped the institutions avoid bankruptcy pressures (Greider 1987, 432–40, 484–87, 520, 545–51; Wolfson 1994a, 108–9). The collapse of the Continental Bank illustrates the overenthusiastic lending of major banks to the energy sector. The bank's failure spurred a multi-billion-dollar bailout for its depositors with public funds to prevent panicked withdrawals from other banks (Wolfson 1994a, 94–99).

5. Galbraith reports that excess capacity was so severe that it was expected to take about a dozen years to work it off (John Kenneth Galbraith 1994, x–xi).

6. The real estate bubble repeated the speculative excesses surrounding the real estate investment trusts (REITs) of the 1970s.

7. Galbraith begins his narrative with the tulip mania (Tulipomania) that swept Holland in the early seventeenth century and turned a rather obscure agricultural product (on par with vegetables) into a speculative asset worth tens of thousands of (current) dollars—until prices collapsed in 1637 (John Kenneth Galbraith 1994, 26–34). He ends his account with the stock market crash of 1987, almost exactly 350 years later.

8. Charles Kindleberger of MIT offers a similar picture of speculative behavior in his classic study *Manias, Panics, and Crashes: A History of Financial Crises* ([1978] 2000). Shiller (2001) dissects the "new era" justification for the stock market's bubble prior to its collapse in 2000.

9. Shiller's analysis of events preceding the market crashes of 1929 and 1987, for example, found little basis for explaining the crashes as rational responses to new information about economic fundamentals (Shiller 2001, chapter 4).

10. Shiller (2001) cites experimental evidence for this claim (144).

11. Drawing on insights from behavioral economics, Mullainathan and Thaler (2000) reach similar conclusions about the inability of arbitrage and learning to force actual markets to perfect information outcomes. Shiller similarly rejects the claims of "efficient markets theory" "that all financial prices accurately reflect all public information at all times" (Shiller 2001, pp. 171–73).

12. Another way to conceptualize Minsky's cycle theory is to think about it in terms of the changing value of liquidity premiums. Minsky suggests that investors confront a spectrum of assets with differing degrees of liquidity. Investment in physical capital tends to be the most illiquid, while holding cash is the most liquid. Minsky suggests that over the course of the business cycle the value of liquidity changes. In the initial periods of an expansion liquidity premiums are small. Real-sector investment is an attractive opportunity. Eventually, however, the tables turn and liquidity pressures depress real investment, choking aggregate demand and recessing the economy.

13. See for example Himmelweit, Simonetti, and Trigg (2001, chapter 17), Epstein (1992), and Henwood (1997, 174–75).

14. See, for example, Bernstein and Baker 2001, 2003.

15. See Furman and Stiglitz 1998 for a similar argument.

16. It may also be helpful to think about the implications of full employment in terms of a shift in relations between consumers and producers analogous to that between capital and labor. In many contexts, market competition tends toward a race to the bottom in the labor market in order to lower prices in the goods market, sacrificing work-lives to consumption patterns. Heterodox economists explore the "social logic," rather than simple free choice, behind this trade-off. One of the "unintended consequences" of capitalism may be the emergence of a harsher labor process than people would voluntarily select, in exchange for a higher level of goods production. Like the prisoner's dilemma and the contradictions of positional competition, the degradation of work (facilitated by lax labor markets) suggests that the invisible hand often misses its mark.

17. Interestingly, voting records for the Open Market Committee from the 1960s and 1970s reveal that the district bank presidents were significantly more likely to vote for tighter monetary policy than the Board of Governors, even though the latter was a relatively conservative and business-friendly group (Greider 1987, p. 313).

18. Financial Markets Center, "Who Directs the Federal Reserve Banks? A Survey of Reserve Bank Board Composition: 1991–1996," Southern Finance Project, November 1996.

19. The Financial Markets Center (FMC) offers a good analysis of the background of the directors of the Fed district banks (see, for example, "Reserve Bank Boards in 2003," available on the FMC web site). Despite a significant improvement from twenty-five years ago, the boards are still dominated by corporate and financial interests, with less than 10 percent of the 108 slots filled by labor, consumer, and community representatives.

20. Greider's book *Secrets of the Temple* (1987) is especially good at conveying this asymmetry.

21. By "market cornucopia" views I mean an implicit faith that markets, left to themselves, produce

wealth and solve complicated social engineering problems in ways that are beyond the imagination of policy makers.

22. Greider's 750-page *Secrets of the Temple* offers some fascinating institutional detail about the workings of the Fed. Joined with current analyses from the Financial Markets Center, the material offers a good starting point for institutionalist analyses of how external structural forces (such as "the capital markets"), the Fed's internal institutional history, and ideological beliefs chisel monetary policy into deep, narrow channels that are extremely resistant to change.

23. Puzzlingly, principles texts often reinforce the popular image of the Fed chair as the second most powerful person in the United States, without any attention to the "political" nature of that power. People assume that the president is a political animal, but they put the Fed above the fray, perhaps even more than the Supreme Court, a puzzling but perhaps ideologically revealing deference.

24. In practice almost all economists now agree that the Fed has no reliable way of predicting and measuring the precise impact of its actions on the money supply. It thus necessarily manages monetary policy by targeting the federal funds rate and the level of short-term interest rates in the economy.

25. Incomes policies involve the use of tax incentives and/or government regulatory authority to influence wage- and price-setting behavior. Pattern bargaining attempts to arrange major wage agreements in the private and public sector so they are negotiated at a common time, preceded by a period of national discussion of noninflationary wage and price guidelines. See, for example, Pollin (1998b, 10–11; 1998a), Baker et al. (2004).

26. Discussions of global finance are more nuanced. Although deregulation is generally praised, more blemishes are acknowledged. Concerns are sometimes raised about the potentially destabilizing effects of short-term cross-border movements of financial capital. Heterodox economists tend to be even more skeptical of the merits of unregulated international capital markets.

27. Shoch reports that the Heritage Foundation commissioned more than two dozen papers attacking industrial policy. The Federal Reserve Bank of Kansas City sponsored an influential conference that was also critical of industrial policy. He adds, "The most damaging of the economists' attacks on Democratic industrial policy thinking came from within the ranks of the liberal Brookings Institution. While the Brookings analysts, many of whom had been long-time Democratic advisors, had been moving steadily toward fiscal conservatism since the stagflation of the 1970s, they became almost apoplectic on the issue of industrial policy, turning the Institution, in *Fortune's* words, into a 'hotbed of anti-industrial policy work'" (Shoch 1994, 181).

REINTRODUCING AGGREGATE SUPPLY AND AGGREGATE DEMAND

INTRODUCTION: TWO CURVES IN SEARCH OF A THEORY

[The aggregate supply (AS) and aggregate demand (AD) model] as currently presented is seriously flawed. First, it does not fulfill the minimum requirement of a model: logical consistency. Its component parts are derived from models that reflect different, and inconsistent, models of the economy. Second, the appropriate disequilibrium adjustment story with which it is consistent—one in which short-run aggregate adjustment occurs because of price flexibility—is consistent neither with observed reality nor with the disequilibrium adjustment story that most macroeconomists accept. . . .

The result is a model of the worst type—a model that obscures, rather than clarifies, that invites students to make the incorrect logical jump that AS/AD analysis is similar to partial equilibrium supply demand analysis, and that discourages thinking deeply about the inner workings of the model.

—David Colander (1995, 170)

The history of the AS-AD model is interesting. The framework's widespread adoption in the late 1970s and early 1980s coincided with a "laissez-faire" counterattack in politics and in economic theory on Keynesian economics and the latter's support for government intervention in the economy to maintain full employment. The AS-AD model also grew out of dissatisfaction with the treatment of the "supply side of the economy" in Keynesian theory and a need to develop better tools to understand the causes and dynamics of inflation. Standard uses of the AS-AD framework often nullify many of the implications of Keynesian economics by subtly revising the rationale for Keynesian macro policies and by forcing economic analysis into an equilibrium framework.

The aggregate supply and aggregate demand curves look familiar, recalling the old workhorse of micro theory: supply and demand. This familiarity invites acceptance. The rationales for the slopes of the curves and their equilibrium resolution, however, are very different from the micro case. What is common across many textbooks is an attempt to migrate students' acceptance and comfort in using supply and demand models at the firm level to the macro level.

In this way the AS-AD framework tends to institutionalize the fallacy of composition.[1] A model intuitively helpful for analyzing one market has been extended to all markets in a way that can obscure the difference between a single market and a system of markets. It is almost as if there were two curves (supply and demand) and an *equilibrium* notion in search of a theory that

Figure 12.1 **Aggregate Supply and Aggregate Demand**

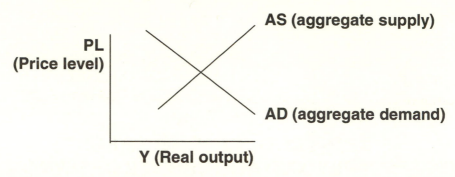

would allow us to talk about macroeconomics as if it were microeconomics. The problem is that macroeconomics is not microeconomics in the aggregate. To the extent that the AS-AD framework encourages such thinking, it misleads readers.

The AS-AD framework is introduced very early in most standard macro principles texts. It often serves as an organizing framework well before its derivation can be fully explained. This encourages a habit of fuzzy thinking about aggregate supply and aggregate demand that we want to challenge in this chapter. We have delayed discussing the AS-AD framework until now because it is necessary to understand the logic behind the Keynesian Cross model of aggregate demand and the manner in which monetary phenomena affect the economy to understand and critique the derivation of the AS-AD model. Given our work in the last three chapters, we are now prepared to assess the AS-AD framework.

Heterodox economists have taken two different tacks in critiquing the AS-AD framework. One group of economists has sought to work within the AS-AD model. They have tried to derive alternative slopes and properties for the AS and AD curves. We will explore these efforts in this chapter. These critiques tend to flatten the AS curve, steepen the AD curve, emphasize the instability of both curves, and undermine laissez-faire macro policy recommendations. Other heterodox economists have sought to develop alternative frameworks to the AS-AD model for studying the integrated logic of the economy as a whole. We will look at these efforts in chapter 13. Both heterodox approaches are very critical of the usual discussion of the AS-AD framework found in most textbooks.

The structure of the remaining parts of this chapter is as follows. The next section reviews the standard presentation of the AS-AD framework in macro textbooks. This is followed by several sections that critique the framework from a heterodox perspective and explore the policy implications of heterodox concerns. The last section of the chapter introduces the themes of chapter 13. Since both chapters 12 and 13 discuss heterodox critiques of the AS-AD framework, we have postponed until chapter 13 our usual concluding threads.

REVIEW OF STANDARD TEXTBOOK TREATMENTS OF AS-AD

Before exploring heterodox economists' objections to standard deployments of the AS-AD framework, we will quickly review the main features of the AS-AD model to make sure we are all on the same page. The first thing to remember is that the AS-AD graph has the *price level* (rather than the price of any particular good) on its vertical axis. Although most texts formally warn students about the novelty of this construction, the warnings are minimally elaborated and probably poorly understood. The decision to hinge the behavior of key variables in the economy on their response

Figure 12.2   **The Impact of a Decline in the Price Level on GDP in the Keynesian Cross Framework**

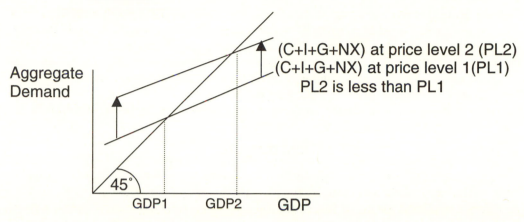

to changes in the price level is an odd one. The choice tends to undermine students' ability to intuitively grasp what is being argued about the behavior of the economy. It also deflects economic analysis from other potentially illuminating topics.

Derivation of the Aggregate Demand Curve

You might recall that the AD curve is almost always drawn with a downward slope. The message conveyed is that the "quantity of demand" in the economy increases (all other things equal) when the price level falls.[2] Most standard texts derive the AD curve by asking what would happen to the level of equilibrium income (Y) determined in the Keynesian Cross diagram if the price level fell.[3]

Three main reasons are usually given for expecting that national income (Y) (as determined by the intersection of the C+I+G+NX line and the 45-degree line) would increase as the price level fell: (1) the *interest rate effect*,[4] (2) the *wealth effect*,[5] and (3) the *net export effect*.[6] (Notes 4–6 review these arguments. We will return to them later in the chapter.)[7]

Derivation of the Aggregate Supply Curve

Although almost all texts share a common explanation for the slope of the AD curve in the AS-AD graph, they differ in rationales for the shape of the AS curve. Most texts derive two aggregate supply curves, distinguishing between the short- and long-run AS curves. A few texts distinguish three separate regions of a single AS curve (flat, rising, and vertical). We will briefly review the short run/long run dichotomy and a bit later comment on the three-region model.

Long-Run AS Curves

Virtually all standard texts assert a vertical aggregate supply curve "in the long run." That is, they argue that the level of output in the economy is determined by factors unaffected by the level of aggregate demand or the inflation rate; among these factors are the size of the labor force and the stock of capital.[8] Most texts also assert that this level of output guarantees full employment. As we shall see, this aspect of the AS-AD framework tends to "prove," by assumption, that markets automatically guarantee full employment.

Short-Run AS Curves

Although almost all neoclassical textbooks agree on the character of the long-run AS curve, they disagree on the shape and stability of the short-run AS curve. The most common version of the short-run AS curve is an upward-sloping curve. The most popular rationale for this shape is that input prices (like money wages) tend to be stickier than output prices (like the cost of shirts). This stickiness reflects phenomena like yearlong wage agreements and multiyear rental agreements. Thus, in the short run (when existing contracts are in force), inflationary pressures might cause higher prices in output markets without proportionally increasing input costs, thereby increasing profits and encouraging higher levels of output. A second theory, called "misperceptions theory," suggests that inflation increases supply by misleading producers into thinking that the relative price for their product has increased.

The short-run textbook AS curve is unstable. When existing input contracts expire, input suppliers (such as workers or landlords) bargain for payments that include adjustments for higher price levels. The initial ability of higher price levels to increase output thus disappears. The assumptions responsible for the upward slope of the short-run AS curve therefore automatically imply a shifting short-run and vertical long-run AS curve. The same conclusion holds for "misperception theories" of the short-run AS curve. When producers realize the real price for their good has not changed they return to pre-inflation levels of output.

Using the AS-AD Framework

Most standard texts argue that the short-run AS curve shifts downward when the economy is operating at less than full capacity (indicated by the vertical long-run AS curve). The presence of unemployed workers or unsold goods is said to cause both workers and firms to offer their products at lower prices. The resulting *decline in the price level* stimulates aggregate demand (as represented by the downward-sloping AD curve) and moves the economy to full employment.

For example, imagine an economy operating at full employment as represented by point A in Figure 12.3. Assume that a fall in business confidence lowers investment spending and shifts back the AD curve to AD_2, moving the economy from point A to point B. Textbook theory assumes that in the long run the AS curve will shift downward, restoring full employment at point C.

Exactly the reverse happens if the intersection of the short-run AS and AD curves temporarily exceeds the full-employment level of income (Yf) (represented by the long-run AS curve). Workers and firms respond to excess demand by raising their prices, which increases the price level and thus moves the short-run AS curve up the AD curve.

Many proponents of this way of thinking about the short-run AS curve portray the debate between "the New Keynesians" and "the new classicals" as a debate over how fast the price level adjusts to changing economic conditions. The New Keynesian economists are portrayed as believers in sticky prices and long adjustment periods and the new classical economists are portrayed as believers in flexible prices and rapid adjustments.

Returning to the scenario depicted in Figure 12.3, the New Keynesian challenge to general equilibrium (GE) theory is claimed to involve the assumption of sluggish price adjustments and a slow-moving AS curve. Figure 12.4 depicts the economy's temporary disequilibrium at point B' due to sticky prices.

One of the appeals of the AS-AD framework is its alleged ability to quickly illuminate the impact of changes in aggregate demand or changes in input costs on the economy's price and output levels. Any factor that might affect the level of aggregate demand in the economy (e.g., a fall in investor confidence, a change in government spending or taxes, an increase in the money

Figure 12.3   **Equilibrium Adjustments of Aggregate Supply and Aggregate Demand**

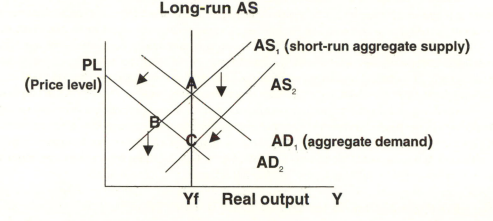

Figure 12.4   **New Keynesian Models of Aggregate Supply and Aggregate Demand**

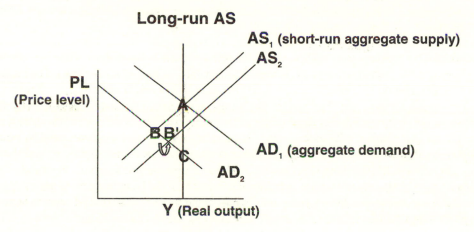

supply, etc.) can be interpreted as shifting the AD line. Any factor that might affect the costs of production (such as an OPEC price hike or an increase in environmental protection requirements) can be interpreted as shifting the AS curve. The initial effects of the changes can be modeled by the new AS-AD intersection, with the long-run impacts modeled by the short-run AS curve's adjustment to output levels above or below Yf.

OVERVIEW OF HETERODOX CRITIQUES OF
THE AS-AD FRAMEWORK

With the flick of a pen and *the addition of a vertical long-run AS curve,* the AS-AD framework scratches out much of Keynesian economics and its concern about serious economic downturns. From a heterodox perspective, this is an astounding and appalling maneuver. All aforementioned heterodox-Keynesian concerns about the impact of expectations, animal spirits, liquidity demand, imperfect information, dynamic feedback, etc. have been obliterated without even a word of discussion. In the long run, there is automatic full employment. To the extent that we have short-run problems, they are due to sticky nominal wages and prices. The world of insufficient aggregate demand is gone. The rhetoric remains, but declines in aggregate demand (due, for example, to collapses in business and consumer confidence or lenders' willingness to extend credit) do not cause economic contractions or unemployment. These macro problems result from the failure of wages and prices to fall together and create deflation when demand falls. The original problems identified by Keynesian economics on the demand side of the economy have not been solved; they have been obscured.

The textbook AS-AD framework also abstracts from the drama of real-life economies on the supply side. The AS-AD framework gives too little attention to the macroeconomic implications of the emergence of large oligopolistic firms and the distinctive characteristics of labor markets in comparison with inanimate input markets. Both oversights can cause market adjustments to behave differently than predicted by the AS-AD framework.

HETERODOX CRITIQUES OF TEXTBOOK AD CURVES

Introduction

If you look closely at the AS-AD framework, a surprising feature emerges. The key macro-adjusting thermostat in the economy that guarantees full employment is the price level! Declines in economic activity are presumed to cause deflation (falling price levels), which reinvigorates the economy. This salutary view of deflation is reflected in the AS-AD framework by the downward slope of the AD curve. Heterodox economists reject this view of deflation, its image of the AD curve, and its picture of automatic economic recovery for several reasons.[9]

First of all, the price level in the U.S. economy has not fallen since the 1950s, despite several serious economic contractions. During the 1974–1975 and 1981–1982 recessions, for example, unemployment reached 9.2 percent and 10.8 percent, respectively. The price level did not fall (although inflation slowed) and deflation did not engineer the recovery.

Most importantly, deflation lacks automatic restorative properties. Even if it occurred (which it has not for a half a century) it could not renew the economy if the underlying problems of aggregate demand were unresolved. For example, the price level did fall during the Great Depression by 20 to 25 percent, but the U.S. economy averaged more than 17 percent unemployment during the 1930s!

Recall that proponents of the AS-AD framework offered three major reasons for why aggregate demand increased as the price level fell (or, graphically, why the AD curve had a downward slope): the "interest rate effect," the "wealth effect," and the "trade" or "net export effect." All three can fail during a serious recession or depression. Let us look at why.

Interest Rate Effects

Recall that the "interest rate effect" relies on falling price levels to cause the real money supply to increase, interest rates to fall, and spending for some items, like automobiles and business investment, to increase. Several factors might block this road to economic recovery.

1. Serious economic downturns and falling prices may increase people's desire to be "liquid" and cause lenders to ask for higher (rather than lower) interest payments to protect them from increased perceptions of risk.
2. Banks and other lenders may have relatively fixed expectations about long-term (e.g.,

fifteen- to thirty-year) interest rates. They may be unwilling to offer loans at rates much below these expectations, regardless of the current availability of loanable funds. Rather than lowering interest rates, deflation may simply lead banks to hold excess reserves (Keynes's liquidity trap).[10]

3. Finally, even if interest rates fell, if firms and households were pessimistic about the economy's future (a reasonable expectation during a depression) low interest rates might not induce them to borrow money to build new factories or expand consumption.[11]

Wealth Effects

Recall that the "wealth effect" implies that as prices fall, households holding government bonds become richer (because the purchasing power of their savings has increased). This extra wealth is claimed to spur consumption. By almost all accounts the "wealth effect" is very small and completely unable to stabilize a collapsing economy. Even using optimistic assumptions about people's tendency to consume out of wealth, James Tobin (winner of the Nobel Prize in Economics in 1981) found that a 10 percent fall in prices would increase consumption by only 0.06 percent of GNP (McCormick and Rives 1998, 12).

Most importantly, serious deflations would probably be a cure worse than the disease for most modern economies. Any large-scale drop in the price level would increase the real debt burden of many households and corporations, raising the possibility of widespread bankruptcies and serious disruptions in the economy. Although the fall in money wages would be offset by a fall in money prices, preexisting debts would become more difficult to pay off. Although many creditors would receive offsetting windfalls, the macroeconomic effect would likely be highly destructive.[12] As Nobel Prize winner Joseph Stiglitz and coauthor Bruce Greenwald noted in 1993,

> The enormous attention that the real balance effect has received over the years hardly speaks well for the [economics] profession. Quantitatively, it is surely an nth order effect; one calculation put it that, even at the fastest rate at which prices fell in the Great Depression, it would take more than two centuries to restore the economy to full employment. (Greenwald and Stiglitz 1993, 36)

Trade and Other Effects

Several factors weaken the ability of deflation to increase aggregate demand by increasing net exports. The first is the possibility of synchronized global recessions where each country's deflation is matched by those of its trading partners. The second is the tendency for exchange rate adjustments to offset price level changes.

A few other reasons have been offered for suspecting that falling price levels could increase aggregate demand. The "inter-temporal effect," for example, suggests that households might anticipate prices rebounding in the future and shift some planned purchases to the present to take advantage of temporarily depressed prices. Although this behavior could modestly increase aggregate demand, its impact *depends on people's expectations.* It is precisely this contingency that Keynes emphasized. If, for example, falling current prices caused people to anticipate further declines, households might postpone the purchase of expensive consumer goods, such as automobiles.[13] The key conclusion of heterodox economics is that there is *no automatic* assurance that falling prices can increase aggregate demand. Outcomes are contingent and dependent on expectations. Sometimes the economy can "automatically" recover from demand shocks; sometimes it

Figure 12.5 **Hypothetical AS-AD Model of the Great Depression**

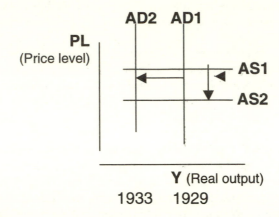

cannot. As illustrated by the Keynesian Cross model, the economy can be mired in a demand crisis. This contingency is lost in the AS-AD framework.

Graphing Heterodox AD Curves

If one wishes to use a graph with the price level on the vertical axis and real output on the horizontal axis (as in the AS-AD framework) to analyze macro conditions *during serious downturns,* heterodox theory suggests it is probably best to assume *vertical aggregate demand lines.* This assumption implies that the economy's return to full employment after a fall in aggregate demand is dependent on a shift of the AD curve rather than a movement along it. Whether the AD curve shifts out when prices fall depends on people's expectations. The AD curve may shift out; it may shift back; it may remain the same. This contrasts with the textbook approach that *assumes* automatic adjustment and guaranteed increases in demand due to deflation. The empirical evidence about the historical relationship between the price level and aggregate demand seems ambiguous at best, and is probably hostile to the claim that deflation is expansionary.[14]

Figure 12.5 illustrates one possible rendition of the economic collapse in the Great Depression. (We will discuss the unorthodox treatment of the AS curve in that graph in the next section.)

KEYNESIAN AND OTHER HETERODOX CRITIQUES OF TEXTBOOK AS CURVES

Introduction

In this chapter we concentrate on critiques of the AS curve that remain within the AS-AD framework. In the next chapter we look at critiques that replace the AS-AD model of supply with a different framework.

The Implicit Supply Curve of the Keynesian Cross

Keynesian economics was born during the Great Depression. It has focused the bulk of its attention on understanding the behavior of economies during economic downturns. Although charac-

Figure 12.6 Increasing Government Spending in the Keynesian Cross

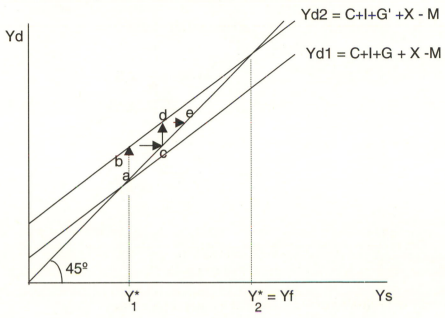

teristics of the supply side of the economy, such as the economy's available labor force, capital stock, resource base, and technological structure, determine its productive potential and output at full employment, Keynesian theory asserts that the demand side of the economy can determine the actual level of output and employment in economies operating at less than full capacity.

In other words, during periods of insufficient aggregate demand, the supply side of the economy can be a passive respondent to the demand side of the economy. This is the picture of the supply curve that is implicit in the Keynesian Cross and the multiplier concept. When demand increases, supply automatically increases, which in turn increases demand and then supply again, in diminishing increments. The logic of this process is illustrated in Figure 12.6. It depicts the impact of an increase in government spending on an economy producing less than its full-employment level of output.

The increase in government spending shifts up the Yd curve; supply responds horizontally (the movement from point b to point c); the higher level of output generates a higher level of income and a second increase in aggregate demand (the movement from point c to point d); supply responds with an increase in output from point d to point e, etc. What does this story imply about the shape of the aggregate supply curve (AS) in a graph with the price level and real income on the vertical and horizontal axes? In the simplest case, this story implies a flat supply curve until output reaches full employment, at which time the supply curve becomes vertical.[15]

In Figure 12.7 increases in aggregate demand from AD1 to AD2 cause increases in output. Once the economy reaches full-employment output (Yf), however, increases in demand only cause inflation. It is more realistic to imagine that labor markets and other markets across the economy "fill up" at different rates. Thus, as the overall level of output approaches full-employment levels, some markets experience inflationary pressures before others. As you get closer and closer to full employment, more and more markets translate increases in demand into increases in prices, rather than increases in output. This analysis implies an up-

Figure 12.7   **AS–AD Implications of the Keynesian Cross**

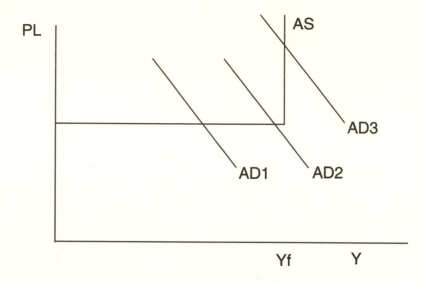

Figure 12.8   **Refined AS-AD Implications of the Keynesian Cross**

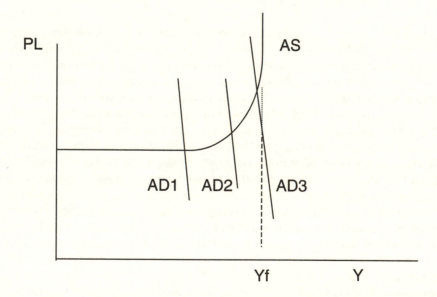

ward-sloping aggregate supply curve near full employment, like the AS curve depicted in Figure 12.8.

In a tilt toward traditional Keynesian theory, some neoclassical textbooks include a "three-region" AS curve similar to the one in Figure 12.8. They call the flat region the Keynesian region. They term the upward-sloping portion the intermediate region and name the vertical portion the classical region. There is almost no discussion, however, of why the economy might get stuck in the first two regions. The relationship between the three-regions approach and the short-run/long-run AS curve distinction is also not fully specified. The profound difference between the disequilibrium ideas underlying the combination curve and the equilibrium ideas underlying the rest of the textbook (including the short-run/long-run model) are not acknowledged.

It is easy for students to assume that the intermediate region of the combination curve mimics the transitory behavior of the short-run AS curve built around price stickiness (rather than insufficient aggregate demand). This interpretation continues the textbooks' habit of obscuring Keynesian ideas within a general equilibrium framework. Heterodox economists reject this approach and highlight the potentially distinctive disequilibrium aspects of the three-region model.

The full "theory of supply" in Keynesian and heterodox economics is more complicated than the reasoning behind Figure 12.8 that derives from the Keynesian Cross. Heterodox analyses of supply build on heterodox ideas about the nature of the firm, the nature of competition between firms, and the nature of decision making within firms. These ideas, in turn, reflect familiar heterodox challenges to the textbooks' assumptions of *homo economicus,* perfect information, and perfect competition.

The discussion below focuses on the implications of the emergence of the giant corporation and the uniqueness of the labor market for the determination of production levels and output prices in key areas of the economy. It concludes that there is good reason for expecting that wages and prices in parts of the economy will be a lot stickier than usually suggested by the textbooks' AS-AD model.

The Implications of the Large Corporation

Introduction

The emergence of mass production technologies and the large corporation at the end of the nineteenth century significantly changed the nature of the firm and the behavior of supply in many areas of the economy.[16] Recognizing this, many heterodox economists have found it helpful to divide the economy into two sectors: the "planning sector," organized by these large firms, and the market sector," populated by smaller firms. The planning sector involves about 1,000 firms, each with more than 10,000 employees, collectively employing about one-quarter of the workforce. The firms own a large share of the nation's business assets and have relatively lengthy planning horizons.[17] The cost of an extra unit of production (i.e., the marginal costs of production) are generally flat or declining as output increases. The relative share of national employment provided by these firms seems to be declining (Bowles, Edwards, and Roosevelt 2005, 280–81). The market sector is composed of about 5.5 million firms with employees and 18 million business establishments without employees, generally producing in relatively competitive markets.[18]

Exercise of Power

The massive size of major corporations often endows them with significant market and sociopolitical power. Many planning-sector firms have huge marketing departments designed to influence consumer behavior.[19] The firms actively lobby the executive and legislative branches of government for favorable policies and have a revolving door relationship with government bureaucracies.[20] The companies use their large purchasing power to impose favorable contractual arrangements on smaller firms in input markets (as illustrated by requirements of just-in-time inventory services that can shift the burden of fluctuating levels of aggregate demand from planning- to market-sector firms).

Oligopolistic Market Structure

The relatively small number of firms in planning-sector markets undermines the assumptions of perfect competition. Unlike small competitive firms (like family farms) who "take" the price for their goods from the market and decide how much to produce, oligopoly firms[21] decide on how much to produce and what to charge. They also have to consider the effect of their actions on the small number of rivals (and an ambiguous number of potential rivals) with whom they share the market. The concentrated structure of oligopoly industries creates the potential for higher-than-average profits. It also creates the need to design business strategies with a view toward the reactions of rival firms and the joint result likely to emerge from pursuing each strategy.

These features tend to reduce price competition in favor of other forms of competition, such as product differentiation.[22] They also encourage firms to respond to changes in demand with changes in output rather than changes in price, quite different from the behavior of market-sector firms and the implications of much of textbook macroeconomic theory.

Tendency for "Managerial Firms" with Bureaucratic Decision Making

"Managerial firms" are firms effectively governed by management rather than shareholders, partially due to the dispersed nature of stock holdings in large firms. Although the increasing role of institutional investors, such as mutual funds, has reduced the degree of management independence in the last few decades, it remains an important attribute of the planning sector. It implies a modest change in corporate objectives. Although corporate managers still have to provide an "acceptable" rate of profit for stockholders, they need not attempt to maximize profits or dividends. They are able to pursue business strategies that maximize managerial well-being. Typically, this appears to involve maximizing the size of the firm, as managerial prestige, salary, and economic security seem to be correlated with firm size.[23] The enormous scale of planning-sector firms also creates a bias for bureaucratic forms of decision making. This encourages the use of "rules of thumb" rather than optimizing models to make many business decisions (such as pricing decisions).

Commitment to Planning

As many economists have noted, the firm is an alternative to the market. Inside the firm, economic activity is coordinated by administrative decisions rather than market prices. These decisions reflect management's strategies for dealing with an uncertain world and the vagaries of human nature. The strategies adopted for tasks like output pricing and wage setting are frequently shaped by the desire to cultivate long-term relationships with the firm's customers and employees. The decisions also reflect the bureaucratic (i.e., rule governed—routinized) character of decision making within large organizations.

Price Stickiness

If we put the characteristics of large firms together, several important conclusions follow for macroeconomics. The starting point is that prices in the planning sector are "administered," that is, set by bureaucratic decision rather than short-term market forces. These decisions are conditioned by the nature of large-scale production and the logic of oligopolistic competition (especially in terms of the desire of firms to cultivate long-term relationships with customers).[24]

The complexity of oligopolistic competition makes it difficult to deduce simple behavioral rules for oligopoly firms. The form taken by and outcome of competition are quite sensitive to industry characteristics and the "strategic" decisions made by firms. Despite the diversity and contingency of oligopolistic markets, some generalizations about firms' behavior in the current institutional environment are possible. There are strong empirical evidence and good theoretical reasons for concluding that planning-sector firms are slower to change output prices when demand changes than implied by most standard macro textbooks.[25] One important reason for sticky output prices and relatively flat AS curves is that many firms use "cost-plus" or "mark-up" pricing.[26] The companies' relatively flat marginal costs of production (or average costs at an expected capacity rate) are "marked up" by a relatively stable multiplier.

There are many reasons why firms might adopt a mark-up or cost-plus rule for pricing decisions, rather than rely on more market-oriented responses that would lower prices in slack markets and raise them in tighter markets.[27] One interesting hypothesis, backed by survey data, suggests that firms have informal understandings ("implicit contracts") with long-term customers that permit them to raise prices when costs increase but not when markets are tight.[28]

What about downward price changes? Why don't firms in oligopoly markets respond to declines in demand with lower prices? Sometimes, of course, they do cut prices. Consumers' experience in markets with highly publicized price wars, like air travel, misleadingly suggests that most markets have flexible prices. In fact, they do not. Firms seem hesitant to quickly cut prices when demand falls for several reasons. The most important impediment is probably fear of mutually destructive price wars. This would be especially relevant in industries where firms maintain excess capacity.[29] Other deterrents to price cuts include firms' expectation that discounting would probably not increase sales significantly (due to brand loyalties) and fears that price cuts will tarnish the perceived quality of their product.[30]

The bottom line is that competition in oligopoly markets often takes non-price forms, which in the AS-AD framework implies a relatively flat AS curve. Thus contractions in demand do not necessarily lead to rapid price level declines that reinvigorate aggregate demand as implied in mainstream textbooks.

We turn next to heterodox analyses of the labor market, which provide additional reasons for expecting supply-side behavior at odds with the automatic full-employment picture of the AS-AD framework.

The Labor Market

Introduction

Heterodox economics explains why many firms, especially planning-sector firms, follow labor policies that tend to insulate their own wage structure from the implications of excess supply or excess demand in external labor markets. As a result unemployed workers may not be able to find work, even if they are willing to accept wages below the going rate for their occupation. Heterodox analysis of labor markets also helps explain why there can be conflicts of interest and political debates over what is the ideal unemployment rate.

Methodological Roots of Heterodox Labor Market Analysis

Heterodox economists have a much more complicated image of human beings than that suggested by rational, isolated economic man and the engineering models of production common in macro textbooks. Heterodox analyses give more attention to the "social aspect" of the labor process, in terms of both its cooperative and its conflictual dimensions, than the largely inanimate, atomistic metaphors and analysis of orthodox economics.

Cooperative Dimensions

While there are many "note but ignore" qualifiers and ad hoc appendages scattered throughout standard macro textbooks (especially in "New Keynesian" models), their take-away message treats the labor market analogously to other inanimate input markets. The productivity of labor is taken as a given, much like the energy content of a pound of coal (and is the basis of the demand curve for labor). The willingness of individuals to work a certain number of hours at a certain intensity is also taken as given (and is the basis for the supply curve of labor). The intersection of these supply and demand curves determines the long-run equilibrium wage and precludes unemployment.

Heterodox theory asserts the qualitative distinctiveness of labor as an economic category, rejecting its "commodified" treatment in standard theory. How hard people work, how careful they are about the quality of their work, how innovative they are, and so on are open issues, resolved daily. Firms buy "labor power" (essentially labor time) in the labor market. They have to transform that productive potential into real output in the workplace. The psychology and sociology of this transformation influences employment and wage policies and can shift market outcomes away from the dictates of the simple supply-and-demand models underlying most introductory macro texts.

Firms need to mobilize the voluntary cooperation of workers and to do so often requires them to think about motivation in more complicated ways than suggested by *homo economicus*. In response, firms set up wage scales that diverge from the simple rules of supply and demand. In contrast to the gasoline market, for example, the price paid for labor (wages) can affect the value of labor (workers' output). High wages can increase productivity rather than simply reflect it. Perceptions of fairness (or unfairness) can also affect productivity.

If the price of tomatoes falls relative to carrots, consumers may temporarily substitute tomatoes for carrots in their salads. If prices reverse, consumers may shift back to carrots without concern for their earlier "disloyalty." Labor markets are more linked in time. Labor market policies today may affect labor productivity in the future. Hirings, firings, pay cuts, pay raises, and so on often need to be integrated across time in a long-term management strategy. What constitutes the best strategy is much less obvious than how many extra tomatoes another dose of fertilizer might produce. Current wages may be in "disequilibrium" vis-à-vis short-term labor market conditions but in line with management's long-term assessment of profit maximization.

The collective or team nature of work often makes it difficult to assign marginal productivities (i.e., individual contributions) to specific people. Wage rates may therefore reflect group productivities and concerns about the impact of the structure as well as the level of wages on group productivity. The mixing of individual and group productivities makes the task of changing wages especially tricky.

A number of other factors make it difficult to measure workers' individual (and even collective) output. How much mentoring and on-the-job training (called "human capital formation" in economic theory) went on within a firm; how much cultivation of client good will; and how much brainstorming for future innovations are difficult to measure. Designing wage structures to facilitate these outcomes is challenging. These problems add to the indeterminacies of the labor market.

Many conclusions follow from these observations that are at odds with simple supply-and-demand theory. For example, employers may not hire workers outside the plant gates who are willing to work for less than those already employed because of a fear that doing so could damage company morale. Firms may be reluctant to offer higher (or lower) wages for some job slots, despite shortages (or surpluses) of workers to fill these positions. This reluctance may reflect a hesitancy to overturn workers' perceptions of fairness in relative wages and company traditions about the relative compensation of different positions. As such, firms' pay scales may be partially insulated from the pressures of supply and demand and may differ across companies.

Within a single firm there may be more than one wage profile that could conceivably maximize profits. The choice of which labor policy to pursue may be determined by the sociology of the firm rather than the logic of the market. For example, it may be relatively common for firms to face a choice between low wage/low productivity bundles of labor policies and high wage/high productivity bundles. Public policy may be able to play an important role in encouraging firms to choose the "high-road" strategy.

What are the macroeconomic implications of these complexities? One key conclusion is that many wages in planning-sector firms are "administered," much like output prices. They are the product of corporate strategies and not merely downloaded from the market. Of course, firms' wage and employment policies are influenced by changes in external market conditions. But the impact of external events is mediated by firms' customs, long-term implicit contracts between employers and employees, and other labor-market institutions.[31]

For a variety of reasons these factors can lead to sticky wages, especially in downward directions. What are the implications of sticky wages for the AS-AD curves? Perhaps the most important implication is that a fall in aggregate demand may lead to a fall in output and a fall in employment rather than a fall in wages. Workers willing to accept the existing market wage for their occupation (or even a lower wage) may not be able to find a job (the classic definition of unemployment).

At first this may seem counterintuitive. Why would firms interested in maintaining company morale lay off workers rather than impose wage cuts? The answer seems to partially lie in historically given institutional arrangements and the culture of planning-sector firms. To some extent, labor policies and worker loyalty in planning-sector firms have traditionally been built around the seniority system, under which both workers and firms make a long-term commitment to each other. Some of the costs of business cycles are absorbed by firms, who, for example, maintain a larger payroll than would be dictated by pure short-run profit calculations. Other costs of business cycle fluctuations are pushed onto the shoulders of input suppliers (who are more likely to be non-planning-sector firms) and the "last hired." After a probationary period, the latter can hope to become part of the core workforce and be relatively insulated from the vicissitudes of the business cycle. Arthur Okun, chair of the Council of Economic Advisers under President Johnson, developed the concepts of "implicit contracts" and "implicit handshakes" to characterize the long-term understanding between workers and employees. This "understanding" is much weaker in the market than the planning sector. Thus the cost of economic contractions tends to be borne disproportionately by market-sector workers.

Conflictual Dimensions

While highlighting the incentives for firms to adopt management strategies that maintain worker morale, many heterodox economists perceive the workplace as a "contested," as well as cooperative, terrain. Workers and employers battle over the pace and conditions of work as well as over wages and benefits. These battles are felt by some heterodox economists (especially radical economists and Marxist economists) to be inherent in capitalism. This is because the ownership of firms by nonworkers transforms labor into a commodity that is purchased by firms and "managed" by them. This arrangement disenfranchises most workers from democratic participation in the organization of work and the distribution of company profits.[32]

Many heterodox economists argue that, although subsiding in periods of relative cooperation and muted by the logic of implicit contracts, battles between employers and employees are always simmering. This aspect of labor markets (conflict) gets suppressed in textbook analyses by the image of harmonious exchange.

In heterodox accounts, firms threaten to go to Mexico (and sometimes do) in search of cheap labor. Workers collectively go on strike or individually jump ship for a better job. Employee well-being is treated by the managers and owners of firms as a "means," not an end in itself. When "shareholder value" and employee well-being conflict, heterodox and standard economic theory expect that managers will look after shareholders. The macroeconomic implications of this potential conflict of interest are explored in heterodox theory.

Unlike neoclassical theory's engineering model of the determination of wages and profits (which finds wages equal to the marginal product of labor and the rate of return on capital equal to the marginal product of capital), the "conflictual model" of capital/labor relations asserts that there is a range of indeterminacy in how firms' income will be divided between workers, managers, stockholders, creditors, and other potential uses, such as reinvestment to expand firms' capital stock. The key aspect of this perspective for our current discussion is the claim that unemployment levels affect the relative bargaining power of labor and capital and thereby influence the distribution of income. In particular, full employment tilts power toward labor, raises wages, increases labor's share of national income, and promotes the trade-offs labor favors in economic priorities. Unemployment shifts power toward employers and the owners of capital.[33] (You may recall that we first discussed the implications of this relationship in chapter 10 in our analysis of potential conflicts of interest over monetary policy and what the Fed's target unemployment rate should be.)

How this plays out in the economy is complicated. The trick is to figure out the macroeconomic implications of microeconomic intuitions. The basic microeconomic intuition behind the heterodox position is easy to illustrate. When there is full employment, workers can credibly threaten to "go across the street" and search for better offers. The logic of "implicit contracts" suggests that planning-sector workers restrain some (though not all) of their labor demands during boom periods in exchange for protection during downturns. The full pressure of tight labor markets, however, asserts itself in the market sector.

If you have ever looked for a job, you probably have an intuitive sense that your bargaining position with an employer is much weaker if there are four hundred rather than four other people who would like the same job. In a booming economy you may be offered a higher wage and more attractive working conditions. The company will be grateful to have you join it. In a slack economy, gratitude flows from the applicant to the employer.

The key question is what happens next. If firms are forced to offer workers better working conditions and higher wages in tight labor markets, do they simply pass on associated cost increases as higher prices? Do higher wages spur productivity and finance themselves? Do the costs of higher wages and better working conditions reduce corporate profits and come out of stockholder dividends, "retained earnings" (funds the firm would have used to expand its capital stock), or the salaries of upper management? Or, perhaps, in an indirect sense, do higher payments to labor somehow reduce the share of national income going to creditors (financial capital)?

And one final complicating question: is there a difference between the short- and long-run response of economic agents to the higher wages and better working conditions that accompany a booming economy? For example, if firms pass on wage increases as price increases, what happens next? Do workers demand new wage increases to compensate them for price increases; and if so, are these new costs passed on? Do firms cut back their level of investment in new equipment beyond the amount shifted to wages due to lower profit incentives (thereby causing a fall in aggregate demand and an eventual decline in employment and wages)? If firms reduce the payment of dividends to stockholders in order to pay for higher wages and better working conditions, do savers stop funneling money through the stock market to firms for new investment (thereby causing a fall in aggregate demand and an eventual decline in employment and wages)?

Different heterodox theorists lean in different directions,[34] but a reasonably good picture of heterodox thinking can be suggested by assuming that a little of all of these things happen: (1) productivity gains tend to finance part of the increase in labor costs; (2) there is a shift in relative income shares toward workers from the owners of firms, the owners of financial capital, and upper management; (3) there is a shift in the economy's trade-off between "goods today" and "goods tomorrow" (which refers to the extra output made possible by the accumulation of capital); (4) there is a shift in the "bundle of goods" workers receive from the economy from cheaper consumer goods to higher-quality work lives;[35] (5) there is a fall in investment, a reduced demand for workers, and a decline in wages from their peak levels. The balance between these outcomes depends on many phenomena, differs across historical periods, and varies among heterodox paradigms.

What does this conclusion imply about the shape of the AS curve? Recall that heterodox theory frequently posits a cost-plus model of output pricing. This suggests that as markets near genuine full employment and nominal wages begin to rise, so will output prices. This behavior implies an AS curve similar to that illustrated by Figure 12.8.

GAPS AND OVERLAPS BETWEEN TEXTBOOK AND HETERODOX THEORY

As you may have noted, there is some overlap between heterodox thinking and the textbooks' elaboration of New Keynesian explanations for unemployment. There are some additional similarities between heterodox and textbook discussions of pricing pressures near full employment. There are also very important differences.[36] Heterodox economists link wage and price stickiness to a deeper analysis of the implications of uncertainty and the institutional specificities of large firms than is common in standard textbooks. Heterodox economists also link wage-price pressures at full employment to different theories of the labor market from the perfect competition, engineering-oriented theories of most macro textbooks. Most importantly, heterodox economists emphasize that:

1. Even if prices were flexible, pessimistic business and consumer expectations, liquidity crises, and elastic price expectations could create serious problems of insufficient aggregate demand and involuntary unemployment (leaving the economy stuck in the flat portion of a heterodox AS curve).
2. Even during economic expansions, laissez-faire outcomes and/or market results conditioned by textbook estimates of the non-acceleratng inflation rate of unemployment (NAIRU) (~5 percent to 6 percent unemployment) are unlikely to capture the large social benefits of genuine full employment.

POLICY IMPLICATIONS

Introduction

We come now to the key *so what* question. What difference does it make if the AD curve is steeper and the AS curve flatter in heterodox economics than in textbook economics, or if there is more conflict between labor and capital in heterodox economics than in textbook economics? Let us see.

Need for Government Demand Management During Economic Downturns

Unlike the AS-AD curves of most orthodox economic textbooks, the longer flat portion of the AS curve and more vertical AD curve of heterodox economics (see Figure 12.8) imply that serious contractions in aggregate demand can cause sustained periods of unemployment. During recessions and/or depressions heterodox economics justifies a much more activist government role in the economy than standard texts do.

Need for Government Policy During Economic Expansions

Because heterodox economists expect rising wages to squeeze profits if unemployment falls to low levels, they foresee market turbulence and political battles over macro policy when unemployment rates fall below 5 to 6 percent. Orthodox textbooks imply that there is an ideal or optimal macro policy that is in everyone's best interest. Many heterodox economists disagree, finding that there are political battles during economic expansions over how tightly to run the economy. These battles often pit the interests of employers against those of employees, and the interests of creditors against those of debtors.

Because heterodox economists conceive of the benefits of low unemployment rates more broadly than orthodox economists do (recall chapter 8) and prioritize the achievement of more egalitarian economic outcomes, heterodox policy thinking is geared toward achieving lower unemployment rates than most textbook targets. The problem from a heterodox perspective is that alongside redistributing national income and societal bargaining power, low unemployment rates can create inflationary pressures. The challenge for macro policy is to contain these pressures.

Orthodox thinking implies that there is a "natural unemployment rate," such that the appearance of inflation is usually a signal of excess demand in the economy. Although orthodox economists acknowledge that government policies, such as unemployment insurance and the minimum wage, can influence the "natural rate," the imagined laissez-faire rate has a benevolent legitimacy to it. Heterodox economists usually find the conventional NAIRU, or orthodox interpretation of the "natural rate," unacceptable.[37] From a heterodox perspective it condones intolerably high unemployment rates and job loss anxieties in order to discipline labor and contain inflation. What are the practical implications of these differences?

Expanded Policy Tools

Because heterodox economists perceive barriers to genuine full employment in the structure of the economy (which necessitates unemployment to contain inflation and strengthen profits), they tend to favor more generous safety nets for the unemployed and a more rigorous search for new ways to reduce unemployment than many orthodox economists do. Among the activist policies recommended by heterodox economists are:

1. Expansion of unemployment benefits and other safety net programs, such as subsidized health insurance for unemployed workers.
2. Assumption of the role of Employer of Last Resort (ELR) by the government (akin to the Fed's role as lender of last resort).
3. An array of policies that would mute full-employment inflationary pressures without cramping aggregate demand and raising unemployment, including (a) formal "incomes policies," whereby the government creates incentives (such as tax breaks) for wage- and price-setting behaviors at full employment that aren't inflationary; (b) pattern bargaining, which attempts to informally accomplish the same end by having major labor agreements between employers and employees expire at a common time, preceded by a national discussion of what would be reasonable nominal wage increases; and (c) encouragement of worker-owned firms.[38]

Expanded Experimentation and Tolerance of Higher Average Inflation Rates

Heterodox economists are willing to experiment on how far the unemployment rate can be lowered before unacceptable inflationary pressures emerge. They are also more willing to tolerate higher temporary or permanent inflationary costs for lower unemployment rates than most orthodox economists are. From a heterodox perspective, even short periods of high or low unemployment can have enduring effects. In very tight labor markets firms learn how to employ people they would have otherwise ignored. They do not unlearn these lessons. In labor markets with high unemployment, workers' skills and work habits may erode. Potentially employable people may drop out of the labor force and lose their ability to take full advantage of better job opportunities when they emerge. Thus short-term trade-offs can have enduring echoes.[39]

The psychology of wage adjustments also suggests that it may be easier for firms to lower relative wages (when market pressures dictate this) by failing to keep pace with inflation than by cutting nominal wages. One would thus expect lower levels of unemployment with inflation rates of 2 to 4 percent than with inflation rates of 0 percent.

CONCLUSION

The debate between orthodox and heterodox economists over the AS-AD framework is a subset of the larger debate between the paradigms over the merits of general equilibrium models of the economy and a 95 percent laissez-faire-oriented macro policy. The typical deployment of the AS-AD framework in orthodox textbooks tends to minimize the problems of economic downturns and narrow the scope for expansionary macro policy during upswings. Heterodox economists find the logical and empirical rationale for textbook renditions of the AS-AD framework unconvincing and offer alternative variants of the curves.

In this chapter we have focused on heterodox critiques of the AS-AD framework that seek to retain the framework but modify it. In the next chapter we will explore alternative frameworks to the AS-AD model for studying the integrated logic of the economy as a whole. We will defer until the end of chapter 13 our usual discussion of distributional, gender, environmental, and metaphorical threads, as well as our illustrative quotations from heterodox economists.

STUDY QUESTIONS

Review Questions

1. Why do heterodox economists argue that the textbooks' deployment of the AS-AD framework often returns economics to pre-Keynesian contexts of analysis?
2. What economic arguments are offered by heterodox economists for drawing the AD curve steeper than textbook renditions do?
3. What economic arguments are offered by heterodox economists for drawing the AS curve flatter than textbook renditions do?
4. What policy implications flow from the alternative treatment of the AS-AD framework in heterodox economics?
5. Briefly explain what is meant by the following terms or phrases: (a) wealth effect, (b) liquidity trap, (c) oligopolistic competition, (d) non-price competition, (e) implicit contracts, (f) implicit handshakes; (g) efficiency wages, (h) full-employment profit squeeze, (i) the natural rate of unemployment, (j) the disciplinary rate of unemployment, (k) incomes policies.

Discussion Questions

1. What do you think is the strongest evidence in favor of textbook images and analyses of the economy? What do you think is the strongest evidence in favor of heterodox images and analyses of the economy?
2. Why do you think empirical data has been unable to resolve debates over the nature of the AS and AD curves?

NOTES

1. Recall that the fallacy of composition involves mistakenly assuming that what is true for the part is automatically true for the whole. If we are all seated and I stand up, I will see better. It is mistaken, however, to conclude that if everyone stands up, everyone will see better.

2. This depiction of the AD curve is the message that students hear. Some textbooks are careful to define the AD curve as a hypothetical "aggregate equilibrium" (AE) curve, rather than as an "aggregate demand curve." The alternative definition treats the curve as a collection of hypothetical price level–output combinations for which the goods and money market clear. Although more accurate, the definition still invites erroneous assumptions about the dynamic properties of the model. The framework invites misleading analogies to the equilibrium resolution of excess demand or excess supply in micro markets. The general equilibrium case is profoundly different from the partial equilibrium case and frameworks that blend the two mislead students. For an excellent discussion of this issue see Colander and Sephton 1998 in Rao 1998.

3. Recall that the level of equilibrium income is solved graphically in the Keynesian Cross diagram by finding the intersection of the aggregate demand line (i.e., the C+I+G line or C+I+G + NX [Net Export] line) and the 45-degree line. This intersection identifies the level of production at which all of the income generated in production is used to buy back the goods produced in production, without any unintended change in inventories.

4. The interest rate effect: As the price level falls, individuals and firms need to keep less actual money in their pockets or checking accounts to carry out transactions. This leaves more funds available for loans (in the same way a Fed increase of the money supply might make more funds available for loans). The increased supply of loanable funds lowers borrowing costs (the interest rate) and encourages business investment and consumer spending.

5. The wealth effect: The wealth effect is also known as the "real balance effect" and the "Pigou effect"

(named after an important economist who used the idea to "prove" that markets automatically generate full employment). All other things equal, a decline in the price level is said to make people owning government bonds wealthier in real terms. Although this wealth increase is matched by the larger real liability of the U.S. government, taxpayers are thought not to include this liability in private consumption decisions. To the extent that people consume a certain percentage of their wealth or lower their savings rate by reference to their wealth, the increased real value of people's wealth would be expected to increase consumption and the level of aggregate demand in the economy.

6. The net export effect: A fall in the U.S. price level is argued to make U.S. goods more attractive to foreigners. Two reasons are given for this. First, as the dollar price of goods falls they become more attractive to foreign buyers. Second, the fall in interest rates cited above makes foreign purchasers less interested in buying U.S. bonds. This reduces the international demand for dollars and causes the exchange rate for the dollar to fall (meaning it takes less foreign money to buy the same amount of American money). This makes American goods cheaper to foreign consumers.

7. Recently a fourth major rationale has been added to the mix: the *Federal Reserve effect*. This argument implies that the Fed has a target inflation rate. As inflation rises, the Fed reduces the money supply and as it falls, the Fed increases the money supply. The AD curve's slope thus reflects the logic and impact of monetary policy. The treatment of Fed policy as an automatic part of the economy is a major methodological departure for economics. "Endoginizing" Fed policy seems to muddy rather than clarify causal relationships. A medical example can help illustrate the problems with this kind of model.

The Fed has important effects on the economy and body politic, just as dentists do on people's teeth. If we were trying to understand the nature of oral hygiene, gum disease, and tooth decay, we would want to understand how the biochemistry of the mouth worked. If we were interested in treating tooth decay, we would also want to understand how dental fillings worked. But we would not include the dentist's potential intervention as part of how the human body worked. The current integration of very particular images of and theories about the Fed (such as the "Taylor Rule," which relates changes in the Fed's target federal funds rate to current inflation and unemployment rates) into a theory of how the economy works needlessly conflates separate phenomena. Both topics, the logic of macroeconomic dynamics and the behavior of the Fed, can be best studied separately and then recombined. One cannot understand the Fed, for example, without an independent theory of how the economy works.

8. In deriving economic outcomes solely from the "supply side" of the economy, the vertical AS-macro model returns economic theory to the pre-Keynesian days of Says Law, which asserted that supply creates its own demand.

9. For some helpful background reading for instructors see Colander 2001a and 1995; and Rao 1998, especially chapters 1–3.

10. The liquidity trap case implies a "kinked" aggregate demand curve. Aggregate demand increases for a while as the price level falls (represented by the downward-sloping portion of the AD curve), but then remains the same no matter how low the price level falls (represented by the vertical trunk of the AD curve).

11. Fazzari, Ferri, and Greenberg (1998) find little empirical support for the claim that falling prices induce higher investment by lowering interest rates (550–51).

12. Debt deflation would also redistribute income from high-mpc households to low-mpc households, further weakening aggregate demand (Fazzari Ferri, and Greenberg 1998, pp. 548–49).

13. For examples of recent fears of this kind of downward spiral see: "Falling Prices Put Fed on Guard: Policymakers Talk About Dangerous Dynamic for Economy," by Steven Pearlstein, *Washington Post*, November 29, 2002, A1; "Deflation Threat," by Mark M. Zandi, Chief Economist for Economy.com, Inc., Economy.com listerv, vol. 3, no. 2 (May/June 2003). Peter Temin and others have linked deflationary expectations to macroeconomic problems during the Great Depression. Ben Bernanke, the new chair of the Federal Reserve, has also warned about the dangers of deflation.

14. Fazzari, Ferri, and Greenberg, for example, conclude, "we find no empirical basis for the nearly universal [neoclassical] assumption that lower prices stimulate spending" (1998, 551).

15. David Colander has been especially effective in pointing out the frequent logical problems in textbook AS-AD discussions due to the simultaneous presence of two different supply curves in the AS-AD model: the implicit flat supply curve within the Keynesian cross, and the explicit AS curve in the AS-AD graph. See, for example, Colander 1995.

It is interesting to note that the causal logics responsible for the upward slope of the AS curve in the major textbook models run in opposite directions. The "short-run/long-run model" bases the upward slope of the AS curve on sluggish price adjustments. The "three-region model" often bases the upward slope of the AS curve on the law of diminishing returns. The first rationale implies that price level increases cause output increases by lowering real input prices. The second rationale implies that output increases cause price level increases due to rising real costs of production. This difference is obscured in most texts.

Another confusing aspect of many discussions of the AS-AD framework is the slipperiness of the price measure on the vertical axis. The stories told with and about the AS curve often shift the variable on the vertical axis in the middle of the analysis, with the price level, changes in the price level (inflation rate), and changes in the inflation rate all appearing at different moments on the vertical axis. The "rising marginal cost" of production rationale for the upward slope of the AS curve seems to use a labor hours deflator to measure price increases as it refers to real rather than nominal changes in production costs.

Sophisticated defenders of the AS-AD framework acknowledge the logical inconsistencies that often accompany its use. They justify neoclassical textbooks' continued reliance on the framework by suggesting that it conveys the "basic story" of macroeconomic adjustments correctly and concisely. For orthodox theorists, the basic message is that markets gravitate to equilibrium outcomes, though they may briefly stumble along the way. Defenders of the AS-AD framework argue that "Telling little white lies can be the right thing to do if the benefits outweigh the costs" (Kennedy 1998, p. 104). This is a reasonable but debatable claim. It conflicts, however, rather dramatically with the textbooks' mathematical posturing that implies the presence of absolute truth. David Colander has termed these maneuvers "dirty pedagogy" (Colander and Sephton 1998).

16. For some fascinating heterodox studies of the implications and evolution of the large corporation, see Nell 1996; Gordon, Edwards, and Reich 1982; and Galbraith 1973.

17. In 2001 there were 930 firms with more than 10,000 employees. Collectively these firms employed 31,357,579 workers, or about 27 percent of all employees. If firms with 5,000 to 9,999 workers are added, total employment equals 37,813,647, or about one-third of all employees (U.S. Census Bureau. "Statistics of U.S. Business: 2001." Accessed June 11, 2006: http://148.129.75.16/epcd/susb/2001/us/US—.HTM The numbers exclude establishments without payrolls.

In 1984 the largest 200 manufacturing firms owned about 60 percent of all manufacturing assets (Toruno 2003, 75). In the early 1980s, the top 1 percent of corporations owned more than 72 percent of all corporate assets (ibid., 75). Goodwin et al. (2003) cite a study indicating that in the early 1990s, "one-quarter of the world's productive assets were held by just 300 corporations" (15-4).

18. U.S. Census Bureau. "Statistics of U.S. Business: 2001." http://148.129.75.16/epcd/susb/2001/us/US—.HTM ; U.S. Census Bureau. 2004. "Nation Adds 2.2 Million Nonemployer Businesses Over Five-Year Period." May 21. http://www.census.gov/Press-Release/www/releases/archives/economic_census/001814.html (accessed June 10, 2004).

Even in markets populated by small firms, such as convenience stores, there is more oligopolistic and monopolistic competition than suggested in standard textbooks by the assumptions of perfect competition.

Some comparative statistics can illustrate the organizational size of the large firm. "General" Motors (365,000 employees) and "General" Electric (310,000) "command" about half as many workers as the generals in the Pentagon, whose 1,439,000 active-duty military personnel in 1997 approximated the number of Wal-Mart employees. (Employment figures for Wal-Mart are for 2001 from *Fortune,* July 22, 2002, F1–F13. Active-duty U.S. military personnel in 1997: *Statistical Abstract of the United States 2000,* p. 369, Table 585.)

In the late 1990s Exxon, Citicorp, GE, and Philip Morris together earned more profits ($51.6 billion) than the net income of all (~2 million) American farm operators ($48 billion). (Corporate profits from *Fortune,* July 22, 2002, F-1; number of farms from *Statistical Abstract of the United States 2000,* p. 665, Table 1097).

About 9,000 corporations (all with assets greater than $250 million) held more than 85 percent of corporate assets in 1997, ranging from a low of ~10 percent in the agricultural sector to more than 90 percent in finance, insurance, and real estate (*Statistical Abstract of the United States: 2000,* p. 541, Table 864). Economy-wide concentration levels are somewhat lower due to the addition of data for proprietorships and partnerships.

The size of firms at the top of the pyramid is growing. The increasing size of large firms seems related to the globalization of production. From 1998 to 2000, for example, the ten largest U.S. mergers and acquisitions (M&A) averaged $76 billion, more than five times the size of the second-largest M&A of the "merger mania" of the 1980s. Pfizer bought Warner-Lambert for $116 billion, AOL bought Time Warner for $106 billion, and Exxon bought Mobil for $86 billion (Du Boff and Herman 2001). To put these numbers in perspective: final crop sales for the U.S. agricultural sector were $102 billion in 1998 (*Statistical Abstract of the United States: 2000,* p. 669, Table 1108); total spending for all public universities and colleges in the United States in 1998 was $149 billion (*Statistical Abstract of the United States: 2000,* p. 151, Table 240);

and total research and development spending by private industry in 1998 equaled $151 billion (*Statistical Abstract of the United States: 2000*, p. 603, Table 978).

19. The ten largest advertisers in the United States, for example, spent ~$16 billion in 2003 ("U.S. Advertising Market Exhibits Strong Growth in 2003." TNS Media Intelligence/CMR/News. Available at www.tnsmi-cmr.com/news/2004/030804.html.

20. Although the public image of the relationship between government agencies and the private sector is combative, the reality, as Galbraith noted, is one of "bureaucratic symbiosis." The Defense Department nurtures the well-being of military contractors; the Department of Energy looks out for the well-being of the nuclear industry and fossil fuel firms; the Department of Transportation befriends the automobile industry; and so on. Although, occasionally, government policies do challenge leading firms in very public ways, the far more common case is mutual support.

21. Oligopolistic markets are defined as those having few enough participants that firms can affect the market price. Although these functional characteristics are more important than the actual number of firms in an industry, oligopoly markets are frequently thought to have from two to about ten major firms.

22. The de-emphasis of price competition reflects, in part, firms' realization that competitors can match price cuts. Exacerbating fears of debilitating price wars is the fact that most large firms maintain significant excess capacity over most of the business cycle. They do this, in part, to permit them to respond to demand increases with output increases in order to protect their market share. It is worth noting that oligopoly firms do engage in price competition from time to time, but the logic of this competition is different from the simpler logic of competitive markets.

23. Although the astronomical level of corporate executive salaries in the United States has many causes, managerial control of corporations is probably a contributing factor. The five highest-paid CEOs in 1998 were the heads of Walt Disney ($576 million), CBS ($202 million), Citigroup ($167 million), AOL ($159 million), and Intel ($117 million) (Ackerman et al. 2000, 64).

24. Blinder's research found that 85 percent of sales are with repeat customers (Blinder et al. 1998, 106).

25. For example, a large survey of corporate executives completed in the late 1990s under the direction of former assistant Federal Reserve chairman Alan Blinder concluded that "there certainly appears to be enough price rigidity in most sectors to matter for macroeconomic purposes. . . . the typical commodity is repriced roughly once a year; and more than 75 percent of GDP is repriced quarterly or less frequently" (Blinder et al. 1998, 105). Rao estimates that 87 percent of U.S. GNP transactions take place in sluggish price markets (Rao 1998, 3). Numerous other studies support or are consistent with sluggish price assumptions (Downward and Lee 2001, 477; F. Lee 1996, 89–90).

26. Colander, for example, reports, "About 90% of final goods markets in the United States are oligopolistic with cost-determined prices" (Colander 2001b, 216).

27. Among the reasons given for firms' adoption of mark-up pricing rules are:

(1) The difficulties involved in distinguishing transient from permanent changes in market conditions and the sluggishness of corporate bureaucracies in processing such information. Blinder et al., for example, report that five of the twelve firms with sales above $10 billion in their survey suggested that bureaucratic delays were an important reason for price sluggishness (Blinder et al. 1998, 303).

(2) The economic costs of implementing price changes in response to demand changes (often termed *menu costs* in reference to the cost to restaurants of constantly reprinting menus).

(3) The preference of customers for stable prices, but greater tolerance of price increases due to producers' cost increases than price increases due to demand increases.

(4) The potentially self-destructive impact of price cuts in response to declines in demand due to competitors' ability to match the cuts.

28. Blinder's interviews found that two-thirds of all firms fell into this category (Blinder et al. 1998, 305).

29. As noted earlier, many firms maintain some excess capacity in order to protect market share if demand increases. Aggregate excess capacity in an industry also helps to discourage new entrants and thereby maintain prices above competitive levels.

30. The fear that discounted prices will be taken as signals of lower product quality seems to be more relevant in consumer than business markets. In the latter case, firms seem to have fairly reliable and independent assessments of product quality (Blinder et al. 1998, 303).

31. Based on more than 300 interviews in 1992 and 1993 with key participants involved in wage setting (corporate executives, union leaders, employment counselors, etc.), Truman Bewley concluded that maintaining worker morale was perhaps the guiding principle that conditioned how corporations reacted to market conditions (Howitt 2002, 126).

32. In worker-owned companies, the conflict between workers and management (democratically elected by workers) would presumably be different. Even if workplaces were democratically managed, however, tensions between the individual and the firm might emerge. This would be especially possible if the organization were quite large and as a result individuals felt that their ability to affect company policy was minimal.

33. See for example Bowles, Edwards, and Roosevelt 2005, 448–52.

34. For example, radical economists and Marxist proponents of the "wage/profit squeeze" tend to foresee "investment strikes" when falling unemployment stimulates rising wages and lower profits. These "strikes" reduce aggregate demand and renew unemployment. For Marxists, capitalism and prolonged full employment are incompatible. The functioning of a capitalist economy requires the existence of a "reserve army of the unemployed" to force the employed to accept the conditions of wage labor. Taking an even broader perspective, many Marxists argue that unemployment is a prerequisite for maximizing the political-economic influence of "capital." Reduced environmental protection, lower taxes on corporations, tax breaks for the wealthy, lower workplace safety standards, and so on are all ransom for jobs. In an economy with guaranteed public employment, many social trade-offs, like that between the environment and economic growth, might be made differently. Although many citizens might be willing to accept lower wages for a cleaner environment, they cannot afford unemployment for a cleaner environment.

Not all heterodox economists accept the Marxist notion of wage/profit squeeze. Post-Keynesians and Marxist economists in the tradition of Kalecki believe that firms can generally pass on the costs of higher nominal wages caused by falling unemployment, implying that it is financial capital (creditors who have lent money during periods with lower inflation expectations) who lose out from full employment. Some Keynesian economists imply that government expansionary policies can shift income toward labor (especially at the low end of the wage scale) before wage-price spirals upset the economy.

35. The reasoning behind this dynamic is subtle. The key argument is that the institutional character of the labor market forces "all-or-nothing" choices on workers, that is, workers cannot always trade lower wages for more meaningful work or shorter work hours. They are often left with an all-or-nothing choice, the job or unemployment. Faced with this choice, many workers work longer, harder, and in less satisfying ways than they might choose to if they could voluntarily sacrifice some income for increased leisure and more pleasurable work. Lower unemployment rates tend to offer workers more choices.

36. The partial overlap between aspects of heterodox and Neo-Keynesian theory illustrates a more general relationship between orthodoxy and heterodoxy in economics. Many different sections of standard textbooks temporarily relax one or two of the underlying assumptions of neoclassical macroeconomics (perfect information, perfect competition, *homo economicus,* etc.) challenged by heterodox economics. Subsequent analysis, however, renews the relaxed assumption when analyzing other issues, denying students the ability to develop an alternative way of thinking about economics.

MIT's Nobel Prize–winning economist Robert Solow is a master of the "relax and renew" strategy. In his hands, neoclassical analysis has generated many rich insights without transcending its broader limitations. Some of Solow's most interesting work has dealt with the concept of "efficiency wages." He argues that some firms pay workers higher wages than the market requires in order to motivate their workforce. Explaining this idea, he writes (1990):

> One important tradition within economics, perhaps the dominant tradition right now, especially in macroeconomics, holds that in nearly all respects the labor market is just like other markets... "I want to make the case that the labor market really is different. In particular, I claim that it cannot be understood without taking account of the fact that participants, on both sides, have well-developed notions of what is fair. . . . (3)
>
> If there are any civilians [meaning noneconomists] here they will wonder why I spend so much time and effort, and exhibit so much defensiveness in asserting the obvious. I have already explained why. Among economists, it is not obvious at all that labor as a commodity is sufficiently different from artichokes and rental apartments to require a different mode of analysis. In fact many economists will regard this idea as simply bizarre (p. 4).

Returning to the fold, he adds, "You will notice that I have not uttered the dread P-word, paradigm. That is because, to my way of thinking, none of this is radically subversive of mainstream economic theory . . . . (23) "Let me make one thing perfectly clear. . . . The analysis of a system of well-functioning markets—what we usually call general equilibrium theory—is the main achievement of economics. . . . That achievement is not in question" (Solow 1990, 29–30).

37. Recently, conventional estimates of the NAIRU have been in the neighborhood of 5 to 6 percent unemployment. There has been a troubling tendency for estimates of the NAIRU to place it near whatever current unemployment rates are. During the latter half of the 1990s most neoclassical economists, including those preparing the *Economic Report of the President 1996,* predicted that inflation would pick up if unemployment fell below 5 to 6.5 percent. Unemployment fell to 4 percent without accelerating inflation (Colander 2001b, 223; Thorbecke 2004). Estimates of the NAIRU also fell with a lag. Nobel Prize winner William Vickrey has labeled conventional estimates of the NAIRU one of the great fallacies of financial fundamentalism.

38. See, for example, Bowles, Edwards, and Roosevelt 2005, 472–75.

39. The economy's path dependency and reflection of its history is often termed hysteresis. MIT economist Olivier Blanchard offers a slightly different reason for why periods of high unemployment might ratchet up: long-run unemployment rates (Blanchard 2000, 438).

13

HETERODOX ALTERNATIVES TO
THE AS-AD FRAMEWORK

INTRODUCTION

In chapter 12 we found that there were serious conceptual problems with the AS-AD framework. It encouraged the confusion of micro- and macro-level supply and demand curves. It abandoned Keynes's focus on uncertainty and the vulnerability of the macro economy to aggregate demand problems. It simultaneously used two different aggregate supply curves, the 45-degree line from the Keynesian cross and the AS curve in the AS-AD graph. And, most significantly, it relied on an adjustment mechanism to stabilize the economy (deflation) that had not occurred in half a century and probably would have further destabilized the economy if it had occurred.

In chapter 12 we tried to express heterodox concerns within the AS-AD framework. We found that heterodox ideas would tend to steepen the AD curve, flatten the AS curve, destabilize both curves,[1] and challenge the assumption that the economy automatically moves to long-run full employment. Although it is possible to illustrate some of the differences between heterodox and textbook macro theory by comparing different versions of the AS-AD curves, it is also helpful to look at alternative frameworks for integrating the supply and demand sides of the macro economy. We look at two heterodox alternatives below: the "Circuits of Capital" and the "Social Structures of Accumulation" (SSA) frameworks.

Neoclassical textbooks tend to (1) de-emphasize uncertainty, (2) ground economic outcomes in supply, (3) highlight static equilibrium moments, (4) abstract from the monetary form of economic activity, (5) neglect institutional detail, (6) assume *homo economicus,* and (7) model the economy as a set of harmonious exchanges with little attention to distributional issues. In contrast, the "circuits of capital" and "social structures of accumulation" frameworks (1) highlight the implications of uncertainty, (2) emphasize the importance of aggregate demand, (3) highlight the importance of dynamic and disequilibrium analysis, (4) integrate the "real" and "monetary" sectors, (5) attend to the macroeconomic implications of the large corporation, (6) reject the oversimplified picture of *homo economicus,* and (7) assert the presence of conflict and power relations in the workplace and the labor market.

CIRCUITS OF CAPITAL APPROACH

As noted in chapter 10, the circuits of capital[2] approach to understanding macroeconomic dynamics depicts macroeconomic activity as a cycle divided into three stages. Economic activity begins with financing. A capitalist[3] advances financial capital (i.e., money, or [M]) for the purpose of organizing production. The money (M) is used to buy real inputs or commodities (C), such as raw materials and labor power. In stage two, production occurs. The input commodities (C) are transformed into output commodities (C′). During this stage, the productive potential of labor power is turned into actual work. The last stage in the cycle is "realization," or "remonetization," during which the outputs are sold and the capitalist's financial capital is recovered in augmented form. Thus the entire picture is M-C-$C′$-$M′$.

This progression (M-C-C′-M′) is the "life cycle of capital" that animates capitalist economies. It is a monetized cycle. It is not C-C′ (people exchanging commodities), which is the conceptual story highlighted in standard textbooks. Heterodox theory emphasizes the unique problems that can occur during each phase of the circuit.

For example, firms can have difficulties mobilizing financial capital (M). The liquidity crunch of the early 1990s is a recent example of this. After the savings and loans debacle, regulatory authorities required that banks increase their owners' (rather than depositors') invested capital–to–loan ratios. This temporarily made it difficult for some companies to get loans and contributed to the recession of 1990–1991.

Firms can also encounter problems when trying to purchase inputs. The most common obstacles arise during the expansion phase of the business cycle, when bottlenecks and price increases for inputs, such as labor and raw materials, can disrupt firms' planning. Strikes, of course, can disrupt input markets at any time. Numerous problems can arise in the next phase of the cycle: production. Difficulties at this stage are ignored in most neoclassical textbooks, where production is implicitly treated as an automatic result of the purchase of inputs. In heterodox analyses the conditions of production are often "contested"[4] in informal but frequent battles over the pace and conditions of work.

The last stage in the cycle is realization. Firms must sell their output and "realize" its value in money. Because we live in a monetized economy, firms cannot pay their workers in units of output or meet their debt obligations in units of output. They must transform their output into money. In this phase of the cycle problems in aggregate demand can cripple firms. Problems can be especially severe if firms are burdened by debt from financing arrangements in stage one. Fears of realization problems can also feedback on other stages of the cycle, inhibiting monetary advances or investment spending at the beginning of the cycle.

The circuit of capital framework emphasizes the insatiability of the economy's motive force (the drive to turn M into M′) and the fragility of capital's life cycle, due to the several reincarnations it must complete in order to renew itself. The framework highlights the necessity of integrating the real and monetary sectors in macro analysis and the potential for economic crises.

SOCIAL STRUCTURES OF ACCUMULATION (SSA)

Introduction

The theory of social structures of accumulation[5] is an institutionalist-oriented analysis of macroeconomic behavior that extends the circuits of capital framework. Like the latter, the theory builds on radical, Marxist, and Keynesian insights about the basic structure of the economy. The SSA model emphasizes the need for institutional arrangements to reduce economic uncertainty and to resolve capital/labor (K/L) tensions in the workplace in order for firms to complete the M-C-C′-M′ cycle. SSA theory assumes that capitalist economies are vulnerable to aggregate demand problems, liquidity crises, and profitability problems. The economies must constantly evolve institutional mechanisms for overcoming these problems.

This contrasts with the general equilibrium story underlying standard textbook macro theory. The latter simply assumes that all firms make the average rate of profit.[6] SSA theory problematizes this outcome and explores how institutional arrangements make possible the economic stability and expansion assumed by GE theory. More specifically, SSA theorists argue that it is necessary to explore:

1. the institutional arrangements organizing the work process and governing K/L relations
2. the institutional arrangements governing competition among firms, or K/K relations
3. the institutional arrangements structuring the "monetary sector" and organizing the relationship between "financial" and "real" capital[7]
4. the institutional arrangements organizing the government's role in the economy
5. the institutional arrangements coordinating a country's economic relationships with the rest of the world.

SSA theorists link the cluster of socioeconomic institutions that define a social structure of accumulation to a time period's levels of unemployment, inflation, economic growth, and economic inequality. What this means is best explained by some concrete examples of SSA analysis. We will briefly look at the two different social structures of accumulation that organized the U.S. economy during the second half of the twentieth century. The first SSA grew out of the Great Depression and the social mobilization accompanying World War II. It was consolidated in the immediate postwar period and lasted about twenty-five years. The second SSA was consolidated in the late 1970s and early 1980s and is still with us. The analysis below extends comparisons first raised in chapter 9's discussion of the different investment patterns found in the two periods.

The Postwar SSA

Capital/Labor (K/L) Relations

Capital/labor relations[8] during the first SSA were characterized by two main institutions: the "dual labor market" and a "truce" between labor and management. The dual labor market reflected the different treatment of workers in the planning and market sectors of the economy. The planning sector was dominated by about a thousand large corporations with significant capital investments and relatively long planning horizons. The market sector was populated by millions of small firms. Within the planning (or primary) sector, workers enjoyed union-like protections (whether they were in unions or not). The arrangements of collective bargaining were accepted by management and unions represented about one-third of the nonagricultural labor force in the early to mid-1950s. Many nonunion firms, like IBM, were encouraged by the threat of unionization to match union contracts.

Work was organized by the seniority system and grievances were governed by formal procedures that limited employers' exercise of absolute authority in the workplace. A 1947 agreement between GM and the United Auto Workers set a pattern of tying wage growth to projected productivity growth. By implicitly entitling workers to share in firms' profits and the benefits of technical change, the agreement helped elicit workers' cooperation with technological innovation. The taming of capital/labor relations during this period is often referred to as "the labor accord" or just "the accord." Although the period's implicit and explicit contracts did mute capital/labor conflict, tensions still simmered beneath the surface. Some observers feel that union hierarchies gradually lost touch with these tensions (and the rank and file in general) as labor organizations became bureaucratized.

Within the market (or secondary) sector, labor relations were more conflictual. Although some upper-echelon workers enjoyed "primary"-sector job conditions, most did not. Unions were resisted. Workplace discipline was unilaterally controlled by management. Stable career ladders were absent and relationships were short term. Access to primary- and secondary-sector jobs was partially determined by workers' social identities. Minorities and women were disproportionately represented in the secondary sector. Although, in the aggregate, income inequalities narrowed from 1948 to 1968,[9] racial and gender inequalities increased (Bowles, Gordon, and Weisskopf 1990, 67).[10]

Capital/Capital (K/K) Relations

In the primary sector, the destabilizing aspects of capitalist competition were reduced by the logic of domestic oligopoly market structures and the weakness of foreign competition. Price competition was generally muted. The combination of stable K/L relations and oligopoly market structures permitted an orderly flow of investment. This helped to maintain aggregate demand and productivity growth in the economy.

Monetary Sector Relations (Financial/Industrial Capital Relations)

The monetary sector was highly regulated by today's standards. Alongside more restrictive banking rules,[11] memories of the stock market crash of 1929, thousands of bank failures, and the Great Depression of the 1930s contributed to a conservative business climate. This milieu helped to mute speculative behavior and to limit the buildup of individual and corporate debt. The economy's lack of debt fragility (and therefore reduced lender's risk), along with Federal Reserve policy, helped to keep interest rates relatively low. These rates and various institutional arrangements channeled credit to the housing sector. The international financial sector was highly regulated by a system of fixed exchange rates and de facto limits on capital mobility.

Public-/Private-Sector Relations

The state played a modestly active role in the economy. The growth in federal government spending from less than 5 percent of GNP before World War II to 20–25 percent of GNP in the postwar period tended to stabilize aggregate demand (Papadimitriou and Wray 1999, 2; Stiglitz 1997, 149). In the policy area, mild-mannered Keynesianism ruled. Government was expected to "lean against the wind," to maintain aggregate demand near, but not too near, full employment (in keeping with the "Employment" but not "Full Employment" Act of 1946). Modest efforts were directed at income redistribution through progressive taxation, rising minimum wages, and social welfare spending.[12]

International Economic Relations

The world economy was dominated by Pax Americana (U.S. military power) and U.S. corporations. The world economic order was organized by U.S.-directed institutions (such as the World Bank and the IMF) and operated under fixed exchange rates. The system facilitated U.S. investment abroad and relied on the dollar as the reserve currency. American military power and geopolitical influence were also used to secure cheap raw materials from third world countries (Bowles and Edwards 1993, 453).

Behavior of the Postwar SSA

From 1946 to 1970, the United States experienced five recessions. All were relatively mild. Unemployment rates averaged 4.8 percent from 1948 to 1973 and never exceeded 6.8 percent. GDP and investment growth averaged 3.8 percent and 4 percent per year, respectively. Labor productivity advanced at an annual rate of 2.2 percent from 1948 to 1966 and at 1.3 percent from 1966 to 1973 (Bowles, Gordon, and Weisskopf 1990, 19, 97). Real family income grew at about 2.6 percent per year from 1947 to 1967 and at 2.9 percent from 1967 to 1973 (Mishel, Bernstein, and Boushey 2003, 56). The Gini coefficient for income inequality fell from 0.376 in 1948 to 0.348 in 1968 (Harrison and Bluestone 1988, 130), while the poverty rate fell from 22.4 percent in 1959 to a low of 11.1 percent in 1973 (U.S. Census Bureau 2001, 18). The period is known in retrospect as the "golden age."

Many aspects of the postwar SSA worked together to promote a shared prosperity. The low debt levels of firms and households reduced the risks of serious recession and lowered credit costs. The government's Keynesian macro policies (which shored up aggregate demand) encouraged individual firms to retain workers during relatively mild downturns in order to tap employee loyalty during robust upswings. Strong aggregate demand also encouraged high levels of investment, which helped underwrite continued productivity growth. Government support for basic research, and relatively cooperative labor management relations in the private sector, also aided labor productivity. Government spending for education reduced the frequency of supply bottlenecks for professional workers during economic expansions and, along with cheap raw materials, rising labor productivity, and a relatively strong dollar, helped keep a lid on inflation.

The above analysis suggests a different way of thinking about "supply" from the vertical long-run AS curve and shifting, upward-sloping, short-run AS curve in the textbooks. Supply and demand are interconnected and embedded in interlocking social institutions. Supply is conditioned by demand expectations, by the structure of product markets and the institutions of the labor market, by the organization of the financial sector, and by numerous other "contextual" phenomena. Because of these institutional linkages, economic policy is not simply about finding the "right" rate of growth for the money supply. Macro policy is architectonic in an institutional sense.

SSA analysis can be used to understand the collapse, as well as the success, of the postwar SSA. We turn now to this story, in preparation for a discussion of the SSA that followed "the postwar accord."

The Collapse of the Postwar SSA

By the late 1960s the success of the postwar SSA began to test its limits. The "labor accord" had to be either expanded or abrogated. As we shall see it was abrogated. Strains began to develop at the end of the 1960s. Spending for the Vietnam War pushed the economy toward genuine full employment. From 1966 to 1969, unemployment averaged only 3.7 percent, falling to a low of 3.5 percent in 1969 (U.S. Executive Office of the President 2000, 354).[13] As unemployment fell, wage/profit squeeze dynamics began to reduce profits and increase inflationary pressures.

At the same time that tight labor markets were complicating K/L relations, increased foreign competition was complicating firms' pricing decisions. The recovery of the Japanese and European economies from the devastation of World War II eventually spawned new competitors for U.S. firms at home and abroad. Between 1960 and 1970 the share of imports in the U.S. automobile and consumer electronics markets rose from 4 percent to 17 percent and from 4 percent to 31 percent, respectively (Bowles, Gordon, and Weisskopf 1990, 76). During the 1970s import competition spread across the economy, with the value of manufactured imports relative to domestic production increasing from 14 percent in 1969 to 38 percent in 1979 (Harrison and Bluestone 1988, 8).

And finally, somewhat related to the above developments and partially coincidental, the economy was buffeted by a series of cost shocks in the 1970s. Among these blows were a slow-down in labor productivity growth, a sharp increase in food prices due largely to bad weather,[14] a sharp increase in energy costs due largely to an OPEC price increase during the 1973 Arab-Israeli war,[15] higher production costs due to tighter environmental standards, and higher import prices due to a falling U.S. dollar.[16] The inflationary pressures accompanying these shocks created a minefield for resolving distributional issues. Someone had to bear the burden of higher real pro-duction costs, but everyone thought it should be someone else.[17]

Squeezed by rising unit labor costs and tougher foreign competition, business profits began to fall in the mid-1960s and continued to do so for about seven years (Harrison and Bluestone 1988, 8, 205, 111). Firms appeared to have three choices: (1) expand the accord with labor to include more extensive profit sharing and participatory management in order to increase labor productiv-ity, improve product quality, and contain wage/profit squeeze pressures; (2) elicit government help in finding nonmarket mechanisms to control wage/profit squeeze and inflationary pressures, which would have meant a much more active government role in the economy; or (3) abrogate the "labor accord" and attempt to slash labor's share of national income.

Policy makers similarly faced tough choices. The most pressing problem was how to respond to inflationary pressures in an economy with downwardly sticky wages and prices. The dilemma was complicated by social disagreements over who should bear the burden of the higher real costs of production caused by economic shocks like OPEC price increases and poor global harvests. Policy makers also seemed to have three choices: (1) retain high aggregate demand policies but complement them with aggressive nonmarket mechanisms, such as incomes and industrial poli-cies, to contain inflationary pressures; (2) attempt to muddle through with a little less expansion-ary demand policy and a little more inflation; or (3) retreat from Keynesian full-employment policies and other social programs that strengthened the bargaining position of labor with capital.

The combination of policies ultimately chosen by business and government to respond to these challenges eventually created a new SSA. Business chose to end the labor accord. Firms actively sought to reduce wages and lower workers' bargaining power, adopting a more adversarial stance toward labor relations. Policy makers chose a complementary strategy that reduced spending for social safety nets, tolerated higher unemployment levels, and weakened unions. The conditions for the "new prosperity" would be quite different from those of the "golden age." The economy had shifted from a "high-road" SSA of capital/labor collaboration to a "low road" of capital/labor confrontation.

As we saw in chapter 11, beginning in 1979 the Fed used tight monetary policy to aggressively slow down the economy. It had experimented with harsh measures in 1974 but retreated from them. This time it held firm. The official unemployment rate reached 10.8 percent in the fall of 1982 and averaged 9.65 percent from 1982 to 1983. If one includes the government's estimate of discouraged workers (the unemployed who have given up looking for work) and half of all invol-untary part-time workers, the unemployment rate reached about 15 percent. Even this figure fails to capture the increase in economic insecurity that accompanied anti-inflation macro policy. Since the average duration of unemployment is less than half a year, annual statistics understate the percentage of the labor force who were unemployed during the year. Official statistics also leave out the large number of people anxious about losing their jobs. As noted in chapter 8, the legacy of the new economic insecurity was captured by the New York Times' "Downsizing" articles in 1996, reprinted in a book with the same name (New York Times 1996, 5).[18]

Complementing a public policy retreat from Keynesian commitments to low unemployment were large reductions in the real value of the minimum wage,[19] reductions in unemployment insurance,[20] and reductions in some social programs. There were also increased barriers to unionization.[21] For their part, corporations greatly expanded antiunion efforts, aided by a growing number of antiunion consultants and law firms.[22] At the same time, the companies sought aggressively to cut wages and benefits and speed up the pace of work. The "internal labor markets" of the "accord" were drawn much more narrowly as corporations expanded the use of temporary workers and outsourced production to suppliers in the nonunion market sector (Harrison and Bluestone 1988, 43–47).[23] Firms increasingly played the "Mexico or Indonesia or Thailand card" in formal and informal labor negotiations. The final result was a macro economy with much more inequality and economic insecurity. Those on the top of the pyramid did extremely well; living standards and work life declined or stagnated for most of the population. (See chapter 15 for more detailed data on the increase in inequality in the U.S. economy during the last three decades of the twentieth century.)

Consolidation of the Neoliberal SSA

Capital/Labor (K/L) Relations

The preceding history gives a pretty good idea of what the new SSA turned out to be. Labor relations became much more adversarial. Although dual labor markets and some implicit contracts remain, the number of "partnership" workers in the primary sector has declined. Unionization in the private sector fell from a peak of 35 percent in the mid-1950s to 9 percent in 2001.[24] The tendency to outsource, use temporary workers, and relocate production in third world countries has accelerated, aided by increases in capital mobility and technological revolutions that make coordinating an international workforce much more feasible.[25] Originally justified by claims that dire actions were necessary for firms to survive, wage cuts, speed ups, layoffs, and so on have persisted, even when companies returned to solid profitability.[26] Former cultural pressures within firms and the broader community for sharing prosperity have weakened, as suggested by the ratio of CEO to factory worker pay, which increased from 41:1 in 1960 to 157:1 in 1992, to more than 300:1 in 2001 (Palley 1998, 58; Worldwatch 2003, 91).[27]

Capital/Capital (K/K) Relations

U.S. government policy has promoted deregulation and increased competition, especially globally. The current period is one of competition for international market share among many countries' largest industrial firms. This competition has created a destructive tendency for global excess capacity in mass production industries, which has put downward pressure on profits and spurred wage reductions. The process has kept a lid on inflation. The process of globalization has increasingly tilted power away from U.S. workers toward employers and owners of financial capital by increasing the mobility of capital and opportunities for foreign investment.

Monetary Sector Relations

There has been aggressive deregulation of the domestic banking sector and a surge in speculative behavior of all kinds. Cultural shifts have contributed to higher debt levels among firms and households.

Financial markets and financial firms (such as the creditors who financed the hostile take-over movements of the 1980s) have become much more involved in setting performance goals for nonfinancial companies (like General Motors). The intrusion of financial firms has often encouraged management to shorten planning horizons in order to maintain current stock prices. This has probably had a negative effect on long-term investment and innovation (Crotty 2003).

Public-/Private-Sector Relations

In the macro field, there has been a retreat from activist Keynesianism and a tendency to view whatever the current unemployment rate is as the "natural rate."[28] The Fed's acknowledged priority has shifted from achieving full employment to fighting inflation.[29] Although aggregate government spending for social programs appears to have been maintained, there has been fraying of important parts of the social safety net. Public-sector investment in non-defense-related physical capital, education, and research also fell, from 2.5 percent GDP in the late 1970s to about 1.5 percent in the late 1990s.[30]

International Economic Relations

U.S. policy has increased the mobility of capital, fostering both rapid short-term financial flows around the globe and increased investment in foreign production. Increased capital mobility has increased the bargaining power of capital in conflicts with labor and undermined the ability of national governments to redistribute income. The changes have also tended to destabilize the international economy.

Comparing the AS-AD and SSA Frameworks for Analyzing Macroeconomic Events

In the hands of skilled users, both the AS-AD and SSA frameworks can be used to tell insightful stories about the macroeconomy.[31] The SSA framework tends to give greater attention to issues of power and institutional design than the AS-AD framework does (although all sorts of exogenous shift parameters can be appended on to the latter to discuss many SSA topics). The subtext of most AS-AD discussions is that macroeconomics is a technical field devoted to modeling a mechanical process akin to planetary motions. The policy message, for the most part, is to let the market work. Heterodox economics perceives the economy in more political terms and finds several different macroeconomic paths possible. In heterodox theory, different "kinds of capitalism" are possible. Which kind of capitalism exits in the United States (for example, the high or low labor road variety) is a political choice. In textbook theory there is basically one outcome—and that approximates the hypothetical anchor of general equilibrium.

THREADS

We turn now to a review of the themes developed in chapters 12 and 13 with an eye toward their implications for the treatment of distributional, gender, and environmental issues. We will also briefly summarize some of the memorable differences in metaphors that animate textbook and heterodox treatments of AS-AD topics.

Distributional Themes

As we have often noted, heterodox economics integrates distributional concerns more centrally into economic theory than neoclassical economics does. The textbooks' AS-AD framework, for example, is geared toward modeling aggregate outcomes. It treats overall GDP as the primary economic indicator. It generally abstracts from who receives national income. There are no struggles in the textbooks between labor and capital. "Representative agents," who are neither rich or poor and all have the same marginal propensities to consume, populate the economy. Shifting income distributions do not alter aggregate demand. Macro policy making is portrayed as an apolitical task that aims to find the optimal economic policy that is in everyone's best interest.

The SSA framework, in contrast, integrates distributional issues into the core of economic modeling. Different macro regimes are linked to different strategies for resolving capital/labor tensions. Some important business cycles are tied to battles over the distribution of income among employers, employees, upper management, and creditors. Other business cycles are tied to the aggregate demand implications of shifting distributions of income. Macro policy making is perceived to involve conflicting economic interests. Macro policy choices (like recent decisions to facilitate capital mobility) are linked to issues of power within the economy and broader society. Macro outcomes are often disaggregated by income group, gender, race, and other categories. These issues are explored in depth in chapter 15 ("Reintroducing the Macroeconomics of Inequality").

Gender Themes

Heterodox treatments of the AS-AD framework and the supply side of the economy reflect methodological choices that are similar to many of the principles of feminist economics. Like feminist economics, heterodox macro theory stresses the need to study the concrete, institutionally specific structure of the U.S. economy, through dual sector, SSA, or other institutionally specified models. Heterodox economists criticize the abstract formalism of textbook AS-AD models. The latter often elevate elegant and precise logical deductions about a fictitious economy (based on assumptions of perfect information and perfect competition) over messier, but more accurate, models of the actual economy.

Like feminist economics, heterodox critiques of the AS-AD framework emphasize the complexity of the macro economy. The critiques assert the necessity of using several different kinds of models (including ones without detailed "micro-foundations") instead of a single simple model to understand macro dynamics.[32]

Echoing feminist economists, heterodox economists also criticize the AS-AD framework for its assumption of isolated economic man. Heterodoxy argues that both labor and financial markets can not be understood without attention to the interdependence of human beings and the roles of emotion, herd behavior, habit, and social convention in human behavior. Both heterodox macroeconomics and feminist economics give much greater attention to the significance of people's sense of fairness in terms of relative wages than is suggested by the AS-AD framework. As demonstrated in the last two chapters, the behavior of "real people" rather than *homo economicus* can regularly generate disequilibrium and unemployment in the labor market.

Finally, heterodox discussions tend to give more attention to the gendered experiences of women in dual labor markets and the macro economy in general than invited by the textbooks' use of the AS-AD framework.

Table 13.1

Competing Images of Aggregate Supply and Aggregate Demand

Textbook AS-AD Models	Heterodox Economics
Equilibrium dynamics	Disequilibrium dynamics
Long run dominated short run	Short run determined long run
Vertical AS; downward-sloping AD curves	Relatively flat AS; steeper AD curves
Stable AS and AD curves	Dancing AS and AD curves
Precise mathematical-graphical solutions (Cartesian/Euclidean)	Messy theories (Babylonian)
Homo economicus	Psychologically complex agents
Isolated individuals	Social structures of accumulation
Real-sector economies with monetary shadows	Monetized economies
Consumer sovereignty	Circuits of financial and productive capital

Environmental Themes

Heterodox discussions of the supply side of the economy offer some interesting insights into the historical character of current environmental problems. The circuits of capital approach, for example, emphasizes the relentless pressures for economic expansion that accompany our current organization of production. The SSA framework offers a rich context for thinking about the environmental implications of different macro regimes.

These linkages are pursued more fully in chapter 16 ("Reintroducing Macroeconomics and the Environment").

COMPETING METAPHORS

How Loud Is the Silence?

Neoclassical economists often argue that the points made by heterodox economists can be made within neoclassical economics. We have argued in this book that the differences are more fundamental. The silences in neoclassical economics texts are not accidental. The proof is in the pudding. Heterodox critics argue that heterodoxy offers a different view of the macro economy. You have to be the final judge of this.

IN THEIR OWN WORDS: HETERODOX CRITIQUES OF TEXTBOOK TREATMENTS OF AGGREGATE SUPPLY AND AGGREGATE DEMAND

On the AS-AD Framework and Theories of Unemployment

Undergraduate students receive their first lesson on the theory of unemployment in the Keynesian-Cross, aggregate expenditure chapter of introductory textbooks. These argue that inadequate effective demand . . . causes harmful and wasteful involuntary unemployment. . . .

The chapter on aggregate supply (AS) and aggregate demand (AD) presents students with a different explanation, inconsistent with the first but treated as a further development. A backward shift in AD would only create fleeting unemployment were it not for downward wage (and price) rigidity. . . . This echoes the classical view of the world that Keynes sought to replace with his own theory of chronic involuntary unemployment (109). . . .

Our proposed alternative . . . builds on the original Keynesian-Cross (119). . . .

—Nahid Aslanbeigui and Michele I. Naples (1996a)

[T]he neoclassical theory of agent choice is restricted to a world in which agents' decisions do not "create" the future (108). . . .

In Keynes's model, the future time path of the economy depends on the decisions taken by agents conscious of their ignorance. . . . [T]here is no predetermined future that is independent of the blind groping of ignorant agents (115). . . .

[A] macrotheory that acknowledges the centrality of uncertainty need not be nihilistic provided that it incorporates the sources of conditional stability built into the capitalist system. We identify . . . two such sources . . . "conventional" expectations and confidence formation; and the institutional structure of the economy (and the society). The integrated effects of these two dimensions of economic life generate both the conditional stability and the periods of disorder that characterize the economic record (117).

—James Crotty (1994)

Heterodox Theories of Pricing and Output Behavior

[N]ormal cost and target rate of return pricing are the pricing procedures most used by business enterprises (88). . . .

One feature of stable, cost-based prices is that they are determined before transactions take place, and are administered to the market—hence their name of administered prices.

—Frederic S. Lee (1996, 89)

The law of supply and demand is repealed because rational maximizing behavior by employers and workers will not eliminate unemployment; firms will not accept offers from job seekers wanting to undercut existing wages, for this will reduce effort levels and increase unit labor costs. . . . The law of one price has been repealed because the relationship between wages and productivity may differ from firm to firm, making the cost-minimizing wage different for each one. This reinforces the Post Keynesian emphasis on labor market segmentation and discrimination, and their denial that markets would be perfect in the absence of institutional barriers. Finally . . . because feelings of fairness and justice influence the supply of effort; it is impossible to separate allocative and distributional issues.

—John E. King (2001, 67)

On Institutions and Economics

[W]hen firms become large . . . a transformation in the very nature of economic society occurs.

The critical instrument of transformation is not the state or the individual but the modern corporation. It is the moving force in the change (38). . . .

[G]rowth both enhances power over prices, costs, consumers, suppliers, the community and the state and also rewards in a very personal way those who bring it about (40). . . .

In the United States one may think of one thousand manufacturing, merchandising, transportation, power and financial corporations producing approximately half of all the goods and services not provided by the state. . . .

Making up the remainder of the economy are around twelve million smaller firms, including about three million farmers (42–43). . . .

That the planning system does not conform to the neoclassical model—that its firms are not passive in response to the market or the state—will not be difficult to establish. Mainly it is a matter of breaking with accustomed and stereotyped thought (44).

—John Kenneth Galbraith (1973)

On Feminist Economics

To put it in gender oriented terms, it is only if one believes that the culturally 'masculine' notions of rational individual choice and rigorous formal analysis are definitive of science, that one has to play on the New Classical playground. The feminist analysis of this book, in arguing that emotions and institutions, and rich metaphorical analysis and concrete observation, are equally valid in defining quality economic practice, should help steer macroeconomics back to a more useful path.

—Julie Nelson (1996, 121)

STUDY QUESTIONS

Review Questions

1. From a heterodox perspective what are the advantages and disadvantages of replacing rather than reforming the AS-AD framework?
2. How does the circuits of capital model portray the economy? From a heterodox perspective, what does the model illuminate that is obscured in the textbooks' AS-AD framework?
3. Explain how the SSA framework depicts the economy. From a heterodox perspective, what does the model illuminate that is obscured in the textbook AS-AD framework?
4. Taking an SSA approach, compare the structure and organization of the economy from 1950 to 1975 with the structure and organization of the economy from 1975 to 2000. What do you think are the strengths and weaknesses of looking at the economy in this way?

Discussion Question

1. Why might economists and public policy makers be led to explore different policy options if they viewed the economy from an SSA rather than an AS-AD framework? How do you think economists make decisions about which framework to use to explain the economy and recommend public policy?

NOTES

1. In heterodox models both the AS and AD curves are made sensitive to volatile expectations. Colander, in particular, has experimented with ways of treating business confidence as a shift parameter for the aggregate supply curve.

2. The circuits of capital approach to understanding macroeconomic dynamics is most frequently used by Marxist, Keynesian, and radical economists.

3. By *capitalist* I mean an individual or "corporate persona." Under U.S. law the corporation is treated as a person. This is why stockholders have only "limited liability." If a corporation is sued, its owners are not

personally liable for the corporation's debts or its illegal actions. This is not the case with a partnership, where all of the owners are jointly liable for any business obligations. The corporation "owns" its own assets (including retained earnings). It decides whether to reinvest such earnings or distribute them to shareholders. It also pays income taxes, which partnerships do not.

4. For a powerful Marxist analysis of this contestation see Braverman 1974. For "radical" analyses see Edwards 1979 and Gordon, Edwards, and Reich 1982. Interestingly, both business and Marxist economists give the problem of "management" more attention than neoclassical economists do.

5. The concept of a social structure of accumulation was developed in the late 1970s by the radical economist David Gordon. It was originally used to help understand "long waves" of economic activity, that is, prolonged periods of relative economic success (e.g., 1945–1970) or distress (1970–1995). Good summaries of early work can be found in Gordon, Edwards, and Reich 1982; Kotz, McDonough, and Reich 1994; and Bowles, Gordon, and Weisskopf 1989 and 1990. SSA models have many similarities to French regulation theory; see for example Boyer 1990; Guttmann 1994; O'Hara 2003a; and Kotz 1990. For some more recent studies see Reich 1997; Stanford, Taylor, and Houston 2001; and McDonough 2005. There are also some interesting analogies and many important differences with the work of "new institutionalist" neoclassical economists, such as Douglas North and Oliver Williamson.

6. This is not exactly right. What the textbooks assume is that if any firm is not making the average profit rate, market adjustments occur so quickly (for example, firms exit the industry and prices and profits rise) that all firms are soon making the average profit rate. The textbooks also assume that there are no lasting effects from the disequilibrium moment, i.e., the economy returns exactly to its hypothetical general equilibrium anchor.

7. *Financial capital* refers to money balances. *Real capital* refers to real productive assets, such as machines and structures. Corporations that organize production (coordinate labor, for example) involve units of real capital. These firms interact with banks and other sources of money, who represent units of financial capital. This distinction is blurring.

8. This analysis is limited to the United States. Similar dynamics may have affected some European economies. See for example Corry and Glyn 1994.

9. The Gini coefficient for income inequality, for example, fell from 0.376 at the end of World War II to 0.348 in 1968 (Harrison and Bluestone 1988, 130). For an explanation and definition of the Gini coefficient see chapter 15.

10. In some ways the dual economy was the Achilles' heel of the labor movement. The unions' failure to more actively represent the interests of working people in general, rather than the narrower interests of their members, eventually contributed to the success of antiunion efforts by business interests. Although unions did undertake many projects in the interests of working people in general, such as support for higher minimum wages and government spending for public education, union priorities and public perception painted a different picture.

11. Wolfson indicates that the regulations and sponsoring legislation separated commercial and investment banking, limited the payment of interest on some bank deposits, and established several new regulatory agencies, such as the Securities and Exchange Commission, to monitor the financial sector. The legislation also established the Federal Deposit Insurance Corporation (FDIC), which insured bank deposits and discouraged banking panics. Wolfson concludes, "[These changes] sought to limit the chaos that excess competition and a laissez-faire government policy had produced. This structure had two defining characteristics: a restriction of competition among financial institutions, and government protection to limit further failures." The arrangements also strengthened the powers of the Federal Reserve Board (Wolfson 1994b, 134–35).

12. In addition to large increases in defense spending, Rosenberg (2003) reports a significant increase in social spending from 1965 to 1981, highlighting increased outlays for Medicare, Medicaid, education, training, employment, and income transfer programs (238–39).

13. The unemployment rate in 1969 was 2.1 percent for white males.

14. For example, retail food prices increased by 15–20 percent in 1973 due largely to the poor harvests of 1972 and a combination of institutional phenomena involving the Russian wheat deal, acreage controls, and the liquidation of government food stocks (Blinder 1979, 36, 89; Thurow 1984, 56).

15. Crude oil prices rose from about $4.50/bbl in Oct. 1973 to $8.50/bbl in Feb. 1974, accompanied by a 39 percent increase in the cost of gasoline (Blinder 1979, 78).

16. From June 1971 to June 1973 the dollar fell 19 percent against other currencies on a trade-weighted basis (Blinder 1979, 28). Besides directly increasing import prices, a weaker dollar lessens price competition from foreign firms in U.S. markets.

17. See Thurow 1984 for some interesting observations about the distributional battle.

18. Updating the *New York Times* material, Magdoff and Magdoff (2004) report, "from the spring of 2000 to the spring of 2003, nearly 20 percent of all U.S. workers—and close to one out of four workers earning less than $40,000 per year—were laid off from either full- or part-time jobs" (26).

19. The real value of the minimum wage (in constant 2003 dollars) fell from $7.18/hour in 1975 to $5.50/hour in 2000 (See Table 15.7 in chapter 15). In 1973 the minimum wage was 46.9 percent of the median wage. In 2003 the minimum wage was 38.2 percent of the median wage (Allegreto and Bernstein, "Economic Snapshots," Economic Policy Institute web site, http://www.epinet.org/printer.cfm?id=1532& content_type=1).

20. In the 1960s about 40–45 percent of the unemployed received unemployment insurance. Coverage reached 76 percent of the unemployed in 1975. By 1987, this number had fallen to 32 percent (Rosenberg 2003, 245).

21. Among the most important antiunion measures was the appointment of pro-business people to the regulatory agency (the National Labor Relations Board) overseeing U.S. labor laws (Harrison and Bluestone 1988, 15, 100–101; Rosenberg 2003, 247–49). The board's decisions have armed employers with powerful new tools to divert production from unionized plants and to defeat unionization drives. Symbolic of government efforts to dismantle the unionized structure of production was President Reagan's use of permanent (rather than temporary) replacement workers in response to the air traffic controllers' strike. Prior to the strike by the Professional Air Traffic Controllers Association (PATCO) there had been an unwritten rule in American labor relations that firms rehired striking workers after a strike was resolved (Palley 1998, 31). Concerns about long-term worker morale and the company's image in the community had protected striking workers. Reagan's action helped redefine what was thought of as "socially acceptable behavior" (Rosenberg 2003, 266).

22. A major business survey, for example, reported that 45 percent of firms indicated that "operating union free" was a labor policy goal in 1983, compared with 31 percent in 1977 (Rosenberg 2003, 267). AFL-CIO economist Thomas Palley (1998, 95–98) and Harrison and Bluestone (1988, 49) offer strong evidence indicating that firms were increasingly willing to violate labor laws in carefully designed strategies to defeat unionization drives. Rosenberg reports that one out of every three union elections were found to include illegal employee terminations by the relatively conservative National Labor Relations Board (Rosenberg 2003, 267).

23. Palley notes that temporary agencies increased their share of total employment from 0.3 percent in 1973 to 2.1 percent in 1995. "Though not a huge number, the effect of this new industry comes from its threat effect: firms do not actually have to use such services; they just need them available as an option" (Palley 1998, 30). See also Rosenberg 2003, 264–65.

24. *Statistical Abstract of the United States 2002*, 411 and Demographia (http://www.demographia.com/ lm-unn99.htm) citing 1/19/2000 BLS release by Troy and Sheflin.

25. Among the technological changes that have facilitated increased use of third world and temporary labor are (1) the communications revolution (better phone, fax, etc. communications, and the Internet); (2) dramatic declines in shipping costs (from 5–10 percent of the value of freight to ~1.5 percent); and (3) reengineered production processes that permit the use of less-skilled labor in production (Palley 1998, 81–82).

26. Before-tax profit rates reached or approached postwar highs (depending on how calculated) in about 1996–1997 (Palley 1998, 113; Baker 2002).

27. From 1970 to 1999 top CEO pay increased from $1.26 million per year to $37.5 million (Crotty 2003, 274), while median family income grew by significantly less than 50 percent (Mishel, Bernstein, and Boushey 2003, 37). With the collapse of the stock market and devaluation of CEO stock options, average CEO income had fallen to $11 million in 2001 (Worldwatch 2003, 91). See also Jacoby 2005, especially p. 70.

28. As unemployment rose in the economy, the imagined full-employment rate of unemployment increased from 3.8 percent in 1970, to 5.1 percent in 1979, to 6–7 percent in 1983 in the annual *Economic Report of the President* prepared by the Council of Economic Advisors (Palley 1998, 109). The Fed departed from this trend in the late 1990s in an experiment that "tolerated" lower unemployment rates than most proponents of the non-accelerating inflation rate of unemployment (NAIRU) thought possible.

29. In the 1990s fiscal policy (government spending and taxes) took a backseat to monetary policy. The potentially stimulative role of government spending was almost abandoned amid debates over balanced budget constitutional amendments.

30. Harms and Knapp 2003, 433. Lester Thurow (1999), former dean of the School of Management at

MIT, is especially alarmed by the fall in government investment in human capital and public infrastructure.

31. For some interesting recent SSA-oriented analyses of the U.S. and global macro economy see several articles in the *Review of Radical Political Economics* 35(3) Summer 2003; O'Hara 2003a; and, to some extent, Brenner 2003.

32. Sheila Dow (1996) has termed this methodological pluralism "Babylonian," as opposed to Cartesian/Euclidean, thinking. She writes, "the Cartesian/Euclidean mode of thought . . . . involves establishing basic axioms, which are either true by definition or 'self evident,' and using deductive logic to derive theorems, which are not self-evident (11). . . .

"[Babylonian thought] starts from the view that it is impossible in general to establish watertight axioms (12). . . .

"Argument in the Babylonian style is thus conditioned by the problem at hand, employs a range of methods suited to the problem, and these methods cannot be combined into one formal deductive argument without drastically changing their nature (13). . . .

"The rationale for the Babylonian mode of thought is that reality is too complex to yield much certain knowledge. . . . As Keynes . . . put it: 'As soon as one is dealing with the influence of expectations and of transitory experience, one is, in the nature of things, outside the realm of the formally exact'" (18).

14

REINTRODUCING INTERNATIONAL
ECONOMIC ISSUES

*Many primers in economics make the point that where trade between individuals is
voluntary, except in cases where people act in error or are deceived about the facts, every
such exchange must provide mutual benefits. Even a child, so the story goes, will not
swap a bag of marbles for a playmate's toy truck unless she prefers the truck to the
marbles, and the other child will not agree to the exchange unless he prefers the marbles
to the truck. These discussions in elementary economics then sometimes jump, erroneously, to the conclusion that same must be true of voluntary trade between nations. . . .*
—Gomory and Baumol 2000, 25

INTRODUCTION

Chapter Outline

Up until now we have usually discussed the domestic economy as if it were a closed economy. In
this chapter we add an international dimension. The next section reviews the treatment of international trade and finance issues in neoclassical textbooks. This is followed by heterodox critiques
of the textbook approach. The next sections link debates over international economics to our
usual threads of the environment, distribution, gender, and economic rhetoric. The last two sections summarize the chapter, ending with quotations from heterodox economists.

Paradigmatic Differences

As we have noted many times, learning a paradigm is like putting on a pair of glasses, or theoretical spectacles. Learning a paradigm is like learning a language with which to talk about the world
in a particular way. Learning a paradigm is like adopting a *certain* research agenda, which illuminates some issues and shadows others.

When you master a paradigm, you gain a sense of its perspective. You can think about new
topics, such as international trade, by drawing analogies to old topics, such as the domestic economy.
From a student perspective, you know "what is going to be on the test"; you know "what the
teacher wants," which is a colloquial way of saying you know what is important from that
paradigm's perspective.

Hopefully, by now, you have a sense of the basic differences between neoclassical and heterodox economic paradigms. Let us test that hypothesis. Before going any further, write down what you think are the main analytical points and subtexts neoclassical textbooks try to convey when discussing international economic issues. Next, write down the main objections and subtexts you think make up heterodox critiques of this approach to international economics. Let us see how you did.

TEXTBOOK PRINCIPLES OF INTERNATIONAL ECONOMICS

Basic Images

Neoclassical textbooks extend the optimality and self-regulating image of market outcomes to the international sector. The texts usually remind readers of the "gains from trade" that motivate voluntary exchange. Just as individuals are better off because of exchange, so are nations. Similarly, just as domestic markets naturally reach equilibrium, so do international markets, be they product markets, currency markets, or asset markets. There is a seamless extension of the basic story of principles textbooks from domestic to international markets.

Subtexts

The textbooks offer strong support for "free trade" policies and warn against protectionism, industrial policy, and other government "interventions" in international markets. Deregulated international markets (lower tariffs, less restrictions on capital mobility, etc.) are seen as promoting economic efficiency and economic growth. Free trade is portrayed as the main hope for third world economic development and a necessary component of a "healthy" developed economy. Favoring free trade is portrayed as "forward looking" and "rational." Skepticism about free trade is portrayed as parochial or uninformed. Some exceptions are noted to this general rule, but the overriding message is "let the global market work."

Summary Picture

There is a beautiful simplicity to the textbook picture of international markets. The logic of "comparative advantage" (whereby each country concentrates its economic efforts in the areas of production in which it is relatively more efficient) demonstrates how global output increases through the specialization that trade makes possible.

David Hume's 250-year-old explanation for how trade imbalances automatically cure themselves (due to an increase in the price level of goods in countries running a balance of payments surplus (as a result of money flowing into the country) and a decline in the price level of goods in countries running a deficit (due to the outflow of money) demonstrates how balance of payments disequilibria are automatically eliminated under a gold standard or other fixed-rate exchange systems.

The workhorse of supply and demand is used to show how a balance of payments deficit automatically cures itself under flexible exchange rates. When more dollars are flowing out of the United States to buy foreign goods and assets than are flowing back to buy American goods and assets, the value of the dollar automatically falls, making our goods cheaper and foreign goods more expensive. The decline continues until equilibrium is restored.

Many additional benefits from "unfettered" global markets are celebrated in standard texts. Free trade cleans clogged economic arteries by bringing increased competitive vitality to economies and technological upgrading. Free trade offers producers new opportunities for specialization and the capture of scale economies. Free trade offers consumers increased product diversity and individual choice. And implicitly, in some accounts, free trade brings democracy and world peace through economic growth and an interweaving of common economic interests.

OVERVIEW OF HETERODOX CRITIQUES

Heterodox objections to textbook treatments of international economic issues build on familiar heterodox themes, indicting the chapters on trade and international finance especially severely for:

1. misplaced concreteness
2. insufficient attention to distributional issues
3. use of static rather than dynamic analysis
4. insufficient attention to the implications of uncertainty in financial markets
5. inadequate treatment of sluggish and non-equilibrating price adjustments
6. insufficient attention to problems of weak aggregate demand and
7. neglect of meta-externalities

The thrust of heterodox thinking is that textbook economics oversimplifies international economic questions. The textbooks tend to excise trade issues from concrete contexts, ignore how the presence of unemployment might alter the analysis, and de-emphasize who benefits and who loses under free trade. In so doing, the textbooks encourage oversimplified endorsements of deregulated international markets. These endorsements have unwisely promoted global international orders that encourage (and to some extent impose) laissez-faire-oriented economic policies in international *and* domestic matters.[1]

The subtext of heterodox analysis is that economic relations need to be re-embedded in a system of social governance at both the international and the domestic levels. Although increased international trade and globalization can be beneficial, this outcome depends on appropriate institutional and regulatory environments. The next several sections elaborate the implications of each of the seven criticisms listed above.

HETERODOX CRITIQUES: MISPLACED CONCRETENESS

Loss of Context

Neoclassical textbooks tend to leap from examples that illustrate "the gains from trade" among individuals to conclusions about the automatic benefits of free trade among nations. From a heterodox perspective much more attention is needed to the context of trade. For example, is it between two developed nations or a first and third world nation; are there competitive or concentrated market structures; are there diminishing or increasing returns in production; are the economies at full employment, and so on.

The textbooks' message, accompanied by the usual "note but ignore" qualifiers, is that free trade and deregulation of international markets inevitably promote economic growth. In some cases, free trade and deregulation are portrayed as the only road to economic growth. Heterodox economists challenge these claims. Although it is hard to disentangle the many factors that affect international economic activity, it is notable that the global economy grew roughly half as fast over the last two decades of the twentieth century under deregulated (neoliberal) free trade policies than it had grown in the previous twenty years.[2] Numerous countries and regions that followed neoliberal policies fared badly, as is the case with Latin America (Chang 2005, 125–29; Stiglitz 2003, 86).

Although it is true that many rapidly growing countries like the Asian tigers did tie their economies to the world market, they did so in a partially state-directed rather than laissez-faire free trade fashion. Their governments pursued industrial policies with protectionist and other interventionist dimensions in their interactions with the world economy. They did not rely totally on the invisible hand to pull up their boot straps. While expanded trade can be desirable, the devil is in the details and particular contexts of trade.

Case Study: NAFTA

Introduction

Consider, for example, analyses of the 1993 North American Free Trade Agreement (NAFTA), which reduced tariffs and other trade restrictions among the United States, Canada, and Mexico. Heterodox economists challenge the tendency of macro principles textbooks to dismiss skeptic concerns about the trade agreement with little attention to concrete particulars. We will concentrate our critique on an excerpt from N. Gregory Mankiw's popular introductory textbook, as his analysis seems fairly typical, his textbook is widely used,[3] and he was recently the chair of President Bush's Council of Economic Advisers. Mankiw writes:

> Economists and the general public often disagree about free trade. In 1993, for example, the United States faced the question of whether to ratify the North American Free Trade Agreement. . . . Opinion polls showed the general public in the United States about evenly split on the issue. . . . By contrast, [neoclassical (*not in original*)] economists overwhelmingly supported the agreement. They viewed free trade as a way of allocating production efficiently and raising living standards in all three countries.
>   Economists view the United States as an ongoing experiment that confirms the virtues of free trade. . . . [T]he United States has allowed unrestricted trade among the states. . . . The world could similarly benefit from free trade among countries (Mankiw 2001, 197–98).

The first thing to note is that Mankiw's arguments for NAFTA rely on general arguments about the benefits of free trade rather than detailed analysis of the reality of inter-American trade. They also rely heavily on analogy. Mankiw compares trade among states within the United States, for example, to trade among nations and predicts the world will prosper as the United States has from free trade.[4] Heterodox economists want to complicate the analysis with concrete details. Although the difference between heterodox and orthodox economists on the need for "context" is one of degree (heterodox economists admit you cannot analyze every situation as a special case and orthodox economists recognize the need for some specific information), the difference in degree is enough to be a difference in kind.[5]

Assessments of NAFTA need to look at the agreement from the perspective of people in all three NAFTA countries. We will look at the agreement from Mexican perspectives in this section to illustrate the problem of misplaced concreteness. We will address more familiar concerns raised from U.S. perspectives in later sections.

Building on textbook trade theory, NAFTA supporters promised it would bring Mexico large economic benefits. A flood of foreign investment was expected to increase employment (especially in the manufacturing sector and the maquiladora plants along the U.S. border), raise wages, and reduce inequality. Although some expectations have been fulfilled (there has been significant U.S. investment and some new job creation), the overall outcome has been disappointing. Real wages in the maquiladora plants fell about 20 percent from 1980 to 1996 (Larudee 1998, 279). The real minimum wage in Mexico has fallen by 60 percent since 1982 and by 23 percent since NAFTA (Wise 2003, 2). Inequality and poverty have increased (Larudee 1998, 281, 289; T. Lee 1998, 294–95).[6] A survey taken in October 2003 found that only 45 percent of Mexicans said NAFTA had benefited their economy (Smith and Lindblad 2003).

Heterodox Analyses of NAFTA

Why hasn't NAFTA lived up to earlier expectations? The answers imply that the benefits of trade depend heavily on the context of trade. Among the key factors limiting NAFTA's ability to improve the lives of many Mexicans are: (1) the negative effects of the agreement on peasant agriculture and rural village life; and (2) the weakness of the Mexican labor movement.[7]

The Decay of Rural Life. Although it has helped some urban consumers through lower food prices, the increased importation of cheap American foodstuffs under NAFTA has reduced the competitiveness of small Mexican farmers, driving many campesinos into crowded urban slums.[8] NAFTA has also encouraged the expansion of cattle ranching (especially by large landowners) for export to the U.S. market. Through normal market mechanisms (rising land prices), local political maneuvering, and extra-market intimidation, these cattlemen have forced additional peasant farmers and de facto squatters off of the land.[9]

From a heterodox perspective, the weakening of rural "village life" that has accompanied urban migration is a key cost of NAFTA. This cost does not show up in the GDP statistics relied on by neoclassical economists to measure relative well-being. From a heterodox perspective, this is poor accounting. Reflecting on the loss of village life, Tom Barry writes:

> The disintegration of campesino villages and loss of communal structures . . . have economic and social implications. Although inefficient in terms of percapita productivity, the commitment of traditional peasant agriculture to provide work and subsistence for all family and community members has helped alleviate the burden of unemployment and poverty in Mexico. . . . Rural life is undeniably harsh, but the poverty of the countryside is not as degrading and ultimately debilitating physically and mentally as the destitution of impoverished urban life, where cash income may be higher but quality of life lower. (Barry 1995,147)

Robin Hahnel adds,

> [W]hen corn is grown in Mexico farmers live in traditional Mexican villages that are relatively disease and crime free and where centuries-old social safety nets exist when family members fall on hard times. Whereas producing shoes, for example, in Mexico requires a Mexican to live in an urban slum or maquiladora zone where disease and crime are higher and social safety nets absent. The positive external effects of rural village life when corn is produced in Mexico are undercounted [181]. . . .
>
> Political economists like David Barkin . . . do not claim that trade liberalization has not created some new jobs in Mexican manufacturing. . . . Instead Barkin . . . point[s] out that disastrous changes in Mexican agriculture, induced in part by terms of the NAFTA agreement, negate any small beneficial . . . effects on employment and wages . . . (Hahnel 2002,190).

Defenders of deregulated economic policies sometimes argue that urban migration is voluntary and "reveals" people's preferences for urban life. Heterodox economists are not so sure. The most important question is not whether people prefer urban migration to desperate conditions in the countryside. The key question is whether alternative economic policies could have produced better choices than post-NAFTA choices.[10]

The Structure of Labor Markets. Many heterodox economists have emphasized the sensitivity of NAFTA outcomes from a Mexican perspective to the institutional characteristics of Mexican labor markets. Among the questions that need asking are: How collusive are employer hiring strategies? What kind of opportunities exist for collective bargaining in the maquiladora plants? How successful is the Mexican government in capturing some of the productivity gains from increased foreign investment for social infrastructure spending and so on? Can the Mexican economy and labor force move up the value-added pyramid from a maquiladora manufacturing base?

Assessments of Mexican labor markets vary. Some accounts stress the "high-road" appearance of Mexican labor markets, which include relatively generous state-mandated severance agreements and required profit sharing. Others accounts find emaciated unions, weak enforcement of progressive labor laws, and a government retreat from redistributive policies. With a strong labor movement and redistributive state policies, the hypothetical benefits of increased foreign investment could be shared among a wide group of Mexicans. Absent such market and political power, the benefits to most Mexicans could be small.[11]

Mehrene Larudee's work suggests that Mexico's embrace of NAFTA reflects a political decision to adopt the "low-road" macroeconomic strategy described in chapter 13 (involving low wages and conflictual labor markets). International capital is less likely than domestic capital to nurture long-term relationships with employees, communities, and other national constituencies. International capital is notoriously "foot loose and fancy free." Larudee writes,

> A strategy focused on exports implies maintaining competitive labor costs. And as MNCs [multinational corporations] produce an increasing share of value-added, their influence is likely to strengthen political pressure to keep real wages down, for example by allowing the nominal minimum wage to lag behind inflation. There will be pressure, too, to "flexibilize" labor markets by reducing labor rights and benefits. (Larudee 1998, 289)

Heterodox economists are just as skeptical of the benefits of low-road macroeconomic strategies abroad as they are at home.

The Political Economy of Global Trade

Heterodox economists also criticize the textbooks' treatment of international trade for de-emphasizing the geopolitical context of free trade rhetoric. Trade patterns and other international economic relations have always been deeply influenced by geopolitical factors, exemplified by colonialism, persistent threats of military or covert interventions over economic issues, and the use of foreign aid as a lever for structuring trade relations. This continues today.

The deposit of Saudi oil revenues in U.S. banks and the Saudis' moderation of OPEC price increases, for example, reflect geopolitical forces (such as our military help in maintaining the Saudi regime) as much as market forces. One of the hidden pressures for NAFTA similarly involved U.S. government efforts to gain privileged access for U.S. firms and financial interests to Mexican oil. The latter has been insulated from foreign ownership by Mexican law.[12]

The recent push for a neoliberal version of "free trade" (which, for example, often strives to protect intellectual property rights much more vigorously than labor rights) is as laden with nationalist geopolitical agendas as past global trading orders. It is also just as laden with the objectives of private corporations and economic interests in the host nations pushing different policies.

Both presidents Nixon and Reagan, for example, filled key trade posts with employees from Cargill, the world's largest grain exporter. The CEO of Monsanto chemical corporation served as the U.S. trade representative to the World Trade Organization under President Clinton, alongside many insiders from U.S. financial firms (Daly and Farley 2004, 330). Joseph Stiglitz, chair of the Council of Economic Advisers during the Clinton years, notes, for example, that U.S. treasury secretary Robert Rubin (one of the key people pushing for deregulating global financial markets during the Clinton administration) came from Goldman Sachs, the largest investment bank in the United States, and returned to Citigroup, which controlled the largest commercial bank. The deputy director of the IMF similarly went to work for Citigroup after leaving the IMF. Stiglitz and others do not argue that these individuals' personal support for particular policies was explicitly "bought" by promises of lucrative employment. Stiglitz and others do claim that corporate pressures on politicians force them to fill key policy posts with individuals who have the good fortune of believing that what is good for financial capital is good for the economy, and good for them as well.[13]

HETERODOX CRITIQUES: DISTRIBUTIONAL ISSUES

Neoclassical textbooks emphasize the "net" gains from free trade. They argue, for example, that although there are groups (such as semiskilled factory workers in the United States or peasant farmers in Mexico) who may be harmed by NAFTA, the beneficiaries of free trade (such as consumers in both countries and workers in expanding industries) could conceivably compensate the losers and still enjoy positive benefits. Some discussions move on to other topics at this point, leading many students to assume that compensation is actually paid or that uncompensated adjustment costs are small compared to the gains from trade. These assumptions allow supporters of free trade to assert its benefits without fully addressing distributional issues.

Heterodox economists want more emphasis placed on distributional questions. They call for more attention to actual outcomes (full compensation is rarely paid) rather than potential outcomes.[14] They find that recent increases in global trade have tended to increase social inequality within nations[15] and perhaps between them.[16] A key factor behind these increases has been increased pressures (as in Mexico) for adoption of low-road macroeconomic strategies.

Heterodox theorists emphasize that "unmediated" free trade policies tend to increase the relative bargaining power and share of national income going to owners of capital and their direct representatives (upper management). This is because these policies tend to increase capital mobility. The threat of capital flight tends to depress wages and benefits, discourage government efforts to redistribute income and wealth, and weaken local and national governments' regulatory options, especially within the developed world. Recent trade patterns have also tended to increase inequality within first world labor markets, due in part to greater foreign competition in low- than high-skill labor markets. Although it is also true that free trade has weakened domestic oligopolies' pricing power, this effect has been less potent.

It is difficult to measure the "threat effect" on labor market outcomes of employers' enhanced ability to move production overseas. Globalization's effect on unionization suggests the impact is significant. One study, for example, found that between 1993 and 1995 over 50 percent of all

U.S. employers threatened to shut down facilities if workers unionized (Bronfenbrenner 1996, 1997).[17] Similar results were reported by an official review board created by the NAFTA agreement (Palley 1998, 170).

Estimates vary of how large a contribution international pressures have made to the growing inequality of income in the United States. Most analysts seem to attribute about 10 to 20 percent of increasing inequality to international factors (Stiglitz 1997, 937; Rodrik 1998, 83, 88; Williamson 1997 [in Ackerman et al. 2000, 303]; Belman and Lee 1992 [in Ackerman et al. 1998, 79–80]).[18] Chapter 15 ("Reintroducing the Macroeconomics of Inequality") explores the causes of growing inequality in more detail.

Besides reducing the market wages of low-skilled workers in the advanced economies (with potentially positive impacts on low-wage workers in the developed countries contingent upon contextual factors), unconstrained free trade can also spawn a "race to the bottom" in terms of the "social wage" (e.g., public provision of basic services through taxation) and regulatory environments. This outcome reflects the potential "prisoner's dilemma" problem of unconstrained market competition to attract global capital. To draw a sports analogy, unregulated global trade can force steroids on economic competitors.[19] The environmental implications of this problem are potentially troubling.

Heterodox economists call for greater attention to issues of fairness and inequality in macroeconomic analysis and policy for two main reasons. The first rationale is familiar and involves conceptions of social justice and revisions of GDP data to include distributional concerns. The second rationale is less well known. Contrary to many political economic theories that find an inherent trade-off between "equity and efficiency," heterodox economists generally believe that large divides between rich and poor can destabilize social orders, erode social capital, and weaken aggregate demand. Thus trade policies that increase inequality can simultaneously harm economic growth. For example, the lack of reduction (and in some cases actual increases) in poverty and the weakening of the middle class that has often accompanied IMF trade policies has often derailed developing economies. As nobel laureate Joseph Stiglitz writes,

> [T]here is a "social contract" that binds citizens together, and with their government. . . .
> Part of the social contract entails "fairness." . . . The Washington Consensus policies paid little attention to issues of distribution or "fairness." If pressed, many of its proponents would argue that the best way to help the poor is to make the economy grow. They believe in trickle-down economics. . . .
> The history of the past fifty years has, however, not supported these theories and hypotheses. (Stiglitz 2003, 78–79)[20]

HETERODOX CRITIQUES: DYNAMIC VERSUS STATIC ANALYSIS

Textbook discussions of international trade usually assume "constant or decreasing returns to scale" in markets for tradable goods. Although these assumptions may seem like technical details that readers can skip, they are not. The assumptions have major policy implications. Markets with economies of scale (such as mass production economies or learning curve economies) can have path-dependent outcomes. This means that the "winners" in these markets are not necessarily determined in advance by exogenously given factors like geography and natural resource endowments. The latter is usually assumed or implied, however, in textbook discussions of comparative advantage.

If there are special opportunities for profit in some markets (such as the long-run potential for "oligopoly profits" in the global automobile industry) or if there are societal benefits to different patterns of production (such as the benefits of a more egalitarian income distribution from national competitiveness in semiskilled industries), government policy may be able to improve a country's quality of life by helping domestic firms capture path-dependent positions in these markets. This is the insight behind "strategic trade theory."

Textbook discussions of trade do not totally neglect these possibilities. There are usually "note but ignore" references to "infant industries," and path dependencies. The full implications of these phenomena, however, are not explored. The textbooks tend to give the impression that recently successful third world economies grew because they deregulated their economies. Actually, the opposite is more accurate. Beginning with England and the United States, and followed by Japan and more recently other East Asian states like Korea and Taiwan, nearly all economic success stories have included aspects of protectionist policies and/or state-directed economic growth.[21]

As Crotty, Epstein, and Kelly note, development in these countries, "has been guided in every case by some form of state-led industrial policy, utilizing credit allocation, regulated and differential interest rates, government-controlled central banks, regulation of labor markets, high state spending on education and infrastructure, managed trade, and controls over the movement of money capital and inward and outward FDI [foreign direct investment]" (Crotty, Epstein, and Kelly 1998, 135).[22]

Although it is true that a "parasitic state" that tilts public resources toward industries based on cronyism and bureaucratic self-interest can generate economic outcomes inferior to deregulated markets, a prudent state can do better than laissez-faire. The debates over strategic trade policy, and industrial policy more generally, are ultimately debates about the feasibility of a "thoughtful" state. This is an historical and institutional question. Answering it requires more than a priori judgments. The analysis is necessarily messier than the simple and/or pristine graphical-mathematical models of free trade that dominate the textbooks.

HETERODOX CRITIQUES: UNCERTAINTY AND FINANCIAL MARKETS

Since the 1970s there has been an accelerating deregulation of global financial markets. The world has moved from a regime of fixed exchange rates and regulations inhibiting the movement of financial capital across national boundaries to a world of "hot money." Prior to 1975 most financial capital stayed at home. The parties to most loans lived within the same country and the sale of most financial assets (such as stocks, bonds, and real estate) did not involve foreign currency exchanges. In 1977 there were about $18 billion a day of currency trades in the global economy. This number grew to $83 billion a day by 1983, $590 billion a day by 1989, and about $1.5 trillion a day by 1998 (Crotty 2000a, 8). Movement of these funds is often governed by volatile short-term sentiments.

In the tradition of Minsky and Keynes, heterodox economists worry about the problem of speculative excesses in global financial markets. They fear bubbles followed by panics in global currency markets. They fear increased volatility in domestic financial markets (such as stock, bond, and real estate markets), due to the fickle behavior of international capital. The problem of uncertainty and herd behavior in global financial markets is exacerbated by the exoticness of foreign markets for many investors, even larger imperfect information problems than those common in national markets, and the absence of an international institution akin to the Federal Reserve. Heterodox economists fear that deregulating global finance will destabilize the "real sector" and undermine global economic performance. Recent economic events have tended to support heterodox concerns. Even many neoclassical supporters of free trade in goods and services are increasingly questioning the wisdom of a parallel deregulation of financial markets.

For example, Jagdish Bhagwati, a strong supporter of free trade and a well-known opponent of the Seattle protests against the World Trade Organization (WTO), writes, "Theoretically there are similarities between free trade and free capital flows. . . .

"But the problem is that when you recognize that capital flows are subject to speculation, manias, panics, and crashes, there is simply no counterpart in trade" (Bhagwati 2001,14).

The dangerous implications of global financial fluctuations were illustrated by the "peso crisis" in Mexico in the mid-1990s. Partially due to the public relations campaign selling NAFTA, the peso had become overvalued by 1994. The speculative bubble burst and was replaced by an investor panic. The exchange rate of the peso against the dollar fell by more than 50 percent from November 1994 to September 1995. Short-term interest rates skyrocketed, and the Mexican economy fell into a sharp recession (Sharma 2001, 59–60).

Similar financial crises severely damaged many of the East Asian economies in the late 1990s. The scenario was strikingly similar to the Mexican case. Low interest rates in the United States and Japan helped turn investor attention to recently opened financial markets in Asia. The rush to buy Asian assets bid up their price and invited new speculative capital flows. This in turn helped spark a Minsky-like speculative boom, which was followed by the inevitable collapse.[23] Unemployment increased significantly in Thailand, South Korea, and Indonesia. The poverty rate doubled in Indonesia and almost tripled in urban South Korea (Stiglitz 2003, 97).[24]

The "Tequila Crisis" and "Asian Flu" ultimately spread to other countries, causing unemployment and other economic disruptions as far away as Brazil and Russia. A hastily arranged $50-billion bailout from the United States helped limit the contagion from the Mexican crisis and a $184-billion IMF bailout helped combat the Asian Flu. As Joseph Stigliz writes,

> Capital market liberalization made the developing countries subject to both the rational and the irrational whims of the investor community, to their irrational exuberance and pessimism. Keynes was well aware of the often seemingly irrational changes in sentiments. . . . [H]e referred to these huge and often inexplicable swings in moods as "animal spirits." Nowhere were these spirits more evident than in East Asia. (Stiglitz 2003, 100)

HETERODOX CRITIQUES: SLUGGISH PRICE ADJUSTMENTS AND INSUFFICIENT AGGREGATE DEMAND

Heterodox economists extend their theories of sluggish price adjustments in modern economies to international markets, noting, for example, that long-term contracts are even more common in international trade than in domestic markets.[25] Most importantly, heterodox economists criticize standard textbooks for using trade models that *assume* full employment. The stories told demonstrating the gains from trade, for example, almost always assume both economies are on their production possibilities frontier before and after trade. From a heterodox perspective, this puts the cart before the horse. The models assume the result they are often used to "prove."[26]

Although heterodox economists agree that deregulating international markets could at times increase aggregate demand, they find that free trade policies could also (1) weaken private-sector demand, (2) undermine the ability of national governments to adopt expansionary monetary and fiscal policy, and (3) in the presence of certain structural economic problems (such as surplus labor in the countryside) destabilize economic relations in ways that exacerbate unemployment.

Free trade regimes could depress private-sector demand in two main ways. By increasing capital mobility free trade policies could reduce labor's share of national income and thereby weaken consumer demand. Deregulating international markets could also increase uncertainty and thereby depress investment demand.[27]

Free trade policies could also weaken the ability of central banks (such as the Federal Reserve) to lower interest rates during recessions. This is because current free trade policies have made it easier for domestic investors to move funds to other countries in search of higher interest rates. Expansionary fiscal policy could be similarly discouraged by fears that footloose investors will become anxious about rising wages, inflation, or currency depreciation as the economy moves toward full employment.[28]

HETERODOX CRITIQUES: META-EXTERNALITIES

General Claim

Because heterodox economists generally use a holist rather than methodologically individualistic approach to study international economic issues, they explore the feedback effects of international trade more broadly than the textbooks do. We have called these feedback effects meta-externalities, as they have important societal implications that are not included in market calculations.

Neoclassical economists acknowledge a limited number of these factors in an ad hoc way without acknowledging the general principle of meta-externalities. Standard textbooks, for example, admit that the benefits of free trade do not necessarily apply to jet fighters and other markets whose outcomes could affect national defense. The texts endorse government purchasing practices and other policies that ensure that important military goods are produced at home. Heterodox economists extend the meta-externality rationale for overriding the world market's division of labor to non-defense industries.

Among candidates for social support are the family farm and manufacturing industries with "good jobs" for blue-collar workers. The rationale for aiding the family farm is the traditional Jerffersonian claim that communities with family farmers develop social institutions conducive to democratic cultures, community well-being, and environmental consciousness. Similar notions about the societal benefits of more egalitarian income distributions underlie recommendations for government support of industries with "good blue-collar jobs." Interesting arguments can be raised for and against government support of these industries on the basis of meta-externalities. The point here is not that the industries should (or should not) be protected, but that the issue should be analyzed more extensively in the textbooks.

Political Externalities

Heterodox economists also focus analytical attention on the "political externalities" of different global trading arrangements. They find current practices creating enormously large and powerful multinational corporations (MNCs) at the same time as disabling the ability of national governments to act as a countervailing force in domestic economies. There is tremendous pressure on national governments to approve mergers of their nations' largest firms because of the threat of competition from super-sized foreign firms. The U.S. Justice Department, for example, approved the merger of the two largest American grain trading companies in 1999, despite concerns that small farmers might find themselves in a weaker bargaining position with these companies (Daly and Farley 2004, 324). Heterodox economists worry about the enormous political and market power that large firms acquire simply by being large. As noted in earlier chapters, heterodox conceptions of corporate power extend beyond the ability of firms to collude in order to set monopoly-like prices. Massive size also confers on firms the ability to influence government policy and public opinion through political action and "education campaigns," the ability to influence consumers through advertising, and the ability to influence technological development through funding path-dependent research.

As noted earlier, heterodox economists also worry that the enhanced mobility of financial capital under current "free trade" policies is weakening governments' ability to redistribute income or fight unemployment with expansionary Keynesian macro policy. The threat of capital flight may also be undermining governments' ability to regulate environmental and other hazards.

Potential Benefits of Localism

There tends to be a preference among many heterodox economists for localizing the division of labor when the financial costs of doing so are relatively modest. When a division of labor is more visible, it is easier to remember that economic relations are a subset of human relations. In contrast, the extreme impersonality of the world market helps erode social norms that restrain inequality and humanize economic relations. As many observers have noted, markets allow strangers to exchange, but they also "make strangers of exchangers." Citing the work of other heterodox economists, for example, Baker, Epstein, and Pollin write,

> [M]arkets do indeed promote efficiency and change, but they achieve this through undermining social coherence and solidarity. Markets must therefore be embedded within social institutions that mitigate their negative consequences. (Baker, Epstein, and Pollin 1998b, 20)[29]

Sounding a somewhat similar theme, Harvard political economist Dani Rodrik (1998) writes,

> Very few economists that I know would condone the idea of recruiting 15-year-old Guatemalan women for work in sweatshops in the United States. Yet, when American companies or their affiliates or their subcontractors outsource, we have essentially the same outcome. . . . The tendency of most trade economists is to say: "Well, that's just trade; it's none of our business." (86)

Nobel Laureate Joseph Stiglitz (2003) writes,

> Domestic firms may at least be attuned to the social context and be reluctant to fire workers if they know there are no alternative jobs available. (I saw this forcefully in my discussions in Korea . . .).[30] Foreign owners, on the other hand, may feel a greater obligation to their shareholders to maximize stock market value. . . . (57)

Stiglitz adds that local banks may be also more responsive to local policy makers' requests to ease credit during economic downturns and to direct credit to underserved groups (Stiglitz 2003, 69–70). Keynes (1933) similarly writes,

> There may be some financial calculation which shows it to be advantageous that my savings should be invested in whatever quarter of the habitable globe shows the greatest mar-

ginal efficiency of capital or the highest rate of interest. But experience is accumulating that remoteness between ownership and operation is an evil in the relations among men, likely or certain in the long run to set up strains and enmities which will bring to nought the financial calculation.

I sympathize, therefore, with those who would minimize, rather than with those who would maximize, economic entanglement among nations. Ideas, knowledge, science, hospitality, travel—these are the things which should of their nature be international. But let goods be homespun whenever it is reasonably and conveniently possible, and, above all, let finance be primarily national. (758)

Drawing on work by Herman Daly, Eban Goodstein (1988) adds,

"By spatially separating the costs and benefits of environmental exploitation, international trade makes them harder to compare. It thereby increases the tendency for economies to overshoot their optimal scale." . . .

Restricted trade keeps the consequences of our actions close to home, where we have both the community of interest and the political tools to manage them. Restricted trade also forces us to develop the recycling, treatment, and waste reduction technologies needed for sustainable development. (301–2)

Many heterodox economists also argue that public policies promoting localized production are necessary to level the playing field due to the large subsidies the energy sector enjoys. These subsides artificially lower transportation costs and bias the global economy toward an overextended division of labor (Daly and Farley 2004, 312).[31]

In closing, it is important to note that while recognizing the meta-externalities of local production and small size, heterodox economists do not deny the possible payoffs to economies of scale, regional specialization, and even the anonymity offered by the world market. The point is to include all important phenomena in an accounting of the costs and benefits of expanding the global division of labor in order to generate a more complete and reliable analysis. It may be the case that increasing global trade is beneficial.

THREADS: TRADE AND THE ENVIRONMENT

We turn now to the implications of heterodox theory for the discussion of international macroeconomic issues related to our three threads: environmental, distributional, and gender concerns. The discussion of environmental issues below expands points made earlier in this chapter and foreshadows longer analyses contained in chapter 16's discussion of macroeconomics and the environment.

Kuznets Curves

Proponents of free trade often argue that it indirectly promotes environmental quality because it promotes economic growth, which promotes environmental quality. They appeal to what has come to be called an "Environmental Kuznets Curve (EKC),"[32] which suggests that pollution levels initially increase as economies industrialize, but then turn downward as economic growth continues. Heterodox economists question whether laissez-faire versions of free trade lead to faster economic growth. Heterodoxy also understands the environmental implications of economic growth differently from orthodox theory, but we will defer discussion of that aspect of Kuznets curves until chapter 16.

Races to the Bottom

The fear that corporations will be able to play national governments against each other in pursuit of lower environmental protection standards is one of the most well-known environmentalist reservations about free trade. Proponents of free trade tend to minimize this concern. They argue that all declines in aggregate output and employment caused by the contraction of industries facing competition from more polluting foreign firms would be automatically eliminated by adjustments in exchange rates. This is because an increase in imports of polluting goods, all other things equal, would lead to a greater supply than demand for dollars. This imbalance would cause the value of the dollar to fall until U.S. exports increased or imports decreased by the exact amount of the growth in polluting industry imports.

The pristine logic of this argument is not reassuring to many heterodox economists. Although such claims may be true in the hypothetical long run and in the aggregate, they are unlikely to address the immediate concerns of the workers, owners, and communities losing jobs to the polluting exporter. These constituencies are likely to press for reductions in U.S. environmental standards to preserve their occupations, communities, and investments.

Somewhat surprisingly, however, most research seems to have found that firms are not relocating production activities in pollution havens (Cosbey 2006,140). This may be because environmental costs remain a small part of total production costs, or due to lags in business location decisions. Imagined business hostility to tough environmental regulations, however, can be a serious problem independent of actual business sensitivity to environmental policies. As Goodstein reports, "in spite of solid economic evidence to the contrary, the frightening perception of global competition for dirty industry has induced very real downward leveling pressures on environmental protection regulation" (Goodstein 1998, 312).

Reconciling Trade and Environmental Regulations

Heterodox economists have expressed concern about the environmental implications of the emerging governance structure of international trade. The key institutions, the IMF, the World Bank, and the World Trade Organization (WTO), lack democratic accountability and have given relatively little weight to environmental interests in the past. Drawing on his experience as chair of the Council of Economic Advisers for President Clinton and three years as chief economist and senior vice president of the World Bank, Joseph Stiglitz depicts these institutions as overseen by the finance and trade ministers of the leading industrialized countries, who in turn represent key corporate and financial interests. The ideology of these institutions tends to be, what is good for multinational corporations is good for world trade and the global economy and thus good for the environment. As Stiglitz writes, "Just as at the IMF it is the finance ministers that are heard, at the WTO it is the trade ministers. No wonder, then, that little attention is often paid to concerns about the environment" (Stiglitz 2003, 225).

The legacies of the General Agreement on Tariffs and Trade, numerous bilateral and multilateral trade agreements (like NAFTA), the policies of the World Trade Organization, and the lending policies of the IMF and the World Bank have been creating a set of rules for international trade that constrain the ability of individual countries to define their own environmental policies. Although most trade agreements formally retain the participating countries' ability to regulate environmental and health hazards within their borders (as long as they treat domestic and foreign firms equally) many features of the agreements have the potential to curb environmental initiatives. The emerging trade authorities have been especially wary of what has been called "green protectionism" and have overturned a number of countries' environmental rules on the grounds that they discriminated unfairly against or intruded on the prerogatives of foreign firms. For example, a GATT panel ruled that the United States cannot limit foreign tuna imports for failing to observe U.S. safeguards against dolphin kills, as required under the Marine Mammal Protection Act (if the foreign catch is made outside of U.S. territorial waters) (Starke 2004, 158).[33] A WTO ruling similarly prevented the United States from prohibiting shrimp imports from companies that use technologies endangering sea turtles, as was required under the U.S. Endangered Species Act (ibid.). A European Union court invalidated a Danish law requiring returnable bottles (Harris 2002, 417).[34] The United States has attempted to prevent European nations from restricting the importation of U.S. beef raised with growth hormones.[35] In February of 2006, the United States won a preliminary ruling from the WTO that weakened European limitations on the importation of genetically modified crops (*Washington Post,* February 8, 2006). A battle over the right of countries to impose labeling requirements about the use of genetically modified materials is likely in the future.

Environmentalists also worry that trade rulings will restrict the ability of countries to promote technological developments in areas deemed socially desirable, such as the development of environmentally friendly energy technologies. Goodstein indicates that the use of government spending, technology-forcing regulations, and direct subsidies to promote clean energy technologies could face potential legal challenges under trade agreements (Goodstein 1998, 316).

Although it is possible that trade rules could be written and interpreted to permit greater local autonomy with respect to environmental goals, and that the environmental objectives challenged in the rulings cited above might be pursuable through other means, heterodox economists fear that the current course of world trade is likely to weaken environmental protection efforts. Harvard political economist Dani Rodrik writes,

> [T]here is an interesting paradox in that the whole GATT-WTO system is built on the notion that we have to avoid regulatory capture by special interest groups so that we do not slide down the slippery slope toward protectionism. Yet in practice it turns out that the agenda of trade globalization, trade expansion, and trade pacts has been captured largely by business interests. (Rodrik 1998, 94)[36]

Some heterodox economists have called for the creation of a World Environmental Organization (WEO), with enforcement powers rivaling the WTO, to counterbalance the elevation of trade objectives over social objectives in the current global order.

Pareto Optimal or Intolerable Exchanges

The race to the bottom debate also raises a second issue about the situations in which it may or may not be desirable to permit countries to compete on the basis of differing environmental standards. The prisoner's dilemma critique of free trade is based on the assumption that both parties would prefer to maintain higher environmental standards but are forced to mutually lower them in self-defeating competition. In the second case, the developing countries "voluntarily" assume some of the pollution burden created by first world consumption in exchange for higher employment and income levels.

Much ink has been spilled over a related remark by Harvard University's former president (and former economics professor) Lawrence Summers, that the third world is "under-polluted." Summers's thinking (in its most attractive light) is that it is rational for third world governments and populations to make different trade-offs between environmental quality and other economic outcomes (like jobs and income) than made in wealthy countries. For example, if environmental quality is viewed as a "luxury good," it may be sensible for third world populations to "purchase less of it" than first world populations do, thus permitting a mutually beneficial exchange of environmental quality for other economic goods between the first and third worlds.

Although many heterodox economists might support this reasoning in limited cases, most would restrict its applicability. This delimitation is due in part to (1) the treatment of some environmental conditions as "human rights" rather than commodities and (2) the need to look at trade choices in dynamic rather than static terms.

Heterodox economists often distinguish between environmental issues involving human health (such as exposure to toxic waste) and environmental issues involving social amenities (like enjoyment of pleasant vistas or river sports). Heterodox economists generally treat freedom from exposure to toxic waste as a human right that cannot be bartered through markets.[37] The full rationale for this position is developed in chapter 16. It is analogous to the reasons for heterodox opposition to the development of markets in body parts (like kidneys) or the allowance of people to sell themselves into slavery. Heterodox thinking draws on a holist and dynamic view of what adopting certain institutions and practices implies over time for the evolution of society.

Heterodox thinking also requires that judgments about the merits of what might be called "toxic trade" (the acceptance of serious environmental and health hazards by the third world in exchange for economic benefits) be made "in context" rather than in the abstract. This requires asking: (1) who benefits from, who bears the costs of, and who makes the decisions about toxic trades in the third world; (2) what kind of information is available to the people affected by these decisions; and (3) what alternatives exist to these choices. In line with heterodox thinking, as of 1994, all of the twenty-four nations of the OECD (the Organisation for Economic Co-Operation and Development, basically the advanced industrial countries), with the exception of the United States, had signed the Basel Convention, prohibiting the export of toxic waste from advanced to developing economies (Tietenberg 2003,489).

Obscuring Natural Limits

Ecological economists and other advocates of sustainable development also fear that expanded trade will make it easier for the advanced economies to escape natural constraints on production. This is because of trade's ability to augment domestic natural resources and shift the burden of assimilating the waste products of production to foreign shoulders. In a world economy with an equitable income distribution and adequate environmental protections, this flexibility would be desirable. In a highly unequal global economy with a bias toward careless economic growth, this flexibility may accelerate excessive resource depletion and waste production.

Consumers in the first world and their imitators among the elites in the third world are becoming habituated to patterns of consumption that will be very difficult to sustain globally. These lifestyles are possible now because of the first world's absorption of productive capacities from the third world.[38] This habituation is likely to create adjustment problems in the future and pressures to relax environmental standards.[39] In similar fashion, the advanced countries' ability to scour the globe for petroleum and other resources may be orienting technological change down dead-end streets. Having to confront more stringent materials and waste assimilating boundaries in the present might create a much more environmentally friendly development path for the future.[40]

THREADS: DISTRIBUTION

As noted above, heterodox economists criticize most textbooks for de-emphasizing distributional issues when discussing trade issues. Heterodox economists are especially concerned about (1) the growth in global inequality facilitated by increasing capital mobility, (2) the growing size and power of multinational corporations, and (3) the erosion of egalitarian social norms, all of which appear to have been encouraged by recent free trade policies. Although heterodox economists generally find that trade liberalization has increased inequality, they recognize countertendencies, such as the ability of foreign competition to weaken the power of domestic monopolies, and the possibility that employment in the manufacturing sector (and other jobs financed by foreign investment) might weaken oppressive patriarchal exploitation of women and young people in the countryside.

Heterodox economists also recommend giving greater attention to the costs as well as the benefits of increasing the global scope of intellectual property rights.[41] Recent trade agreements, for example, have had the effect of limiting access to inexpensive generic drugs in countries like Brazil and India. The most well-known controversies have involved the ability of poor African nations to produce generic versions of AIDS drugs. Because the developed nations own the vast majority of the world's patents (some sources estimate 97 percent) (Daly and Farley 2004, 326), tightening the global reach of intellectual property rights will mean a transfer of income from poor to rich countries. Because of the low incomes in the third world, patent protection may not increase patent owners' revenues very much. The higher prices of patent-protected products, however, will limit their availability in the third world.

The rhetoric of "freedom" often mobilized by advocates of "free trade" is slippery here. The extension of intellectual property rights is a restriction on freedom. It may or may not be wise policy, but it no doubt protects a monopoly and limits people's ability to use available knowledge. It could also slow economic growth in the third world.

There are legitimate economic reasons for generally rewarding inventors with exclusive rights over their discoveries for a fixed period of time. The main question posed by heterodox economists with respect to trade and intellectual property rights involves an "in-context" assessment of the treatment of third world markets.

THREADS: GENDER

Heterodox economists criticize the textbooks for giving insufficient attention to the impact of international economic policies on women and the household sector. Since the 1980s, for example, "structural adjustment policies" (SAPs) have often called for third world governments to curb government deficits by cutting government spending for social services and reducing government subsidies for basic commodities. Economists' traditional neglect of the household sector has tended to conceal the gendered impact of these policies and their full effect on human capital formation in the family. Feminist economists have emphasized that government cutbacks frequently lead to more self-provisioning in the household. The extra work required by SAPs is usually performed disproportionately by women. One especially unfortunate side effect of some structural adjustment policies may be the withdrawal of young women from school to help shoulder the load of expanded family labor. The interruption and/or termination of young girls' education (and retarding of human capital accumulation in economic terms) does not show up as a cost of SAPs in the GDP accounts, but it is likely to slow economic growth.

There is significant gender segregation in third world labor markets. For women, free-market globalization often involves expanded home production with very low compensation and little job security, migration and employment as household domestic laborers, and concentration in "feminized occupations." Interestingly, more than half of the new jobs created in export-oriented, low-wage industries in the third world, for example, have been filled by women.[42] Various arguments have been offered for the "feminization" of the global assembly line, including the alleged nimbleness and/or docility of female fingers. Regardless of the explanation, it is clear that the global division of labor can not be studied without exploring how norms and social roles influence market behaviors and how market practices help shape norms and social roles.[43]

Many heterodox economists argue that traditional social constraints on women have contributed to the relatively poor working conditions and low compensation in feminized global production. Union efforts, for example, have been weaker among women workers. Women's lack of political power has also made it harder to use the state to protect women workers' interests. In the United States, for example, race, gender, and class issues combined to leave African American domestic workers outside of the protection of federal minimum wage law until the mid-1970s (Peterson and Lewis 1999, 567). This was not a trivial oversight. As late as 1950, 42 percent of all employed African American women worked as domestics (Amott and Matthaei 1991, 173). Similar patterns are repeating themselves on a global scale. Rural women from the third world are replacing wealthier women's labor in the home in the first and third world.[44] The young rural migrants are often isolated in private dwellings and are at a significant cultural disadvantage when bargaining with their employers. There are many opportunities for abusive relations, ranging from excessive hours of work to sexual exploitation. Globalization has also been accompanied by an explicit expansion of the sex industry.

The impact of expanded women's wage employment on the relationship between men and women is complex and seems to defy simple generalizations. Opportunities for factory work seem to reduce the pressures on women to accept domestic service employment or lower-paying home production assignments. There is some evidence that access to market wages increases women's bargaining power in the family. The extent to which this occurs seems conditioned by a society's norms and institutions. In South East Asia increased market liberalization seems to have improved the status of women, while in the former Soviet Union the opposite seems to have occurred (Beneri´a 2003, 77–87). In South East Asia women's wages in export-oriented manufacturing industries appear to have risen over time (Beneri´a 2003, 83). This has not happened in the Mexican maquiladora plants, perhaps because of a much larger pool of surplus labor (Beneri´a 2003, 83; Fussell 2000, 76–77).

Heterodox economists call on economic analysis to study what determines the character of socioeconomic interactions in labor markets. Heterodox economists similarly call for expanded inquiry into how the status of women in society (years of schooling, economic opportunities, retirement security, etc.), rather than simple GDP levels, affect reproduction rates and the so-called "demographic transition."

Lourdes Beneri´a (2003) suggests that economists also study whether increased market participation is universalizing the outlook of *homo economicus*. She writes, "Are women becoming more individualistic, selfish, and less nurturing? Is market behavior undermining 'women's ways of seeing and doing?'" (84) She acknowledges that "the market can have positive effects for women and men, such as the breaking up of patriarchal traditions . . ." and warns against an "essentializing" view of gender that links the tendency for different behaviors among men and women to human nature. Still, she calls for trying to "preserve gender traits that contribute to individual, family, and human welfare without generating or perpetuating gender inequalities based on unequal power relations" (85). She asks," Can women provide different voices as they

Table 14.1

Competing Models and Metaphors of International Trade

Textbook Emphasis	Heterodox Focus
Parsimony (simple models of trade based on the logic of interpersonal exchange)	In-context analysis of concrete conditions of international trade
Automatic gains from trade	Possible gains from trade, potential race to the bottom (prisoner's dilemma)
Invisible hands and social benefits from global corporate profit seeking	Invisible handshakes and concerns about fractured communities
Aggregate gains from trade	Disaggregated effects of trade (distributional concerns)
Global capital mobility as a mechanism for economic efficiency	Global capital mobility as a threat to the social governance of the economy
Rational actor model of global financial markets	Minsky bubbles and hot money
Static efficiency	Dynamic efficiency
Laissez-faire logics	Industrial policy
Parasitic state	Thoughtful state
Perfect competition and powerless firms	Imperfect competition and powerful multinational corporations
Automatic market equilibrium	Potential disequilibrium

become more integrated in the market and public life? Can 'difference' . . . be a source of inspiration for progressive social change?" (88).

In summary, although globalization can improve the economic and social position of women, it can also extend gender inequality into new domains. Understanding the impact of globalization and designing public policies to maximize national welfare require integrating social and economic analysis. Although nothing in this task is inherently inconsistent with textbook economics, the integration often fits much more easily into a heterodox than orthodox agenda and imagination.

ALTERNATIVE IMAGES & COMPETING METAPHORS

Table 14.1 compares and contrasts heterodox and textbook metaphors related to trade issues.

CONCLUSION

Heterodox economists criticize textbook chapters on international economics for familiar methodological problems, especially:

1. misplaced concreteness
2. insufficient attention to distributional issues
3. the use of static rather than dynamic analysis
4. insufficient attention to the implications of uncertainty in financial markets
5. inadequate treatment of sluggish and non-equilibrating price adjustments
6. insufficient attention to problems of weak aggregate demand
7. neglect of meta-externalities

These shortcomings have often led the textbooks to give insufficient attention to the downside of deregulating international markets. The potential problems highlighted by heterodox analysis include:

1. weakened government powers to reduce social inequality, protect the environment, and pursue expansionary macro policies
2. speculative excesses in global financial markets
3. the erosion of important social capital (such as a sense of community)

From a heterodox perspective, the textbooks' discussion of international economic issues is dominated by the subtext of strong support for free trade. What is included and what is excluded from discussion, what stories are told and what simplifications are tolerated, are framed by the desire to teach how "free markets" can organize international economic relations in beneficial ways.

Many economists have commented on the passion that neoclassical economists have for free trade. Princeton University's well-known *New York Times* economist Paul Krugman (1987), for example, has asserted "If there were an Economist's Creed, it would surely contain the affirmations 'I understand the Principle of Comparative Advantage' and 'I advocate Free Trade'" (131). He adds, "[D]efense of free trade [is] as close to a sacred tenet as any idea in economics." And defend free trade the textbooks do.

Harvard political-economist Dani Rodrik has noted that many economists privately acknowledge that the behavior of international markets is much more complicated than generally suggested by most public endorsements of free trade. Rodrik (1988) comments,

> I'm really quite struck by why many things that are often said and repeated and rationally discussed in the seminar room among economists are often taboo in the public arena. I think part of it has to do with the fact that free trade is such a sacrosanct subject among economists. . . . I think there is a tremendous amount of concern in the profession . . . that statements that are okay in the seminar setting might be misinterpreted by the pubic and essentially provide ammunition to the "barbarians." (81–82)

From a heterodox perspective, the textbooks fail to convey a key part of the debate over "free trade." Proponents of deregulating international markets are pursuing the agenda of "classical liberalism."[45] This project has been gathering steam for well over 250 years and seeks to disembed the "perfect"[46] market from systems of social governance. In its ideal form, it atomizes experience and coordinates human action through exchange. It believes that human beings can maximize their happiness and personal freedom by organizing as much of life as possible through markets.

For over 250 years critics of classical liberalism have sought to "humanize" the market, to take advantage of the energies and beneficial by-products that markets can generate while countering the negative meta-externalities markets can produce. Critics of classical liberalism have fought to reduce market-generated inequality, market instabilities, market-produced concentrations of power, market erosion of community, and other market liabilities.[47]

Although many social institutions have been involved in efforts to "humanize" the market, ranging from the kinship ties of extended families to voluntary institutions like churches and labor unions, the most effective countervailing force to market autarky has been the state. Through policies like minimum wages, social security, progressive income taxes, health and safety standards, universal free public education, public provision of common facilities (such as public libraries, public parks, and neighborhood playgrounds), guarantees of the right to collective bargaining, limitations on campaign contributions, and so on, public policy has sought to knit people together in ways that counter the market's centrifugal potential for divisive and inequitable outcomes.

Many heterodox economists fear that current forms of "free trade" threaten to undermine the ability of national and local communities to pursue "market-humanizing" policies. Herman Daly and Joshua Farley have contrasted what they call "internationalization," which links communities together globally but preserves governments' ability to embed markets in systems of social governance, with "globalization," which interconnects individuals through world markets following a classical liberal trajectory.

The debate over which approach to international linkages is best is partly a philosophical debate and partly a political-economic debate. The key difference is whether one sees government involvement in the economy as likely to have positive or negative effects. Free traders come down hard on the negative side. They often acknowledge that a "good government" could improve on the outcome of laissez-faire international trade (for example by protecting infant industries and even looking after the "meta-externalities" of different trade patterns). Free traders, however, expect the capture of government by special interests, incompetent politicians, or inert bureaucracies and therefore call for limited political oversight of international trade.[48]

This position is not indefensible. It has a coherent theoretical basis and some support from empirical data. The problem is, so do contrary interventionist arguments. The heterodox claim is that this debate should be highlighted in the textbooks. From a heterodox perspective, it is misleading to imply that the most important ideas about international trade can be conveyed by a few graphs and simple appeals to the principle of comparative advantage.

In addition to being a debate over the proper division between democratic political and market decision making, the debate over free trade is also indirectly a debate over the degree to which promises of economic growth trump other arguments for social action. Supporters of free trade often assert that increased trade promotes growth, which is the sine qua non for solving most social problems. As we have noted many times in this commentary, growth enthusiasts see an automatic link between higher GDP and greater human happiness, increased environmental protection, lower population growth, reduced poverty rates, and a cornucopia of many other positive effects, ranging from the spread of democracy to the promotion of world peace.

Heterodox critics take issue with both steps in the trade/cornucopia argument. They question whether deregulated international trade accelerates economic growth,[49] and whether maximizing GDP delivers the goods promised. From a heterodox perspective, the success of market democracies has been due to their ability to direct rather than totally defer to markets. The free trade debate also returns us to TINA questions. Advocates of free trade claim that there are no alternatives to deferring to the world market. Free trade is thus both inevitable and optimal, a fortuitous correspondence. Heterodox economists believe there are alternatives to adopting free trade hook, line, and sinker, and that these development paths are sometimes superior to deregulated market outcomes.

What kind of policies would heterodox economists recommend for international markets? There are no automatic answers, as heterodox economists stress the need to design policies "in context." Heterodox economists also have active debates among themselves (a dimension of heterodox economics we have not been able to detail in this commentary). However, the list below illustrates the kinds of policies heterodox economists would explore.

1a. Policies to preserve the ability of national governments to maintain domestic aggregate demand (i.e., policies that would limit fears of capital flight from curbing the use of expansionary monetary and fiscal policies during periods of high unemployment).

1b. Policies to reduce contractionary biases in global balance of payments mechanisms (i.e., policies to balance the contractionary pressures placed on deficit countries with expansionary pressures on surplus countries).

2. Policies that preserve the ability of national governments to address distributional issues (e.g., policies that curb the threat of capital flight from limiting income and wealth redistribution and other egalitarian policies such as tax-funded public education).

3a. Upgraded global labor and environmental standards, defining minimally acceptable working conditions, wages, and environmental practices.

3b. The establishment of a World Environmental Organization with as much oversight and leverage over the organization of international trade as the World Trade Organization.

4. Policies that preserve the ability of national governments to shape their countries' division of labor (such as policies to protect the family farm).[50]

5a. Regulations to stabilize global financial markets, including policies to limit the impact of "hot international money" on domestic economies.

5b. Enhancement of the IMF's power to act as a lender of last resort to avert international monetary panics.

6. Policies to "democratize" the IMF, World Bank, and WTO, by reducing the influence currently exercised by representatives of global finance and multinational corporations.

7. A modest sales tax on international trade, with revenues earmarked for third world economic development and perhaps compensation for workers in the first world harmed by free trade.

IN THEIR OWN WORDS

[S]ystems competition is another example of the prisoner's dilemma. . . . Each country can either maintain standards or cut standards. The social optimum is for both to maintain standards, in which case there is trade with fair work conditions and well-paid employment. However, each country faces an incentive to cut standards a little so as to gain a competitive advantage. . . . The result is that both countries cut standards, resulting in a race to the bottom.

—Thomas Palley (1998, 158)

The radically simplified assumptions about human behavior, the biases against politics, and the ahistorical perspectives that inform the literature of the neoclassical school would be of no concern outside the profession were it not for the increasing presence of economists and their students in the corridors of power [p. 63]. . . .

"Of all the social sciences, economics became the most abstracted from social reality. . . . Economists could recommend free trade without realistically being able to conceive of its consequences for the nation's polity, culture, or social system, since they did not hold themselves responsible for what they considered nontechnical matters.

—Stephen Clarkson (1993, 66)

Equilibrium applies best only to markets that deal with known quantities. But financial markets deal with quantities that are not only largely unknown but unknowable. They discount a future that is contingent on how the financial markets assess it at present. The appropriate concept, in my view, is reflexivity, not equilibrium. Reflexive processes are not just unpredictable; they are genuinely indeterminate because the outcomes depend on the predictions that investors have made. The process may be self-correcting, in which case you tend toward equilibrium, or it can be initially self-reinforcing but eventually self-defeating, in which case you have a boom and a bust. . . .

After each crisis, we made institutional changes. We now have a Federal Reserve system. . . . We have national institutions that keep excesses from going too far. . . . [H]owever, markets have become truly global. And we do not have comparable international institutions to prevent the excesses.

—George Soros (1999, 73–75)

STUDY QUESTIONS

Review Questions

1. Many introductory discussions in economics demonstrate the mutual benefits of voluntary exchange between individuals and extend this conclusion to the benefits of free trade between nations. Why do heterodox economists argue that this analogy can be misleading?
2. What is the subtext of neoclassical textbook discussions of free trade? What is the subtext of heterodox critiques?
3. Why have some "in-context" analyses of the North American Free Trade Agreement suggested that the agreement was not as beneficial for Mexico as originally thought?
4. Why do heterodox economists fear that deregulating global financial markets will increase the instability of the world economy?

Discussion Questions

1. Heterodox objections to the treatment of international economic issues in neoclassical textbooks build on familiar themes. Explain how heterodox concerns about (a) distributional issues, (b) misplaced concreteness, (c) the limits of static analysis, (d) price stickiness, (e) insufficient aggregate demand, (f) uncertainty, and (g) meta-externalities can be linked to heterodox critiques of textbook discussions of international economic issues.
2. Why do many heterodox economists argue that goods should be "homespun" where possible? What benefits do these economists argue accompany local production? Why are these benefits difficult to see when using neoclassical methodologies to view the economy? What do you think are the major weaknesses of the heterodox approach?
3. Why are heterodox economists worried about increased capital mobility in the world economy? What kind of responses do you think neoclassical economists would have to heterodox concerns?
4. Neoclassical defenders of "free trade" (deregulation of international trade) expect it to promote environmental quality. Heterodox critics of "free trade" expect it to probably harm the environment. Explain the basis for each side's argument and link their disagreements to methodological debates between the two paradigms.

NOTES

1. For an excellent analysis of the role of neoclassical economic theory in winning public acceptance of NAFTA see Cypher 1993.

2. See for example Goodstein 1998, 313; Pollin 2003, 131–33; Chang and Grabel 2004, 14–24.

3. Mankiw is considered a superstar among neoclassical textbook writers for having received a $1.4-million advance for his principles text. The book has been the required text in Harvard University's introductory economics classes.

4. Earlier in the text he offers an even simpler analogy to buttress the case for free trade, writing, "Trade between two countries can make each country better off.

"To see why, consider how trade affects your family. . . . [E]ach family in the economy is competing with all other families.

"Despite this competition, your family would not be better off isolating itself. . . . Trade allows each person to specialize in the activities he or she does best. . . .

"Countries as well as families benefit from the ability to trade with one another" (Mankiw 2001, 9).

5. Drawing on his experience as chairperson of President Clinton's Council of Economic Advisers and his service as senior economist at the World Bank, Nobel Laureate Joseph Stiglitz finds that the same misplaced concreteness has marred the economic recommendations of the International Monetary Fund. He notes, for example, that the IMF generally has only one resident economist in many of the countries it advises and often recommends economic policies with little attention to local specificities. He writes, "[T]o the IMF lack of detailed knowledge is of less moment, because it tends to take a 'one-size-fits-all' approach" (Stiglitz 2003, 34).

6. Mexico began orienting its economy toward exports and free trade in the mid-1980s. Since 1984 the number of households living in poverty has grown 80 percent (Wise 2003, 2).

7. We will look briefly at some other problems caused by NAFTA, such as the increased vulnerability of the Mexican economy to instabilities in global currency markets, when the discussion shifts from misplaced concreteness to other critiques of textbook trade theory later in this chapter.

8. *Business Week*'s Geri Smith and Cristina Lindblad report that 1.3 million farm jobs have disappeared since 1993, presumably due to "a flood of subsidized U.S. food imports" (Smith and Lindblad 2003). Earlier studies anticipated that 700,000–800,000 workers would be displaced by U.S. corn imports (Larudee 1998, 281).

9. Barry 1995, 102. The displacement of small peasant farmers growing corn and beans by large landowners growing export-oriented cash crops has occurred throughout Central America and would likely have been accelerated by the proposed Free Trade Agreement for the Americas (Harris 2002, 410). See also Goodstein 1998, 304; and Hahnel 2002, 189.

10. For an interesting, "in-context" account of the impact of free-market trade policies on India, see Pollin 2003, 138–42. For an analysis of events in El Salvador see Kampwirth 2002, 49–51.

11. Nobel Laureate Joseph Stiglitz finds that most of the benefits of globalization and growth on the Mexican side went to the top 30 percent of the Mexican population, especially the top 10 percent. He adds, "Those at the bottom have gained little; many are even worse off" (Stiglitz 2003, 86).

12. As Larudee (2006) makes clear, U.S. trade negotiators put significant pressures on Mexico to open up Mexico's energy sector to foreign investment and to guarantee the supply of Mexican oil to U.S. buyers. These efforts were only partially successful.

13. See, for example, Stiglitz 2003, chapter 8.

14. See, for example, McCloskey 1985, 3–44. The U.S. Trade Adjustment Act, for instance, provides government funds for retraining and other adjustment costs to workers who can demonstrate they were harmed by free trade agreements. Benefits and coverage were expanded in 2002, but still fall short of fully compensating those harmed economically by increased international competition.

15. Daly and Farley report, for example, that trade liberalization in Latin America has been accompanied by a jump in the income gap between the richest and poorest 10 percent of the population from 37:1 to 48:1 (Daly and Farley 2004, 336; see also Stiglitz 2003, 86; Chang and Grabel 2004, 20). The increase in inequality in Russia since "shock therapy" is of course legendary. This increase has many causes, but most are related to laissez-faire-oriented economic policies. Chapter 15 explores the increase in inequality in the United States during the period of trade liberalization.

16. As elaborated in chapter 15 ("Reintroducing the Macroeconomics of Inequality"), constructing aggregate measures of inequality is tricky and making international comparisons even more difficult. Nevertheless, it seems likely that the differences between low- and high-income countries have increased during the liberalization of trade over the last three decades. This is especially apparent if China is deleted from global data (Pollin 2003, 32–37; Daly and Farley 2004, 334).

17. See also Rodrik, in Ackerman et al. 1998.

18. This range may be biased downward, as it likely excludes some ripple effects.

19. Crotty, Epstein, and Kelly (1998) indicate that federal corporate tax rates fell by about a third from the 1970s to the mid-1990s in the United States. While not linking the cut entirely to international economic competition, they draw an analogy to pressures for reduced business taxes within the United States due to

competition among localities to retain or attract new businesses. They estimate that such tax breaks have probably cost communities tens of billions of dollars and cite a call by the Federal Reserve Bank of Minneapolis for federal legislation that would curb such "prisoner's dilemma"-like competition (Crotty et al. 1998, 133).

20. See also Furman and Stiglitz 1998; Wade 2005, 26–33; and Bowles, Edwards, and Roosevelt 2005, 391–92.

21. See Chang 2005 for an excellent historical account.

22. See also Chang 2005; Stiglitz 2003, 91–92; and Shaikh 2003, esp. 12–14.

23. The collapse was like an accident waiting to happen. Japanese economic problems encouraged some Japanese firms to reduce their direct foreign investment in East Asia, which in turn lowered local real estate prices. Falling property values undermined the collateral used to secure many loans. At about the same time, exchange rate shifts weakened local competitiveness and economic recovery in the United States drew capital westward. When Thai monetary authorities allowed their pegged currency to depreciate modestly, investors began to sell Thai assets, sparking an unexpected stampede out of other Asian assets and currencies (Grabel 2000).

24. See also Aslanbeigui and Summerfield 2000.

25. This perspective reinforces criticisms raised in standard textbooks by New Keynesian economists of quickly adjusting general equilibrium models of free trade.

26. Relatedly, Ian Kregel has suggested that the first principle of Post Keynesian economics is to ask, "How would analysis of an issue be different if we acknowledged the potential for insufficient aggregate demand to cause unemployment?" (Eighth International Post Keynesian Summer School, University of Missouri at Kansas City, June 2004, lecture presentation.)

The fallout from economic education's tendency to assume full employment in its models is not limited to introductory economics students. As Stiglitz writes, "[T]oo often the training of the IMF macroeconomists does not prepare them well for the problems that they have to confront in developing countries. In some of the universities from which the IMF hires regularly, the core curricula involve models in which there is never any unemployment. After all, in the standard competitive model—the model that underlies the IMF's market fundamentalism—demand always equals supply. If the demand for labor equals supply, there is never any involuntary unemployment" (Stiglitz 2003, 34–35). Acting on this conclusion can have costly consequences. Stiglitz offers several case studies of how the IMF's neglect of the aggregate demand implications of its austerity "medicine" aggravated unemployment problems in the third world.

Many heterodox economists also argue that an asymmetry in the organization of world trade depresses aggregate demand. Countries running balance of payments deficits are usually under strong market pressure to eliminate those deficits and frequently adopt contractionary monetary and fiscal policies to do so. Surplus countries face no parallel pressures to expand their economies in order to eliminate their surplus. To eliminate this imbalance, Keynes and several other heterodox economists have called for a system of "trade clearing" that charges both debtors and surplus countries "interest" on their net balances. Keynes, in fact, urged shifting "'the onus of adjustment from the debtor to the creditor position. . . . aiming 'at the substitution of an expansionist, in place of a contractionist, pressure on world trade'" (in Davidson 2002, 486).

27. If the increased share of national income going to the owners of capital under free trade policies increased investment (perhaps due to the lure of higher returns), the tilt of national income from labor to capital need not weaken aggregate demand. Heterodox economists tend to be skeptical of this outcome, however, due to the fickleness of investment and the tendency for reductions in popular consumption to encourage businesses to invest less rather than more.

28. Fears of currency depreciation reflect, in part, expectations that rising domestic income will spur increased imports and worsen the balance of trade.

29 Eban Goodstein draws an environmental analogy, noting that American citizens appear to be willing to pay a much higher price to protect the Alaskan Arctic National Wildlife Refuge than to protect other environmental sites around the world damaged in the course of meeting American import demand. The reason, according to Herman Daly: "out of sight, out of mind" (Goodstein 1998, 301).

30. The sentence in the parenthesis was footnoted in the original.

31. Goodstein cites estimates of annual energy industry subsidies of $28 billion (Goodstein 1998, 314). Brian Halweil reports that food typically travels an average of 1,500 to 2,400 miles from "farm to plate" in the United States (Halweil 2002, 5). Halweil offers an interesting "systems analysis" of how current market institutions tilt food and other production toward an elongated international division of labor.

32. As elaborated in more detail in chapter 16 the curve draws its name from an analogy to a theory of

income inequality developed by Simon Kuznets in 1955. Kuznets argued that inequality initially increases during economic growth but then declines as economies mature. This claim led many development theorists to recommend that governments ignore problems of inequality during economic development on the grounds that these problems would resolve themselves. Subsequent economic developments have contradicted this reasoning (Ackerman et al. 2000, 292).

33. There appears to be some confusion over the influence of this decision, as its implementation seems to have been blocked by the United States (Cosbey 2006, 137).

34. Goodstein reports that a deposit requirement was upheld but requirements that containers be reusable were weakened (Goodstein 2005, 502).

35. Several other similar cases have been reported by other heterodox economists. For example, Daly and Farley report that the United States was forced to allow the importation of gasoline from Venezuela that did not comply with the U.S. Clean Air Act. The WTO similarly rejected an Australian limitation on raw salmon on the grounds that the risk of infecting domestic stocks was acceptably low. Daly and Farley imply that the WTO's ruling denied Australia the right to follow the precautionary principle and restrict imports on the grounds of risk-averse responses to uncertainty (Daly and Farley 2004, 328). Goodstein reports that Canadian efforts to slow the development of Canada's natural gas resources and to require the monitoring of fish catches in depleted areas have been undermined by the U.S.-Canadian Free Trade Agreement (Goodstein 1998, 304). Harris reports that a U.S. challenge successfully overturned a Canadian ban on the importation of a gasoline additive (Harris 2002,412). Cosbey (2006) suggests there is a modest possibility that labeling activities by voluntary organizations (such as "Fair Trade" coffee labeling) could be reviewed by the WTO.

36. Many heterodox economists criticize introductory textbooks for appearing to endorse this outcome in the name of economic growth. Summing up their analysis of international trade in one of the best-selling macro principles texts, for example, McConnell and Brue write, "Economists agree that labor protections such as workplace safety, enforcement of child labor laws, and collective bargaining rights, as well as environmental concerns such as protection of forests and fisheries, are legitimate issues. But most economists believe these causes should not be used to slow or reverse trade liberalization. . . . Trade liberalization is too important in its own right to be linked to a host of other, sometimes conflicting, political and economic causes" (McConnell and Brue 2002, 391).

37. This argument could also be conceivably made within neoclassical theory, though there tends to be a much greater willingness among neoclassical economists to commoditize aspects of life and celebrate their rearrangement through markets.

38. Consider for example the problem of global warming. Most scientists are convinced that current levels of greenhouse gas (GHG) emissions need to be significantly reduced in order to avoid serious problems with global warming. China, with a population more than four times that of the United States, currently produces about one-eighth the GHG emissions per person as the United States. If the Chinese were to imitate U.S. production and consumption patterns, the trajectory of global GHG emissions would present very serious hazards.

39. It is sometimes argued that a key reason for turning points in the EKC is a tendency for highly polluting industries to be exported to the third world, a process that cannot be duplicated when economic growth occurs in these countries. Empirical tests of this hypothesis have produced mixed results. They seem to indicate that there may have been some pollution shifting, but this has not been the major reason for the appearance of an EKC for some pollutants (Rothman 1998).

40. In an interesting twist on this observation, Michael Porter of the Harvard Business School suggests that stricter regulations can sometimes force firms to think more carefully about production techniques. This review can accelerate innovation and lower firms' production costs. In other words, tougher regulations may actually improve companies' long-run profitability. One study attempting to test the Porter hypothesis found that states with stricter environmental regulations generally had better economic performance. It was not clear, however, which way the causality flowed (Tietenberg 2000, 555).

41. See, for example, Chang and Grabel 2004, 92–104.

42. For example, although women made up only 33–40 percent of the wage labor force in Malaysia, South Korea, and the Philippines, they accounted for 53–77 percent of the workers in export processing zones in the early 1990s (Beneri´a 2003, 79).

43. A good source for current heterodox thinking about the intersection of macroeconomics, gender, and international economics is the Levy Institute's program on gender equality and the economy. Levy publications can generally be accessed online (www.levy.org). The International Working Group on Gender, Macroeconomics and International Economics is another useful source.

44. In Brazil, for example, 16–20 percent of all women workers are employed in domestic service (Benería 2003, 79).

45. The term *classical liberalism* is an important term to learn. It has a confusing lineage. In today's language, classical liberals like Milton Friedman would be called *libertarians* or *conservatives*. Classical liberals basically believe in laissez-faire economic policies and the idea of limited government. The early giants of classical liberalism, however, had a much more supple and sophisticated idea of the social context of experience than many of today's proponents of classical liberalism.

46. By *perfect,* economists mean markets conforming to their assumptions (well-defined property rights, perfect competition, no externalities, etc.).

47. See, for example, Pieper and Taylor 1998; Costanza et al. 1997, 156–74.

48. The textbooks' treatment of potential problems with free trade offers another example of "note but ignore" pedagogy. As William Cline of the Institute for International Economics notes, the same attitude pervaded more high-brow neoclassical discussions of trade. The implications of two key neoclassical conclusions about international trade were de-emphasized when they appeared able to undermine the political case for free trade. Both the "Stolper-Samuelson theorem" and the "factor-price equalization" theorem tended to predict falling relative wages for unskilled labor in the first world in a free-trading global economy. Cline writes, "[I]t has been a triumph of economic theory to install as the dominant public policy precept the somewhat counterintuitive notion that the nation will be better off under free trade than under protection. To keep this policy achievement intact, the most convenient attitude toward the Stolper-Samuelson and factor price equalization theorems was that their necessary assumptions were so unrealistic as to turn the theorems into mere curiosities. . . . An alternative approach, however, would have been to interpret the theorems as meaningful long-run tendencies and, therefore, important grounds for formulating trade policy with key side measures to ensure equitable distribution of the gains from trade" (Cline 1997, 36). Cline also notes that Samuelson's original paper (which implied that protectionism could raise the wages of unskilled workers in first world countries) was apparently rejected for publication in the leading neoclassical economic journal, the *American Economic Review* (AER), partially "because of concern that the article could be read as a sellout to protectionism" (ibid., 43). Incredibly, the editors criticized Samuelson's paper for unrealistic assumptions, a concern of little import for numerous other AER articles.

49. Recent work by researchers at the Global Development and Environment Institute (GDAE) casts further doubt on the claim that increased trade liberalization will bring large benefits to the developing nations. See, for example, Frank Ackerman. "The Shrinking Gains from Trade: A Critical Assessment of the Doha Round Projections," http://ase.tufts.edu/gdae/Pubs/wp/05–01ShrinkingGains.pdf.

50. There are mixed feelings about this plank among heterodox economists, due to fears of protectionism (based on special interests rather than national priorities) and retaliatory trade wars, as emphasized in neoclassical analyses.

REINTRODUCING THE MACROECONOMICS OF INEQUALITY

No country not experiencing a revolution or a military defeat with a subsequent occupation has probably ever had as rapid or as widespread an increase in inequality as has occurred in the United States in the past two decades.
—Lester Thurow (1996, 42), former dean of the MIT School of Management

We are richer than any other nation in the world—richer, by far, than any nation in the history of the world. And yet a significant portion of our population has become poorer over the last two decades. . . . This is the biggest economic and social—and, perhaps, moral—challenge we face as a society. And yet there is remarkably little public discussion about it.
—Former secretary of labor Robert Reich (R. Freeman 1999, ix)

The discipline and profession of economics has a long tradition of acquiescence in the existing social order, punctuated only rarely by rebellion. We need a rebellion now. . . . [T]he great rise in inequality from 1970 onward has been . . . catastrophic.
—James K. Galbraith (2000, 263), professor of economics, University of Texas

INTRODUCTION

Most neoclassical macro courses and macro principles texts give only modest attention to distributional issues. The absence is especially striking given the unusually large increase in economic inequality that occurred during the last quarter of the twentieth century. The textbooks' relative disinterest in distributional issues is partially due to neoclassical economists' tendency to treat these topics as subjects for micro- rather than macroeconomics. This decision reflects neoclassical theory's tendency to analyze and explain income inequality, poverty, and other distributional outcomes in terms of the distribution of individual traits rather than the structure of the macro economy.

Heterodox macro economists tend to devote more attention to distributional issues than neoclassical economists do. They also tend to look for structural rather than individual roots for economic outcomes. The subtext of neoclassical macroeconomics makes maximizing current and future GDP the chief goals of economic knowledge and economic policy. Heterodoxy has a broader set of goals, high among which is promoting increased economic equality.

230

Table 15.1

Quintile Shares of National Income*

Year	Lowest 20%	Second 20%	Third 20%	Fourth 20%	Top 20%	Gini coefficient**
1967	4.0	10.8	17.3	24.2	43.8	0.399
1975	4.4	10.5	17.1	24.8	43.2	0.397
1985	4.0	9.7	16.3	24.6	45.3	0.419
1995	3.7	9.1	15.2	23.3	48.7	0.450
2000	3.6	8.9	14.9	23.0	49.7	0.460
2003	3.4	8.7	14.8	23.4	49.8	

*Income refers to money income before taxes, including government cash transfers such as social security, but excluding the value of non-cash benefits such as food stamps. Income also excludes unrealized capital gains.

** In 1993 new survey methods increased the Gini coefficients by about 0.02 (Mishel, Bernstein, and Boushey 2003, 53).

Source: 1967–2000 data from: U.S. Census Bureau, Current Population Reports, *Money Income in the United States: 2000* (September 2001), p. 8. http://www.census.gov/prod/2001pubs/p60–213.pdf. 2003 Data from: U.S. Census Bureau, Press Briefing, August 26, 2004, "2003 Income and Poverty Estimates."

The rest of the chapter proceeds as follows. We begin with several sections that present statistics about economic inequality. This is followed by a comparison of neoclassical and heterodox analyses of the general causes of inequality. Thereafter we explore the narrower question of what caused the large increase in inequality over the last thirty years and what to do about it. The chapter concludes with our usual threads and quotations.

MEASURING INEQUALITY: "LIES, DAMN LIES, AND STATISTICS" (BENJAMIN DISRAELI)

Introduction

As the British statesman Benjamin Disraeli complained, it is easy to mislead with statistics. This is especially true when dealing with abstract, multidimensional concepts like economic inequality.

Measures of Income Inequality

Income inequality fell significantly in the United States from the late 1920s until the mid-1970s and has risen significantly since then.[1] The top 20 percent of the income ladder received about ten times the share of national income received by the bottom 20 percent in 1975, and about fourteen times the bottom quintile's share in 2000 (U.S. Census Bureau 2001, 8). In 2003, the bottom quintile's share of national income fell to 3.4 percent, the lowest level in over fifty years (U.S. Census Bureau 2004, 36, Table A-3; Mishel, Bernstein, and Boushey 2003, 54)[2] (see Table 15.1).

The income of chief executive officers (CEOs) increased from forty-two times that of average hourly workers in 1980, to eighty-five times in 1990, to several hundred times in 2000 (Gill 2001).[3] From 1979 to 2000 the top 5 percent of households captured 52 percent of the increase in national income, compared with less than 1 percent for the bottom 20 percent of households (Mishel, Bernstein, and Allegretto 2005, 62).[4] One of the most common statistical measures of inequality is the "Gini coefficient." Box 15.1 explains its derivation. The Gini coefficient for national income increased from 0.397 in 1975 to 0.460 in 2000 (U.S. Census Bureau 2001, 8).

Box 15.1
The Gini Coefficient

The Gini coefficient is one way of measuring overall inequality. It is best defined geometrically. Imagine a graph with a horizontal axis representing the percentage of American households (from 0% to 100%), ranked in ascending order of income. The vertical axis measures the percentage of income held by any percentage of the population identified on the horizontal axis. A perfectly equal income distribution would trace out a 45-degree line from the origin (see Figure 15.1). The percentage of national income received by any group of people would match their percentage of the population. Thus 30 percent of the population would earn 30 percent of the nation's income and 86 percent of the population would earn 86 percent of the nation's income.

On the other hand, if all of the nation's income were earned by one person, the graph would look like a reverse "L," registering 0 percentage income for all of the population until the last person, at which point the vertical height would leap to 100%. One can imagine intermediate cases where some people earn very little of the nation's income, others a bit more, and finally a small percentage earns a high percentage of the nation's income (see the curve below the 45-degree line in Figure 15.1). The figure traced out by connecting the dots on the graph is called a Lorenz curve.

Figure 15.1   **Lorenz Curve for National Income, 2003**

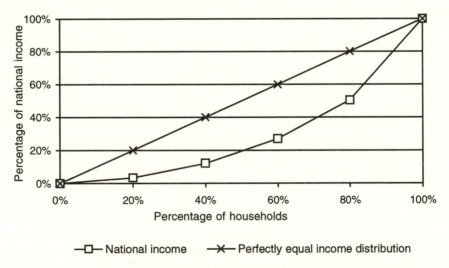

The Gini coefficient measures the area between the Lorenz curve and the 45-degree line and compares it to the area of the triangle formed by the points (0%,0%), (100%,0%), and (100%,100%). A perfectly equal income distribution would have no area between the Lorenz curve and the 45-degree line, so it would have a Gini coefficient of 0. A perfectly unequal distribution would have a Gini coefficient of 1. The higher the Gini coefficient, the more unequal the income distribution.

Table 15.2

Distribution of Wealth 2001

Asset	Top 1% of Families	Next 4%	Next 5%	Top 10%	Bottom 50% of Families
Net worth*	32.7	25	12.1	69.8	2.8
Total financial assets**	31.5	26.6	14.1	72.2	2.5
Stocks***	52.9	25.3	9.9	88.1	0.5
Bonds***	64.3	22.7	8.8	95.8	0.3
Houses	9.0	16.0	12.2	37.2	12.3
Vehicles	5.1	9.3	9.5	23.9	27.9
Overall debts	5.9	11.6	8.6	26.1	25.9
Credit card balances	0.5	4.9	3.2	8.6	49.8

* Total assets minus debts.

**Includes a long list of financial assets, including bank accounts, direct holdings of stocks and bonds, cash value of life insurance policies, and pension accounts where withdrawals or loans are permitted.

***Direct holdings of publicly traded stocks and bonds.

Source: Kennickell 2003, p. 21.

Note: For slightly different figures, indicating somewhat lower shares of stock ownership for the top 1 percent, but similar concentrations at the 10 percent level, see Mishel, Bernstein, and Allegretto 2005, p. 287.

Measures of Wealth Inequality

Income is a flow. Wealth is a stock, representing accumulated net income. Wealth confers economic security, independence, and potential social and political power. Concentrations of wealth facilitate the intergenerational transmission of social position. The distribution of wealth in the United States is significantly more unequal than the distribution of income.[5] (See Table 15.2.)

The recent trends in wealth and income distribution are fairly similar. Wealth inequality decreased significantly from the late 1920s until World War II. Wealth inequality increased modestly in the 1950s, fell significantly in the 1960s, and then increased substantially from 1976 to 2000.[6] From 1983 to 2001, the richest 1 percent and 20 percent of the population captured about 33 percent and 89 percent, respectively, of the total growth in net worth in the economy (Wolff 2004, 31, Table 3).[7]

Heterodox economists tend to explore the linkages between economic and social structures and the feedback between political and economic events more actively than neoclassical economists do. For example, heterodox economists often focus on who owns "productive," as opposed to "consumptive," property. *Productive property* refers to resources that generate income, while *consumptive property* refers to resources that provide their owners with consumer services, like a house, a car, or a wardrobe. Ownership of productive property frequently (but not always) bestows control over the labor process involved with producing that income. Thus, wealth in the form of "productive property" often involves a social relationship (command over labor) as well as ownership of physical things.[8]

The ownership of productive property in the U.S. economy is very unequal. In 2003 a senior economist at the Federal Reserve Board estimated that the top 5 percent and 10 percent of the population held 78 percent and 88 percent, respectively, of all directly held stocks (Kennickell 2003, 21).[9] These numbers challenge the frequent image in the press that more widespread ownership of stocks has altered the basic character of the U.S. economy. Although about half of all American families now own stock directly, or through pension accounts, the average holding of the bottom 60 percent in 1998 was only $4,000 (Mishel, Bernstein, and Boushey 2003, 27).[10] Even including pension accounts and other indirect mechanisms of stock ownership, the top 10 percent of the population still held more than three quarters of all stocks (Wolff 2000, 15; 2004, 25).

A somewhat similar picture emerges if we look at the ownership of private businesses.[11] Although a surprisingly high percentage of families (11.5 percent) held equity in unincorporated businesses in 1995, the value of these holdings were distributed very unequally (Toruno 2003, 27). The top 1 percent and 10 percent of families owned 70 percent and 92 percent of all business equity (Wolff 1998, 140). As Ackerman has observed, "few of the facts about wealth are as unexpected as the monopolization of 'small business' equity by the rich" (Ackerman 2000, 39).

The distribution of wealth, along with the level of job security in the economy and the strength of the social safety net (unemployment insurance, food stamp provisions, etc.) can also throw light on the general level of economic security in the economy.[12] Many studies have found increasing anxiety among workers about job loss.[13] Less than half of all American households headed by a person in middle life have enough financial resources (such as savings accounts and stocks and bonds) to sustain their families at 125 percent of the poverty level for five months (Wolff 2000, Table 13).

POVERTY: DEFINITION, MEASUREMENT, AND SIGNIFICANCE

Introduction

There has been an implicit tendency in much of neoclassical economics (made explicit in some political-economic programs, like supply-side economics) to assume a reliable inverse relationship between GDP levels and poverty rates. In colloquial terms the saying is, "when the tide comes in, all boats rise." Heterodox economists find reality more complicated and stress that maximizing GDP is not an adequate antipoverty strategy.

Defining and measuring poverty is a tricky task. There tend to be two basic approaches, the "absolute" and the "relative" approach. The former conceives of poverty in terms of some minimum (or subsistence) standard of living, while the latter defines poverty in relationship to other people's standard of living. Since the mid-1960s, the U.S. government's poverty statistics have been based on an "absolute" definition of poverty, based on the cost of a nutritionally adequate food budget for different family sizes and a multiplier for nonfood expenses. The poverty line is adjusted annually for changes in the consumer price index, but not adjusted for changes in per capita income or social expectations about minimally acceptable lifestyles. For the first part of this discussion we will work with official statistics that adopt an absolute approach to poverty. We will then look at the implications of some alternative definitions of poverty. Table 15.3 lists some key poverty statistics.

"Absolute" Definitions of Poverty: Historical Trends

From 1959 to 1973, per capita income increased in the United States by 48.6 percent and official poverty rates declined dramatically, falling from 22.4 percent of the population in 1959 to 11.1 percent in 1973. From 1973 to 1993, GDP per capita increased by 42 percent, but the poverty rate did not decline; in fact it increased from 11.1 percent to 15.1 percent (fluctuating between 11.3

Table 15.3

Incidence of Poverty 2003

	Overall	White	Non-Hispanic White	Black	Hispanic	Asian
National poverty rate	12.5%	10.5%	8.2%	24.4%	22.5%	11.8%
Children's poverty rate	17.6%	14.3%	9.8%	34.1%	29.7%	12.5%

	Overall	Among married couples	Among male householders, no wife present	Among female householders, no husband present
Family poverty rate	10%	5.4%	13.5%	28.0%

Overall rate among native born	11.8%
Overall rate among foreign born*	17.2%
Number (and percent) of people with incomes less than half the poverty line	15.3 million (5.3%)
Number (and percent) of people with incomes less than 125% of the poverty line	48.7 million (16.9%)
Number (and percent) of people without health insurance	45 million (15.6%)

*The impact of new immigrants on poverty rates is probably exaggerated in the public's mind. Eighty-eight percent of those below the poverty line in 2003 were native born Americans (U.S. Census Bureau 2004, 11).

Sources: U.S. Census Bureau 2004, Tables 3, B-1, B-2, B-3, *Income, Poverty, and Health Insurance Coverage in the United States: 2003.*

percent and 15.2 percent).[14] The poverty rate in 2003 was 12.5 percent. It would have taken about $105 billion (or about 1 percent of GDP) in 2003 to raise all individuals above the poverty line.[15] The poverty rate increased to 12.7 percent in 2004.

Over the last two decades, poverty rates have varied more directly with the unemployment rate than with GDP.[16] One area where there has been a large decline in poverty attributable to social policy is poverty among the elderly, which fell from about 30 percent in 1967 to about 10 percent in 2003.[17]

"Relative" (Non-Subsistence) Definitions of Poverty

Many heterodox economists and poverty theorists have offered "relative" rather than "absolute" definitions of poverty. Amartya Sen, winner of the Nobel Prize in Economics in 1998, and others have analyzed poverty and inequality in terms of human capacities and access to full participation in society (quaintly expressed in Adam Smith's time as the ability to appear in public without embarrassment). The daunting task is how to "operationalize" these definitions, that is, how to measure people's access to life's possibilities.

One quick-and-dirty measure looks at the number of people below one-half the median in-

Table 15.4

Key Poverty Statistics for 2003

U.S. Census Bureau: Poverty Income Thresholds	
One person (under 65 years old)	$9,393
Two persons (householder under 65)	$12,015
Three persons	$14,680
Four persons	$18,810
Cost of Annual College Tuition, Fees, and Room and Board at:	
Four-year private institutions	$26,854
Four-year public institutions	$10,636
Two-year private institutions (2001)	$15,217
Two-year public institutions (just tuition and fees)	$1,905
Median Household Income 2003	$43,318
Per Capita GDP, Third Quarter of 2003	~$36,000
2003 Poverty Level for a Single Person as a Percent of Per Capita GDP	24.3%

Sources: U.S. Census Bureau, *Income, Poverty, and Health Insurance Coverage in the United States 2003*, p. 39, Appendix B; College Board, "Trends in College Pricing 2003." http://www.collegeboard.com/prod_downloads/press/cost03/cb_trends_pricing_2003.pdf; *Economic Report of the President, 2004.*

come. In the mid-1990s about 17 percent of the population and 22 percent of all children were poor by this standard (Mishel, Bernstein, and Boushey 2003, 416 [Table 7.13]). The official poverty threshold in 2006 stood at about one-third the median family income. A much more complicated approach tries to estimate key expenditures (for nutrition, health care, housing, education, etc.) necessary for realistic participation in contemporary American life (or for the development of people's capacity to participate in American life). The Economic Policy Institute's family budget project estimates that most families need about twice the poverty thresholds to meet their "basic needs and achieve a safe and decent standard of living" (Bernstein, Brocht, and Spade-Aguilar, 2000).[18] Table 15.4 lists some recent poverty thresholds in comparison with college tuition and other fees.

RACIAL AND GENDER INEQUALITIES

Racial Inequalities

Despite some genuine progress culturally, politically, and economically, there remains an enormous racial divide in the United States. From 1939 to 1979 African Americans made significant gains in relative income. Since 1980, progress has been modest (Bowles, Edwards, and Roosevelt 2005, 346). The median African American household income in 2003 was slightly less than two-thirds the median white household income (U.S. Census Bureau 2004, 4). Tables 15.5a and 15.5b document this divide. The unemployment rates for African Americans have for decades been twice the rate among whites. Over the last thirty years, the poverty rate among African American children has ranged from 30 percent to 47 percent (U.S. Census Bureau 2004, Table B-2). The rate was 34 percent in 2003. The median financial wealth of black families in 2001 was less than

Table 15.5a

Racial and Ethnic Income Inequalities 2003

Population Group	Median Income
All groups	$43,318
White	$45,631
Non-Hispanic white	$47,777
Black	$29,645
Hispanic	$32,997
Asian	$55,699

Source: U.S. Census Bureau, Income, Poverty, and Health Insurance Coverage in the United States 2003 (August 2004), p. 4.

Table 15.5b

Racial Differences in Wealth

Type of Wealth	Mean Value Non-Hispanic Whites	Mean Value Non-Hispanic Blacks	Median Value Non-Hispanic Whites	Median Value Non-Hispanic Blacks
Net worth 1995	$242,400	$40,800	$61,000	$7,400
Financial wealth 1995	$188,400	$21,200	$18,100	$200

Year	Median Non-Hispanic Black Net Worth / Median Non-Hispanic White Net Worth	Median Non-Hispanic Black Financial Wealth / Median Non-Hispanic White Financial Wealth
2001	~10%*	3%
1995	12%	1%
1989	3%	0%
1983	7%	0%

Source: Edward Wolff, "Recent Trends in the Size Distribution of Household Wealth," *Journal of Economic Perspectives* 12(3) (Summer 1998): 141.
   *Mishel, Bernstein, and Allegretto 2005, p. 285.

3 percent of the median financial wealth of white families (Mishel, Bernstein, and Allegretto 2005, 285). The economic situation of young African Americans without a high school diploma is especially disastrous.[19]

To some extent, the relative position of middle- and upper-income African American families to white families has improved or remained the same over the last few decades, while the position of the least-well-off African American families and young African American males, especially in the inner city, seems to have deteriorated.[20] This has created a bifurcation in the black community. The income of the richest 20 percent of African American households was more than seventeen times that of the poorest 20 percent of African American households in 2003.[21] As noted in chapter 8, many scholars have written about the serious impacts of very high African American unemployment rates in the inner city. It is unlikely that inequalities within the African American community, or inequalities between blacks and whites, can be addressed without increasing employment opportunities for African Americans in the inner city.

Gender Inequalities

Although women have made significant economic progress over the last few decades, there are still serious gender inequalities. The ratio of median female to male wages for full-time workers, for example, increased from 62.5 percent in 1979 to 79.5 percent in 2003 (U.S. Bureau of Labor Statistics 2004, 29).[22] Occupational segregation, while declining, remains high in some areas of the economy, generally clustering women in less-well-paying jobs. In 2000, for example, more than 95 percent of the economy's 3.75 million secretaries and administrative assistants were women, as were more than three-quarters of the economy's 4.5 million teachers (primary, secondary, and special ed.). On the other hand, only about 10 percent of all engineers, and a quarter of all top executives, physicians, and lawyers, were women (Caiazza, Shaw, and Werschkul 2004, Table 3).[23]

In much the same vein, although women composed 46 percent of the labor force, 58 percent of those earning the minimum wage in the late 1990s were women (Mishel, Bernstein, and Boushey 2003, 197, 252; U.S. Executive Office of the President 2000, Table B-35). Similarly, although the overall poverty rate among families was 10 percent in 2003, and 13.5 percent for single-parent families headed by a man, 28 percent of all single-parent families headed by a woman were poor.[24] On the other hand, unemployment rates have been slightly lower for women than men since 1989, reversing the trends of the 1960s and 1970s (Mishel, Bernstein, and Boushey 2003, 219; U.S. Executive Office of the President 2004, 335).

The upshot of these statistics is that improving the status of women in the economy will require targeted as well as general macroeconomic policy measures. Although policies that tighten labor markets do benefit women, other policies, such as increasing the minimum wage, providing universal publicly funded preschool, increasing public expenditures in sectors staffed by women (such as education), and increasing aid to families with children would address many women's economic difficulties even more directly.

Women also continue to do a disproportionate share of household labor, even when working outside the home. Although calculating precise numbers is difficult, it seems likely that women spend at least one and a half hours more per day on domestic chores than men do.[25]

TAXES AND INEQUALITY

Over the last twenty-five years the progressivity of the tax system[26] and its ability to counteract growing inequality in pretax income has waxed and waned. Macroeconomic arguments and policies have often influenced the distributional design of tax policy. The redistributive impact of the tax system fell during the 1980s due to supply-side tax cuts, which went disproportionately to upper-income groups. Tax changes in the 1990s increased the system's progressivity, while the tax cuts from 2001 and 2003 reduced it.[27] Changes in inheritance taxes have also tended to increase wealth inequality.

The key egalitarian mechanism of the 1990s was expansion of the earned income tax credit (EITC). The EITC is somewhat like a negative income tax (a government subsidy rather than tax of labor earnings) primarily for low-income workers with children. The EITC matches a portion of low-income families' market wages with tax credits, or direct payments if a family's tax burden is less than the credit. In 1999 the EITC lifted about five million working families out of poverty. In recent years funding has been in the range of thirty to thirty-five billion dollars per year.[28]

INTERNATIONAL COMPARISONS

Because of contextual differences, interpreting and drawing inferences from international comparisons is a risky enterprise. By most measurements, however, it appears that the United States has more unequal economic distributions than other industrialized democracies. The Gini coefficient for income distribution and the ratio of the top 10 percent of households' income to the bottom 10 percent's income are both significantly higher in the United States than in most OECD[29] countries. Poverty rates (as measured by the number of families with incomes less than half the national median income) are higher in the United States, as is the level of chronic poverty (poverty incomes for three or more years in a row). And despite the fact that the median income of American households is higher than the median income of households in most OECD countries, the bottom 10 percent of American households still have lower absolute real income than the bottom 10 percent of households in most other OECD countries (Mishel, Bernstein, and Allegretto 2005, 403). The equality gap between the U.S. and OECD states is even larger than the above statistics suggest, as most OECD countries have more generous publicly provided services, such as national health care and subsidized higher education, than the United States.

These numbers pose some interesting questions, which we will pursue later in this chapter. Among these questions are: why does it appear that U.S. capitalism is more unequal than other capitalisms? What kind of macroeconomic policies might bring U.S. experience in line with OECD experience? Are there any social costs (such as higher unemployment, or lower average per capita incomes) to increasing economic equality, and is the greater equity of OECD capitalism offset by greater social mobility in the United States?

The greatest economic divide is clearly that between the first and third world. More than one billion people lived on less than one dollar per day in 2001.[30] About 2.7 billion people lived on less than two dollars a day, which has become a rough-and-ready global poverty line.[31] From 1981 to 2001 the percentage of the world's population living on less than two dollars a day fell from 67 percent to 53 percent, though the absolute number of people living on less than two dollars a day grew by three hundred million (Wade 2005, 22–23). The economic performance of China and parts of India are bright spots in the battle against world poverty; while the trends in sub-Saharan Africa are alarming.

MEASURING SOCIAL MOBILITY

Unfortunately, the practical and methodological problems associated with measuring social mobility are even more daunting than the difficult problems associated with measuring income, wealth, and the other distributional variables discussed above. Most judgments must therefore be very tentative. There seems to be little evidence that social mobility is increasing in the United States, and some reason to think it may be declining (Mishel, Bernstein, and Boushey 2003, 75–78; Rose 1996; Mazumder 2004). Although America is a land of opportunity for some, it is likely that economic mobility is much less than imagined by popular stories of rags to riches.

One of the best ways to measure social mobility is to compare people's relative position in the income ladder over time, holding constant age cohorts. A recent study analyzing data from 1969 to 1994 found that 41 percent of the families in the bottom fifth of the income ladder in 1969 were still there twenty-five years later (Mishel, Bernstein, and Boushey 2003, 76).[32] Only about one in twenty of this group (5.8 percent) managed to reach the top quintile of the income ladder, compared with about eight in twenty (38.8 percent) of those who began in the top fifth. Overall, it appears that 40 percent to 60 percent of parents' income advantage is passed on to their children (Wessel 2005, A7; Mazumder 2002 and 2004).

Estimates of economic mobility in the United States have declined since 1990. This decline appears to reflect an actual decline in economic mobility and a reassessment of economic mobility by scholars. The reassessment was facilitated by the collection of better data, in particular by better adjustment for reporting errors and the impact of temporary fluctuations in income (Bowles and Gintis 2001, 2002; Mazumder 2002 and 2004).

It is especially difficult to find reliable statistics on international comparisons of social mobility. It seems unlikely that the U.S. economy's relatively high level of inequality is offset by unusually high levels of social mobility (Mishel, Bernstein, and Boushey 2003, 431). In fact, a recent review of dozens of studies of the United States, Canada, and Europe summarized in the *Wall Street Journal* concluded, "The U.S. and Britain appear to stand out as the least mobile societies among the rich countries studied. . . ."[33]

INTERMISSION

Review Questions

1. Why do heterodox macroeconomists tend to give greater attention to economic inequality than standard textbooks do?
2. What has been the overall trend in inequality in the U.S. economy since World War II?
3. What is meant by the Gini coefficient and the Lorenz curve?
4. What is the impact of taxes on inequality in the United States and how has this impact varied over time?
5. Which is more equally distributed in the United States, wealth or income?
6. What are the two basic approaches to defining poverty rates? What arguments have been offered for adopting each approach?
7. Briefly discuss the trend in the U.S. poverty rate over the last fifty years.
8. Roughly speaking, in 2001:
   a. What was the ratio of median African American income to median white income?
   b. What was the ratio of median Hispanic income to median white income?
   c. What was the ratio of median African American net worth to median white net worth?
   d. What was the ratio of African American to white poverty rates?
   e. Over the last fifty years unemployment among African Americans has averaged what percent of unemployment among white Americans? What is the ratio today?
9. Briefly discuss the trend in gender inequality over the last several decades.
10. How does the level of inequality in the United States compare with that in other industrialized countries?

Discussion Questions

1. What kind of obligations do you think we have as a society to each other and to each other's children?
2. What are the boundaries of obligation; do they cross national borders?
3. If you were asked by the president of the United States to measure poverty and changes over time in the poverty rate, how would you do it?
4. What is your family's pretax income? What decile of the income ladder does that income place you in?

THE MACROECONOMICS OF INEQUALITY

Neoclassical Approaches

Neoclassical theorists tend to think about inequality in terms of the distribution of income and wealth, and ultimately in terms of the distribution of consumption (which is thought of as the final goal of all economic activities). They usually do not actively explore other dimensions of inequality involving social and political phenomena. For the neoclassicals, the distribution of income is based on the distribution of the factors of production (e.g., land, labor, and capital) and their relative productivity. People who own a lot of fertile land or possess valuable labor skills, for example, will enjoy higher market rewards than people who are landless and unskilled.

The shifting conditions of supply and demand alter the market's rewards for different factors and thus alter income distributions. In this vision, the market functions like a giant computer that allows people to trade and recombine the assets they have, such as their labor time, in ways that leave both parties to an exchange better off. The level of inequality in the economy reflects the characteristics of the economy's participants. To draw an academic analogy, the distribution of income in the economy, like the distribution of grades in a class, reflects the students' and economic agents' talents and choices.

Heterodox Alternatives

Introduction

While not rejecting the neoclassical image entirely, heterodox economists add other important dimensions to the neoclassical picture. The economic implication of individual characteristics is placed in a social context. The observed pattern of market exchange is tied to larger institutional and political blueprints that influence people's trading strategies and the value of people's assets. Market outcomes reflect both people's individual characteristics *and* the reproducing logic and distributions of power of various institutional, ideological, and political contexts.

To draw an academic analogy, imagine a course graded on a curve. People's individual grades would still be heavily influenced by their individual characteristics. The distribution of grades, however, would also reflect a structural logic, the shape of the curve imposed by the faculty member. Heterodox economics spends more time exploring "the shape of the curve" than neoclassical theory does. To take the academic analogy one step further, course grades can also reflect the kinds of teaching and exams used (e.g., large lecture classes and multiple choice tests versus small classes with group work and essay exams). If some students do better in one context than another, final grades will reflect students' individual characteristics and the social structure of education. So too for participants in the economy; different structures benefit different groups. Heterodox economics explores the institutional logics that benefit some parts of the economy over others.

Heterodox Challenges to Naturalizing Inequality

There is a tendency within neoclassical theory to "normalize" inequality. There is, for example, a "natural rate" of unemployment. Notable differences in wealth and income are portrayed as a "natural" result of voluntary exchange among diverse individuals. Equity and efficiency are generally assumed to be inherently conflicting macroeconomic goals. Redistributing income, through mechanisms such as a progressive income tax, is thought to dull economic incentives. From a neoclassical perspective, the job of economists is to explore what the equity/efficiency trade-offs are (i.e., to determine how much the pie shrinks as we try to make the slices more equal). It is up to the political process and people's normative judgment to decide what trade-offs to make.

Heterodox economists challenge the way neoclassical theorists have framed distributional issues. They replace images of natural occurrence with images of social construction. They reject ahistorical claims about the inevitability of equity-efficiency trade-offs. They link distributional outcomes to the logic of social contexts as much as to individual characteristics. Different heterodox paradigms and heterodox theorists perceive different structural logics at work in the economy. We explore some of these logics below. Often they overlap rather than contradict each other.

The Distributional Implications of Full Employment

While neoclassical subtexts tend to prioritize maximizing GDP as an economic goal, heterodox economists tend to give equal or more weight to the goal of full employment. This is largely due to the social and distributional implications of full employment. As noted in chapter 8, heterodox economists tend to emphasize the broader social, psychological, and community implications of work experience more than neoclassical economists. This tends to make the cost of unemployment and the benefits of full employment seem higher to heterodox than to neoclassical economists.

As noted in earlier chapters, heterodox theories of wage and profit determination give more weight to the impact of bargaining power on income distributions and working conditions than neoclassical introductory textbooks. Many heterodox economists believe that tight labor markets significantly tilt bargaining power away from employers and toward workers, especially the least advantaged workers. This tilt improves wages, fringe benefits, job security, and working conditions, partially at the expense of profits and real interest payments, and partially due to the higher rates of capacity utilization and economic efficiency achieved at full employment.[34] Conversely, slack labor markets increase the bargaining power of employers and their influence in and outside of labor markets.

Given this dynamic, many heterodox economists perceive a conflict of interest between workers and property owners (recipients of profits and interest payments) over how "tightly" to run the economy. Although no one benefits from prolonged periods of high unemployment, owners of firms (who receive profit income) and owners of financial capital (who receive interest payments) generally favor running the economy with somewhat higher levels of unemployment (~5–6 percent currently) than workers (~3–4 percent). Rather than perceiving macro policy makers as apolitical experts who strive to determine the "correct" macro policy that would benefit "everyone," many heterodox economists see macro policy making as partially "political," that is, as a task that involves and resolves conflicts of interest. This is perhaps most clearly visible in the difference between heterodox and neoclassical analyses of Federal Reserve policy making (recall chapter 11).

Besides increasing labor's share of national income, falling unemployment tends to raise the wages of lower-paid workers faster than those of higher-paid workers, adding a second avenue by which full employment reduces inequality. Institutionalist economist James Galbraith estimates that "[m]ovements of the unemployment rate alone account for 79 percent of all variation in wage inequality [1924–1992]. . . . It is, above all, the low rates of unemployment in the 1920s, during World War II, and in the late 1960s that bring inequality in the wage structure down. Nothing else in our history has had a comparable effect" (James K. Galbraith 2000, 147).

Recent data seem to support Galbraith's claim. For example, from 1995 to 2000 unemployment fell from 5.6 percent to 4.0 percent, approaching full employment (less than 4 percent unemployment) for the first time in thirty years. Real wages for the bottom 30 percent of hourly workers rose faster than wages for the top 30 percent, reversing the pattern of the previous twenty

Table 15.6

The Equalizing Impact of Full-Employment

Category/Group	1995	2000
Unemployment rates*		
National rate	5.6%	4.0%
White	4.9%	3.5%
Black or African American	10.4%	7.6%
Hispanic	9.3%	5.7%
Poverty rates**		
National rate	13.8%	11.3%
White Non-Hispanic	8.5%	7.4%
Black	29.3%	22.5%
Hispanic American	30.2%	21.5%
Family income growth***		1995–2000
White families		+11%
African American families		+16%
Hispanic families		+25%

*Unemployment Rates: *Economic Report of the President* 2005, p. 260, Table B-42.
**Poverty Rates: U.S. Census Bureau, "Poverty in the United States 2001," pp. 20–24. (http://www.census.gov/prod/2002pubs/p60–219.pdf).
***Mishel, Bernstein, and Boushey 2003, p. 5.

years. As Table 15.6 indicates, socially disadvantaged groups were especially helped. For example, median family income grew 11 percent for white families, 16 percent for African American families, and 25 percent for Hispanic families.

Galbraith finds 5.5 percent unemployment to be a hinge for macro levels of inequality. He writes, "the change in inequality will equal zero, on average in this century, when unemployment averages about 5.5 percent. When unemployment is below 5.5 percent, inequality is likely to fall. . . . A 5.5 percent rate of unemployment may therefore be called the *ethical rate of unemployment* [italics in original] for the Unites States over most of the twentieth century. For those who are concerned with inequality, it should be an article of policy that unemployment be kept below this value" (James K. Galbraith 2000, 148–49).

Dual Labor Markets and Inequality

As previously noted heterodoxy links some of the inequalities in the economy to the uneven structure of labor markets. Dual labor market theory is a very common approach. Dual labor market theory posits the existence of two different kinds of jobs in two different kinds of markets. Primary-sector jobs have relatively high wages and benefits, good working conditions, good job security, job ladders (with payoffs to seniority, opportunities for advancement, and business investment in employees), and formal governance procedures that limit the arbitrary exercise of power by supervisors. Secondary-sector jobs are pretty much the mirror image of primary-sector jobs. They have low compensation, poor working conditions, little job security, little opportunity for advancement, close supervision, and autocratic discipline. Although sometimes the difference between primary- and secondary-sector jobs is linked to the nature of the work (such as the different activities required of engineers and sales clerks), sometimes the same job (janitor or cafeteria worker) will be organized very differently if the firm is a primary-sector employer (like IBM) or a secondary-sector employer (like a small local restaurant). Because primary-sector jobs pay above market wages, there are more people willing and qualified to work in this sector than there are jobs. Positions are rationed in many different ways, including by race and gender.

Why do segmented labor markets exist; why do not employers lower the perks that primary-sector workers receive and hire qualified workers willing to work in primary-sector jobs for less than the going wage; and why is assignment to each sector often done by group characteristics like race, ethnicity, and gender?

Heterodox theorists give several different reasons for the existence of distinct labor markets. The first rationale is similar to the concept of "efficiency wages" offered by some neoclassical theorists.[35] It suggests that some firms choose to pay higher than market wages in order to increase labor productivity by winning worker loyalty, reducing labor turnover, and reducing supervision costs. This management strategy makes the most sense for workers whose replacement would involve expensive searches, whose labor is hard to monitor, and whose voluntary cooperation is essential for the firm's success.

The second rationale for segmented labor markets is more historical. It suggests that many firms had the option in the past to employ "high-road" or "low-road" labor strategies. Low-road strategies rely more on the "stick" of close supervision and threats of dismissal to discipline and motivate workers. High-road strategies rely more on the "carrot" of above-market compensation and worker identification with the firm to motivate voluntary cooperation. Once a strategy is in place it is hard (but not impossible) to make changes, as both worker and management culture, and the firm's technology, tend to lock the enterprise into a certain cluster of practices. Current inequalities may thus have more to do with past than current choices.

A third rationale for labor market segmentation suggests that firms try to differentiate the working conditions among employees in order to discourage collective action by employees. The isolation of privileged primary-sector workers from the larger cohort of employees is especially helpful in reducing the latter's bargaining strength.

Why is assignment to primary or secondary jobs often done by race and gender, with African Americans, Hispanics, and women disproportionately represented in secondary-sector jobs? Many heterodox economists argue that racial and gender channeling reinforces the barriers to inter-sector cooperation, strengthening employers' hands in bargaining with labor. A second interpretation suggests that firms defer to social prejudice (which might make employing a woman or African American in a management position more contentious than employing a white male) in making management decisions.

Dual labor market theory has important implications for the economics of inequality. It suggests that economists need to look at the structure of labor markets (analogous to the grading curve discussed above), as well as individual workers' productive capacities, to understand income distributions. Dual labor market theory also invites attention to holist dynamics. Heterodox theorists stress the feedback effects of labor policies. They explore how job structures coevolve with employees' work habits and complementary social institutions in the community (such as informal networks and school systems). Many heterodox theorists worry that prolonged employment in secondary jobs can make transitions to primary-sector employment difficult. When secondary-sector jobs dominate a social-geographic niche, like the inner city, they may make their perpetuation a self-fulfilling prophecy.

From the perspective of dual labor market theory, the decline in the number of primary-sector jobs available to less educated blue-collar workers has been one of the major contributors to increased inequality in the economy. The loss of jobs in the primary sector has been accompanied by an expansion of several forms of secondary employment, including: temporary employment (through companies like Manpower, which is now the largest single employer in the United States), contingent employment (where firms have workers on call but not in stable employment), and outsourcing of formerly primary-sector jobs to secondary-sector subcontractors.

Macro Regimes and Inequality

As noted in chapter 13, many heterodox economists analyze macroeconomic events in terms of institutional conjunctures. The most well known of these approaches is the Social Structures of Accumulation (SSA) school. SSA theorists argue that different combinations of socioeconomic institutions lead to different distributional outcomes. You many recall from chapter 13 the difference between "high- and low-road" macro regimes. High-road economies have been called "capitalism with a human face," "welfare state capitalism," and "Nordic capitalism." Low-road strategies are currently associated with neoliberalism and "the Anglo-American model."

High Roads

High roads involve:

- Active government demand management policies to limit the severity of recessions
- Collaborative labor strategies by major firms (frequently involving high unionization rates, significant business investment in job training, and reliance on internal job ladders rather than pure market forces to structure compensation)
- High levels of business investment
- Cooperative labor policies toward business
- High levels of government investment in infrastructural projects (like the Internet) and human capital (such as education, health, and nutrition spending)
- High levels of government regulation of financial markets (to curb speculation and market volatility)
- Mildly progressive government distribution policies (such as relatively progressive tax rates)

Low Roads

Low roads involve:

- A shift in government policy from prioritizing full employment to prioritizing low inflation as macroeconomic goals
- Corporate labor strategies congenial with periods of relatively high unemployment, such as strategies that reduce long-term labor commitments and attempt to benefit from labor's weakened position during economic downturns
- Less government support for the social safety net, especially policies that would decrease the costs of job loss
- Reduced government regulation of business, such as weaker occupational health and environmental regulation
- Reduced government efforts to redistribute income
- Reduced public investment

Path Choices

High-road economic strategies try to resolve some of the inherent uncertainties in capitalism around wage/profit issues and investment decisions through social policies that encourage and reward cooperation. High-road economic strategies also reduce the inequalities generated by unconstrained markets. Low-road economic strategies celebrate the benefits of market competition and the unbridled pursuit of self-interest in resolving uncertainties and setting an economic course.

Heterodox economists portray the choice between these different capitalisms as a political choice. Textbook economics ignores or denies the choice, or implies that the market inherently makes the "optimal" choice on its own. As explained in the next section, heterodox economists tie the large increase in inequality in the United States over the last thirty years to the American economy's turn onto the "low road." The choice of this path was facilitated by macro policies that retreated from full-employment goals and public responsibility for the social shape of the economy.

WHY DID INEQUALITY INCREASE FROM 1973 TO 2003?

Neoclassical Explanations

Many common factors appear in both neoclassical and heterodox explanations for the causes of rising inequality, but the weighting tends to be different. Heterodox explanations also include factors often absent in neoclassical stories. Conventional neoclassical textbooks tend to link rising inequality to "technical factors," such as changes in production technologies and product mixes, and noneconomic factors, such as demographic shifts. The most important of these are:

- An increase in the demand for skilled relative to unskilled workers driven largely by technological changes, especially computerization (the "skills biased technical change" hypothesis)
- A shift in the mix of economic output from manufactured goods (with relatively high-paying blue-collar jobs) to services (with relatively low-paying white-collar jobs)
- Changes in family structure, both an increase in the number of single-parent, female-headed households at the bottom of the income ladder and an increase in the number of two-income households at the top of the ladder (the "family structure hypothesis")
- Increased globalization, which forces low-skilled American workers to compete with third world workers, be they new immigrants or workers in foreign plants of domestic firms.

Most of these factors also play a role in heterodox explanations, but their relative importance is often reduced and they are situated in a larger context.

Heterodox Explanations

Introduction and Overview

Heterodox explanations for rising inequality tend to be more "politicized." The explanations reject the "naturalness" and appearance of inevitability and optimality present in neoclassical stories. The market's path is tied in part to the economic strategies pursued by powerful economic interests and to the design of public policy.

Heterodox accounts criticize neoclassical texts for overemphasizing the impact of skill-rewarding-technological change and demographic factors on wage dispersion. They point out, for example, that wage inequality increased significantly before the onset of the widespread use of computers in about 1983–1984.[36] Although the increase in female-headed single-parent families did contribute to rising inequality, this increase was slowing down when inequality was accelerating. Heterodox accounts also note that inequality increased within most job categories and family types in the United States, suggesting that something else, besides family structure and computerization, was an underlining cause of growing inequality.

What replaces, or more accurately complements, demographics and technically determined explanations in heterodox approaches? The answer is institutional and policy changes. Many heterodox economists give special attention to changes in the organizational, regulatory, and cultural norms structuring the labor market. Five key areas stand out:

1. Declines in the real value of the minimum wage
2. Declines in the influence of labor unions
3. Shifts in cultural norms and business strategies
4. Shifts in government macro priorities from maintaining employment to fighting inflation
5. Shifts in regulatory policy

Heterodox economists also tend to give greater weight to the impact of globalization in explaining growing inequality than neoclassical economists do, in part because of greater attention to the impact of "free trade" policies on institutional environments.

Falling Minimum Wages

About twenty million workers (~17.5 percent of all workers) were earning between the old federal minimum wage and a dollar above the new higher minimum wage in 1996.[37] Thus shifts in the minimum wage and their ripple effects on workers earning near the minimum wage impact a fairly large group of workers (Mishel, Bernstein, and Boushey 2003, 196–203). As Table 15.7 indicates, the federal minimum wage, measured in constant 2003 dollars, fell from a peak of $8.46/hour in 1968 to $4.77/hour in September 2005.[38] There was about a 25 percent decline in the real value of the minimum wage between the early 1970s and the 2000s. The current ratio of the minimum wage to the average hourly wage of nonsupervisory workers (~33 percent) is the lowest percentage in fifty-five years.[39]

Mishel, Bernstein, and Boushey estimate that about one-third of the increase in inequality in the 1980s was due to falling minimum wages and de-unionization.[40] Other economists have compared the wage dispersions in states with different state-mandated minimum wages, such as Mississippi and New Jersey, and found similar levels of impact (Gordon 1996, 218, 228). The minimum wage has an especially large impact on low-skilled women workers. Mishel, Bernstein, and Boushey (2003) found that 90 percent of the increasing inequality between women's wages at the fiftieth and tenth percentile of wages would have disappeared if the minimum wage had kept pace with inflation (200–201).[41]

Declining Union Influence

Union membership peaked at 35 percent of the workforce in 1953. Despite falling from 35.7 percent to 29.1 percent of the workforce from 1953 to 1970, union influence remained strong economically and politically. Over the last three decades of the twentieth century, however, this influence eroded. Table 15.8 details the collapse in union membership.

Table 15.7

Federal Minimum Wage Rates: 1960–2003

Year	Minimum Wage in Historical Dollars	Minimum Wage in Constant 2003 Dollars
1960	1.00	6.22
1965	1.25	7.30
1968*	1.60	8.46
1970	1.60	7.59
1975	2.10	7.18
1980	3.10	6.92
1985	3.35	5.73
1990	3.80	5.35
1995	4.25	5.13
2000	5.15	5.50
2005	5.15	4.77 (through 9/2005)

* Peak year for the real value of the minimum wage.

Sources: Minimum Wage in Current Historical Dollars: U.S. Census Bureau, *Statistical Abstract of the United States 2004–2005,* p. 413, Table 626, Federal Minimum Wage Rates; Adjustment to 2003 $ based on the Consumer Price Index-All Urban Consumers series, Bureau of Labor Statistics (BLS) 1980–2003 and *The Economic Report of the President* (2000), p. 373, Table B-58, CPI-U 1960–1980. 2004–2005 data from BLS 10/14/2005 CPI-U series. Some economists believe that the CPI-U series overestimates inflation. Using a different CPI deflator (CPI-URS) earlier minimum wages are somewhat lower: ~18 percent lower in 1960, 10 percent lower in 1980, and the same in 2000 (private correspondence with Jared Bernstein of the Economic Policy Institute). The fall in the peak real value of the minimum wage also declines from a drop of ~44 percent to a drop of ~31 percent.

Many heterodox economists argue that strong unions increase labor's share of national income, reduce wage dispersion among wage and salary earners, and tilt political outcomes toward greater social equality. The economic arguments underlying the first two conclusions are complicated and involve several different effects. Among these are claims that:

1. unions force firms with above-average profits to share those "economic rents" with workers
2. unions force shareholders to accept the lower range of "acceptable" returns
3. unions impose "high-road" labor strategies on firms that partially finance themselves through efficiency wage effects
4. unions encourage firms to smooth out wage inequalities inside companies (through policies like seniority, common compensation, and limits on top management salaries)

Unions have other economic effects with more ambiguous implications for inequality. Unions may restrict access to certain occupations and lower employment levels in those jobs. This effect raises the wages of union members, but by crowding remaining workers into nonunion jobs it may lower nonunion wages. On the other hand, the "union threat" effect tends to raise wages and improve working conditions in nonunion firms within the same industry. Union contracts have also tended, with a lag, to set norms for working conditions and fringe benefits (such as pension and health benefits) across the economy.

Unions can also raise operating costs and force consumers to pay higher prices for final products. The overall impact of these effects on inequality depends partially on the industry and occu-

Table 15.8

Labor Union Membership 1950–2000

Percentage union members	1950	1955	1960	1965	1972	1978	1983	1985	1990	1995	2000
Total labor force	22.0	24.4	23.6	22.4	21.8	19.7					
Nonagricultural employment	31.5	33.2	31.4	28.4	26.4	23.6					
Wage and salary workers							20.1	18.0	16.1	14.9	13.5
Private sector							16.5	14.3	11.9	10.3	9.0
Public sector							36.7	35.7	36.5	37.7	37.5

Sources: 1950–1978: U.S. Census Bureau, *Statistical Abstract of the United States 1980,* p. 429, Table 714; 1983–2000: U.S. Census Bureau, *Statistical Abstract of the United States 2002,* p. 411, Table 628. There is a modest shift in categories between the two series (1950–1978 and 1983–2000).

pation involved. For example, unionization of domestic workers (maids etc.) might raise wages for household workers and increase the costs for cleaning services, with only modest employment effects. This could reduce inequality. Unionization of highly paid airline pilots may have increased inequality. Unions can also influence other kinds of inequalities, such as gender and racial inequalities. The record of unions in these areas is mixed.

Alongside the direct economic impact of unions, heterodox economists stress the political and cultural importance of unions. Many observers feel that a strong labor movement is essential if the United States is to have a more equal health care system, greater aid to education, progressive tax rates, and other egalitarian social policies.

Changing Cultural Norms and Business Strategies

Because the economy involves social relationships, social mores and social expectations infuse market supply and demand curves. Heterodox theories of the workplace stress the socially contingent aspect of what is an "efficient wage structure," or a "profit-maximizing business strategy." For example, cooperative management styles and the image of a "community-oriented firm" may aid or hurt the bottom line, depending on the larger social context. Thus, the loosening of cultural constraints against the unbridled pursuit of self-interest by firms, CEOs, and privileged workers since the 1980s has had economic consequences. These changes have encouraged firms to adopt "low-road" business and labor relations strategies, characterized by aggressive antiunion policies, less compunctions about plant closings, increased use of "contingent workers" (such as temps, part-time workers without full benefits, and outsourcing), greater emphasis on the short than long run, and larger inequalities in compensation within the firm.[42]

Shifting Macro Policies and Unemployment Levels

As noted above, heterodox economists argue that high levels of employment tend to reduce inequality. The shift in government monetary and fiscal policy after the mid-seventies from prioritizing full employment to prioritizing low inflation thus tended to increase inequality by increasing unemployment. From 1974 to 2003, unemployment averaged a full point and a half higher (6.4 percent) than from 1948 to 1973 (4.8 percent), increasing wage dispersion and poverty rates.

Shifting Regulatory Policies

Government policies have also helped reshape labor markets. Many observers feel that political appointees to the National Labor Relations Board (NLRB), which interprets and enforces the rules governing labor disputes, have become more pro-business since 1980. Harvard economist Richard Freeman, for example, criticizes the NLRB for allowing companies to illegally threaten workers with dismissal if they attempt to form a union. He suggests that this kind of intimidation helps explain why less than 10 percent of the private sector is unionized, despite polling data indicating that 20 to 30 percent of private-sector workers want to be represented by unions (R. Freeman 1999, 25–26).[43] Many other NLRB decisions about issues ranging from sympathy strikes to misleading company statements have similarly tilted the playing field toward antiunion election outcomes.[44]

Government policy has also led by example. One of the unwritten rules of U.S. labor relations from approximately 1950 to 1980 was that firms did not hire permanent replacement workers during a strike. When job actions ended, regardless of who won, the firms' old workers went back to work under the new contract. When the Federal Air Traffic Controllers struck in 1981 (despite laws prohibiting such strikes by public employees) President Reagan permanently replaced the 11,000 striking workers. This action seemed to encourage private companies to threaten striking workers with similar fates, tilting the balance of power in labor disputes toward business.[45]

The biggest shift in bargaining power in U.S. labor markets probably involves U.S. firms' increased ability to shift production overseas.[46] Although the major causes of globalization have probably involved technological changes (such as improved communications and information-management resources), government policies (as noted below) have also made it easier to shift production overseas. Other government policies, such as reductions in unemployment insurance,[47] have also weakened labor's bargaining position. Some changes in the tax structure have also increased social inequality.

Trade Effects

Many heterodox economists find that recent shifts toward "freer trade" have tended (1) to loosen the cultural obligations of business to anyone besides stockholders, (2) to weaken the "social constraints" on wage inequality within firms, and (3) to equalize the wages of similarly skilled workers throughout the world, thereby depressing the wages of unskilled labor in the United States.

Heterodox economists also stress the impact of increased capital mobility, which has accompanied the expansion of trade, on firms' bargaining power with local and national governments. The threat of capital flight has tended to reduce the ability of public policy to redistribute income and to regulate corporate behavior in environmental, health and safety, and other areas.

It is difficult to derive a quantitative estimate for the relative contribution of increased international trade to growing inequality in the United States. Rough calculations tend to assign 10 to 20 percent of the increase in inequality to international factors. Heterodox estimates would probably trend higher than neoclassical estimates.

Conclusion

Heterodox economists challenge the thesis that rising inequality reflects the inevitable implications of technological change and other forces beyond social governance, as is often implied in neoclassical analyses. Paul Krugman, an independent-minded neoclassical economist, has depicted the debate between heterodox and orthodox economists over the reasons for increased inequality quite clearly. In a recent column in the *New York Times* (Krugman 2006) Krugman criticized Ben Bernanke, the new chair of the Federal Reserve, for claiming that the primary reason for rising inequality is a rising skill premium for educated labor. Krugman writes,

> Why would someone as smart and well informed as Mr. Bernanke get the nature of growing inequality wrong? Because the fallacy he fell into tends to dominate polite discussion about income trends, not because it's true, but because it's comforting. The notion that it's all about returns to education suggests that nobody is to blame for rising inequality, that it's just a case of supply and demand at work. . . .
>
> The idea that we have a rising oligarchy is much more disturbing. It suggests that the growth in inequality may have as much to do with power relations as it does with market forces. Unfortunately, that's the real story. (A19)

POLICY RESPONSES TO INEQUALITY

Introduction

Heterodox economists criticize standard macro texts for giving insufficient attention to policy responses to inequality. They replace the economic fatalism of the textbooks with images of competing macro regimes and recommend that public policies shift the economy from a "low-road" to a "high-road" macroeconomic strategy. These recommendations often include a much broader range of policy options than considered in standard textbooks.

When neoclassical textbooks discuss macroeconomic policy debates about inequality, the discussion tends to be dominated by debate between mainstream and conservative voices. The mainstream perspective urges a "steady-as-you-go" policy framework, while the conservative perspective (represented by supply-side economics) urges increases in inequality to spur economic growth. Heterodox analyses add a third, more egalitarian perspective. We look at each of these views below.

"Steady-As-You-Go" Policy Recommendations

This perspective treats existing levels of inequality as a natural and more-or-less inevitable reflection of the market implications of the distribution of human talents and individual motivations. The posture assumes that economic growth benefits everyone and tends to be relatively tolerant of inequality as long as it is accompanied by economic growth. The Fed and other economic policy makers are assumed to design macro policy to maximize the general welfare. There is little portrayal of macro policy making as a political battle that may benefit some groups at the expense of others. Debates over macroeconomic policy are presented as debates about technical issues in economic theory. While noting the public's perception of large disagreements among economists, the texts imply that the range of disagreement among "reputable [i.e., neoclassical] economists" is smaller than it often seems.

The steady-as-you-go stance notes there are "positive" debates among economists over what happens to economic efficiency when egalitarian policies are pursued and "normative" debates about what combination of economic efficiency and economic equality are desirable. The range of combinations discussed, however, is relatively narrow.

The steady-as-you-go stance highlights several policy responses to macroeconomic inequality. Among these are:

- efforts to offset the distributional implications of skill-biased technological change by increasing low-income families' access to education and job training
- efforts to offset the distributional implications of free trade agreements (like NAFTA) by giving special retraining assistance to workers who lose their jobs as a result of these agreements
- efforts to redistribute income through progressive tax policies and means-tested social programs, such as the food stamp program and other "welfare" assistance

These redistributive programs are constrained in the textbooks, however, by the assumption that too much redistribution will dull economic incentives. The books' take-away message tends to endorse policies fairly close to the status quo.[48]

Supply-Side (SS) Macroeconomic Policy Recommendations

Supply-side macroeconomics arose in the late 1970s and early 1980s. It was a policy-oriented theory designed to explain and respond to the stagflation of the 1970s. Unlike mainstream theory, which tends to downplay distributional issues, supply-side economics highlights them. It calls for greater changes in redistributive policies and larger increases in inequality than common in the steady-as-you-go approach.

From a supply-side perspective, inequality in a competitive market economy primarily reflects differences in ability and effort.[49] It is a necessary part of a healthy economy and not a cause for concern. Unemployment in an economy with few market imperfections is voluntary and caused by individuals' refusal to accept the market wage. Inflation is caused by the Federal Reserve. It arises when the money supply grows faster than real output. It could be eliminated if the Fed set monetary growth roughly equal to GDP growth. The Fed's failure to do this reflects a misguided attempt to fight unemployment.

Thus far, supply-side economics looks quite similar to traditional general equilibrium (GE) theory. It assumes that perfect markets automatically produce full employment without government efforts to maintain aggregate demand. Supply-side economists part company with GE economists, however, over whether the actual economy is close enough to the idealized economy to behave as GE theory predicts. The supply-siders argue that many government policies designed to reduce inequality, such as minimum wages and unemployment insurance, interfere with market mechanisms and dull economic incentives. They favor reducing these "market imperfections." Their policy recommendations fall into three areas: policies to reduce labor market imperfections, policies to reduce incentives for not working, and policies to increase incentives for working.

The major supply-side recommendations for restructuring labor markets are reductions in the minimum wage, reductions in union power, and deregulation of labor markets. The major supply-side recommendations for decreasing the incentives for voluntary unemployment are reductions in unemployment insurance, reductions in public assistance programs, and cutbacks in other safety net programs. These policies are often called the "stick" part of supply-side economics.

The "carrot" in the supply-side program involves direct and indirect measures to increase the rewards for working. The direct effects lead immediately to higher wages. The indirect effects involve policies that supporters claim would eventually lead to higher wages. There are surprisingly few policies with direct effects. Although tax cuts play a big role in the supply-side program, most of them are received by higher-income groups who have low labor-market unemployment rates.

The indirect effects, colloquially called "trickle-down" economics, or "feed the horses to feed the sparrows," embody the bulk of supply-side policy recommendations. The causal logic behind these policies is often quite complicated and is explored in more detail in footnote 50.[50] The basic chain of argument calls for government efforts to increase business profits, in order to increase business investment, in order to increase labor productivity, in order to increase wages, in order to decrease voluntary unemployment. Supply-side economists argue that reducing corporate income taxes, subsidizing business investment, and reducing required business spending for environmental protection and occupational health and safety measures will increase business profitability and thereby spur investment. Supply-side economists also favor cutting taxes on the income that the owners of corporations receive (as dividends or capital gains) and cutting taxes on interest payments that bondholders receive when they loan money to businesses. The supply-siders argue that these tax cuts will cheapen the cost of capital to business and provide an additional spur for investment.

As John Kenneth Galbraith has observed, the distributional problem to supply-side economists is that the poor have too much money and the rich not enough. The supply-side program lobbies for large increases in inequality in exchange for promises of lower unemployment rates and faster economic growth.[51] Ironically, the supply-siders share the perspective of some Marxist economists, that a more egalitarian capitalism is impossible. Many non-Marxist heterodox and non-supply-side neoclassical economists disagree and search for wider ranges of potential capitalisms.

Heterodox Policy Recommendations

Overview

Heterodox economists expand the list of policy responses to inequality found in neoclassical texts. They highlight:

1. The vigorous pursuit of full employment
2. Economic policies that create incentives for business to adopt high- rather than low-road labor relations strategies
3. Economic policies that regenerate social capital and egalitarian cultural norms
4. Specially targeted programs to deal with disadvantaged groups and dual labor markets
5. Innovative ways of responding to equity/efficiency trade-offs in contexts where they occur

Taken as a group, the policies compose a market-oriented form of economic planning, or what is sometimes called "industrial policy." Some heterodox economists, such as Marxist economists, are pessimistic about the possibilities of significantly reducing inequality within a capitalist economy. These economists urge more fundamental social changes.

Full-Employment Policies

Heterodox economists recommend the aggressive use of monetary and fiscal policy to maintain full employment (~3–4 percent unemployment).[52] They reject macroeconomic speed limits of 5–6.5 percent unemployment set by conventional estimates of the non-accelerating inflation rate of unemployment (NAIRU). They favor "restructuring the Fed" and shifting its priorities from fighting inflation to fighting unemployment. They also recommend expanded public employment programs and greater public spending for infrastructural investment.

There is debate within the heterodox community over whether low unemployment generates inflationary pressures. Heterodox economists who are concerned about tight labor markets' generating inflation urge the adoption of innovative anti-inflation policies. Among these are TIPS (Tax-Based Incomes Policies) that offers tax breaks to firms for noninflationary pricing behavior and forms of collective bargaining that reduce wage pressures near full employment.

Economic Planning

Because of heterodox economic theory's conception of macro regimes, heterodox policies attempt to create a "high-road" macro development path. Among the kinds of policies discussed are:

1. High minimum wages
2. Legislation to strengthen unions
3. Tax incentives for firms that invest in employee training, involve workers in corporate governance, and moderate intra-firm wage differentials.[53]
4. Government aid for industries with desirable employment profiles, such as traditional blue-collar industries and businesses employing disadvantaged residents from the inner city
5. Limits on capital mobility
6. Macro policies that keep unemployment rates low and thereby reward firms that pursue long-term relationships with their employees

Taken together these policies attempt to foster a planning environment that turns management's attention to how to organize production in ways that presume high-wage, long-term employment relations. Laissez-faire-oriented economists are skeptical of the benefits of forcing social agendas on private managers. They argue that if solving such problems were an efficient use of managers' time they would already be addressing these issues. Heterodox economists disagree. Appealing to the concept of meta-externalities, they argue that the market's calculus of economic efficiency leaves out distributional and cultural concerns. It is up to social policy to create capitalism with a human face.

Regenerating Social Capital and Recreating a Sense of Community

Because of heterodoxy's holist methodology, heterodox macro policy recommendations include a broader range of goals and tools than standard textbook discussions do. Among these add-ons are proposals to reduce inequality by regenerating social capital.[54] One line of thinking favors greater efforts to regenerate egalitarian social norms through increased funding of preschools and public schools (which besides educating children create a sense of community). Another strategy calls for greater spending for tax-supported free goods, like public beaches, local playing fields for community recreation, public libraries, free concerts, and pleasing vistas in urban environments. The provision of these goods lowers the stakes of market competition and offers people a sense of a shared future.

Neoclassical textbooks tend to find these projects economically inefficient.[55] The textbooks imply that public provision forces a bundle of socially determined consumer goods on individuals, while market provision tailors products to people's preferences. Heterodox economists acknowledge the benefits of market allocation for many commodities, but argue that the meta-externalities of public provision heavily outweigh these advantages in some cases.

Heterodox economists often worry about the collapsing vision of a shared future in the U.S. economy. The logic of neoclassical textbooks would appear to treat the rise of gated communities,[56] which remove public streets from shared consumption, as a move toward economic efficiency, while heterodoxy perceives their expansion as a troubling symbol of the decline of our life as one people. In a similar vein heterodox economists worry about the effects of privatizing social security or expanding the voucher system in precollege education. The fear is that the rich and the upper middle class will opt out of a system of social reciprocity, leaving the middle and lower middle classes in a mean-spirited competition with their better-funded "superiors" and needy "subordinates."

Helping Disadvantaged Groups and Dealing with Dual Labor Markets

Although heterodox economists stress the importance of reducing unemployment for improving the economic conditions of African Americans, Hispanics, and women, they also argue that the special circumstances of these groups require additional targeted policies.[57] This is especially true for young African American males without a high school diploma and for female-headed single-parent families with children. Heterodox economists often criticize standard macro texts for giving insufficient attention to the design of economic policies to aid these groups. This inattention often reflects the texts' preoccupation with GDP as a measure of economic performance and national welfare. Free and universal child care, along the lines of the public school system, paying decent wages to caregivers (likely to be women) might be one of the most effective policies for reducing inequality.[58]

Innovative Responses to Potential Equity/Efficiency Tradeoffs

While rejecting the claim that equity and efficiency are inherently at odds with each other, heterodox economists recognize that these goals do conflict in some important contexts, and search for innovative ways to mitigate those conflicts. Some heterodox economists, for example, argue that subsidizing a more egalitarian distribution of assets, like human capital, is preferable to redistributing income through the tax system as an egalitarian strategy. They favor expanded government job training programs and aid to education over expanded transfer payments as a way of equalizing market outcomes. They similarly favor subsidizing home ownership, as opposed to rent control or rental assistance grants, for low-income families. Proponents of subsidizing more equal asset distribution also argue that these policies are likely to win greater political support than income transfers, due to their strategy of helping people help themselves.[59] Many neoclassical economists would be comfortable with these policies.

Heterodox Critiques of Supply-Side Economics

To its credit supply-side economics put distributional issues back into a prominent role in macroeconomic theory. Unfortunately, from a heterodox perspective, supply-side theory calls for more rather than less inequality in the economy. Heterodox economists perceive supply-side economics in two ways: (1) as a political program representing the interests of certain groups (e.g., high-income families and the owners of financial assets) and (2) as a macroeconomic theory asserting certain ideas about the relationship between economic inequality and macro-economic performance.

Heterodox economists criticize standard textbooks for ignoring the first dimension of sup-ply-side economics. As we have noted many times, standard textbooks often give the impres-sion that macro policy making and macro policy debates are primarily intellectual and highly technical debates about how to achieve the best outcome for everyone. Heterodox analyses add a political dimension to these controversies, portraying them as both technical *and po-litical* debates in which different groups may have different interests. Heterodox economists are quite explicit about their political objectives, which include a more equal distribution of economic outcomes.

From a heterodox perspective, supply-side economics was a Trojan horse designed to redis-tribute income upward.[60] In the name of the "general interest," many supply-side policies pro-moted the special interest of the well to do. The purported goal of many supply-side policies was to lower voluntary unemployment by increasing wages through incentives to business to increase investment. At first hearing, this seems a plausible policy. If employees are working with more capital they will be more productive and perhaps earn higher wages.

But the same logic applies, even more directly, to policies that subsidize workers' accumula-tion of more human capital through government subsidies for education and job training. These policies benefit workers directly and increase their relative share of national income. These poli-cies were often cut during the years of supply-side economics and were not a major part of the supply-side program (Ackerman 1984, 101–2, 110).[61]

Even more telling was the relative silence of supply-siders about social security taxes, which are a special tax on labor income. Absent from the supply-side program was a call for reduc-tions in "labor taxes" by financing part of social security from general tax revenues. In fact, during the 1981–1985 halcyon days of supply-side economics, when personal income and busi-ness taxes were cut dramatically, labor taxes were scheduled to rise.[62] More than 70 percent of all households now pay more in social security and Medicare taxes on labor income than fed-eral income taxes.[63]

Besides castigating standard textbooks for downplaying the politics of supply-side economics, heterodox economists join many mainstream economists in criticizing supply-side theory for neglecting aggregate demand issues and mis-specifying the causes of investment and savings.

For example, heterodox economists argue that because the supply-side tax cuts went chiefly to upper-income groups,[64] they had smaller effects on aggregate demand than similar sized tax re-ductions would have had if targeted at low-income families (such as tax rebates or increases in the standard deduction).[65] While acknowledging that investment tax credits and accelerated depre-ciation allowances can sometimes have modest effects on investment levels, heterodox econo-mists emphasize the key role that demand expectations play in investment decisions. They find supply-side income transfers to business and the owners of capital regressive and expensive ways of increasing investment.

Heterodox economists are similarly skeptical of supply-side arguments that justify large tax breaks for wealthy individuals on the grounds that lower taxes will spur the rich to save a greater percentage of their income, leading to lower interest rates and greater incentives for investment. The supply-side claim contradicts the bulk of economic research, which finds that "take home" rates of return on savings have very small effects on savings rates.[66]

Figure 15.2 **The Laffer Curve**

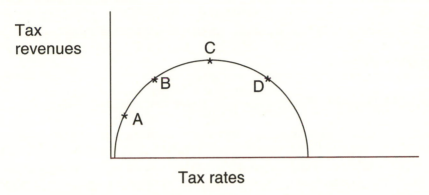

The implication of many heterodox criticisms of supply-side policies is that they are primarily income-transfer programs, benefiting high-income taxpayers. These rebates create government budget deficits and increased pressures for cutbacks in government spending, especially for social programs. The supply-siders' response to deficit concerns was contained in the "Laffer Curve," which was used to imply that supply-side tax cuts would be "self-financing."

Figure 15.2 illustrates the Laffer Curve. Tax rates are measured on the horizontal axis and tax revenues on the vertical axis. As we move from A to B, tax rates rise along with tax revenues. As we move from C to D, however, higher tax rates are accompanied by falling tax revenues (as higher taxes discourage economic activity). Supply-side advocates such as Art Laffer and George Gilder popularized the notion that tax levels in the U.S. economy were high enough to allow tax cuts to finance themselves (i.e., we could move from point D to point B without loss of government revenue).

The large budget deficits of the 1980s discredited self-financing claims. Although tax cuts do recoup some lost government revenue through higher economic activity, they do not pay for themselves. The break-even points are different for different kinds of taxes. It now appears that income tax rates need be as high as 80 percent before tax cuts do not cause revenue losses. Effective rates during the supply-side years were only in the neighborhood of 33 percent (Thurow 1984, 135).[67]

To sum up, heterodox economists challenge both the microeconomic reasoning underlying supply-side economics (such as the assumption that cutting taxes on interest income will cause upper-income households to save a higher percentage of their income) and the meta-economic assumptions justifying the need for significant economic inequality to motivate economic activity. Although the specificity of historical contexts makes it difficult to generalize from past macroeconomic events, the historical record strongly suggests that economic growth and economic vitality are possible with much more egalitarian outcomes than are present in today's economy. Both the "golden age" in the U.S. economy and similar experiences in Europe and elsewhere contradict the supply-side assumption of an enduring trade-off between equity and efficiency.[68]

The debate over supply-side economics remains very relevant to contemporary macro policy making. Heterodox analysis challenges many recent proposals of supply-side theorists, such as recommendations to end the inheritance tax, lower the capital gains tax, lower taxes on stock dividends, lower corporate income taxes, shift from a graduated federal income tax to a flat tax, and replace the income tax with a national sales tax.

THREADS: GENDER

We turn now to our familiar threads. We begin with gender issues and feminist economics' contribution to analyses of inequality. The discussion draws together ideas developed earlier in the text and breaks some new ground.

Level of Attention to Equity Issues

Like almost all heterodox economists, many feminist economists urge greater attention to equity issues. Feminist economists complement the neoclassical concepts of "economic man" and the "separative self" with personas that include the "relational dimension" of behavior. Once human action and well-being are thought to partially depend upon social linkages, such as perceptions of fairness and status competition, the need to attend to distributional outcomes becomes more pressing.

Standard economics textbooks tend to prioritize discussions of economic efficiency and economic growth over distributional and equity concerns. The texts also highlight the Pareto principle when discussing distributional issues. Martin Feldstein, a leading neoclassical economist,[69] reflects a strong version of this tendency. Feldstein (1998) writes,

> When professional economists think about economic policies, we generally start with the Pareto principle that *a change is good if it makes someone better off without making anyone else worse off* . . . .
>
> A change that increases the incomes of high-income individuals without decreasing the incomes of others meets that test. . . .
>
> There has no doubt been a relatively greater increase in higher incomes in recent years in the United States. . . .
>
> [T]here is nothing wrong . . . with an increase in inequality that results from a rise in higher incomes. (357–58)[70]

Feminist economists tend to utilize more complicated measures of well-being than the Pareto optimality principle favored by Feldstein. Some feminist economists worry about potential shifts in political and social power that increasing economic inequality may cause, having used "bargaining models" to demonstrate how wage inequalities in the market can spur inequalities in power relations inside the household.

Empathy and Interpersonal Utility Comparisons

Neoclassical economists frequently emphasize that it is impossible to make "scientific statements" about the change in overall well-being that might result from redistributing income from very wealthy to very poor people. The problem arises due to the impossibility of measuring interpersonal utility on a common scale. This incommensurability seems to discourage the textbooks from discussing equity issues.

While noting the special challenges involved with interpersonal comparisons, feminist economists argue that we can make rational and useful judgments about others' well-being based, in part, on our capacity for empathy. They criticize standard theory for failing to utilize this faculty in assessing macro outcomes.

Challenging Equity Efficiency Trade-Offs

In rejecting inherent trade-offs between equity and efficiency, many feminist economists point out that high levels of inequality can erode the social solidarity and social capital necessary for economic efficiency. Albelda and Tilly (1999) write, for example,

> [T]here is new empirical evidence that greater equality leads to greater growth, not the other way around (459) . . ." They add, "Supply-side and New Classical economists . . . . argue that the best way to achieve growth is to enrich the wealthy, whose investments will spur economic expansion. Bolstered by these ideas, governments in industrialized countries cut back welfare state redistribution programmes while reducing taxes on the rich over the past 20 years. . . .
>
> Feminist economists have marshaled empirical research to contest these policies. (462)

Gender Inequalities

Feminist and other heterodox economists recommend disaggregating macro outcomes by gender and urge increased attention to social phenomena in addition to traditional productivity variables in explaining gendered outcomes. For example, heterodox economists tend to give greater weight than neoclassical economists do to structural explanations, such as dual labor market theory, when explaining the gender gap in wages. Feminists also highlight the role of cultural prejudices in devaluing women's labor and lowering wages for "women's work" within firms' internal job ladders. The legacy of these practices has tended to make occupations such as preschool teaching and day-care work low-paying jobs.[71] It has also tended to depress women's wages for seemingly equal tasks (such as different forms of unskilled labor in a grocery store) when one is performed predominantly by men and another predominantly by women (Spitz 1991).

Inequality and the "Caring Economy"

As we have noted many times, neoclassical textbooks focus chiefly on formal market relations. There have been only modest studies of the distribution of household labor. Existing research appears to indicate that women spend at least 1.5 hours per day more on domestic chores than men do.[72] Feminist economists call for expanded research of the household and voluntary sectors, especially with respect to the care of children, the aged, and the ill.

This perspective has several implications for the macroeconomics of inequality. The rise of the two-income family has allowed GDP and family income to continue to grow over the last twenty-five years, while the real wages of more than 50 percent of husbands in families with children fell or stagnated (Mishel, Bernstein, and Boushey 2003, 106). The expansion of market opportunities for women has also improved the lives of many women and tended to make intra-family relations more equal.

Higher rates of female labor force participation, however, have also tended to create a time crunch at home. From 1979 to 2000, the average middle-income married couple with children added twelve and one-half weeks of market labor to the household's work year (Mishel, Bernstein, and Allegretto 2005, 4). This has sometimes undermined the family's ability to take care of some of its members. The shift of talented women out of the home and the voluntary sector has also drained the informal sector's caring institutions of key resources. In the absence of major injections of public funds for caring labor (such as expanded public expenditures for preschool and nursing services) there will continue to be a hidden increase in inequality due to higher unmet caring needs. There will also be a hidden "tax" on the remaining providers in and outside the market of caring labor. This burden will fall mainly on women. Although men are doing modestly more domestic labor at home, cultural mores still hold women more accountable than men for unmet domestic tasks. Women working outside the home are thus under more psychological stress due to perceived gaps in domestic performance.

THREADS: ENVIRONMENTAL ISSUES

Heterodox critiques of neoclassical analyses of the linkages between macroeconomic outcomes, inequality, and the environment tend to run along two tracks. The first track involves debates over the impact of inequality on environmental quality. The second track involves attention to the distribution of environmental burdens.

Neoclassical economists tend to imply that economic inequality has little impact on or is beneficial for environmental quality. This was most strongly argued by supply-side economists, who portrayed increasing inequality (in the name of increasing economic incentives) and decreasing government regulations (including some environmental regulations) as a spur to economic growth. The latter was seen as the magic bullet for protecting the environment. Most neoclassical economists support weaker versions of supply-side arguments, or find no connections between macroeconomic levels of inequality and environmental protection.

Many heterodox economists suspect that high levels of inequality are bad for the environment. There are two main reasons for this. First, inequality tends to spur emulative behavior and competitive consumption, encouraging lower-income groups to imitate the lifestyles of upper-income groups. Second, inequality tends to generate political pressures for GDP growth in order defuse the social tensions created by economic inequality. Both of these phenomena artificially tilt political-economic decisions toward higher resource use and more environmental pollution than would occur in a more equal economy. We will pursue these ideas further in chapter 16.

Heterodox economists also tend to give greater attention to who bears the costs of environmental degradation. Not surprisingly, they find that pollution burdens are disproportionately borne by poor communities, especially in terms of siting decisions for LULUs (locally unwanted land uses, like toxic waste dumps). As inequality increases, heterodox economists fear that poorer communities (such as Indian reservations or inner-city neighborhoods) will be pressured to accept environmental burdens (waste products, etc.) in order to survive. The availability of a bottom tail to the income and wealth distribution thus artificially lowers the costs of pollution to many consumers, thereby increasing the amount of pollution produced.

CONCLUSION

Holism, Methodological Individualism, and Inequality

The major difference between how heterodox and neoclassical economists think about the macroeconomics of inequality probably involves dynamic issues. Heterodoxy thinks about major socioeconomic phenomena, such as inequality, in "path" terms, where many factors are "variables" and open to change. The neoclassical and textbook approach tends to assume more fixed environments and relationships.

Heterodox economists tend to favor inserting "social constraints" into the economy, such as the requirement of a "living wage." They assume that once the requirement is in place it will spur feedback pressures to fulfill it. For example, if a higher minimum wage creates unemployment problems, heterodox economists expect social pressures for increased public employment, or increased public spending for job training and other skill-enhancing programs to make people employable at higher wages, or increased management attention to how to utilize minimum-wage employees in more efficient ways, and so on.[73] There is obviously a limit to what social engineering can accomplish, but heterodox economists expect much more flexibility than acknowledged in the textbooks.

The neoclassicals tend to be wary of "interfering" in markets. They assume that underlying technical forces, like technological change or demographics, drive market outcomes. They are instinctively skeptical about explanations for rising inequality that appeal to changes in social constraints, like the minimum wage, union strength, and social norms about fairness. They suspect instead that shifts in these phenomena reflect lagged responses to market forces (i.e., the decline in the minimum wage and unionization was an effect, not a cause, of changing market conditions in low-wage and union industries), and manipulating them will not bring desired results.

International Comparisons

Both neoclassical and heterodox economists often appeal to international comparisons to bolster their claims. These comparisons are fraught with methodological difficulties. Because each country has a different history and different social conditions, it is potentially misleading to attribute differences in economic outcomes to differences in current economic policy. Observed correlations are at best suggestive, but they do provide food for thought.

Defenders of the U.S. model of capitalism (with its high levels of inequality) frequently claim that the higher standard of living in the United States in comparison with more egalitarian OECD countries confirms the inevitable trade-off between equity and efficiency cited in the textbooks. Heterodox economists read the data differently. They point to the high wages, high social services, and historically low unemployment rates in many Western European countries and Japan as evidence for the viability of "high-road" capitalism. Both sides can marshal data in support of their claims.

Per capita income data probably provide the strongest evidence for the U.S. model. Interpreting comparative income statistics, however, is tricky. To keep things simple, we compare U.S. income with three different groups of countries: four large industrial democracies with modestly more egalitarian economies than the United States (Japan, Germany, France, and Italy); five European countries with significantly more egalitarian economies (Denmark, Finland, the Netherlands, Norway, and Sweden); and a larger group of nineteen OECD states that includes the above countries.[74]

There is little difference in average per capita income in the year 2000 between the U.S. and the five Nordic countries and 3 industrial democracies listed above using market exchange rates to translate national incomes into a common metric (Mishel, Bernstein, and Boushey 2003, 397). There is, however, about a 30 percent U.S. advantage with purchasing power exchange rates (ibid, 398).[75] For our purposes, the key questions are: (1) is this 30 percent difference an accurate representation of the quality of economic life in the United States and other countries, and (2) if there is a difference, is this difference due to the greater inequality in the U.S. economy?

Several factors make the use of per capita income at best an incomplete measure of national economic welfare. First, because of differing levels of inequality among countries, the median rather than average income would give a better measure of the market experiences of most people. Replacing average with median income reduces the U.S. income advantage.

Second, much of the higher per capita income in the United States reflects the fact that Americans work more weeks and longer days per year than workers in almost all industrialized democracies. Americans work 13 percent more hours (1,877/year) than workers in the nineteen OECD countries in our sample (1,629/year) (Mishel, Bernstein, and Boushey 2003, 425). It is difficult to praise or criticize economies' labor/leisure choices, if they are voluntary.[76] It is not sensible to judge the U.S. economy as 13 percent better for having its workers labor 13 percent longer hours than workers in OECD countries.[77]

Because of the problems associated with using per capita income as a measure of economic success, some economists find wages per hour a better measure of economic performance. The wage and productivity picture is mixed, but it is clear that there are a number of western European countries with much more egalitarian social and economic policies than those of the United States (France, Norway, the Netherlands, and the former West Germany) whose workers produce more GDP per hour than U.S. workers (Mishel, Bernstein, and Boushey 2003, 399–400). Real hourly compensation for manufacturing workers in the nineteen countries in our sample was also close to the U.S. rate (93 percent) in 2000 (Mishel, Bernstein, and Boushey 2003, 405). Finally, the growth in labor compensation per year for Japan, Germany, France, and Italy (1979–2000) was higher than in the United States, despite (or perhaps because of) these countries' more egalitarian labor policies.[78]

Although the picture is murky and changes from decade to decade (with, for example, the continental European economies having lower unemployment rates than the United States in 1974–1990 and higher rates in 1991–2003 (Boltho 2003, 13), it seems likely that the Europeans' more equal economic arrangements have not seriously harmed their economies, and may have helped them.[79] More importantly, it is clear that it is possible to run an economy more equally than the U.S. economy and produce a high standard of living. This does not mean that this is an easy thing to do.

Coda

The debate between neoclassical and heterodox economic theories over how to understand the interaction between social and technical variables deserves more attention in the textbooks. Both heterodox and supply-side economics return political issues to macroeconomics courses. As we begin the twenty-first century, we face some basic choices about the level of economic inequality we want to have in American society. Students in principles of macroeconomics classes should be able to participate in these discussions.

IN THEIR OWN WORDS

The achievement and sustaining of tight full employment could do almost all of the job of eliminating poverty.

—Hyman Minsky (quoted in Bell and Wray 2004, 21)

Using Pareto-optimality as the criterion of efficiency derives at least in part from the assumption that interpersonal utility comparisons are impossible. . . .

How does the feminist critique of separation/connection relate to interpersonal utility comparisons? The assumption that interpersonal utility comparisons are impossible flows from assuming a separative self. . . . and denying the possibility of an empathic, emotionally connected self. But if we assume instead that individuals can make interpersonal utility comparisons, then surely we would conclude that as scholars we, too, are capable of making such comparisons. . . .

The tendency to eschew interpersonal utility comparisons is part of why positive neoclassical theories harmonize so well with conservative normative positions on distributional issues.

—Paula England (2003, 40–41)

Reigning interpretations of economic inequality . . . trace social inequalities back to different individual choices, abilities, and resources. Analyses that follow this logic are, in our view, thinly disguised apologies for the existing social hierarchies of gender, class, privilege, and power. Feminist economists reject such essentialist justifications and instead root economic inequality in social processes. . . .

—Drucilla K. Barker and Susan Feiner (2004, 2)

[P]eople are considerably more generous than the model in economics textbooks allows, and they are equally unselfish in seeking to punish, often at great cost to themselves, those who have done harm to them and others. . . .

"An impressive body of evidence . . . has served to bury [*homo economicus*]. . . . In its place this body of evidence suggests a new *persona,* whom we may call *Homo reciprocans. Homo reciprocans* comes to new social situations with a propensity to cooperate and share, responds to cooperative behavior by maintaining or increasing his level of cooperation, and responds to selfish, free riding behavior . . . by retaliating against the offenders, even at a cost to himself, and even when he could not reasonably expect future personal gains from such retaliation.

—Samuel Bowles and Herbert Gintis (1998, 369–70)

Economic theory offers us some indispensable tools for organizing our joint endeavors. That's why it's so important to get economics right—to ensure that it includes careful consideration of love, obligation and reciprocity, as well as self-interest. We must stop assuming that norms and preferences of caring for others come from 'outside' our economic system and can therefore be taken as a given. We must start thinking about care as a propensity that can be defended and developed—or weakened and wasted. . . .

—Nancy Folbre (2001, 210)

FINAL STUDY QUESTIONS

Review Questions

1. What are the basic causes of economic inequality according to neoclassical economics?
2. How does heterodox thinking about the causes of economic inequality differ from textbook analyses?
3. Briefly explain the impact of unemployment rates, dual labor markets, and "macro regimes" on economic inequality from the perspective of heterodox economic theory.
4. Compare and contrast textbook and heterodox explanations for the large increase in inequality at the end of the twentieth century in the United States.

Discussion Question

1. How do current debates between neoclassical and heterodox economists over the causes of increasing inequality re-illustrate the basic methodological differences between heterodox and textbook economics?

NOTES

1. The biggest declines in income inequality occurred from the late 1920s to the mid-1940s and during the 1960s. In between these periods there were some years of increasing and decreasing inequality. See Harrison and Bluestone (1988, 7), Wolff (1996, 28), U.S. Census Bureau (2001).

2. Mishel, Bernstein, and Allegretto (2005, 67) calculate the share of income going to the lowest quintile to be 4.1 percent in 2003, tying 1993 as the lowest year. The authors warn, however, that methodological changes in how income shares are measured from 1993 forward may have increased reported inequality.

3. Due to the burst of the stock market bubble during 2000–2001 and the accompanying decline in the value of stock options, the ratio of CEO pay to that of a typical worker had fallen to 185:1 in 2003 (Mishel, Bernstein, and Allegretto 2005, 7).

4. In 2003, the top one tenth of one percent of all taxpayers (129,000 taxpayers) had more income than the bottom third of all taxpayers (~42,570,000). In contrast, in 1979 the bottom third totaled two and one-half times the income of the top 0.1 percent (*New York Times*, October 4, 2005, C1).

5. The Gini coefficients for net worth in the late 1990s, for example, tended to be about 30 percent higher than the Gini coefficients for income.

6. See for example, Wolff 1996, 78, 82–83; and Wolff 2004.

7. Net worth subtracts debt from a household's total assets. There was a modest reduction in wealth inequality along some dimensions at the end of the last economic expansion.

8. This concept lies behind a strange-sounding Marxist claim, that "capital" is a "social relationship." In neoclassical economics, capital is generally portrayed as an asset that generates a stream of outputs. The image of capital tends to be objectified as a thing (physical asset) or a skill (human capital). The Marxist concept adds a social-structural notion involving control of the division of labor.

9. This kind of ownership, unlike indirect stock ownership through a pension plan, confers formal control over corporate decision making. See also Toruno 2003, 29.

10. See also Guo 2001.

11. The Federal Reserve Board's 1998 Survey of Consumer Finances "defines a private business as consisting of single proprietorships, partnerships, and non-publicly traded corporate stock" (Toruno 2003, 27).

12. For a helpful discussion of the linkages between wealth distributions and poverty see Caner and Wolff 2004.

13. See, for example, Mishel, Bernstein, and Boushey 2003, 273.

14. Population statistics from *Statistical Abstract of the United States 2000*, Table 2; GDP Statistics from *The Economic Report of the President February 2000*, Table B2; poverty rates from U.S. Census Bureau (2001, 18).

15. In 2003 there were ~7,607,000 families below the poverty line with an average income deficit of $7,627, and ~9,713,000 unrelated individuals below the poverty line with an average income deficit of $5,024. Sources: Current Population Survey: *Annual Demographic Survey*, Table pov28 (2003).

16. The drop in unemployment at the end of the last business expansion (peak in March 2001) was correlated with an impressive decline in poverty and a strong improvement in the economic position of African and Hispanic Americans. During the last recession and relatively jobless recovery (2000–2003), the number of Americans below the poverty line increased from ~31.5 million to ~36 million. U.S. Census Bureau, *Income, Poverty, and Health Insurance Coverage in the United States: 2003*, p. 40, Table B-1.

17. Daniel H. Weinberg, http://www.census.gov/hhes/income/income01/prs02asc.html; and U.S. Census Bureau 2004, 46.

18. See also Mishel, Bernstein, and Allegretto 2005, 309–10.

19. As Darity and Myers note, in 1970 both white and black high school dropouts earned about 25 percent of the wages of white and black college graduates. In 1988 white high school dropouts still earned about one-quarter of the wage of white college graduates. Black high school dropouts, however, earned only 5 percent the wage of black college graduates (Darity and Myers 1998, 10–11).

20. For example, the income of the eightieth-percentile black household in both 1973 and 2003 was 68.5 percent of the income of the eightieth-percentile white household (Census Bureau, Historical Income Tables: H2, www.census.gov/hhes/income/histinc/h02w.html). The lowest 20 percent of black households' share of black income, however, fell more sharply than the lowest 20 percent of white households' share of white income over the same period. The bottom quintile's share of black income fell from 4.1 percent to 2.9 percent, or a drop of ~29 percent. The bottom quintile's share of white income fell from 4.4 percent to 3.6 percent, for a drop of ~11 percent (ibid.).

21. U.S. Census Bureau, Historical Income Tables: H2, www.census.gov/hhes/income/histinc/h02w.html. The ratio of the top income quintile to bottom income quintile among white Americans in 2003 was 13.7 (see Table I1).

22. See also Mishel, Bernstein, and Boushey 2003, 171; Institute for Women's Policy Research, Fact Sheet: "The Gender Wage Ratio." The ratio for people 16–24 was 93 percent in 2003 (Bureau of Labor Statistics 2004, 9). The female/male ratio fell from 1955 until the early 1970s and then turned upward. The initial decline probably reflected the effects of the postwar dual labor market. Also, while some of the improvement in the wage ratio has been due to higher wages for women, much of the increase has been the result of falling male wages, especially in blue collar sectors.

23. It is likely that statistics for more recent entrants into these fields would be more equal than aggregate statistics. See also Bowles, Edwards, and Roosevelt 2005, 367.

24. The situation of minority women is especially difficult. More than 35 percent of single-parent African American families headed by a woman were in poverty (Caiazza, Shaw, and Werschkul 2004).

25. Barker and Feiner (2004), for example, cite studies that estimate married women spend eighteen to twenty-three hours per week on household labor compared with seven to twelve hours per week for their husbands. One especially interesting finding was that women working outside the home spent about as much time with their children as women not in the labor market, with the adjustment variable being sleep, free-time activities, and voluntary activities (32, 150). Wolff, Zacharias, and Caner (2003) find that women average thirty-one hours a week on housework compared with nineteen hours per week for men (8). Guzman and Jekielek report that mothers spend from forty to ninety minutes more time per day with their children than fathers do, though the gap is narrowing (Guzman and Jekielek n.d.).

26. Taxes are progressive if the percentage of income paid rises as income rises, neutral if all people pay the same percentage of their income, and regressive if the percentage of income paid falls as income rises.

27. Mishel, Bernstein, and Allegretto (2005) indicate that the tax savings for the top 1 percent of households from 2001 to 2003 averaged $67,000. This compares with tax savings of about $600 per household for middle-income families and $61 per household for the bottom 20 percent of households (3).

28. "Making Wages Work: Earned Income Tax Credit & Other Tax Benefits" (Making Wages Work web site, accessed March 22, 2005) and United States Government Accountability Office: GAO-05-92 Earned Income Tax Credit, http://www.gao.gov/new.items/d0592.pdf. The growth of payroll taxes (social security and Medicare) has offset some of the EITC effect. Seventy-one percent of all households now pay more in social security and Medicare taxes than federal income taxes. These taxes are regressive, in that the tax rate, as a percentage of income, rises as income falls. This is because the tax only applies to labor income and richer households have a greater percentage of their income coming from non-labor sources (such as stock dividends) than lower income households. In addition, social security taxes are only paid on the first $87,900 of labor income (as of 2004).

29. OECD stands for Organization for Economic Cooperation and Development. The member countries included in the sample are Australia, Austria, Belgium, Canada, Denmark, Finland, France, Germany, Ireland, Italy, Japan, the Netherlands, New Zealand, Norway, Portugal, Spain, Sweden, Switzerland, the United Kingdom, and the United States.

30. The World Bank, Poverty.net website, "Overview" section, available at www.worldbank.org under site map—"Topics in Development." Due to the nature of subsistence economies, the implication of this statistic is not fully analogous to its meaning in a developed market economy. Nevertheless the statistic does capture the dire economic circumstances of the world's poor.

31. The World Bank, "PovertyNet: Overview: Measuring Poverty at the Global Level." Available at www.worldbank.org. Accessed June 5, 2005.

32. Mishel, Bernstein, and Allegretto (2005) add that the percentage of families in the bottom quintile of the income ladder who are still there ten years later increased from 49.4 percent (1969–1979), to 50.4 percent (1979–1989), to 53.3 percent (1989–1998) (p. 75). Race seems an especially important barrier to social mobility. Tom Hertz, for example, found that 42 percent of black families in the bottom 10 percent of the income distribution were still in the lowest decile thirty-two years later, compared to 17 percent of white families (Hertz 2003, 1).

33. Wessel 2005, A7, citing Corak 2004. See also Solon (2002, 64) and Erikson and Goldthorpe (2002, 36).

34. Jared Bernstein and Dean Baker offer two additional hypotheses for why full employment is able to raise wages for the lowest-paid workers. They argue that the higher wages won by low-income workers spur employers to restructure jobs in order to use those workers more efficiently (Bernstein and Baker 2003, 3).

This causality expands the textbook story, which usually has the relationship between marginal productivity and wages running in only one direction, from productivity to wages. Similar ideas were developed by Rudolf Meidner, a Swedish economist who helped establish the institutions and economic theory of Sweden's high-wage egalitarian economy after World War II.

Bernstein and Baker also claim that tight labor markets can force employers to overcome stereotypes and prejudices, allowing productive contributions from previously stigmatized groups, such as former welfare recipients. They write, "Anecdotal evidence and some polling found that employers' preconceptions about these workers' abilities made them hesitant to hire former welfare recipients. But given economic conditions at the time, they either took the chance or cut production. As it turned out, the majority of these employers found these workers to be as good or better than their current workforce, a discovery they would not have made if demand had been weaker" (Bernstein and Baker 2003, 11–12).

35. See endnote 36 in chapter 12, which discusses Robert Solow's work.

36. Mishel, Bernstein, and Boushey argue, "One explanation that does not hold up is that the growth of wage inequality reflects primarily a technologically-driven increase in the demand for 'educated' or 'skilled' workers. Economists have found that the overall impact of technology on wages and employment structure was no greater in the 1980s or 1990s than in the 1970s" (Mishel, Bernstein, and Boushey 2003, 7). Galbraith similarly finds major flaws in the computer revolution hypothesis (James K. Galbraith 2000, 31–35). Many heterodox economists also note that the increase in inequality in the United States was generally much greater than that in many foreign economies, despite a global spread of modern information and communication technologies. See also Howell 2002.

37. The split is pretty even, with 9.9 million workers earning the minimum and another 9.6 million within $1/hour of the minimum (Mishel, Bernstein, and Boushey 2003, 199). David Gordon's estimate of the impact of changes in the minimum wage is a bit higher. He calculates the direct and ripple effects of the fall in the minimum wage from 1979 to 1993 to be 18.9 percent and 4.6 percent respectively, implying that 23.5 percent of all private nonfarm wage and salary employees felt the effects of a drop in the wage floor (Gordon 1996, 215–16).

In the mid-1990s about half of all minimum wage earners worked full time and 80 percent worked at least twenty hours a week. Their wages provided 54 percent of their family's income (Mishel, Bernstein, and Boushey 2003, 197). Only about 12 percent of the recipients were teenagers from families with above-average incomes (Schafer and Faux 1996, 165).

38. Some economists believe that the CPI-U deflator overestimates inflation. If the CPI-URS series is used to measure inflation, the peak minimum wage falls by about 8.5 percent. The fall in the minimum wage since the early 1970s is roughly two-thirds as large.

39. Economic Policy Institute, www.epinet.org/issueguides/minwage/figure2.gif.

40. Mishel, Bernstein, and Boushey estimate the impact of declining minimum wages on inequality by recalculating various measures of inequality assuming a constant real minimum wage (2003, 7). Their projection offers an upper bound estimate of the impact of minimum wages on low-wage incomes, as it seems to ignore the impact of the earned income tax credit and assumes that raising the minimum wage would not significantly reduce low-wage employment. This assumption is consistent with many research findings on the minimum wage, but is contradicted by findings in the immigration literature (Bernstein and Baker 2003, 66–67).

Research by David Card and Alan Kreuger on the lack of employment effects on fast food workers from increases in the minimum wage in New Jersey has been especially important in reducing estimates of the employment impact of modest increases in the minimum wage. The hike in the minimum wage required to match its peak value in the late 1960s might exceed these margins.

41. See also Gordon 1996, 219.

42. See Gordon 1996, chapter 8 for a discussion of changing corporate management strategies, especially vis-à-vis unions. Piketty and Saez's (2003) analysis also emphasizes the importance of shifting social norms and institutional phenomena in explaining the sharp increase in inequality over the last three decades of the twentieth century.

43. See also Palley (1998, 95–98), Bowles, Edwards, and Roosevelt (2005, 165), and Gordon (1996, 210).

44. See, for example, Rosenberg 2003, 247–249.

45. See Rosenberg 2003, 266.

46. For example, a 1996 study by Kate Bronfenbrenner found that over half of all employers threatened to close part or all of a plant during union organizing drives.

47. The share of the unemployed receiving unemployment insurance payments fell from 76 percent in

1975, to 45 percent in 1987 (Rosenberg 2003, 245), to 37.2 percent in 1999; while the percentage of weekly wages replaced by unemployment insurance fell from 36.6 percent in 1980 to 31.6 percent in 1999 (*Statistical Abstract of the United States 2001*, p. 351, Table 537).

48. Samuelson and Nordhaus's macro principles text nicely illustrates this position. They write, "A cautious verdict is that there are but modest losses to economic efficiency from redistributional programs of the kind used in the United States today. . . . But countries whose welfare-state policies have gone far beyond those in the United States see major inefficiencies." They then warn against imitating the generous social policies of Sweden and the Netherlands and conclude, "Countries need to design their policies carefully to avoid the extremes of unacceptable inequality or great inefficiency" (Samuelson and Nordhaus 2001a, 398).

49. See, for example, Weiner and Monto's summary of Martin Feldstein's explanation for recent increases in economic inequality (Weiner and Monto 1998, 8).

50. Much of supply-side economics rests on ten assumptions: (1) there are no problems of aggregate demand in the economy; (2) much perceived unemployment is voluntary; (3) higher wages would reduce voluntary unemployment; (4) higher labor productivity would increase wages; (5) increased business investment would increase workers' productivity; (6) investment is primarily determined by the expected rate of profit per unit on production; (7) expected profit rates are insensitive to concerns about future aggregate demand (because there are no such concerns), and quite sensitive to the level of government regulation, business taxes, and interest rates; (8) interest rates are quite sensitive to the level of saving and fall as savings rise; (9) savings rates are quite sensitive to the after-tax return on savings, which is sensitive to tax rates; and (10) supply-side tax cuts will not cause budget deficits because economic growth will allow the government to collect the same level of tax revenues from lower tax rates. Critics of supply-side economics challenge many of these assumptions.

51. In the words of supply-side critic James Tobin (winner of the Nobel Prize in Economics in 1981), "The only sure results of supply-side policies are redistribution of income, wealth, and power—from government to private enterprises, from workers to capitalists, from poor to rich" (Tobin 1982b, 138).

52. Although most heterodox economists probably cluster toward the high end of this range, Post Keynesian economists like Wray, Bell, and Minsky, and perhaps Nobel Prize–winner William Vickrey, have tended toward the lower end. See, for example, Bell and Wray 2004.

53. One interesting suggestion calls for terminating the deductibility of executive salaries above a certain multiple of a firm's lowest-paid full-time employees. The current tax code caps the deductibility of an executive's salary at $1,000,000 per year and does not appear to include indirect compensation, such as stock options. The "Income Equity Act," proposed by Congressman Martin Olav Sabo, would cap the deductibility of executive salaries at twenty-five times that of the firm's lowest-paid worker (www.house.gov/sabo/ie.htm#HR687). See Gordon 1996, chapter 9, for some other suggestions.

54. Some of the most interesting recent research in economics involves the intersection between culture and the economy. One fascinating line of inquiry explores the cultural, biological, and economic components of sharing and reciprocity. Samuel Bowles and Herbert Gintis, radical economists at the University of Massachusetts, argue that human beings have a strong tendency for social reciprocity. People are quite willing to share with others provided that the recipient "plays by the rules." (See, for example, Bowles, Edwards, and Roosevelt 2005, chapter 2.) The cultural and institutional challenge is to create a social context that offers everyone real as well as hypothetical membership in the group.

55. The textbooks tend to limit support for public provision of goods and services to situations of market failure. The classic case is "public goods," where the nature of the product makes charging for use impractical. The classic example is a lighthouse. Although the benefits of a lighthouse may outweigh the costs of construction and operation, no private company will build one because they can not charge users for light house services. This is not the case for beaches, or libraries, or many of the items favored for public provision by many heterodox economists.

56. In 1997, Blakely and Snyder (Fortress America) estimated that 8.4 million Americans lived in gated communities (*St. James Encyclopedia of Popular Culture*, 2002).

57. Bell and Wray (2004), for example, demonstrate why traditional antipoverty policies, designed to increase low-wage and unemployed workers' skills and to maintain aggregate demand, are likely to fail workers in the inner cities without a public employment program.

58. Heidi Hartmann argues similarly for paid family leave as a way of improving the living conditions of families with children (Hartmann 1997).

59. Samuel Bowles and Herbert Gintis have done especially interesting work in this area. See for example *Recasting Egalitarianism: New Rules for Communities, States and Markets* (1998).

60. The allusion to a Trojan horse was first popularized by David Stockman, director of the Office of Management and Budget under President Reagan, in an interview in the *Atlantic,* where he opined, "Kemp-Roth was always a Trojan horse to bring down the top rates" (Kimzey 1983, 89).

61. A similar argument can be made about supply-side economics' lack of support for the expansion of publicly owned infrastructural capital (Tobin 1982a, 220).

62. There was some discussion of reducing social security taxes by cutting benefits (especially by raising the age for receiving social security from sixty-five to sixty-eight). Discussion of financing social security from general tax revenues was foreclosed by the huge deficits that accompanied the supply-side tax cuts for high-income taxpayers.

63. This calculation combines the employer and employee portion of the tax, as the bulk of economic research implies that this tax comes out of wages (U.S. Congressional Budget Office 2003, 2–3).

64. For a heterodox analysis of the details of the tax cuts of the early 1980s, see Ackerman 1982.

65. Interestingly, the Reagan supply-side tax cuts did not adjust the personal exemption and standard deduction for the high rate of recent inflation. This tended to especially disadvantage low-income tax payers (Ackerman 1982, 42).

66. While some families may save more when after tax interest rates rise (due to the higher reward for saving), other families may save less, as accumulating any target sum, like school tuition, requires less saving. More importantly, most savings decisions seem dictated by custom and income (i.e., people save a certain percentage of their income), rather than by the rate of return on savings.

67. Defending the Bush administration's supply-side tax cuts, Vice President Cheney reiterated the claim that tax cuts finance themselves and indicated that the Bush administration was establishing a half-million-dollar research project in the Department of the Treasury to prove it (*Washington Post,* February 11, 2006, A11). The administration's claim is not supported by many economists of any type.

68. Corry and Glyn, for example, cite a number of studies finding a positive correlation between economic equality and economic growth, and economic equality and macroeconomic stability. The World Bank's *World Development Report* of 1991, for instance, found "there is no evidence . . . that income inequality leads to higher growth. If anything, it seems that inequality is associated with slower growth" (Corry and Glyn 1994, 214). Cory and Glyn speculate that the positive effect of economic equality on aggregate demand and labor productivity may be responsible for its macroeconomic benevolence. They acknowledge, however, that the data is inconclusive, warning, for example, that causality may run from growth to equality, rather than from equality to growth.

69. Feldstein has been the main instructor for Harvard's introductory economics courses, president of the prestigious National Bureau of Economic Research, and a former chair of the Council of Economic Advisers under President Reagan. He was also one of the leading candidates to replace Fed Chair Alan Greenspan.

70. Feldstein does not rule out possible welfare gains from redistributing income from the rich to the poor (due to the declining marginal utility of money). He is quite dismissive, however, of those who worry about growing inequality due to massive increases in wealth and income at the high end of these distributions, calling them "spiteful egalitarians" (Feldstein 1998, 358).

71. The median preschool teacher's salary in 2002 was $21,332. Preschool teacher's assistants had a median salary of $14,162, less than that of parking attendants (Barnett 2003).

72. See note 25.

73. Chris Tilly makes a similar argument, terming the feedback from wage-forcing policies "pressure effects." Tilly writes, "Policies that close off the low-road strategy . . . create pressure effects, driving economic elites to search for investment opportunities that pay off by boosting productivity rather than squeezing the have-nots harder" (Tilly 2004).

74. The nineteen countries are: Australia, Austria, Belgium, Canada, Denmark, Finland, France, Germany, Ireland, Italy, Japan, Netherlands, New Zealand, Norway, Portugal, Spain, Sweden, Switzerland, and the United Kingdom.

75. "Per capita income based on market exchange rates" is derived by translating each country's national income into U.S. dollars at the current market exchange rate and dividing by the country's population. Purchasing power parity exchange rates convert foreign income into U.S. dollars in a slightly different way. Because the price of commodities varies across countries (with land and housing prices, for example, much higher in a densely populated country like Japan than in the United States), purchasing power parity exchange rates adjust currencies for what they can buy in each country by comparing the cost of a standard bundle of commodities. The methodology for revising exchange rates for purchasing power parity does not adjust, however, for the implicitly lower costs to median households for health care, day care, higher educa-

tion, etc. in economies where significant dimensions of these goods are provided publicly. The adjustments would thus seem to overstate the per capita difference between the median American and OECD household (though a full analysis would require inquiry into the median household's tax burdens for those services).

76. It is a different matter if the difference in working hours is involuntary, due, for example, to higher unemployment rates or more discouraged workers.

77. Robert Gordon also notes that making purchasing power parity (PPP) adjustments can be tricky, because it is hard to determine what a comparable market basket is. Gordon suggests that there are aspects of American life, like higher energy consumption, that are best understood as intermediate goods rather than final goods. Thus, the fact that Americans are able to consume more gasoline than Europeans (and need to because of dispersed settlement patterns) is not translatable on a 1:1 basis into a higher standard of living. Gordon suggests that America's apparent 25 percent per capita income advantage over Europe deflates to about a 10–15 percent advantage if PPP adjustments and longer work hours are taken into consideration (R. Gordon 2004).

78. The United States lagged the four countries by ~1.25 percent per year in 1979–1989 and 0.725 percent per year in 1989–1995. The United States led the four countries by 1.6 percent per year in 1995–2000 (Mishel, Bernstein, and Boushey 2003, 403).

79. After making many of the changes noted above, Boltho (2003) suggests that differences in living standards between continental Europe and America appear minimal, ranging from parity to a 10 percent U.S. advantage (11).

REINTRODUCING MACROECONOMICS AND THE ENVIRONMENT

INTRODUCTION

What does economics have to say about environmental and natural resource issues? How can understanding macroeconomics contribute to understanding the causes of and solutions to environmental problems? What kind of macro policies would best promote human welfare, protect the environment, and fulfill our ethical obligations to each other, future generations, and other living things? This chapter summarizes heterodox critiques of the answers to these questions found in standard macro principles texts. It builds on arguments raised in earlier chapters and offers an alternative to neoclassical environmental economics.

Environmental issues receive relatively little attention in most neoclassical introductory macro texts.[1] When environmental issues are discussed, the assumptions behind the texts' conclusions are not always elaborated. Thus it is helpful to begin our discussion of macro textbooks' treatment of the environment with a brief summary of the main ideas of neoclassical environmental economics. We then criticize these ideas from a heterodox perspective and draw implications for macroeconomic analysis. Most heterodox economists find neoclassical theory a useful lens for viewing *some* environmental problems, but criticize the paradigm for having large blind spots.

THE NEOCLASSICAL MODEL OF ENVIRONMENTAL ECONOMICS

Subtexts

The subtext of neoclassical environmental economics is: "let the *perfect market* work" and "economic growth is the answer" (regardless of the question).

Basic Logic and Assumptions

The logic of neoclassical environmental and resource economics is built on six premises:

1. Natural resources and environmental phenomena can and should be treated as commodities, amenable to analysis by the same analytic tools used to analyze the economy's treatment of other commodities.
2. The "perfect market" would automatically allocate natural resources (such as fossil

fuels) and environmental resources (such as the earth's ability to absorb and recycle waste materials) efficiently.

3. The need for government "intervention" in the market in environmental and resource areas arises from market imperfections and the need to address equity issues.

4. The goal of government policy should be to "correct market failures," in order to allow perfect markets to determine how natural resources and the environment will be used.

5. Equity concerns associated with environmental issues can be dealt with separately from efficiency concerns. Most discussions of environmental economics can ignore equity questions by assuming they have been dealt with elsewhere (for example, by the tax system's redistribution of income). This is not necessarily the case for intergenerational equity concerns.

6. Probably the most effective way to sustain the environment is to promote economic growth, as it will provide the resources and technology necessary to protect the environment.

Let us explore what these premises mean and imply. The claim that environmental resources can be conceptualized as normal commodities implies that the value of environmental phenomena (such as biodiversity, wilderness areas, and clean air) can be determined by people's willingness to pay for them as revealed by market behavior and as measured in market prices. The claim that "perfect" markets produce optimal outcomes rests on a number of familiar assumptions about the nature of "perfect markets" and their participants.

Consumers are assumed to (a) rationally maximize utility, (b) have perfect information, (c) have exogenous and stable tastes and preferences, and (d) have desires that are independent of other peoples' desires and social position.

Firms are assumed to (a) maximize profits, (b) have perfect information, and (c) lack influence over government policy and consumer tastes.

Markets are assumed to have (a) well-defined property rights, (b) perfect competition among firms, (c) equilibrium outcomes, (d) the absence of positive or negative externalities,[2] (e) the absence of public goods,[3] and (f) the existence of perfect "futures markets" that permit contracting to buy and sell commodities in the future.

Joined with a few additional technical assumptions, these preconditions imply that the supply-and-demand curves for a commodity represent the marginal costs and marginal benefits of production for that commodity. As such, the market level of output (determined by the curves' intersection) is the "optimal" level of output. Extending this argument, the neoclassicals conclude that if markets can be established for environmental commodities, they will produce the ideal or "optimal"[4] level of environmental services.

From a neoclassical perspective, environmental problems are caused by "market imperfections," that is, violations of one or more of the above assumptions necessary for perfect markets. Environmental problems can be "solved" by eliminating these imperfections or by offsetting their distorting effects. For example, the problem of air pollution can be solved by charging polluters an emission fee equal to the economic value of the damage caused by the pollution.

There are no inherent physical limits to growth in most neoclassical models. Technological change, substitutability, and price signals free the economy from quantity constraints. U.S. and global GDP can expand endlessly by substituting abundant for scarce materials on the input side of production and shifting to less material-intensive products on the output side. If markets are allowed to "get the prices right," they can govern themselves. Thus, from a neoclassical perspective, environmental concerns are not really relevant for macro economists (Daly 1996, 45).

Let us see how these ideas play out in practice by looking at neoclassical explanations for two environmental and resource problems: overfishing and air pollution.

Examples of Neoclassical Environmental Analysis

Fishing Stocks

Traditionally, property rights have not been well defined for most coastal or oceanic fishing stocks. This violates one of the assumptions of perfect markets. It means that no one owns the fishing stock. Because of this and the large number of fishing boats, there is little incentive for self-interested individuals to independently and voluntarily limit their catch to efficient and sustainable levels. As a result overfishing occurs. This is often referred to as the "tragedy of the commons," drawing analogy to the overgrazing that sometimes occurred on town commons when all citizens had unrestricted grazing rights to common pasture lands.[5]

In order to avoid the wastefulness of overfishing, neoclassical economists have recommended privatizing fishing areas, that is, letting people own, and therefore restrict access to, areas of the sea with self-contained fishing resources, like lobster beds.[6] Where privatization is impractical, due to the mobility of fishing stocks, the neoclassicals have recommended establishing tradable rights to harvesting fixed amounts of fish. Only those owning these rights would be allowed to fish. The aggregate catch permitted would be set at the level of fishing that a profit-maximizing firm would undertake if it owned the entire resource and wanted to maximize the value of its output over time.

Coal Combustion and Sulfur Dioxide Pollution

Let us look at a second example of an environmental problem that can be treated as a market failure, the problem of air pollution, and in particular the release of sulfur dioxide (SO_2) from burning coal. The emission of SO_2 causes human health problems and also damages lakes by causing acid rain. These costs have traditionally been a negative externality (i.e., they were not borne by the polluter or the consumer of the product). This has led to "excessive pollution."

From a neoclassical perspective there are costs and benefits to air pollution. The costs are the harm done by the pollutant. The benefits are the reduced cost of production made possible by the polluting technology (i.e., avoidance of the extra costs that would be incurred to produce the good without the pollution). The key economic task is to ensure that the benefits of pollution exceed the costs of pollution. This is hard to do when the costs of pollution are not paid for by the polluter and thus are treated as zero by polluting firms. The goal of neoclassical SO_2 policy is to "internalize" the cost of SO_2 releases, that is, to charge polluters for the damages that SO_2 causes. If, after including those costs, it is profitable for some plants to burn coal and release SO_2, the emissions have the blessing of neoclassical theory. Recent EPA regulations have had the effect of imposing a price on SO_2 emissions. From a neoclassical perspective, the regulations have sought to generate the "optimal level of SO_2 pollution."

Virtually all concerns about natural resource use and environmental degradation can be posed in neoclassical terms. The problem of water pollution can, like air pollution, be understood as a market failure involving negative externalities. The loss of biodiversity due to habitat destruction can be treated as a market failure involving imperfect property rights and/or positive externalities. The depletion of the ozone layer and disruption of the earth's climate system can be treated as public-goods problems, and so on.

The solution to these problems, according to the logic of neoclassical theory, is to figure out what a perfect market would do and impose that outcome on the economy. Thus, from a neoclassical perspective, there are no "limits to growth." Prices, in a properly functioning market economy, will carve out a growth path sensitive to environmental and resource constraints.

Box 16.1
Thinking like a Heterodox Economist

Before we begin, see if you can anticipate how a heterodox economist might expand the realm of discourse defined by the neoclassical examples discussed above. Try to recall the arguments underlying the environmental threads woven through earlier chapters.

How might heterodoxy's methodological critiques of neoclassical economics apply to environmental economics?

What are the implications of heterodoxy's objections to methodological individualism and misplaced concreteness for understanding environmental and resource economics?

How might heterodoxy's assumption of a more complicated economic persona than *homo economicus* affect environmental economics?

How might heterodoxy's greater focus on the implications of equity issues, uncertainty, and path dependency affect environmental and resource economics?

What are the limits of market-based environmentalism?

Why might environmental economics be more relevant to heterodox than neoclassical conceptions of macroeconomics?

FUNDAMENTAL PROBLEMS WITH NEOCLASSICAL ENVIRONMENTAL ECONOMICS

Introduction

There are many different heterodox views on environmental issues and many different environmental topics. This discussion must necessarily homogenize a diverse set of perspectives and comment on a relatively narrow set of environmental issues. I have emphasized topics that reflect common methodological concerns across many heterodox paradigms and de-emphasized some important debates among heterodox paradigms.

At first glance, the examples of neoclassical analysis discussed above suggest that the paradigm offers powerful explanations for the existence of environmental problems and helpful recommendations for their solution. We will try to show why this appearance captures only part of the story.

As noted earlier, heterodox economists find that neoclassical theory provides a useful lens for viewing *some* environmental problems. Neoclassical textbooks, however, tend to present their incomplete perspective as a totalizing-perspective. This viewpoint carries enormous blind spots. The analysis below explores those blind spots.

Competing Subtexts

Most heterodox economists reject the subtexts of neoclassical environmental analysis that markets are the ideal social mechanism to organize almost any area of societal life, and economic growth is the most urgent goal for social policy. Behind this rejection is heterodoxy's attention to:

1. the biases markets impose on activities they organize and their inability to capture and integrate some of the key dimensions of important societal and ecological choices

2. the limitations of GDP-maximizing strategies for increasing human well-being
3. the importance of addressing equity issues for understanding and solving environmental problems, and
4. the need to analyze capitalism as a social system in order to fully understand and respond to environmental challenges.

Limitations of Market Rationality and Market Mechanisms

There is a much greater willingness among heterodox than orthodox economists to question the "wisdom" of market choices and the adequacy of maximizing GDP as the centerpiece of macroeconomic policy. Heterodox economists, for example, are more willing than neoclassical economists to reflect on the environmental and cultural implications of the large advertising and marketing campaigns (greater than 2 percent of GDP) maintained in modern capitalist economies.[7]

In addition, rather than simply assuming that the best measure of the relative value of different uses of the environment is automatically signaled by "perfect market" prices, heterodox economists ask what available research indicates about market valuations of environmental resources. While there are different interpretations of the data, many findings suggest that people make "predictable errors" that lead them to overvalue consumer goods and tolerate excessive environmental damages to acquire them (Gardner, Assadourian, and Sarin 2004, 12).

The logic of positional competition, for example, gives good reason for suspecting that market choices will lead households to sacrifice excessive resources to wasteful competitive consumption. Heterodox economists also appeal to introspection (reflection on our own feelings and subjective experience) to support notions of overconsumption. They find many instances of "impulse buying" and "buyer remorse" (post-purchase regrets).

Citizens Versus Consumers

One of the implications of heterodox analyses of consumer behavior is that market choices may not always reflect people's "deepest" sentiments or preferences. Therefore perfecting or shadowing the market may not be the ideal mechanism for designing environmental policy. Heterodoxy challenges neoclassical theory's tendency to portray market behavior as more informed and rational than political behavior. Sometimes the exact opposite seems true. Mark Sagoff (1982), for example, notes that the same individuals who buy unrecyclable goods may vote for policies that require them to recycle. The same individuals who do not inquire about the environmental impacts of the goods they buy may favor imposing environmental conditions on producers. Which behavior should guide public policy? Neoclassical theorists most often prefer market shadows (after correcting for market failures). Heterodox economists favor increasing the scope for political judgments. At the very least heterodoxy calls for posing the choice in economics textbooks.

Path Choices

Reflecting heterodoxy's commitment to dynamic rather than static analysis, heterodox economists emphasize the importance of thinking about economic outcomes in terms of path choices. Two of the economic sectors with the largest environmental implications are the energy and agricultural sectors. Many heterodox economists think about both sectors in terms of "hard" versus "soft" path choices.

"Hard" energy paths rely on increases in large centralized energy supply technologies, like those associated with fossil fuels and nuclear power, to meet large increases in energy demand.

"Soft" energy paths rely on increased efficiency in energy use (e.g., more miles to the gallon) and expanded use of small-scale decentralized energy technologies, such as wind, biomass, and solar energy, to meet energy needs.

Hard agricultural paths rely on energy-intensive cultivation techniques with heavy doses of chemical inputs (nitrogen fertilizers, herbicides, pesticides, antibiotics, growth hormones, genetically engineered seeds, etc.). These strategies also involve mono-cropping and large-scale animal confinement techniques (factory farming). Soft agricultural paths involve more integrated and diversified output mixes, smaller-scale operations, and less chemical-intensive production techniques.

Although it is possible for individuals to combine aspects of the different paths at a point in time, the systems logic of the different paths, reflecting phenomena like economies of scale and learning curves, tend to channel the economy into one or the other strategy over time. Heterodox economists believe that path choices in modern economies are influenced by many factors besides engineering estimates of economic efficiency. There is a large literature that finds that past tilts toward the hard path have been significantly influenced by the growth strategies of major firms and public bureaucracies, an inertia in business and consumer expectations, and numerous market imperfections (such as skewed subsidies and neglected externalities). Taking the hard path has hurt the environment and undermined economic sustainability (see for example Hawken, Lovins, and Lovins 1999; Jackson 1984, 1980).[8] Heterodox economists are interested in how public policy can tilt development paths in more environmentally friendly directions.

Meta-Externalities

Reflecting holist methodologies, many heterodox economists investigate how feedback from economic decisions affects social structures and culture. Sometimes the most important implications of our economic choices are the unintended consequences of market choices. This is especially true when these effects help select socioeconomic development paths.

Heterodox economists want policy makers to reflect on the indirect consequences of economic policies for the environment. For example, it appears that a highly mobile, footloose and fancy-free economy erodes people's sense of community and attachment to the land. There seem to be many positive externalities (indirect benefits) to stable communities and "landed identities." As such, economic incentives that reward employment stability might be able to increase economic efficiency, environmental protection, and the humaneness of the economy at the same time.

In a similar vein, family farmers with historic ties to local communities may adopt a longer-term perspective on farming choices than factory farms organized by outside investors might. Although family farmers sometimes participate in franchise farming under the supervision of vertically integrated factory farm operations, the locus of control in these enterprises has shifted from the farmer to the franchiser. It is likely that the franchisers feel much more comfortable externalizing costs to the local community (vis-à-vis externalities like odor and waste burdens) than traditional family farmers do. Protection of the family farm from absorption into agribusiness may thus indirectly protect the environment from short-term thinking.

In the latter chapters of this book we have argued that our society faces a number of choices about how it will evolve. We have to think about the level of equality we wish to promote, the opportunities for community and common futures we wish to preserve, and the character of our relationship to the land, to nature, and to future generations. Neoclassical theory tends to remove these choices from economic discussion and democratic decision making. It favors letting the market dictate outcomes. Heterodox economists call for open discussion of these choices and tend to favor a more varied group of mechanisms (certainly including markets) for making these decisions.

Figure 16.1 **Traditional Circular Flow Design**

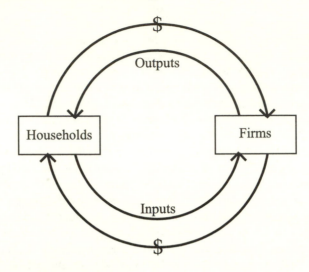

Scaling Effects and Qualitative Change

Many heterodox economists believe that the scale of the global economy passed critical thresholds in the twentieth century. Heterodox analyses often illustrate this by revising the textbooks' circular flow diagram to situate the economy in relationship to the ecosystem. As figures 16.1 to 16.3 illustrate, there is a profound difference between the pre-1900 period, when human economic activity had only modest impacts on the global environment, and the current period, where the by-products of economic activity seem to be pressing up against ecological limits.

Heterodox economists tend to believe that current environmental risks are orders of magnitude more hazardous than in the past. To illustrate this, they point to many concrete phenomena, such as the hole in the earth's ozone shield caused by chlorofluorocarbons (CFCs), the threat of climate change caused by greenhouse gases, the annual extinction of at least 5,000 species (a rate about 10,000 times the pre–human species extinction rate), and the human use of more than 50 percent of the earth's accessible surface freshwater and about 40 percent of the output of terrestrial photosynthesis (Costanza et al. 1997, 8, 13; Hawken, Lovins, and Lovins 1999, 8). Reviewing these totals, ecological economists (a school of heterodox theory) argue that the "throughput" of the economy, that is, the size of the economy in physical terms (pounds of material reorganized, BTUs of energy consumed, etc.) relative to the earth's natural systems has reached dangerous proportions. They expect harmful disruptions of the earth's natural systems if economic activity continues to expand.

While acknowledging that it is theoretically possible that economic growth could occur without increasing "throughput," many ecological economists do not find this likely. They are skeptical that technological change and shifts by consumers and producers toward less material-intensive products and production processes will allow GDP to grow without a corresponding growth in physical inputs. For example, although the amount of energy (measured in physical terms) needed to produce a dollar's worth of GDP has fallen over time, energy consumption has still continued to rise, due to GDP growth.[9] Two leading ecological economists, Herman Daly and Joshua Farley, criticize weightless images of the "information economy" that portray economic activity as floating above material requirements. They point out that information technologies currently consume

Figure 16.2   **The Circular Flow Within a Geological and Ecological Envelope: "Empty Pond" Case**

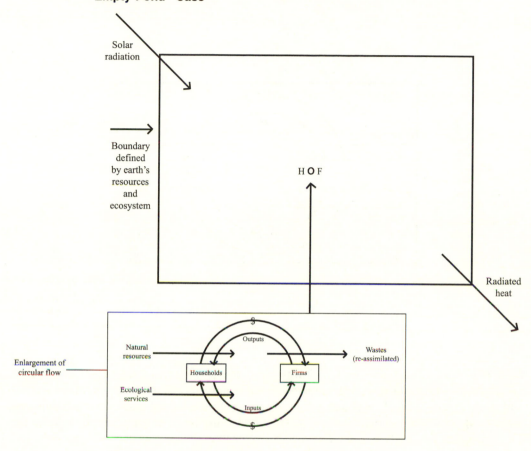

about 13 percent of U.S. electricity. They also note that in the next five years about three hundred million personal computers, each containing seven to ten pounds of toxic metals, will find their way into the nation's landfills (Daly and Farley 2004, 40).[10]

Many ecological economists worry about running out of resources as well as environmental limits to growth, but we shall concentrate on environmental issues here. The argument for environmental limits to growth is more widely shared in heterodox circles than are concerns about resource limits to growth.

ECONOMIC GROWTH AND ENVIRONMENTAL QUALITY

Neoclassical Inquiry: Is There an Environmental Kuznets Curve?

There is an implicit tendency among many neoclassical economists to assume an "environmental Kuznets curve (EKC)." As noted in chapter 14, this view extends the payoffs of economic growth to environmental protection. The curve implies that pollution levels initially increase as

Figure 16.3 **Full Earth Visible Lily Pads Case**

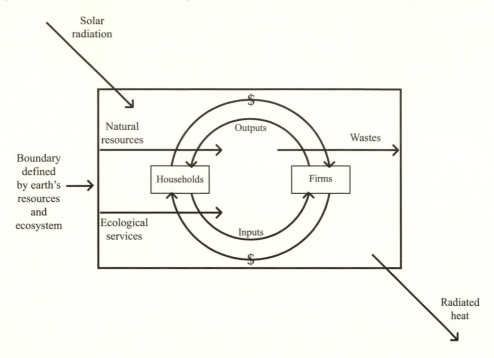

economies industrialize, but then turn downward as economic growth continues. The downturn is tied partially to consumers' growing interest in environmental quality as they become wealthier and partly to the ability of economic growth to promote technological innovation (which lowers the cost of maintaining a clean environment and repairing past environmental blunders). The EKC metaphor fits nicely with neoclassical theory's subtext promoting economic growth.

Testing for the presence of an environmental Kuznets curve empirically is tricky.[11] Some environmental indicators do seem to indicate that economic growth improves environmental quality. Among these indicators are measures of urban sanitation, access to clean water, and urban air quality (with respect to smoke, carbon monoxide, lead, and sulfur dioxide). Other pollutants, however, such as greenhouse gases, nitrogen oxides, and some toxic chemicals, have increased with economic growth.

Technological optimists expect new innovations to eventually address these latter problems.[12] Some recent work by neoclassical economists is cautiously optimistic about the presence of an environmental Kuznets curve and the likelihood that technical change will lower the EKC's turning points, permitting countries to have both economic growth and better environments in much shorter time frames (see, for example, Dasgupta et al. 2002). Although opinion is not unanimous within the neoclassical community, the dominant stance is optimistic about the long-term ability of economic growth to improve (or at least not damage) the environment.

Heterodox Inquiry: Are There Limits to Growth?

Although there are debates within both the orthodox and the heterodox camps between the "Malthusians" (who fear resource and environmental limits to growth) and the "Cornucopians" (who foresee limitless market expansion), heterodox economists tend to be more attentive to limits-to-growth concerns than neoclassical economists are. This is perhaps because of heterodoxy's greater attention to (1) the unique aspects of environmental resources, (2) the implications of uncertainty, (3) the tendency for predictable errors in conventional reasoning about scarcity and environmental hazards, and (4) the ability of political economic interests to frustrate hypothetical price and regulatory adjustments to scarcity and market failures.

Heterodox economists often stress that the logic of exponential growth (where a variable, such as GDP or energy consumption, grows annually in percentage terms) is quite different from the linear logic of much of human experience. Adjustment in the latter case is generally gradual enough to permit feedback from current experience to guide future behavior. In contrast, exponential growth can "sneak up on you." It can seem to explode all at once, creating discontinuities that make the inertias of everyday life and institutional structures very costly.

The classic example used to illustrate the surprises caused by exponential growth involves lily pads. Let us imagine a pond where the lily pads double in surface area every week and initially only 1/400,000 of the pond is covered by the pads. They are virtually invisible. After one week, 1/200,000 of the pond is covered and after one month (~four weeks), 1/25,000 of the pond is covered. The pads are still almost invisible.

After two months (eight weeks), the pads cover about 1/16 of 1 percent of the pond and are still hard to see. After three months the pads finally cover 1 percent of the pond. They are easy to spot, but hardly a major presence in the pond. After four months the pads cover 1/6 of the pond and have finally become a concern. The problem is that in less than three weeks they will totally cover the pond. While it took sixteen weeks to cover 1/6 of the pond, it will take less than three weeks to cover the remaining 5/6 of the pond. It is the explosiveness of the growth at the end of the process that can catch people by surprise.

Market economies tend to be exponential economies. Global GDP, for example, has grown at about 3.5 percent per year over the last two decades.[13] At this rate global output would double every twenty years. Heterodox economists worry that the environmental burdens and resource demands of global economic growth can be likened to lily pads. Appealing once again to notions of misplaced concreteness (abstraction from key details), many heterodox economists argue that the neoclassicals' a priori faith in market rationality needs to be tempered when thinking about the implications of exponential growth at this point in human history. In particular, many heterodox economists worry:

1. that market participants (like everyone else) have a psychological tendency to expect that the future will be more like the recent past than is objectively "rational," despite incentives for other views.[14]
2. that, as noted above, the global economy has recently passed (or is rapidly approaching) key thresholds that make the environmental dangers of continued economic growth qualitatively different and orders of magnitude more troubling than previous hazards
3. that we are likely to have to make key environmental decisions before we have full information about the implications of these decisions, and
4. that political-economic interests tied to existing patterns of economic growth can overwhelm market feedback and frustrate both market-based (price-induced) conservation efforts and public policy rationales for curbing pollution and resource use.

Heterodox theorists emphasize that most important environmental issues, such as the dangers of global warming, the probability of serious nuclear accidents, the hazards of toxic chemicals, and the risks of genetic engineering, are surrounded by uncertainty. Many factors are responsible for this, including the complexity of the earth's ecosystem, the potential for discontinuous threshold effects rather than linear hazard risks, the long time horizons involved in many environmental problems, the latency and interactive aspects of human health hazards, and the novelty of the literally hundreds of new chemicals produced annually by the economy (Meadows, Meadows, and Randers 1992, 91).[15] Heterodox economists find textbook environmental discussions marred by a tendency to "note but not fully explore" the implications of these uncertainties. This outcome may be a legacy of the neoclassical paradigm's habit of assuming totally rational economic agents, perfect information, non-path-dependent outcomes, and significant substitutability among inputs in general equilibrium portraits of economic life.

We will focus on the issue of energy to get a feel for the heterodox perspective. In many ways, energy is the all-purpose natural resource. Abundant and relatively cheap energy, for example, relaxes scarcity constraints for numerous other materials by permitting the mining of low-grade ores on land and in the ocean. Neoclassical theory argues that market feedback (e.g., relative price changes and profit incentives) and government policy designed to eliminate market failures in the energy area are sufficient to govern the complex way energy is used in the economy. Heterodox economists are not so sure.

They raise two main concerns. The first involves the environmental problems associated with increased energy use, and the second the scarcity of fossil fuels. We will look primarily at the first concern here. Energy production and consumption has traditionally been the cause of many environmental problems, such as oil spills, smog, and acid rain (as noted above in the SO_2 discussion). The most serious current energy-related environmental problem, global climate change, is at least an order of magnitude more serious than previous problems associated with the burning of fossil fuels.

The exponential growth in energy consumption has caused an exponential growth in carbon dioxide (CO_2) emissions. These emissions have exceeded the environment's ability to recycle carbon and begun to alter the earth's climate. The lily pads are now clearly visible. Continued "business as usual" policies in the developed world and/or economic growth along traditional paths by countries such as China threaten serious environmental disruptions.

Especially troubling is the possibility that attempts to reduce greenhouse gas emissions without curbing energy consumption will simply shift rather than solve environmental problems. One popular suggestion, for example, is to replace fossil fuels with massive increases in the use of nuclear energy. Nuclear power, however, has its own environmental problems, such as the risk of serious nuclear accidents, nuclear waste disposal, and the proliferation of nuclear weapons materials. Many environmentalists, including most ecological economists, fear that all alternatives to conventional fossil fuels able to support continued exponential growth in energy consumption are likely to risk serious hazards.[16] These observers also warn that greenhouse abatement strategies designed to permit exponential increases in fossil fuel consumption through high-tech means (such as injecting reflective materials into the atmosphere to decrease the influx of solar radiation, or altering the chemistry of the earth's oceans to accelerate photosynthesis and the aquatic sequestering of carbon) carry equally burdensome side effects.

Herman Daly, probably the most famous "ecological economist," treats the problem of global warming as a warning signal that suggests the need for a macro limit on the scale of "throughput" in the economy. He acknowledges that it would be very difficult to determine the appropriate limits for permissible consumption of different materials, but claims that finding those limits should be on the agenda of economic theory and economic instruction. Heterodox economists suggest that introductory macro courses give greater attention to how macroeconomic policy can address limits to growth concerns.

Heterodox economists tend to emphasize two initiatives for responding to resource scarcity and environmental hazard concerns: (1) the precautionary principle and (2) sustainability requirements.

The Precautionary Principle

Most environmentalists and ecological economists urge the adoption of the "Precautionary Principle." The latter considers technologies that could be extremely harmful to the environment "guilty until proven innocent." Heterodox economists fear that political pressures for continued economic growth, and social lags in the popular comprehension of new problems, will force the adoption of the inverse policy, "innocent until proven guilty." Many environmentalists fear a long period of expanding energy consumption and accommodative public policy, during which the earth's eco-systems will suffer serious damage. The Bush administration's support for expanded oil drilling in the arctic wildlife preserve and opposition to U.S. participation in the Kyoto Treaty, which limits greenhouse gas emissions, illustrate the fears of ecological economists.

The main problem with the precautionary principle is its ambiguousness. It is not clear when to invoke it or how to satisfy it.

Sustainability Conditions

Defining Sustainability

In 1987, the World Commission on Environment and Development (the Brundtland Commission) defined sustainable development as "development that meets the needs of the present without compromising the ability of future generations to meet their own needs" (Tietenberg 2003, 553). As with the precautionary principle, exactly what this means is ambiguous, as is determining what is a sustainable or not a sustainable economic activity. For our purposes, however, the issue is whether sustainability should be part of the subject matter of introductory macroeconomics. The answer from a heterodox perspective is yes.

At present there are three major policy stances toward sustainability. The first stance is to let the market determine the level of resource conservation. For the most part this is current U.S. policy. It does not recognize any obligation on the part of resource owners or current consumers to future generations. It implies that in the absence of market failures, the private interest of resource owners in capturing the highest value for their asset will lead to the optimal level of conservation. This may or may not mean sustainability. If resource owners believe we are running out of a resource they will probably anticipate higher prices for the resource in the future. This may cause some suppliers to defer production into the future, reducing current output, raising current prices, and naturally conserving some of the resource. If the expected price in the future is not enough to compensate producers for the lost opportunity to produce today and put their profits in the bank at the going rate of interest, then production will not be deferred and the resource could be exhausted.

Market imperfections, like insecure property rights, however, can undermine the market's potential for conservation. The Saudi royal family, for example, may not be confident that it will control Saudi Arabia and its oil fields fifty years from now. It may, therefore, decide to produce more oil today than would be economically efficient if it were sure it could capture the higher prices for oil in the future. In this scenario, the world could end up using oil for less-valuable purposes in the present than in the future. Appealing to the familiar rationale of "market imperfections" (in this case insecure property rights), some neoclassical economists argue that there is a need for public policy to slow down world oil consumption in order to reproduce "perfect market outcomes." It is important to emphasize, however, that the basis for government intervention is to correct a market failure (insecure property rights), not to ensure sustainability.

The second and third positions assert that current generations have an ethical obligation to future generations to leave them with as valuable an economic inheritance as we received from our predecessors. The first of these two positions is called "weak sustainability." It suggests that we should use resources in a way that preserves our productive capacity and allows future generations to achieve GDP per capita levels equal to our own. This stance permits the depletion of exhaustible resources like fossil fuels if we leave an equivalent endowment of productive capacity (such as better computer technology) to future generations. Defining an equivalent endowment is tricky. Under weak sustainability, equivalency is generally measured in terms of the monetary value of the natural resource used up and capital stock passed on.[17]

The final position is called "strong sustainability." It also requires we leave our offspring with at least the same productive capacity we inherited. The notion of equivalence in this case assumes a more physical than monetary form. This stance would prohibit using exhaustible resources. It implies that market prices are not an adequate measure of economic inheritance. It suggests that human-made capital (like machines) is not fully substitutable for "natural capital" (like ecosystems and species diversity). It requires each generation to leave the next with a certain set of physical assets as well as endowments denominated in monetary terms.

There is a middle ground between weak and strong sustainability that can be thought of as "moderately strong sustainability." This condition requires that the productive capacity replacing an exhaustible resource (like oil or phosphorous) have properties "equivalent" to the depleted resource. Thus improved solar energy technology might be seen as an offsetting legacy to fossil fuel consumption, while the development of advanced video games would not be acceptable, even if the market value of that innovation were equal to the market value of the fossil fuels consumed.

How might economic policy promote sustainable economic practices? Public policy could increase the cost to consumers of using exhaustible resources. In the current political environment, however, it seems unlikely that initiatives like increasing gasoline taxes will find much political support. More promising would seem to be government efforts to finance research and development for better windmills, more efficient automobile engines, and less environmentally burdensome agricultural technologies. Part of the focus of our national income accounts could be measurement of the economy's current degree of sustainability, with an eye toward the level of R&D investments necessary to maintain "moderately strong sustainability." Heterodox analyses of resource use would also tend to support the protection of some public lands from resource extraction, in order to ensure the provisioning of future generations.

The Discount Rate

Another way of illuminating the different treatment of sustainability in neoclassical and heterodox theory is to analyze the different treatments of the role of real interest rates in making intertemporal decisions. To explain heterodox concerns, we need to review how interest rates might affect resource use and environmental protection.

If you put $100 in the bank today (with a 6 percent interest rate), you would receive $106 dollars next year. If you kept the money in the bank for two years (at 6 percent interest), you would receive $112.36 at the end of two years.[18] The accumulation from your original $100 deposit until any year in the future can be calculated by multiplying $100 times (1+ the interest rate)^t, where t equals the years to receipt of the money.

A sum of money received in the future can similarly be "discounted" back to its "present value" by dividing it by $(1+ \text{the interest rate})^t$. The interest rate in this case is known as the discount rate.[19] The calculation indicates how much money would need to be deposited in the bank today in order to accumulate to the sum receivable in the future.

Present value calculations have very important implications for inter-temporal resource use. High interest rates quickly devalue incentives for conserving resources or for avoiding future environmental harms. For example, at a 6 percent interest rate, standard economic calculations imply that it would be unwise to spend $300 million today to avoid greenhouse damages of $30 trillion (an amount roughly equal to current global GNP) two hundred years from now.[20]

Heterodox economists reject this conclusion and the appropriateness of using current long-term market interest rates to make economic decisions that extend more than three or four generations. They offer four main reasons for expecting market interest rates to excessively discount the future. First, heterodox economists believe that market contexts orient behavior toward excessive present mindedness and short-term thinking, which bias interest rates upward. Although some of this bias is captured in neoclassical theory through appeal to market imperfections (such as insecure property rights), some of the bias is neglected (such as pressures for current consumption created by advertising).

Second, echoing concerns raised by supporters of "strong" and "moderately strong" sustainability, heterodox economists question whether it makes sense to use current market measures like the interest rate to homogenize different kinds of resources, over long periods of time.

Third, heterodox economists warn that current "long-term" interest rates reflect relatively short planning horizons (~ twenty to fifty years) and somewhat longer historical experience (at most a few hundred years). It seems unwise to assume that past rates of productivity growth (which are partially responsible for positive interest rates) will continue indefinitely into the future. As such, market interest rates seem much more legitimate for making intra-generational decisions (or at least decisions among overlapping generations) than intergenerational decisions over more than one hundred years. Finally, heterodox economists raise ethical questions about the "right" of our generation to "discount" future costs and benefits based on our current preferences.

Although many of these concerns have also been raised by some neoclassical economists, the neoclassical paradigm's tendency to defer to the market causes these reservations to get less attention in orthodox than heterodox macroeconomic discussions. If one takes seriously the conclusion that market interest rates are too high from the point of view of long-run economic planning, there is a need for greater government intervention in long-term decision making.

EQUITY AND ENVIRONMENTAL ECONOMICS

Is Inequality Good, Bad, or Irrelevant for the Environment?

Heterodox economists argue that large economic inequalities promote environmental degradation by increasing the number of communities willing to trade environmental amenities (like the absence of polluting industries) for employment and local income.[21] Poverty can similarly force people to make very short-term-oriented choices with respect to sustainability. This is quite evident in third world economies, where a lack of economic alternatives is often correlated with environmentally destructive treatment of marginal agricultural lands.[22]

High levels of economic inequality also create artificial political pressures for economic growth. This is because large disparities in wealth and income are more easily tolerated by less-advantaged groups if they expect that economic growth will offer access to the current privileges of the wealthy in the not-so-distant future. Absent growth, the "social bargain" of capitalist societies can break down. Inequality thus encourages macroeconomic strategies that expand production in order to defuse social tensions. This expansion can overtax the environment.

Heterodoxy also finds that inequality spurs imitation by each subgroup of its proximate superiors. This tends to ratchet up popular consumption levels, with attendant burdens on the environment. Many heterodox economists suspect that a more equal economy with higher levels of publicly supplied goods would have a gentler effect on the environment.

Although neoclassical textbooks do not usually highlight the linkages between inequality and environmental protection they sometimes imply that inequality is good for the environment. Supply-side economists, for example, argue that inequality spurs economic growth and, assuming an environmental Kuznets curve, protects the environment. A similar argument can be used to argue that environmental protection regulations hurt the environment, if one argues that these regulations slow economic growth. This type of reasoning illustrates the radically conservative potential applications of the growth subtext in standard neoclassical theory.

Is There a Trade-off Between Protecting Jobs and the Poor and Protecting the Environment?

In the United States there is often a political undertow around environmental regulation that suggests a tradeoff between jobs and environmental protection. Although neither heterodox nor neoclassical theory supports this conclusion in the long run, heterodox theory recognizes the political impact of the perception. This leads heterodox economists to suspect that policies that promote full employment would make it easier to protect the environment.

The most common discussion of the impact of environmental concerns on inequality involves fears that conservation and environmental protection may hurt the poor. Enthusiasts for economic growth sometimes warn that the tightening of environmental regulations threatens to kill the goose that lays the golden egg of GDP growth, condemning many to permanent poverty.

Heterodox economists challenge these claims. Although they acknowledge that reducing environmental pollution and conserving natural resources may increase some production costs, they reject the idea that environmental degradation is the necessary ransom for increasing the standard of living for low-income families. As detailed in chapter 15, the persistence of poverty in America has nothing to do with decisions about the level of environmental protection. Globally, there are more genuine choices between meeting environmental or other human needs. But even in the third world, the choices between increasing environmental quality and meeting other development goals are a very minor part of antipoverty challenges.

Ethics, Economic Methodology, and the Environment

As we have noted many times, neoclassical economics' scientistic self-image encourages textbook writers to deflect ethical issues to other disciplines. The claim that no scientifically based conclusions can be made about the benefits of transferring a dollar of income from a rich to a poor person frequently seems to justify inattention to distributional issues. Concerns about sustainability, however, presuppose the relevance and discussability of equity concerns. Raising the topic thus invites broader attention to distributional issues than is common in standard textbooks.[23]

For example, if one asserts that our generation should bequeath future generations an equal chance for economic well-being (the logic behind sustainability), it can seem inconsistent to deny such egalitarian beginnings to poor children alive today.[24] In addition, taking a long view of economic outcomes, as required by sustainability goals, often illuminates the limitations of methodological individualism as way of thinking about social choices. The world inherited by future generations will be shaped as much by our culture as by individual choices. Issues of sustainability thus turn attention to holist methodologies of social explanation.

What is the implicit textbook rationale for giving greater attention to intergenerational equity issues (i.e., economics of sustainability) than intra-generational equity issues (i.e., the economics of poverty and inequality) in macroeconomic discussions? The answer to this question suggests how ideology helps determine scholarly agendas. The growth subtext of neoclassical economics (which implies that the contribution of economics to human well-being is its ability to facilitate economic growth) is often complemented in political discussions by the claim that individuals' economic success is largely determined by their own efforts. Poverty, in other words, is an individual rather than a system failure. Viewed in this light, macro economists need to think about how to preserve the system's ability to create wealth. The economics of sustainability is about how to handle this task. Macro economists need not think about issues of poverty and inequality, as they are more matters of individual determination.

This line of reasoning is highly ideological, that is, it is impossible to prove or disprove empirically and reflects broader views, similarly beyond proof or disproof, about the nature of human nature, capitalism, and other "big topics." Some readers may find the reasoning attractive and "true." Others may find it offensive and "false." What I would like you to see most of all is that it is not a scientific perspective. The vision probably infuses your textbook, but is not really argued. The assumptions behind the vision have important implications for what is covered and not covered in macroeconomics courses.

"Environmental Justice" Issues

As noted in chapter 15, environmental burdens tend to be borne disproportionately by the poor and disadvantaged minorities, especially with respect to the siting of toxic waste dumps.[25] The environmental justice movement tries to address this issue. Neoclassical economists have contributed many useful studies on the incidence of pollution burdens.

Heterodox economists tend to be uneasy with aspects of neoclassical theory's preference for market distributions of "environmental amenities." The neoclassical perspective invites the poor to trade environmental quality for economic benefits. Although this may make sense with respect to some "environmental amenities," like a lakeside view, it is not acceptable to many heterodox economists for other environmental phenomena, such as the distribution of health hazards accompanying toxic waste dumps or air pollution. Why not?

Many heterodox economists analogize the neoclassical model's celebration of the "freedom" of poor people and poor countries to sell assets like pollution and public health standards to the "freedom" we might give people to sell bodily organs. Taking a neoclassical perspective, it could be argued that the poor would be better off if a market in kidneys and other body parts were organized. The change might be judged a "Pareto optimal" change, as no one would be any worse off than before the market was created, since no one would be forced to participate in the market.

Taking a more holistic view, heterodoxy raises the possibility that contemporary culture dictates a certain minimal standard of living for fellow citizens. The ability to sell one's organs or exposure to pollution might simply replace part of the social safety net, rather than augment the poor's income. In this sense, the existence of the option imposes it on the least well-to-do. Thus rather than commodifying clean air, clean water, and protection from harmful chemicals, and permitting individuals to "sell" their "property rights" to these "amenities," some heterodox economists favor nonnegotiable standards for environmental quality.

"SOCIAL LOGICS" AND THE ENVIRONMENT

Social Systems and the Environment

Heterodox economics asks questions about the environmental implications of "our way of life." Rather than simply interpreting market outcomes as the summation of randomly given individual tastes and preferences, heterodox economics investigates whether there are larger logics at work. What is meant by "our way of life" is of course an open-ended question. Different social theories perceive different social logics at work. Two of the most popular theories tie contemporary environmental outcomes to the logic of modern technology or the logic of capitalism.

The first approach adopts a somewhat technologically deterministic view of culture and institutions. It depicts "industrial civilization" as an interlocking combination of political, economic, and ideological responses to modern technology. For example, it links technologically determined phenomena, like the existence of large economies of scale in manufacturing production, to social outcomes, such as the rise of the large corporation. This approach treats modern technology as a naturally expanding system whose physical productivity requires expanding levels of consumption for social stability. Adherents of this approach perceive an inevitable tension between the economic growth spawned by this system and the limiting envelope of the natural environment. They point to the presence of serious environmental problems in both the former Soviet Union and capitalist countries as evidence of the universality of this process (see for example Schnaiberg and Gould 1994).

Is Capitalism Sustainable?

The second perspective argues that the implications of technology and the direction of technical change are always shaped by social institutions. The most common application of this perspective links the nature of contemporary social institutions to the logic of capitalism. Exploring the nature of capitalism as a social system is a project beyond the scope of neoclassical economics. To the extent that our environmental problems are a product of capitalism they will be obscured by textbook economics.

From the perspective of Marxist and radical economics, organizing the economy in a competitive capitalist fashion creates strong pressures in favor of economic growth, even at high environmental costs. This outcome has several causes. One of the most important is capitalism's tendency to tie many people's access to employment to the expansion, rather than the maintenance, of the economy. In a similar vein, most firms in a capitalist economy must strive to grow in order to survive, as they must capture economies of scale. Firms are also encouraged to constantly incite the appetites of consumers through advertising and other marketing efforts to ensure customers for their products.

Wealth holders in capitalism similarly seek expanded outlets for their growing money balances. From a Marxist and radical economics perspective, the owners of financial capital play a special role in modern society. As discussed in chapter 13, their unique project is to change M into M'. This project is the wellspring of change in the modern world. It is different from the motivation of insatiable consumer desires depicted in neoclassical theory. It is more like a miser's pursuit of money for its own sake. It is a historically created logic, reflective of a particular social system.

From a radical and Marxist perspective, the incentives for economic expansion and environmental risk-taking in capitalism emerge from the supply rather than the demand side of the economy. The incentives reflect the nature of employment and competition in capitalism and the projects of financial capital. They reflect the structure of production, not consumer preferences. They create an expansionist and commercial civilization that "commodifies" the natural world.[26] Although there are also aspects of modern capitalism that promote environmental protection (such as the great wealth created by capitalism), most radical and Marxist economists doubt that these forces will be strong enough to create an environmentally sustainable capitalism.

From a Marxist and radical perspective, the quintessential organization in a capitalist society is the corporation. It is the mover and shaker of societal life, economically, technologically, and, increasingly, politically. It has the status of a person in law and is the active "agent" in the economy. The purposes of "for-profit" corporations (by far the dominant form of corporations) are beautifully simple: to "maximize shareholder value."

From a Marxist and radical perspective, one of the best ways to understand the logic of a capitalist society is to "think like a corporation," that is, to imagine how the world would look if your only objective was to maximize "shareholder value." The trajectory of such a world is the trajectory radical and Marxist economists expect for capitalism. It is a slash-and-burn path. From the perspective of Adam Smith and classical liberalism, the war of all against all is guided by the invisible hand of competition to serve the general welfare. For radical and Marxist economists, a social system that relies mainly on greed to protect the environment will destroy it.

Let us return to the economics of fishing discussed earlier in this chapter. Neoclassical analyses tend to portray the privatization of fishing resources and the evolution of modern fishing technology as a triumph of economic rationality and technological productivity. Heterodox economists are more skeptical of emerging fishing practices. Like "factory farming" on land (with immobilized hogs and chickens), modern aquaculture, typified by shrimp farming, threatens to overwhelm local ecosystems. The pattern in Taiwan and Thailand, for example, has been for outside investors to establish shrimp farms in coastal areas. These investors destroy coastal wetlands; pollute and exhaust local environments by discharging biological wastes, chemicals, and fertilizers beyond the area's natural assimilating capacity; and then move on to the next site. This has been especially harmful to mangrove forests, which purify local water sources and serve as nurseries for a high percentage of wild fish. Fish farming has also encouraged unsustainable biomass fishing for fish food (see for example McGinn 1998; Harris 2002, 292; and Skladany, Belton, and Clausen 2005).[27]

Aldo Leopold, a famous ecologist, has argued for environmental strategies that are fundamentally different from those encouraged by market rationality. Leopold challenges the ability of enlightened self-interest to protect the environment. Rather than "thinking like a corporation," his "land ethic" recommends "thinking like a mountain" as the necessary vantage point for environmental survival. To think like a mountain, he suggests, is to take a long view of human beings' interconnectedness to each other and to the ecosystem. Leopold ([1949] 1966) is careful to include economic considerations in humans' relationship to the natural world, but he refuses to reduce the natural world to economic inputs and outputs. He writes,

> The Golden Rule tries to integrate the individual to society. . . . There is as yet no ethic dealing with man's relation to land and to the animals and plants which grow upon it. . . . The land-relation is still strictly economic (238). . . .
>
> The extension of ethics to this third element in human environment is, if I read the evidence correctly, an evolutionary possibility and an ecological necessity. . . .

An ethic may be regarded as a mode of guidance for meeting ecological situations so new or intricate, or involving such deferred reactions, that the path of social expediency is not discernible to the average individual. . . .

The land ethic simply enlarges the boundaries of the community to include soils, waters, plants, and animals, or collectively: the land. (239)

One way of reading Leopold is to say he expresses much more poetically and ecologically heterodox economists' ideas about the implications of environmental complexity, uncertainty, and holism for understanding economic systems and designing economic policies. He warns that the invisible hand is an insufficient guardian of the environment and reminds policy makers that nature's economy is too important to be left to the economists.

CONCLUSION: POINT AND COUNTERPOINT

We will review some of the major issues raised in this chapter by looking at neoclassical responses to heterodox critiques and heterodox replies. Defenders of neoclassical macro textbooks argue that they address the relevant portions of heterodox concerns about environmental and conservation issues. When interesting topics are omitted, the neoclassicals imply it is often due to space limitations and the need for a division of labor between macroeconomics and other economics courses.

For example, some textbooks briefly acknowledge efforts to include changes in the level of natural resources available to the economy in the GDP accounts (Samuelson and Nordhaus 2005, 99). They do not, however, explore this topic. There are similarly brief references in most textbooks to debates over limits to growth, with little elaboration. Mankiw's (2001) text, for example, states,

> Many commentators have argued that natural resources provide a limit to how much the world's economies can grow. . . .
>
> Despite the apparent appeal of such arguments, most [*neoclassical* (not in original)] economists are less concerned about such limits to growth than one might guess. They argue that technological progress often yields ways to avoid these limits. . . .
>
> One way to answer this question is to look at the prices of natural resources. In a market economy, scarcity is reflected in market prices. If the world were running out of natural resources, then the prices of those resources would be rising over time. But, in fact, the opposite is more nearly true. (248–49)

The implicit message is that concerns about resource limits to growth need to be noted but can be ignored. There is, in fact, some disdain for such concerns, due to a sense of having been "snookered" in the past by careless arguments.[28] The textbooks' stance toward potential environmental limits to growth is similar, but more respectful. There is no evidence of concern about generalized environmental crises. It is likely that many neoclassical authors are sympathetic to the idea of an environmental Kuznets curve.

The debate over how much attention to give to potential resource and ecological constraints on the scale of macroeconomic activity partially involves differing intuitions about the reliability of the past for forecasting the future. It is also a debate over the ability of markets to correctly interpret scarcity data and a debate over the adequacy of our geological, engineering, and ecological expectations. The textbooks are confident that previous patterns of technological change and resource substitutability will prevail.

Mankiw's argument illustrates the self-referenced dimension of aspects of the neoclassical position. Concern about market failures can be dismissed because market prices reveal no such concern. To be fair to Mankiw and the textbooks, there are many nonmarket indicators of resource availability and environmental health that can be also used to support optimism about the economic growth (see for example Tietenberg 2003, ch. 14). The problem is that there are counter-indicators as well. Good evidence can be marshaled for either side of this debate. I personally find the case for ecological constraints on economic growth compelling and the case for resource constraints unconvincing. But the real issue is whether the topics deserve serious exploration in macroeconomics courses, and here there seems little ambiguity to me; the answer is yes.

To some extent, the different subtexts of neoclassical and heterodox paradigms explain the different macroeconomic treatments of environmental issues. Neoclassical theory's celebration of economic growth as the enabler of human possibility (and economists as the engineers of economic growth) makes it very difficult for the paradigm to conceive of limits to growth. Neoclassical theory's view of markets as ingenious pieces of social machinery that transform inputs into their highest-valued output makes it similarly difficult to challenge "perfect market outcomes."

For the neoclassicals, growth is like a breeder nuclear reactor; it creates more fuel for human possibility than it consumes. Markets are like programmable machine tools; you turn them on and they produce what you want. From this perspective the ideal environmental policy is one that lets the perfect market work and turns the benefits of economic growth to whatever people wish, including producing environmental quality.

Heterodoxy desanctifies the market, perfect market outcomes, and market-organized economic growth. Because heterodoxy has a more complex view of human psychology than *homo economicus,* a more complicated notion of human well-being than maximizing GDP, and a more complex view of the relationship between the economy and the rest of society than assumed by methodological individualism, heterodoxy has a more complicated view of the process of economic growth and its relationship to the environment.

Many heterodox economists are not convinced that current market trajectories will maximize human well-being and the sustainability of the environment over time. Because heterodox economists look at the economy as part of a larger social process that creates tastes and preferences as well as satisfies them, creates development paths as well as discovers them, and influences culture and political life as well as responds to them, heterodoxy asks broader questions about the relationship between macroeconomic outcomes and the environment than neoclassical theory does.

As E.F. Schumacher has written, it is not obvious that encouraging the unbridled pursuit of self-interest is currently the best organizing principle for the social division of labor. He warns, "An attitude of life which seeks fulfillment in the single-minded pursuit of wealth—in short, materialism—does not fit into this world, because it contains within itself no limiting principle, while the environment in which it is placed is strictly limited" (Schumacher 1973, 27).

Heterodoxy worries about the economy's tendency to incite consumption, to create political pressures for unwise environmental policies, and to take short-sighted views on long-term resource and ecological issues. Neoclassical critics of heterodoxy warn that its elevation of environmental goals is presumptuous and perhaps elitist. The neoclassicals criticize heterodox economists for appearing to substitute their own environmentalist valuations of wilderness, species diversity, natural vistas, and so on for the market's aggregation of popular opinion.

I think there is an element of truth in neoclassical claims. Environmentalists do assert that markets make some predictable errors and that it is sometimes wise to ask whether there are nonmarket standards (like the UN's human development index, notions of sustainability, and principles of distribution) that trump hypothetical perfect-market outcomes. There is an underlying unease beneath many heterodox imaginations that the "economic system" may be out of control. This is, of course, exactly the opposite of the optimality images underlying neoclassical theory. Many heterodox economists worry that the invisible hand has gone astray, much like the sorcerer's apprentice in Walt Disney's movie *Fantasia*.

IN THEIR OWN WORDS

The reason that environmental macroeconomics is an empty box lies in what Thomas Kuhn calls a paradigm, and what Joseph Schumpeter more descriptively called a preanalytic vision. . . . [A]nalysis has to start somewhere—there has to be something to analyze. That something is given by a preanalytic cognitive act that Schumpeter called 'Vision.' . . .

The vision . . . of macroeconomics, is the familiar circular flow diagram. . . . The macroeconomy is seen as an isolated system (i.e., as having no exchanges of matter or energy with its environment) in which exchange value circulates between firms and households in a closed loop. . . . Since analysis cannot supply what the preanalytic vision omits, it is only to be expected that macroeconomics texts would be silent on environment, natural resources, depletion and pollution.

—Herman Daly (1996, 46–47)

[A]s Gandhi said . . . "Earth provides enough to satisfy every man's need, but not for every man's greed." . . .

The cultivation and expansion of needs is the antithesis of wisdom. . . . (31)

Until fairly recently the economists have felt entitled, with tolerably good reason, to treat the entire framework within which economic activity takes place as *given* [italics in original], that is to say, as permanent and indestructible. . . . Since there is now increasing evidence of environmental deterioration . . . the entire outlook and methodology of economics is being called into question. The study of economics is too narrow and too fragmentary to lead to valid insights, unless complemented and completed by a study of meta-economics.

—E.F. Schumacher (1973, 48–49)

Our species' activities on the planet have now become so large a scale that they are beginning to affect the ecological life-support system itself. The entire concept of economic growth (defined as increasing material consumption) must be rethought. . . . (4)

Can we be humble enough to acknowledge the huge uncertainties involved and protect ourselves from their most dire consequences? Can we effectively develop policies to deal with the tricky issues of wealth distribution, population prudence, international trade, and energy supply in a world where the simple palliative of 'more growth' is no longer a solution? (5)

It took all of human history to grow to the $600 billion/yr scale of the economy of 1900. Today, the world economy grows by this amount every two years . . . (7).

—Robert Costanza et al. (1997, 4, 5, 7)

Capitalism, as practiced, is a financially profitable, nonsustainable aberration in human development. What might be called 'industrial capitalism' does not fully conform to its own accounting principles. It liquidates its capital and calls it income. It neglects to assign any value to the largest stocks of capital it employs—the natural resources and living systems, as well as the social and cultural systems that are the basis of human capital.

—Hawken, Lovins, and Lovins (1999, 5)

STUDY QUESTIONS

Review Questions

1. From a heterodox perspective compare and contrast the subtexts of neoclassical and heterodox environmental economics.
2. List the six basic premises of neoclassical environmental economics.
3. What is the basis for government action in the environmental area according to the logic of neoclassical economics?
4. Outline the kinds of policies neoclassical economists would recommend for dealing with the problems of acid rain, the greenhouse effect, and the depletion of fishing stocks.
5. Briefly define what is meant by the terms listed below and their relevance to environmental economics: (a) negative externality, (b) public good, (c) Environmental Kuznets Curve, (d) positional competition, (e) precautionary principle, (f) weak sustainability, (g) strong sustainability, (h) moderately strong sustainability, (i) threshold effects.
6. Marxist and radical economists assert that capitalism is not sustainable. Why do they claim this? What do you think? Explain your answer.

Discussion Questions

1. From a heterodox perspective, list some of the major methodological differences between heterodox and neoclassical economics and illustrate how these differences find expression in heterodox critiques of the treatment of environmental issues in macroeconomics textbooks.
2. What do you find to be the most convincing heterodox critique of the treatment of environmental issues in your textbook? What do you think is the least convincing heterodox critique? Explain your answers.
3. Why might heterodox analysis lead to different kinds of environmental policies? Illustrate your answer with some specific examples.
4. Neoclassical economists often see economic growth as the solution to social and economic problems. What social problems do you think economic growth can help address? What problems do you think economic growth will not be able to address? Explain your answers.

NOTES

1. Environmental issues tend to receive more attention in neoclassical micro than macro principles texts. This is due to neoclassical economic theory's treatment of environmental problems as the result of micro-level market failures (such as negative externalities) rather than macro-level systems effects.

2. Negative externalities (like soot from a factory smokestack) are costs associated with the production or consumption of a good that are not included in its price and thus not borne by the good's consumers. Positive externalities are benefits from a good's production that are not captured by the good's purchaser, such as the climatic benefits society enjoys from the capture and storage of the greenhouse gas carbon dioxide by the trees around your home. From the point of view of economic efficiency, markets will overproduce goods with negative externalities and underproduce goods with positive externalities.

3. A public good is a good that is hard to charge for because providing it to one person automatically provides it to others. The earth's ozone layer, which protects living things from the harmful effects of ultraviolet radiation, is a good example of a public good.

4. For the neoclassicals, "optimal" outcomes mean "Pareto-efficient" outcomes. These are outcomes in

which no person could be made better off without making another person worse off. A less technical way of saying this is to claim that "perfect markets" exhaust the benefits of voluntary exchange. Still another way of putting this is to say that markets allow people to rearrange resources efficiently. Thus, if we imagine the environment as a resource, we can expect the perfect market to use it efficiently. Neoclassical economists recognize that Pareto-efficient outcomes may not be socially desirable if the distribution of resources preceding exchange is highly unequal. They usually argue, however, that questions of efficiency and equity can be addressed separately. The usual strategy of neoclassical textbooks is to assume that equity issues have already been resolved through the political process (through mechanisms like the progressive income tax or subsidized public education) and focus economic discussion on efficiency issues.

5. As many heterodox economists have noted, the claim that common property is always misused is an overgeneralization. Although it is true that common property resources invite misuse in a competitive market culture, they have survived quite well in traditional cultures where custom and other informal means of organizing community behavior oversaw land use. See, for example, work by Bonnie M. McCoy and E.P. Thompson.

6. All paradigms agree that it is important to determine how the property rights (i.e., ownership rights) to fishing resources are distributed. The three most popular options are to treat the fishing stock as: public property; the property of fishing boat owners; or the property of boat owners and crew. Under public ownership, the government receives the revenues from the fishing stock's sale to the highest bidders at public auction. In the second and third cases, title to the fishing stock is divided among boat owners and crew, who may fish or sell their rights. Heterodox economists suggest that the equity implications of privatization have to be looked at dynamically rather than statically, suggesting that over time a privatized fishing industry may generate a more unequal social structure than some other alternatives, such as community ownership.

7. In the year 2002, $446 billion was spent on advertising worldwide, almost nine times the level in 1950. Although about half of this sum was spent in the United States, the cultivation of consumption outside the United States is accelerating, increasing by more than 350 percent over the last twenty years (Gardner, Assadourian, and Sarin 2004, 14).

8. See also work by Kendall M. Thu and William J Weida.

9. For example, despite a decline in energy intensity of 1.9 percent/year since 1992, U.S. energy consumption grew by about 10 percent over the last decade (*Annual Energy Outlook 2005*, U.S. Department of Energy). The Department of Energy forecast an increase of 0.5 percent/year in energy use in the United States over the next twenty years, despite continued efficiency gains in the level of output produced per unit of energy consumed.

10. Other heterodox economists are more optimistic about the ability of major technological shifts to reduce the amount of materials used to produce goods and services. Peter Dorman and researchers at the Rocky Mountain Institute, for example, foresee the possibility of a 75 percent reduction in the amount of materials used per dollar of GDP.

11. The empirical literature is quite murky and contested. Since many variables are correlated with time (such as GDP and advances in knowledge), it is difficult to isolate their specific impacts on environmental quality. Although cross-sectional studies escape this problem they face other difficulties. To the extent that high-income countries are shifting some pollution burdens to low-income countries, the data will exaggerate the ability of economic growth to reduce pollution. The major problem, however, is how to aggregate different kinds of environmental hazards in order to arrive at an overall assessment.

12. Different researchers have calculated different "turning points" for when economic growth begins to help rather than hurt the environment. There are also different turning points for different pollutants. Many advocates of an EKC report turning points ranging from $2,000 per capita to $12,000 per capita (Harris 2002, 414). Average global income, measured in purchasing power parity terms, around the turn of the century was $5,533 and median income $1,700 (United Nations Development Programme, *Human Development Report 2005*, 36).

13. For the purpose of understanding the implications of exponential growth, it is often helpful to think in terms of doubling times. For relatively small growth rates the doubling time can be estimated by dividing 70 by the growth rate. At a 1 percent growth rate, for example, doubling takes ~70 years. Doubling takes ~14 years at a 5 percent annual growth rate and ~7 years at a 10 percent growth rate.

14. Some neoclassical economists accept this hypothesis, but argue that public policy makers are prey to the same errors. Given the potential for political as well as market failures, they find market mechanisms more likely to weed out "predictable mistakes." Heterodox economists tend to reject "lesser of two evils" kinds of justifications for market authority. Instead, they call for structural changes to improve public-policy decisions.

15. There are currently about 55,000 potential substances in active use that could prove toxic (Tietenberg 2003, 497).

16. Of necessity these energy sources would probably have to be nonrenewable, non-solar-based energy sources (such as nuclear fission, nuclear fusion, unconventional fossil fuels, coal, or geothermal) in order to permit exponential growth in energy consumption. Although it is feasible to run an industrial civilization on incoming solar energy, using biomass, hydroelectric, solar thermal, photovoltaic, wind, and other renewable energy, these sources would not seem to permit continuous exponential increases in energy consumption.

17. Norway's management of its oil revenues is often cited as an example of policies meeting the criterion of weak sustainability.

18. This calculation assumes that interest payments are compounded only once a year.

19. Note that this is a different use of the word "discount" from the phrase "discount rate," which refers to the interest rate the Fed charges member banks for short-term loans.

20. \$30 trillion/$(1.06)^{200}$ = ~\$260 million. Daly and Farley note that a 6 percent discount rate was used in one cost-benefit study of what to do about global warming (Daly and Farley 2004, 272).

21. See Boyce 1994 for elaboration. Efforts to site nuclear waste dumps on American Indian reservations offer a classic example of this phenomenon.

22. This point is also often made by neoclassical economists.

23. As also noted earlier, there are many neoclassical economists who care deeply about distributional issues and have spent their careers studying inequality. This focus is rarer, however, in neoclassical than heterodox economics. The attention given distributional issues in standard introductory texts, which tend to mirror the neoclassical paradigm as whole, is therefore relatively modest.

24. Interestingly, the longer perspective one takes the more it appears that redistribution of income in the present optimizes intergenerational utility, as one's progeny are likely to be mixed descendants from many backgrounds. For an interesting discussion of this idea see Daly 1999, 114–18.

25. See Bullard 2000 for helpful background information.

26. From a Marxist and radical perspective, economic growth is also required politically in capitalist societies to defuse the social tensions created by significant economic inequality. Growth also maximizes the social surplus available to governments for use in interstate rivalries.

27. Environmentalists have drawn up similar indictments for salmon farming and open-ocean shrimp fishing. Without a social morality it is extremely difficult for regulators to turn "bottom line"–oriented corporate planning toward environmentally sustainable practices.

28. In the early 1970s the Club of Rome's computer models seemed to predict relatively imminent disaster for the world's economy. This impression relied heavily on a forecasting methodology that compared current consumption of a natural resource to proven reserves of that resource. Using this metric it was not hard to demonstrate that an exponential growth in resource use would exhaust resource stocks relatively quickly, even if reserves had been estimated relatively conservatively. The model de-emphasized the implications of technological change and the impact of rising prices on resource use and reserves. It was not a very good measure of scarcity.

REINTRODUCING CURRENT POLICY DEBATES IN MACROECONOMICS

INTRODUCTION

Most introductory textbooks have a "taking-stock" chapter near or at the end of the book that reviews the basic ideas of neoclassical macroeconomics and discusses recent debates in macro theory and macro policy. This chapter critiques those discussions from a heterodox perspective.

Neoclassical Subtexts

The subtexts of different macro paradigms animate the chapters on current macro policy debates. Standard neoclassical texts are dominated by the theme of market optimality. Most of the important debates highlighted in standard macroeconomics texts involve arguments about whether to maintain or reduce the level of government "intervention" in the macro economy. Very limited attention is given to the merits of expanding the "social governance" of the economy. Other issues are also slighted. There is usually little discussion of distributional and equity issues, with the exception of supply-side economists' call for increasing inequality in the name of increasing economic incentives. There is seldom significant discussion of environmental or gender issues. There is no serious discussion of what we mean by economic well-being.

Heterodox Subtexts

In contrast, heterodoxy expands the range of issues considered appropriate or relevant subject matter for macroeconomics and macro policy. Heterodox economists call for greater attention to issues of economic inequality and environmental sustainability, to developments in the household and voluntary sectors, to conditions in the workplace, and to non-GDP-based measures of macro performance. Heterodox economists also expand the policy options considered when analyzing potential government responses to unemployment, inflation, and globalization.

From a heterodox perspective, the range of disagreement in standard texts is just large enough to give the appearance of exhausting debate but small enough to preclude discussion of any serious changes in government policy. It is, to paraphrase Robert Lucas, a conservative Nobel Prize–winning macroeconomist from the University of Chicago, a debate over whether a 95 percent or 100 percent laissez-faire economic policy is best (Lucas 1979, 5). Heterodoxy challenges these boundaries with its own subtext that capitalist economies need strong systems of social governance in order to promote widespread economic well-being.

Many students studying economics for the first time often feel uncomfortable with the "let the market work" policy implications of their textbooks, but most are unable to formally justify their uneasiness. Unless very careful attention is paid to the methodological assumptions of textbook economics it is very difficult to get out of the analytical box these assumptions create. And if one remains "inside the box," it is difficult to avoid reaching neoclassical policy conclusions.

One of the goals of this commentary is to enable readers who may be experiencing some skepticism about laissez-faire economic policies to "talk back to the textbooks." I have tried to develop a pattern of critique that explicitly stresses methodological issues (such as criticisms of methodological individualism, *homo economicus,* the assumptions of perfect information and perfect competition, etc.) in order to empower such readers to begin their exploration of alternative economic policies by asking the right questions. We review these ideas in this chapter.

Differences Among Heterodox Paradigms

Because of page constraints and the introductory nature of this commentary, it has been difficult to discuss differences among heterodox economists. I have emphasized instead their common ground. That is, I have stressed their shared critiques of textbook economics rather than the different ways different heterodox paradigms (and even different theorists within these paradigms) often develop these critiques. This chapter follows the same strategy. It is thus important to note that not all heterodox economists would agree with all of the policies mentioned in this chapter. There would be more consensus about the nature of the problems present in the economy and in economic theory than about their solutions.

Chapter Outline

The rest of this chapter builds on earlier discussions of macro policy. The initial sections summarize heterodox critiques of textbook discussions of how to respond to unemployment and inflation. The next few sections compare and contrast heterodox and textbook policy recommendation on a wider range of issues. The final sections conclude the chapter with our usual threads, contrasting metaphors, and quotations.

TEXTBOOK PORTRAYALS OF POLICY DEBATES: GENERAL EQUILIBRIUM (GE) AND KEYNESIAN POSITIONS

Unemployment

Prominence of GE Claims

The major debate at the end of most textbooks is whether there is a need for even modest government "intervention" in the economy to maintain full employment. The laissez-faire position tends to occupy the high ground of theoretical rigor in debates among neoclassical economists. This is because of the peculiar assumptions of neoclassical theory about the nature of economic behavior and economic argument. These assumptions favor explanations of market outcomes that are expressed in simple mathematical models utilizing the psychology of *homo economicus* to explain individual behavior.

More complicated and interdependent psychological models of behavior are discouraged, as are holist inquiries into the social origin of tastes, preferences, and expectations. The assumptions of perfect competition and perfect information tend to be perceived as valuable simplifications rather than as dubious starting points. When viewed from this vantage point, the simple models of general equilibrium theory often seem compelling, while the disequilibrium models of Keynesian theory appear ad hoc and lacking in firm foundations.

In a nutshell, general equilibrium theory (also known as new classical economics) "fits" better than Keynesian disequilibrium theory with the broad subtexts of neoclassical economics. As Alan Blinder, a thoughtful Neo-Keynesian economist, has observed, "the ascendancy of new classicism in academia was . . . a triumph of *a priori* theorizing over empiricism, of intellectual aesthetics over observation. . . ." (Blinder 1988, 278).

From a heterodox perspective, it is remarkable how many new wrinkles can be crafted and extraordinary assumptions tolerated in order to fit observed macro fluctuations into hypothetical general equilibrium models. In the "new-old" models of GE theory, deviations from optimality are either quickly corrected by the market or beyond improvement by public policy. For example, when analyzed according to the general equilibrium model:

- Business downturns and business cycles are said to reflect new production conditions and shifting levels of optimal output and employment (*Real Business Cycle Theory*) rather than economic failures. Current output becomes the best estimate of potential output, and actual unemployment becomes the best estimate of the "natural rate of unemployment."
- People are assumed to behave as if they had extraordinary amounts of information and/or knowledge of economic theory (*Rational Expectations Theory*), pushing actual market outcomes toward general equilibrium outcomes almost instantaneously.
- Government tax policy is held unable to increase consumption demand because people automatically increase savings by the exact amount of any deficit-financed tax cut. This strange behavior results from assuming that taxpayers anticipate future tax increases to pay for the tax cuts. Thus, according to this theory, people can be expected to save their entire tax cut to pay for future tax increases (*"Ricardian" View of Fiscal Policy*).
- Unemployment is said to be mainly voluntary. Increases in unemployment are caused by people voluntarily quitting jobs (due to unrealistically high wage expectations), while increases in employment are due to people accepting surprisingly low wage offers (*Misperceptions Theories of the Business Cycle*).

Like many intellectual fads, some of these theories have had only five minutes of fame. What is interesting about them is their reincarnations. The Monetarists, for example, warned in the late 1960s and early 1970s that the Fed should adopt a more laissez-faire-oriented policy toward the economy because of the practical difficulties posed for monetary policy making by lag times. Similar arguments reappeared in the late 1970s in game theoretic garb for quite different reasons.[1] And they are echoed again today in arguments against using fiscal policy to stimulate the economy. Walras's auctioneer now appears in "rational expectations" garb, while Says Law (the notion that supply creates its own demand) reappears in supply-side economics.

The general pattern is for a laissez-faire-oriented theorist to begin by asserting a reasonable claim about economic behavior. The rational expectations theorists, for example, argued that people tend to make use of new information in making decisions, including information about government macro policy. This initial and reasonable inference is then expressed mathematically and combined with "simplifying assumptions" in the construction of an economic model. From a heterodox perspective, it is these extra assumptions that ensure that the resulting model generates classical macroeconomic conclusions.

In the case of rational expectations theory, these assumptions implied that everyone in the economy had the ability to translate available information into perfect market prices, much like the auctioneer. Thus, although the initial idea of "rational expectations" (that people make use of new information) was reasonable, the laissez-faire policy implications generated by rational expectations models of the economy were not.

Five years from now when you are reading newspaper accounts of the latest economic theories, heterodox economics invites you to look very skeptically at the newest version of classical economics. Look at the whole model and try to identify the key assumptions that are responsible for its optimality claims about unimpeded market outcomes.

Heterodox economists also warn against accepting the "end of the business cycle" claims that tend to appear during the latter part of most healthy economic upturns. The most recent examples of this rhetoric were the "new economy" claims of the 1990s that foresaw uninterrupted economic expansion. From a heterodox perspective, both business cycles and mistaken claims of their disappearance are likely to be with us for as long as we have a capitalist economy. When the conventional wisdom forgets this, hold on to your wallet, and beware of speculative bubbles followed by financial crises.

Softened Keynesian Claims

The textbooks contrast GE/classical theory with a watered-down version of Keynesian economics, what we have termed "Neo-Keynesianism" (NK). Under the latter banner the texts emphasize the overlapping work of the New Keynesians, asymmetric information theorists, and efficiency wage theorists. These economists' potentially interesting objections to GE theory are usually reduced to the assumption of "sticky wages and prices." Absent is any serious reference to Keynes's ideas about fundamental uncertainty, animal spirits, pessimistic expectations, social conventions, speculative bubbles, liquidity panics, and so on.

There is a further tendency for the texts to portray a narrowing of debate between Keynesian and GE theory. Since the textbook disagreement is basically about how flexible prices are, it encourages the reader to contemplate a middle ground, where classical theorists admit some price stickiness and Keynesian theorists admit faster adjustment than acknowledged in the past. Hence, readers are left with a sense that there are minor but discernable disagreements among economists, which are sometimes exaggerated by the media.

Shifts to Long-Run Views of Macro Outcomes

The textbooks' tilt toward GE theory over the last few decades has been accompanied by a rhetorical shift in emphasis from the short run to the long run. Because of the odd way that neoclassical theory conceives of the long run (see below), this shift frequently reinforces the assumptions necessary for laissez-faire macroeconomic policies.

Many potential problems posed by uncertainty for macroeconomic performance are deflected in the textbooks' long-run analysis by arguing that markets eventually find their natural equilibrium. This shift to long-run frameworks also tends to elevate supply- over demand-side concerns. Since long-run equilibrium *presupposes full employment* and high-capacity utilization, the only way that output can be increased is to increase potential supply. Textbook discussions of supply tend to give special attention to laissez-faire-oriented policies, such as "trickle-down" economics.

To some extent, the debate between GE and Keynesian theorists is a debate over "how long is short" and an argument about the relationship between the short and long runs. GE theorists tend to argue that the short run is pretty short and inconsequential. Keynesian economists disagree. As Keynes quipped, "In the long run, we are all dead," implying that life is lived in the short run.

GE theorists tend to think of long-run outcomes independently of short-run moments. They presume a hypothetical long-run "center of gravity" for the economy that persists independently of actual short-run moments. The economy necessarily gravitates to this long-run condition relatively quickly in GE theory. In contrast, Keynesian and heterodox theorists think of the long run as the cumulative implications of actual short runs. Rather than a static general equilibrium center of gravity, they perceive a partially contingent development path.

To draw an analogy, the GE model implies that individuals have an ideal job that they search for and eventually find. This ideal job remains the same independent of the discovery process. Heterodox theory implies that people's work experiences partially change them so that one's life course is path dependent. The long run is not independent of and prior to the short run.

The formal definition of the long run in most economic textbooks *assumes equilibrium*. The time frame involves hypothetical rather than historical time. The long run is the hypothetical time necessary for all of the implications of an economic shock to transpire and create a new general equilibrium. For example, one could ask the question, "what would the economy look like if the price of oil tripled and all economic decisions sensitive to oil prices worked themselves out, holding all other variables constant?" Short-run changes would involve adjustments consistent with the existing capital stock, such as a reduction in the miles driven by existing automobiles. Long-run changes would include all adjustments to the capital stock, as people slowly purchased more energy-efficient automobiles.

The textbooks' concept of the long run is very paradigmatic. It assumes inevitable equilibrium. It includes a tendency for comparative static analysis (the comparison of two different equilibrium states). It reinforces an equilibrium and optimality picture of the economy. It need not do this. For example, if long-run analysis included attention to how economic choices create development paths, the shift from a short- to long-run perspective could lead to greater attention to holist issues. Long-run analysis could explore how many of the variables taken as given in neoclassical models (such as tastes and preferences and institutional structures) evolve. Heterodox economics tilts long-run thinking toward these issues.

The textbooks lean in the opposite direction, deploying a fairly odd hybrid of assumptions. Textbook models posit that people remain exactly the same, but markets spin through lengthy periods of adjustment (renegotiating labor and other multiyear contracts, adding to or reducing the capital stock to its equilibrium level, and so on) in order to arrive at textbook notions of long-run outcomes. The latter are basically what would happen if people had perfect information in the short run.

The bottom line is that the paradigmatic structure of neoclassical economics tends to orient policy discussions of unemployment toward minimal government initiatives. The framework leaves just enough room for a debate between mild-mannered Keynesianism and laissez-faire policies.

Inflation Policy

The textbooks teach that *in the long run* inflation is caused by excessive growth of the money supply. The obvious solution is to slow monetary expansion. There is modest debate between the GE and NK schools over how quickly monetary contraction can lower inflation rates. The NKs tend to worry about sticky inflationary expectations. When the Fed slows monetary growth, these expectations can lead some workers and businesses to overprice their services, resulting in unsold goods and unemployed workers. GE economists, such as rational expectations theorists, tend to predict quick adjustments to monetary contractions, while NK economists find longer periods of adjustment and accompanying unemployment and reduced output. The textbooks implicitly encourage readers to migrate to the "rational middle" between the two schools' adjustment assumptions.

The textbooks also teach that *in the short run* the economy can suffer from demand-pull or cost-push inflation. Demand-pull inflation occurs when there is an increase in demand in an economy already at full employment. Because the economy is operating at full capacity, increases in demand translate into increases in prices rather than output. Cost-push inflation is caused by an economic shock on the supply rather than the demand side of the economy. The OPEC oil price shock in the mid-1970s and ensuing inflationary pressures is a classic example of cost-push inflation.

The textbooks are relatively unanimous about the need to respond to demand-pull inflation with contractionary macro policy. The texts note modest debates, however, between GE and NK economists (and among NK economists) over how to respond to cost-push inflationary shocks. The GE economists recommend a laissez-faire stance. They acknowledge that cost-push shocks, like an OPEC oil price increase, will initially cause a rise in the prices and a fall in output and employment (stagflation).[2] But, they claim, this effect will quickly pass. Producers (with unsold goods) and unemployed workers (with unsold labor) will lower their prices and wages, ridding the economy of inflationary pressures, unemployment, and excess capacity.

The NK economists sometimes disagree due to concerns about sticky wages and prices. They warn that expansionary government policy might be necessary to lower unemployment, if wages do not fall quickly enough. They acknowledge this would exacerbate inflationary problems. Thus the NK economists are left with the dilemma of trading temporary increases in unemployment or inflation for temporary decreases in the other variable. Almost all of the textbooks portray Paul Volcker as an economic hero who broke the back of inflation in the early 1980s by biting the bullet and accepting several years of high unemployment.

The "technical" or "practical" debates related to monetary policy highlighted in the textbooks usually involve proposals that call for more laissez-faire-oriented constraints on policy initiatives. Two of the most popular are calls for "monetary rules" and calls for zero inflation. Monetary rules would require the Fed to set a target rate of growth for the money supply and adhere to it regardless of subsequent economic conditions, including rising unemployment. A zero inflation policy would encourage the Fed to contract the money supply whenever price levels rose.[3] The textbooks do not endorse or oppose these proposals, but by focusing significant attention on these laissez-faire-oriented policies they "crowd out" attention to heterodox responses to inflation.

Financial Sector Regulation

There is some debate in the textbooks over the wisdom of the recent deregulation of the financial sector. Neoclassical theory's faith in market optimality, however, limits textbook discussion of regulatory oversight to modest proposals, such as minor taxes on financial transactions to reduce short-term speculative activity.

Globalization

The textbooks strongly promote free trade and free capital mobility. There are usually a few "note but ignore" qualifications (such as brief comments on potential problems related to infant industries, military industries, and "unfair competition") but these problems are treated as minor concerns. Slightly more attention is given to the "temporary adjustment problems" that workers in industries harmed by free trade might encounter. Like all "disequilibrium" moments in GE-oriented analyses, however, these problems are portrayed as modest and self-liquidating.

Most other sociopolitical impacts of free trade are given little attention, except for the texts' approving citation of the world market's ability to impose competitive discipline on firms and workers, who might otherwise be able to use the political process to protect inefficient industries and parochial interests. The main debate portrayed in the textbooks tends to be between enlightened support of and short-sighted opposition to free trade. There is also attention to more technical issues, such as whether fixed or flexible exchange rates, or joining currency unions, such as the European Union, are best for particular countries.

HETERODOX ALTERNATIVES

Introduction

How do heterodox economists pose current macro theory and policy issues? Heterodox economists do not challenge everything claimed in standard texts. They accept, for example, the possibility of demand-pull inflation, cost-push inflation, equilibrium moments, and sticky prices. They add, however, dimensions to these concepts and often situate them within broader causal logics. They also add additional topics to the scope of economic analysis. Most importantly, they tend to denaturalize and de-optimize laissez-faire outcomes.

Unemployment

By taking the implications of uncertainty seriously, heterodox economics provides a micro foundation for Keynesian economics. At the most basic level, heterodox economists warn that capitalist economies can suffer from high voluntary unemployment and low-capacity utilization rates due to *insufficient aggregate demand*—and, as a corollary, that expansionary monetary and fiscal policy can help the economy by increasing aggregate demand. This rationale complements the weaker Neo-Keynesian (NK) justification for expansionary macro policy, which ultimately rests on increasing the price level to get around sticky wages and prices.

Heterodox economists also challenge the textbooks' tendency to prioritize fighting inflation over fighting unemployment. Although the textbooks do a fair job of discrediting some myths about inflation that exaggerate its harmfulness, they do not do enough from a heterodox perspective. For example, there is a tendency to discuss hyperinflation in ways that allow readers to overestimate the probability that low levels of inflation will turn into run-away inflation. There are also insufficient efforts to dispel the notion that inflation seriously hurts most people's real wages.

Public opinion polls suggest that many people suffer from the fallacy of composition in assessing the impact of inflation. They believe that if inflation fell, their nominal wages (or prices if they are firms) would be little changed, while all other prices would fall, a mutually inconsistent outcome. When inflation occurs during a period of falling real wages, people tend to conflate the two phenomena. Even though the underlying problem is falling real wages, people blame inflation for the decline in their standard of living. Without inflation nominal wages would have fallen; with inflation, nominal wages fail to keep up with increases in the price level. Ending inflation will not increase real wages.

There can be some real costs to even moderate levels of inflation. Many, however, are trivial, like the alleged "shoe leather costs" of trying not to hold one's wealth in money very long in an inflationary environment. Some costs are more substantial, like arbitrary income transfers and increases in economic uncertainty. From a heterodox perspective, however, many of these real costs would be even higher if rising unemployment were the mechanism used for reducing inflation.[4]

The textbooks' tilt toward prioritizing fighting inflation over fighting unemployment is subtle but pervasive. It includes normalizing relatively high unemployment rates (5–6 percent) under standard uses of the NAIRU concept (see below). It is also reflected in the textbooks' simultaneous turn against using fiscal policy to stimulate aggregate demand[5] and recommendation that fighting inflation be the first priority of monetary policy. Although this stance still permits the Fed to use monetary policy to combat unemployment during serious recessions (when fears of inflation are very low), it restricts expansionary policy in most other contexts. It is a strategy consistent with a 95–100 percent laissez-faire vision of the economy. Heterodox economists urge policy makers to prioritize fighting unemployment whenever it exceeds 3–4 percent.

Heterodox economists tend to look more favorably on fiscal policy than the textbooks do. They urge consideration of a wider range of fiscal stimuli, especially the expanded use of public employment, including proposals for the government to act as an employer of last resort. Heterodox economists also favor higher levels of government spending for infrastructural projects, public education, child care, elder care, and environmental protection. They find revenue sharing at the state and local levels an attractive option for decentralizing fiscal policy's impacts.

Inflation

Many heterodox economists believe that it is often necessary to look at "distributional struggles" in the real sector in order to understand some of the underlying pressures that are responsible for inflation.[6] Two scenarios are especially important, price spirals kicked off by an increase in the costs of production (such as a surge in oil prices) and price spirals arising from wage-push pressures near full employment. Endnote 7 briefly explores the oil shock case.[7] We concentrate here on wage-push pressures.

In the wage-push case, falling unemployment leads to rising wages and inflationary pressures. This is due to two assumptions in many heterodox macro models: first, that wage rates are sensitive to workers' bargaining power, which depends partly on unemployment rates; and second, that many firms set prices by marking up average production costs by a fixed amount. Thus as the unemployment rate falls, inflationary pressures may increase.

Standard textbook theory recommends that the Fed respond to wage-push inflationary pressures by slowing the growth of the money supply. There are two rationales for this policy. The first rationale asserts that inflation is "always and everywhere" a monetary phenomenon. It is ultimately caused by an imbalance between the growth of the money supply and real output. It can always be curbed by slowing monetary growth. The second rationale is more ad hoc. It equates full employment to the highest level of employment that avoids wage-push pressures, calling the accompanying unemployment rate the "Non-Accelerating Inflation Rate of Unemployment," or NAIRU. It treats wage-push inflationary pressures as evidence of excess demand in the economy and recommends contractionary monetary policy. The spirit of the analysis is best captured by the normative title coined initially by Milton Friedman for the NAIRU, the "natural rate" of unemployment.

From the perspective of heterodox theory, this strategy accepts the need for socially unacceptable levels of unemployment and job insecurity in order to fight inflation. Economist Ellen Frank terms the Fed's willingness to throw people out of work in order to fight inflation "sado-monetarism" (E. Frank 2004, 123). To draw an imperfect analogy from academia, it would be as if colleges and universities decided the best way to respond to excess demand for popular courses was to have the classes meet at 7:00 A.M. This would probably keep enrollments down, but would be a clumsy way to solve the problem; so too with using unemployment and excess production capacity to fight inflationary pressures.

Heterodox economists insist on finding ways to contain inflationary pressures without relying on socially destructive rates of joblessness and labor market insecurity. The general goal is to find ways to ensure that wages grow at about the rate of productivity growth when labor markets tighten. Heterodox economists have explored several different mechanisms to accomplish this, including (1) "incomes policies" that use tax incentives and public opinion to mitigate price increases above productivity increases; (2) "pattern bargaining," which attempts to use major union and public-sector wage agreements to set a noninflationary benchmark for other wage and price increases; (3) the articulation of a new "social contract" with high levels of "social protections" (such as national health insurance, subsidized higher education, and job security guarantees) that make moderating wage demands at full employment a more palatable quid pro quo; and (4) expansion of participatory management and worker ownership of businesses (as a means of reducing wage/profit squeeze pressures).[8] Heterodox economists acknowledge that finding alternatives to economic contraction as a means of fighting inflation is difficult, but claim that is precisely why the subject deserves greater attention in the textbooks.

Financial Sector Regulation

Heterodox economists tend to recommend more regulatory oversight of the financial sector than usually considered in standard textbooks. This is partially due to heterodoxy's greater attention to the economic implications of uncertainty and the assumption of a more volatile and nonrational economic actor than *homo economicus*. The combination makes the potential for financial market crises much greater in heterodox than orthodox macro theory.

Heterodox economists, for example, anticipate periodic runs on banks or currencies, speculative bubbles and busts in asset markets, and domino effects from the collapse of overindebted consumers and firms. They recommend regulatory firewalls to reduce the spread and impact of related financial crises. Domestically, for example, heterodox economists tend to favor limitations on banks' lending practices to reduce risk taking (such as traditional restrictions on the lending options of savings and loan associations). Internationally, heterodox economists favor regulations that would curb the destabilizing effects of short-term international capital flows.

Heterodox economists also support increased regulation of the financial sector for equity reasons. They tend to favor limitations on international capital mobility in order to protect the capacity of national governments to pursue redistributive economic policies. Unrestricted capital mobility enhances the bargaining power of the owners of financial wealth. It permits them to threaten capital flight in response to progressive income taxes, inheritance taxes, pollution taxes, and profit squeeze pressures near full employment. Carefully designed and internationally coordinated barriers to capital flight may be able to reduce this bargaining power.

Heterodox economists also draw attention to the disproportionate influence that financial interests have domestically over the governance of the Fed, and, by extension, over monetary policy (especially over the selection of the district bank presidents who sit on the Open Market Committee). Heterodox economists have proposed reforms that would democratize the governance of monetary policy and criticize the textbooks for truncating debates over the governance of the Fed.

Globalization

As noted above the textbooks strongly promote unregulated trade and unrestricted capital mobility. Heterodoxy dissents, finding that the global economy needs a system of social governance even more than domestic economies do in order to best meet human needs. Heterodox economists favor rules for international trade that reduce the negative consequences of capital mobility and maintain individual governments' ability to redistribute income and wealth, maintain health and safety standards in the workplace, maintain stable communities, and pursue other societal objectives, such as high-road labor policies.

Heterodox economists challenge the implication in many textbooks that countries with the most laissez-faire-oriented trade relations have grown the most rapidly. Heterodox authors find, instead, that most successful trading countries, such as the Asian tigers, have had partially state-directed interactions with the world economy. Heterodox economists similarly find that unregulated short-term capital flows have caused many serious financial crises in recent years that have harmed real-sector growth. Heterodox economists do not oppose the expansion of world trade, but they do oppose policies that would allow increased world trade to serve as a Trojan horse for imposing laissez-faire economic policies around the globe.

HETERODOX EXPANSION OF POLICY AGENDAS

Introduction

As we have noted many times, heterodox economists measure macroeconomic outcomes with broader indices than GDP statistics. To some extent this outlook reflects the holist methodology of many heterodox economists. This methodology links macroeconomic outcomes to numerous sociopolitical phenomena, such as the level of social inequality, environmental sustainability, the viability of democratic politics, and the health of nonmarket sectors of the economy, like the household. We have termed the impacts of economic phenomena on these social and cultural outcomes meta-externalities. Heterodox economics recommends that economic theory and economic policy analyze and respond to meta-externalities. We explore the implications of this recommendation with respect to industrial policy below.

Industrial Policy

Industrial policy refers to a wide range of government initiatives aimed at channeling economic activity in targeted directions. Potential policies include:

- government spending for research and development and for infrastructural investments for industries with positive meta-externalities (such as high-tech manufacturing industries with good blue-collar jobs or family farms that preserve local communities)
- government subsidies and tax incentives for industries with positive meta-externalities (such as government tax aid to higher education)
- trade policies that seek to capture path-dependent economies of scale and other benefits for industries with positive meta-externalities
- policies that channel credit toward outcomes with positive meta-externalities (such as lending restrictions and asset-based reserve requirements that tilt credit to the housing industry, due to the meta-externalities believed to be associated with home ownership).

Standard macroeconomics textbooks give relatively little attention to debates over industrial policy. The books' subtexts, however, are generally critical of government-influenced economic development and often point out the alleged failures of such projects in the third world, the former Soviet Union, and, more recently, Japan. Heterodox economists paint a much more complicated picture of the history of industrial policy. They find many important successes in Japanese, U.S., and South Korean history, as well as some notable failures. Heterodox economists generally urge expanded use of industrial policy to orient the economy in desirable directions.

STRUCTURALIST MACROECONOMICS: MACRO REGIMES AND MACRO POLICY

Most heterodox macro economists believe that market outcomes cannot be fully explained by starting with isolated individual tastes and preferences and aggregating them into supply-and-demand curves in all input and output markets. This is because individual behaviors build on or presuppose the larger macro context they participate in and help reproduce. Thus macro causality has to be studied as an interactive process between the logic of an institutional and expectational context and individual strategies pursued within that context. Key parts of the larger context involve institutional mechanisms to reduce uncertainty and defuse potentially disruptive tensions between capital and labor. The shape of these institutions varies over time, inevitably stamping every period's macroeconomic outcomes with the implications of its institutional arrangements.

While occasionally noting the importance of institutional variables, textbook macro models tend to take contextual phenomena as given. Macro outcomes are conceived of as "micro founded." Little attention is given to "macro logics." Readers are led to ignore the question of where institutions and most expectations come from or to imagine that institutions evolve naturally in response to isolated market decisions. This approach differs sharply from heterodox theory, which stresses the ability of private-sector initiatives and public policy to influence macro outcomes by shaping macroeconomic institutional contexts.

This emphasis has led heterodox theorists to develop "structuralist" models of the economy. These models tie macro outcomes to sociopolitical phenomena, such as the distribution of income in a society, the degree of government support for full employment, and the inherited social conventions used by people for responding to uncertainty. This approach highlights the importance of government policies in constructing macro development paths and puts debates over these policies at the center of macro policy making.

Heterodox economists tend to think about institutional-expectational phenomena in systemic terms, that is, they tend to look for clusters of phenomena that interactively fit together to define a "macro regime." In chapters 13 and 15 we illustrated this idea by using the concept of Social Structures of Accumulation (SSAs) to analyze the different macro logics (or macro regimes) organizing U.S. macroeconomic activity in the second half of the twentieth century. Heterodox economists see one of the major tasks facing macro policy makers to be the construction of a new egalitarian, "high-road" macro development path.

THREADS: DISTRIBUTIONAL ISSUES

We close the chapter with our usual threads, beginning with distribution. As we have frequently noted, heterodox economists tend to give greater attention to distributional issues and a higher policy priority to reducing inequality than most (though not all) neoclassical economists do. This attention reflects heterodox economists' holist methodology, rejection of *homo economicus,* and willingness to raise ethical issues in economic analysis.

Heterodox economists tend to be more comfortable than neoclassical economists with raising ethical issues in economics classes. This is partly due to heterodoxy's rejection of the rhetorical strategy used by many neoclassical economists to increase belief in economic theory and gain social prestige for economists. This strategy has been to represent economics as a technocratic discipline that is similar in practice to engineering and similar in theory to physics.

Standard texts, for example, commonly refer to the "law of supply and demand" as if they were discussing the "law of gravity." For the most part, textbooks are written in the passive voice. This means that the claims made transcend the author. They are not matters of personal or paradigmatic judgment. They are matters of scientific truth. Raising ethical questions reminds readers that we are dealing with different entities from inanimate objects and that there is a human author behind the text. This can invite debate.

Interestingly, despite the textbooks' concern for maximizing the total utility produced by an economy and the texts' assumption of the declining marginal utility of money (i.e., the assumption that the marginal utility of an extra dollar of income falls as people gain higher incomes), there is minimal discussion of the possibility that more equal distributions of income might increase aggregate utility. Instead the textbooks stress the impossibility of "scientifically" making interpersonal utility comparisons. Heterodox economists believe that meaningful discussions, even if not "scientific" in the narrowest sense of the term, can and should be offered about the implications of different income distributions for national well-being.

Standard macro textbooks' reticence on distributional issues can appear to endorse the status quo, if by nothing else than by signaling students that equity issues are not worth attending to. Heterodoxy's focus on the surge in economic inequality over the last thirty years in the United States signals students that this is a major dimension of macroeconomic performance.

Heterodoxy's holist, as opposed to methodologically individualistic, methodology also contributes to heterodox economists' heightened attention to distributional issues. Holism encourages economists to look for connections between levels of economic equality and other societal outcomes, such as the health of the public schools or the vitality of democratic political institutions. Research on these linkages suggests that more equal economic outcomes can generate "social capital" by reinforcing the bonds of community, reciprocity, trust, and cooperation.[9] Besides being valuable in themselves, these attributes can increase economic efficiency by lowering the "transaction costs" of market exchange, for example, by lowering the amount of resources used to measure and monitor everyone's fulfillment of expected obligations (see, for example, Epstein and Gintis 1995, section V). A more equal, honest, and cooperative society, can, for example, produce goods in the workplace with fewer supervisors, coordinate exchange with fewer lawyers, run retail stores with lower surveillance costs, and adopt new technologies with less resistance from those disadvantaged by the innovation in the short run.[10]

Heterodoxy's rejection of *homo economicus* also recommends attention to distributional issues and raises the likelihood of positive payoffs to redistributive macro policies. The textbooks' "economic man" is an isolated, rational maximizer who gets utility from privately consuming goods and services. Heterodoxy's "socioeconomic person" is an interdependent individual with empathy, a potential interest in reciprocity and altruism, and a capacity for envy and positional competition. This view of economic agents invites exploration of egalitarian initiatives, such as more progressive taxation and the use of luxury taxes to reduce the waste of positional competition.

In sum, heterodox theory recommends that macro texts give greater attention to the feasibility of an egalitarian "macro regime." Among the policy options that might be discussed are:

1. Aggressive monetary and fiscal policies to promote genuine full employment (3–4 percent unemployment) accompanied by innovative anti-inflation policies.
2. Industrial policies that orient government R&D spending, tax breaks, regulatory incentives, credit assistance, and so on toward industries with egalitarian implications.
3. Labor market policies that would raise the minimum wage, facilitate unionization, and encourage firms to adopt high-road labor strategies. Among the latter initiatives would be macroeconomic policies aimed at keeping recessions short and shallow and tax policies that rewarded businesses for investing in employee training.
4. Public policies to regenerate social capital and egalitarian social norms, such as expanded support for public education and community schools, and expanded provision of tax-supported free goods, such as public libraries, public parks, local playgrounds, and civic events.
5. Public policies to increase the economic assets of disadvantaged groups, such as land redistribution (especially in third world economies) and increased public spending for education from preschool through university and job training.
6. A national health insurance system and retention of progressive social security mechanisms that engender a popular sense of shared futures.
7. Progressive taxation and an expanded social safety net.
8. Restrictions on capital mobility.

THREADS: GENDER ISSUES

General Inequality

Feminist economists share heterodoxy's criticism of textbook policy discussions for giving insufficient attention to distributional issues.

Gendered Economic Experience

Feminist and other heterodox economists often favor disaggregating macroeconomic outcomes to ensure that adequate attention is given to the distinctive experiences of women in the economy (see for example Himmelweit 2002). This frequently involves giving greater attention to macroeconomic policies that address (1) gender discrimination; (2) the household, voluntary, and informal sectors of the economy; (3) "secondary" labor markets (such as those organizing part-time employment); and (4) caring labor anywhere in the economy.

For example, heterodox economists often urge greater attention in the textbooks to policy debates over universal preschool funding, child care subsidies, public support for female-headed families (especially those in poverty), and the nurturing of stable communities to reinforce the informal networks of neighborhood child care. The activist policy recommendations of feminist economists represent a heterodox version of supply-side economics that would increase human (rather than physical) capital on the supply side of the economy.

All GDP Is Not Created Equal

Heterodox and feminist economists offer a second reason for greater attention to economic policies affecting elder and child care. Unlike textbook economics, which as a matter of principle treats all GDP as of equal value, many heterodox analyses take a "human needs" approach and prioritize the production of certain goods and services over others. From this perspective both the measurement of and delivery of "caring services" and the development of human capacities (which includes but is not limited to economic notions of human capital) need a higher priority in the textbooks and public policy.[11] Possible policy initiatives include expanded public provision of caring services, public subsidies for caring labor, universal health insurance, and general incentives for the development of social norms and institutional arrangements (such as parental leaves) that promote caring practices. From a gendered and feminist perspective, these concerns are macro concerns, as they assess and relate to the aggregate performance of the economy, albeit using a different metric than GDP.

THREADS: ENVIRONMENTAL ISSUES

Sustainability

Heterodox economists urge greater attention to environmental and sustainability issues in discussions of macro policy. Like many neoclassical economists, they support expanded efforts by the Department of Commerce to include resource depletion and environmental outcomes in the National Income and Product Accounts (GDP statistics). Heterodox economists also urge greater discussion of the plusses *and minuses* of slowing down the "material throughput" of the economy. Among potential policies that could slow down materials use are limitations on resource extraction from public lands, a "natural capital depletion" tax on the consumption of exhaustible resources, and increased research funding for renewable materials technologies (financed, perhaps, by the tax just cited, as recommended by the principle of weak sustainability).

As we have frequently noted, two of the distinctive aspects of heterodox economics are its holist methodology and its interest in and support for forms of economic planning. Holism causes heterodox economists to look for more underlying causes of environmental stress (such as the pressures for consumerism created by advertising) than are explored in neoclassical theory. Heterodoxy's interest in economic planning recommends policies that would shift the economy toward development paths with lower environmental burdens.

More heterodox than neoclassical economists, for example, recommend that governments explore how economic policies can reduce positional competition and competitive consumption. They suspect that social policies, such as higher taxes on luxury goods and advertising, greater government provision of free goods (such as public beaches), and incentives for shorter work weeks, might reduce pressures for competitive consumption and its attendant environmental burdens.

Heterodox economists emphasize that public policy can influence the broad planning contexts, expectations, and assumptions that shape decentralized economic decision making. If it were clear, for example, that public policy was going to encourage reductions in materials throughput, numerous industries would begin to explore ways that they might better compete in such an environment.

Equity and the Environment

As noted in chapter 16, heterodox economists see important links between distributional and environmental issues. They find that inequality leads in subtle ways to pressures for higher consumption

Table 17.1

Competing Macro Policy Metaphors

Textbook Metaphor	Heterodox Alternative
Macro policy as government intervention in the economy	Macro policy as social governance of the economy
Macro policy making as an engineering enterprise	Macro policy making as a political enterprise
Long-run general equilibrium anchors	Path-dependent outcomes
Narrowing policy differences	Persisting policy differences
Emerging GE-Keynesian consensus	Neoclassical/heterodox divide
GDP yardsticks	Multidimensional metrics
All GDP dollars are equal	All GDP dollars are not equal
Market optimalities	Meta-externalities
Equity/efficiency tradeoffs	Equity/efficiency complementarities
Inflation as always a monetary phenomenon	Inflation as sometimes a shadow of distributional conflict
Fed chairs as superheroes (or at least tough-minded fathers)	Sado-monetarism
Relatively stable financial markets	Casinos and animal spirits
The foolishness of the "command economy"	Benefits of democratic planning
Genderless outcomes	Gendered outcomes
The gains from trade	The risks of trade
Free trade	Fair trade
TINA (There Is No Alternative)	Macro regimes

and increased stress on the environment and resource stocks. They anticipate that more egalitarian macroeconomic policies will indirectly protect the environment. They also expect that increased gender equity will tend to reduce population growth and its pressures on the environment.

Trade and the Environment

Heterodox economists tend to urge stronger international environmental standards in order to reduce the risks of a global "race to the bottom" in environmental protection.

COMPETING METAPHORS

The comparisons in Table 17.1 juxtapose textbook and heterodox metaphors for thinking about macro policy.

IN THEIR OWN WORDS

We conclude this chapter with a few quotes on the aims of macro policy from heterodox perspectives.

> Neoclassical economists look at the economy as something external with a fixed structure and so focus on the supply-side and on trying to get prices right. In contrast, for Post

Keynesians, public policy can shape the structure of the economy and future economic performance through monetary and fiscal policies that can affect potential rates of economic growth. The openness and dynamic nature of the Post Keynesian macroeconomic model also opens the door for a state that can promote growth by its ability to affect fundamental economic relationships.

—Richard Holt and Steven Pressman (2003, 182)

The cornerstone of an alternative policy approach in the United States . . . is to promote full employment at decent wages [p. 177]. . . .

There is no question that [these] programs . . . need to take account of the problems associated with inflation [p. 186]. . . .

[But] if workers were living within a framework of basic social protections . . . they should then be much more amenable to moderating their wage demands in situations where inflationary pressures threatened prospects for economic stability and growth.

—Robert Pollin (2003, 188)

[A] sound long-term macroeconomic strategy should contribute at least to the macroeconomic objectives of assuring employment opportunities for everyone and promoting high rates of environmentally sustainable productivity growth in ways which directly foster the broader social goals of greater equity and greater democracy.

—David Gordon (1995, 335)

STUDY QUESTIONS

Review Questions

1. What are the subtexts of textbook and heterodox economics, according to heterodox economics?
2. Why do heterodox economists feel that the range of policy debate in introductory macroeconomics textbooks is relatively narrow? What would heterodox economists add to this debate?
3. Heterodox economists argue that the textbooks soften Keynesian claims. What do they mean by this?
4. From a heterodox perspective, why has the shift from short- to long-run analysis in many introductory textbooks tended to reinforce laissez-faire macroeconomic policy recommendations?
5. What are the major differences between textbook and heterodox discussions of policy debates over inflation? What do heterodox economists mean by "sado-monetarism?"
6. What are the major differences between textbook and heterodox discussions of policy debates over financial sector regulation?
7. Heterodox economists tend to raise a broader list of issues for macro policy than highlighted in the textbooks. Identify some of these extra issues and explain why the logic of heterodox paradigms recommends more attention to them than usually found in neoclassical textbooks.
8. What are the major differences between heterodox and textbook discussions of macro policy debates about distributional issues? In what ways do these differences illustrate basic methodological differences between orthodox and heterodox economic analysis? What kind of distributional policies do heterodox economists tend to favor?

9.   Compare and contrast textbook and heterodox attitudes toward industrial policy.
10.   What do heterodox economists mean by the term *macro regimes*? How do some heterodox economists use the concept of macro regimes to organize their approach to macro policy?
11.   What are the major differences between textbook and heterodox discussions of international macro policy?
12.   How do you think macroeconomic policy should address concerns about economic sustainability? What do you think are the strongest and weakest aspects of heterodox thinking about sustainability?

Discussion Questions

1.   What do *you* think the major objectives should be for macroeconomic policy? Defend your answer from criticisms by textbook and/or heterodox economists.
2.   From a heterodox perspective, compare and contrast the main policy recommendations of textbook and heterodox economics. Discuss how these recommendations reflect the distinctive frameworks each uses to think about the macro economy.
3.   Juxtapose three metaphors from textbook and heterodox economics and explain how the contrast illustrates some of the basic differences between the two approaches to economic theory.

NOTES

1. See Mayer (1993) for an interesting discussion of the rhetorical treatment of the "time inconsistency" problem in monetary policy. Mayer demonstrates that the turn against discretionary monetary policy based on game theory had little empirical content (63–65).

2. This can be modeled within the AS-AD framework as a backward shift of the short-run AS curve.

3. The laissez-faire spirit behind these proposals is echoed in calls for a constitutional amendment requiring a balanced federal budget. This requirement would prevent policy makers from using tax and spending policies to manage the level of aggregate demand in the economy.

4. See E. Frank 2004, chapter 4, for a good heterodox discussion of inflation myths.

5. In recent years the textbooks have increasingly highlighted problems with implementing fiscal policy, citing, for example, potentially long lead times to pass legislation; misguided tax and spending decisions (based on political rather than economic criteria); "crowding out" (due to expansionary policy's effect on interest rates); and, more recently, concerns about huge government deficits. The textbooks also frequently imply that public spending is inherently less valuable than private spending. Many different reasons are casually offered for this conclusion, including claims that people behave less rationally in political contexts than market contexts, and the fact that public expenses are often financed by taxation, which can dull economic incentives. Contrary arguments about the irrationality of consumer behavior and the possibility that people reflect on issues more deeply when making political as opposed to market decisions are given less attention.

6. Heterodox economists agree that inflation could be caused by the Fed unintentionally increasing the money supply faster than the growth of output in the real sector, as suggested by GE theory. Heterodox economists also agree that stagflation could result from efforts by the Fed to quickly curb inflation, as suggested by NK theory. But, more often than not, heterodox economists want to push the analysis of inflation into deeper waters. They want to look for and address the "real-sector" origin of pricing pressures.

7. Heterodox economists share NK reservations about automatically responding to input cost shocks (like an oil price increase) with aggressive contractions of the monetary supply. Heterodox macro models reject the common textbook assumption of perfect competition. Firms in oligopoly markets are thought to be able to pass on a higher percentage of input cost increases (such as oil price increases) to customers than is implied in typical textbook models. The result can be stagflation, whereby cost shocks cause rising prices and unsold goods in some industries, with cost increases persisting despite excess supply. (In NK models this is equivalent to assuming a backward-shifting and sticky short-run AS curve.)

Heterodox economists warn that combating cost-push inflation is a tricky matter. This is due to the need to prevent sticky prices and anti-inflation policies from disrupting business and consumer confidence and causing a crisis in aggregate demand. This fear is downplayed in the textbooks.

8. When similar concerns are raised in the textbooks about inflationary pressures near full employment the policy suggestions tend toward laissez-faire changes that would reduce the social safety net, such as lowering unemployment insurance and reducing social spending.

9. In neoclassical economics the term *social capital* is sometimes used to refer to the intangible cultural assets a society has that facilitate economic activity and promote individual well-being. Because of the methodological individualism of neoclassical theory, the concept has an ad hoc quality. Every now and then it is appealed to explain some phenomenon (such as the failure of the former Soviet Union to make a successful transition to capitalism), but since it requires a holist sense of how a society reproduces itself, the concept is underdeveloped in neoclassical analysis. It is sometimes mentioned in discussions of the "transaction costs" involved with market activity, but it is not given much attention in macro texts.

10. Many heterodox economists also expect more equal income distributions to reduce unemployment. This is because they expect stronger aggregate demand to accompany increased income equality due to the relatively low marginal propensity to consume among high-income groups.

These economists also include distributional variables (such as the share of national income going to different income deciles or the split of national income between labor and property income) in macroeconomic forecasting models. This strategy differs from that of typical textbook macro models, which abstract from distributional issues by assuming that the rich and the poor consume and save the same percentages of their income. Many advanced neoclassical models make similar assumptions by working with "representative agents," who are neither rich nor poor.

11. There are many ways to "justify" weighting goods and services related to child care at higher values than the market price generated by parents' and other overseers' willingness to pay. Using the language of neoclassical theory, feminist economist Nancy Folbre has suggested treating aspects of child care as public goods, from which everyone benefits without paying "user fees." Folbre and others have written about the social capital produced by good child care. We have used the term *positive meta-externalities* to describe the beneficial sociocultural effects associated with some economic practices. Market valuation can also be challenged by appealing to the declining marginal utility of money (which implies that necessities have higher use values than luxuries), the irrationalities of positional competition (which may draw monies away from child care), or cultural notions of value that contradict market orderings. The market may, for example, bias "demand" toward goods amenable to marketing campaigns by large-scale organizations. This may lead to higher expenditures for manufactured toys than after-school care providers. For a highly accessible article on feminist economics' thinking about child and other caregiving services see Folbre 1998. For a good discussion of "family policy issues" see *Feminist Economics* 6(1), special issue on children and family policy, March 2000.

18

CONCLUSION: RETHINKING MACROECONOMICS

Heterodox Versus Textbook Economics

The purpose of studying economics is not to acquire a set of ready-made answers to economic questions, but to learn how to avoid being bedeviled by economists.
—Joan Robinson (1955, 30)

INTRODUCTION

This chapter reviews the debate between textbook and heterodox macroeconomics, giving each side the opportunity to respond to the other. The last part of the chapter explores where to look in the library and on the web for additional information about heterodox economics. Neoclassical economic theory offers a formidable framework for thinking about macroeconomic events. Even if one finds its view of the economy lacking, it is important to understand this perspective, as it frames the thinking of most economists. Hence we begin with a review of textbook macroeconomics.

TEXTBOOK MACROECONOMICS

Textbook economics presents itself as *the* science of economics, with an equivalent ability to command belief to a physics textbook. The textbooks' subtext is that markets usually produce optimal outcomes. The textbooks' definition of economic success is maximizing economic efficiency and economic growth. Besides maximizing consumer satisfaction by maximizing consumer purchasing power, economic growth is expected to eliminate poverty, take the sting out of inequality, solve the population problem, provide the resources necessary to protect the environment, and provide the social basis for democracy and world peace.

The government's main economic task according to the textbooks is to provide a framework for market activity to take place. Governments do this primarily by defining and enforcing property rights, by managing the money supply, and by filling in for markets in areas where the conditions necessary for efficient exchange break down, as in the case of negative externalities, such as pollution.

The textbooks acknowledge that markets left to themselves may generate undesirable levels of inequality, justifying government redistributive efforts. The textbooks suggest that there is a trade-off between more equal economic outcomes and the overall level of economic output. The more equal the pieces of the pie, the smaller the size of the pie. The texts argue that the proper role for economists is to study the cause and effect of inequality (a positive question), recognizing that decisions about what is an acceptable level of inequality involve moral judgments (a normative question), which are outside the purview of economics. Most textbooks imply, however, that the range of inequality in the United States over the last fifty years provides a reasonable estimate of acceptable levels of inequality.

Markets are portrayed as basically self-regulating. Movements away from equilibrium automatically create pressures to return to equilibrium. There is modest debate in the textbooks over how fast markets correct themselves. The Neo-Keynesians argue that careful government monetary and fiscal policy can sometimes accelerate the market's return to full employment. General equilibrium (GE) or classical economists doubt that policy makers can improve on the market.

Although the textbooks acknowledge that markets make errors, their track record is generally portrayed as far superior to government efforts at economic planning. Industrial policy, credit channeling, protectionism, and other attempts by governments to shape economic development are either ignored or treated very skeptically in the texts.

Although there are some references to the importance of social institutions in determining macroeconomic outcomes, there is relatively little exploration of the institutional requirements or choices facing capitalist economies. Good institutions tend to be ones that mesh seamlessly with "free markets." Although the process is never explored explicitly, textbooks often hint that good institutions emerge naturally from routine market dynamics, such as well-ordered stock exchanges, innovative financial assets, or the modern multinational corporation.

Economic policy making tends to be treated as a problem of economic engineering. There are few political battles where the preferred policies depend on whose interest is being protected. There is little attention in the textbooks to the role of political and economic power in making macro policy decisions. Macro issues are treated as technical questions where the right policy benefits everyone, rather than political questions that have distributional implications. The Fed is portrayed as an institution governed by apolitical technical experts who design monetary policy to promote the general welfare.

Although many of the above claims are qualified by briefly noting exceptions and complexities, there is a tendency to imply that more advanced discussion would not alter the basic argument.

The spirit of the textbooks is captured by their approach to globalization. The dominant message is that policy makers should let the market work. Free trade and free capital mobility are portrayed as powerful mechanisms for maximizing global economic efficiency and global economic growth. Furthermore, even if policy makers did have doubts about the potential impacts of free trade and unlimited capital mobility on their countries, there would not be anything they could productively do about it. There Is No Alternative (TINA), the textbooks argue, to deferring to the world market.

From a heterodox perspective, the textbooks' account is very paradigmatic; that is, it is highly dependent on seeing the world through a particular lens. Although it remains a plausible system of explanation, textbook economics is nevertheless very contestable.

HETERODOX MACROECONOMICS

Heterodox economics stresses the paradigmatic nature of all economic theory and urges students to think about the basic methodological assumptions and subtexts underlying different paradigms. Heterodox analysis both expands the questions asked in textbook macroeconomics and offers different answers to familiar questions.

The subtext of heterodox macroeconomics is that capitalist economies need strong systems of social governance in order to meet human needs. Heterodox economists accuse textbook economics of assuming what it claims to have proved (the wisdom of 95–100 percent laissez-faire economic policies) by the way it goes about doing economic analysis.

Heterodox economics challenges the basic methodology of textbook economics. For example, heterodox economics rejects methodological individualism in favor of holism, replaces "rational economic man" with a more complicated and interconnected human psychology, and jettisons the assumptions of perfect information and perfect competition. As a result of these and other methodological differences with neoclassical economics, heterodoxy denies market outcomes the naturalness and automatic optimality they enjoy in the textbooks.

The key task for macro policy, from a heterodox perspective, is to create a desirable institutional and expectational context for macro choices. The goals of heterodox macro policy are therefore broader than maximizing GDP and include promoting "high-road" labor policies, more equal economic and social outcomes, environmental sustainability, and other positive meta-externalities. Included within the latter category would be nurturing the next generation, maintaining viable communities, and increasing social capital. In other words, heterodox economists see the macro economy as part of a larger reproducing social whole and want to promote macro development paths that reflect democratically chosen goals. Textbook economics claims that markets automatically do this; heterodox economists disagree.

From a heterodox perspective, textbook economics masks the inherent political implications of its analysis, claiming an apolitical status that does not accurately reflect the consequences of its implementation. That is, it portrays as "natural" aspects of the economy that could be changed, endowing the status quo with a necessity it does not have.

Besides altering the goals and topics addressed by macroeconomics, heterodox economics also offers a different take on familiar subjects. For example, heterodoxy's heightened attention to the implications of uncertainty leads to different rationales for insufficient aggregate demand and voluntary unemployment from those highlighted in the textbooks. Rejection of the assumption of perfect information also leads to a different view of the monetary sector. The heterodox perspective highlights the potential for speculative manias, financial panics, and liquidity crises. Heterodoxy's demand for institutional detail (especially its attention to the implications of the large corporation) also undermines the textbooks' general equilibrium picture of the economy, which usually assumes perfect competition among countless small firms.

In sum, heterodox economics moves away from the ideal world of general equilibrium theory. In doing so it opens up a much larger role for government policy.

TEXTBOOK RESPONSES TO HETERODOX CRITIQUES

Although heterodox economics raises many different kinds of objections to different parts of textbook economics, defenders of textbook economics tend to have four basic responses to most criticisms. These responses merit careful consideration. They are summarized below, with heterodox rejoinders offered in the next section.

(1) Identification of Neoclassical Economics with Science, Mathematics, and Empirical Verification

Neoclassical economists often respond to epistemological challenges (that is, to claims that neoclassical theory represents a paradigm rather than a universal approach to economics) by claiming that their critics reject the notion of science. From the neoclassical perspective, there are accurate and inaccurate economic theories, rather than competing paradigms. From this perspective, the choice is between thinking about economic knowledge as a science (analogous to the laws of nature presented in a physics textbook), or reducing economics to the level of literature, where knowledge is a matter of opinion.

The defenders of neoclassical theory celebrate the use of mathematics as a language of clarity that forces otherwise hidden assumptions into the open and allows discovery of uncontestable truths. They criticize heterodox economics for often failing to utilize psychological theories or institutional analyses that can be expressed in simple mathematical terms. They also claim that heterodox economics lacks serious empirical support. Heterodoxy may tell some good stories, they argue, but in contrast with neoclassical economics, heterodox accounts lack empirically testable hypotheses.

(2) Rejection of Heterodox Critiques as Attacks on a Straw Man

The textbooks' defenders argue that all theories must simplify reality, especially at the introductory level. The key question is, what are legitimate simplifications? What are the fundamental ideas that need to be conveyed? The common textbook assumptions of perfect competition, perfect information, and *homo economicus* are legitimate simplifications, they suggest, because they permit more fundamental ideas, such as market optimality and the resilience of competition, to be communicated.

The textbooks' defenders also argue that it is impossible at the introductory level to seriously address most of the issues raised in heterodox critiques. They are left out of the textbooks not because discussion would threaten ideological subtexts, as heterodox economists imply, but because they cannot be dealt with adequately at an introductory level. The textbooks usually assume markets with countless small firms and perfect competition, for example, because modeling competition in markets with a few firms is extremely complicated. When more advanced analyses are performed, however, the neoclassicals claim that most of the important conclusions derived from simpler models are still valid.

Defenders of the textbooks buttress their claims by pointing out that the limitations of introductory analysis are duly noted in the textbooks, even if they cannot be explored. For example, the limitations of GDP as a measure of economic welfare are acknowledged. The concept of GDP is nevertheless highlighted as a welfare measure in introductory courses, they argue, because ideal measures of economic well-being are likely to be correlated with GDP. Similar arguments are made about the treatment of uncertainty and other phenomena highlighted by heterodoxy. In short, heterodox critiques of introductory textbooks are portrayed as attacks on a straw man.

(3) The Long-Run Anchor of General Equilibrium

Defenders of neoclassical theory tend to argue that many heterodox phenomena are best understood as short-run phenomena, whose import need not be addressed in introductory courses. For example, in the short run people may rely on rules of thumb and social conventions for making some decisions rather than rationally calculating the costs and benefits of different actions. In the long run, however, these conventions themselves change in ways that conform behavior to the logic of neoclassical models. It is thus appropriate for the textbooks to give little attention to social conventions in explaining important economic outcomes. In the long run, general equilibrium values anchor the economy, and it is the primary task of introductory courses to explain the nature and implications of this anchor.

(4) The "Relative Optimality" of Market Outcomes

While acknowledging that markets have their blemishes, neoclassical economists argue that heterodoxy gives too little attention to "government failures." Virtually all of the problems with market mechanisms identified by heterodoxy, such as those caused by uncertainty or concentrations of power, accompany the public policy initiatives recommended by heterodox economists. For example, why should government policy makers in the Fed or on the Council of Economic Advisers be better able to address uncertainty than participants in the economy? Why should the Fed realize that stocks are "overvalued" before the market does? Why should the government be better able to pick winning industries for the economy than the private sector?

One need not believe that the market has perfect information, they point out, in order to recommend relatively laissez-faire macro policy. All that is necessary is the belief that the government has no better handle on the situation than market participants do. Because of the spur of self-interest and hands-on knowledge of concrete situations, it is reasonable to expect that market decision makers will do better than government functionaries in addressing phenomena like uncertainty.

As to meta-externalities, defenders of the laissez-faire flavor of economic orthodoxy argue that we simply do not know what the unintended consequences are of economic policies. Attempting to address them is a Trojan horse for the imposition of authoritarian or special-interest policies on everyone else.[1]

Finally, neoclassical economists criticize heterodox policy recommendations for being utopian. Whatever their flaws, you cannot repeal the laws of the market, they argue, any more than you can repeal the laws of nature. Similarly, you cannot repeal the law of supply and demand, alter the existence of a NAIRU, or even alter very much the distribution of income without seriously disrupting the economy. Heterodox claims that government policy can reconstruct macro contexts are simply unrealistic. Human nature is much more "hard wired" than heterodoxy seems to imply; social capital is more exogenous; and the market is more uncontrollable than heterodox theory suggests. As in the old science fiction movies where the mad scientist meets his end for tampering with God's domain, neoclassical economists warn heterodox theorists to leave the market alone.

HETERODOX REJOINDERS

(1) Paradigmatic Nature of Knowledge

Heterodox economists criticize opponents of paradigmatic theories of economics for oversimplifying the nature of economic inquiry and utilizing theories of knowledge that have largely been rejected in philosophy for decades.[2] To argue that knowledge is paradigmatic does not reduce economic argument to random opinion or imply the absence of criteria to distinguish good from bad arguments. Asserting a paradigmatic theory of knowledge does imply, however, that there could be more than one system of explanation that meets the rigorous criteria of good arguments.

It is true that paradigmatic theories of knowledge offer no automatic criteria for choosing among competing paradigms. This indeterminacy poses an intellectual dilemma, but it reflects the nature of knowledge, rather than a weakness of heterodox theory. The proper teaching strategy is to present competing paradigms as fairly as possible, rather than to pick a single paradigm, as most neoclassical textbooks do, and present it as economics.

Heterodox economists defend their use of diverse modes of inquiry by noting that all economic paradigms use a wider range of reasoning techniques than that formally approved by textbook economics. Neoclassical theorists imply that all economic argument must follow the scientific method used in physics, whereby hypotheses are deduced logically from axiomatic principles and then tested experimentally. This is a noble aspiration. In practice, however, controlled experiments for major propositions in economics are impossible. Neoclassical economists themselves do not and could not live up to the rules of argumentation they attack other paradigms for not adopting.[3]

Heterodox economists also reject neoclassical demands that economic argument revolve around simple mathematical models, criticizing neoclassical theory for elevating a technique of inquiry over the substance of inquiry. Although heterodoxy finds mathematical argument attractive when situations permit its use, it does not limit economic inquiry to those questions that can be posed and answered in mathematical terms. Heterodox economists unapologetically urge that economic argument use a broad range of deliberative techniques to answer economic questions, including introspection, empathy, interviews, detailed case studies, reasoning by analogy, statistical and econometric analysis, and simulation.

(2) Fair Target or Straw Man?

Heterodox economists reject the claim that their criticisms of neoclassical analysis are either already explored in introductory textbooks or because of their complexity deferred to upper-level classes, where they are fully rebutted. From a heterodox perspective, most heterodox concerns are either seriously neglected or treated superficially with "note but ignore" qualifiers in introductory textbooks. You can judge for yourself whether this is a fair description of the treatment of heterodox ideas in your text.

Heterodox economists maintain that heterodox concerns, such as the potential for uncertainty to cause aggregate demand problems, can be addressed at an introductory level. The absence of serious engagement with heterodox ideas in neoclassical textbooks is due to paradigmatic decisions about what is important to discuss in introductory courses, rather than pedagogical judgments about what is possible to discuss with introductory students.

Heterodox economists also find continuing inattention to heterodox ideas in upper-level classes. You might ask your friends who have taken these classes whether the heterodox ideas you encountered this term (topics such as holism, positional competition, the meaning of economic well-being, the determination of tastes and preferences, the impact of fundamental uncertainty on aggregate demand, the special influence of financial interests on Federal Reserve policy, etc.) are seriously addressed in more advanced classes. I think you will find that they are largely ignored there as well. The treatment of heterodox ideas in introductory textbooks and courses is fairly representative of their treatment in neoclassical theory as a whole. Introductory textbooks are a worthy adversary.

Heterodox economists are especially troubled by introductory textbooks' assertion of laissez-faire policy conclusions based on models that involve limited definitions of economic and social well-being and unrealistic assumptions (such as perfect information and perfect competition). Defenders of laissez-faire policies do have rationales for their conclusions that can be argued in more realistic contexts. These rationales, however, rest on contestable theories of human nature and human social organization, value judgments, and other factors quite different from the mathematical claims of Pareto optimality. These claims deserve to be honestly debated.

(3) Long-Run Anchors or Floating Hypotheticals?

Heterodox theory rejects the textbook image of hypothetical GE outcomes as an inert anchor for actual market outcomes.[4] The heterodox picture of macroeconomic evolution asserts a more dynamic and path-dependent image of the economy's performance. From a heterodox perspective actual economic outcomes can be heavily influenced by popular expectations and self-fulfilling prophecies, by the exercise of power, by institutional inertia, by social conventions, and by random historical accidents.

In the neoclassical and textbook picture of the long run, all fundamental causal variables (such as individuals' tastes and preferences or technology) are held constant until the general equilibrium implications of the short run are achieved. In heterodox theory, the long run is the working out of actual short runs, which can take the economy down paths quite different from hypothetical GE results.

From a heterodox perspective, neoclassical theory's explanation of actual economic outcomes with reference to hypothetical general equilibrium outcomes in an environment of perfect competition and perfect information is akin to explaining political outcomes in the United States by assuming perfect information on the part of voters, the absence of campaign financing effects, and electoral results that automatically mirror the deepest preferences of all American citizens. This is a comforting image, but not a realistic one.

(4) Relative Optimality

Heterodox economists agree that political alternatives to market mechanisms can suffer from the same problems as market decision making. Which mechanism is preferable depends on the context of the decision. For example, the shift from market mechanisms to political decision making does not reduce environmental uncertainty. It may, however, alter the impact of uncertainty on economic outcomes due to the different social conventions, incentive structures, and risk averseness of public and private decision makers. Heterodox economists tend to think that people often reflect more deeply on the implications of environmental uncertainties in political contexts than they do in economic contexts.

In a similar vein, we may not want to rely on the market and isolated individuals' private decision making in areas where the pressures of positional competition could influence people's behavior. We may want to maintain "forced savings," such as mandatory social security contributions, in order to prevent reciprocal pressures for current consumption from undermining everyone's retirement security. We may similarly want to withdraw some stock of resources, such as Alaskan oil reserves, from market allocation.

As for the charge of being utopian, heterodox economists find standard textbooks' laissez-faire commitment to the "perfect market" much more doctrinaire and akin to a religious faith than heterodoxy's messy willingness to rely on many different strategies for solving economic problems.

CONCLUSION

Beyond Laissez-Faire "Lite"

Heterodox economics criticizes standard introductory economics classes and introductory textbooks for narrowing the questions asked in economics, the methodologies used to explore these questions, and the public policies considered for responding to economic problems. The market optimality and laissez-faire subtext of standard textbooks is very hard to contest if readers do not escape the paradigmatic boundaries of argument imposed by neoclassical theory. As Joan Robinson (one of the giants of heterodox economics) noted in the quote beginning this chapter, a major reason for studying economics is to avoid being fooled by economists. It is the thesis of this book that attending to paradigmatic issues can break the hold of neoclassical economics on economic discussion and liberate economic policy from its 95–100 percent laissez-faire straitjacket.

The neoclassical vision warns policy makers against interfering with the market. Heterodox economists warn policy makers that the current path of the world economy, dictated by laissez-faire-oriented logics, is a dangerous one and unlikely to maximize human welfare.

Building on Common Ground

The historical development of heterodox economics has been characterized by limited communications across most heterodox paradigms, but the current period offers an opportunity to change this. The Internet has greatly expanded the possibilities for cross-fertilization among heterodox thinkers. Several new organizations and publications, such as ICAPE and the *Post Autistic Economic Review,* are actively trying to create a pan-heterodox community. This commentary has tried to demonstrate that there is indeed a large common ground for these efforts to build upon. It will take cultivation of that common ground to free economics from the limits of neoclassical theory. Economics has a major contribution to make toward a better world and it is time for us to make it.

STUDY QUESTIONS

Review Question

1. Neoclassical macro economists tend to offer four main responses to heterodox critiques of standard introductory textbooks. Outline these responses and heterodox rejoinders.

Discussion Questions

1. What do you think are the most convincing aspects of heterodox critiques of standard introductory macroeconomics textbooks? What do you think are the least convincing aspects of heterodox critiques? Explain your answer.
2. Do you think the concept of "paradigm debate" is a useful way to describe disagreements between heterodox and neoclassical economists? If so, why; if not, why not?
3. If you were encountering a macroeconomic theorist for the first time and someone asked you whether the economist was a neoclassical or heterodox economist, what kinds of things might you look for in the economist's work to identify their paradigmatic leanings?

FURTHER READING

I hope that this commentary has whetted your interest in heterodox economics. It is a vibrant field and with a little practice you should be able to find heterodox analyses of most economic subjects.

General Sources of Information

One good place to start looking is the website of the Heterodox Economics Web, which is available at www.orgs.bucknell.edu/afee/HetAssns.htm. The web site includes information about and links to heterodox economic journals, heterodox newsletters and other publications, heterodox discussion groups, heterodox think tanks, heterodox course syllabi, and heterodox associations.

The Heterodox Newsletter, edited by Frederic Lee, http://1.web.umkc.edu/leefs/htn12.htm, is intended mainly for professors, but also has some items of interest to students.

The *Post Autistic Economics Review* is an online heterodox journal that specializes in short articles accessible to students and scholars from other fields interested in heterodox economics. Its URL is http://www.paecon.net/.

As noted on the Heterodox Economics web site, many heterodox paradigms have scholarly journals that often include articles accessible to students. *The Review of Radical Political Economics* (radical economics), *Feminist Economics* (feminist economics), *The Journal of Economic Issues* (institutionalist economics), *Monthly Review* (Marxist economics) and *Challenge* (Post Keynesian oriented economics) (http://www.challengemagazine.com/) are especially reader friendly.

There are also many good online or print sources that offer heterodox takes on recent macro events. These include

1. The Center for Economic and Policy Research, http://www.cepr.net. This is a good web site for heterodox policy discussions. The center formerly published "The Economic Reporting Review," a heterodox commentary on the week's major business and economics articles in the *New York Times* and the *Washington Post.* The commentary has recently shifted to a blog format.

2. The Financial Markets Center, http://www.fmcenter.org/. This is a good web site for heterodox analyses of the monetary sector and the Federal Reserve.

3. *Left Business Observer,* http://www.panix.com/~dhenwood/LBO_home.html. This is a good web site for heterodox analysis of current economic issues; some material is available to subscribers only.

4. *Dollars and Sense,* http://www.dollarsandsense.org/index.html. This is a monthly magazine and a good source of heterodox macro- and microeconomic analysis. The Dollars and Sense group also publishes a series of "readers" (such as *Real World Macro*) intended for introductory economics courses.

5. Jerome Levy Economics Institute, http://www.levy.org/. This a good web site for data and analysis on current macroeconomic events, frequently from a Post Keynesian perspective.

6. The Economic Policy Institute, http://www.epinet.org/. This is a good web site for macro data. This site is an especially good source for information about economic inequality.

7. The Global Development and Environment Institute (GDAE), http://ase.tufts.edu/gdae/. This is a good web site for contextual economics and institutionalist-oriented heterodox materials on macroeconomics, microeconomics, and the economics of the environment.

There are also several heterodox economics discussion lists. The Progressive Economists Network List (PEN-L) is a good place to ask for advice on heterodox sources for research topics, from undergraduate course papers to Ph.D dissertations. To subscribe, send a message to listserv@sus.csuchico.edu In the body of the message, type the following command: sub pen-l your name.

Femecon-L, (Feminist Economists Discussion Group) is a good list to join for perspectives on feminist economics. To subscribe, mail to: Listserv, Command: Subscribe Femecon-L <<Your First and Last Name>>.

There are also a growing number of heterodox textbooks and surveys of heterodox economics. I've listed a few below. There are many other good texts as well.

Introductory Macroeconomics and Microeconomics Textbooks

1. *Economics: A New Introduction,* by Hugh Stretton (2000) (covers both micro and macro).
2. *Microeconomics in Context,* by Neva Goodwin, Julie A. Nelson, Frank Ackerman, and Thomas Weisskopf (2005) (first edition). A *Macroeconomics in Context* is also planned. A preliminary version is available at: http://www.ase.tufts.edu/gdae/publications/text-books/macroeconomics.html
3. *Economics: A Tool for Critically Understanding Society* (7th ed.), by Tom Riddell, Jean Shackelford, Steve Stamos, and Geoffrey Schneider (2005).
4. *Economics: An Introduction to Traditional and Radical Views* (6th ed.), by E.K. Hunt and Howard J. Sherman (1990).
5. *Neoclassical and Institutionalist Perspectives on Economic Behavior: Microeconomics,* by Susan Himmelweit, Roberto Simonetti, and Andrew Trigg (2001). (Intermediate-level text.)

Introduction to Political Economy

1. *Understanding Capitalism: Competition, Command, and Change* (3rd ed.), by Samuel Bowles, Richard Edwards, and Frank Roosevelt (2005).
2. *Introduction to Political Economy* (3rd ed.), by Charles Sackrey and Geoffrey Schneider (2002).
3. *The Political Economics of Capitalism,* by Mayo Toruno (2003).

Introduction to Radical Economics

1. *Understanding Capitalism* (Bowles, Edwards, and Roosevelt 2005)
2. *Political Economy for the 21st Century: Contemporary Views on the Trend of Economics,* edited by Charles J. Whalen (1996).
3. *Political Economy and Contemporary Capitalism: Radical Perspectives on Economic Theory and Policy,* edited by Ron Baiman, Heather Boushey, and Dawn Saunders (2000).

Introduction to Institutionalist Economics

1. *The Theory of Economic Progress,* by Clarence E. Ayres (1962). 1996 Internet edition available at http://www.orgs.bucknell.edu/afee/InstReadings/AYRES_TEP/TEPHome.htm.
2. *The Discretionary Economy: A Normative Theory of Political Economy,* by Marc R. Tool (2000).
3. *The Theory of the Leisure Class,* by Thorstein Veblen ([1899] 1973).
4. *Economics and the Public Purpose,* by John Kenneth Galbraith (1973).

Introduction to Feminist Economics

1. *Beyond Economic Man: Feminist Theory and Economics,* edited by Marianne A. Ferber and Julie A. Nelson (1993b). Second edition: *Feminist Economics Today: Beyond Economic Man,* edited by Marianne A. Ferber and Julie A. Nelson (2003).
2. *Out of the Margin: Feminist Perspectives on Economics,* edited by Edith Kuiper and Jolande Sap with Susan Feiner, Notburga Ott and Zafiris Tzannatos (1995).

3. *The Invisible Heart: Economics and Family Values,* by Nancy Folbre (2001).
4. *The Elgar Companion to Feminist Economics,* edited by Janice Peterson and Margaret Lewis (1999).

Introduction to Post Keynesian Economics

1. *A New Guide to Post Keynesian Economics,* edited by Richard Holt and Steven Pressman (2001).
2. *Alternative Principles of Economics,* by Stanley Bober (2001). (Intermediate level.)
3. *Introduction to Post Keynesian Economics (2003),* by Frederic S. Lee (available electronically from the author, leefs@umkc.edu. For a more advanced discussion see Lee's *Post Keynesian Price Theory* (1998).

Introduction to Marxist Economics

1. *Marxism For and Against,* by Robert L. Heilbroner (1980).
2. *The Theory of Capitalist Development: Principles of Marxian Political Economy,* by Paul M. Sweezy ([1942] 1968).
3. *Economics: Marxian Versus Neoclassical,* by Richard D. Wolff and Stephen A. Resnick (1987).
4. *Labor and Monopoly Capital: The Degradation of Work in the Twentieth Century,* by Harry Braverman (1974).

Introduction to Ecological Economics

1. *Ecological Economics: Principles and Applications,* by Herman E. Daly and Joshua Farley (2004).
2. *An Introduction to Ecological Economics*, by Robert Costanza, John Cumberland, Herman Daly, Robert Goodland, and Richard Norgaard (1997).
3. *For the Common Good: Redirecting the Economy Toward Community, the Environment, and a Sustainable Future,* by Herman E. Daly and John B. Cobb Jr. (1994).
4. *Small is Beautiful: Economics as if People Mattered,* by E.F. Schumacher (1973).

Introduction to Social Economics

1. *Economics for the Common Good: Two Centuries of Social Economic Thought in the Humanistic Tradition,* by Mark A. Lutz (1999).
2. *Teaching the Social Economics Way of Thinking: Selected Papers from the Ninth World Congress of Social Economics,* edited by Edward J. O'Boyle (1999).
3. *The Moral Dimension: Toward a New Economics,* by Amitai Etzioni (1988).

More Advanced Discussions of Heterodox Critiques of and Alternatives to Neoclassical Theory

1. *Frontier Issues in Economic Thought.* This is a series of six edited volumes by researchers associated with the Global Development and Environment Institute. Each volume contains about fifty to one hundred short summaries of key book chapters and journal

articles presenting largely heterodox views of the volume's topic area. The individual volume titles are: *A Survey of Ecological Economics* (Krishnan, Harris, and Goodwin 1995), *The Consumer Society* (Goodwin et al. 1997), *Human Well-Being and Economic Goals* (Ackerman et al. 1997), *The Changing Nature of Work* (Ackerman et al. 1988), *The Political Economy of Inequality* (Ackerman 2000), and *A Survey of Sustainable Development: Social and Economic Dimensions* (Harris et al. 2001).

2. *Debunking Economics: The Naked Emperor of the Social Sciences,* by Steve Keen (2002).

3. *Foundations of Economics: A Beginner's Companion,* by Yanis Varoufakis (1998).

4. *Anti-Samuelson* Volumes I and II (1977), by Marc Linder with Julius Sensat Jr. These texts present a Marxist critque of introductory economics textbooks.

NOTES

1. Informally, neoclassical economists tend to imply that markets and market economies have very desirable meta-externalities. "Free markets" are portrayed as the foundation of a free society. They are celebrated for decentralizing political power, promoting a culture of choice, and instilling a sense of personal responsibility among people. These claims are necessarily argued "between the lines" of neoclassical texts, as they formally contradict the logic of methodological individualism underlying the neoclassical paradigm. MI principles require that people precede institutions rather than partially reflect them.

2. For an excellent summary of these arguments see *The Rhetoric of Economics* by McCloskey (1985). McCloskey is a free market, feminist, neoclassical economist from the University of Chicago.

3. Defenders of neoclassical theory sometimes argue that the textbooks use "softer arguments," such as arguments by analogy and introspection, only to illustrate propositions that have been "proved" more formally. The rub is that the formal methods do not and could not really prove the propositions argued, such as claims that markets are efficient; that there is a trade-off between equity and efficiency; or that the NAIRU is between 5 and 6 percent. Thus there is a sleight of hand. The real action is in the metaphors and stories told, in the case studies and pattern of analogy developed, but the rhetoric of proof continues to cite the scientific method.

4. Ironically, heterodox economists note that the latest advanced mathematical treatments of GE theory (see for example Ackerman 1999) reject the claim that markets automatically gravitate or return to general equilibrium.

GLOSSARY

Absolute Definitions of Poverty: Definitions of poverty based on a fixed subsistence level of income (as opposed to **Relative Definitions of Poverty**).

Accumulation: A heterodox term for increases in investment and expansion of the level of economic activity within capitalism.

Administered Prices: Prices set by firms' bureaucratic decisions rather than by short-term market forces.

Aggregate Demand: The level of intended spending in an economy, frequently represented as C + I + G + NX (consumer demand, plus investment demand, plus government spending, plus net exports).

Anglo-American Capitalism: A relatively laissez-faire form of capitalism; contrasted with "**Nordic capitalism**" and the "European welfare state."

Animal Spirits: Keynes's term for business expectations based on gut feelings, especially important for Keynesian theories of investment amid uncertainty.

Arguments by Introspection: Arguments that ask what you would do in a similar situation in order to understand others' behavior and assess the reasonableness of an economic model.

Asymmetric Information Theory: Analyses of economic behavior that assume participants in an exchange may possess different information; used by some Neo-Keynesian economists to explain some disequilibrium phenomena.

Auctioneer Metaphor: A metaphor featuring a fictitious person (the auctioneer) who oversees the elimination of excess supply or excess demand in the market by changing prices to equilibrium prices before any trades take place; a metaphorical expression of the **perfect information assumption** or instantaneous price adjustment assumption; challenged in heterodox theory by the assumption of **imperfect information** and exploration of the implications of uncertainty.

Babylonian Methodology: The use of a variety of methods in economic analysis, ranging from surveys and introspection to mathematical deduction and experiments; more pluralistic than neoclassical methodology.

Bads: Undesirable side effects of economic activities; the opposite of "goods."

Bargaining Theories of Wages: A theory of wage determination that finds wages are not fully determined by the marginal productivity of labor and reflect, in part, the relative bargaining strength of workers and employers.

Behavioral Economics: A relatively new research agenda in economics that seeks to understand how people actually behave in the economy rather than simply assume the implications of *homo economicus;* sometimes involving experiments.

Blank Slate Theories of Knowledge: An alternative to paradigmatic theories of knowledge implying that researchers can escape the boundaries of paradigmatic thinking and develop universal, **paradigm**-free knowledge.

Bounded Rationality: The tendency of decision makers to explore a subset of options and information rather than all possible options and available information when making decisions.

Bureaucratic Decision Making: The tendency for large firms to rely on preset rules and other forms of "routinized behavior" to make decisions rather than relying on optimizing models and managers' independent judgment to make business decisions.

Capital as a Social Relation: A Marxist metaphor noting that ownership of financial capital often carries with it control over the labor process.

Capital Mobility: The ability of investors to move their financial capital, and to a lesser extent their real physical capital, in search of the highest returns. All other things being equal, increased capital mobility tends to increase the share of national and/or global output going to the owners of capital.

Capitalism: an economic and social system characterized by the private ownership of the means of production, the widespread organization of work by wage labor, the coordination of the division of labor between companies by markets with monetized exchange, and the motivation of economic activity by profit seeking.

Caring Labor: Labor performed in market and nonmarket settings that takes care of others, such as child care, elder care, and care for the ill and disabled; often involving (and perhaps requiring, in order to be successful) intrinsic motivation.

Casino Image: A Keynesian metaphor portraying aspects of the economy as being like a casino due to participants' need to make decisions amid uncertainty; a counterimage to the **general equilibrium**, **perfect information auctioneer metaphor**.

Ceteris Paribus Trick (or the "Cet Par Trick"): Holding "all things constant," except a single shifting variable, when it is inappropriate to hold all things constant.

Circuits of Capital: See **M-C-C′-M′**.

Circular Flow Model: Empty Pond Case: Production unconstrained by environmental limits and rising natural resource prices.

Circular Flow Model: Visible Lilly Pads Case: Production constrained by environmental limits and rising (or anticipation of rising) resource costs.

Citizen/Consumer Distinction: The idea that the same individual might behave differently in the voting booth than in the marketplace when assessing economic matters, such as the value of environmental protection.

Class: A category of analysis used differently in different paradigms; in Marxist theory it signifies a group's relationship to the means of production and social surplus, rather than a group's income level.

Conditional Stability: A period of market stability due to stable expectations.

Contextual Economics: A new **heterodox economics** paradigm that attempts to situate economic analysis within social, psychological, and ecological contexts, and that also includes attention to ethical issues and the question of what we mean by **economic well-being**.

Coordination Problem: The disequilibrium potential created by imperfect feedback among the economy's linked markets, especially with respect to aggregate demand and the market's difficulty registering the potential demand of unemployed workers.

Cornucopians: Forecasters who anticipate that technological change and input and output substitutability will permit endless economic growth; opposite of **Malthusians**.

Credit Crunch: A decline in the availability and/or increase in the cost of credit, especially during periods of increased demand for credit.

Crisis Theory: A Marxist set of theories that attribute the causes of periodic and long-term macroeconomic problems, such as high unemployment, low capacity utilization, and widespread bankruptcies, to the internal workings of capitalism.

Defensive Expenditures: spending to offset difficulties caused by other economic activities, such as the purchase of a bigger car for safety reasons when other drivers purchase SUVs.

Demand Gap: A situation where the level of aggregate demand is insufficient to produce full employment, often used in conjunction with the **Keynesian Cross** to graphically illustrate aggregate demand problems.

Disciplinary Rate of Unemployment: A heterodox term for the economy's tendency to generate involuntary unemployment in order to reduce pressures for rising wages and (perhaps) rising prices; a heterodox alternative to the textbooks' concepts of the "natural rate of unemployment" or "Non-Accelerating Inflation Rate of Unemployment" (NAIRU).

Discouraged Workers: Workers who would like a job at the existing market wage for their skills, but have given up looking for work due to poor economic conditions. These workers are not included in the official unemployment rate.

Disequilibrium: Persistent excess supply or excess demand in a market.

Disproportionality Problems: A Marxist term for macroeconomic disequilibria arising from imperfect information, such as a mismatch among the economy's industries that leads to over- or underproduction of capital goods versus consumer goods.

Distributional Issues: Fairness questions involving the distribution of income, the distribution of wealth, and other equity issues.

Downward Spiral: A contagious collapse in aggregate demand that spreads across linked industries and the economy as a whole.

Dual Economy: The division of the economy into two sectors, with the core (sometimes called the **planning sector**) inhabited by large oligopoly firms, and the periphery (sometimes called the **market sector**) inhabited by small competitive firms.

Dual Labor Markets: The separation of labor markets into (1) "primary markets" with implicit long-term commitments between employer and employees, relatively high wages, job security, opportunities for advancement, and formal governance procedures and (2) "secondary markets" that lack these features.

Duesenberry Hypothesis: The idea that an individual's marginal propensity to consume (mpc) is influenced by their relative as well as real level of income, with increases in an individual's relative income lowering their mpc, but proportional increases in everyone's real income not changing national mpcs.

Dynamic Analysis: Analysis that looks at how an economy moves from one state to another, often finding that the adjustment process and adjustment path can influence the economy's final outcome; contrasted with static (or comparative static) analysis.

Earned Income Tax Credit (EITC): Tax breaks for low-income workers (especially significant for families with children) that can result in "negative" income tax payments, that is, government payments to working families.

Ecological Economics: A **heterodox economic paradigm** that emphasizes the need for economic analysis to give greater attention to the economy's embeddedness in the natural world.

Economics: The study of how groups of people reproduce the material bases for life and the complicated interaction between economic activities and the rest of social life.

Economic Well-Being: A heterodox concept that attempts to explore and assess economic outcomes along more dimensions than GDP.

Economies of Scale: A decline in per-unit costs of production as output increases.

Economies of Scope: A decline in per-unit costs of production when two or more products are produced together rather than separately.

Efficiency Wages: Wages set above equilibrium wages in order to win employee loyalty and motivate work effort.

Elastic Price Expectations: Expectations that prices will continue to move in the direction they have been moving, in excess of hypothetical equilibrium price adjustments; when in a downward direction, sometimes a spur for **downward spiral**s.

Empathy: The ability to put yourself in another's shoes; employed by some heterodox economists, such as feminist economists, to help make interpersonal utility comparisons.

Endogenous Money: A heterodox term that calls attention to the idea that the banking sector has a much greater ability to create money (and credit) and retire money (and credit) than most neoclassical models suggest.

Endogenous Variable: A dependent variable whose value is determined within an economic model. Distinct from an **exogenous variable**.

Environmental Kuznets Curve (EKC): The hypothesis that economic growth in a country initially worsens environmental quality but then improves it.

Epicycle: An adjustment made within a **paradigm** to reconcile it to new data or resolve existing anomalies.

Epistemology: The study of the nature of knowledge, especially with respect to its grounds and limitations.

Equity-Efficiency Complementarities: The idea that equity and efficiency are mutually compatible goals with gains in one facilitating gains in the other.

Equity-Efficiency Tradeoffs: The idea that equity and efficiency are competing goals, with increases in one necessarily requiring decreases in the other.

Exacerbating Errors Model: The possibility that a market with excess supply or excess demand will move away from rather than toward equilibrium.

Exogenous Variable: A variable whose value is taken as given (i.e., independent and prior to the economy) in economic analysis; distinct from an **Endogenous Variable**. Heterodox economists find economic influences on many variables that are treated as exogenous by neoclassical theory (such as tastes and preferences).

Exponential Growth: Proportional rather than linear rates of growth, implying increasing increments of growth and the potential appearance of "explosive growth" in relationship to fixed boundaries.

Fallacy of Composition: Assuming that what follows for one person taking an action (such as increased sales for a firm lowering its price) automatically follows for an entire group taking the same action.

Fallacy of Misplaced Concreteness: Analysis that mistakenly abstracts from essential institutional and substantive details; a claim often made by ecological economists about the treatment of environmental and natural resources in **neoclassical economics**.

False Trading: Trades executed at nonequilibrium prices.

Federal Reserve District Bank Presidents: Rotating members of the Federal Reserve's Open Market Committee, traditionally selected with special attention to the opinions of banking and business interests.

Feminist Economics: A **heterodox economic paradigm** that criticizes aspects of neoclassical theory methodologically (rejecting, for example, the psychology of *homo economicus*) and topically (for giving incomplete and sometimes misleading analysis of the experience of women in the economy). There are competing uses of the term *feminist economics,* with **neoclassical** feminists simply calling for more attention to the experiences of women in the economy.

Financial Dementia: John Kenneth Galbraith's characterization of the tendency for financial markets to experience periods of irrational behavior.

Financial Panic: A rush to hold money and other safe assets, often involving sudden large withdrawals of funds from the banking system and/or the selling of other assets to raise cash in depressed market conditions.

Freedom To (as opposed to Freedom From): Possession of the material resources necessary to exercise free choice in a situation.

Fundamental (as opposed to Probabilistic) **Uncertainty**: Uncertainties that lack probability distributions (distinct from the uncertainty accompanying the roll of dice).

GE Theory: An abbreviation for **general equilibrium theory**.

General Equilibrium Theory: A theory of market outcomes that portrays the economy as a linked set of markets all operating at their equilibrium price and quantity.

Genuine Progress Indicator (GPI): A heterodox measure of economic well-being descended from the Index of Sustainable Economic Welfare (**ISEW**) that attempts to add some heterodox concerns to the national income accounts.

GINI Coefficient: A measure of inequality related to the **Lorenz Curve** and varying from 0 (complete equality) to 1.

Government as the Employer of Last Resort: Guaranteed public employment.

Great Depression: A global economic collapse from roughly late 1929 to 1940, during which the unemployment rate in the United States averaged more than 17 percent.

Growth Subtext: The idea that economic growth provides the resources necessary to meet most human needs and that the special contribution of economics to human welfare is to facilitate economic growth; a key **subtext** of **neoclassical economics**.

H: An abbreviation for **Holism**.

Hamlet Without the Prince: Analyses of the monetary sector that do not highlight the implications of uncertainty.

Hermeneutics of Suspicion: A skepticism toward the conventional wisdom due to the latter's historical biases, as exemplified by feminist concerns about the legacy of sexism in economic analyses of women's experience.

Heterodox Economics: A collection of economic paradigms that share many of the same methodological objections to neoclassical theory, such as objections to **methodological individualism**, to *homo economicus*, to the **fallacy of misplaced concreteness**, and to insufficient attention to the implications of uncertainty. Among the most well-known heterodox economic paradigms are **institutionalist economics**, **radical economics**, **Marxist economics**, **Post Keynesian economics**, **feminist economics**, **ecological economics**, Neo-Ricardian economics, **social economics**, and **socioeconomics**. Most of these paradigms find that the economy needs more social governance than implied by the **neoclassical paradigm**. Some alternative definitions of heterodoxy would also include Austrian economics and **behavioral economics**.

High-Road Labor Strategies: Use of the carrot rather than the stick to motivate labor and lower per-unit labor costs; often involving **implicit contracts**, **efficiency wages**, and significant employer investment in employee training; contrasts with **low-road labor strategies**.

High-Road Macro Regimes: Macro contexts characterized by active government policies to maintain full employment, **high-road labor strategies**, high levels of business investment and government infrastructural spending, active government policies to redistribute income, and government regulation of financial markets to curb destabilizing speculation.

Hinge Rate of Unemployment: The level of unemployment at which wage inequality usually begins to fall, estimated by James Galbraith to be 5.5 percent.

Holism (or Holist-Structuralism): An approach to social science that studies societal outcomes in terms of the characteristics of a social system, situating individual behavior within a reproducing social logic; contrasted with **methodological individualism**.

Homo Economicus: The assumption of "rational economic man," implying that economic actions can be understood as if undertaken by isolated, rational agents trying to maximize their self-interest; contrasted with *homo reciprocans* and other more complex economic psychologies in **heterodox economics**. See also **Separative Self**.

Homo Reciprocans: A **heterodox economic** psychology that presumes humans have a natural tendency for reciprocity, as well as egoism, with the former facilitating voluntary cooperation and retribution against free riders even when cooperation or retribution is not in an individual's immediate self-interest.

Hot Money: Highly mobile short-term movements of international financial capital.

Household Sector: The nonmarket production of goods, services, and other outcomes of value in the household; generally not included in GDP.

HS: An acronym for **Holist Structuralism**.

Human Development Index: A statistic developed by the United Nations Development Programme to measure a country's economic performance in terms of basic societal outcomes, such as adult literacy rates and life expectancy.

Hysteresis: **Path dependency**, the idea that the economy's short-run moments influence its long-run outcomes; implying that "history matters" and diversions from hypothetical **GE** outcomes may have enduring results. See also Dynamic Analysis.

IEESA: Integrated Environmental and Economic Satellite Accounts; additional statistics developed by the Department of Commerce that complement the core national income accounts and address some heterodox concerns about the limitations of GDP as a measure of economic welfare. Also known as "augmented national accounts" and "green accounting."

Imperfect Information: The absence of perfect information, raising the possibility that market participants will expect prices and market conditions that are different from hypothetical equilibrium prices and will therefore behave differently than supposed in **GE** theory.

Implicit Contracts: Informal understandings, often between employers and employees (**invisible handshakes**), implying that firms will not cut wages during hard times; sometimes between suppliers and long-term customers allowing firms to raise prices in response to rising costs but not in response to rising demand.

Incomes Policies: Government policies that attempt to control inflation by influencing firms' wage and price-setting behavior.

Industrial Policy: Government policies aimed at influencing the structure of the economy, often for the purpose of addressing **meta-externalities**.

Inelastic Price Expectations: The expectation that prices will return to previous levels after an exogenous shock has generated a new hypothetical equilibrium price.

Infant Industry Argument for Protectionist Trade Policies: The idea that a country's industries need to be protected from international competition until they can capture economies of scale and other **path-dependent** economic advantages.

Instantaneous Adjustment: A key assumption of **GE theory**, implying that markets can be modeled as if they responded instantaneously to excess supply or excess demand with equilibrium price and quantity adjustments; similar to the assumption of perfect information or the implications of the **auctioneer metaphor**.

Institutionalist Economics: A **heterodox economic** paradigm that emphasizes the need for economists to study the way institutions and social conventions shape economic life.

Insufficient Aggregate Demand: The idea that the structure and level of **aggregate demand** can be insufficient to maintain full employment.

Inter- vs. Intra-Generational Discount Rates: The idea that it may be appropriate to use a different interest rate for making inter-temporal choices across a few overlapping generations than for much longer time periods.

Interdependent Consumer Preferences: A situation where people's preferences for goods are influenced by what other people are buying, as with bandwagon effects, snob effects, and **positional goods**.

Intermediate Good Expenditures: Spending for goods and services, such as commuting costs, in order to acquire other goods and services, such as a large house.

Internal Labor Markets: Job ladders and compensation schedules within firms that are partially insulated from external market forces.

Interpersonal Utility Comparisons: Comparisons of the relative value of an additional dollar of income to different people, especially people with different incomes; generally precluded in **neoclassical** theory and pursued in **heterodox** theory.

Introspection: See **Arguments by Introspection**.

ISEW: Index of Sustainable Economic Welfare; a heterodox measure of economic welfare created by **ecological** economists Herman E. Daly and John B. Cobb, Jr.

Invisible Handshake: Informal long-term commitments between employers and employees involving a sense of shared mutual interests. See also **implicit contracts**.

Involuntary Part-Time Workers: Workers who would prefer full-time work but have accepted part-time work due to poor economic conditions. These workers are not counted in the official unemployment rate.

Irrational Exuberance: Alan Greenspan's characterization of the stock market's excessive valuations in the mid-1990s.

Keynesian Cross: A graphical and algebraic model for determining expected GDP from the structure of aggregate demand by locating the intersection of the aggregate demand line and the 45-degree line.

Labor Accord (or "The Accord"): Part of the post–World War II **social structure of accumulation** that managed capital/labor conflict within the **planning sector** of the U.S. economy from approximately 1946 to 1970.

Labor/Labor Power Distinction: The idea that firms purchase labor power (i.e., labor time or labor potential) rather than actual labor in the labor market and then extract an indeterminate amount of labor from that potential through management techniques during production.

Land Ethic: A term coined by ecologist Aldo Leopold calling for a sense of stewardship toward the environment and warning that "enlightened self-interest" is likely to be insufficient to protect the environment and our self-interest.

Learning Curve Cost Reductions: The tendency for costs to decline as firms gain experience with a technology.

Limits to Growth: The idea that current environmental and/or resource constraints imply that future economic growth cannot follow the trajectory of the past, often linked with fears that market institutions will not be able to lead the economy to a **sustainable development** path.

Liquidity: The ability to transform assets into money (and subsequently into whatever one wishes) without delay or loss of equilibrium value; modeled after the ability of liquids to assume different forms in different vessels.

Liquidity Premium: The shifting worth of **liquidity** in asset valuations.

Liquidity Trap: A situation where interest rates have fallen to or below many people's long-term interest rate expectations, encouraging lenders to accumulate excess reserves rather than offer loans at lower rates, thus limiting the ability of monetary policy to spur the economy by lowering interest rates on bank loans or long-term bonds.

Liquifier of Last Resort: The ability of the Federal Reserve to transform all kinds of assets into money during **liquidity** crises, often undertaken in order to prevent **downward spiral**s induced by the need to sell assets in depressed market conditions.

Lorenz Curve: A way of graphically representing the distribution of an economic asset, such as income or wealth, with the percentage of families on the horizontal axis and percentage of ownership of the asset on the vertical axis. Complete equality would trace out the 45-degree line. Complete inequality would trace out a reverse L.

Low-Road Labor Strategies: Use of the stick rather than the carrot to motivate labor and lower per-unit labor costs; often involving low wages, minimal firm investment in employee training, high labor turnover, and adversarial labor relations; contrasts with **high-road labor strategies**.

M-C-C'-M': The circuit of capital. The circuit begins with the advance of money (M) and purchase of input commodities (C), proceeds through production to C' (a new commodity), and ends with the sale of that commodity and the remonetizing of capital, from which point the process begins again.

Macroeconomic Foundations of Microeconomics: The macroeconomic conditions and expectations that provide the context for microeconomic decisions, which in turn create macroeconomic outcomes.

Macro Regimes: Macro contexts for micro decision making, characterized by alternative labor market arrangements, industry structures, government macro policies, and so on.

Malthusians: Forecasters who anticipate significant limits on future economic growth due to environmental and resource constraints; opposite of **Cornucopians**.

Managerial Firms: Firms in which management has a relatively large degree of independence from direct oversight by stockholders.

Mark-Up (or cost-plus) **Pricing**: A theory of price determination that asserts that firms set prices by adding a "markup" to their costs often associated with constant average variable costs in the short run.

Market Sector: The sector of the economy dominated by small firms, as distinct from the **planning sector**. See also **Dual Economy**.

Marxist Economics: A **heterodox economics paradigm** that emphasizes **holism** and the need to study **capitalism** as a social system in order to understand economics.

Menu Costs: The financial costs of changing prices, such as the cost of printing new menus in restaurants.

Meta-Externalities: The unintended consequences of economic activities for social and cultural phenomena, such as the viability of democracy or ease of voluntary cooperation among individuals.

Methodological Individualism: The attempt to explain societal outcomes by explaining and then aggregating individual behavior; a form of reductionism; a contrasting theory to **holism**.

MEW: Measure of Economic Welfare; a more comprehensive measure of **economic well-being** than GDP, devised by neoclassical economists James Tobin and William Nordhaus.

MI: An acronym for **Methodological Individualism.**

Minsky Cycles: A theory of business cycles that emphasizes the tendency of financial markets to oscillate between excessively optimistic and excessively pessimistic swings of opinion.

Misplaced Concreteness: See **Fallacy of Misplaced Concreteness**.

Moderately Strong Sustainability. A theory of economic sustainability that requires each generation to pass on to the next an equal endowment of **natural capital**, defining equality in functional rather than monetary or physical terms; permitting the use of exhaustible resources if offset by the development of a renewable source for the same use.

Monetary Sector: Reference to the circulation of pieces of paper representing claims on the real sector.

Monetized Exchange: The need to use money to buy commodities and meet economic obligations (in contrast with barter); linked in heterodox analyses to some unique kinds of **disequilibrium** dynamics.

Multinational Corporation (MNC): A corporation that operates in at least two countries, sometimes termed a transnational corporation.

Multiple Equilibria: The existence of several possible outcomes for an economic situation, with the actual outcome determined by the subjective expectations and strategic behavior of decision makers.

Natural Capital: An economic concept that characterizes the earth's natural resources (such as the stock of oil in the ground) and environmental capacities (such as the atmosphere's ability to recycle a certain amount of carbon dioxide) as economic assets that provide a flow of valuable services.

Necessarily Psychologically Complex Individual: A heterodox alternative to *homo economicus* that assumes that individuals respond to uncertainty in complex ways involving, among other things, **bounded rationality** and deference to social conventions.

Negative Externalities: Costs of production not borne by the producer or consumer of a product, such as pollution damages.

Neoclassical Economics: The currently dominant **paradigm** in **economics**, built around concepts such as **methodological individualism**, *homo economicus*, **general equilibrium**, and market optimality.

Neo-Keynesian (NK) Analysis: Versions of Keynesian theory that link unemployment to short-term wage and price **stickiness** rather than to the implications of uncertainty, softening Keynes's methodological break with **GE** theory; the portrayal of Keynesian economics in most **neoclassical** macro textbooks, termed "bastard Keynesianism" by some heterodox critics; contrasts with **Post Keynesian analysis**.

NK: Abbreviation for **Neo-Keynesian**.

Nordic Capitalism: Capitalism as found in many Scandinavian countries, with a larger public sector and greater social governance of markets than in **Anglo-American capitalism**.

Normal Science: Research conduced within the boundaries of an existing **paradigm**.

Note but Ignore Motif: A heterodox characterization of **neoclassical** theory's tendency to offer formal qualifications of many claims that are, in practice, employed in an unqualified way.

Oligopoly Markets: Markets with a relatively small number of firms who act strategically with respect to each other; distinct from perfectly competitive markets.

Ontology: The study of the nature of being, involving debates in economics between **methodological individualism** and **holism**.

Paradigm: A conceptual framework organizing thought and research.

Path Dependency: The idea that different technologies and economic strategies may turn out to be competitively dominant depending upon which option accumulates scaling-type economies. See also: **Dynamic Analysis** and **Hysteresis.**

Pattern Bargaining: The establishment of a common bargaining outcome; when used to help contain inflation the strategy is oriented toward establishing shared guidelines for wage and price behavior.

Perfect Competition (PC) Assumption: The assumption that all markets are composed of countless small firms, who produce homogeneous products and are forced by vigorous price competition to charge identical prices; contrasted with the assumption that many markets are dominated by large firms who attempt to influence their environment and act strategically with respect to a small number of relevant competitors.

Perfect Information Assumption: A similar assumption to the assumption of instantaneous price adjustments (or the **auctioneer metaphor**) that guarantees markets operate at equilibrium prices and quantities; challenged in heterodox theory by the assumption of **imperfect information** and the exploration of the implications of uncertainty.

Planning Contexts: The background conditions and expectations that create the context for economic decisions.

Planning Sector: The sector of the economy dominated by large firms, employing about one-quarter to one-third of the workforce. See also **Dual Economy**.

Porter Hypothesis: The hypothesis that strong environmental regulations can force firms to innovate and thereby improve, rather than reduce, their competitiveness.

Positional Competition: Competition for social status, often discussed in economics in terms of competitive consumption.

Positional Goods: Goods purchased at least in part for their status value, rather than for their direct use value.

Positive Externalities: Benefits from production not captured by the purchaser of a good or service, such as the benefits to neighbors of a homeowner's external improvements.

Positive/Normative Distinction: Positive claims involve issues of fact and can be either true or false. Normative claims involve ethical judgments and can be right or wrong in a moral sense. Although they are separate kinds of claims, positive claims often influence normative claims by establishing a context for making such judgments.

Post Keynesian Economics: A **heterodox paradigm** emphasizing the implications of uncertainty, the importance of monetary phenomena, and the potential for problems of **insufficient aggregate demand** in the economy; contrasts with **Neo-Keynesian analysis**.

Precautionary Principle: The idea that added weight should be given to the high end of risk estimates when dealing with potentially serious and possibly irreversible environmental hazards.

Prisoner's Dilemma: A situation where the isolated pursuit of self-interest by separate individuals prevents those individuals from maximizing their self-interest; a contrasting perspective to the optimality properties suggested by the invisible hand metaphor.

Progressive Tax Rates: Tax rates that increase as your income increases.

Protectionist Policies: The insulation of domestic industries and workers from foreign competition.

Provisioning: A **feminist economics** term for the subject matter of economics.

PQLI: Physical Quality of Life Index, a statistic that measures a country's economic success by its literacy rate, infant mortality rate, and life expectancy at age one.

Race to the Bottom: A situation where economic competition leads to an erosion of environmental, health and safety, and other regulatory standards. See also **Prisoner's Dilemma**.

Radical Economics: A **heterodox economic paradigm** that combines many of the insights from other **heterodox paradigms**, such as **Marxist economics** and **institutionalist economics**.

Rational Expectations Theory: A theory claiming that people make rational use of all available information in making economic forecasts and economic decisions, often fused with other assumptions to support **general equilibrium** models of the economy and laissez-faire-oriented macroeconomic policies.

Real Sector: Reference to the circulation or exchange of commodities (real goods and services) for other commodities; distinct from the **monetary sector** involving the circulation of pieces of paper representing claims on the real sector.

Reserve Army of the Unemployed: A Marxist concept asserting that **capitalism** requires a sizable number of unemployed workers and/or a widespread fear of unemployment to maintain employer authority in the workplace and acceptable profit rates for investors, implying that enduring full employment is impossible within **capitalism**.

Relative Definitions of Poverty: Definitions of poverty in terms of a percentage of a society's mean or median income (as opposed to **absolute definitions of poverty**).

Scarcity-Efficiency Discourse: The assumption that human beings naturally have an insatiable desire for goods and services and that the primary economic challenge is to allocate scarce resources among these infinite appetites.

Scientific Revolution: A **paradigm** shift.

Self-Fulfilling Prophecies: Situations where participants' subjective expectations significantly influence economic outcomes, challenging the perfect information determinism of **general equilibrium** models, frequently linked to **downward spirals** and speculative bubbles.

Separative Self: A feminist characterization of the economic psychology implied by *homo economicus;* contrasted with heterodox notions of **interdependent consumer preferences**, empathetic capacities, and relational selves.

Shared Exemplars: The **paradigm**atic solution to classical problems in a field of study. By mastering these problems and learning to draw appropriate analogies, students learn to see the world in **paradigm**atic terms.

(The) Social Bargain in Capitalist Countries: The justification of significant inequalities in capitalist countries in the name of economic efficiency and future economic growth.

Social Capital: Cultural habits and institutions that increase societal well-being by lowering the transaction costs of economic activities and by providing direct benefits to individuals (such as a sense of community).

Social Economics: A **heterodox economic paradigm** that explores the ethical foundations of economic analysis and focuses on both the individual and the social dimensions of economic problems.

Social Governance of the Economy: Active government involvement in the economy to achieve social goals, such as full employment, increased equality, greater democracy, environmental sustainability, and the expansion of **social capital**.

Social Limits to Growth: A heterodox concept that finds that the payoffs to GDP growth decline as a society becomes richer due to the increasing importance and waste of **positional competition** and the erosion of **social capital**.

Social Structures of Accumulation: An institutionalist and neo-Marxist concept that refers to an interrelated set of institutions, government policies, and socially grounded expectations that reduce uncertainty, manage capital/labor conflict, and provide stable contexts for long-term investments and economic evolution.

Socioeconomics: A **heterodox economic paradigm** that situates economic activity in a social context with more complex economic agents than *homo economicus*.

Speculative Bubbles: Inflated asset prices.

Stakeholder Governance: The idea that diverse interests, including those of workers, input suppliers, and financiers, should be represented as stakeholders alongside stockholders on the boards of directors of major corporations.

Sticky Wages and Prices: Wages and prices that are slow to change in response to market disequilibrium.

Strategic Trade Theory: The theory that competitive advantage in international trade can sometimes be created by government policies that capture **path-dependent** economic advantages for domestic firms, such as **economies of scale** and **economies of scope**, and **learning curve cost reductions**.

Strong Sustainability: A theory of economic sustainability that requires each generation to pass on to the next an equal endowment of **natural capital**, defining equality in physical rather than monetary terms and implying no consumption of exhaustible resources.

Structural Choices: Basic (often infrastructural) choices that influence the path taken by an economy.

Subtexts: The basic assumptions underlying a **paradigm** and the projects the **paradigm** is meant to facilitate.

Supply-Side Economics: A macroeconomic theory that rejects the need for government policy to maintain **aggregate demand**, but urges lower taxes and reduced regulatory requirements in order to increase economic incentives for supply; colloquially known as "trickle-down" economics because most of the direct benefits accrue to higher income groups.

Sustainable Development: As defined by the World Commission on Environment and Development (the Brundtland Commission): "development that meets the needs of the present without compromising the ability of future generations to meet their own needs." (See also **Weak Sustainability**, **Moderately Strong Sustainability**, and **Strong Sustainability**.)

Thick Curves: A graphic rendering of supply and demand curves that emphasizes a range of likely outcomes rather than an equilibrium point.

Throughput: A term from **ecological economics** referring to the size of an economy in physical rather than price terms.

TINA: "**There Is No Alternative**" (to contemporary **capitalism**). The claim that the only viable way to organize a modern economy is to participate in the global division of labor as a capitalist society (frequently implying **Anglo-American capitalism**).

TIPS: **Tax Based Incomes Policies**. Government policies that attempt to control inflation by using tax incentives to influence firms' wage and price setting behavior.

Underconsumptionist Theories of Unemployment: Theories that tie unemployment to problems of **insufficient aggregate demand** caused by weak consumer demand; sometimes fused with analyses of how the distribution of income affects consumer demand (due to the tendency of richer households to have lower marginal propensities to consume than poorer households).

Underemployment Rate: A measure of labor market difficulties that includes the official unemployment rate, **discouraged workers**, **involuntary part-time workers**, and other marginally employed workers.

Unemployment Equilibrium: The presence of involuntary unemployment without automatic pressures for movement to full employment.

Wage/Profit Squeeze Business Cycles: A theory of business cycles with the following stages: (1) Expansionary Phase: rising investment, rising **aggregate demand**, falling unemployment, rising wages, falling profits, falling investment; (2) Contractionary Phase: falling investment, falling **aggregate demand**, rising unemployment, falling wages, rising profits, rising investment; (3) Expansionary phase, etc.

Weak Sustainability: A theory of economic sustainability that requires each generation to pass on to the next generation an equal endowment of capital, aggregating and measuring all kinds of capital, such as physical capital, human capital, and natural capital, in monetary terms.

WORKS CITED

Ackerman, Frank. 1982. *Reaganomics Rhetoric vs. Reality.* Boston: South End Press.
———. 1984. *Hazardous to Our Wealth: Economic Policies in the 1980s.* Boston: South End Press.
———. 1997a. "Consumed in Theory: Alternative Perspectives on the Economics of Consumption." *Journal of Economic Issues* 31(3) (September): 651–64.
———. 1997b. "Critiques and Alternatives in Economic Theory: Overview Essay." In Goodwin, Ackerman, and Kiron 1997, pp. 189–200.
———. 1997c. "Foundations of Economic Theories of Consumption: Overview Essay." In Goodwin, Ackerman, and Kiron 1997, pp. 149–59.
———. 1999. "Still Dead After All These Years: Interpreting the Failure of General Equilibrium Theory." GDAE Working Paper 99-01. Medford, MA: Global Development and Environment Institute. Available at www.ase.tufts.edu/gdae/publications/working_papers/index.html.
———. 2000. "Distribution of Wealth and Power." In Ackerman et al. 2000.
Ackerman, Frank, Neva R. Goodwin, Laurie Dougherty, and Kevin Gallagher, eds. 1998. *The Changing Nature of Work.* Washington, DC: Island Press.
———. 2000. *The Political Economy of Inequality.* Washington, DC: Island Press.
Ackerman, Frank, David Kiron, Neva R. Goodwin, Jonathan M. Harris, and Kevin Gallagher, eds. 1997. *Human Well-Being and Economic Goals.* Washington, DC: Island Press.
Albelda, Randy, and Chris Tilly. 1999. "Income Distribution." In Peterson and Lewis 1999, pp. 457–63.
Amott, Teresa, and Julie Matthaei. 1991. *Race, Gender, and Work.* Boston: South End Press.
Anderson, Perry. *Passages from Antiquity to Feudalism.* 1978. New York: Verso.
Aslanbeigui, Nahid, and Michele Naples. 1996a. "Is There a Theory of Involuntary Unemployment in Introductory Textbooks?" In Aslanbeigui and Naples, 1996b.
———. eds. 1996b. *Rethinking Economic Principles.* Chicago: Irwin.
Aslanbeigui, Nahid, and Gale Summerfield. 2000. "The Asian Crisis, Gender and the International Financial Architecture." *Feminist Economics* 6(3): 81–103.
Ayres, Clarence E. [1962] 1996. *The Theory of Economic Progress: A Study of the Fundamentals of Economic Development and Cultural Change.* New York: Schocken Books. Internet edition: www.orgs.bucknell.edu/afee/InstReadings/AYRES_TEP/TEPHome.htm.
Baiman, Ron, Heather Boushey, and Dawn Saunders, eds. 2000. *Political Economy and Contemporary Capitalism: Radical Perspectives on Economic Theory and Policy.* Armonk, NY: M.E. Sharpe.
Baker, Dean. 1996. "The Inflated Case Against the CPI." *The American Prospect* 7(24) (December 1): 86–89.
———. 1998a. "The Boskin Commission After One Year." *Challenge* 41(2) (March–April): 6–11.
———. 2002. "Business Week Restates the Nineties—Incorrectly?" *Challenge* 45(4) (July–August).
Baker, Dean, ed. 1998b. *Getting Prices Right: The Debate over the Consumer Price Index.* Armonk, NY: M.E. Sharpe.
Baker, Dean, Gerald Epstein, and Robert Pollin, eds. 1998a. *Globalization and Progressive Economic Policy.* New York: Cambridge University Press.
———. 1998b. "Introduction." In Baker, Epstein, and Pollin 1998a, pp. 1–34.

Baker, Dean, Andrew Glyn, David Howell, and John Schmitt. 2004. "Unemployment and Labor Market Institutions: The Failure of the Empirical Case for Deregulation." New York: Center for Economic Policy Analysis. www.newschool.edu/cepa/papers/archive/cepa200404.pdf.

Barker, Drucilla K., and Susan Feiner. 2004. *Liberating Economics: Feminist Perspectives on Families, Work, and Globalization.* Ann Arbor: University of Michigan Press.

Barnett, W. Steven. 2003. "Low Wages = Low Quality: Solving the Real Preschool Teacher Crisis." *Preschool Policy Matters* (3) March.

Barry, Tom. 1995. *Zapata's Revenge: Free Trade and the Farm Crisis in Mexico.* Boston: South End Press.

Bartlett, Bruce. 1982. *Reaganomics: Supply-Side Economics in Action.* New York: Quill.

Bartlett, Robin. 1995. "Attracting 'Otherwise Bright Students' to Economics 101." *American Economic Review* 85(2) May, 362–66.

———, ed. 1997. *Introducing Race and Gender into Economics.* New York: Routledge.

Bell, Stephanie, and L. Randall Wray. 2004. "The War on Poverty after 40 Years." Public Policy Brief No. 78. Annandale-on-Hudson, NY: The Levy Institute.

Belman, Dale, and Thea M. Lee. 1992. "International Trade and the Performance of U.S. Labor Markets." Summarized in Ackerman et al. 1998, pp. 76–77.

Benería, Lourdes. 2003. *Gender, Development, and Globalization: Economics as if All People Mattered.* New York: Routledge.

Bernstein, Jared, and Dean Baker. 2001. "Full-Employment at Risk." *The American Prospect* 12(19) November.

———. 2003. *The Benefits of Full Employment: When Markets Work for People.* Washington, DC: Economic Policy Institute.

Bernstein, Jared, Chauna Brocht, and Maggie Spade-Aguilar. 2000. *How Much Is Enough: Basic Family Budgets for Working Families,* "Executive Summary." Washington, DC: Economic Policy Institute. Available at www.epinet.org/content.cfm/books_howmuch#anchor812851.

Bernstein, Jared, and Lawrence Mishel. 2003. "Labor Market Left Behind." Economic Policy Institute Briefing Paper. Washington, DC: Economic Policy Institute, August.

Bhagwati, Jagdish. 2001. "Responding to Seattle: Interview with Jagdish Bhagwati." *Challenge* 44(1) (January–February): 6–18.

Blanchard, Olivier. 2000. *Macroeconomics* (2nd ed.). Upper Saddle River, NJ: Prentice Hall.

Blaug, Mark, ed. 1986. *Who's Who in Economics: A Biographical Dictionary of Major Economists, 1700–1986.* Boston: MIT Press.

Blinder, Alan. 1979. *Economic Policy and the Great Stagflation* (student edition). New York: Academic Press.

———. 1988. "The Fall and Rise of Keynesian Economics." *The Economic Record* 64(187) December.

———. 1992. "A Keynesian Restoration Is Here" (Interview). *Challenge* 35(5) (September–October): 11–18.

Blinder, Alan, Elie R.D. Canetti, David E. Lebow, and Jeremy B. Rudd. 1998. *Asking About Prices: A New Approach to Understanding Price Stickiness.* New York: Russell Sage.

Bober, Stanley. 2001. *Alternative Principles of Economics.* Armonk, NY: M.E. Sharpe.

Boddy, Raford, and James Crotty. 1975. "Class Conflict and Macro Policy: The Political Business Cycle." *Review of Radical Political Economics* 7(1): 1–19.

Boltho, Andrea. 2003. "What's Wrong with Europe?" *New Left Review* 22 (July–August).

Bond, James T., Ellen Galinsky, and Jennifer E. Swanberg. 1998. "1997 National Study of the Changing Workforce, Executive Summary." New York: Families and Work Institute.

Bond, James T., Cindy Thompson, Ellen Galinsky, and David Prottas. 2003. "Highlights of the National Study of the Changing Workforce: Executive Summary." New York: Families and Work Institute.

Boskin, Michael J., Ellen R. Dulberger, Robert J. Gordon, Zvi Griliches, and Dale W. Jorgenson. 1998. "Consumer Prices, the Consumer Price Index, and the Cost of Living." *Journal of Economic Perspectives* 12(1): 3–26.

Bowles, Samuel, and Richard Edwards. 1993. *Understanding Capitalism: Competition, Command, and Change in the U.S. Economy* (2nd ed.). New York: HarperCollins.

Bowles, Samuel, Richard Edwards, and Frank Roosevelt. 2005. *Understanding Capitalism: Competition, Command, and Change* (3rd ed.). New York: Oxford University Press.

Bowles, Samuel, and Herbert Gintis. 1998. *Recasting Egalitarianism: New Rules for Communities, States and Markets.* New York: Verso.

———. 2001. "Schooling in Capitalist America Revisited." November 8 (available at www.umass.edu/preferen/gintis/soced.pdf). Accessed May 17, 2005.

———. 2002. "The Inheritance of Inequality." *Journal of Economic Perspectives* 16(3): 3–30.

Bowles, Samuel, Herbert Gintis, and Melissa Osborne Groves, eds. 2005. *Unequal Chances: Family Background and Economic Success.* Princeton: Princeton University Press.

Bowles, Samuel, David M. Gordon, and Thomas E. Weisskopf. 1989. "Business Ascendancy and Economic Impasse: A Structural Retrospective on Conservative Economics 1979–87." *Journal of Economic Perspectives* 3(1): 107–34.

———. 1990. *After the Wasteland: A Democratic Economics for the Year 2000.* Armonk, NY: M.E. Sharpe.

Boyce, James K. 1994. "Inequality as a Cause of Environmental Degradation." *Ecological Economics* 11, pp. 169–78.

Boyer, Robert. 1990. "Regulation." In Eatwell, Milgate, and Newman 1990, pp. 331–35.

Braverman, Harry. 1974. *Labor and Monopoly Capital: The Degradation of Work in the Twentieth Century.* New York: Monthly Review Press.

Brenner, M. Harvey. 1979. "Influence of the Social Environment on Psychopathology: The Historic Perspective." In *Stress and Mental Disorder,* edited by James E. Barrett, pp. 161–77. New York: Raven Press.

Brenner, Robert. 2003. *The Boom and the Bubble: The U.S. in the World Economy.* New York: Verso.

Bronfenbrenner, Kate. 1996. "Final Report: The Effects of Plant Closing or Threat of Plant Closing on the Right of Workers to Organize." Ithaca, NY: Cornell University ILR School. Available at http://digitalcommons.ilr.cornell.edu/intl/1/.

———. 1997. "We'll Close! Plant Closings, Plant-Closing Threats, Union Organizing and NAFTA." *Multinationtal Monitor* 18(3): 8–14.

Bullard, Robert D. 2000. *Dumping in Dixie: Race, Class, and Environmental Quality.* Boulder, CO: Westview.

Caiazza, Amy, April Shaw, and Misha Werschkul. 2004. "Women's Economic Status in the States: Wide Disparities by Race, Ethnicity, and Region." Washington, DC: Institute for Women's Policy Research.

Campen, Jim, John Miller, and Abby Scher, eds. 1999. *Real World Banking* (4th ed.). Somerville, MA: Dollars and Sense.

Caner, Asena, and Edward D. Wolff. 2004. "Asset Poverty in the United States." Public Policy Brief, Highlights No. 76A. Annandale-on-Hudson, NY: The Levy Institute.

Chang, Ha-Joon. 2005. *Kicking Away the Ladder: Development Strategy in Historical Perspective.* London: Anthem Press.

Chang, Ha-Joon, and Ilene Grabel. 2004. *Reclaiming Development: An Alternative Economic Policy.* New York: Zed Books.

Clarkson, Stephen. 1993. "Economics: The New Hemispheric Fundamentalism." In Grinspun and Cameron 1993, pp. 61–69.

Cline, William R. 1997. *Trade and Income Distribution.* Washington, DC: Institute for Institutional Economics.

Cohn, Steven. 1997. *Too Cheap to Meter: An Economic and Philosophical Analysis of the Nuclear Dream.* Albany: State University of New York Press.

Colander, David. 1995. "The Stories We Tell: A Reconsideration of AS/AD Analysis." *Journal of Economic Perspectives* 9(3): 169–88.

———. 1996a. "The Macrofoundations of Micro." In Colander 1996c, pp. 57–68.

———. 1996b. "Overview." In Colander 1996c, pp. 1–17.

———. 2001a. "Effective Supply and Effective Demand." *Journal of Post Keynesian Economics* 23(3): 375–82.

———. 2001b. *Macroeconomics* (4th ed.). New York: McGraw Hill.

Colander, David, ed. 1996c. *Beyond Microfoundations: Post Walrasian Macroeconomics.* New York: Cambridge University Press.

———. 2000. *The Complexity Vision and the Teaching of Economics.* Northampton, MA: Edward Elgar.

Colander, David, and Peter Sephton. 1998. "Acceptable and Unacceptable Dirty Pedagogy: The Case of ADAS." In Rao 1998, pp. 137–54.

Committee on the Status of Women in the Economics Profession (CSWEP). 2004. "Report of the Committee on the Status of Women in the Economics Profession." *CWEP Newsletter* (Winter): 5.

Corak, Miles. 2004. *Generational Income Mobility in North America and Europe.* New York: Cambridge University Press.

Corry, Dan, and Andrew Glyn. 1994. "The Macroeconomics of Equality, Stability and Growth." In Glyn and Miliband 1994, pp. 205–16.

Cosbey, Aaron. 2006. "Reconciling Trade and Sustainable Development." In *State of the World 2006,* ed. Linda Starke. New York: Norton.

Costanza, Robert, Ralph d'Arge, Rudolf de Groot, Stephen Farber, Monica Grasso, Bruce Hannon, Karin Limburg, Shahid Naeem, Robert V. O'Neill, Jose Paruelo, Robert G. Raskin, Paul Sutton and Marjan van den Belt. 1997. "The Value of the World's Ecosystem Services and Natural Capital." *Nature* 387 (6630): 253–60.

Costanza, Robert, John Cumberland, Herman Daly, Robert Goodland, and Richard Norgaard. 1997. *An Introduction to Ecological Economics.* Boca Raton, FL: St. Lucie Press.

Crotty, James. 1994. "Are Keynesian Uncertainty and Macrotheory Compatible? Conventional Decision Making, Institutional Structures, and Conditional Stability in Keynesian Macromodels." In Dymski and Pollin 1994, pp. 105–39.

———. 2000a. "The Case for Capital Controls." Amherst, MA: Political Economy Research Institute.

———. 2000b. "Structural Contradictions of the Global Neoliberal Regime." *Review of Radical Political Economics* 32(3) (September): 361–68.

———. 2003. "The Neoliberal Paradox: The Impact of Destructive Product Market Competition and Impatient Finance on Nonfinancial Corporations in the Neoliberal Era." *Review of Radical Political Economics* 35(3): 271–79.

Crotty, James, Gerald Epstein, and Patricia Kelly. 1998. "Multinational Corporations in the Neo-Liberal Regime." In Baker, Epstein, and Pollin 1998a, pp. 117–43.

Crotty, James, and Don Goldstein. 1993. "Do U.S. Financial Markets Allocate Credit Efficiently? The Case of Corporate Restructuring in the 1980s." In Dymski, Epstein, and Pollin 1993, pp. 253–86.

Cypher, James M. 1993. "The Ideology of Economic Science in the Selling of NAFTA: The Political Economy of Elite Decision Making." *Review of Radical Political Economics* 25(4): 146–63.

Daly, Herman E. 1995. *Developing Ideas.* Interview, February 8. Available from the International Institute for Sustainable Development (IISD) web site www.iisd.org.

———. 1996. *Beyond Growth: The Economics of Sustainable Development.* Boston: Beacon Press.

———. 1999. *Ecological Economics and the Ecology of Economics: Essays in Criticism.* Northampton, MA: Edward Elgar.

Daly, Herman E, and John B. Cobb Jr. 1994. *For the Common Good: Redirecting the Economy Toward Community, the Environment, and a Sustainable Future.* Boston: Beacon Press.

Daly, Herman E., and Joshua Farley. 2004. *Ecological Economics: Principles and Applications.* Washington, DC: Island Press.

Darity, William Jr., and Arthur H. Goldsmith. 1996. "Social Psychology, Unemployment and Macroeconomics." *Journal of Economic Perspectives* 10(1): 121–40.

Darity, William A. Jr., and Samuel L. Myers Jr. 1998. *Persistent Disparity: Race and Economic Inequality in the United States Since 1945.* Northampton, MA: Edward Elgar.

Dasgupta, Susmita, Benoit Laplante, Hua Wang, and David Wheeler. 2002. "Confronting the Environmental Kuznets Curve." *Journal of Economic Perspectives* 16(1): 147–68.

Davidson, Paul. 1996. "What Revolution? The Legacy of Keynes." *Journal of Post Keynesian Economics* 18 (Fall): 47–60.

———. 2002. "Globalization." *Journal of Post Keynesian Economics* 24 (3): 475–92.

de Graaf, John. 2003. "Workweek Woes." *New York Times* (April 12): A13.

Demaree, Allan T. 1970. "G.E.'s Costly Ventures Into the Future." *Fortune* (October): 88–93, 156, 158.

Devine, James. 2001. "The Cost of Living and Hidden Inflation." *Challenge* 44(2): 73–84.

Dorman, Peter. 2001. "Waiting for an Echo: The Revolution in General Equilibrium Theory and the Paralysis in Introductory Economics." *Review of Radical Political Economics* 33(3): 325–33.

Dow, Sheila. 1996. *The Methodology of Macroeconomic Thought.* Northampton, MA: Edward Elgar.

Downward, Paul, and Frederic S. Lee. 2001. "Post Keynesian Pricing Theory Reconfirmed? A Critical Review of *Asking About Prices.*" *Journal of Post Keynesian Economics* 23(3): 465–83.

Du Boff, Richard B., and Edward S. Herman. 2001. "Mergers, Concentration, and the Erosion of Democracy." *Monthly Review* 53 (1): 14–29.

Dymski, Gary, Gerald A. Epstein, and Robert Pollin, eds. 1993. *Transforming the U.S. Financial System: Equity and Efficiency for the 21st Century.* Armonk, NY: M.E. Sharpe.

Dymski, Gary, and Robert Pollin, eds. 1994. *New Perspectives in Monetary Economics: Explorations in the Tradition of Hyman P. Minsky.* Ann Arbor: University of Michigan Press.

Easterlin, Richard A. 2000. "Where Is Economic Growth Taking Us?" Paper delivered at the Mount Holyoke Conference on "The World Economy in the 21st Century: Challenges and Opportunities." February 18–19.

———. 2003. "Explaining Happiness." *Proceedings of the National Academy of Sciences* 100 (19): pp. 11,176–83.

Eatwell, John, Murray Milgate, and Peter Newman. 1990. *The New Palgrave: Marxian Economics.* New York: Macmillan.

Edwards, Richard. 1979. *Contested Terrain: The Transformation of the Workplace in the Twentieth Century.* New York: Basic Books.

Ehrlich, Everett. 1997. "The Downside of Bad Data." *Challenge* 40(2): 13–37.

Eichner, Alfred S. 1985. *Towards a New Economics: Essays in Post-Keynesian and Institutionalist Theory.* Armonk, NY: M.E. Sharpe.

Eisner, Robert. 1988. "Extended Accounts for National Income and Product." *Journal of Economic Literature* 26(4): 1611–84.

Engemann, Kristie, Leora Friedberg, and Michael T. Owyang. 2005. "Keep Your Resume Current: The Causes Behind Declining Job Tenure." *The Regional Economist* (January).

England, Paula. 2003. "Separative and Soluble Selves: Dichotomous Thinking in Economics." In Ferber and Nelson 2003, pp. 33–59.

England, Richard W. 1997. "Alternatives to Gross National Product: A Critical Survey." In Ackerman et al. 1997, pp. 373–405.

Epstein, Gerald A. 1992. "Political Economy and Comparative Central Banking." *Review of Radical Political Economics* (24)1, 1–30.

Epstein, Gerald A., and Herbert M. Gintis, eds. 1995. *Macroeconomic Policy After the Conservative Era.* New York: Cambridge University Press.

Erikson, Robert, and John H. Goldthorpe. 2002. "Intergenerational Inequality: A Sociological Perspective." *Journal of Economic Perspectives* 16(3): 31–44.

Etzioni, Amitai. 1988. *The Moral Dimension: Toward a New Economics.* New York: The Free Press.

Fazzari, Steven M., Piero Ferri, and Edward Greenberg. 1998. "Aggregate Demand and Firm Behavior: A New Perspective on Keynesian Microfoundations." *Journal of Post Keynesian Economics* 20(4): 527–59.

Feather, Norman T. 1990. *The Psychological Impact of Unemployment.* New York: Springer-Verlag.

Feldstein, Martin. 1998. "Overview: Is Income Inequality Really a Problem?" Comments delivered at the Federal Reserve Bank of Kansas City's 1998 Symposium entitled "Income Inequality: Issues and Policy Options."

Ferber, Marianne A. 1997. "Gender and the Study of Economics: A Feminist Critique." In R. Bartlett 1997, pp. 147–55.

Ferber, Marianne A., and Julie A. Nelson. 1993a. "Introduction." In Ferber and Nelson 1993b, pp. 1–22.

———. 1993b. *Beyond Economic Man: Feminist Theory and Economics.* Chicago: University of Chicago Press.

Ferber, Marianne A., and Julie A. Nelson, eds. 2003. *Feminist Economics Today: Beyond Economic Man.* Chicago: University of Chicago Press.

Folbre, Nancy. 1998. "The Neglect of Care-Giving" (Interview). *Challenge* 41(5) (September–October): 45–58.

———. 2001. *The Invisible Heart: Economics and Family Values.* New York: The New Press.

Frank, Ellen. 2004. *The Raw Deal: How Myths and Misinformation About the Deficit, Inflation, and Wealth Impoverish America.* Boston: Beacon Press.

Frank, Robert H. 1985. "The Demand for Unobservable and Other Nonpositional Goods." *American Economic Review* 75(1) (March): 101–16.

———. 1999. *Luxury Fever: Money and Happiness in an Era of Excess.* Princeton, NJ: Princeton University Press.

———. 2005a. "How the Middle Class Is Injured by Gains at the Top." In Lardner and Smith 2005, pp. 138–48.

———. 2005b. "The Mysterious Disappearance of James Duesenberry." *New York Times* (June 9): C–2.

Freeman, Richard B. 1999. *The New Inequality: Creating Solutions for Poor America.* Boston: Beacon Press.

Frey, Bruno S., and Alois Stutzer. 2002. "What Can Economists Learn from Happiness Research?" *Journal of Economic Literature* 40(2): 402–35.

Friedman, Milton. (1962) 1982. *Capitalism and Freedom.* Chicago: University of Chicago Press.

Fullbrook, Edward, ed. 2003. *The Crisis in Economics: The Post-Autistic Economics Movement: The First 600 Days.* New York: Routledge.

Furman, Jason, and Joseph E. Stiglitz. 1998. "Economic Consequences of Income Inequality." Paper delivered at the Federal Reserve Bank of Kansas City's 1998 Symposium entitled "Income Inequality: Issues and Policy Options."

Fussell, Elizabeth. 2000. "Making Labor Flexible: The Recomposition of Tijuana's Maquiladora Female Labor Force." *Feminist Economics* 6(3): 583–602.

Galbraith, James K. 2000. *Created Unequal.* Chicago: University of Chicago Press.

Galbraith, John Kenneth. 1955. *The Great Crash.* Boston: Houghton Mifflin.

———. [1958] 1998. *The Affluent Society* (40th anniversary ed.). Boston: Houghton Mifflin.

———. 1973. *Economics and the Public Purpose.* Boston: Houghton Mifflin.

———. 1994. *A Short History of Financial Euphoria.* New York: Whittle.

Galinsky, Ellen, James T. Bond, Stacy S. Kim, Lois Backon, Erin Brownfield, and Kelly Sakai. 2005. "Overwork in America: When the Way We Work Becomes Too Much (Executive Summary)." New York: Families and Work Institute.

Gardner, Gary, Erik Assadourian, and Radhika Sarin. 2004. "The State of Consumption Today." In Starke 2004, pp. 5–21.

Garson, Barbara. 2002. *Money Makes the World Go Around: One Investor Tracks Her Cash Through the Global Economy.* New York: Penguin.

Gill, Jennifer. 2001. "Why Do They Want So Much Dough, Anyway?" *Business Week* April 9.

Glyn, Andrew, and David Miliband. 1994. *Paying for Inequality: The Economic Cost of Social Injustice.* London: Rivers Oram Press.

Gneezy, Uri, and Aldo Rustichini. 2000. "A Fine Is a Price." *Journal of Legal Studies* 29(1): 1–17.

Gomory, Ralph E., and William J. Baumol. 2000. *Global Trade and Conflicting National Interests.* Cambridge: MIT Press.

Goodstein, Eban. 1998. "Malthus Redux? Globalization and the Environment." In Baker, Epstein, and Pollin 1998a, pp. 297–318.

———. 2005. *Economics and the Environment* (4th ed.). Hoboken, NJ: John Wiley and Sons.

Goodwin, Neva R., Frank Ackerman, and David Kiron, eds. 1997. *The Consumer Society.* Washington, DC: Island Press.

Goodwin, Neva R., Julie A. Nelson, Frank Ackerman, and Thomas Weisskopf. 2003. *Microeconomics in Context* (preliminary edition). New York: Houghton Mifflin.

Gordon, David M. 1995. "Growth, Distribution, and the Rules of the Game: Social Structuralist Macro Foundations for a Democratic Economic Policy." In Epstein and Gintis 1995, pp. 335–83.

———. 1996. *Fat and Mean: The Corporate Squeeze of Working Americans and the Myth of Managerial Downsizing.* New York: The Free Press.

Gordon, David M., Richard Edwards, and Michael Reich. 1982. *Segmented Work, Divided Workers: The Historical Transformation of Labor in the United States.* New York: Cambridge University Press.

Gordon, Robert J. 2004. "The Slippery Art of Measuring Living Standards" (Interview). *Challenge* 47(2) (March–April): 70–80.

Gosselin, Peter G. 2002. "Enron a Rerun of History." *Los Angeles.Times* (February 22): A1.

Gould, Stephen Jay. 1981. *The Mismeasure of Man.* New York: Norton.

Grabel, Ilene. 2000. "The Asian Financial Crisis: What Went Wrong." In Baiman, Boushey, and Saunders 2000, pp. 218–24.

Greenwald, Bruce, and Joseph Stiglitz. 1993. "New and Old Keynesians." *Journal of Economic Perspectives* 7(1): 23–44.

Greider, William. 1987. *Secrets of the Temple: How the Federal Reserve Runs the Country.* New York: Simon and Schuster.

Grinspun, Ricardo, and Maxwell A. Cameron, eds. 1993. *The Political Economy of North American Free Trade.* New York: St. Martin's Press.

Guo, Hui. 2001. "Stockholding Is Still Highly Concentrated." *National Economic Trends* (June): 1. St. Louis: Federal Reserve Bank of St. Louis.

Guttmann, Robert. 1994. *How Credit-Money Shapes the Economy.* Armonk, NY: M.E. Sharpe.

Guzman, Lina, and Susan M. Jekielek. n.d. "Family Time." In *Indicators of Child, Family, and Community Connections: Companion Volume of Related Papers.* Washington, DC: U.S. Department of Health and

Human Services. Available at http://aspe.hhs.gov/hsp/connections-papers04. Accessed October 3, 2005.

Hahnel, Robin. 2002. *The ABCs of Political Economy.* Sterling, VA: Pluto Press.

Hailstones, Thomas J., ed. 1982. *Viewpoints on Supply-Side Economics.* Richmond, VA: Robert F. Dame.

Halweil, Brian. 2002. "Home Grown: The Case for Local Food in a Global Market." Worldwatch Paper 163 (November). Washington, DC: Worldwatch Institute.

Harms, John B., and Tim Knapp. 2003. "What's New, What's Not." *Review of Radical Political Economics* 35(4): 413–36.

Harris, Jonathan M. 2001. "Trade and the Environment." Medford, MA: Global Development and Environment Institute.

———. 2002. *Environmental and Natural Resource Economics: A Contemporary Approach.* Boston: Houghton Mifflin.

Harris, Jonathan M., Timothy Wise, Kevin Gallagher, and Neva R. Goodwin, 2001. *A Survey of Sustainable Development: Social and Economic Dimensions.* Washington, DC: Island Press.

Harrison, Bennett, and Barry Bluestone. 1988. *The Great U-Turn: Corporate Restructuring and the Polarizing of America.* New York: Basic Books.

Hartmann, Heidi. 1997. "Through a Gendered Lens: A Response to Richard Freeman's 'Solving the New Inequality.'" From the December–January 1996–97 *Boston Review.* Available at www.bostonreview.net/BR21.6/hartmann.html.

Hausman, Daniel M., and Michael S. McPherson. 1996. *Economic Analysis and Moral Philosophy.* New York: Cambridge University Press.

Hawken, Paul, Amory Lovins, and L. Hunter Lovins. 1999. *Natural Capitalism: Creating the Next Industrial Revolution.* Boston: Little, Brown and Company.

Heilbroner, Robert L. 1967. *The Worldly Philosophers: The Lives, Times, and Ideas of the Great Economic Thinkers* (3rd ed.). New York: Simon and Schuster.

———. 1980. *Marxism For and Against.* New York: Norton.

Henwood, Doug. 1997. *Wall Street.* New York: Verso.

Hertz, Tom. 2003. "Rags, Riches and Race: The Intergenerational Economic Mobility of Black and White Families in the United States." Available at http://nw08.american.edu/%7Ehertz/HERTZ%20Rags%20Riches%20and%20Race%20April%202003.pdf.

Hewitson, Gillian. 1999. *Feminist Economics: Interrogating the Masculinity of Rational Economic Man.* Northampton, MA: Edward Elgar.

Himmelweit, Susan. 2002. "Making Visible the Hidden Economy: The Case for Gender-Impact Analysis of Economic Policy." *Feminist Economics* 8(1): 49–70.

Himmelweit, Susan, and Roberto Simonetti, and Andrew Trigg. 2001. *Neoclassical and Institutionalist Perspectives on Economic Behavior: Microeconomics.* London: Thompson Learning.

Hirsch, Fred. 1976. *Social Limits to Growth.* Cambridge: Harvard University Press.

Hirsh, Richard F. 1989. *Technology and Transformation in the American Electric Utility Industry.* New York: Cambridge University Press.

Hodgson, Geoffrey. 1986. "Behind Methodological Individualism." *Cambridge Journal of Economics* 10(3) (September): 211–23.

———. 1998. "The Approach of Institutional Economics." *Journal of Economic Literature* 36(1): 166–92.

Holt, Richard, and Steven Pressman. 2003. "Teaching Post Keynesian Economics to Undergraduate Students." *Journal of Post Keynesian Economics* 26(1) (Fall): 169–86.

Holt, Richard, and Steven Pressman, eds. 2001. *A New Guide to Post Keynesian Economics.* New York: Routledge.

Howell, David. 2002. "Increasing Earnings Inequality and Unemployment in Developed Countries: Markets, Institutions, and the 'Unified Theory.'" *Politics and Society* 30(2): 193–243.

Howitt, Peter. 2002. "Looking Inside the Labor Market: A Review Article." *Journal of Economic Literature* 40(1) (March): 125–38.

Hulten, Charles. 1997. "Quality Change in the CPI: Some Missing Links." *Challenge* 40(2) (March–April): 48–74.

Hunt, E.K., and Howard J. Sherman. 1990. *Economics: An Introduction to Traditional and Radical Views* (6th ed.). New York: Harper and Row.

Hymer, Stephen. 1971. "Robinson Crusoe and the Secret of Primitive Accumulation." *Monthly Review* 23(4): 11–36.

Jackson, Wes. 1980. *New Roots for Agriculture.* Lincoln: University of Nebraska Press.

————. 1984. *Meeting the Expectations of the Land: Essays in Sustainable Agriculture and Stewardship.* San Francisco: North Point Press.

Jacoby, Sanford. 2005. "Corporate Governance and Society." *Challenge* 48(4) (July–August): 69–87.

Kahan, Dan M. 2002. "The Logic of Reciprocity: Trust, Collective Action, and Law." Yale Law School, John M. Olin Center for Studies in Law, Economics, and Public Policy Working Paper Series. Paper 281. Available at http://lsr.nellco.org/yale/lepp/papers/281.

Kahneman, Daniel, and Alan B. Krueger. 2006. "Developments in the Measurement of Subjective Well-Being." *Journal of Economic Perspectives* 20(1): 3–24.

Kalecki, Michal. 1971. *Selected Essays on the Dynamics of the Capitalist Economy.* New York: Cambridge University Press.

Kampwirth, Karen. 2002. *Women and Guerilla Movements: Nicaragua, El Salvador, Chiapas, Cuba.* University Park: Pennsylvania State University Press.

Keen, Steve. 2002. *Debunking Economics: The Naked Emperor of the Social Sciences.* New York: Zed.

Kennedy, Peter. 1998. "Defending ADAS: A Perspective on the ADAS Controversy." In Rao 1998, pp. 95–106.

Kennickell, Arthur. 2003 "A Rolling Tide: Changes in the Distribution of Wealth in the U.S., 1989–2001." March 3 Available at www.Federalreserve.gov/pubs/oss/oss2/papers/concentration.2001.pdf.

Keynes, John Maynard. [1931] 1963. "Economic Possibilities for Our Grandchildren." In *Essays in Persuasion*, pp. 358–73. New York: Norton.

————. 1933. "National Self-Sufficiency." *The Yale Review* 22(4) (June): 755–69.

————. [1936] 1964. *The General Theory of Employment, Interest and Money.* New York: Harcourt.

Kimzey, Bruce. 1983. *Reaganomics.* New York: West Publishing.

Kindleberger, Charles P. [1978] 2000. *Manias, Panics, and Crashes: A History of Financial Crises* (4th ed.). New York: John Wiley.

King, J.E. 2001. "Labor and Unemployment." In Holt and Pressman 2001, pp. 65–78.

Kotz, David. 1990. "A Comparative Analysis of the Theory of Regulation and the Social Structure of Accumulation Theory." *Science and Society* 54(1): 5–28.

Kotz, David, Terrence McDonough, and Michael Reich, eds. 1994. *Social Structures of Accumulation: The Political Economy of Growth and Crisis.* New York: Cambridge University Press.

Krishnan, Rajaram, Jonathan M. Harris, and Neva R. Goodwin, eds. 1995. *A Survey of Ecological Economics.* Washington, DC: Island Press.

Krueger, Alan. 2005. "Economic Scene." *New York Times* (January 6): C2.

Krugman, Paul R. 1987. "Is Free Trade Passe?" *Journal of Economic Perspectives* 1(2): 131–44.

————. 2006. "Graduates Versus Oligarchs." *New York Times* (February 27): A19.

Kuhn, Thomas. 1970. *The Structure of Scientific Revolutions* (2nd ed.). Chicago: University of Chicago Press.

Kuiper, Edith, and Jolande Sap, with Susan Feiner, Notburga Ott and Zafiris Tzannatos, eds. 1995. *Out of the Margin: Feminist Perspectives on Economics.* New York: Routledge.

Lardner, James, and David A. Smith, eds. 2005. *Inequality Matters: The Growing Economic Divide in America and Its Poisonous Consequences.* New York: The New Press.

Larudee, Mehrene. 1998. "Integration and Income Distribution under the North American Free Trade Agreement: The Experience of Mexico." In Baker, Epstein, and Pollin 1998a, pp. 273–92.

————. 2006. "The Political Economy of NAFTA: What's Oil Got to Do with It?" Paper Delivered at the 2006 meetings of the Allied Social Science Associations (January).

Lavoie, Marc. 1994. "A Post Keynesian Approach to Consumer Choice." *Journal of Post Keynesian Economics* 16(4): 539–62.

————. 2003. "The Tight Links Between Post-Keynesian and Feminist Economics." In Fullbrook 2003, pp. 189–92.

————. 2004. "Post-Keynesian Consumer Theory: Potential Synergies with Consumer Research and Economic Psychology." *Journal of Economic Psychology* 25(5): 639–49.

Lee, Frederic. 1996. "Pricing and the Business Enterprise." In Whalen 1996, pp. 87–102.

————. 1998. *Post Keynesian Price Theory.* New York: Cambridge University Press.

Lee, Thea. 1988. "Comment on Larudee 1998." In Baker, Epstein, and Pollin 1998a, pp. 293–95.

Lekachman, Robert. 1966. *The Age of Keynes.* New York: Random House.

Leopold, Aldo. [1949] 1966. *A Sand County Almanac.* New York: Oxford University Press.

Levin, Lee B. 1995. "Toward a Feminist Post-Keynesian Theory of Investment: A Consideration of the

Socially and Emotionally Constituted Nature of Agent Knowledge." In Kuiper and Sap 1995, pp. 100–119.

Linder, Marc. 1994. *Labor Statistics and Class Struggle*. New York: International Publishers.

Linder, Marc, with Julius Sensat, Jr. 1977a. *Anti-Samuelson Volume I: Macroeconomics: Basic Problems of the Capitalist Economy*. New York: Urizen Books.

————. 1977b. *Anti-Samuelson Volume II: Microeconomics: Basic Problems of the Capitalist Economy*. New York: Urizen Books.

Lucas, Robert E. Jr. 1979. "The Death of Keynes." In Hailstones 1982, pp. 3–5.

Lutz, Mark A. 1999. *Economics for the Common Good: Two Centuries of Social Economic Thought in the Humanistic Tradition*. New York: Routledge.

MacDonald, Martha. 1995. "The Empirical Challenges of Feminist Economics." In Kuiper and Sap 1995, pp. 175–97.

Magdoff, Fred, and Harry Magdoff. 2004. "Disposable Workers." *Monthly Review* 55(11) April 18–35.

Magdoff, Harry. 1971. "Economic Myths and Imperialism." *Monthly Review* 23 (7) (December): 1–17.

Mankiw, N. Gregory. 1992. "The Reincarnation of Keynesian Economics." *European Economic Review* 36 (July): 559–65.

————. 2001. *Principles of Macroeconomics* (2nd ed.). Fort Worth, TX: Harcourt.

Manning, Linda M., and Patricia Graham. 1999. "Banking and Credit." In Peterson and Lewis 1999, pp. 27–32.

Maurer, Harry. 1979. *Not Working: An Oral History of the Unemployed*. New York: Holt, Rinehart and Winston.

May, Ann Mari. 2002. "The Feminist Challenge to Economics." *Challenge* 45(6): 45–69.

Mayer, Thomas. 1993. *Truth Versus Precision in Economics*. Brookfield, VT: Edward Elgar.

Mazumder, Bhashkar. 2002. "Analyzing Income Mobility over Generations" *Chicago Fed Letter* # 181, September. Chicago: Federal Reserve Bank of Chicago.

————. 2004. "What Similarities Between Siblings Tell Us About Inequality in the U.S." *Chicago Fed Letter* # 209, December. Chicago: Federal Reserve Bank of Chicago.

McCloskey, Donald N. 1985. *The Rhetoric of Economics*. Madison: University of Wisconsin Press.

McConnell, Campbell R., and Stanley L. Brue. 2002. *Macroeconomics: Principles, Problems, and Policies* (15th ed.). New York: McGraw-Hill.

McCormick, Ken, and Janet Rives. 1998. "Aggregate Demand in Principles Textbooks." In Rao 1998, pp. 11–23.

McDonough, Terrence. 2005. "Social Structures of Accumulation: The Last Ten Years." Paper delivered at the Allied Social Science Associations Meetings in Philadelphia, January.

McGinn, Anne Platt. 1998. "Rocking the Boat: Conserving Fisheries and Protecting Jobs." Worldwatch Paper # 142, June.

Meadows, Donella H., Dennis L. Meadows, and Jorgen Randers. 1992. *Beyond the Limits: Confronting Global Collapse, Envisioning a Sustainable Future*. Post Mills, VT: Chelsea Green Publishing Company.

Miringoff, Marque-Luisa, Marc Miringoff, and Sandra Opdycke. 2001–2002. "A Social Report on America's Well-Being." *Indicators: Journal of Social Health* 1(1): 50–89.

Mishel, Lawrence, Jared Bernstein, and Sylvia Allegretto. 2005. *The State of Working America 2004/2005*. Ithaca, NY: Cornell University Press.

Mishel, Lawrence, Jared Bernstein, and Heather Boushey. 2003. *The State of Working America 2002/2003*. Ithaca, NY: Cornell University Press.

Mullainathan, Sendhil, and Richard Thaler. 2000. "Behavioral Economics." MIT Department of Economics, Working paper 00-27, September.

Myrdal, Gunnar. 1978. "Institutional Economics." *Journal of Economic Issues* 12(4) 771–83.

Nell, Edward. 1996. *Making Sense of a Changing Economy*. New York: Routledge.

Nelson, Julie A. 1995. "Feminism and Economics." *Journal of Economic Perspectives* 9(2): 131–48.

————. 1996. *Feminism, Objectivity & Economics*. New York: Routledge.

New York Times. 1996. *The Downsizing of America*. New York: Times Books.

Nordhaus, William D. 1998. "Quality Changes in Price Indexes." *Journal of Economic Perspectives* 12(1) (Winter): 59–68.

Nordhaus, William D., and Edward C. Kokkelenberg, eds. 1999. *Nature's Numbers: Expanding the National Economic Accounts to Include the Environment*. Washington, DC: National Academy Press.

Nordhaus, William D., and James Tobin. 1972. "Is Growth Obsolete?" In *Economic Growth* (Volume 5:

Economic Research: Retrospect and Prospect). New York: National Bureau of Economic Research/ Columbia University Press.

North, Douglas C. 1981. *Structure and Change in Economic History.* New York: Norton.

Norwood, Janet. 1997. "How Right Is the Boskin Commission?" *Challenge* 40(2): 38–47.

O'Boyle, Edward J., ed. 1999. *Teaching the Social Economics Way of Thinking: Selected Papers from the Ninth World Congress of Social Economics.* Lewiston, NY: Edwin Mellen.

O'Hara, Phillip Anthony. 2003a. "Deep Recession and Financial Instability or a New Long Wave of Economic Growth for U.S. Capitalism? A Regulation School Approach." *Review of Radical Political Economics* 35 (1): 18–43.

———. 2003b. "Principles of Political-Economy: Integrating Themes from the Schools of Heterodoxy." Paper delivered at the ICAPE conference on the Future of Heterodox Economics (June).

Palley, Thomas. 1997. "How to Rewrite Economic History." *The Atlantic Online* (April).

———. 1998. *Plenty of Nothing: The Downsizing of the American Dream and the Case for Structural Keynesianism.* Princeton: Princeton University Press.

Papadimitriou, Dimitri B., and L. Randall Wray. 1999. "Minsky's Analysis of Financial Capitalism." Jerome Levy Institute Working Paper No 275, July. Annandale-on-Hudson, NY: The Levy Institute.

Perelman, Michael. 2000. *Transcending the Economy: On the Potential of Passionate Labor and the Wastes of the Market.* New York: St. Martin's Press.

Persky, Joseph. 1998. "Price Indexes and General Exchange Values." *Journal of Economic Perspectives* 12(1): 197–205.

Peterson, Janice, and Margaret Lewis, eds. 1999. *The Elgar Companion to Feminist Economics.* Northampton, MA: Edward Elgar.

Piachaud, David. 1997. "A Price Worth Paying? The Costs of Unemployment." In *Working for Full Employment,* ed. John Philpott, pp. 49–62. New York: Routledge.

Pieper, Ute, and Lance Taylor. 1998. "The Revival of the Liberal Creed: The IMF, the World Bank, and Inequality in a Globalized Economy." In Baker, Epstein, and Pollin 1998a, pp. 37–63.

Piketty, Thomas, and Emmanuel Saez. 2003 "Income Inequality in the United States 1913–1998." *Quarterly Journal of Economics* 118(1): 1–39.

Pollin, Robert. 1998a. "Can Domestic Expansionary Policy Succeed in a Globally Integrated Environment? An Examination of Alternatives." In Baker, Epstein, and Pollin 1998a, pp. 433–60.

———. 1998b. "The 'Reserve Army of Labor' and the 'Natural Rate of Unemployment': Can Marx, Kalecki, Friedman, and Wall Street All Be Wrong?" *Review of Radical Political Economics* 3(30): 1–13.

———. 1999. "Transforming the Fed." In Campen, Miller, and Scher 1999, pp. 8–10.

———. 2003. *Contours of Descent: U.S. Economic Fractures and the Landscape of Global Austerity.* New York: Verso.

Rao, B. Bhaskara, ed. 1998. *Aggregate Demand and Supply: A Critique of Orthodox Macroeconomic Modeling.* New York: St. Martin's Press.

Ravetz, Jerry. 1995. "Economics as an Elite Folk Science: the Suppression of Uncertainty." *Journal of Post Keynesian Economics* 17(2): 165–84.

Reich, Michael. 1997. "Social Structure of Accumulation Theory: Retrospect and Prospect." *Review of Radical Political Economics* 29(3): 1–10.

Revkin, Andrew C. 2005. "A New Measure of Well-Being from a Happy Little Kingdom." *New York Times* (October 4): D-1.

Riddell, Tom, Jean Shackelford, Steve Stamos, and Geoffrey Schneider. 2005. *Economics: A Tool for Critically Understanding Society* (7th ed.). New York: Pearson Addison-Wesley.

Riegle, Donald W. Jr. 1982. "The Psychological and Social Effects of Unemployment." *American Psychologist* 37(10) (October): 1113–15.

Robinson, Joan. 1955. *Marx, Marshall and Keynes.* Delhi, India: The Delhi School of Economics.

Robson, Denise. 1999. "Wherefore Art Thou. . . . Women and Minorities in Economics Textbooks." Paper prepared for the International Atlantic Economic Society meeting, October 7–10.

Rodney, Walter. 1981. *How Europe Underdeveloped Africa.* Washington, DC: Howard University Press.

Rodrik, Dani. 1997. "Consequences of Trade for Labor Markets and the Employment Relationship." Summarized in Ackerman et al. 1998, pp. 88–91.

———. 1998. "Has Globalization Gone Too Far?" *Challenge* 41(2) (March–April): 81–94.

Rose, Stephen. 1996. "The Truth About Social Mobility." *Challenge* 39(3) (May–June): 4–8.

Rosenberg, Samuel. 2003. *American Economic Development Since 1945.* New York: Palgrave Macmillan.

Rothman, Dale S. 1998. "Environmental Kuznets Curves—Real Progress or Passing the Buck? A Case for Consumption-Based Approaches." *Ecological Economics* 25 (2): 177–94.

Roush, Wade. 1997. "Ecological Economics: Putting a Price Tag on Nature's Bounty." *Science* 276 (5315) 1029.

Ruggles, Richard. 1983. "The United States National Income Accounts, 1947–1977: Their Conceptual Basis and Evolution." In *The U.S. National Income and Product Accounts: Selected Topics,* ed. Murray F. Foss, pp. 15–49. Chicago: University of Chicago Press.

Sackrey, Charles, and Geoffrey Schneider. 2002. *Introduction to Political Economy* (3rd ed.). Cambridge, MA: Economic Affairs Bureau.

Sagoff, Mark. 1982. "At the Shrine of Our Lady of Fatima, or Why Political Questions are Not All Economic." *Arizona Law Review* 23(4): 1283–98.

Samuelson, Paul A., and William D. Nordhaus. 2005, 2001a, 1998a. *Macroeconomics* (18th, 17th, 16th eds.). New York: McGraw-Hill.

———. 2001b. *Economics* (17th ed.). New York: McGraw-Hill.

Schafer, Todd, and Jeff Faux, eds. 1996. *Reclaiming Prosperity: A Blueprint for Progressive Economic Reform.* Armonk, NY: M.E. Sharpe.

Schmitt, John, and Dean Baker. 2006. "Missing Inaction: Evidence of Undercounting of Non-Workers in the Current Population Survey (CPS)." CEPR Briefing Paper. Washington, DC: Center for Economic and Policy Research.

Schnaiberg, Allan, and Kenneth Alan Gould. 1994. *Environment and Society: The Enduring Conflict.* New York: St. Martin's Press.

Schor, Juliet. 1991. *The Overworked American: The Unexpected Decline of Leisure.* New York: Basic Books.

———. 2000. *Do Americans Shop Too Much?* Boston: Beacon Press.

Schor, Juliet, and Samuel Bowles. 1987. "Employment Rents and the Incidence of Strikes." *Review of Economics and Statistics* 69(4): 584–92.

Schumacher, E.F. 1973. *Small Is Beautiful: Economics as if People Mattered.* New York: Harper and Row.

Schutz, Eric A. 2001. *Markets and Power: The 21st Century Command Economy.* Armonk, NY: M.E. Sharpe.

———. 1997. "Inequality, Unemployment and Contemporary Europe." *International Labor Review* 136(2): 155–71.

Shaikh, Anwar. 2003. "Globalization and the Myth of Free Trade." Paper prepared for the Conference on Globalization and the Myths of Free Trade (April). Available at http://homepage.newschool.edu/~AShaikh/

Shaikh, Anwar, and E. Ahmet Tonak. 1994. *Measuring the Wealth of Nations: The Political Economy of National Accounts.* New York: Cambridge University Press.

Sharma, Shalendra. 2001. "The Missed Lessons of the Mexican Peso Crisis." *Challenge* 44(1): 56–89.

Shiller, Robert J. 2001. *Irrational Exuberance.* New York: Broadway Books.

Shoch, Jim. 1994. "The Politics of the US Industrial Policy Debate, 1981–1984 (with a note on Bill Clinton's 'industrial policy')." In Kotz, McDonough, and Reich 1994, pp. 173–90.

Siegfried, John J. 1999. "Trends in Undergraduate Economics Degrees, 1997–1998." *Journal of Economic Education* (Summer): 325–28.

Skidelsky, Robert. 2005. *John Maynard Keynes, 1883–1946: Economist, Philosopher, Statesman.* New York: Penguin.

Skladany, Mike, Ben Belton, and Rebecca Clausen. 2005. "Out of Sight & Out of Mind: A New Oceanic Imperialism." *Monthly Review* 56(9): 14–24.

Smith, Adam. [1776] 1965. *An Inquiry into the Nature and Causes of the Wealth of Nations.* New York: Random House.

Smith, Geri, and Cristina Lindblad. 2003. "Mexico: Was NAFTA Worth It?" *Business Week,* December 22 Available at http://businessweek.com/magazine/content/03_51/b3863008.htm.

Snowdon, Brian, and Howard R. Vane. 1999. *Conversations with Leading Economists: Interpreting Modern Macroeconomics.* Northampton, MA: Edward Elgar.

Snowdon, Brian, Howard R. Vane, and P. Wynarczyk. 1994. *A Modern Guide to Macroeconomics: An Introduction to Competing Schools of Thought.* Brookfield, VT: Edward Elgar.

Solnick, Sara J., and David Hemenway. 1998. "Is More Always Better? A Survey About Positional Concerns." *Journal of Economic Behavior and Organization* 37 (3): 373–83.

Solon, Gary. 2002. "Cross-Country Differences in Intergenerational Earnings Mobility." *Journal of Economic Perspectives* 16(3): 59–66.

Solow, Robert. 1990. *The Labor Market as a Social Institution.* Cambridge, MA: Basil Blackwell.

Soros, George. 1999. "An Interview with George Suros." *Challenge* 42(2) (March–April): 58–76.

Spitz, Janet. 1991. "Productivity and Wage Relations in Economic Theory and Labor Markets." Ph. D. Dissertation. Palo Alto, CA: Stanford University.

Stanford, Jim, Lance Taylor, and Ellen Houston, eds. 2001. *Power, Employment, and Accumulation: Social Structures in Economic Theory and Practice.* Amonk, NY: M.E. Sharpe.

Starke, Linda, ed. 2004. *State of the World 2004.* New York: Norton.

Stiglitz, Joseph E. 1997. *Economics* (2nd ed.). New York: Norton.

———. 2002. "The Roaring Nineties." *Atlantic Monthly* 290 (3) (October): 75–89.

———. 2003. *Globalization and Its Discontents.* New York: Norton.

Strassmann, Diana. 1999. "Feminist Economics." In Peterson and Lewis 1999, pp. 360–73.

Stretton, Hugh. 2000. *Economics: A New Introduction.* Sterling, VA: Pluto.

Sweezy, Paul M. (1942) 1968. *The Theory of Capitalist Development: Principles of Marxian Political Economy.* New York: Monthly Review Press.

Terkel, Studs. 1970. *Hard Times: An Oral History of the Great Depression.* New York: Random House.

Thorbecke, Willem. 2004. "Inflation Targeting and the Natural Rate of Unemployment." Public Policy Note 2004/1. Annandale-on-Hudson, NY: The Levy Institute.

Thurow, Lester C. 1984. *Dangerous Currents: The State of Economics.* New York: Vintage.

———. 1996. *The Future of Capitalism: How Today's Economic Forces Shape Tomorrow's World.* New York: Penguin.

———. 1999. "Building Wealth." *The Atlantic Monthly* 283 (6): 57–69.

Tietenberg, Tom. 2003, 2000. *Environmental and Natural Resource Economics* (6th and 5th eds.). Boston: Addison Wesley.

Tilly, Chris. 2004. "Geese, Golden Eggs, and Traps: Why Inequality Is Bad for the Economy." *Dollars and Sense* 254 (July–August).

Tobin, James. 1982a. "The Reagan Economic Plan—Supply-Side, Budget and Inflation." In *Hailstones* 1982, pp. 207–20.

———. 1982b. "Supply-Side Economics: What Is It? Will It Work?" In *Hailstones* 1982, pp. 132–38.

Tool, Marc R. 2000. *The Discretionary Economy: A Normative Theory of Political Economy.* New Brunswick, NJ: Transaction Publishers.

Toruno, Mayo. 2003. *The Political Economics of Capitalism.* Cincinnati: Atomic Dog Publishing.

U.S. Bureau of Labor Statistics (BLS). 2004. *Highlights of Women's Earnings in 2003.* Washington DC: Department of Labor, Bureau of Labor Statistics.

U.S. Census Bureau. 2001. *Money Income in the United States: 2000.* Current Population Reports, P60-213. Washington, DC: Government Printing Office. Available at www.census.gov/prod/2001pubs/p60-213.pdf.

———. 2001. *Poverty in the United States: 2000.* Current Population Reports, Series P60-214. Washington, DC: Government Printing Office. Available at www.census.gov/prod/2001pubs/p60-214.pdf.

———. 2004. *Income, Poverty, and Health Insurance Coverage in the United States: 2003.* Current Population Reports, P60-226. Washington, DC: Government Printing Office. Available at www.census.gov/prod/2004pubs/p60-226.pdf.

———. *Statistical Abstract of the United States* (various years). Washington, DC: Government Printing Office.

U.S. Congressional Budget Office. 2003. *Effective Federal Tax Rates 1997 to 2000.* Washington, DC: Congressional Budget Office.

U.S. Executive Office of the President. 1997. *The Economic Report of the President.* Washington, DC: Government Printing Office. Available at www.gpoaccess.gov/usbudget/fy97/pdf/erp.pdf.

———. 2000. *The Economic Report of the President.* Washington, DC: Government Printing Office. Available at www.gpoaccess.gov/usbudget/fy01/pdf/2000_erp.pdf.

———. 2003. *The Economic Report of the President.* Washington, DC: Government Printing Office. Available at www.gpoaccess.gov/usbudget/fy04/pdf/2003_erp.pdf.

———. 2004. *The Economic Report of the President.* Washington, DC: Government Printing Office. Available at www.gpoaccess.gov/usbudget/fy05/pdf/2004_erp.pdf.

———. 2005. *The Economic Report of the President.* Washington, DC: Government Printing Office. Available at www.gpoaccess.gov/eop/2005/2005_erp.pdf.

Varoufakis, Yanis. 1998. *Foundations of Economics: A Beginner's Companion.* New York: Routledge.

Veblen, Thorstein. [1899] 1973. *The Theory of the Leisure Class.* Boston: Houghton Mifflin.

Vickrey, William. 1993. "Today's Task for Economists." *Challenge* 36(2): 4–14.

Wade, Robert Hunter. 2005. "Does Inequality Matter?." *Challenge* 48(5): 12–38.

Weiner, Stuart E., and Stephen A. Monto. 1998. "Income Inequality: A Summary of the Bank's 1998 Symposium." *Economic Review* 1998 (4): 1–8.

Wessel, David. 2005. "As Rich-Poor Gap Widens in the U.S., Class Mobility Stalls." *Wall Street Journal* (May 13): A1, A7.

Whalen, Charles J. 1996. *Political Economy for the 21st Century: Contemporary Views on the Trend of Economics.* Armonk, NY: M.E. Sharpe.

White, Michael. 1982. "Reading and Rewriting: The Production of an Economic Robinson Crusoe." *Southern Review: Literary and Interdisciplinary Essays* 15(2): 115–42.

Williamson, Jeffrey G. 1997. "Globalization and Inequality, Past and Present." Summarized in Ackerman et al. 2000, pp. 303–5.

Wilber, Charles K., and Robert S. Harrison. 1978. "The Methodological Basis of Institutional Economics: Pattern Model, Storytelling, and Holism." *Journal of Economic Issues* 12(1) (March): 61–89.

Wilson, William Julius. 1996. *When Work Disappears: The World of the New Urban Poor.* New York: Knopf.

Wise, Timothy A. 2003. "NAFTA's Untold Stories: Mexico's Grassroots Response to North American Integration." Americas Program Policy Report, June 10. Silver City, NM: Interhemispheric Resource Center.

Wolff, Edward N. 1996. *Top Heavy: A Study of the Increasing Inequality of Wealth in America and What Can Be Done About It.* New York: New Press.

———. 1998. "Recent Trends in the Size Distribution of Household Wealth." *Journal of Economic Perspectives* 12(3): 131–50.

———. 2000. "Recent Trends in Wealth Ownership, 1983–1998." Working Paper No. 300, April. Annandale-on-Hudson, NY: The Levy Institute.

———. 2004. "Changes in Household Wealth in the 1980s and 1990s in the U.S." Working Paper No. 407, May. Annandale-on-Hudson, NY: The Levy Institute.

Wolff, Edward N., Ajit Zacharias, and Asena Caner. 2003. "Levy Institute Measure of Economic Well-Being: United States 1989 and 2000." Annandale-on-Hudson, NY: The Levy Institute.

Wolff, Richard D., and Stephen A. Resnick. 1987. *Economics: Marxian Versus Neoclassical.* Baltimore: Johns Hopkins.

Wolfson, Martin H. 1994a. *Financial Crises: Understanding the Postwar U.S. Experience* (2nd ed.). Armonk, NY: M.E. Sharpe.

———. 1994b. "The Financial System and the Social Structure of Accumulation." In Kotz, McDonough, and Reich 1994, pp. 133–45.

Worldwatch. 2003. *Vital Signs 2003.* New York: W.W. Norton and Company.

Wray, L Randall, and Marc-Andre Pigeon. 2000. "Can a Rising Tide Raise All Boats?" *Journal of Economic Issues* 34(4): 811–45.

Yates, Michael D. 2003. *Naming the System: Inequality and Work in the Global Economy.* New York: Monthly Review Press.

INDEX

ABOUT THE AUTHOR

Steve Cohn is a professor of economics at Knox College. His work on heterodox economics has appeared in the *Review of Radical Political Economics*, the *Journal of Economic Issues*, and the *Post Autistic Economics Review*. He has served on the steering committee of the Union for Radical Political Economics and is a co-director of the heterodox web site project. He is also the author of *Too Cheap to Meter: An Economic and Philosophical Analysis of the Nuclear Dream*.